Informed Design of Educational Technologies in Higher Education:

Enhanced Learning and Teaching

Anders D. Olofsson
Umeå University, Sweden

J. Ola Lindberg
Mid Sweden University, Sweden

Information Science
REFERENCE

Senior Editorial Director:	Kristin Klinger
Director of Book Publications:	Julia Mosemann
Editorial Director:	Lindsay Johnston
Acquisitions Editor:	Erika Carter
Development Editor:	Mike Killian
Production Editor:	Sean Woznicki
Typesetters:	Christopher Shearer
Print Coordinator:	Jamie Snavely
Cover Design:	Nick Newcomer

Published in the United States of America by
Information Science Reference (an imprint of IGI Global)
701 E. Chocolate Avenue
Hershey PA 17033
Tel: 717-533-8845
Fax: 717-533-8661
E-mail: cust@igi-global.com
Web site: http://www.igi-global.com

Library of Congress Cataloging-in-Publication Data

Informed design of educational technologies in higher education: enhanced learning and teaching / Anders D. Olofsson and J. Ola Lindberg, editors.

p. cm.

Includes bibliographical references and index.

Summary: "This book presents recent and important theoretical and practical advances in educational technology design in higher education, examining their possibilities for enhancing teaching and learning"--Provided by publisher.

ISBN 978-1-61350-080-4 (hardcover) -- ISBN 978-1-61350-081-1 (ebook) -- ISBN 978-1-61350-082-8 (print & perpetual access) 1. Education, Higher--Computer-assisted instruction. 2. Education, Higher--Effect of technological innovations on. 3. Educational technology. I. Olofsson, Anders D., 1973- II. Lindberg, J. Ola, 1966-

LB2395.7.I546 2012

378.1'734--dc22

2011013012

British Cataloguing in Publication Data

A Cataloguing in Publication record for this book is available from the British Library.

Editorial Advisory Board

Table of Contents

Detailed Table of Contents

trends. It is argued that this way to carry out education instills in students the skills needed in order to become informed citizens in an ever-changing and networked world.

Focusing on the challenges of developing an activity– driven design method for online resources in an education programme for school leaders, this chapter uses an experimental design method grounded in Cultural–Historical Activity Theory (CHAT), and contributes within CHAT in terms of moving from the current use of CHAT as a descriptive evaluation tool between analysis and design or design and redesign towards a more developmental model.

Due to the internet, possible arenas for students and professionals to meet have grown rapidly. This chapter is based on findings from a case study concerning participation in a professional Online Learning Community (OLC) in general medicine. Discussed are design implications for organizing online educational activities in higher education that will intentionally engage medical students and professionals in the field.

This chapter discusses the application of a transactional approach to educational design, in the chapter applied to the practice of supervision in a thesis course. Inspired by scholars such as Bakhtin, Dewey, and Vygotsky the applied transactional approach expands on ideas such as dialogues and educational settings. The author argues that such a theoretical approach will support the students in conducting dialogues around problems related to research tasks in combination to enhance the practice of supervision.

This chapter presents an exploration of the design and methods of two instantiations of authentic learning tasks in online learning environments. The chapter demonstrates a range of possibilities for the instructor interested in more informed design of technology-based learning environments in higher education, and in particular, the design and creation of authentic learning tasks.It is argued that there is a need for a critical analysis of existing educational technologies to promote a learning environment that is engaging students in meaningful learning activities.

Section 3
Emerging Educational Technologies

The last ten years has seen an increase of available educational technologies, technologies becoming more and more advanced and offering greater possibilities for innovative educational activities than ever before. In this section, some of these emerging educational technologies and practices are presented. Throughout the included chapters it is stressed that teaching and learning in higher education but must be supported by informed design and use of available technologies.

This chapter concerns designing for learning in educational computer-assisted simulations (ECAS) in health care education (HCE). Drawing upon the works of Luckin (2008, 2010) empirical data from two studies from the Learning Radiology in Simulated Environments project, are discussed. More specifically, the authors argue for the need of an informed design of simulations and its use in higher medical and health care education.

This chapter addresses the more prevalent usage of simulation in education. A case study of a specific computer-based instructional simulation, the Virtual Audiometer, and instructor and student perspectives regarding the simulation use's effects on teaching and learning is presented. Findings are described within a model of five areas in which technology can effect education: visualization, authentic engagement, quality and quantity of practice and feedback, interaction and collaboration, and reflection.

3D virtual worlds have rather rapidly made its way into the educational arena.This chapter makes a contribution towards an understanding of how 3D virtual worlds can be designed and deployed effectively in the education domain by reporting on three notable case studies at the authors' own institutions, which have pioneered the use of Second Life, a 3D virtual world, in higher education.

By describing how theoretical frameworks including the Ecology of Language Learning (van Lier, 2004), the Five Stage Model of Computer Supported Collaborative Learning (Salmon, 2004) and Activity Theory (Leont'ev, 1978) can be used in order to address different aspects of the design of virtual world environments such as Second Life® (SL), this chapter reports on a case study aimed at the design and initial implementation of a telecollaborative language learning activity between four universities.

The last five years or so has seen an increased interest from higher education institutions in social media. In this chapter, much of the existing research on eLearning, mobile learning and multimodal learning are discussed and reviewed and a framework based on Activity Theory (AT) and Experiential Learning Theory (ELT).for designing and analyzing learning activities in learning ecosystems that are based on mobile and social media is presented.

Mobile learning offer new technical capabilities for higher education. This chapter focuses on various dimensions of mobile learning, including definitions, theoretical dimensions, mobile learning applications in higher education, and provides broad definitions and discussions of mobile learning drawing upon existing work. By exploring the experiences and views of various researchers, the chapter reveals the opportunities and challenges involved with mobile learning.

This chapter will focus on the design, implementation and evaluation of a recent location based, context aware system for urban education students, trainee teachers and language learning students. A major conclusion is that there is much to commend the Zone of Proximal Development context sensitive design as a catalyst for active learning.

Section 4
Informed Design Models and Educational Technology

Over the years, research and practices related to instructional design and educational technology design have often been demonstrated through the use of different kind of models. In this section, five chapters provide innovative and challenging design models to enhance teaching and learning in higher education in theoretically informed ways.

The focus of this chapter is a specific proposal aimed to foster the wide diffusion of Educational Technology (ET) and Networked Collaborative Learning (NCL) in higher education (HE). In this perspective the chapter analyses the main barriers that limit the diffusion of Network-Based Educational Technology (NBET) approaches, in particular NCL, and then, in order to overcome them, presents an innovative approach to faculty training in Educational Technology Instructional Design.

There exists a rather extensive body of research on social network. This chapter draws on this research and discusses and illustrates how knowledge of social networks can be used to inform social and technical design for learning and teaching in higher education. The chapter introduces the social network perspective and how this can be used to explore learning teaching and professional development with educational technology.

In this chapter, the authors introduce and discuss the informed design of a specific pedagogical model in the context of higher education, the model of Enhanced Teaching and Meaningful e-Learning. Presented is first a theoretical framework for the design of the model, taking into account previous models and characteristics of meaningful learning, and the possibilities to design, implement, and evaluate the use of educational technology in the context of higher education is given.

Foreword

HOW DO WAVES SHAPE THE LITTORAL?

Every few years, a technology wave reaches the beaches of higher education. Mobile technologies, social software, Web 2.0, and e-portfolios are recent waves addressed in this book. Every wave brings novelty: it affords new learning activities and hence generates expectations, often over-expectations. When the wave returns to the ocean, it leaves behind it some tears of disappointment. If one considers a single wave, the educational landscape remains somehow similar to what it was before it. There has been (fortunately) no educational tsunami. Nonetheless, over a longer term, waves do somehow shape the littoral. Higher education is not the same as 30 years ago, partly due to technologies, partly to other factors. This book contributes to our understanding of our technologies have influenced the complex ecosystems of higher education institutions.

The contributions reflect the emergent maturity in the field of technology-enhanced learning. The book escapes from a discourse that would consider learning technologies as intrinsically innovative and adopts a more rigorous approach that editors labeled “informed design.” The word “design” partly refers to the old tradition of instructional design: some contributions stress the importance of analyzing learning goals when preparing an educational intervention. However, the word “design” has evolved. Since some chapters address informal learning, the word “design” cannot refer to the sequencing of interventions (questions, exercises, feedback, …), but to more subtle ways of shaping social interactions through technology. Most of Web 2.0 technologies addressed in this book are not suitable tools to implement lessons plans, but introduce changes in the institutional ecosystems that might indirectly change instruction. The status of university lectures illustrates this point. Lecturing is not a sandy beach that waves easily reshaped; it is much closer to rather rocky cliffs that learning technologies have never destabilized. Recording lectures does not intrinsically change the pedagogy – a recorded lecture is a lecture – but simply provides a few extra features (navigation, search, subtitles, …) that may have indirect effects. It is per not a pedagogical innovation but yet, some features many change the processes. The term “informed design” hence takes two meanings. Not only must design be enriched by the understanding of the cognitive outcomes of learning activities, but it must also be influenced by the understanding of how a technology answers to the needs of the teachers, the students, and the institutions. Technologies are more innovative when they address real problems than when they simply aim to be innovative. The maturity of our field requires understanding the constraints that shape teachers’ daily work: the curriculum constraints, the time segmentation, the workload for students, et cetera...

Actually, other waves reach university beaches every year: new students enter the system, as well as new teachers. While many teachers pessimistically argue that students are "less" than before (lower in maths, working less, …), many technologists expect that the last generation – the digital natives – have a new relationship to learning, to knowledge, to social interaction. Myth or reality? This book includes different voices, some supporting, some questioning the existence of generational effects. What is important is that one cannot anymore claim that the situation will simply change the day all teachers will be familiar with technologies (new teachers are digital natives), or the day when Internet will be accessible anytime, anywhere, or the day when students will be able to access knowledge across the world, or the day where teachers will have access to on-line repositories of educational resources. These days are today, at least in the industrial countries. If, on the one hand, these days have come while, on the other hand, technologies are still under-exploited in higher education, our mature community has to learn from this disappointment. The lessons learned, collected in this book, will inform the design of technologies that penetrate educational ecosystems.

Pierre Dillenbourg
Swiss Federal Institute of Technology in Lausanne (EPFL), Switzerland

Preface

INTRODUCTION

Higher education is surrounded by expectations and demands from various stakeholders. When it comes to higher education and information and communication technologies (ICT), at least two types of formulation and realization arenas can be identified. A first arena, in a nonacademic context, mirrors the development of a tremendous growth in the belief in the power of ICT demonstrating itself through e-learning. This is present in relation to the so-called market as well as in the context of governmental instances such as the European Union (EU). They seem to share an idea of ICT in higher education, embodied in the concept of e-learning as the savior that will pave the way for a more democratic and tolerant world inhabited by humans with high digital competence ready to lead the world into the future. Within such a development, a possible scenario could be that ethical issues of e-learning become a question of instrumentalism and design in the sense that several general principles are constructed with the aim of directing how students should act and learn together in, for example, Virtual Learning Environments (VLE) in normative and unreflected ways.

A second arena, not necessarily opposite to the first, is placed in an academic context and holds the practices of both education and research. These practices can be located inside the walls of the universities as well as on the Internet. It will likely be increasingly important to include ethical aspects when educating students in technology-rich environments, in online environments, and, not the least, in the research of such environments and related educational activities. The case will most likely be the same regardless of whether the research carried out is conducted in terms of, for example, developmental, design-based, or interpretational research. To point to precisely what this will mean seems difficult, but nonetheless it seems crucial that both practices consider that being a human is always also a being-for-the-other (Lévinas, 1969, 1981, 1986; Olofsson & Lindberg, 2008). Education as well as research can never be reduced to merely providing the "right" teaching methods; depicting the "right" guidelines; or suggesting the "right" technologies. Rather it is a question of identifying and being aware of different, inherently ethical needs in democracy and the privilege to participate in higher educational activities on equal terms for all included. In relation to designing educational technology, Mor and Winters (2007) state that "Every piece of technology designed for education assumes, and therefore supports, a particular organizational structure and a specific prioritization of knowledge. Yet these assumptions are often left unmentioned" (p. 67). It is for reasons such as the one mentioned by Mor and Winters that we will argue that issues of informed and reflected design focusing on the use of educational technology in higher education needs to be constantly addressed. Researchers, teachers, and other stakeholders in higher education must be prepared to meet institutional changes and demands from present and future students. Teachers need to be able to make informed choices among the variety of educational technologies available. Choices need to be explained, and not only in relation to curricula and instruction. To provide programs and courses in higher education in the most developed, productive, and at the same time ethical way possible, teachers have to make informed choices scaffolding the possibilities for students to attain both formal learning outcomes as well as students' own informal, or personalized, goals. Learning and teaching in higher education must continuously be enhanced in a sound and sustainable way (Looi, Toh, & Milrad, 2010). Teachers' theoretical and practical skills when it comes to the design of educational technologies are therefore always in constant need of rethinking and improvement, and research needs to embrace such a perspective. This book shall be read as a contribution to such activities and processes.

Informed Design and Learning: A Question of Moving From Technology Toward Educational Technology?

Thus far, the question of design in relation to learning and teaching within higher education seems to not be thoroughly addressed, especially in relation to educational technologies (Der-Thanq, Hung, & Wang, 2007). In trying to find a possible answer regarding why this seems to be the case, one can start by considering design as a science and why design issues seem to have become increasingly attractive in relation to higher education and educational technologies during the last 10 years. According to Mor and Winters (2007), design approaches in learning and teaching with technology are under the strong influence of Professor Herbert A. Simon (1916–2001). Simon differentiated between natural sciences, or the behavioral science paradigm, and the sciences of the artificial, whereas the former is about the question of what is, and the latter deals with the question of what ought to be. The same underlying rhetoric of the possibilities to create, develop, and change through design can be found in Walls, Widmeyer, and El Sawy (1992) arguing that design is both a noun and a verb, both a product and a process. That is, it embodies a set of both activities and artifacts (compare Hevner, March, Park, & Ram, 2004; March & Smith, 1995) that could be implemented and used in educational activities. Most likely, this ambiguity makes it rather attractive for higher education institutions and teachers wanting to develop and facilitate the learning and teaching practices. Hokanson, Miller, and Hooper (2008) points at an important factor, that is—design activities in relation to education should "focus on creating rich and innovative learning *experiences*, as opposed to simply developing instructional products through staid processes. Advancing design innovation through use of a new set of design lenses and perspectives" (p.37). In other words, to create innovative and enhanced learning experiences for the students, the design process must involve informed choices. Der-Thanq, Hung, and Wang (2007) uses a similar argumentation saying that often when it comes to educational design, the theoretical foundation for the design process and its implementation is not congruent; there is a lack in the epistemological logos between the learning theories behind a certain educational design. Mor and Winters (2007) follow this line of thought in addressing the fact that design studies should yield theoretical contributions when bringing up the gap between theory and practice. Theory is also said to be crucial when providing new constructs for describing and thinking about the consistently value-driven educational practices and related questions. In their words, it all seems to be a question of "to what extent are we driven by a pure quest for knowledge and to what extent are we committed to influencing educational practice?" (p. 64).

In the previous paragraph, we tried to sketch a possible relation between design and education. Next, we will attempt to connect technology to design and education. Mitcham (1994) claims that one of the most significant aspects of being human is the use of technology. Technology can be understood in different ways, but in one sense it is enough to consider it merely as a tool, an artefact, to realize its importance. At the same time, it might be enough to merely consider the development of technology as a tool in education to realize how the transformed use of technology has affected education. According to Laurillard (2008a), technology, per se, does little for education and can never be the whole solution for providing high-quality higher education. In addition, technology in education is not an uncomplicated affair. Laurillard makes the point that "The recent history of technology in education always tells us that however good it is, it achieves little without the complementary human and organizational changes needed, and these are always more difficult. Using technology to improve education is not rocket science. It's much, much harder than that" (p. 320). When providing a critique of too technology-friendly e-learning initiatives, Dillenbourg (2008) agrees with Laurillard, saying that technology is not in itself innovative, but innovation germs may be hidden in specific details. Dillenbourg continues in his critique by claiming that during the last years, too much focus has been on online learning, e-learning, and other such conceptualizations. Dillenbourg's argument is that "the place of technology in educational activities is not a dichotomy (*with* vs. *without*). Most spaces include some technology" (p.132). In this book, we try to follow Dillenbourg not only by including a number of chapters that provide examples of educational technologies integrated in physical higher education contexts, as well as higher education practices carried out in an online context, but also, through different chapters, by highlighting human, organizational, educational, and informed design-related factors involved when searching for important knowledge to enhance learning and teaching in higher education. Laurillard (2008b) gives us further support for such an approach in talking about the relationship between learning and technology. Her opinion is that "Learning complex concepts and mastering difficult procedures and processes, will always require effortful thinking. Technology will probably not change what it takes to learn, therefore, but it may change how the process of learning is facilitated" (p. 527).

Therefore, concurring with the researchers referred to above, there is a clear connection between education and technology. That is—today, educational technology plays an important role in modern higher education and will do so also in the future (see also Lindberg & Olofsson, 2010). But there is also criticism toward some of the research being conducted on educational technologies and on related educational practices. For example, Bebell, O'Dwyer, Russell, & Hoffmann (2010) claim that often in such research there seems to be a lack of theory guiding the studies and that these studies repeatedly fail to provide sufficient empirical evidence in relation to its outcomes. They use such strong words as "Even today, little empirical research exists to support many of the most cited claims on the effects of educational technology" (p. 31). Dillenbourg (2008) claims that educational technology research needs to more often consider multiple factors such as context, software, students' motivation, organizational constraints, and so on. Mor and Winters (2007) argues for a better and more effective communication and exchange between research communities primarily interested in the technology aspects of educational technology and those primarily interested in the educational aspects of educational technologies. In addition, they mean that the design process requires input from many diverse areas of expertise. It is our ambition in this multidisciplinary book to take on such challenges and to present research with solid empirical results. Included in the book is therefore research that is concerned with the complex practice of educational technologies in higher education and related questions of informed design. The outspoken intention is that this book can function as a bridge between the two research communities described by Mor and Winters (2007), providing new insights and knowledge that contribute to the process of closing the gap.

Learning and Teaching with Educational Technology in Higher Education

In seems rather uncomplicated to claim that two important actors or parts in higher education are teachers and students. But do these two parts uphold an unproblematic relationship? According to one strand of the research literature, it is sometimes said that there is a gap or digital divide between them when it comes to their use of technology. One often cited idea is of the students as so-called digital natives (Prensky, 2001) born into a world with ICT and related digital technologies that rapidly become an apparent part of their everyday life. Today, students belong to a generation that have been immersed in digital technology all their lives. Implied is that those digital natives, when entering higher education in the role of students, expect to carry out their studies with tools they are used to—that is, various forms of digital technology. This expectancy, research tells us, may cause difficulty when meeting university organizations and teachers not familiar with the implementation and use of ICT in their educational planning and teaching practices. In another strand of research, the concept coined by Prensky seems to be receiving critique. For example, one critique is that not all students of today can be understood as digital natives (e.g., age factors, socioeconomic differences, cultural differences, and so on may make the digital natives heterogeneous as a group), and another critique is that many universities and their teachers are today fairly well orientated in the use of ICT and other digital technologies. Bennett, Maton, and Kervin (2008), in relation to the academic discussion of the concept and inherent meaning of digital natives, add "that rather than being empirically and theoretically informed, the debate can be likened to an academic form of a 'moral panic'" (p. 775). A possible question to pose seems to be if it matters whether or not digital natives exist, or if that concept is overestimated when it comes to learning and teaching with educational technologies in higher education. Maybe the important issue to recognize is that higher education institutions today are crowded not only with teachers and students but also with many educational technologies that in various ways provide possibilities, and sometimes constraints, for the educational practices both on campus and online. The important thing might be to design educational technologies in the most informed way possible that can contribute to enhance learning and teaching as well as develop the university on an organizational level.

Another aspect important in relation to the discussion in the previous paragraph is that education and educational design are ongoing processes (Wang, 2008). However, Schneckenberg (2009) warns us that the current educational design of most curricula applies a traditional model of knowledge transmission of specific subject matter and leads in the best way to the acquisition of a qualification. Therefore, an urgent and constant need seems to exist for teachers to select learning goals in an informed, systematic, and well-analyzed way, to address what kind of content is appropriate for framing these goals, and to choose educational technology tools in relation to the three questions of what, when, and why. Further, it seems important to create active and collaborative orientated-learning processes among the students that also scaffold the students' own learning. Last but not least, the question remains of how the assessment practices shall be constructed in order to evaluate the learning goals (Lindberg, Olofsson, & Stödberg, 2010; Olofsson, Lindberg, & Stödberg, 2011).

In line with the points made by Dillenbourg (2008), we claim that educational technologies are becoming, in a way, an invisible part of educational practices framed in a higher education context. They are becoming integrated in students' learning activities, using Dillenbourg's words, which are being orchestrated by the teachers (see also Sorensen & Ó Murchú, 2006). Therefore, it seems to be more important than ever to make explicit the theoretical foundations that our design of educational technologies rests on to provide for transparency between the design approaches used and the choices made, and to make explicit how they support the teachers' work and the students' learning. For that reason, the call for chapters for this book invited authors from different academic backgrounds and disciplines, with different focuses in their research, ready to go beyond what so far has been reported in the research literature in this field. Together in this book, we create a body of research-based knowledge paving the way for informed design of educational technology in higher education for the cause of enhanced learning and teaching. Next, we will introduce the section themes presented in the book along with some words about each of the included chapters.

Section 1: Aspects of the Research Field

This section introduces the different themes of the book and the various aspects present within each theme. The four chapters included offer a solid foundation for understanding this particular field of research. It provides insight into important issues brought up by the different authors, and it will help to frame the reading of the other chapters in the book. Specifically, this section includes chapters dealing with learning and teaching, educational planning and assessment, and educational technology and the relation to instructional design. The first chapter, "*The Influence Upon Design of Differing Conceptions of Teaching and Learning with Technology*," written by Adrian Kirkwood and Linda Price from The Open University, UK, includes some of the theoretical foundations of teaching and learning in higher education. It is stressed by the authors that informed design in the use of technology is underpinned by conceptions of teaching and learning with technology. If academic teachers consider their own conceptions of teaching and learning with technology, it could imply a move toward learner-centered pedagogies and user-led conceptions of technology. In chapter 2, "*The Outcomes-Based Approach: Concepts and Practice in Curriculum and Educational Technology Design*," Maureen Tam from The Hong Kong Institute of Education, China, concentrates on an emerging trend of an outcomes-based approach to curricula improvement in higher education, which is captured in this chapter. Provided is a critical review of this approach as well as practical considerations and examples for curricula and educational technology design. It is argued that learning outcomes can make important contributions to better curricula and student learning. Chapter 3, "*Instructional Design for Technology-Based Systems*" written by Gary R. Morrison, of the Old Dominion University, USA, and Gary J. Anglin, of the University of Kentucky, USA, bring forth the risk for instructional designers to be seduced by the possibilities of the technologies of today. Instructions that might seem to be appealing to the learner could instead become inefficient. It is demonstrated in the chapter that effective instruction results from designing instructional strategies based on research rather than from specific educational technologies. Finally in Chapter 4, "*The Next Generation: Design and the Infrastructure for Learning in a Mobile and Networked World*," Agnes Kukulska-Hulme and Chris Jones, of The Open University, UK, bring together some of the fast and growing bodies of research on learner practices and networked learning. They argue for an integrated pedagogical design approach that includes learner practices, spaces for learning, and technologies. The authors stress that a major challenge for the future will be to design for learning in contexts in which educators have increasingly limited control.

Section 2: Integrating Arenas Through Designed Learning and Teaching

The second section in this book includes five chapters that in various ways show how educational technologies can be used to integrate different arenas related to higher education. They demonstrate and exemplify the ways learning and teaching processes can be enhanced through theoretically informed, systematic, and research-based design of the educational activities and can show how different participants or group of participants in higher education can share common spaces for educational purposes. In these chapters, the Internet plays an important role in the education delivery as can be seen in chapter 5, "*Using Online Data for Student Investigations in Biology and Ecology*," written by Nancy M. Trautmann, Cornell Lab of Ornithology, USA, and Colleen M. McLinn, Cornell Lab of Ornithology, USA. They take on the challenge to enhance undergraduate students' research experiences in large higher education classes. It is shown that the use of online databases, including ecological data derived through citizen science, can help to overcome that challenge. Informed design of educational technology in combination with the use of well-analyzed learning theory will provide possibilities for the students to obtain access to research experiences. It is argued that this method of carrying out education instills in students the skills needed to become informed citizens in an ever-changing and networked world. In chapter 6, "*Towards an Activity-Driven Design Method for Online Learning Resources*," written by Trond Eiliv Hauge, and Jan Arild Dolonen, University of Oslo, Norway, the authors address how Cultural-Historical Activity Theory (CHAT), which has a strong position in research on educational technologies, can be used as the foundation for a developmental design model in higher education. Through empirical examples collected from school leaders in education in Norway, an activity-driven design method for creating online learning resources is revealed. It is argued that understanding the interplay between cultural artifacts leads to contradictions in design activities and creates opportunities for the transformation of the design as a whole. Chapter 7, "*Informed Design of Educational Activities in Online Learning Communities,*" written by Urban Carlén, University of Skövde, Sweden, and Berner Lindström, University of Gothenburg, Sweden, consider how the Internet has provided different arenas for higher education students and professionals during the last 10 years. Through the use of so-called professional Online Learning Communities, the authors demonstrate how medical students embrace and learn from discussions with doctors in the medical area of general medicine. An informed design for such educational activities through technologies can contribute both to foster students in becoming doctors and to create and sustain relationships important for their future careers as doctors. In the following chapter 8, "*Boundless Writing: Applying a Transactional Approach to Design of a Thesis Course in Higher Education*," Jimmy Jaldemark of Mid Sweden University, Sweden, takes on the issue of supervising students in thesis writing. Today, universities all over the world offer different online courses in which the students are supposed to write their own independent thesis. In this chapter, a design of a thesis course in higher education online informed by a transactional perspective is presented. The author argues that such a theoretical approach will support the students in conducting dialogues around problems related to research tasks as well as enhance the practice of supervision. In the final chapter of this section, "*Authentic Tasks Online: Two Experiences*," written by Tel Amiel, Universidade Estadual de Campinas, and Jan Herrington, Murdoch University, Australia, the authors give two accounts of authentic learning tasks in online learning environments. One is an experiential e-learning model focused on preservice teachers and multicultural education; the other is focused on a scenario-based model in relation to mathematics and preservice teachers. Throughout the chapter, the authors provide various possibilities for instructors with regard to the design and creation of authentic learning tasks. They also argue that there is a need for a critical analysis of existing educational technologies to promote a learning environment that engages students in meaningful learning activities.

Section 3: Emerging Educational Technologies

During the last 10 years or so, the number of available educational technologies has increased. The technologies have become more and more advanced, and the possibilities for innovative educational activities through, for example, the Internet is today larger than ever before. In this section, some of these emerging educational technologies and practices are presented. It is stressed throughout the chapters that the educational technologies, per se, will hardly enhance learning and teaching in higher education and must be supported by informed design and use of the technologies. In the first chapter in this section, chapter 10, "*Designing for Learning in Computer-Assisted Health Care Simulations*" Lars O. Häll and Tor Söderström, Umeå University, Sweden, address the fact that simulations have become increasingly important in medical and health care education. This chapter presents possibilities with regard to how to train complex medical activities in a safe environment. With a base in the work of Luckin (2008, 2010), this chapter proposes an Ecology of Resources framework for analyzing and designing health care simulations. Two empirical cases focusing on how to learn radiology with simulations are presented and discussed. The authors argue for the need for an informed design of simulations and for its use in higher medical and health care education. The next chapter, chapter 11, "*The Impact of Instructional Simulation Use on Teaching and Learning: A Case Study*," is written by Michael C. Johnson, Charles R. Graham, and Su-Ling Hsueh, Brigham Young University, USA. They report on a case study conducted on a computer-based instructional simulation—the Virtual Audiometer. The authors stress the importance of analyzing the use of simulations in higher education in relation to learning and teaching. Five areas in which educational technology of this kind can effect and enhance education are presented in this chapter. It is argued that empirical studies can reveal important knowledge of the impact of simulations on learning and teaching as well as knowledge that can inform design of both the simulations as such and its implementation in educational practices. In chapter 12, "*3D Virtual Worlds in Higher Education*," Lucia Rapanotti, Shailey Minocha, and Leonor Barroca, all of The Open University, United Kingdom, and Maged N. Kamel Boulos, of University of Plymouth, United Kingdom, and David R. Morse, The Open University, United Kingdom, beginning with the development of more powerful computers, high-speed broadband, and other developments, conclude that 3D virtual worlds have rather rapidly made their way into the educational arena. They provide new possibilities for educators to teach and for students to learn in creative digitalized environments. In this chapter, three case studies report on the use of one type of 3D virtual worlds, Second Life, in higher education. The authors take the challenge of providing a better understanding of how to design and deploy 3D virtual worlds. They argue that one important area for improvement through research is the understanding of pedagogical affordances of 3D virtual worlds. Chapter 13, "*Debating Across Borders*," written by Mats Deutschmann, Umeå University, Sweden, reports a case study aimed at the design and initial implementation of a telecollaborative language learning activity between four universities. The activities were carried out in Second Life. The use of three different theoretical frameworks informed the design process, and the empirical data collected was analyzed to discover affordances and constraints related to the learning activities. One important conclusion drawn in the chapter is that traditional forms of examination must be reviewed and revised to better reflect new learning practices such as those emerging in Second Life. Then chapter 14, "*Designing Learning Ecosystems for Mobile Social Media*" by Jari Multisilta, University of Helsinki, Finland, is concerned with how social media has been given increased attention by higher education institutions. However, there are some knowledge gaps that still to be filled by research. One of the most important gaps is addressed in this chapter—designing learning activities for learning ecosystems based on mobile social media. Two theoretically informed examples using a framework based on Activity Theory (AT) and Experiential Learning Theory (ELT) are presented. It is argued that this framework can lead to improvements in designing future learning activities and learning ecosystems in higher education based on mobile social media. In chapter 15, "*Mobile Learning in Higher Education,*" Rui Zeng, University of Texas Health Science Center at Houston, USA, and Eunice Luyegu, Franklin University, USA, provide an account of how mobile learning offers new technical capabilities for higher education. This chapter provides insight into various dimensions of mobile learning. Broad definitions and discussions of informed mobile learning are presented in a review of much of the existing work in the field. The authors argue that mobile learning is still an emerging and immature field and that the pedagogical use of mobile devices is not widespread in higher education. The final chapter of the section, chapter 16, "*Designing for Active Learning: Putting Learning into Context with Mobile Devices*" Carl Smith, Claire Bradley, and John Cook, London Metropolitan University, together with Simon Pratt-Adams, Anglia Ruskin University, United Kingdom focuses on the design of active and collaborative learning in urban settings through the use of context sensitive technologies in terms of mobile devices. The empirical studies presented show that Design-Based research can be used in order to tailor the use of mobile educational technology in higher educational practices. The authors argue that social media and augmented reality are important to pay attention in urban education projects of the future.

Section 4: Informed Design Models and Educational Technology

Over the years, research and practices related to instructional design and educational technology design have often been demonstrated through the use of various types of models. These models often describe the way a certain educational activity or sequence ought to be carried out. In addition, the questions of what, when, and why certain educational technologies ought to be used are addressed. The models are used for various purposes, on the one hand, to suggest ways to attain better practices, and on the other hand, to function as a tool for understanding practice. In this section, five chapters provide in theoretically informed ways innovative and challenging design models to enhance learning and teaching with educational technology in higher education. Beginning with chapter 17, "*Fostering NCL in Higher Education: New Approaches for Integrating Educational Technology Instructional Design into Teachers' Practices,*" Serena Alvino and Guglielmo Trentin, Institute for Educational Technologies—National Research Council, Italy, depart from the increased use of the Internet for educational purposes, arguing that networked collaborative learning (NCL) is an important factor in higher education. The authors demonstrate how to foster a wide diffusion of educational technology and NCL in higher education. In addition, they provide an approach to faculty training in educational technology instructional design that provides the teachers with possibilities for designing active and collaborative learning practices. The authors argue the importance of giving the teachers direct and indirect scaffolding when designing for NCL activities. In chapter 18, "*Social Network Informed Design for Learning with Educational Technology*" Caroline Haythornthwaite, University of British Columbia, Canada, and Maarten DeLaat, Open Universiteit Nederland, The Netherlands, introduce the social network perspective and ways to use such a perspective to explore and understand learning. In addition, they provide research demonstrating how knowledge of informal learning networks can facilitate informed design for learning, teaching, and professional development with educational technology. Chapter 19, "*Designing a Model for Enhanced Teaching and Meaningful E-Learning,*" written by Heli Ruokamo, Päivi Hakkarainen, and Miikka Eriksson, University of Lapland, Finland, introduces and discusses a pedagogical model the authors have developed. They continuously revise it to make it even more useful for designing educational activities that are supported by educational technologies—the model of Enhanced Teaching and Meaningful e-Learning. The model provides possibilities to design, implement, and evaluate the use of educational technology in the context of higher education. A research study related to the model is presented, and suggestions for related course developments are articulated. Then in chapter 20, "*An Ecological Approach to Instructional Design: The Learning Synergy of Interaction and Context*," Paul Resta and Debby Kalk, The University of Texas at Austin, USA, describe possibilities for engaging students in authentic learning experiences that can help them to develop a deep understanding of their learning objectives. These experiences are often facilitated and mediated through the use of educational technologies. In this chapter it is argued that to afford such learning experiences, the instructional designer needs to move beyond existing and traditional sequences of design and instead use a nonlinear approach or model. The authors present and suggest the ecological approach to instructional design as one possible and fruitful approach. Finally in chapter 21, "*Multi-Faceted Professional Development Models Designed to Enhance Teaching and Learning within Universities*," Donald E. Scott and Shelleyann Scott, University of Calgary, Canada, draw from results generated from two mixed-method case studies on online and blended learning and from two informed models to promote pedagogical-focused professional development and design. Also discussed is the way educational technology can be integrated to facilitate model-related activities.

Section 5: Changing Educational Practices through Informed Choices of Design

To change the educational practices and activities embraced by educational technologies in higher education in a positive and productive way, there is a constant need for well-informed decisions. Deep knowledge is required to support this kind of decision, and there are quite a few ways to generate or build such knowledge. In this fifth and final section of the book, three different approaches for promoting successful changes in educational, technology-rich contexts are presented. The chapters, one by one and together as a triad, communicate a rationale for change through informed design. Examples come from online, blended, and physical environments and practices in higher education beginning with chapter 22, "*The Design of Learning Materials within Small-Scale Projects: What is the Value of an Action Research Approach?*" It is written by Michael Hammond, University of Warwick, UK, and Jie Hu, University of Chongqing, China. In this chapter, the authors' focus is on the design of learning materials in small-scale projects, and they present a case on how to support academic reading skills on a university level. The authors demonstrate that using an action-research approach can be a powerful way to facilitate learning, teaching, and designing of related material in higher education. At the same time, they stress that there is always a need to pay close attention to the tension between the different stakeholders involved in an action research process. Then in chapter 23, "*Instructional Technical and Pedagogical Design: Teaching Future Teachers Educational Technology*," Anne T. Ottenbreit-Leftwich, Mark O. Millard, and Peter van Leusen, Indiana University, USA, address an important task for universities around the globe—to prepare future teacher education students to use educational technology. An equally important task is for university teachers to select the most appropriate technologies in the learning and teaching activities together with the students. In this chapter, it is discussed how a conceptual guide for technology teacher experiences informed the educational technology design in a teacher education course. In the chapter, the importance of the instructional design is continuously assessed and evaluated is stressed. Finally, in the last chapter of the book, chapter 24, "*Priorities in the Classroom: Pedagogies for High Performance*

Learning Spaces," authors Robert Emery Smith, Helen L. Chen, Menko Johnson, Alyssa J. O'Brien, and Cammy Huang-DeVoss, Stanford University, USA, take up the challenge of what the future will demand from higher education institutions. The importance of current designs, implementations, and various possible scenarios for the future classroom and learning spaces, embraced by advanced educational technologies, is stressed. Informed by the Technology, Pedagogy, and Content Knowledge (TPACK) model, the authors design and demonstrate a three-level categorization of teaching innovation. They argue that it is of great importance that informed teachers' classroom priorities be kept on the pedagogy, not on the latest educational technologies.

Scholarly Value and Contribution of the Book

It is our hope that this book will contribute to a wider, deeper, and informed understanding of the current state and future potential of informed design of educational technology in higher education. The underlying idea of using educational technology in informed ways is to actually enhance learning and teaching in higher education through encouraging a reflected approach in which ethical issues are always considered. In addition, we believe that informed understanding will pave a productive way of developing the higher educational system to better cater to a future workforce. The content of this volume is useful at the policy-making level as well as at actual university researcher and teacher level; the content provides and demonstrates productive ways of bridging the otherwise often separated groups of professionals concerned with learning and teaching using educational technologies in higher education.

CONCLUSION

This book presents interesting aspects regarding enhancing learning and teaching in higher education through the informed design and use of educational technology. Each section or chapter can be read separately as a stand-alone contribution, but all can be read as a whole as well; each is connected and informs the sections or chapters to come. We are convinced that the book covers many important aspects of informed design of educational technologies in higher education, and these are aspects that are thoroughly presented, discussed, and reflected upon in the chapters. Altogether, such informed elaborations provide a solid platform for both educational practice and related future research. It is important to address the potential for informed design of educational technology. Its use in policies and in learning and teaching activities enhances the insight of the impact that learning, teaching, and related educational technologies, in combination with learning arenas, can have in enriching and cultivating the practices of students and staff. As a reader, you will be provided with a framework of theoretical ideas of possible understanding and implementations of the design of educational technology. You will acquire access to research-based knowledge that can be used to reflect or act upon in relation to your own professional context or practice. In this way, the book will expand the field of research and provide both theoretical support and practical examples to the reader.

REFERENCES

Bebell, D., O'Dwyer, L. M., Russell, M., & Hoffmann, T. (2010). Concerns, considerations, and new ideas for data collection and research in educational technology studies. *Journal of Research on Technology in Education, 43*(19), 29–52.

Bennett, S., Maton, K., & Kervin, L. (2008). The digital natives debate: A critical review of the evidence. *British Journal of Educational Technology, 39*(5), 775–786. doi:10.1111/j.1467-8535.2007.00793.x

Der-Thanq, C., Hung, D., & Wang, Y.-M. (2007). Educational design as a quest for congruence: The need for alternative learning design tools. *British Journal of Educational Technology, 38*(5), 876–884. doi:10.1111/j.1467-8535.2006.00675.x

Dillenbourg, P. (2008). Integrating technologies into educational ecosystems. *Distance Education, 29*(2), 127–140. doi:10.1080/01587910802154939

Hevner, A. R., March, S. T., Park, J., & Ram, S. (2004). Design science in information systems research. *Management Information Systems Quarterly, 28*(1), 75–105.

Hokanson, B., Miller, C., & Hooper, S. (2008). Role-based design: A contemporary perspective for innovation in instructional design. *TechTrends, 52*(6), 36–43. doi:10.1007/s11528-008-0215-0

Laurillard, D. (2008a). Open teaching: The key to sustainable and effective open education . In Iiyoshi, T., & Vijay Kumar, M. S. (Eds.), *Opening up education: The collective advancement of education through open technology, open content, and open knowledge* (pp. 319–336). Cambridge, MA: The MIT Press.

Laurillard, D. (2008b). Technology enhanced learning as a tool for pedagogical innovation. *Journal of Philosophy of Education, 42*(3-4), 521–533. doi:10.1111/j.1467-9752.2008.00658.x

Lévinas, E. (1969). *Totality and infinity*. Pittsburgh, PA: Duquesne University Press.

Lévinas, E. (1981). *Otherwise than being or beyond essence*. Pittsburgh, PA: Duquesne University Press.

Lévinas, E. (1986). The trace of the other . In Taylor, M. (Ed.), *Deconstruction in context* (pp. 345–359). Chicago, IL: University of Chicago Press.

Lindberg, J. O., & Olofsson, A. D. (Eds.). (2010). *Online learning communities and teacher professional development: Methods for improved education delivery*. Hershey, PA: IGI Global.

Lindberg, J. O., Olofsson, A. D., & Stödberg, U. (2010). Signs for learning in a digital environment. *Australasian Journal of Educational Technology, 26*(7), 996–1011.

Looi, C.-K., Toh, Y., & Milrad, M. (2010). Nurturing sustainable learning eco-systems. In T. Cerratto-Pargman, P. Hyvönen, S. Järvelä, & M. Milrad (Eds.), *The First Nordic Symposium on Technology-Enhanced Learning (TEL)* (pp. 3-5). Växjö, Sweden: Linnaeus University.

March, S., & Smith, G. F. (1995). Design and natural science research on information technology. *Decision Support Systems, 15*, 251–266. doi:10.1016/0167-9236(94)00041-2

Mitcham, C. (1994). *Thinking through technology: The path between engineering and philosophy*. Chicago, IL: The University of Chicago Press.

Mor, Y., & Winters, N. (2007). Design approaches in technology-enhanced learning. *Interactive Learning Environments*, *15*(1), 61–75. doi:10.1080/10494820601044236

Olofsson, A. D., & Lindberg, A. D. (2008). An ethical perspective on ICT in the context of the other . In Hansson, T. (Ed.), *Handbook of digital information technologies: Innovations, methods and ethical issues* (pp. 504–519). London, UK: Information Science Publishing. doi:10.4018/978-1-59904-970-0.ch032

Olofsson, A. D., Lindberg, J. O., & Stödberg, U. (2011). Shared video media and blogging online: Educational technologies for enhancing formative e-assessment? *Campus-Wide Information Systems*, *28*(1), 41–55.

Prenksy, M. (2001). Digital natives, digital immigrants: Do they really think differently? *Horizon*, *9*(6), 1–6. doi:10.1108/10748120110424843

Schneckenberg, D. (2009). Understanding the real barriers to technology-enhanced innovation in higher education. *Educational Research*, *51*(4), 411–424. doi:10.1080/00131880903354741

Sorensen, E., & Murchú, Ó. D. (Eds.). (2006). *Enhancing learning through technology*. London, UK: Information Science Publishing.

Walls, J. G., Widmeyer, G. R., & El Sawy, O. A. (1992). Building an information system design theory for vigilant EIS. *Information Systems Research*, *3*(1), 36–59. doi:10.1287/isre.3.1.36

Wang, Q. (2008). A generic model for guiding the integration of ICT into teaching and learning. *Innovations in Education and Teaching International*, *45*(4), 411–419. doi:10.1080/14703290802377307

Acknowledgment

This book is the hard work of many people who, in various and important ways, have supported the process from start to finish. In particular we will say a genuine thank you to all the authors of the individual chapters for their excellent contributions. We will also thank our brilliant colleagues around the globe who, with their deep knowledge in this research area, have participated in the review process. Without your support this book project could for sure not have been satisfactorily completed. In this respect special gratitude shall be given to Professor, Ph.D. Gregory Anderson, Professor, Ph.D. Marcie Boucouvalas, Assistant Professor, Ph.D. Erik Borglund, Professor, Ph.D. Henk Eijkman, Associate Professor, Ph.D. Stefan Hrastinski, Professor, Ph.D. Jianli Jiao, Assistant Professor, Ph.D. Monica Liljeström, Professor, Ph.D. Simon Lindgren, Assistant Professor, Ph.D. Ġorġ Mallia, Professor, Ph.D. Guy Merchant, Associate Professor, Ph.D. Urban Nuldén, Assistant Professor, Ph.D. Carl-Johan Orre, Assistant Professor, Ph.D. Hans Rystedt, and Associate Professor, Ph.D. Tor Söderström. We will of course also say thank you to the contributing authors in this book that in a productive way have peer-reviewed the chapters. Before giving credit to some other important persons in this process we will point out that it is our hope that this book will serve as a platform for future network building and joint research projects.

A special note of thanks is due to the staff at IGI whose support throughout the process has been most valuable. In addition we will thank the Faculty of Social Sciences, Department of Education, Umeå University, Sweden, and the Faculty of Social Sciences, Department of Education, Mid Sweden University, Sweden, for providing both of us generous opportunities for working with this book. We will also say thank you our local research groups, LICT (Learning & ICT) and HEALTH (Higher Education And Learning through Technology enHancement) and for encourage and academic support. Finally, we would like to thank our families for their love, understanding and patience throughout this book project. In Anders case his fiancée Tina Collryd and their children Neo "Yoda" Collryd and Wille "Skywalker" Collryd. For Ola his former wife Anne, and their children Joakim, Sanna, and Martin.

Anders D. Olofsson
Umeå University, Sweden

J. Ola Lindberg
Mid Sweden University, Sweden

Section 1
Aspects of the Research Field

This first section introduces the different themes of the book, and offers a solid foundation for understanding this particular field of research. It will help to frame the reading of the other chapters in the book, in specific this section includes chapters dealing with learning and teaching, educational planning and assessment, as well as educational technology and the relation to instructional design.

Chapter 1
The Influence Upon Design of Differing Conceptions of Teaching and Learning with Technology

Adrian Kirkwood
The Open University, UK

Linda Price
The Open University, UK

ABSTRACT

This chapter considers some of the theoretical foundations of teaching and learning in higher education and how these are reflected in practice. We consider how varying conceptions of teaching and learning with technology have an impact upon how teachers design teaching and learning. This chapter reviews why these variations are important and how they can affect the design of the curriculum and ultimately what and how students learn. We conclude that promoting increased use of technology does little, if anything, to improve student learning. It is only by attending to higher education teachers' conceptions of teaching and learning with technology and supporting change in this area that significant progress will be achieved. In this chapter we advocate that informed design in the use of technology is underpinned by beliefs about (conceptions of) teaching and learning with technology. To this end the chapter explores some of the theoretical underpinnings of these conceptions and argues that they are fundamental to driving well-informed practice in the use of technology to support student learning.

DOI: 10.4018/978-1-61350-080-4.ch001

INTRODUCTION AND BACKGROUND

There is much hope and promise that accompanies the use of technologies for teaching and learning in higher education, but it is challenging to consider what the best possible uses of technology might be in the design of student learning. Why is it that, in certain cases, technology supported learning is successful in actively engaging students and in improving the learning experience, while in other cases it does not? What is informing the design of successful learning experiences with technologies? We suggest that teachers in higher education need to be informed not only about the technologies available and their potential uses for teaching and learning, but also about other important factors that have considerable influence upon those processes.

University teachers' views of technology have a fundamental relationship with how they use them and what they consider to be a successful use (Kirkwood & Price, 2005). As higher education institutions strive to embrace societal changes in the use of technology and a range of other influences on how they operate, it is important to recognise what factors affect the use of technology for teaching and learning and what may be done about supporting and improving the practices of academic staff.

To date there has been an over-emphasis on technological manifestations (in other words what technologies are used in educational settings) and this has led to the neglect of pedagogical considerations (Katz, 2010; Kirkwood & Price, 2005). For example, why and how might students and teachers benefit from using technologies (Beetham & Sharpe, 2007; Conole *et al.*, 2008; Kirkwood, 2009)? Reviews of technology use in universities in Westernised countries have repeatedly revealed that, despite the widespread adoption of e-learning technologies and online learning environments, the associated *pedagogical* issues have been of secondary concern (e.g. Becker & Jokivirta, 2007; JISC/UCISA, 2003; Zemsky & Massy, 2004; Zenios *et al.*, 2004).

There is nothing novel about this perplexity. When television was a relatively new medium, McLuhan's assertion that 'the medium is the message' (1964) summarised his view that communication technologies exerted influence upon society to a greater extent through the characteristics of the media themselves than by the content they conveyed. His technologically deterministic view over-simplified the complexity of the social relationship between *medium* and *message* and with society more widely. This is particularly relevant in education, where the deterministic view suggested that media themselves had a greater influence on outcomes than the efforts of teachers and educational designers. However, it is rarely a case of medium *OR* message, but rather the interplay between the two and other factors as well.

In the 1970s Schramm reviewed several decades of educational media research and concluded that there was little evidence to suggest that any particular medium or technology could, in or of itself, account for enhancing learning outcomes. Rather, he pointed out "a common report among experimenters is that they find more variance *within* than *between* media – meaning that learning seems to be affected more by what is delivered than by the delivery system" (1977, p. 273). While Clark and his associates (see Clark, 2001) sought to identify how media contributed to education by reviewing comparative studies (that is, projects in which various media had been used to *replicate* classroom practices), other researchers focussed on the unique contributions to educational processes and outcomes made possible by different forms of representation through various media technologies (see, for example, Saloman, 1997).

The advent of the Internet and World Wide Web has not only made technologies more ubiquitous in educational contexts, but has been accompanied by the development of an expanding range of media technologies, each with its own particular characteristics and potential for educational use. While any specific technology can facilitate *and* constrain the educational activities that it makes possible, each has the potential to be used for significantly different pedagogical purposes; it is not associated with just one approach and multiple designs can be employed. As Phipps and Merisotis noted in their review of technology-enabled distance education (1999, p. 8), "many of the results seem to indicate that technology is not nearly as important as other factors, such as learning tasks, learner characteristics, student motivation, and the instructor".

Underpinning variations in the use of technology in teaching and learning is a conflation of two distinct aims:

- changes in the *means* through which university teaching happens; and
- changes in *how* university teachers teach.

The ways in which teachers in higher education conceptualise both the nature of learning technologies and the role of teaching have significant (and interrelated) impacts upon the way that they and their students are likely to make use of devices and software tools in the design of teaching and learning; that is their *approach to teaching with technology*. In our research and in reviewing the use of technologies in higher education over many years we have found that teachers and managers tend to focus primarily on technology as the means by which university teaching happens. This tends to be driven by a technological deterministic view of its use, in other words that the use of technology *in and of itself* will improve student learning. Thus the *approaches* to using technology in teaching and learning appear to be underpinned by *conceptions* about the use of technology in teaching and learning. We use 'conception' to refer to an individual's views or beliefs about a particular phenomenon or the meaning they attach to it (Kember, 1997).

We draw upon the 4P model developed by Price and Richardson (2004) to illustrate the relationships between *conceptions of and approaches to teaching and learning with technology* and more fundamental *conceptions of and approaches to teaching*. The 4P model builds upon Dunkin and Biddle's (1974) model, the original Presage-Process-Product (3P) model of Biggs (1985) and research by Prosser and Trigwell (see for example, Prosser & Trigwell, 1999). As the focus of this chapter is on conceptions of teaching and learning with technology we shall draw out this aspect of the model to illustrate relations with conceptions of teaching. Richardson (2008) has made similar connections between conceptions of teaching and conceptions of sign language interpreting for deaf students. He shows that interpreters' conceptions of interpreting influence their approaches to interpreting. This is similar to the relationship between teachers' *conceptions of teaching* and teachers' *approaches to teaching* (their practices). From our review of the literature we posit that there are similar relations between conceptions and approaches to teaching and learning with technology and with more fundamental beliefs and practices in teaching. We have attempted to show these relationships in Figure 1.

(At present some of the relationships in this model are shown as dotted lines as more research is required to establish their causality and direction).

In the following section we will explore variations in the conceptions of teaching with technology and the relationship with approaches to teaching with technology. In a subsequent section we will consider variations in the conceptions of teaching held by academics and the impact they have upon the approaches to teaching adopted and, consequently upon student learning.

Figure 1. Relationships between academics' conceptions, approaches and teaching practices

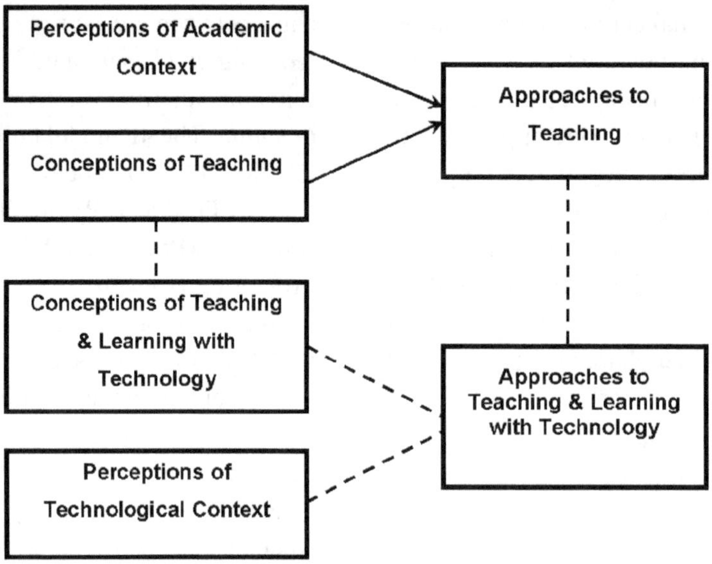

WHAT PERCEPTIONS DO TEACHERS HAVE OF TECHNOLOGY?

Here we use 'perception' to refer to the awareness that people have of a phenomenon; their interpretation of what they experience. It can be difficult to discern what perceptions people hold about technology without careful investigation. However, the ways in which people talk about devices and the ways in which they use them may reflect the ways in which they think about and perceive them and the context of use. In Figure 1 we have illustrated this awareness about technology as 'perceptions of the technological context'. We will start by looking at the terms used to describe technologies before moving on to consider the implications for how technologies are used.

How are Technologies and Tools Described: What's in a Name?

In some parts of the world there is a device known as a *cellular phone*, while in other countries the same device is known as a *mobile phone*. It is one of the most ubiquitous digital technologies in the world and has achieved high levels of access in both developed and developing nations. So, is there any significance to the fact that different names have been ascribed to the same device? We believe there is and we consider this to be illustrative of the technological context.

The coining of the term *cellular phone* primarily focuses on the technical characteristics that enable the device to work: messages are relayed over a cellular network that enables wireless coverage to be achieved over a wide geographical area. In contrast, the name *mobile phone* focuses on the manner in which people can use the device for communication; in other words how humans have appropriated the device to allow them to communicate with others wherever they happen to be located. People who use one (or more) of these devices are much more likely to be aware of the fact that they can exploit its functions almost anywhere they happen to be situated (in other words a user-led focus), rather than understanding the technical means by which communication is made possible (that is, a technology-led focus). We are not suggesting that the ways in which cellular/mobile phones are used by people are shaped by the term used to describe that particular technology, but we do feel that the original naming provides insights into the differing conceptions of the technical developers.

Throughout the educational world the term *technology enhanced learning* is used extensively: in strategy and policy documents, in institutional promotional outputs as well as in the research and evaluation literature. It is the latest in a variety of terms that have been used to describe the application of information and communication technologies to teaching and learning. Other terms include *Computer-assisted learning*, *e-Learning*, *Networked learning*, *Online learning*, *Telelearning, and Web-based learning.* In other words, the particular term used reflects perceptions of the technological context. Each term has been applied in an imprecise way to describe a diverse range of educational activities and imply a technology-led rather than a user-led focus. For example, the term *networked learning* has sometimes been used to refer to uses of technology to enable communication between geographically distributed learners; in other contexts the term refers to networks of learners working together on collaborative learning activities (Steeples & Jones, 2002). Any reference to the intended users is derived indirectly through the ubiquitous use of the word 'learning'. More often than not, however, it is 'teaching' rather than 'learning' that is the focal point of the educational activity being described.

Unlike the other terms, *technology enhanced learning* implies a value judgement: 'enhanced' suggests that something is improved or superior in some way. However, it is rare to find explicit statements about what the term is actually supposed to mean. How does technology *enhance* learning – what is the 'value added'? What *learning* is being enhanced and in what ways – quantitative and/or qualitative? Is there a widely shared view of what constitutes *learning* in higher education and how it can be *enhanced*? This lack of precision and clarity about the application of technology to educational processes suggests that technology-led conceptions are predominant among higher education teachers in the design and implementation of new forms of academic practice. The implications of this are considered next.

Technology-Led and User-Led Conceptions: Teaching and Learning with Technology

When teachers in higher education consider the ways in which they might exploit digital technologies and tools in designing teaching and learning, some adopt a *technology-led conception*: "What can I use this technology or tool for?" Others may adopt a *user-led conception*: "How can I enable my students to achieve the learning that is necessary?" Those who espouse a *technology-led conception* are likely to think about the optimum technical affordances of any particular technology or tool and assume that use of that particular device or tool will *in itself* bring about the desired behaviours and outcomes in learners. It is not hard to find examples of teachers making statements of this kind: 'The use of computer-mediated communication (or a social networking site) will engage students in collaborative working fostering the development of a learning community'. This represents a technologically deterministic conception of the educational process (that is, the idea that technological developments are the central determinants of social change rather than social contexts shaping the ways in which technological tools are used). Very often it results in disappointment for both teachers and their students (Kirkwood, 2009).

In contrast, where teachers exhibit a *user-led conception* their primary concern is with the activities that they and their students have to do to enable the achievement of valued outcomes from learning through the use of digital devices or tools. How best can they design activities for learning that allow their students to engage with technologies or tools to work in appropriate ways towards significant goals?

Many assertions have been made about the disruptive (Blin & Munro, 2008) or transformative (Garrison & Anderson, 2000; Garrison & Kanuka, 2004) potential of technology in relation to teaching and learning practices in higher education. Technologies are often described by enthusiasts seeking to foster educational reforms as catalysts that contribute to radical changes being brought about in university practices and processes: changes not only in the manner in which teaching and learning take place, but also in the nature of the students' engagement and learning. Some descriptions of the *potential* for technologies to help foster active student learning or promote a constructivist approach to educational activities accentuate the role of technology in bringing about such changes, while under-emphasising the responsibility of the teacher in designing appropriate tasks or processes to enable the desired outcomes to be achieved.

In the following sections we shall explore the first of two aspects of university teachers' conceptions of, and relationships with, technologies for teaching and learning: *agency* and *control.*

WHERE DOES AGENCY RESIDE?

The *Oxford English Dictionary* defines the term *agent* as "a person or thing that takes an active role or produces a specified effect" and the associated term *agency* as an "action or intervention producing a particular effect". We think that it is important to consider *who* or *what* takes the active role when teaching innovations are introduced. For more than 20 years much has been written about the potential for technologies to transform educational practices, not only in higher education and not only in developed countries (for example, see http://www.tessafrica.net/). Very often, the potential agent for change is assumed to be the technology itself (device and/or software); if teachers get their students to use a particular technology, then certain educational outcomes will follow. This is a form of 'technological determinism'. Sometimes *technology as agent* is explicit within statements about changes in teaching and learning practices; more often it is implicit within statements that are clearly 'technology-led'. Here are some examples from the web sites of companies or organisations that offer technologies for use in universities:

- At Elluminate, we unify your enterprise technologies (video and web conferencing, instant messaging, phone, learning and content management systems, social networks, and more) *to make learning and collaboration happen better, faster, and more efficiently*. (http://www.elluminate.com/) [Italics added]
- Built by educators for educators, Sakai *provides a student-centered platform* for learning that can *transform the educational experience*. Its customizable and easy to use interface enables effective and efficient development, delivery and management of courses, course content, and collaborative efforts. (http://sakaiproject.org/using-sakai) [Italics added]

In the research literature it is not uncommon to find expressions of *technology as agent.* For example, one study undertaken with teaching staff in a North American university (Ajjan & Hartshorne, 2008, p. 79) provided evidence that most [teachers in that university] feel that integrating Web 2.0 technologies such as blogs and wikis into the classroom learning environment can be effective at increasing students' satisfaction with the course, improve their learning and their writing ability, and increase student interaction with other students and [teaching staff]; thus changing the students' role from passive to active learners, allowing them to better create and retain knowledge.

Less frequently is it recognised that the main agent for change is the teacher, through what they are trying to achieve by using a technological tool. In contrast with the statements from Elluminate and Sakai above, the developers of Moodle™ (an open source course management system) are aware that the teachers who use that system can employ the component tools and facilities in differing ways:

Many of our users love to use the activity modules (such as forums, databases and wikis) to build richly collaborative communities of learning around their subject matter (in the social constructionist tradition), while others prefer to use Moodle as a way to deliver content to students (such as standard SCORM packages) and assess learning using assignments or quizzes. (From the Moodle™ website: http://moodle.org/about/).

This statement emphasises the fact that technology can be used in different ways for a variety of educational purposes and that the *agent* is the academic as user and creator of opportunities in designing teaching and learning.

The next illustration is drawn from outside the higher education sector. Within the schools sector in Western countries there has been considerable expenditure in recent years on the acquisition of digital interactive whiteboards for classroom use. But as Haldane (2007) has pointed out, it is the teacher rather than the technology that is the agent:

Of course, the digital whiteboard in itself is not and cannot be 'interactive'; it is merely a medium through which interactivity may, to a greater or lesser extent, be afforded. It is the user of the board who chooses whether or not to take full advantage of the digital whiteboard's interactive potential. The digital board simply provides an opportunity for interactivity to occur; it is a medium, a mere carrier of information and messages, not the creator of the messages or the one to decide how the messages will be conveyed (pp. 259–259).

We argue that the agent is the teacher rather than the technology and that "although ICT can *enable* new forms of teaching and learning to take place, they cannot *ensure* that effective and appropriate learning outcomes are achieved" (Kirkwood & Price, 2005, p. 260). In other words, the use of technologies for teaching does not *in and of itself* lead to improved educational practices. What really matters is the manner in which teachers – as *agents* – have chosen to design teaching and learning with technology, using tools as appropriate to achieve the outcomes that are significant and valued. We will look at the impact of these differing views and conceptions by contrasting some examples of technologies that are used in various ways within higher education.

RELATIONSHIPS BETWEEN CONCEPTIONS OF AND APPROACHES TO TEACHING AND LEARNING WITH TECHNOLOGY

We illustrated in Figure 1 how university teachers' *conceptions* of teaching and learning with technology relate to their *approaches* to teaching and learning with technology. In the following sections we draw upon two examples of technology being used in differing ways to demonstrate variations in design and impact.

Example 1: Podcasting: An Educational Innovation?

For many years radio and recorded audio have been used to reach people learning outside educational institutions (Buck, 2006; Schramm, 1977). Over recent decades, the development of new means of delivering audio recordings (for example from records, cassette tapes, audio CDs to iPods/MP3 players) has given learners much greater control over *where*, *when* and *how* they listen to audio resources. In turn, the increased control that learners can exercise over how they chose to listen has enabled those creating audio resources for learners to change the format and presentation style to exploit those characteristics. So audio sequences no longer need to resemble a linear talk or lecture, but can, for example, consist of several separate sections interspersed with appropriate activities for the learner to undertake or perhaps present primary source material or an audio 'case study' for learners to interpret or analyse using knowledge and skills they have acquired in other aspects of their studies. Educational audio sequences can be created in which the voice of the 'teacher' is implicit rather than explicit; in fact, it might not be heard at all. Within the context of open and distance learning worldwide, considerable expertise has been developed in the preparation of audio resources that actively engage learners and contribute to them feeling connected to their teachers, even when separated by time and location (e.g. Rowntree, 1994; Thomas, 2001).

Digitisation has not only made it easier to distribute and listen to audio resources across a range of educational contexts, it has also enabled individuals to cheaply and easily record and edit their own audio files. Basically, *podcasting* refers to the on-line distribution of audio files (sometimes enhanced with visuals) to which users can listen via a desktop or laptop computer or a portable digital audio device (iPod or mp3 player). The term *podcast* was introduced in 2004 to indicate the combination of 'broadcast' and 'iPod' (a portable, digital audio playback device). Podcasting brought the use of audio resources to the wider higher education community. Duke University in the USA distributed iPods to over 1600 entering first-year students in 2004 and encouraged teaching staff to make their lectures available as podcasts (Duke University, 2005). Other universities tried similar schemes and with the launch of sites such as Apple's iTunes U ("Learn anything, anytime, anywhere," http://www.apple.com/education/itunes-u/) no self respecting western university wants to be without a podcasting presence, even if their students are predominantly on-campus.

However, the vast majority of 'podcasts' available from sites such as iTunes U or from an institutional Learning Management System (LMS) or Virtual Learning Environment (VLE) take the form of recorded lectures or presentations – teacher-led didactic presentations (see Rossell-Aguilar, 2007). It is difficult to discern whether or not the academics responsible for creating these audio recordings have been informed by pedagogical approaches for promoting active learning.

Differing Ways of Conceptualising Educational Audio

The euphoria that accompanies the commercial launch of any new technological device or software tool is of great interest to technophiles, or what Rogers (1995) has referred to as *Innovators* and *Early Adopters*. However, enthusiasm with the novelty and potential of new devices and tools seems to induce amnesia among educational managers and teachers about existing research and evaluations of effective educational use of pre-existing media (e.g. Edirisingha *et al.*, 2010; Kirkwood & Price, 2005). Over the last 5 years, the educational podcasting literature has tended to be dominated by technology enthusiasts and new converts to the potential use of audio in university teaching, primarily for making available recorded lectures or supplementary/revision talks. Very often the focus has been technological, with an emphasis on how audio files are distributed and can potentially be accessed in a variety of locations and circumstances. Much is made of 'mobile learning' and 'portability', while evidence from studies of actual student use indicates that a large proportion of campus-based students do not listen to these resources while on the move (Evans, 2008; Lonn & Teasley, 2009; Walls *et al*, 2010). Similarly, while people with a technology-led conception stress the importance of automated syndication (RSS) that distinguishes podcasts from mere audio files/downloads, it is difficult to find evidence that this feature is considered important by students.

The technology-led focus of podcasting (foregrounding aspects of production, distribution and replay) masks consideration of the content or message conveyed and the educational purpose(s) being served. There is relatively little in the literature that:

- demonstrate a user-led conception,
- report on student-generated audio material created for the benefit of either their peers or their teachers (Lazzari, 2009; Lee, McLoughlin & Chan, 2008; Middleton, 2009), or,
- consider audio to provide personalised feedback to students on their assignments (e.g. Merry & Orsmond, 2008).

Some published reports discuss appropriate pedagogies for promoting active learning (see examples on students' digital storytelling) and supporting collaborative and reflective learning in Salmon and Edirisingha (2008). Newton and Middleton (2009) caution that "understanding educational podcasting as a mechanism for adding new content channels to a teaching system, established many centuries ago, neglects the real opportunity." (p. 238)

These relatively recent studies have concentrated on the new educational opportunities that podcasting offers to university teachers keen to transform the student learning experience; the "real opportunity" to which Newton and Middleton refer. Primarily, these innovations are less about the technological aspects involved and more about engaging students in activities that have been designed to be learner-centred to a much greater extent (in other words, are user-led). In general, digital technologies can be utilised for a range of broad educational purposes. Kirkwood (2009) suggests that technologies for teaching and learning have very often been adopted to enable one or more of these functions:

- *Presentation*: making materials and resources (text, data, sounds, still and moving images, etc.) available for students to refer to, either at predetermined times or 'on demand',
- *Interaction*: enabling learners to actively engage with resources, to manipulate or interrogate information or data, etc,
- *Dialogue:* facilitating communication between teachers and learners or between peers for discussion, co-operation, collaboration, etc,
- *Generative activity*: enabling learners to record, create, assemble, store and retrieve items (text, data, images, etc.) in response to learning activities or assignments and to evidence their experiences and capabilities. (p. 108)

Although podcasting is essentially a one-way medium unable to support true *dialogue*, there is great potential for audio or video podcasts to contribute not only to the *presentation* of information, but also to promoting *interaction* and *generative activities*. Unfortunately, the technology-led conceptions that many teachers exhibit, confine them to perceiving podcasts as being primarily about replicating or augmenting their predominantly presentational approach to teaching.

Example 2: Communication and Collaboration: What Are They For?

Interpersonal communication is an essential element of university learning and it takes place in a variety of contexts, both formal and informal, and fulfils a number of different purposes. It might involve just two people or many and can engender the academic and social integration that is important for student retention (Tinto, 1997). The main educational intention of a dialogue might be *convergent* (for example when a learner asks their teacher – or fellow students – to explain or clarify something they have misunderstood) or *divergent* (as when learners compare, discuss or debate their different perspectives or experiences relating to a particular event, concept, principle or theory). The tutorial or small group discussion has been a key element of university education for many years, although the roles of the participants and the types of interaction that take place need to be carefully handled to optimise effective outcomes (e.g. Abercrombie, 1974; Anderson, 2005; Northedge, 2003).

With the increased use of blended learning and learning environments in campus-based universities, online communication has become a feature of many programmes throughout higher education. The advent of new interactive technologies enable universities to overcome the lack of (or reduced) direct teacher-student and student-student communication that exist in supporting learners who may study in a remote or blended learning context. Considerable research has explored the *potential* educational benefits of online communication as a means to provide more personalised support (Mason & Kaye, 1989; Budman, 2000; Houston, 2008; Joinson, 2003, 2005; McKenna, Green, & Gleason, 2002; Parks & Floyd, 1996; Walther, 1992). This illustrates the flexibility of technology in supporting online learning while increasing contextuality for learners (Koole, McQuilkin & Ally, 2010).

Many terms have been used to refer to text-based, asynchronous communication between learners and with their teachers: computer mediated communication, asynchronous conferencing, bulletin boards, discussion boards, forums, online discussion groups, and threaded discussions. Some of these emphasise the means by which communication is enabled (a technology-led conception), while others highlight the purpose of the communication (a user-led conception). While campus-based students might have ample opportunities to engage in interpersonal communication – both formal and informal – with their teachers and fellow students, there is an increasing realisation that asynchronous text-based communication which is not transient, but extended over a period of time can have a number of advantages. For example

- Participants can contribute 'anytime and anywhere', within the constraints of the particular system used.
- There is time for individuals to consider their question/contribution/response and to review their posting before it is communicated to the recipient(s).
- It enables those students who are less likely to speak in class to contribute.
- A record of the interactions or discussion is retained within the system that can be accessed for review, analysis and future reference.

However, there are differing understandings and views held by both teachers and students in higher education about the role of communication and collaboration (Ellis & Calvo, 2006; Ellis, Goodyear, Prosser & O'Hara, 2006). These give rise to differing expectations among learners and variability in the extent and value of contributions to such events. When communication and collaboration take place online, learners and teachers lack the cues that are often so valuable in face-to-face contexts (Price, Richardson, & Jelfs, 2007).

Differing Ways of Conceptualising Online Communication

In their review of literature about social interaction in computer supported collaborative learning environments, Kreijns, Kirschner & Jochems (2003) identified a common pitfall:

A majority of educators – consciously or unconsciously – take social interaction for granted. They think that because in face-to-face learning groups social interaction is 'easy' to achieve if not already there, the same patterns will be encountered in distributed learning groups. (p. 340)

Concerns have been expressed, both in campus-based and distance-learning contexts, about how best to encourage learner participation in online discussions. A recent review (Hrastinski, 2008) identified six differing conceptions of 'online learner participation' within 36 research articles. The researchers had looked for different forms of learner activity as evidence of 'online participation'. These ranged from simple criteria such as 'Participation as accessing e-learning environments' and 'Participation as writing' to more complex criteria reflecting the purpose of the participation:

It was found that research is dominated by low-level conceptions of online participation, which relies on frequency counts as measures of participation. However, some researchers aim to study more complex dimensions of participation, such as whether participants feel they are taking part and are engaged in dialogues, reflected by using a combination of perceived and actual measures of participation. (p. 1761)

The educational purpose of online communication and collaboration appears to be of secondary importance to educators with a technology-led conception. Sometimes online communication has been added to existing distance-learning courses with the technology-led expectation that extensive discussion would result, and that 'learning communities' would develop: in practice, the anticipated outcomes often fail to be realised (Erlich, Erlich-Philip & Gal-Ezer, 2005; Fung 2004).

When the operation of online communication or collaboration is informed by a user-led conception of technology use, ample consideration will be given to the purpose(s) to be achieved and to ensuring that learners understand the individual and collective benefits that can be achieved through a reasonable level of participation. Further, the assessment criteria will reflect an appropriate weighting for both the process and the product for the activity (Russell, Elton, Swinglehurst & Greenhalgh, 2006).

WHO HAS CONTROL IN EDUCATIONAL TRANSACTIONS?

In an earlier section we examined *agency* as the first of two highly significant aspects of university teachers' conceptions of, and relationships with, technologies for teaching and learning. This section we turn our attention to *control* in educational processes and to what conceptions teachers in higher education hold about teaching and learning.

University models of teaching are rooted in historical models prevalent in the 1920s in Westernised school systems. These were not underpinned by research into how people learned, but by assumptions about learning based around transferring collections of facts and procedures from the teacher to the learner (Sawyer, 2006), which Papert (1993) characterised as *instructionist* approaches to learning.

Failures in the instructivist approach to education are characterised by differences between what is 'taught' by teachers and what is 'learned' by students (Snyder, 1971). The memorisation of facts and figures is ill-matched to the needs of a knowledge-based economy (Bereiter, 2002; Hargreaves, 2003), which requires learners to act as professionals, able to construct new knowledge and ideas and to take responsibility for their own continual learning during their lifetime (Sawyer, 2006; Sharples, 2000). By the 1980s it became recognised that higher education learners could generalise their learning and apply it to a greater range of contexts when they engaged in learning the concepts rather than memorising facts and procedures (Entwistle & Ramsden, 1983; Marton & Säljö, 1976; Sawyer, 2006; Richardson, 2000). The challenge for learners has shifted from being able to remember and repeat information, to being able to find it and use it appropriately (Bransford, Brown, & Cocking, 2000), and our goal as educators is to support them in that task. Unfortunately, learning in higher education is rarely evaluated in terms of qualitative changes in individual learners.

For many decades educators such as Malcolm Knowles (1975, 1990) argued that most of the learning activities undertaken by adults are conducted in an independent, self-directed manner. The learner takes responsibility for facilitating the learning process, from start to finish. Knowles identified five important steps, although these do not necessarily progress in a neat, linear way. The learner:

- Diagnoses their learning needs
- Formulates learning needs
- Identifies human and material resources for learning
- Chooses and implements appropriate learning strategies
- Evaluates learning outcomes.

Higher education students need to become increasingly self-directed in their learning in preparation for their future personal, social and work-related lives. Higher education processes require deliberate opportunities for the promotion of self-direction and independence in learners. Hence, learners should be empowered to take responsibility for decisions relating to their learning; including acquiring appropriate resources and determining that their own learning outcomes have been met. Boud (2000) argues that "in order for students to become effective lifelong learners, they need also to be prepared to undertake assessment of the learning tasks they face throughout their lives" (p. 152) and that the existing assessment practices in most educational institutions do little to prepare learners for this. University education should prepare students to fully participate within a 'community of practice' related to their profession or discipline area (Lave & Wenger, 1991).

This has prompted a shift towards the greater use of learner-centred approaches to teaching and expanding the role of constructivism (including social constructivism) (Bruner, 1990). However, many teachers are uncomfortable about developments that would change their role from being *the sage on the stage* to the *guide on the side*. These are interpreted as stripping academics of the control and authority they have traditionally enjoyed and that the balance of power in relationships with their students would shift away from them (Eynon, 2008; Katz, 2010). It is possible that the 'threat' is perceived as being much more detrimental than it actually is, due to their lack of understanding of what is involved in approaches that are alternative to traditional didactic teaching. Hence in order to resist what might be perceived as an eroding of the academic role, transmissive approaches to teaching are more dominant, allowing academics to retain control.

Most of the decisions about *what, where, when* and *how* students undertake their studies are controlled by teaching staff of the institution and this has significant impact upon the design of the curriculum. Even work undertaken during 'independent' or 'private study' time is predominantly directed towards tasks or activities that have been determined by the teachers, who also formulate the means by which an assessment of the learning achieved will be made. Although student learning is ultimate aim, a large proportion of academic practices in higher education remain transmissive and teacher-centred. This also impacts upon technology use, as providing added freedom to the student in terms of access to and use of technology further challenges their position by going beyond their sphere of control.

What Conceptions do Higher Education Teachers Have of Teaching and Learning?

The teaching approaches of academics in higher education and their underlying conceptions and models of the teaching process have been the subject of considerable investigation (Kember, 1997; Kember & Kwan, 2000; Lindblom-Ylänne *et al.*, 2006; Trigwell *et al.*, 1999). Teaching tends to be conceptualised in a range of ways that can be differentiated in terms of two broad categories; either as the *transmission of knowledge* or as the *facilitation of learning*. Those teachers who hold the first of these conceptions concentrate on conveying knowledge for students to assimilate and absorb. Their teaching practices emphasise presentational methods that provide students with the necessary knowledge, skills and procedures. In contrast, teachers who conceptualise teaching as the facilitation of learning are much more likely to pay attention to learners' needs, thus helping develop their own conceptions, understanding of the subject, and their capacity to become autonomous and self-directed. Figure 1 illustrates this relationship between teachers' *conception of teaching* and their *approach to teaching*.

While digital technologies can be used in a variety of different ways, more often than not higher education teachers use them to support or reinforce their particular conception of teaching (Gonzalez, 2009). However, contrary to the views expressed by some educational policy makers, when technology is used to mediate teaching and learning practices it does not, *in itself*, change the underlying model of teaching. For example, delivering a lecture using PowerPoint or a video-enhanced podcast does not make it anything other than a lecture – often a *transmissive* pedagogy. It might make it accessible to learners in varying locations and at different times, but fundamentally it remains a lecture. Similarly, on-line discussion within a course is unlikely to promote co-operative or collaborative working, if the teaching is predominantly transmissive in its approach and only the products of individual students is assessed. Only when existing educational beliefs and practices are questioned and re-assessed is there the potential for a teacher's use of technology to reflect a more transformative stance.

CHANGES IN HIGHER EDUCATION: THE CONFLATING AND CONFOUNDING OF ISSUES

Despite much talk about the 'transformative' or 'disruptive' potential of technologies for teaching and learning, there is little evidence of university teachers' practices being changed greatly by the use of technologies – in fact, non-transformation (Roberts, 2003; Blin & Munro, 2008) might be more commonly found (Price *et al.*, 2007). Even though higher education institutions have expended enormous amounts on the introduction of learning environments and content management systems, there has been relatively little change in the educational methods and processes. Content-based resources predominate on many systems and "activities that demand collaboration or reflection ... are used less frequently than those activities that replicate face-to-face teaching" (Blin & Monroe, 2008, p. 488).

In contrast, Hiltz and Turoff (2005, p. 60) claim that the evolution of online learning is linked to a transformation in higher education. They suggest that:

We are in the process of moving:

- From: face-to-face courses using objectivist, teacher-centred pedagogy, and offered by tens of thousands of local, regional, and national universities;
- To: online and hybrid courses using digital technologies to support constructivist, collaborative, student-centred pedagogy, offered by a few hundred "mega-universities" that operate on a global scale.

This line of thought confounds at least three different types of change in higher education and implies that each is bound up with the others. The first type of change concerns the nature of knowledge, teaching and learning processes (epistemology, learning and pedagogy). Another type of change refers to the means by which the teaching and learning take place (face-to-face or technology mediated). The third type of change refers to the organisational structure for higher education (an issue that we do not address in this chapter). These first two changes are often conflated in higher education policy documents and in accounts of innovations aimed at changing teaching and learning in universities. However, we suggest that these changes are *not* inextricably linked: it is quite possible for changes to take place in one area (in other words the means by which teaching and learning take place) without being accompanied by any significant change in another area (the approach to teaching and learning and associated pedagogy).

The introduction of technologies in the design of university teaching and learning has often been accompanied by rhetoric of increasing *learner engagement*, *active learning* and of more *learner-centred* approaches. But any review of how technologies are actually used in higher education reveals that, more often than not, they supplement or replace prevalent didactic teaching practices (for example lectures). *Technology-enhanced* usually means providing more teaching, often intended to compensate for reduced contact time or larger class sizes. Less commonly does *technology-enhanced* signify that the curriculum and teaching approach has been redesigned to increase learner's opportunities to achieve greater 'self direction' by exercising more control over their learning activities.

Katz (2010) has suggested that teaching and learning in higher education will change as the result of a transition following an innovative shock or disturbance. While in the first phase technologies were predominantly used as instruments or tools to supplement existing practices, the second phase will be one in which "some people cease to use the [technology] as a tool in support of historically defined approaches and begin to reconsider the approaches themselves" (p. 44). In contrast, we have argued in this chapter that technologies are much more likely to enhance the learning experience when higher education teachers do not accept a technologically deterministic view of the process. Instead they need to recognise the centrality of their role in devising and designing activities to promote learning and to use technologies in ways that enable students to achieve desired educational ends. Further, in order to better serve the needs of the current generation of learners their pedagogic practices need to be reconsidered so that they actively *promote learning* in their students, particularly in relation to the use of technology.

FURTHER RESEARCH DIRECTIONS

Most of the research that has been conducted into conceptions of teaching and approaches to teaching of university teachers has not specifically considered these in relation to technology use and their design of the curriculum (for an exception, see Bain & McNaught, 2006). We have illustrated in our review of the literature that there are grounds for arguing *that conceptions of teaching and learning with technology* are related to *approaches to teaching and learning with technology* and that these are influenced by *perceptions of the technological context*. We feel that this omission is in need of attention as it influences and informs the design of the learning. Much of the research into technology use in education is under-theorised and is evaluated in terms of itself rather than in relation to pre-existing research teaching and learning. In particular it warrants an examination of teachers' conceptions of teaching and learning with technology in order to understand the variation and how these might be related to more fundamental conceptions of teaching. This encompasses an examination of approaches to teaching and learning with technology and with more fundamental approaches to teaching. The role of context in influencing perceptions of technology is also necessary. Designs for the use of learning technologies need to take account not only of *institutional* contexts (including the specific characteristics of learning activities, courses, disciplines, departments, etc.), but also the wider contexts associated with *individual learners* in our 'networked' world (Luckin, 2010). Furthering our understanding of these complex relationships is essential if the potential of teaching and learning with technology is to be realised.

CONCLUSION

Conceptions of teaching and learning with technology in higher education tend to focus on *improving the means through which teaching happens*; these are not focused on student learning and enhancements are *process-driven* as opposed to *learner-driven*. In comparison, conceptions of teaching and learning with technology that are focused upon *improving how university teachers teach* are more likely to be underpinned by pedagogical considerations of how such changes enhance student learning. If we are going to employ technology in a way that enhances student learning, then understanding the variations in conceptions is fundamental to appreciating how we might effect change and how we better design higher education.

Future development for academics needs to consider their underpinning beliefs about teaching and learning using technology and, more fundamentally, their conceptions about teaching. This is important in order to devise strategies that support staff in the difficult task of changing entrenched views toward using technology so that they make better-informed decisions when designing learning activities. For many teachers this would mean a transition from teacher-centred to learner-centred pedagogies and from technology-led to user-led conceptions of technology.

REFERENCES

Abercrombie, M. L. J. (1974). *Aims and techniques of group teaching*. Guildford, UK: Society for Research into Higher Education.

Ajjan, H., & Hartshorne, R. (2008). Investigating faculty decisions to adopt Web 2.0 technologies: Theory and empirical tests. *The Internet and Higher Education, 11*(1), 71–80. doi:10.1016/j.iheduc.2008.05.002

Anderson, C. (2005). Enabling and shaping understanding through tutorials. In F. Marton, D. Hounsell, & N. Entwistle (Eds.), *The experience of learning: Implications for teaching and studying in higher education* (3rd ed., pp. 184-197). Edinburgh, UK: University of Edinburgh, Centre for Teaching, Learning and Assessment. Retrieved July 8, 2010, from http://www.tla.ed.ac.uk/ resources/ ExperienceOfLearning/ EoL12.pdf

Bain, J. D., & McNaught, C. (2006). How academics use technology in teaching and learning: Understanding the relationship between beliefs and practice. *Journal of Computer Assisted Learning, 22*(3), 99–113. doi:10.1111/j.1365-2729.2006.00163.x

Becker, R., & Jokivirta, L. (2007). *Online learning in universities: Selected data from the 2006 observatory survey*. A report from the Observatory on borderless higher education, London. Retrieved July 8, 2010, from http://www.obhe.ac.uk/ documents/ view_details?id=15

Beetham, H., & Sharpe, R. (Eds.). (2007). *Rethinking pedagogy for a digital age: Designing and delivering e-learning*. Abingdon, UK: Routledge.

Bereiter, C. (2002). *Education and mind in the knowledge age*. Mahwah, NJ: L. Erlbaum.

Biggs, J. (1985). The role of metalearning in study processes. *The British Journal of Educational Psychology, 55*, 185–212. doi:10.1111/j.2044-8279.1985.tb02625.x

Blin, F., & Munro, M. (2008). Why hasn't technology disrupted academics' teaching practices? Understanding resistance to change through the lens of activity theory. *Computers & Education, 50*(2), 475–490. doi:10.1016/j.compedu.2007.09.017

Boud, D. (2000). Sustainable assessment: Rethinking assessment for the learning society. *Studies in Continuing Education, 22*(2), 151–167. doi:10.1080/713695728

Bransford, J., Brown, A., & Cocking, R. (Eds.). (2000). *How people learn: Brain, mind, experience, and school*. Washington, DC: National Academy Press.

Bruner, J. (1990). *Acts of meaning*. Cambridge, MA: Harvard University Press.

Buck, G. H. (2006). The first wave: The beginnings of radio in Canadian distance education. *Journal of Distance Education, 21*(1), 75–88.

Budman, S. (2000). Behavioral health care dot-com and beyond: Computer-mediated communications in mental health and substance abuse treatments. *The American Psychologist, 55*, 1290–1300. doi:10.1037/0003-066X.55.11.1290

Clark, R. E. (Ed.). (2001). *Learning from media*. Greenwich, CT: Information Age Publishing.

Conole, G., de Laat, M., Dillon, T., & Darby, J. (2008). Disruptive technologies, pedagogical innovation: What's new? Findings from an in-depth study of students' use and perception of technology. *Computers & Education, 50*(2), 511–524. doi:10.1016/j.compedu.2007.09.009

Duke University. (2005). *Duke University iPod first-year experience: Final evaluation report*. Retrieved July 8, 2010, from http://cit.duke.edu/pdf/ reports/ ipod_initiative_04_05.pdf

Dunkin, M., & Biddle, B. (1974). *The study of teaching*. New York, NY: Holt, Rinehart and Winston.

Edirisingha, P., Hawkridge, D., & Fothergill, J. (2010). A renaissance of audio: Podcasting approaches for learning on campus and beyond. *The European Journal of Open, Distance and E-Learning*. Retrieved July 8, 2010, from http:// www.eurodl.org/ ?article=393

Ellis, R. A., & Calvo, R. A. (2006). Discontinuities in university student experiences of learning through discussions. *British Journal of Educational Technology, 37*(1), 55–68. doi:10.1111/j.1467-8535.2005.00519.x

Ellis, R. A., Goodyear, P., Prosser, M., & O'Hara, A. (2006). How and what university students learn through online and face-to-face discussion: Conceptions, intentions and approaches. *Journal of Computer Assisted Learning, 22*(4), 244–256. doi:10.1111/j.1365-2729.2006.00173.x

Entwistle, N., & Ramsden, P. (1983). *Understanding student learning*. London, UK & Canberra, Australia: Croom Helm.

Erlich, Z., Erlich-Philip, I., & Gal-Ezer, J. (2005). Skills required for participating in CMC courses: An empirical study. *Computers & Education, 44*(4), 477–487. doi:10.1016/j.compedu.2004.04.010

Evans, C. (2008). The effectiveness of m-learning in the form of podcast revision lectures in higher education. *Computers & Education, 50*(2), 491–498. doi:10.1016/j.compedu.2007.09.016

Eynon, R. (2008). The use of the World Wide Web in learning and teaching in higher education: Reality and rhetoric. *Innovations in Education and Teaching International, 45*(1), 15–23. doi:10.1080/14703290701757401

Fung, Y. H. (2004). Collaborative online learning: Interaction patterns and limiting factors. *Open Learning, 19*(2), 135–149. doi:10.1080/0268051042000224743

Garrison, D. R., & Kanuka, H. (2004). Blended learning: Uncovering the transformative potential in higher education. *The Internet and Higher Education*, *7*(1), 95–105. doi:10.1016/j.iheduc.2004.02.001

Garrison, R., & Anderson, T. (2000). Transforming and enhancing university teaching: Stronger and weaker technological influences. In Evans, T., & Nation, D. (Eds.), *Changing university teaching* (pp. 24–33). London, UK: Kogan Page.

Gonzalez, C. (2009). Conceptions of, and approaches to, teaching online: A study of lecturers teaching postgraduate distance courses. *Higher Education*, *57*(3), 299–314. doi:10.1007/s10734-008-9145-1

Haldane, M. (2007). Interactivity and the digital whiteboard: Weaving the fabric of learning. *Learning, Media and Technology*, *32*(3), 257–270. doi:10.1080/17439880701511107

Hargreaves, A. (2003). *Teaching in the knowledge society: education in the age of insecurity*. New York, NY: Teachers College Press.

Hiltz, S. R., & Turoff, M. (2005). Education goes digital: The evolution of online learning and the revolution in higher education. *Communications of the ACM*, *48*(10), 59–64. doi:10.1145/1089107.1089139

Houston, M. (2008). Tracking transition: Issues in asynchronous e-mail interviewing. *Qualitative Social Research*, *9*, 55.

Hrastinski, S. (2008). What is online learner participation? A literature review. *Computers & Education*, *51*(4), 1755–1765. doi:10.1016/j.compedu.2008.05.005

Joinson, A. (2003). *Understanding the psychology of internet behavior: Virtual worlds, real lives*. Basingstoke, UK: Palgrave Macmillan.

Joinson, A. (2005). Internet behavior and the design of virtual methods. In Hine, C. (Ed.), *Virtual methods: Issues in social research on the internet* (pp. 21–34). Oxford, UK: Berg.

Joint Information Systems Committee (JISC) and the Universities and Colleges Information Systems Association. (UCISA). (2003). *Managed learning environment activity in further and higher education in the UK*. Retrieved July 9, 2010, from http://www.jisc.ac.uk/ uploaded_documents/mle-study-final-report.pdf

Katz, R. (2010). Scholars, scholarship, and the scholarly enterprise in the digital age. *Educause Review, 45*(2). Retrieved July 4, 2010, from http://www.educause.edu/ EDUCAUSE+Review/EDUCAUSEReviewMagazineVolume45/ ScholarsScholarshipandtheSchol/202341

Kember, D. (1997). A reconceptualisation of the research into university academics' conceptions of teaching. *Learning and Instruction*, *7*(3), 255–275. doi:10.1016/S0959-4752(96)00028-X

Kember, D., & Kwan, K.-P. (2000). Lecturers' approaches to teaching and their relationship to conceptions of good teaching. *Instructional Science*, *28*(5), 469–490. doi:10.1023/A:1026569608656

Kirkwood, A. (2009). E-learning: You don't always get what you hope for. *Technology, Pedagogy and Education*, *18*(2), 107–121. doi:10.1080/14759390902992576

Kirkwood, A., & Price, L. (2005). Learners and learning in the 21st century: What do we know about students' attitudes and experiences of ICT that will help us design courses? *Studies in Higher Education*, *30*(3), 257–274. doi:10.1080/03075070500095689

Knowles, M. S. (1975). *Self-directed learning. A guide for learners and teachers*. Englewood Cliffs, NJ: Prentice Hall.

Knowles, M. S. (1990). *The adult learner: A neglected species* (4th ed.). Houston, TX: Gulf Publishing.

Koole, M., McQuilkin, J. L., & Ally, M. (2010). Mobile learning in distance education: Utility or futility? *Journal of Distance Education, 24*(2), 59–82.

Kreijns, K., Kirschner, P. A., & Jochems, W. (2003). Identifying the pitfalls for social interaction in computer-supported collaborative learning environments: A review of the research. *Computers in Human Behavior, 19*(3), 335–353. doi:10.1016/S0747-5632(02)00057-2

Lave, J., & Wenger, E. (1991). *Situated learning: Legitimate peripheral participation*. Cambridge, UK: Cambridge University Press.

Lazzari, M. (2009). Creative use of podcasting in higher education and its effect on competitive agency. *Computers & Education, 52*(1), 27–34. doi:10.1016/j.compedu.2008.06.002

Lee, M. J., McLoughlin, C., & Chan, A. (2008). Talk the talk: Learner-generated podcasts as catalysts for knowledge creation. *British Journal of Educational Technology, 39*(3), 501–521. doi:10.1111/j.1467-8535.2007.00746.x

Lindblom-Ylänne, S., Trigwell, K., Nevgi, A., & Ashwin, P. (2006). How approaches to teaching are affected by discipline and teaching context. *Studies in Higher Education, 31*(3), 285–298. doi:10.1080/03075070600680539

Lonn, S., & Teasley, S. D. (2009). Podcasting in higher education: What are the implications for teaching and learning? *The Internet and Higher Education, 12*(2), 88–92. doi:10.1016/j.iheduc.2009.06.002

Luckin, R. (2010). *Re-designing learning contexts*. London, UK: Routledge.

Marton, F., & Säljö, R. (1976). On qualitative differences in learning: I - Outcome and process. *The British Journal of Educational Psychology, 46*(1), 4–11. doi:10.1111/j.2044-8279.1976.tb02980.x

Mason, R., & Kaye, A. (Eds.). (1989). *Mindweave: Communication, computers and distance education*. Oxford, UK: Pergamon.

McKenna, K., Green, A., & Gleason, M. (2002). Relationship formation on the Internet: What's the big attraction? *The Journal of Social Issues, 58*(1), 9–31. doi:10.1111/1540-4560.00246

McLuhan, M. (1964). *Understanding media: The extensions of man*. New York, NY: McGraw Hill.

Merry, S., & Orsmond, P. (2008). Students' attitudes to and usage of academic feedback provided via audio files. *Bioscience Education eJournal, 11*(June). Retrieved June 23, 2010, from www.bioscience.heacademy.ac.uk/ journal/ vol11/ beej-11-3.pdf

Middleton, A. (2009). Beyond podcasting: Creative approaches to the design of educational audio. *ALT-J, 17*(2), 143–155. doi:10.1080/09687760903033082

Newton, J., & Middleton, A. (2009). Podcasting for pedagogic purposes: The journey so far and some lessons learned. In T. Mayes, D. Morrison, H. Mellar, P. Bullen, & M. Oliver (Eds.), *Transforming higher education through technology-enhanced learning* (235-248). York, UK: The Higher Education Academy.

Northedge, A. (2003). Enabling participation in academic discourse. *Teaching in Higher Education, 8*(2), 169–180. doi:10.1080/1356251032000052429

Papert, S. (1993). *The children's machine: Rethinking school in the age of the computer*. New York, NY: BasicBooks.

Parks, M., & Floyd, K. (1996). Making friends in cyberspace. *Journal of Computer-Mediated Communication, 1*(4). Retrieved October 19, 2004, from http://www.ascusc.org/ jcmc/ vol1/ issue4/ parks.html

Phipps, R., & Merisotis, J. (1999). *What's the difference? A review of contemporary research on the effectiveness of distance learning in higher education*. Washington, DC: Institute for Higher Education Policy.

Price, L., & Richardson, J. (2004). Why is it difficult to improve student learning? In C. Rust (Ed.), *Proceedings of the 11th Improving Student Learning Symposium: Theory, Research and Scholarship* (pp. 105-120). Oxford, UK: The Oxford Centre for Staff and Learning Development.

Price, L., Richardson, J. T. E., & Jelfs, A. (2007). Face-to-face versus online tutoring support in distance education. *Studies in Higher Education, 3*(1), 1–20. doi:10.1080/03075070601004366

Prosser, M., & Trigwell, K. (1999). *Understanding learning and teaching: The experience in higher education. SRHE and Open University Press.*

Richardson, J. (2000). *Researching student learning: Approaches to studying in campus-based and distance education*. Buckingham, UK: SRHE and Open University Press.

Richardson, J. T. E. (2008). Approaches to studying among deaf students in higher education. In Marschark, M., & Hauser, P. C. (Eds.), *Deaf cognition: Foundations and outcomes* (pp. 387–410). New York, NY: Oxford University Press.

Roberts, G. (2003). Teaching using the Web: Conceptions and approaches from a phenomenographic perspective. *Instructional Science, 31*(2), 127–150. doi:10.1023/A:1022547619474

Rogers, E. M. (1995). *Diffusion of innovations* (4th ed.). New York, NY: Free Press.

Rossell-Aguilar, F. (2007). Top of the pods – In search of a podcasting "podagogy" for language learning. *Computer Assisted Language Learning, 20*(5), 471–492. doi:10.1080/09588220701746047

Rowntree, D. (1994). *Teaching with audio in open and distance learning*. London, UK: Kogan Page.

Russell, J., Elton, L., Swinglehurst, D., & Greenhalgh, T. (2006). Using the online environment in assessment for learning: A case-study of a Web-based course in primary care. *Assessment & Evaluation in Higher Education, 31*(4), 465–478. doi:10.1080/02602930600679209

Salmon, G., & Edirisingha, P. (Eds.). (2008). *Podcasting for learning in universities*. Maidenhead, UK: Open University Press.

Saloman, G. (1997). Of mind and media: How culture's symbolic forms affect learning and thinking. *Phi Delta Kappan, 78*(5), 375–380.

Sawyer, R. (2006). Introduction: The new science of learning. In Sawyer, R. K. (Ed.), *The Cambridge handbook of the learning sciences* (pp. 1–19). New York, NY: Cambridge University Press.

Schramm, W. (1977). *Big media, little media*. London, UK: Sage.

Sharples, M. (2000). The design of personal mobile technologies for lifelong learning. *Computers & Education, 34*(3-4), 177–193. doi:10.1016/S0360-1315(99)00044-5

Snyder, B. (1971). *The hidden curriculum* (1st ed.). New York, NY: Knopf.

Steeples, C., & Jones, C. (Eds.). (2002). *Networked learning: Perspectives and issues*. London, UK: Springer.

Thomas, J. (2001). *Audio for distance education and open learning*. Vancouver, Canada: Commonwealth of Learning. Retrieved July 8, 2010, from http://www.col.org/ resources/ publications/ operational/ Pages/ audioDEOL.aspx

Tinto, V. (1997). Classrooms as communities: Exploring the educational character of student persistence. *The Journal of Higher Education*, *68*(6), 599–623. doi:10.2307/2959965

Trigwell, K., Prosser, M., & Waterhouse, F. (1999). Relations between teachers' approaches to teaching and students' approaches to learning. *Higher Education*, *37*(1), 57–70. doi:10.1023/A:1003548313194

Walls, S. M., Kucsera, J. V., Walker, J. D., Acee, T. W., McVaugh, N. K., & Robinson, D. H. (2010). Podcasting in education: Are students as ready and eager as we think they are? *Computers & Education*, *54*(2), 371–378. doi:10.1016/j.compedu.2009.08.018

Walther, J. (1992). Interpersonal effects in computer-mediated interaction: A relational perspective. *Communication Research*, *19*(1), 52–90. doi:10.1177/009365092019001003

Zemsky, R., & Massy, W. F. (2004). *Thwarted innovation: What happened to e-learning and why?* A report from the Learning Alliance, University of Pennsylvania. Retrieved July 8, 2010, from http://www.irhe.upenn.edu/ WeatherStation.html

Zenios, M., Goodyear, P., & Jones, C. (2004). Researching the impact of the networked information environment on learning and teaching. *Computers & Education*, *43*(1-2), 205–213. doi:10.1016/j.compedu.2003.12.014

KEY TERMS AND DEFINITIONS

Agent / Agency: An *agent* is a person or thing that takes an active role and/or produces a specific effect. *Agency* is an action or intervention producing a particular effect.

Approach to Learning / Teaching: The *approach* of teachers to their teaching and of learners to their learning refers to the behaviours and practices that they adopt in respect of those activities.

Conception of Learning / Teaching: The *conceptions* that teachers and learners hold about learning and teaching refer to an individual's views or beliefs about the particular phenomenon or the meaning they attach to it.

Conceptions of Learning and Teaching with Technology: The views or beliefs individuals hold about the phenomenon of learning and teaching with technology or the meaning they attach to it.

Control in Educational Transactions: This refers to whom or what has responsibility in the social process of learning and teaching.

Perceptions: This refers to the awareness that people have of a phenomenon or their interpretation of what they experience of the phenomenon.

Teacher-Centred / Learner-Centred: A *teacher-centred* approach is one in which the teacher's concerns determine the nature and form of the educational process, while a *learner-centred* approach concentrates on the development of learning in each individual.

Chapter 2
The Outcomes-Based Approach:
Concepts and Practice in Curriculum and Educational Technology Design

Maureen Tam
The Hong Kong Institute of Education, Hong Kong

ABSTRACT

This chapter aims to discuss the emerging trend of an outcomes-based approach to curriculum improvement in higher education in recent decades; consider its practical considerations for curriculum and educational technology design; critically review the advantages and disadvantages of adopting an outcomes-based approach; and finally discuss the caveats of inappropriate use in curriculum and instructional design in higher education. As any other models of educational or instructional design, the outcomes-based approach has limitations, as well as promises for guiding better instruction and curriculum. It remains as a matter of how skillfully it is used to maximize its benefits and value while diminishing its limiting effects that could educationally trivialize the kind of learning and education that it purports to promote in the first place.

INTRODUCTION

The outcomes-based approach is completely student-centred, which focuses on what students know and can actually do. Sharpening the focus onto student learning outcomes goes beyond mere tinkering with traditional structures and methods; it really constitutes a paradigm shift in educational philosophy and practice. To discuss and critically review such paradigm shift from teaching to learning, this chapter is organized around four objectives. Firstly, it begins with a summary of

DOI: 10.4018/978-1-61350-080-4.ch002

developments in institutional assessment and curriculum improvement in higher education in recent decades. Secondly, it identifies instructional principles that characterize the outcomes-based approach for curriculum design in higher education. Thirdly, practical pedagogical considerations are drawn from the outcomes-based approach for curriculum and instructional design, providing an example in the context of educational technology for effective assessment of outcomes. Fourthly, the approach is critically reviewed for its value from the perspectives of both practical and philosophical considerations. In so doing, it is directed to the heightening of sensitivity as to the manner and situations in which the outcomes-based approach may be employed.

BACKGROUND

In recent decades there is a widespread interest in the outcomes of educational experiences and how those outcomes meet a variety of societal needs.

Learning outcomes are important for recognition ... The principal question asked of the student or the graduate will therefore no longer be 'what you do to obtain your degree?' but rather 'what can you do now that you have obtained your degree?' This approach is of relevance to the labour market and is certainly more flexible when taking into account issues of lifelong learning, non-traditional learning, and other forms of non-formal educational experiences. (Purser, Council of Europe, 2003)

International trends in higher education show a shift away from the teacher-centred model that emphasizes what is presented, towards the learning-based model focusing on what students know and can actually do. As aptly pointed out by Ewell (2008), the vogue of outcomes-based approaches in higher education is in fact arising from the so-called 'assessment movement' that began in the mid-1980s in the United States with government calls to examine the effectiveness of the funds invested in public institutions of higher education by looking at how much graduates had learned by the point of graduation. With the assessment movement in higher education focusing on student learning outcomes as the emerging measure of institutional excellence and effectiveness, ideas about what constitutes a high-quality education have shifted from the traditional view of what teachers provide to a practical concern for what learners actually learn, achieve, and become. Indicators of student learning outcomes as part of the larger accountability framework have become prominent in the early 1990s first in the United States, which then spread to many countries including Australia, New Zealand, the United Kingdom and South Africa.

The outcome-based approach has been increasingly adopted within credit frameworks and by national quality and qualifications authorities such as the QAA (Quality Assurance Agency for Higher Education) in the UK, the Australia, New Zealand and South African Qualification Authorities. (Gosling & Moon, 2001)

One recent example of the widespread international interest in outcomes-based approaches is the cross-national effort at standards alignment currently underway in Europe under the auspices of the Bologna Process that seeks to create a common model for higher education in Europe, in which learning outcomes should play an important role (Adam, 2004, 2006). As a result, the directive is that, by 2010, all programs offered by higher education institutions should be based on the concept of learning outcomes, and that curriculum should be redesigned to reflect this. Through the development of national frameworks of qualifications, all degrees (Bachelor and Masters) would be described in terms of learning outcomes, workload, level, competences and profile (Kennedy, Hyland & Ryan, 2006).

Central to the outcomes-based approach are the performance indicators of efficiency and effectiveness as the means of attaining the specified ends in a system of 'outcomes-driven education' (Bagnall, 1994). This is congruent with the aforementioned assessment movement in higher education worldwide, where accountability in terms of effectiveness and efficiency is defined as the function to maximize the attainment of individual educational goals and societal outcomes (such as employment gains, reduced criminality).

To maximize educational effectiveness, it requires:

1. The prior specification of the intended educational outcomes (as goals or objectives) or their consequences;
2. The management of the ensuing education in such a way as to maximize the attainment of those desired ends; and
3. The evaluation of that education and its entailed learning in such a way as to assess the extent to which the desired ends have been realized in actual educational outcomes or their consequences. (Bagnall, 1994, pp. 20-21)

Similarly, to maximize educational efficiency, it requires:

1. That all educational activity be directed maximally towards the attainment of the specific desired ends;
2. That any educational activity that is directed towards the attainment of other ends, or for the satisfaction of other interests, be minimized; and
3. That educational success be seen as the ratio of (1) the extent to which the desired ends have been attained as a result of those particular educational activities, and (2) the total educational costs (time spent, materials used, other activities foregone, etc.). (Bagnall, 1994, pp.21)

By achieving effectiveness and efficiency in attaining the specified ends, educational institutions are seen to have fulfilled their particular institutional tasks and outcomes. Efficiency and effectiveness are thus the central concepts of outcomes-based approaches in higher education, providing the impetus for curriculum improvement at the levels of the individual student, program and institution.

THE OUTCOMES-BASED APPROACH

Different Levels of Outcomes

The word 'outcomes' will mean different things depending on the level of analysis and the kind of results of an academic experience that we are talking about. In fact, learning outcomes approaches have been used at many levels, ranging from that of instructional design where the individual student is the object of interest, through institutions and programs where the prominent concerns are evaluation-based program improvement and quality assurance (Ewell, 2008). At this juncture, it is necessary to define 'outcomes' in relation to the context in which they are used.

At the individual student level, learning outcomes are used to express what learners are expected to achieve and how they are expected to demonstrate that achievement. Learning outcomes are here defined as student attainment as a result of engagement in a particular set of teaching and learning experiences. The classical work of Benjamin Bloom (1913-1993) has identified three broad categories of learning outcomes at the student level – cognitive, affective and psychomotor (Bloom et al., 1956). Cognitive outcomes generally refer to the content knowledge that students can comprehend, explain, analyze and apply. Skills outcomes refer to the capacity to do things, including problem solving, communicating effectively, or performing certain technical procedures in a task. Affective outcomes are related to attitudes which usually involve changes in beliefs or the development of certain values such as ethical behavior, empathy, or respect for others.

At the program or course level, learning outcomes are more broadly defined as development or growth as a result of studying a particular course or program (Ewell, 2008). Student development can take the form of employability and increased career mobility, enhanced lifestyle, the opportunity for further studies, or simply a more fulfilled and happier life. However, in more pragmatic terms, learning outcomes at this level are also referred to as the certification of specific levels of knowledge, skill, or ability for a given profession. Simply put, student learning outcomes at this level refer to the attainment of the particular competencies acquired by students on completion of an academic program or course.

Outcomes at the institutional level are generally more broadly defined and are related to the assessment of institutional performance for quality assurance (Ewell, 2008). To this end, institutions need to collect evidence about student abilities to prove that the institution-level outcomes or goals are achieved. Evidence here embraces the results of both quantitative and qualitative approaches to gathering information about student learning outcomes either in absolute or value-added terms. In absolute terms, outcomes are referred to as attainment against established standards (criterion-referenced assessment) or as the performance of an individual or group compared to others (norm-referenced assessment). Here outcomes extend beyond student learning outcomes to provide quantitative measures to allow assessment of institutional performance. In value-added terms, outcomes can refer to the 'before-after development' or 'enhancement' as a result of a student's attendance at an institution of higher education. These outcomes may include things like enhanced income, changes in career, or even increased student satisfaction and motivation. Self-reports provided by students and alumni about their development and satisfaction with the university experience by way of surveys and interviews could also be counted as evidence of student learning outcomes for the purpose of examining institutional-level effectiveness.

The above delineation of the terminology provides the distinctions between the different units of analysis for learning outcomes ranging from individual students to aggregates of students grouped by an academic program or institution. As the focus of this chapter is outcomes-based approach for enhanced curriculum and student learning, the emphasis is hence not to assess institutional effectiveness in relation to outcomes, but rather to identify those instructional principles that characterize the outcomes-based approach and its pedagogical considerations for curriculum and educational technology design in higher education.

The Paradigm Shift

Sharpening the focus of higher education onto student learning outcomes goes beyond mere tinkering with traditional structures and methods; it really constitutes a paradigm shift in educational philosophy and practice. The traditional way of curriculum design, the teacher-centred approach focuses on the teacher's input and on assessment in terms of how well the students absorb the materials taught. A departure from this traditional paradigm is the student-centred approach where the emphasis is on what the students are expected to be able to do at the end of the learning experience. This approach is also referred to as an outcomes-based approach with statements used to express what knowledge students have actually acquired, and what abilities they have actually developed. Implicit in the student-centred model is the idea that teachers are facilitators of learning, who create and sustain an effective learning environment and experience based on a wide range of best practices in teaching and learning. And the fundamental role of assessment is to monitor, confirm and improve student learning.

Such radical shift from teacher delivery to student learning is resonant with Biggs' (2003) theory of constructive alignment. Central to this theory is the claim that any learning or meaning is constructed by the students in the course of their learning experience. Simply put, learning is a product of the student's activities and experiences, rather than the tutor's. The emphasis is on what students can actually do at the end of the learning experience. So when designing a learning experience, the focus should be on learning outcomes and the key questions to consider will include:

1. What should the student be able to understand or perform at the end of the learning experience?
2. What activities would the student have to undertake in order to learn this?
3. How can the tutor find out if the student has learned successfully?

To answer these three questions, we need to draw up (a) learning outcomes; (b) teaching and learning activities; and (c) assessment. It is important that there is agreement between the learning outcomes, the teaching and learning activities, and the assessment to make sure that the three elements should all be aligned (Biggs, 1999). Aligning these three elements will ensure compatibility and consistency within the curriculum where the desirable learning outcomes agree with the teaching and learning activities and the assessment tasks in a coherent manner. This model of constructive alignment focuses on learning outcomes which specify the achievement of the desired kind of learning, while the teaching and learning activities and assessment are the means to achieve the ends. When the three elements are working in synergy, the learning outcomes are in fact driving the curriculum design, with the other elements including teaching and assessment falling in place dictated by the results of the desired learning experience of students.

When designing outcomes-based instruction, planning begins by determining what should be learned. It is results-oriented and the primary measure of curriculum success is what graduates actually know and are able to do. It is also competency-based when learning outcomes specified at the very outset are tied to the most important skills and knowledge in a program or course. Most importantly, it is dedicated to continual improvement through ongoing assessment of student learning. As the outcomes-based approach requires the demonstrated achievement of specified learning outcomes, designs of this kind are usually termed 'competency-based' or 'mastery' programs with focus on what the learner can demonstrate at the end of a learning activity.

Adopting the outcomes-based approach in curriculum planning, the first step is to identify the desired levels of student learning after engaging in a meaningful learning experience. The action verbs used in writing the outcomes statements define the required level of understanding and competence. The precise verbs chosen will drive and suggest the type of teaching and learning activities that students need to undertake in order to achieve the level of sophistication at which they are expected. For example, action verbs such as 'explain', 'diagnose' or 'problem solve' call for very different learning outcomes at various levels that need to be very specific at the outset for both students and curriculum designers to have a clear idea of what is expected at the end of the learning experience.

Having decided on the level and nature of learning outcomes, the second step is to consider what students need to do to be able to achieve the outcomes. This process informs the kind of student activity that is linked to the level of each learning outcome for curriculum designers and teachers to plan and select teaching and learning activities appropriate to the expected outcomes. It is no longer enough for designers and teachers to be competent in their discipline; they are required to create, develop, and manage stimulating learning environments, using a variety of resources, methods, and technologies, including assessment resources in order to deepen and enrich student learning. Such a shift for the role of designer or teacher from subject expert to facilitator of learning implies that teaching and learning activities are designed to reflect this relationship to focus more on the educational process rather than subject content.

What follows from the stage of designing appropriate teaching and learning activities is the very important part played by assessment to demonstrate that students have achieved in the end the kind and level of learning expected of them. As the design of teaching and learning activities takes messages from the declared outcomes in the early stages of curriculum planning, assessment should also be the starting point to be considered for how learning is to be assessed and evaluated. The outcomes-based approach, coupled with Biggs' constructive alignment theory, in fact calls for virtually simultaneous consideration of the desired learning outcomes, the planning of appropriate teaching and learning activities and the proposed means of assessment to aim at the desired level cognitive and affective outcomes which are declared as results from a worthwhile learning experience.

Outcomes-Based Design Model

As a departure from the traditional way of curriculum and instructional design which emphasizes subject content, the outcomes-based approach focuses on the student and learning, rather than on subject matter and teaching. The outcomes-based design model provides much clearer links between the desired outcome of an educational experience and its design of teaching and learning. It also encourages the discussion of appropriate assessment, including its kind and level for measuring achievement of the desired outcomes. The outcomes-based approach and the requirement of compatibility between the learning outcomes, teaching and learning activities and appropriate assessment provide a system which helps structure learning in a coherent and meaningful way to result in an enhanced learning experience for students.

The traditional model of curriculum and instructional design follows a rather linear or chronological process (Figure 1). The different components in the design process receive attention in the order in which they are considered by teachers and learners in the form of a sequence.

Such conventional model has been described in detail by curriculum planners and researchers (for example Davies, 1971; Romiszowski, 1981;

Figure 1. Traditional model of curriculum and instructional design

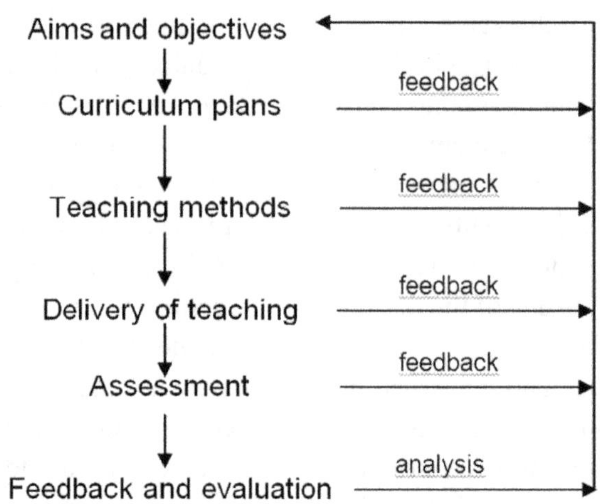

Tookey, 1999), who conceptualize the process as a linear sequence in which:

1. Aims and objectives are first identified
2. Curriculum plans are mapped out
3. Teaching methods are selected
4. Teaching is delivered
5. Teachers assess learning
6. The course is evaluated providing feedback for revisions at various stages
7. The cycle reiterates.

This linear process is, however, fraught with problems because it assumes that aims, objectives or outcomes are only considered at the beginning of the process and then reviewed at the end, once per cycle. Besides, it focuses on teaching, not learning, with the curriculum plans and the delivery of teaching structured around topics or content to be covered. It also assumes that learning will take place after the delivery and be best assessed at the end of the teaching and learning process. Most importantly, the process ignores the interaction and relationships between the different elements and the combined influences that the various elements may have on the design of the curriculum, the specification of learning outcomes and the selection of assessment tasks.

The integrated model of outcomes-based learning plus Biggs' constructive alignment, however, provides a different approach, which is interactive and non-linear (Figure 2).

In this model, the intended learning outcomes are central, and are assumed to interact with and influence the design of the teaching and learning activities and assessment that occur during the processes of planning, delivery and evaluation. In addition to the three key components, evaluation is crucial to provide feedback and analysis of data which inform the level and kind of learning by students and their overall learning experience. Decisions for change and revisions will then be considered and implemented in an interactive and integrated manner. By monitoring the effects of interactions among the various elements in the curriculum and instructional design process, designers and teachers are able to identify problem areas and to design improvements. By adopting this outcomes-based curriculum design model, the principles of alignment and the intricate relationships between outcomes, teaching and learning, and assessment can be translated into practice. The pedagogic implications of outcomes-based and alignment within a curriculum are more likely to result in improving the quality of students' learning experience than the traditional chronological model of curriculum and instructional design. And the major tenet is that the outcomes-based model truly sets the learning experience highest in the curriculum and instructional devel-

Figure 2. Outcomes-based model of curriculum and instructional design

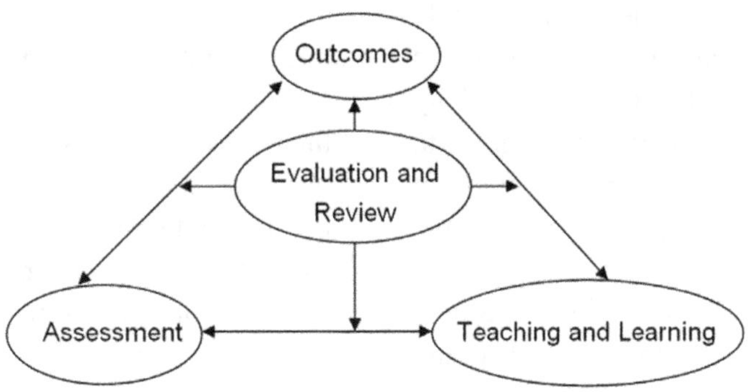

opment agenda, allowing the learning outcomes to drive the design of teaching and learning and assessment in the light of the expected outcomes.

In summary, when adopting the outcomes-based model in curriculum and instructional design, teachers are expected to be clear about what they want students to learn and what students would be able to do in order to demonstrate that they have learned at the required level. They are also expected to know and deploy strategies and methods of getting their students to learn effectively, to be more student-centred in their teaching and learning activities, and more learning-oriented, authentic in their assessments. By aligning the three elements – outcomes, teaching and learning, and assessment, the outcomes-based model provides a framework for systematically operationalizing these pedagogic principles and considerations to result in programs and courses that are designed with student learning as the centrality.

Integrating Educational Technology with the Outcomes-Based Approach

When implementing the outcomes-based approach, teachers often find the consideration of appropriate assessment to effectively measure the achievement of the learning outcomes (how do we know our students have learned?) the biggest challenge. This is particularly true in the assessment of affective outcomes in the form of values, attitudes, behaviours and related attributes or dispositions which have consistently been proved difficult to be assessed by traditional assessment methods like examination or assignment (Shephard, 2009). In this part of the chapter, an example is provided to illustrate the use of educational technology to enable teachers and instructional designers to better assess aspects of learning that could not be effectively assessed using more conventional means.

This example is an e-portfolio assessment system for higher education to evaluate learning outcomes, in particular, those affective attributes such as teamwork, creativity, lifelong learning, which can rarely be assessed with the same level of objectivity as those cognitive ones. How can educational technology help with the assessment of affective outcomes? This section presents an example of using educational technology to support the assessment of affective attributes by way of e-portfolios.

Portfolios are becoming more widely used in student assessment especially for outcomes that are affective in nature. Baume (2007) has aptly identified a few reasons for portfolio assessment:

In producing a portfolio, the student assembles smaller pieces of work into a large whole; makes connections among the items of work they have done; and gives a critical overview of their work and learning. In marking a portfolio, the lecturer sees a coherent and reflective picture of the student's work and development. '(Baume, 2007, pp. 1)

When developing a portfolio, students are required to analyze and critically reflect on evidence of a wide range of learning outcomes, including skills related to the application of knowledge, as well as affective attributes indicative of values, attitudes and dispositions. Unlike paper-based portfolios, e-portfolios, because of their ability to integrate student learning with the virtual learning environments and student record systems within institutions, are more versatile in allowing information to be stored, accessed, updated, and presented in various electronic formats to record student achievements (Tubaishat et al., 2009). For students, the e-portfolio provides many opportunities for online reflective writing to document the process of learning and to showcase their achievements with respect to the intended outcomes. For the teachers, the e-portfolio allows them to better manage, review, and comment on students' work. On a broader scale, setting up an e-portfolio assessment system will allow the institution to measure whether the curriculum meets institution learning outcomes, resulting in improvements to the curriculum, and teaching and learning practices.

The deployment of educational technology, such as information and communication technologies (ICT), in setting up the e-portfolio assessment system will add flexibility (allowing adaption and exploration), interactivity (allowing links between different elements of the same work and to different works in multiple media) and connectivity (allowing interactions between multiple players) (Shephard, 2009). Harnessing the flexibility and interactivity of ICT, the e-portfolio assessment system can support students to include in their e-portfolio a variety of digital artifacts such as projects, term papers, photos, web pages, or case studies in various media. And because of its connectivity, ICT allows teachers to post comments on student work on the system, enabling students to access the teacher's comments and update their work and reflect on their learning. The ICT-supported system also allows teachers and program/course coordinators to assess specific components of student work that includes various learning outcomes. Data thus obtained from the system will contribute to the evaluation of how courses/programs are meeting their intended learning outcomes and, more broadly, the institutional goals.

In summary, an ICT-supported e-portfolio assessment system is one example of using educational technology to support student assessment in outcomes-based instruction. Students compile key learning experiences to showcase their work in the e-portfolios, providing evidence in a variety of digital artifacts, including comments from teachers of what students have submitted. The reflective aspect of the e-portfolio assessment system facilitates the review and revision process, allowing students to complete the reflective cycle of planning, doing, recording and reviewing. Finally, course/program coordinators and teachers can use information generated from the system to assess curricular efficiency and to evaluate the effectiveness of the learning outcomes for the course/program in question. With the support of ICT, the e-portfolio assessment system provides a vehicle, not just for the assessment of individual criterion-referenced outcomes, but more importantly, for the evaluation of broader and affective outcomes that traditional assessment methods find difficult to determine. This is exactly an example of how educational technology design can benefit from the characteristics of the technology that has created the opportunities.

Benefits and Limitations

As with any other models of educational and curriculum design, the outcomes-based approach has limitations, as well as promises for guiding better instruction and curriculum. In this section, the benefits and limitations of outcomes-based approaches will be identified and reviewed first from a practical implementation perspective, then through a philosophical analysis in broader terms.

At the level of implementation, the outcomes-based approach are considered to offer benefits including clarity, flexibility, comparison and portability (Ewell, 2008).

Clarity

Focusing on outcomes can help communicate clearly between various stakeholders the kind of learning expected at the end of a learning program or course. Students will know what is expected of them; same as teachers about the level and standards at which they need to teach the intended outcomes. This is particularly important when there is team teaching which involves diverse teaching staffs across departments and schools. At the institutional level, requirements and standards of a certain program or credential can be articulated in the form of a qualifications framework for benchmarking with similar credentials offered by other institutions. By the same token, employers and even educational policymakers will know more precisely the standards and competencies of graduates for employment and accountability purposes.

Flexibility

Although the intended outcomes are specified, the means to achieve the ends are fairly open in an outcomes-based approach. For the same or similar outcomes, a variety of teaching and learning activities, methods and even modes of delivery can be deployed to suit different circumstances. A great deal of flexibility is built in the model for the selection of the means of instruction so long as the same intended level of knowledge and skills are resulted. In this regard, different abilities and backgrounds of students can be accommodated through the different instructional paths, technologies and modes that are allowed in an outcomes-based approach. There is also flexibility with recognizing prior student learning through assessment against the various levels of learning outcomes within the framework.

Comparison

With the outcomes-based approach, it is more plausible to establish comparable standards across programs and even institutions, for accreditation, benchmarking, as well as accountability purposes. These summative and formative comparisons will help institutions to check standards against each other and benchmark for improvement as they learn from each other through the cross-checking of outcomes. Comparison is also possible among students from different institutions or backgrounds by way of comparing assessed outcomes against recognized standards or certain qualifying criteria as in professional qualifications and credentials. Such comparative data will provide useful information for admission, placement or certification of students with reference to their level of standards and outcomes achieved.

Portability

As the word 'portability' suggests, students can earn and transfer credits from a program offered by one institution to another program in a different institution. This is made possible by having articulated the learning outcomes in different programs using clear criteria and credible standards. It will also allow increased mobility and exchange of students in this age of growing student mobility and modularity of instructional provision, not just locally, but internationally.

Despite the many benefits it promises, the outcomes-based approach is not without problems. Further on the issue of benefits and problems, Ewell (2008) completes his analysis by cautioning against four major drawbacks – definition, legitimacy, fractionation, and serendipity, which may emerge when efforts are made to operationalize outcomes at the implementation level.

Definition

Definitions of learning outcomes are subject to the context of their application and the judgment made by a specific team or group of people involved. Outcomes identified for a particular course or program could not be generalized across contexts largely due to the sufficient precision and consistency required for a valid and reliable judgment about the ability or characteristic in question. Simply put, it is not easy to obtain agreement or consensus about the definition and meaning of learning outcomes across different course or program teams, and even more so, across different disciplines and subject areas.

Legitimacy

Many academics opine that learning outcome statements are inadequate to capture those 'ineffable' aspects of learning which may result in 'reductionism' and 'reification' (Ewell, 2008). By their very nature, outcome statements tend to break down holistic conceptions of learning, and reduce them to learning abilities or changes in behavior that are specific, observable and measurable. As a result, outcomes schemes still fall short of being widely accepted and recognized in academia as a valid way of conceptualizing what learning is all about.

Fractionation

The way assessment works in outcomes schemes may sometimes found to be too narrow and even mechanical in assessing learning, missing the essence of integrated ability that is supposed to unite many discrete skill elements into expert practice (Ewell, 2008). From the operational perspective, assessment for outcomes could become too focused on the student's acquisition of skills and knowledge that other more important developmental outcomes over time are ignored. Also, there may be a lack of coherence among smaller components in an instructional program as a result of fractionation that breaks down both learning and assessment in small units of incremental progress.

Serendipity

In a similar vein, outcomes-based approaches are criticized for their constrained serendipity which presumes that all of the valued and important ways that a learner can construct meaning in the context of a particular discipline or ability are known in advance (Ewell, 2008). This problem is conceived to be more pronounced in advanced levels of study and in certain disciplines such as fine arts where unexpected important learning may occur during the instructional process.

There are both advantages and disadvantages associated with adopting outcomes-based approaches. An understanding of both benefits and limitations will help make the principles and concepts of outcomes schemes more concrete in the form of application in curriculum and educational technology design. In a broader perspective, Bagnall (1994) has examined the benefits and limitations presented by outcomes-based approaches through a philosophical analysis, from a lifelong education perspective. Building on the work of earlier critiques (such as those by Apling, 1989; Ashworth & Saxton, 1990; Hyland, 1991), Bagnall questions the efficacy of outcomes-based approaches which in practice may be more likely to diminish precisely those qualities that it is intended to enhance.

In his philosophical discussion, Bagnall has aptly pointed out that in order to maximize efficiency and effectiveness, outcomes-based education is in fact constraining and limiting; trivial and mechanical; inflexible and conservative with too much emphasis on attribution and consequence; promoting egoistic maximization of individual self-interests; and not as empowering to both the students and educators as it claims because it dehumanizes students as resources to be enhanced and promotes dependence of the learners on the educators.

A learning outcome, in order to be useful and practical, has to be clearly and validly specifiable, reliably observable, quantifiable and essentially unchanging over the course of the instructional experience. In most cases, many worthwhile educational outcomes can satisfy these requirements without compromising their value. But for educational outcomes of a more liberal nature, such as creativity, intellectual virtues, respect for self and others, responsibility and self-sufficiency, are not easily amenable to concrete specification and quantifiable measurement in the form of behavioral learning outcomes. Because of its nature to constrain, to focus rather than to liberate, to broaden, an outcomes-based approach may work against, ironically, many of its ideals of enhancement of excellence, individual freedom, liberation, individuality, plurality, creativity, innovativeness and responsiveness, towards a system of encouraging the development of relatively closed, self-serving, bureaucratic systems of education (Bagnall, 1994). Failure to achieve what it purports to do in relation to these education ideals, outcomes schemes are prone to becoming dehumanizing and educationally trivializing to result in curricular fragmentation and simplification; the externalization of educational reward; student dependence; and educational conservatism, tokenism, inflexibility, centralization, instrumentalism and functionalism (ibid).

Application to Curriculum and Educational Technology Design

Despite these criticisms, there is no doubt that learning outcomes as measures of learning effectiveness and instructional quality can make an important contribution to the improvement of that quality. As any other models of curriculum or educational technology design, the outcomes-based approach has limitations, as well as promises for guiding better instruction and curriculum. It remains as a matter of how skillfully it is used to maximize its benefits and value while diminishing its limiting effects that could possibly dehumanize and educationally trivialize the kind of learning and educational principles cognizant to it. While the intention here is not to discourage the use of outcomes-based approaches, the caveat is that we must heighten our sensitivity as to the manner and situations in which the approach may be employed.

The main recommendation is that a working model of outcomes-based approaches be integrated with curriculum and educational technology design at three crucial points: the curriculum or unit objectives are clearly stated in terms of concrete intended learning outcomes that imply appropriate performances; the teaching methods, including the use of technology, are deployed to enable effective learning of the outcomes; and the assessment tasks address those same outcomes to elicit performances from students at the end of the learning experience. On the basis of constructive alignment between the three components – outcomes, teaching and assessment, the outcomes-based approach, both in theory and practice, provides a powerful teaching and learning model for curriculum and educational technology design.

FUTURE RESEARCH DIRECTIONS

This chapter has addressed the potential application of outcomes-based approaches to curriculum and educational technology design, as well as the issues, controversies, problems associated with them. As outcomes schemes have become more popular and widely adopted in higher education internationally, it is important that deliberate discussions and due consideration be given to the following questions:

- How are learning outcomes approaches already being used in curriculum and educational technology design in higher education? Are there ways these applications might usefully be evaluated? What lessons can be drawn from these experiences for improvement both in terms of theory development and implementation?
- What areas of studies or types of programs might benefit particularly from applying learning outcomes concepts and approaches to curriculum planning and educational technology design?
- How might greater use of the language of learning outcomes in program and course descriptions help students understand better what is expected of them? How might it have an impact on student learning?
- How will the alignment between learning outcomes, teaching methods and assessment help to improve the quality of teaching and learning through outcomes-based curriculum and educational technology design?
- Is there a need for staff development and what specific implications are there for development programs and activities to

familiarize staff with the outcomes-based approach to curriculum and educational technology design?

- How might learning outcomes concepts and approaches be useful to curriculum reform and development in higher education? What specific implications are there for quality reviews at the levels of institution, program and individual students?
- What specific implications are there for instructional and educational technology designs, such that appropriate technologies and media are deployed to achieve the intended learning outcomes for a course or program?

CONCLUSION

This chapter is about the concepts and applications of outcomes-based approaches to curriculum and educational technology design. The widespread interest in the outcomes of educational experiences has resulted in a shift away from the teacher-centred model that emphasizes what is presented, towards the learning-based model focusing on what students know and can actually do. Learning outcomes are defined according to the context in which they are used. Learning outcomes at the individual student level help students understand what is expected of them at the end of an educational experience. At the course or program level, learning outcomes are useful to guide curriculum, learning and assessment to aim at the achievement of those competencies or abilities by students enrolled in a particular course or program. Outcomes at the institutional level are often linked to institutional performance in terms of the efficiency and effectiveness towards achieving the institutional-level outcomes or goals. In this chapter, the outcomes-based approach is mainly applied at the course and program level to elicit both pedagogic principles and practical considerations for implementation at this level.

Learning outcomes together with the theory of constructive alignment are found to be the essential components in an outcomes-based design model. In it the three elements – outcomes, teaching and learning, and assessment need to be aligned to achieve consistency and coherence in the design process, resulting in instruction and assessment that are designed to address the intended learning outcomes. In this light, the adoption of the learning outcomes approach has the potential to help embrace a more systematic approach to the design of programs and courses. As an illustration of its application in the context of educational technology, an example in the form of ICT-supported e-portfolios is suggested to enable teachers and students to better review and assess learning outcomes that could not be effectively assessed using more conventional means.

Despite its usefulness, the outcomes-based approach is subject to criticism and cautionary use. Some critics have found outcomes schemes to be overly specifiable, observable, quantifiable and so narrow that they can be limiting rather than liberating, which may result in reductionism, reification, fractionation, serendipity, and may fail to achieve the kind of learning and education that it purports to promote in the first place. Despite these criticisms, outcomes-based learning appears to be premised on the belief that it is by nature empowering to its participants – both students and educators. There is no doubt that learning outcomes as measures of learning effectiveness and instructional quality can make an important contribution to the improvement of that quality by way of better curriculum and student learning. A final note is that while learning outcomes approaches are useful, care is needed to take into account the different views and perceptions of those involved in defining learning outcomes and to keep the ultimate goal of improving student learning clearly in mind. Care must also be taken to avoid rigidity and conceptual reification during implementation in curriculum and educational technology design.

REFERENCES

Adam, S. (2004, July). *Using learning outcomes: A consideration of the nature, role, application and implications for European education of employing learning outcomes at the local, national and international levels.* Report on United Kingdom presented at the Bologna Seminar, Herriot-Watt University, U.K.

Adam, S. (2006). An introduction to learning outcomes. In E. Froment, J. Kohler, L. Purser, & L. Wilson (Eds.), EUA Bologna Handbook *(B2.3-1)*. Berlin, Germany: Raabe.

Apling, R. N. (1989). *Vocational education performance standards*. Washington, DC: Congressional Research Service, The Library of Congress.

Ashworth, P. D., & Saxton, J. (1990). On competence. *Journal of Further and Higher Education, 14*(2), 3–25.

Bagnall, R. (1994). Performance indicators and outcomes as measures of educational quality: A cautionary critique. *International Journal of Lifelong Education, 13*(1), 19–32. doi:10.1080/0260137940130103doi:10.1080/0260137940130103

Baume, D. (2007). *Portfolios for learning and assessment*. Higher Education Academy. Retrieved October 5, 2008, from http://www.palatine.ac.uk/files/936.pdf

Biggs, J. (1999). *Teaching for quality learning at university*. Buckingham, UK: Society for Research in Higher Education and Open University Press.

Biggs, J. (2003). Enhancing teaching through constructive alignment. *Higher Education, 32*(3), 347–364. doi:10.1007/BF00138871doi:10.1007/BF00138871

Bloom, B. S., Engelhart, M. D., Furst, E. J., Hill, W., & Krathwohl, D. (1956). *Taxonomy of educational objectives.: Vol. 1. The cognitive domain.* New York, NY: McKay.

Davies, I. K. (1971). *The management of learning*. London, UK: McGraw Hill.

Dick, W., & Carey, J. (2004). *The systematic design of instruction* (6th ed.). Boston, MA: Allyn & Bacon.

Ewell, P. (2008, June). *Building academic cultures of evidence: A perspective on learning outcomes in higher education*. Paper presented at the symposium of the Hong Kong University Grants Committee on Quality Education, Quality Outcomes – the way forward for Hong Kong, Hong Kong. Retrieved September 15, 2010, from http:www.ugc.edu.hk/eng/ugc/activity/outcomes/symposium/2008/present.html

Goodman, G. (Ed.). (2008). *Educational psychology: An application of critical constructivism.* New York, NY: Peter Lang.

Gosling, D., & Moon, J. (2001). *How to use learning outcomes and assessment criteria*. London, UK: SEEC Office.

Hyland, T. (1991). Taking care of business: Vocationalism, competence and the enterprise culture. *Educational Studies, 17*(1), 77–87. doi:10.1080/0305569910170106doi:10.1080/0305569910170106

Kennedy, D., Hyland, A., & Ryan, N. (2006). Writing and using learning outcomes: A practical guide. In E. Froment, J. Kohler, L. Purser, & L. Wilson (Eds.), EUA Bologna handbook *(C3.4-1)*. Berlin, Germany: Raabe.

Purser, L. (2003). Report on Council of Europe Seminar on Recognition Issues in the Bologna Process, Lisbon, April 2002. In Bergan, S. (Ed.), *Recognition issues in the Bologna process.* Retrieved July 20, 2009, from http://book.coeint/EN/ficheouvrage.php?PAGEID=36&lang=EN&produit_aliasid=1618

Romiszowski, A. J. (1981). *Designing instructional systems*. London, UK: Kogan Page.

Shephard, K. (2009). E is for exploration: Assessing hard-to-measure learning outcomes. *British Journal of Educational Technology*, *40*(2), 386–398. doi:10.1111/j.1467-8535.2008.00927.xdoi:10.1111/j.1467-8535.2008.00927.x

Toohey, S. (1999). *Designing courses for higher education*. Buckingham, UK: Society for Research in Higher Education and Open University Press.

Tubaishat, A., Lansari, A., & Al-Rawi, A. (2009). E-portfolio assessment system for an outcome-based information technology curriculum. *Journal of Information Technology Education: Innovations in Practice*, *8*, 43–54.

Willis, J. W. (Ed.). (2009). *Constructivist instructional design (C-ID): Foundations, models, and examples*. Charlotte, NC: Information Age Publishing, Inc.

ADDITIONAL READING

Astin, A. W. (1977). *Four critical years*. San Francisco: Jossey-Bass.

Banta, T. W., & Associates. (1993). *Making a difference: Outcomes of a decade of assessment in higher education*. San Francisco: Jossey-Bass.

Biggs, J. B., & Moore, P. J. (1993). *The process of learning*. Sydney: Prentice Hall.

Blackmur, D. (2004). A critique of the concept of a national qualifications framework. *Quality in Higher Education*, *10*(3), 267–284. doi:10.1080/1353832042000299559doi:10.1080/1353832042000299559

Bloom, B. S. (1975). *Taxonomy of educational objectives, Book 1 Cognitive domain*. Longman Publishing.

Brown, S., & Knight, P. (1994). *Assessing learners in higher education*. London: Kogan.

Burke, J. C. (2005). Reinventing accountability: From bureaucratic rules to performance results. In J. C. Burke, & Associates. (Eds.), *Achieving accountability in higher education* (pp. 216–245). San Francisco: Jossey-Bass.

Cowan, J. (2000). *Curriculum development. A booklet to support staff development workshops*. Aveiro: Universidade de Aveiro.

Dill, D. (2000). Designing academic audit: Lessons learned in Europe and Asia. *Quality in Higher Education*, *6*(3), 187–208. doi:10.1080/13538320020005945doi:10.1080/13538320020005945

Duffy, T. M., & Jonassen, D. (Eds.). (1992). *Constructivism and the technology of instruction: A conversation*. Hillsdale, NJ: Erlbaum.

Entwistle, N. J., & Ramsden, P. (1983). *Understanding student learning*. London: Croom Helm.

Erwin, T. D. (1991). *Assessing student learning and development*. San Francisco: Jossey-Bass.

Ewell, P., & Ries, P. (2000). *Assessing student learning: A supplement to measuring up 2000*. San Jose, CA: National Center for Public Policy in Higher Education.

Ewell, P. (2001). *Accreditation and student learning outcomes: A proposed point of departure*. Washington, DC: Council on Higher Education Accreditation (CHEA).

Feldman, K. A., & Newcomb, T. M. (1969). *The impact of college on students*. San Francisco: Jossey-Bass.

Gibbs, G. (1992). *Improving the quality of student learning*. Bristol: Technical and Educational Services.

Harvey, L., & Newton, J. (2004). Transforming quality evaluation. *Quality in Higher Education*, *10*(20), 149–166. doi:10.1080/1353832042000230635doi:10.1080/1353832042000230635

Heywood, J. (1989). *Assessment in higher education* (2nd ed.). Chichester: Wiley.

Mager, R. F. (1984). *Preparing instructional objectives* (2nd ed.). Belmont, California: Pitman Learning.

Marton, F., Hounsell, D., & Entwistle, N. (1997). *The experience of learning*. Edinburgh: Scottish Academic Press.

Miller, M. A., & Ewell, P. T. (2005). *Measuring up on college level learning*. San Jose, CA: National Center for Public Policy in Higher Education.

Pace, C. R. (1979). *Measuring college outcomes*. San Francisco: Jossey-Bass.

Prosser, M., & Trigwell, K. (2000). *Understanding learning and teaching*. Buckingham: Society for Research in Higher Education and Open University Press.

Schon, D. (1983). *The reflective practitioner: How professionals think in action*. London: Temple Smith.

Shuell, T. J. (1986). Cognitive conceptions of learning. *Review of Educational Research, 56*, 411–436.

Tam, M. (1999). Managing change involves changing management: Implications for transforming higher education. *Quality in Higher Education, 5*(3), 227–232. doi:10.1080/1353832990050304 doi:10.1080/1353832990050304

Tam, M. (1999). Quality assurance policies in higher education in Hong Kong. *Journal of Higher Education Policy and Management, 21*(2), 215–226. doi:10.1080/136008099021020 8doi:10.1080/1360080990210208

Tam, M. (2001). Measuring quality and performance in higher education. *Quality in Higher Education*, *7*(1), 47–54. doi:10.1080/1353832 0120045076doi:10.1080/13538320120045076

Tam, M. (2002). Measuring the effect of higher education on students. *Quality Assurance in Education, 10*(4), 223–228. doi:10.1108/096848 80210446893doi:10.1108/09684880210446893

Tam, M. (2002). University impact on student growth: a quality measure? *Journal of Higher Education Policy and Management, 24*(2), 211–218. doi:10.1080/1360080022000013527d oi:10.1080/1360080022000013527

Tam, M. (2004). Using students' self-reported gains as a measure of value-added. *Quality in Higher Education, 10*(3), 253–260. doi:10.1080/135383204 2000299531doi:10.1080/1353832042000299531

Tam, M. (2006). Assessing quality experience and learning outcomes, Part 1: instrument and analysis. *Quality Assurance in Education, 14*(1), 75–87. doi:10.1108/09684880610643629doi:10. 1108/09684880610643629

Tam, M. (2007). Assessing quality experience and learning outcomes, Part II: Findings and discussion. *Quality Assurance in Education, 15*(1), 61–76. doi:10.1108/09684880710723034doi:10. 1108/09684880710723034

Tam, M. (2009). Constructivism, instructional design, and technology: implications for transforming distance learning. In J. W. Willis (Ed.), *Constructivist instructional design (C-ID): Foundations, models and examples* (pp. 61–80). Charlotte, NC: IAP – Information Age Publishing.

Terenzini, P. T. (1989). Outcomes assessment with open eyes: Pitfalls in studying student outcomes. *The Journal of Higher Education, 60*, 644–664. doi:10.2307/1981946doi:10.2307/1981946

Webb, G. (1996). *Understanding staff development*. Buckingham: Society for Research in Higher Education and Open University Press.

Westerhiejden, D. F. (2001). Ex Oriente Lux?: National and multiple accreditation in Europe after the fall of the wall and after Bologna. *Quality in Higher Education*, *7*(1), 65–76. doi:10.1080/13538320120045094doi:10.1080/13538320120045094

KEY TERMS AND DEFINITIONS

Constructive Alignment: Constructive alignment requires virtually simultaneous consideration of the intended learning outcomes, the planning of appropriate teaching and learning activities and the proposed means of assessment to aim at the desired level of student learning. Aligning these three elements will ensure compatibility and consistency within the curriculum where the desirable learning outcomes agree with the teaching and learning activities and the assessment tasks in a coherent manner.

Educational Effectiveness: It is a performance indicator to assess the extent to which the intended educational outcomes are achieved by an institution through its programs and activities.

Educational Efficiency: It refers to the ability of an institution to maximize the attainment of the intended educational outcomes while minimizing the educational costs involved.

E-Portfolios: E-portfolios are electronic versions of paper portfolios which provide students with the opportunity to compile, document, review, reflect, revise, and showcase what they have learned and achieved. Because of the ability to integrate student learning with the virtual learning environments and student record systems within the institution, e-portfolios are more versatile in allowing information to be stored, accessed, updated, and presented in various electronic formats to record student achievements.

Information Communication Technologies (ICT): These are technologies that can be used to enable and enhance flexibility (allowing adaptation and exploration), interactivity (allowing links between different elements of the same work and different works in multiple media) and connectivity (allowing interactions between multiple players).

Learning Outcomes: Learning outcomes are defined as student attainment as a result of engagement in a particular set of teaching and learning experiences. They are what learners are expected to achieve and how they are expected to demonstrate that achievement.

Outcomes-Based Approach: The outcomes-based approach focuses on the student and learning, rather than on subject matter and teaching. Teachers are facilitators of learning, who create and sustain an effective learning environment and experience based on a wide range of best practices in teaching and learning. And the fundamental role of assessment is to monitor, confirm and improve student learning.

Outcomes-Based Design Model: Curriculum and instruction designed with an outcomes-based approach focuses on the student and learning, exhibiting clear links between the desired outcome of an educational experience and its design of teaching and learning and assessment. Outcomes-based design is non-linear and interactive, allowing the learning outcomes to drive the design of teaching and learning and assessment in the light of the expected outcomes.

Student-Centred Approach: The emphasis of the student-centred approach is on what the students are expected to be able to do at the end of the learning experience. Learning is a product of the student's activities and experiences, rather than the tutor's.

Teacher-Centred Approach: It is a traditional educational philosophy and practice that focuses on the teacher's input and on assessment in terms of how well the students absorb the materials taught.

Chapter 3
Instructional Design for Technology-Based Systems

Gary R. Morrison
Old Dominion University, USA

Gary J. Anglin
University of Kentucky, USA

ABSTRACT

As technologies continue to evolve and develop, instructional designers are presented with a growing list of possibilities for designing and delivering instruction. It is easy for an instructional designer to be seduced by a new or even older technology and focus on the affordances of the technology resulting in instruction that is both ineffective and inefficient while appearing to appeal to the learner. In this chapter, we show how existing instructional design models are capable of designing instruction for a variety of technologies. We will address the features of design models, analyze instructional interactions, examine technological affordances, and describe the importance of research-based instructional strategies.

INTRODUCTION

Over the past 75 years, we have witnessed the introduction of numerous technologies into higher education classrooms. These innovations range from lantern slide projectors, 16mm films, programmed instruction, video recordings, main frame computers, personal computers, hypertext, the Internet, netbooks, and m-learning to a variety of Internet-based social media. With each technology, there is a call for new instructional design models that can address the needs of the innovations and produce better instruction that will lead to greater gains in learning. Yet, the research on the effectiveness of these technological innovations during the past 75 years has failed to find any significant learning gains attributable to the technology (Clark, 1983, 1994a; Morrison, 1994). One argument is that existing instructional design models fail to produce designs appropriate for the technology. Another argument is that we have focused too much on the technology rather

DOI: 10.4018/978-1-61350-080-4.ch003

than on the design of the instruction (Morrison, Ross, Kalman, & Kemp, 2011). The focus of this chapter is on designing instruction when employing technology.

What is Instructional Design?

Instructional design has been defined by a number of authors. One recent definition reflects a general consensus, "[a] systematic process that is employed to develop education and training programs in a consistent and reliable fashion" (Reiser & Dempsey, 2007, p. 11). Morrison, et al. (2011) state that instructional design is based on learning theory, information technology, systematic analysis, educational research, and management methods. Instructional design translates learning and perceptual theories and research into instructional applications to address specific objectives. This translation process is what Dewey (1900) describes as a linking science (Snellbecker, 1974). That is, instructional design serves as a link between research and the classroom (or instruction). A design model leads to decisions about instructional strategies that are based on sound research findings. Well-designed instruction is the output of a systematic process that involves analysis of the learner, environment, and content; and the design of appropriate instructional strategies that are tested and revised to produce effective and efficient instruction.

Instructional Design Models

Instructional design models describe a systematic approach to the design of instruction by organizing heuristics and prescriptions for informed decision making. Gropper (1983) identified two characteristics of instructional design models that are relevant for this discussion. First, the analysis of the content and learners allows the instructional designer to create and classify objectives for the instruction. This classification allows the designer to dissect the objective to determine the behaviors and type of content (e.g., fact, concept, principle) required to achieve the objective. Second, the model specifies the conditions that affect the difficulty of achieving of the objective and it prescribes the treatment that will result in efficient and effective instruction. By distinguishing between conditions and treatment, the instructional design model can prescribe a variety of strategies that are address the behavior required to achieve the objective. For example, numerous studies have established the effectiveness of mnemonics for recalling information (Balch, 2005; de Graaff, Verhoeven, Bosman, & Hasselman, 2007; Johnson, 2006; Kuo & Hooper, 2004; Levin, Anglin, & Carney, 1987). According to Gropper, a design model should distinguish between recalling factual information and higher order skills like analysis and problem solving to identify the most appropriate strategies. For example, recent research on problem solving (Hung & Jonassen, 2006; Jonassen & Hung, 2006; Oh & Jonassen, 2007) suggests mnemonics would not be an appropriate strategy for teaching problem solving. Thus, the instructional design model should differentiate between behaviors and prescribe strategies that are appropriate for the behavior the learner is to master. The more finely the model can distinguish between different behaviors, the more effective the resulting instruction. For example, the previous example contrasting factual learning and problem solving ignores many of the behaviors identified in Bloom's (Bloom, Englehart, Furst, Hill, & Krawthwohl, 1956) taxonomy such as comprehension, application, analysis, and synthesis that fall between recall and problem solving. Of particular importance to this discussion is the ability of the design model to distinguish between different learner performances (i.e., behaviors) and to prescribe specific strategies to develop those performances. An instructional design model and instructional designers should have a variety of instructional strategies that address various behaviors rather than simply relying on more traditional practices such as rehearsal, practice, and role play to address all types of objectives. For example, Morrison et al. (2011) distinguish between six different types of content (fact, concept, principle and rules, procedures, interpersonal skills, and attitudes) and two levels of performance (recall and application) when they analyze objectives to prescribe specific instructional strategies. An instructional design model that meets Gropper's criteria is a useful tool for faculty designing their own instruction. First, the specification of objectives and then the distinction between performance behaviors of the objectives can help a faculty member determine if the course is meeting the faculty member's expectations for higher level thinking. Second, the differentiation of objectives can help the faculty member select the appropriate instructional strategy for teaching the content.

Merrill (2002) has taken a different approach and identified five principles of the instruction that he derived from a study of various instructional design models. These five principles are considered to be basic strategies that are prescribed by different instructional design models although none of the models reviewed include all five principles. These principles are general instructional strategies an instructional designer can employ when designing instruction. The following is a summary of the five principles. First, engaging learners in real world problems promotes learning. The simplest implementation of this principle is to illustrate how the learner can solve a problem as a result of the instruction. The focus of this principle is on learning to solve problems rather than problem-based instruction in which content is learned by solving a problem. The second principle states that learning is enhanced when prior knowledge is activated. This principle is an application of schema theory (Anderson & Lebiere, 1998; Anderson & Bower, 1983; Rummelhart & Ortony, 1976) that suggests knowledge structures (e.g., schema) held by the learner are modified when relevant new information is provided. According to Merrill, the instruction should provide a means of recalling this prior knowledge before the instruction. Third, demonstrating what the learner needs to know is more effective than simply telling the learner. Demonstration of the information can include the use of examples and nonexamples when learning concepts, visualizing information to provide concrete images, and modeling an interpersonal communication behavior. The third principle suggests that the instruction should go beyond just a basic presentation and requires thought as to how to visualize the information as well as presenting an adequate number of instances to facilitate learning. Fourth, the instruction should require the learners to apply their knowledge or skill to promote learning. Merrill suggests a variety of strategies ranging from practice requiring recall of information, naming of parts, solving problems, coaching that includes error detection and fading, and solving varied problems. The final principle states that learners should transfer their new knowledge or skill to real world applications to promote transfer of the knowledge or skill. Merrill suggests requiring the learner to demonstrate their knowledge or skill in public, to reflect, and create or invent a way of using the knowledge or skill.

Gropper (1983) and Merrill (2002) both emphasize the need for instructional strategies to address varied learner performances. The emphasis on instructional strategies is consistent with Bruner's (1966) early concept of instructional theory that stated that an instructional theory must be prescriptive. That is, the instructional theory should prescribe an efficient and effective way to design the instruction. It is our belief that these prescriptions should be based on sound research rather than individual observations. Using a heuristic approach (Morrison, et al., 2011), the designer then modifies these prescriptions based on feedback from both formative and summative evaluations. Similarly, a faculty member could use a higher education specific model such as Diamond's (1989) instructional design model to design and test various instructional strategies.

This discussion of instructional design models raises the question of who is responsible for the design task in higher education. For large projects and projects involving complex technology designs (e.g., multimedia and computer-based instruction) the responsibility for instructional design might rest primarily with an instructional designer with the faculty member serving as the subject-matter expert. A faculty member often serves as the instructional designer for individual lessons in a course. How the instructional designer and the faculty member, however, employ the instructional design process may vary as the faculty member usually has limited resources and time which often results in completing fewer steps in the process (Morrison, et al., 2011).

Does Technology Require a Different Approach to Design?

From World War II until the mid-1980's, instructional designers typically used the same instructional design model for any medium ranging from printed instruction to 16mm films. With an increasing focus on computer technology in the 1980's along with distance education, technology specific instructional design models began to appear (Allessi & Trollip, 1985; Dabbagh & Brannan-Ritland, 2005; Moore & Kearsley, 1996). A logical question is whether there is a need for instructional design models specific to a technology, or if a more traditional instructional design model is applicable to most if not all current and new technologies?

Mayer (Mayer, 2001; Mayer & Moreno, 1998, 2002) recently proposed a new theory of multimedia learning that is applicable for designing research as well as a basis for designing instructional strategies in a multimedia environment. The proposed multimedia design model is based on more traditional theories that were developed from research that used printed, projected (e.g., film), and computer-based instruction. Mayer and Moreno (1998) argue that these theories are applicable to a theory of multimedia learning even though they are based on different and often static pictures and printed text. Similarly, the Moore and Kearsley's (1996) distance education design model presents an adapted version of the traditional instructional design model developed by Dick, Carey, and Carey (2008).

An answer to the question of whether technology specific instructional design models are needed may be answered by the results from media comparison studies. Clark and others (Clark, 1983, 1994a; Morrison, 1994, 2001) argue that there are no achievement differences between the multimedia version of instruction and one in print when the instructional strategy is the same in both forms of instruction. Thus, achievement differences for different technologies are due to the instructional strategies employed not the technology. Similarly, Ross and Morrison (1989) proposed a media replication design that allowed a research to contrast similar, but different strategies in two different media. The emphasis of the research, however, was still on the instructional strategy rather than on the technology. Thus, higher education faculty do not need to master a different instructional design model for each technology as the emphasis is on the design of the instructional strategy, not the technology. In the remainder of this chapter, we will examine how instructional strategies are implemented in different technologies. Our discussion will focus on five general topics including engagement, technology affordances, presentation of information, interaction, and pacing.

Engagement

Engaging the learner through interactions is considered one of the essential components of instruction. Interaction with immediate feedback at regular intervals is one of the essential principles of programmed instruction that was based on Skinner's operant conditioning theory (Markle, 1969). Allen (1957) summarized the findings of several studies that found successful use of student interaction while viewing films and filmstrips. Other studies have examined learner interaction with printed materials (Anderson & Kulhavy, 1972; Schultz & Di Vesta, 1972), computer-based instruction (Anderson, Kulhavy, & Andre, 1972) using note taking, imagery, and questions as forms of interaction. Bernard et al.'s (2009) analysis of interaction in distance education courses found a distinct advantage for learner interactions with the content (e.g., answering questions, note taking, paraphrasing, and use of imagery) with learners engaged in learner-content interactions achieving higher grades than students just engaged in only learner-instructor or learner-learner interactions. Learner-content interactions are considered asymmetrical as they are a one-way communication that include strategies such as reading from a textbook or listening to a lecture (Holden & Westfall, 2006). In contrast are interactions that use two-way communication such as discussions either online (asynchronous) or face-to-face (synchronous) are considered symmetrical communication. Holmberg (1989) and Keegan (1996) proposed theories of learner-content interactions in distance education that can mimic learner-instructor interactions through the proper design of the instruction and the activation of inner speech similar to that described by Vygotsky (1962). The task of the instructional designer/faculty member is to design materials in such a manner that they invoke this inner speech interaction in the learner to interact with the instructor's words. Thus, simply posting one's lecture notes or PowerPoint slides on a website is inadequate for instruction as it does not engage the learner to interact with the instructor's words.

One framework for designing these interactions is content-by-treatment interactions (Jonassen & Grabowski, 1993). Content-by-treatment interactions are based on the assumption that the structure of the content provides information the instructional designer can use to sequence and present the instruction. For example, a task analysis reveals the process to achieve the objectives whether psychomotor, cognitive, or affective. This assumption is similar to Gropper's (1983) assumptions about instructional design models. Jonassen and Grabowski's (1993) second assumption suggests that the instruction should reflect the environment similar to the one in which the learner will perform the task or use the information. This assumption is similar to Merrill's (2002) first principle of instruction. The key then to an effective design is to identify the specific behavior or performance of the learner and the content type, then design the instruction (i.e., the treatment) to achieve the objective in a realistic context. Thus, the task of the faculty member when designing individualized materials such as a study guide is to design strategies that initiate this interaction between the learner and the instructional materials.

The focus of instruction is on the learner interactions and primarily those between the learner and the content. This interaction is mediated by the instructional strategy that defines specific tactics the learner can employ either through prompts (i.e., interactions) or on their own as a self-regulated learning strategy (Schunk & Zimmerman, 1998; Zimmerman, 1990) to help learners process and understand the content. A common element across different technologies is the learner-content interactions that are guided by different instructional strategies. These strategies present the learner with a prompt, for example a question or condition such as "increased blood pressure" and the learner must make an input either in the form of an answer to a question or manipulation of equipment or drugs to control the blood pressure. In this case, strategies are used across a variety of technologies with none being unique to a specific technology (Clark, 1983). While the strategies are applied across technologies, each technology affords different but not unique affordances that provide a means of enhancing and making the strategies efficient. We will examine these affordances and different classes of instructional strategies in the next section.

FOCUSING ON TECHNOLOGIES

Media or technologies are described as having attributes or affordances that designers can use to create efficient instructional strategies. Salomon (1970) first described these attributes as one of two intersecting variables that defined a medium, "*an instructional medium is a package of unique modes of presenting information* (which may or may not be a consequence of some attributes of a machine) *which also fulfills a unique psychological function*" (p. 38, italics in original). Several studies have examined strategies that used these attributes including zooming in and laying out an object (e.g., unfolding a box) (Salomon, 1972, 1974). This process of focusing on various media attributes was part of Salomon's (1970) supplanting theory that suggested media could be used to model mental behaviors for the learner, particularly those mental behaviors that the learner was not yet capable of performing. For example, chemistry instructors frequently use molecular models to illustrate the bonding of elements. A naïve student may have difficulty thinking of a complex molecule, thus the plastic model of the molecule is used to supplant an image the student can use for thinking.

Salomon (1979) suggested that many of these attributes were unique to specific media and make a unique cognitive representation. That is, an instructional designer *could not* replicate the instructional strategy that employed the attribute in another medium. As an example of a unique attribute Salomon suggested the use of zooming in (or irising) to focus the learner's attention on a specific attribute of the display in a 16mm film. Clark (1994b) refuted the unique attribute claim by Salomon. The effect of zooming was easily replicated using an iris in a static picture to focus the learner's attention. Thus, it was not the zooming in effect, that is, the media attribute, that produced a unique cognitive effect; but rather the strategy of cueing or focusing the learner's attention on specific attribute of a picture or diagram. Clark argues that there are many different attributes in a variety of media that can help the learner accomplish the same learning goal. We agree with Clark that there are not unique media attributes that make unique cognitive functions.

Technological attributes provide a means for designing *efficient* instruction. For example, a teacher using flash cards with a student is as *effective* a strategy as is a flash card computer program. Both provide immediate feedback and can vary the pace and sequence of presentation. The computer program, however, can adapt the presentation to the learner so that learned items are not presented as often as those that are not learned. Similarly, the computer has unlimited patience and can provide the student with undivided attention most any time (or anytime with a mobile application). In the following pages we will discuss how various technology attributes can be used with different instructional strategies to design effective and efficient instruction.

Technology Affordances

It is beyond the scope of this chapter to discuss the full range of technology affordances. For example, Salomon's (1972, 1974) research focused on zooming in and laying out an object where Suthers (2006) examined the "social affordance of technology" for collaborative learning. Rather, we will examine some of the key affordances that designers can use to design efficient instruction. The following discussion will examine technology affordances and instructional strategies. We have arranged the affordances into three major categories that are applicable across a number of technologies. These categories are presentation of information, interactions, and pacing of the instruction.

Presentation of Information

The first technology affordances focus on the presentation of information or content. Presentations include the information on the page of a textbook whether presented on a printed page or in an e-book as well as the information in a computer-based tutorial. While the overall instructional design model defines this content, the design of the presentation may rely more on message design principles (Fleming & Levie, 1978). Fleming and Levie (1978) define message design as "a pattern of signs (words, pictures, gestures) produced for the purpose of modifying the psychomotor, cognitive, or affective behavior of one or more persons" (p. x). There are three distinct forms of information presentation: text, static pictures, and animations that include multimedia or multiple external representations. These three forms can appear individually or in various combinations.

Text Displays

When designing a textual display, the designer must be concerned with the layout of the page and the selection of a font that is readable and appropriate for the audience. Tinker (1963) provides useful guidelines for font, font size, line length, and leading to produce text that is legible in a printed format. Similarly, Hartley (1994) and Misanchuck (1992) provide research-based heuristics for the layout of the printed page including margins, white space, and headings. However, there is little evidence that these guidelines for printed instruction are transferrable to computer displays. There have been few studies on the design of CBI screens with most articles deferring to those writing about human interfaces. For example, Skaalid (1999) cites several sources describing guidelines for printed instruction as well as sources that focus on human interface design. Other research has focused on the use of color in computer-based instruction (Clariana, 2004; Clariana & Prestera, 2009) while others have examined the amount of information to place on the screen at one time (Ardac & Unal, 2008; Lee, Plass, & Homer, 2006). Other sources of guidelines include web design guidelines (Galdo & Nielsen, 1996; Nielsen, 1990) that often describe accepted practices. Faculty who are designing web-based instruction and websites to support instruction, should follow established guidelines to present a consistent interface for the user. An easy to use interface will allow the learner to focus on the content rather than using valuable cognitive resources trying to navigate the content. The design of electronic textual displays is one area of needed research for the instructional designer.

Static Images

Static images can include both representational (e.g., photographs) and nonrepresentation (e.g., graphs) images. Anglin, Vaez, and Cunningham (2004) define pictures as "illustrations that have some resemblance to the entity that they stand for, whereas nonrepresentational graphics including charts, graphs, and diagrams are more abstract, but do use spatial layout in a consequential way" (p. 865). There are several sources for guidelines for designing instruction using static images. Anglin et al., Levin et al. (1987) and Levie and Lentz (1982) provide detailed summaries of the literature on static images with guidelines of when and how to use images. Similarly, Fleming and Levie (1978) provide multiple heuristics for designing instructional materials that incorporate images. These guidelines for designing pictures appear to apply to multiple technologies unlike the research on text layout which is technology specific. For example, Canham and Hegarty (2010) examined the effect of including irrelevant information on weather maps when presented on a computer monitor. Inclusion of irrelevant information negatively affected achievement. The findings from research on cognitive load theory (Sweller, 1988) provide additional guidelines for the use of images in instruction. Of particular importance is the avoidance of a split-attention effect (Sweller, Chandler, Tierney, & Cooper, 1990). Split attention occurs when the learner must examine both the text where the picture is described and the picture in order to interpret the text. The mental effort required to understand the content due to the two sources of information increases the amount of information to be processed in working memory which then hinders the development of an understanding and schema development or modification. Similarly, two or more sources of textual information are separated and also create a split-attention effect. Another cognitive load effect occurs when there is redundant information in the text and illustration (Chandler & Sweller, 1991). The suggested guideline is to integrate the text with the illustration by using labels and callouts and remove the redundant information from the text (Sweller, 1999). Mayer and Moreno's (2003) research suggests that these guidelines are applicable to both printed and multimedia and computer-based instruction[1]. When designing instructional materials with pictures, faculty should follow several guidelines to effectively use the pictures. First, each picture should perform a specific function such as representing an idea, helping the learner organize information, assisting the learner in interpreting a difficult idea, or transforming the information into a useable format such as mnemonic (Levin, et al., 1987). Second, pictures and narrative explanation should be integrated to avoid split attention and redundant information should be eliminated.

Dynamic Images

Dynamic images include animations and video that are part of instruction. We also include multimedia in this category as much of the multimedia research incorporates both animation and narration. Today, the more common way of presenting dynamic images either via the Internet or from a CD/DVD is with animations. The research on the effectiveness of animations is mixed when compared with static images. Mayer, Hegarty, Mayer, and Campbell (2005) note that there is a general assumption that animations are more effective for instruction than text and illustrations on a printed page. In a study comparing static images (i.e., printed instruction) and animations with narration, Mayer et al. found that the printed instruction with illustrations was more effective than the animations with narration. These results were consistent with previous studies that also found printed instruction superior to animations (Mayer, 1989; Mayer & Gallini, 1990). Animations, however, should not be dismissed according to Mayer et al. as additional research is needed to determine if they are helpful with students who have spatial ability limitations or when used to visualize ideas that are not visible to the human eye such as air pressure or molecules. For faculty who want to design and incorporate multimedia in their instruction, Mayer and Moreno (2002) suggest the following four guidelines. First, the narration should be presented simultaneous rather than before or after the animation. Second, adding embellishments to the audio such as additional information in the narration or background music results in reduced achievement. Third, narration presented as audio is superior to narration presented as text on the screen with the pictures. Fourth, including written narration on the screen simultaneously with the audio narration is detrimental to learning.

Interactions

Interactions are not unique to instruction delivered via computer technology. In 1961, Skinner (1996) described programmed instruction as a "constant interchange between the program and instruction." The research, however, on programmed instruction failed to find a significant effect for the constant interactions (Kulik, Schwalb, & Kulik, 1982; Kulik, Bangert, & Williams, 1983; Kulik, Cohen, & Ebeling, 1980). That is, simply having an interaction for the sake of interaction or even an interaction with feedback is not adequate for learning. For example, one of the most common instructional strategies is the inserted question that was described by Rothkopf (1970) in his concept of mathemagenic behaviors involved the use of adjunct or inserted questions placed before or after the relevant material. Research on inserted questions is mixed and there is a lack of theory that explains or supports the process (Lindner & Rickards, 1985). The design of the interaction should be determined by the differential analysis of the content and objectives described by Gropper (1983). The design model should prescribe effective and efficient strategies that use interactions for each type of objective (Bruner, 1966). That is, the strategies used to help the learner achieve an objective focused on recall of information should be different from an objective that requires the learner to apply a rule or identify examples of a concept. The task is selecting an appropriate strategy for the objective, a prescriptive task, and then selecting an appropriate interaction if needed. The following sections describe how faculty can select appropriate strategies and interactions to enhance learning in the college classroom.

Instructional Strategies

Options for learner-computer interactions and feedback are quite varied and appear to be only limited by new hardware developments. For example, peripheral equipment is easily used to create an environment using a steering wheel, accelerator, and brake pedal that are easily adapted for cars, trucks, and aircraft that can provide interactions and feedback. Similarly, haptic feedback can be given via a mouse in a virtual environment to increase the realism (Kyung, Choi, Kwon, & Son, 2004). There are three common forms of learner-computer interactions in computer-based instruction. First is answer inputting that generally requires the learner to type a response using a keyboard or to speak the response. The learner often must press the enter key or click a button to submit the response. Second is the selection of an object which is often done with a mouse or with a touch screen. Manipulations can include selecting an answer from a list such as a multiple choice test item by clicking a button, clicking on an object, picture, or specific part of a picture or other graphic such as a chart or map. For example, a biology instructor might create a program for students using a graphic image of a single cell or single cell animal and ask them to click on the nucleus or other components. Third is the manipulation of an object. Instructors can design manipulations using computer technology which are typically completed with the use of a mouse or other input device such as a steering wheel. Similarly, a real device such as a microscope or a transit level can provide a realistic form of manipulation although they would require more supervision by the instructor or laboratory assistant than a computer-based manipulation. A learner might be asked to sequence four pictures by dragging them to the correct sequential order using either printed images or graphics on a computer screen. Similarly, a student might enter an appropriate code for a numeric controller by clicking an image of the keys on the controller's keypad. Feedback can include text or images on the screen, audio, and haptic feedback. The key to the use of these forms of interaction and feedback is to design the appropriate instructional strategy using the interaction based on research supporting the strategy. It is the strategy that supports the learning, not the interaction with the technology.

A limited repertoire of strategies consisting of rehearsal practice and answering questions is not adequate to address a diverse set of instructional objectives. One theoretical framework for designing instructional strategies is Wittrock's generative learning strategies (Wittrock, 1974a, 1974b, 1989). These strategies describe learning as the process of activating the learner's existing knowledge structures and then altering those structures. Generative strategies require the learners to consciously and purposefully relate new information to their existing schemas. In contrast, the approach often used with adjunct questions is simply responding to a question with little meaningful thought. Jonassen (1988) classified generative strategies into four groupings of information processing strategies. The first category, recall, includes strategies that help the learner recall specific information. Strategies include rereading, covert and overt rehearsal, and the use of mnemonic devices. Integration strategies comprise the second category and are useful for helping the learner integrate new information with existing schemas to modifying existing schemas. Sample strategies include paraphrasing, creating metaphors, and creating new examples. The third category is organizational strategies which are used to help the learner determine how ideas relate to one another. Example strategies include analyzing key ideas, categorizing examples to compare concepts, and outlining information or creating concepts maps to see the organization. The fourth category is elaboration strategies that are used to make the content more meaningful. Elaboration strategies include the use of analogies and sentence elaborations. For example when using sentence elaborations, the learner might be asked to explain why a fact is true (Woloshyn, Paivio, & Pressley, 1994; Wood, Pressley, & Winne, 1990). These four broad categories of generative strategies provide prescriptive strategies the instructional designer can use to address the performance requirements of a variety of objectives. Similarly, a faculty member can incorporate these strategies in study guides and online instructional materials.

Interactions with Technology

The next task for the instructional designer is to select an appropriate interaction method for the instructional strategy. If the learner is required to recall information, a simple flash card strategy might be used. An organizational strategy that requires the learner to construct a concept map might use an interactive manipulation that allows the learner to drag concept labels or images on the screen and then create links. If the learner is paraphrasing information, then the instructional software would need to provide an input field with the ability to capture the appropriate number of characters. Last, a rehearsal practice strategy might have the learner select answers by clicking a button. To effectively use an interaction, the strategy must first be designed; otherwise the interaction may simply before the sake of interaction with no meaningful learning benefit.

Types of Feedback

There are five general types of feedback used in computer-based instruction. The first, answer until correct requires the learner to continue entering a response until the correct response is given. A math program might use this strategy that requires the learner to enter the correct answer before attempting the next problem. The second type is knowledge of correct response that has two variations. The simplest is informing the learner if the response is correct or incorrect. For example, if a student selected option A, the program might answer "That answer is incorrect." A more complex format informs the learner of the correct response and if the learner entered an incorrect response it requires the learner to enter the correct response before proceeding. A program using this strategy might respond to an incorrect response with the following feedback "The correct answer is nucleus, enter nucleus and press enter." The third type is delayed feedback in which no feedback is given until the instruction is completed, although variations can include a simple knowledge of correct response strategy after each item (Morrison, Ross, Gopalakrishnan, & Casey, 1995). One approach with delayed feedback is to provide the learner with immediate feedback as to the correctness of the response and then provide more detailed information about the correct response *after* the instruction is completed. The fourth type of feedback is explanatory and consists of the software providing explanations beyond a correctness of the response (Moreno, 2004). Elaboration feedback might provide the following response "The downward sloping line is the demand curve." The final type of feedback is response-sensitive feedback that provides a unique form of feedback for each response to help the learner understand why the response was correct or incorrect. Response sensitive feedback requires a careful analysis of errors the learner might make and the development of appropriate feedback. For example, a math program might provide the following response sensitive feedback "Your answer of 15 suggests you added rather than subtracted 5. The correct answer is 5."

Pacing

The last affordance of technology-based instruction is control of the pacing of the instruction. Merrill (1988) described learner control as the process by which learners take control of the instruction in terms of not only how quickly they progressed through the instruction, but also the sequence of the content and number of examples they would complete. Unlike the affordances already discussed, pacing is a macro level rather than a micro level strategy. The research on learner control has produced mixed findings (Corbalan, Kester, & van Merriënboer, 2006; Kopcha & Sullivan, 2008; Swaak & de Jong, 2001; van Gog, Ericsson, Rikers, & Paas, 2005; van Merriënboer, Chuurman, de Croock, & Paas, 2002).

There are three types of pacing. The first is program control in which the computer-based instructional program determines pacing and sequence of the content. That is, each learner receives the same instruction, sequence, and pacing. Second is learner control where the learner determines the pacing, sequence, and amount of instruction. Third, is adaptive control in which the program adapts to each individual learner. Thus, a unique sequence and number of examples are presented to each learner based on either prior achievement or responses during the instruction. The success of research on learner control has been limited (Carrier & Williams, 1988; Ross & Morrison, 1989). The general consensus is that poor learners lack the ability to make decisions concerning sequencing and how to make effective choices for effective and efficient learning (Ross & Morrison, 1989).

FUTURE RESEARCH DIRECTIONS

Future research should continue to focus the effectiveness of instructional strategies using an intervention research approach (Hsieh, et al., 2005). Of particular importance is research that extends studies of strategies in one technology to determine if they are effective in other technologies (Mayer & Moreno, 1998). For example, there is a lack of studies on the display of textual information on computer-based screens. Most of the research is based on Tinker's (Tinker, 1963) classic work on printed materials. Researchers should avoid the seduction of comparing two technologies in a classic media comparison study that have failed to yield meaningful and significant results (Clark, 1983, 1994a). The focus of future research should be on the effectiveness of various strategies in different technologies (Ross & Morrison, 1989).

CONCLUSION

Effective instruction is the result of designing instructional strategies based on findings from the research rather than from specific technologies. In this chapter, we have demonstrated how an instructional designer can use a variety of instructional strategies that are based on the generative learning theory and supported by research to take advantage of the affordances offered by various technologies. When the appropriate instructional strategies selected for specific objectives are used, then effective and efficient instruction is an outcome of the instructional design effort.

REFERENCES

Allen, W. (1957). Research on film use: Student participation. *Educational Technology Research and Development, 5*(2), 423–450. .doi:10.1007/BF02815928

Allessi, S. M., & Trollip, S. R. (1985). *Multimedia for learning: Methods and development* (3rd ed.). Needham, MA: Allyn & Bacon.

Anderson, J. R., & Lebiere, C. (1998). *The atomic components of thought*. Mahwah, NJ: Erlbaum Associates.

Anderson, R. C., & Bower, G. (1983). *Human associative memory*. Washington, DC: Winston.

Anderson, R. C., & Kulhavy, R. W. (1972). Imagery and prose learning. *Journal of Educational Psychology, 63*(3), 242–243. .doi:10.1037/h0032638

Anderson, R. C., Kulhavy, R. W., & Andre, T. (1972). Conditions under which feedback facilitates learning from programmed lessons. *Journal of Educational Psychology, 63*(3), 186–188. doi:10.1037/h0032653

Anglin, G. J., Vaez, H., & Cunningham, K. L. (2004). Visual representations and learning: The role of static and animated graphics. In Jonassen, D. H. (Ed.), *Handbook of research for educational communications and technology* (2nd ed., pp. 865–916). Mahwah, NJ: Lawrence Erlbaum Associates, Publishers.

Ardac, D., & Unal, S. (2008). Does the amount of on-screen text influence student learning from a multimedia-based instructional unit? *Instructional Science: An International Journal of the Learning Sciences, 36*(1), 75–88.

Balch, W. R. (2005). Elaborations of introductory psychology terms: Effects on test performance and subjective ratings. *Teaching of Psychology, 32*(1), 29–34. doi:10.1207/s15328023top3201_7

Bernard, R. M., Abrami, P. C., Borokhovski, E., Wade, C. A., Tamim, R. M., Surkes, M. A., & Bethel, E. C. (2009). A meta-analysis of three types of interaction treatments in distance education. *Review of Educational Research, 79*, 1243–1289. .doi:10.3102/0034654309333844

Bloom, B. S., Englehart, M. D., Furst, E. J., Hill, W. H., & Krawthwohl, D. R. (1956). *Taxonomy of educational objectives: Handbook I. The cognitive domain*. New York, NY: McKay.

Bruner, J. (1966). *Toward a theory of instruction*. Cambridge, MA: Harvard University Press.

Canham, M., & Hegarty, M. (2010). Effects of knowledge and display design on comprehension of complex graphics. *Learning and Instruction, 20*, 155–166. doi:10.1016/j.learninstruc.2009.02.014

Carrier, C. A., & Williams, M. D. (1988). A test of one learner-control strategy with students of differing levels of task persistance. *American Educational Research Journal, 25*(2), 285–306.

Chandler, P., & Sweller, J. (1991). Cognitive load theory and the format of instruction. *Cognition and Instruction, 8*(4), 293–332. doi:10.1207/s1532690xci0804_2

Clariana, R. B. (2004). An interaction of screen colour and lesson task in CAL. *British Journal of Educational Technology, 35*(1), 35–43. doi:10.1111/j.1467-8535.2004.00366.x

Clariana, R. B., & Prestera, G. E. (2009). The effects of lesson screen background color on declarative and structural knowledge. *Journal of Educational Computing Research, 40*(3), 281–293. doi:10.2190/EC.40.3.b

Clark, R. E. (1983). Reconsidering the research on media. *Review of Educational Research, 53*(4), 445–459.

Clark, R. E. (1994). Media will never influence learning. *Educational Technology Research and Development, 42*(2), 21–29. doi:10.1007/BF02299088

Corbalan, G., Kester, L., & van Merriënboer, J. J. G. (2006). Towards a personalized task selection model with shared instructional control. *Instructional Science, 34*, 399–422. doi:10.1007/s11251-005-5774-2

Dabbagh, N., & Brannan-Ritland, B. (2005). *Online learning: Concepts, strategies, and applications*. Columbus, OH: Pearson.

de Graaff, S., Verhoeven, L., Bosman, A. M. T., & Hasselman, F. (2007). Integrated pictorial mnemonics and stimulus fading: Teaching kindergartners letter sounds. *The British Journal of Educational Psychology, 77*(3), 519–539. doi:10.1348/000709906X160011

Dewey, J. (1900). Psychology and social practice. *Psychological Review, 7*, 105–124. doi:10.1037/h0066152

Diamond, R. M. (1989). *Designing and improving courses and curricula in higher education*. San Francisco, CA: Jossey-Bass.

Dick, W., Carey, L., & Carey, J. O. (2008). *The systematic design of instruction* (7th ed.). Columbus, OH: Pearson.

Fleming, M., & Levie, W. H. (1978). *Instructional message design: Principles from the behavioral sciences*. Englewood Cliffs, NJ: Educational Technology Publications.

Galdo, E. D., & Nielsen, J. (Eds.). (1996). *International user interfaces*. New York, NY: John Wiley & Sons.

Gropper, G. L. (1983). A metatheory of instruction: A framework for analyzing and evaluation instructional theories and models. In Reigeluth, C. M. (Ed.), *Instructional-design theories and models: An overview of their current status* (pp. 37–53). Hillsdale, NJ: Lawrence Elrbaum Associates, Publishers.

Hartley, J. (1994). *Designing instructional text* (3rd ed.). East Brunswick, NJ: Nichols.

Holden, J. T., & Westfall, P. J.-L. (2006). *An instructional media selection guide for distance learning*. Boston, MA: United States Distance Learning Association.

Holmberg, B. (1989). *Theory and practice of distance education*. New York, NY: Routledge.

Hsieh, P., Acee, T., Chung, W., Hsieh, Y., Kim, H., & Thomas, G. (2005). Is educational intervention research on the decline? *Journal of Educational Psychology, 97*(4), 523–529. doi:10.1037/0022-0663.97.4.523

Hung, W., & Jonassen, D. H. (2006). Conceptual understanding of causal reasoning in physics. *International Journal of Science Education, 28*(13), 1601–1621. doi:10.1080/09500690600560902

Johnson, G. M. (2006). Online study groups: Reciprocal peer questioning versus mnemonic devices. *Journal of Educational Computing Research, 35*(1), 83–96. doi:10.2190/1G67-HLL5-4172-083U

Jonassen, D. (1988). Integrating learning strategies into courseware to facilitate deeper processing. In Jonassen, D. (Ed.), *Instructional designs for microcomputer courseware* (pp. 151–181). Hillsdale, NJ: Lawrence Erlbaum Associates, Publishers.

Jonassen, D. H., & Grabowski, B. L. (1993). *Handbook of individual differences, learning, and instruction*. Hillsdale, NJ: Lawrence Erlbaum Associates.

Jonassen, D. H., & Hung, W. (2006). Learning to troubleshoot: A new theory-based design architecture. *Educational Psychology Review, 18*(1), 77–114. doi:10.1007/s10648-006-9001-8

Keegan, D. (1996). *Foundations of distance education* (3rd ed.). London, UK: Routledge.

Kopcha, T. J., & Sullivan, H. (2008). Learner preferences and prior knowledge in learner-controlled computer-based instruction. *Educational Technology Research and Development, 56*, 265–286. doi:10.1007/s11423-007-9058-1

Kulik, C. C., Schwalb, B. J., & Kulik, J. A. (1982). Programmed instruction in secondary education: A meta-analysis of evaluation findings. *The Journal of Educational Research, 75*(3), 133–138.

Kulik, J. A., Bangert, R. L., & Williams, G. W. (1983). Effects of computer-based teaching on secondary school students. *Journal of Educational Psychology, 75*(1), 19–26. doi:10.1037/0022-0663.75.1.19

Kulik, J. A., Cohen, P. A., & Ebeling, B. J. (1980). Effectiveness of programmed instruction in higher education: A meta-analysis of findings. *Educational Evaluation and Policy Analysis, 62*(2), 51–64.

Kuo, M.-L. A., & Hooper, S. (2004). The effects of visual and verbal coding mnemonics on learning Chinese characters in computer-based instruction. *Educational Technology Research and Development, 52*(3), 23–38. doi:10.1007/BF02504673

Kyung, K., Choi, H., Kwon, D., & Son, S. (2004). Interactive mouse systems providing haptic feedback during the exploration in virtual environment. *Lecture Notes in Computer Science, 3280*, 136–146. .doi:10.1007/978-3-540-30182-0_15

Lee, H., Plass, J. L., & Homer, B. D. (2006). Optimizing cognitive load for learning from computer-based science simulations. *Journal of Educational Psychology, 98*(4), 902–913. doi:10.1037/0022-0663.98.4.902

Levie, W. H., & Lentz, R. (1982). Effects of text illustrations: A review of research. *Educational Communications and Technology Journal, 30*(4), 195–232.

Levin, J. R., Anglin, G. J., & Carney, R. N. (1987). On empirically validating functions of pictures in prose. In D. M. Willows & H. A. Houghton (Eds.), *The psychology of illustration, volume 1: Basic research* (pp. 51–80). New York, NY: Springer-Verlag.

Lindner, R. W., & Rickards, J. (1985). Questions inserted in text: Issues and implications. In Jonassen, D. (Ed.), *Technology of text* (*Vol. 2*, pp. 131–157). Englewood CLiffs, NJ: Educational Technology Publications, Inc.

Markle, S. (1969). *Good frames and bad: A grammar of frame writing*. New York, NY: Wiley.

Mayer, R. E. (1989). Systematic thinking fostered by illustrations in scientific text. *Journal of Educational Psychology, 81*, 240–246. doi:10.1037/0022-0663.81.2.240

Mayer, R. E. (2001). *Multimedia learning*. New York, NY: Cambridge University Press.

Mayer, R. E., & Gallini, J. K. (1990). When is an illustration worth ten thousand words? *Journal of Educational Psychology, 82*, 715–726. doi:10.1037/0022-0663.82.4.715

Mayer, R. E., Hegarty, M., Mayer, S., & Campbell, J. (2005). When static media promote active learning: Annotated illustrations versus narrated animations in multimedia instruction. *Journal of Experimental Psychology, 11*(4), 256–265. doi:. doi:10.1037/1076-898X.11.4.256

Mayer, R. E., & Moreno, R. (1998). *Learning from multiple representations in a multimedia environment*. Paper presented at the annual meeting of the ACM SIGCHI Conference on Human Factors in Computing Systems, Los Angeles, CA.

Mayer, R. E., & Moreno, R. (2002). Aids to computer-based multimedia learning. *Learning and Instruction, 12*, 107–119. doi:10.1016/S0959-4752(01)00018-4

Mayer, R. E., & Moreno, R. (2003). Nine ways to reduce cognitive load in multimedia learning. *Educational Psychologist, 38*, 43–52. doi:10.1207/S15326985EP3801_6

Merrill, M. D. (1988). Learner control: Beyond aptitude–treatment interactions. *Educational Communications and Technology Journal, 23*, 217–226.

Merrill, M. D. (2002). First principles of instruction. *Educational Technology Research and Development, 50*(3), 43–59. .doi:10.1007/BF02505024

Misanchuck, E. R. (1992). *Preparing instructional text: Document design using desktop publishing*. Englewood Cliffs, NJ: Educational Technology.

Moore, M. G., & Kearsley, G. (1996). *Distance education: A systems view*. Boston, MA: Wadsworth Publishing Company.

Moreno, R. (2004). Decreasing cognitive load for novice students: Effects of explanatory versus corrective feedback in discovery-based multimedia. *Instructional Science: An International Journal of Learning and Cognition, 32*(1-2), 99–113.

Morrison, G. R. (1994). The media effects question: Unresolvable or asking the right question? *Educational Technology Research and Development, 42*(4), 41–44. doi:10.1007/BF02299090

Morrison, G. R. (2001). Equivalent evaluation of instructional media: The next round of media comparison studies. In Clark, R. E. (Ed.), *Learning from instructional media: Arguments, analysis, and evidence*. Greenwich, CT: Information Age Publishers, Inc.

Morrison, G. R., Ross, S. M., Gopalakrishnan, M., & Casey, J. (1995). The effects of feedback and incentives on achievement in computer-based instruction. *Contemporary Educational Psychology, 20*(1), 32–50. .doi:10.1006/ceps.1995.1002

Morrison, G. R., Ross, S. M., Kalman, H. K., & Kemp, J. E. (2011). *Designing effective instruction* (6th ed.). Hoboken, NJ: John Wiley & Sons, Inc.

Nielsen, J. (1990). *Designing web usability: The practice of simplicity*. Indianapolis, IN: New Riders Publishing.

Oh, S., & Jonassen, D. H. (2007). Scaffolding online argumentation during problem solving. *Journal of Computer Assisted Learning, 23*(2), 95–110. doi:10.1111/j.1365-2729.2006.00206.x

Reiser, R. A., & Dempsey, J. V. (2007). *Trends and issues in instructional design* (2nd ed.). Upper Saddle River, NJ: Pearson Education, Inc.

Ross, S. M., & Morrison, G. R. (1989). In search of a happy medium in instructional technology research: Issues concerning external validity, media replications, and learner control. *Educational Technology Research and Development, 37*(1), 19–33. doi:10.1007/BF02299043

Rothkopf, E. Z. (1970). The concept of mathemagenic activities. *Review of Educational Research, 40*, 325–336.

Rummelhart, D. E., & Ortony, A. (1976). The representation of knowledge in memory. In Anderson, R. C., Spiro, R. J., & Montague, W. E. (Eds.), *Schooling and the acquisition of knowledge* (pp. 99–136). Hillsdale, NJ: Erlbaum.

Salomon, G. (1970). What does it do to Johnny? A cognitive-functionalistic view of research on media. *Viewpoints: Bulletin of the School of Educaiton. Indiana University, 46*(5), 33–62.

Salomon, G. (1972). Can we affect cognitive skills through visual media? An hypothesis and initial findings. *Audio Visual Communications Review, 20*(4), 401–422.

Salomon, G. (1974). Internalization of filmic schematic operations in interaction with learner's aptitudes. *Journal of Educational Psychology, 66*(4), 499–511. doi:10.1037/h0036753

Salomon, G. (1979). *Interaction of media, cognition and learning*. San Francisco, CA: Jossey Bass.

Schultz, C. B., & Di Vesta, F. J. (1972). Effects of passage organization and note taking on the selection of clustering strategies and on recall of textual materials. *Journal of Educational Psychology, 63*(3), 244–252. .doi:10.1037/h0032651

Schunk, D. H., & Zimmerman, B. J. (1998). *Self-regulated learning: From teaching to self-reflective practice*. New York, NY: Guilford Publications.

Skaalid, B. (1999). Web design for insruction: Research-based guidelines. *Canadian Journal of Educational Communication, 27*(3), 139–155.

Skinner, B. F. (1996). Teaching machines. In Ely, D. P., & Plomp, T. (Eds.), *Classic writings on instructional technology* (*Vol. 1*, pp. 211–227). Englewood, CO: Libraries Unlimited.

Snellbecker, G. (1974). *Learning theory, instructional theory, and psychoeducational design*. New York, NY: McGraw-Hill.

Suthers, D. (2006). Technology affordances for intersubjective meaning-making. In Mizobuchi, R., Dillenbourg, P., & Zhu, Z. (Eds.), *Learning by effective utilzation of technologies: Facilitating intercultural understanding*. Amsterdam, The Netherlands: IOS Press.

Swaak, J., & de Jong, T. (2001). Learner vs. system control in using online support for simulation-based discovery learning. *Learning Environments Research, 4*, 217–241. doi:10.1023/A:1014434804876

Sweller, J. (1988). Cognitive load during problem solving: Effects on learning. *Cognitive Science, 12*(2), 257–285. doi:10.1207/s15516709cog1202_4

Sweller, J. (1999). Instructional design in technical areas. [Victoria, Australia.]. *Australian Educational Researcher, 43*, 168.

Sweller, J., Chandler, P., Tierney, P., & Cooper, M. (1990). Cognitive load and selective attention as factors in the structuring of technical material. *Journal of Experimental Psychology. General, 119*(2), 176–192. doi:10.1037/0096-3445.119.2.176

Tinker, M. A. (1963). *Legibility of print*. Ames, IA: Iowa State University Press.

van Gog, T., Ericsson, K. A., Rikers, R. M. J. P., & Paas, F. (2005). Instructional design for advanced learners: Establishing connections between the theoretical frameworks of cognitive load and deliberate practice. *Educational Technology Research and Development, 53*, 73–81. doi:10.1007/BF02504799

van Merriënboer, J. J. G., Chuurman, J. G., de Croock, M. B. M., & Paas, F. G. W. C. (2002). Redirecting learners' attention during training: Effects on cognitive load, transfer test performance and training efficiency. *Learning and Instruction, 12*, 11–37. doi:10.1016/S0959-4752(01)00020-2

Vygotsky, L. S. (1962). *Thought and language*. Cambridge, MA: The M.I.T. Press. doi:10.1037/11193-000

Wittrock, M. C. (1974a). A generative model of mathematics education. *Journal for Research in Mathematics Education, 5*(4), 181–196. doi:10.2307/748845

Wittrock, M. C. (1974b). Learning as a generative process. *Educational Psychologist, 19*(2), 87–95. doi:10.1080/00461527409529129

Wittrock, M. C. (1989). Generative processes of comprehension. *Educational Psychologist, 24*, 345–376. doi:10.1207/s15326985ep2404_2

Woloshyn, V. E., Paivio, A., & Pressley, M. (1994). Use of elaborative interrogation to help students acquire information consistent with prior knowledge and information inconsistent with prior knowledge. *Journal of Educational Psychology, 86*(1), 79–90. doi:10.1037/0022-0663.86.1.79

Wood, E., Pressley, M., & Winne, P. H. (1990). Elaborative interrogation effects on children's learning of factual content. *Journal of Educational Psychology, 82*(4), 741–748. doi:10.1037/0022-0663.82.4.741

Zimmerman, B. J. (1990). Self regulated learning and academic achievement. *American Educational Research Journal, 25*, 3–17.

ADDITIONAL READING

Andre, T. (1979). Does answering higher-level questions while reading facilitate productive learning? *Review of Educational Research, 49*(2), 280–318.

Atkinson, R. K., & Renkl, A. (2007). Interactive example-based learning environments: using interactive elements to encourage effective processing of worked examples. *Educational Psychology Review, 19*, 375–386. doi:10.1007/s10648-007-9055-2

Baddeley, A. (1992). Working memory. *Science, 255*, 556–559. doi:10.1126/science.1736359

Bandura, A. (1977). *Social learning theory*. Englewood Cliffs, NJ: Prentice Hall.

Cheon, J., & Grant, M. M. (2009). Are pretty interfaces worth the time? The effects of user interface types on web-based instruction. *Journal of Interactive Learning Research, 20*(1), 5–33.

Clark, R. E. (2001). *Learning from media*. Greenwich, CT: Information Age Publishers Inc.

Clark, R. E., & Feldon, D. F. (2005). Five common but questionable principles of multimedia learning. In Mayer, R. E. (Ed.), *The Cambridge Handbook of Multimedia Learning* (pp. 97–115). New York: Cambridge University Press.

Craik, F. I. M., & Lockhart, R. S. (1972). Levels of processing: A framework for memory research. *Journal of Verbal Learning and Verbal Behavior, 11*, 671–684. doi:10.1016/S0022-5371(72)80001-X

Dillon, A., & Gabbard, R. (1998). Hypermedia as an educational technology: A review of the quantitative research literature on learner comprehension, control, and style. *Review of Educational Research*, (68): 322–349.

Gerjets, P., Scheiter, K., & Schuh, J. (2008). Information comparisons in example-based hypermedia environments: Supporting learners with processing prompts and an interactive comparison tool. *Educational Technology Research and Development, 56*, 73–92. doi:10.1007/s11423-007-9068-z

Grabowski, B. L. (1996). Generative learning: Past, present, and future. In Jonassen, D. (Ed.), *Handbook of research for educational communication and technology* (pp. 897–918). New York: Macmillan Library Reference USA.

Hamilton, R. J. (2004). Material appropriate processing and elaboration: The impact of balanced and complementary types of processing on learning concepts from text. *The British Journal of Educational Psychology, 74*, 221–237. doi:10.1348/000709904773839851

Kulik, J. A., & Kulik, C. C. (1988). Timing of feedback and verbal learning. *Review of Educational Research, 58*, 79–97.

Lowe, R. (2008). Learning from animation. In Lowe, R., & Schnotz, W. (Eds.), *Learning with animations: Research and implications for design* (pp. 49–68). New York: Cambridge University Press.

Markle, S. (1969). *Good frames and bad: A grammar of frame writing*. New York: Wiley.

Mayer, R. E. (2009). *Multimedia learning* (2nd ed.). NY: Cambridge University Press.

Morrison, G. R., & Anglin, G. J. (2006). An instructional design approach for effective shovelware: Modifying materials for distance education. *Quarterly Review of Distance Education, 7*(1), 63–74.

Morrison, G. R., Ross, S. M., & Baldwin, W. (1992). Learner control of context and instructional support in learning elementary school mathematics. *Educational Technology Research and Development, 40*, 5–13. doi:10.1007/BF02296701

Mory, E. H. (2004). Feedback research revisited. In Jonassen, D. H. (Ed.), *Handbook of research on educational communications and technology* (2nd ed., pp. 745–783). Mahwah, NJ: Lawrence Erlbaum Associates.

Renkl, A., Atkinson, R. K., & Grobe, C. S. (2004). How fading worked solution steps works—A cognitive load perspective. *Instructional Science, 32*, 59–82. doi:10.1023/B:TRUC.0000021815.74806.f6

Rickards, J. P. (1979). Adjunct postquestions in text: A critical review of methods and processes. *Review of Educational Research, 49*(2), 181–196.

Ross, S. M., & Anand, P. G. (1987). A computer-based strategy for personalizing verbal problems in teaching mathematics. *Educational Communications and Technology Journal, 35*, 151–162.

Ross, S. M., Morrison, G. R., & O'Dell, J. K. (1989). Uses and effects of learner control of context and instructional support in computer-based instruction. *Educational Technology Research and Development, 37*, 29–39. doi:10.1007/BF02307719

Rummel, N., Levin, J., & Woodward, M. M. (2003). Do pictorial mnemonic text-learning aids give students something worth writing about? *Journal of Educational Psychology, 95*(2), 327–334. doi:10.1037/0022-0663.95.2.327

Tennyson, R. D., & Cocchiarella, M. J. (1986). An empirically based instructional design theory for teaching concepts. *Review of Educational Research, 56*, 40–71.

Tognazzini, B. (2003). *First principles of interaction design*. Retrieved from http://www.asktog.com/ basics/ firstPrinciples.html.

van Gog, T., Ericsson, K. A., Rikers, R. M. J. P., & Paas, F. (2005). Instructional design for advanced learners: Establishing connections between the theoretical frameworks of cognitive load and deliberate practice. *Educational Technology Research and Development, 53*, 73–81. doi:10.1007/BF02504799

van Merriënboer, J. J. G. (1997). *Training complex cognitive skills*. Englewood Cliffs, NJ: Educational Technology Publications.

KEY TERMS AND DEFINITIONS

Affordance: An attribute of a medium or technology that instructional designers can use to enhance the instruction such as judging a response or incorporating an animation.

Feedback: Information provided to a learner after a response indicating correctness. Feedback can vary in the amount of information provided to the learner.

Instructional Design: A systematic process for analyzing content and the learner to design effective and replicable instruction.

Instructional Strategy: A tactic employed to aid the learner in developing an understanding of the content or development of skill needed to master an objective.

Interaction: Interactions can occur between the learner and the technology such as pressing a button to navigate to a new page, or the interaction can occur either overtly or covertly between the learner and the instruction as part of the instructional strategy.

Redundancy: An undesirable outcome of the instruction that occurs when duplicate information is provided in two or more forms such as in a picture or text or when the spoken narration is shown on the computer display.

Split Attention: An effect created when the learner must move his attention between the text narrative and an illustration to understand the content. The result is an overload on working memory that often fails in the learner not being capable of developing appropriate schema.

Technology-based instruction: Instruction that is delivered or communicated by the learner using some form of technology to mediate the instruction.

ENDNOTE

1 We use the term computer-based instruction as generic term that includes web-based and multimedia, that is, any instruction presented via a computer.

Chapter 4
The Next Generation:
Design and the Infrastructure for Learning in a Mobile and Networked World

Agnes Kukulska-Hulme
The Open University, UK

Chris Jones
The Open University, UK

ABSTRACT

Focusing on intermediate and institutional levels of design for learning, this chapter explores how institutional decisions relate to design, using recent experience at The Open University as a case study. To illuminate the relationship between institutional decisions and learner-focused design, we review and bring together some of the research on learner practices in mobile and networked learning. We take a critical stance in relation to the concept of generation, which has been applied to understanding learners of different ages using terms such as net generation and digital natives. Following on from this, we propose an integrated pedagogical design approach that takes account of learner practices, spaces for learning, and technologies. The chapter also proposes future research directions focused on the changing context for learning, a distinction between place and space and an understanding of how the different levels of educational systems interact with mobile and networked technologies.

INTRODUCTION

In recent years a number of studies have investigated how new generations of students, including mature learners returning to study, draw on a range of personal experience with online and mobile tools and services to support their learning (Bullen et al., 2009; Hargittai, 2010; Jones et al., 2010; Kennedy et al., 2008; Pedró, 2009). Although the studies show that students are often adept at using these tools and services in creative ways that benefit their learning, there are also

DOI: 10.4018/978-1-61350-080-4.ch004

strong reminders that not all members of any age-defined 'generation' have the same levels and extent of expertise. In particular, the younger age group is by no means homogenous in its use and understanding of technology. Nevertheless there are significant age-related changes taking place in students' and young peoples' use of new media and digital and networked technologies (Jones et al., 2010; Ofcom, 2009). Bennett et al. (2008) argue that although there are age-related differences they do not lead to a deficit in which teachers can be thought of as simply lagging behind their students in this regard.

The public rhetoric has emphasised the risk that, as a wave of more competent or adventurous learners (spanning all ages) forges ahead with ever more sophisticated uses of technology, taking their peers with them, there will be increasing dissonance between educators' ideas about learning and those of their students. To assess and if necessary manage this risk, we can analyze the characteristics of learning in a mobile and networked world and provide educators, both individuals and institutions, with conceptual tools for more appropriate designs for learning. The groundwork for this has already been done (Beetham & Sharpe, 2007), with a number of conceptual tools being available for mapping mediating technologies onto the tasks they can help support (Laurillard, 2002), analyzing the implications of how people learn (Mayes & de Freitas, 2004) and learner differences (Beetham, 2007), using checklists for activity design (Beetham, 2007) and for course design (Sharpe & Oliver, 2007a), using a taxonomy of learning activities (Conole, 2007) or a typology of effective interventions for e-learning practice (Sharpe & Oliver, 2007b). However, a world in which mobile and networked technologies have gained prominence but are no longer separate entities calls for a new approach, synthesizing research and practice from these two communities to give a more holistic account of learner experience and a perspective on the implications of physical, virtual and 'hybrid' space.

The potential for a mismatch between the technology experience of educators and learners (Becta, 2006) is not the only tension we need to consider. Students' experience with mobile and networked technologies is based partly on everyday interactions for social reasons or informal learning, but it is also influenced by their use of technology in previous formal settings, such as school and college, or work contexts if they are part-time workers returning to study or continuing their professional development. Therefore institutional or organisational views of how technology supports or does not support learning, and the infrastructures provided for learning, are powerful factors. Higher Education institutions are frequently driven by imperatives such as organisational strategy, including IT procurement strategies and plans for the development of their estates. When we confront this with the aspirations of university teachers to try out new technologies or new ways of using technology, it is possible to identify some overlaps, but also some areas of disjunction. We wish to argue that by building continual research on student practices with technology into the practice of teaching, we can create environments where students and teachers are in ongoing dialogue and this in turn has the potential to inform and transform institutional strategy.

This chapter provides a review of recent research relating to the use of networked and mobile technology by learners in different age groups, whilst taking a critical stance in relation to the concept of 'generation'. Our main objectives for this chapter are the following:

- To explore how institutional factors relate to design by setting the parameters within which specific instances of design can take place
- To review and bring together research on learner practices with technology from two communities, namely mobile learning and networked learning

- To formulate implications for the next generation of design for learning in relation to new infrastructures for learning

Against a background of institutional change, illustrated through the experience of The Open University, we identify key findings from a range of studies concerning learner use of technology, including our own research, focusing primarily on use of the web and mobile technologies. We then use these findings to formulate implications for design which should be sensitive to learner practices. We also believe that institutions should embrace more open environments in which these practices can be observed, discussed, and integrated into future designs for learning, creating enhanced conditions for teaching and learning.

BACKGROUND: INSTITUTIONAL CHANGE

Much of the recent work in relation to design has focused on learning design, used in a number of somewhat different ways (Koper & Tattersall, 2005; McAndrew et al., 2006). The stance taken in the chapter is that design for learning is indirect, that is that learning cannot be designed directly but only designed *for* by providing good conditions in which learning can take place (Beetham & Sharpe, 2007; Jones & Dirckinck-Holmfeld, 2009). We explore how institutional factors relate to design for learning by setting the parameters within which specific instances of design can take place. The focus is on intermediate and institutional levels of design that sit between micro levels of design affecting day to day interactions and macro levels of design that affect broad areas of infrastructure at regional, national or global level. The chapter draws on the experience of The Open University (UK) and the implementation of the OU Virtual Learning Environment (VLE) between 2005 and 2009 (Jones, 2009; Sclater, 2008). The university also has an evolving mobile learning strategy and engagement with the potential of social networks for learning.

By taking a single case study of institutional change the chapter examines some general issues affecting the design of an infrastructure for learning (Guryibe, 2005; Guryibe & Lindström, 2009). These include the way that the design of an institutional tool such as a VLE can impact on day to day interaction, the way that the selection of a technological platform can have a lock-in effect and the way that systematic planning at institutional level can be affected by contingent organisational factors. The chapter also examines the limits of institutional design and the impact that universal service infrastructures, such as search engines (e.g. Google™), Wikipedia®, open educational resources, cloud computing and mobile applications can have on local educational practices.

The Open University Case Study

The Open University (OU) adopted Moodle™ as the main platform when it introduced a new Open University Virtual Learning Environment (Jones, 2009; Sclater, 2008). The design of Moodle™ was based around an imagined setting: the classroom and a single academic teaching a cohort of students. The problem for the OU was that the university is based around a pedagogy of 'Supported Open Learning', which relies on support for individual students and groups in large distance education courses that are designed by complex course teams and delivered by a group of Associate Lecturers on separate contracts to the course team. The new platform supporting the change in infrastructure had inscribed into it a notion of how teaching and learning would be done. The Open University has program level structures which are used to integrate courses and the overall student experience. The basic structure of Moodle™ had a limited repertoire of roles and permissions that neither reflected the way in which Open University courses organized themselves nor did it fully support the organizational structures that linked those courses into coherent programs (see Sclater, 2008). Whilst these precise arrangements are particular to the OU, each technological platform has inscribed in it a set of notions about teaching and learning and each institution has its own individual ideas about how teaching and learning should be conducted (see Jones et al., 2009; and for a full case study at another Open University (OUNL), see Hermans & Verjans, 2009).

Lock-in, Contingency and Planning

The starting conditions for a change in infrastructure are rarely clear cut and they usually build on existing systems. The Open University had adopted FirstClass® computer conferencing as a tool for discussion and email and by the time of the changeover to Moodle™, FirstClass® was deeply embedded in the institution and it was obvious that disengagement from FirstClass® would take between 18 months and 3 years. Initially lock-in was observed because many of the OU courses were so dependent upon FirstClass® conferencing and courses had written FirstClass® into their course materials and embedded it at a detailed level. In reality it is only in 2010 (5 years later) that the OU is finally ready to deploy a new email system, part of a wider adoption of Google™ Apps, to replace student FirstClass® email accounts.

The planning for the new VLE was accompanied by changes in senior personnel including the appointment of a temporary Director prior to the appointment of a VLE Director for a fixed term linked to the implementation of the VLE program. It was in the period when the temporary Director was in place that the move towards the crucial decision to adopt Moodle™ took place. This necessarily had two effects. Firstly the new Director largely inherited a major decision that would have a significant influence on later decisions and secondly the decision was taken outside the detailed procedure for setting out the requirements in Phase 1 of the OU VLE project. The planned approach was replaced and Moodle™ was largely selected prior to the appointment of the new Director, although the final decision took place at a Steering Group in the first week after his arrival. The process described here illustrates how contingent the decision making process is. The infrastructure developed at the OU arose out of a combination of structured decision making processes and the day to day contingencies of organisational life and we should expect this contingent element in the development of other large infrastructure projects in universities.

Institutional Limits

Following the introduction of the OU VLE, the university has continued to experiment with the integration of new web services into the university's online infrastructure, such as iTunes™ U and YouTube™. It has gone further than this in the attempt to integrate Web 2.0 technologies with the development of SocialLearn (Walton et al., 2008). The aim of SocialLearn (http://www.open.ac.uk/blogs/sociallearn/) is to apply Web 2.0 technologies to learning and in particular aspects of social networking. There are also universal services that influence universities but sit outside the institution's boundaries such as Wikipedia® and social networking sites like Facebook. The adoption of mobile technologies introduces these influences into the interactions of students in new ways, for example during work-based learning, and makes the boundary of the university less distinct.

This brief case study draws attention to the mediating role of the institution as it selects technologies for deployment in the university. The university puts in place a technological infrastructure, part of which is intentionally linked to the learning process, an infrastructure for learning (Guryibe & Lindström, 2009). This infrastructure is not easily changed and the selection of technologies that are central to the infrastructure brings with it an implicit set of decisions designed in to the system regarding pedagogy and the organization of learning. Finally the kinds of technology that are emerging are of a kind that disrupts the organizational boundary of the university. Universal service infrastructures and cloud computing allow some interactions that are key to learning to reside beyond institutional borders.

NEXT GENERATION LEARNERS

In this section we review some of the literature concerning learner use of technology produced or referenced by two communities, namely researchers in networked and mobile learning. They share many theoretical assumptions and methods, but they have separate conferences (chief among them being Networked Learning and mLearn) and do not habitually refer to the work of the other community. A novel contribution of the chapter is that we bring the research together here for the purpose of abstracting and critiquing key findings relating to learner experience in relation to conceptualizations of learner generations. We believe that these findings have implications for how educators and institutions should create the conditions for appropriate learning.

Learners in a Networked World

When students arrive at university they have developed a variety of practices related to learning and the use of digital and networked technologies. The availability of good broadband network access is becoming nearly universal in advanced industrial countries as are the various devices, laptop computers, mobile devices, etc., connecting to these networks. Because the world that most young people grow up in is filled with new technology, it has become a commonplace to ask whether this new environment is having profound, identifiable and universal impacts on young people. Two of the most common ways to describe the new generation of young people are as the Net Generation (Tapscott, 1998, 2009) and Digital Natives (Prensky, 2001a, 2001b).

As a result of the impact of these terms there is a growing literature that is critical of the Net Generation and Digital Native arguments. There is literature based on empirical research (Bullen et al., 2009; Hargittai, 2010; Jones et al., 2010; Kennedy et al., 2008; Pedró, 2009; Selwyn, 2008) and a smaller number of critics who have taken a more theoretical stance (Bayne & Ross, 2007; Bennett et al., 2008). The research demonstrates that students in advanced industrial countries are far from homogenous in their response to new technologies (see Hargittai, 2010, Jones et al., 2010, and Kennedy et al., 2008), whilst Bayne and Ross (2007) suggest that there is a paradox in the debate because each person is said to be fixed in a generational position but older people are still expected to change and become more like the young.

Prensky has argued that there is a distinct generational boundary and that young people have:

... not just changed incrementally from those of the past, nor simply changed their slang, clothes, body adornments, or styles, as has happened between generations previously. A really big discontinuity has taken place. One might even call it a "singularity" – an event which changes things so fundamentally that there is absolutely no going back. (Prensky, 2001a, p.1)

The generational argument that arises from both the writings of Tapscott (1998, 2009) and Prensky (2001a, 2001b), suggests that a whole generation of students has been affected by their immersion since birth in a world infused with digital and networked technologies. They suggest that it is technological immersion that causes a change in the entire generation of young people in relation to technology and in relation to a range of other activities including learning. Tapscott for example argues that the Net Generation has a tendency towards collaboration:

In education they [the Net generation] are forcing a change in the model of pedagogy, from a teacher-focused approach based on instruction to a student-focused model based on collaboration. (Tapscott, 2009, p.11)

More recently Tapscott and Williams have argued for a radical shift towards collaborative learning, understood as social learning (Tapscott & Williams, 2010, pp.18-21). The empirical research describing the Net Generation suggests another way of understanding the relationship in which the developments in digital and networked technologies allow for, or afford, different patterns of engagement with technology and learning. The way student agency affects engagement with technology has been investigated in a developing economy in which access to technology is not as universal or unproblematic as in advanced industrial settings (Czerniewicz et al., 2009). In this view technologies do not force any particular change, rather they define the range of choices that can be made. For example, students suggest that the new technologies can be distracting when they are working (Jones & Healing, 2010a). Agent driven notifications appear on screen while the students work with multiple applications open at the same time, with some providing educational and work related support whilst others are related to the student's social life and leisure. Students are not passive in response to this tendency to distraction and indeed they actively choose to follow their own strategies for dealing with this technology driven phenomenon (Jones & Healing, 2010a). Choice is not only concerned with the individual student and their relationship with technology because, as we pointed out in the previous case study, universities are also making choices.

We have argued that students are being described as different from their teachers in generational terms and we now go on to relate these arguments to the suggestion that the university as an institution is threatened by Internet based technologies. In these arguments change is not conceived of as a choice, it is described as inevitable:

Universities are losing their grip on higher learning as the Internet is, inexorably, becoming the dominant infrastructure for knowledge—both as a container and as a global platform for knowledge exchange between people— and as a new generation of students requires a very different model of higher education. Many people have written about this topic, in EDUCAUSE Review and other publications. The transformation of the university is not just a good idea. It is an imperative, and evidence is mounting that the consequences of further delay may be dire. (Tapscot & Williams, 2010, p.18)

Bennett et al. (2008) have argued that this kind of discourse resembles an academic 'moral panic' because it restricts critical and rational debate. Moral panic is a term that describes conditions in which an identified group in society is placed in a media spotlight and described in sensationalist terms as a threat to social values and norms. The Net Generation of Digital Natives is identified in this way and they are identified as the cause of fundamental change in universities.

A powerful force to change the university is the students. And sparks are flying today. A huge generational clash is emerging in our institutions. (Tapscott & Williams, 2010, p.29)

Tapscott and Williams argue that it is a generational clash that is a major cause of university transformation.

Bates (2010) has argued that collaborative learning is a long standing aim of educational reform and that: 'The interesting question is not what universities should be doing, but why it isn't happening.' (Bates, 2010). He goes on to question the underlying idea that the problem in Universities is the 'obstructive, non-market-based business models.' (see Tapscott & Williams, 2010, p.29). Tapscott and Williams suggest a neo-liberal market oriented re-organisation of universities whereas Bates identifies cost cutting and resource limitation as organisational factors that restrict the capacity of universities to change. Bates' criticism focuses on three main points:

1. The 'new' constructivism identified by Tapscott and Williams is not in fact new.
2. That constructivist methods require staff student ratios that have been eroded in cost cutting drives for efficiency in universities.
3. That privatization would harm some of the most basic and essential functions of university (e.g. knowledge creation and autonomy).

Bates argues that the future of university provision is a choice not a technological requirement, and that while technological change can help in the reform of university teaching and learning, resistance to change arises more from issues of funding, organization and vision than it does from a non-market form of organization. We have argued above that design has an institutional aspect through the design of infrastructure and infrastructures for learning specifically. We find no evidence that a new Net Generation of Digital Natives are forcing change on institutions, nor that the pressures for change suggest a neo-liberal market response. Pressures for change have a political and ideological source and if there are organisational constraints restricting the ability of universities to design new models of learning, such as collaborative learning, then they are more likely to be resource constraints and the reduction of staff student ratios than a non-market model of university organization.

Learners in a Mobile World

The questions implied in the above analysis are to some extent echoed in the concerns of educators and their institutions when it comes to the challenges posed by mobile learning: 'Is change inevitable?', 'Are Digital Natives causing fundamental change in universities?', 'Is there a generational clash between teachers and learners?'. Although mobile technologies have been around a long time, their impact on university education is much more recent, and the possible extent of this impact is only just being imagined. The use of mobile technologies in teaching and learning began as a set of discrete research projects, followed by a wave of more widespread adoption by a limited number of institutions, some of which have issued laptops, phones, mp3 players or tablet computers to whole cohorts of students. The current situation in the UK and in less developed economies, such as South Africa (Czerniewicz et al., 2009, pp. 77-81) is that the mobile phones owned by the majority of students, due to their improved functionality, are becoming a feasible tool for mobile learning, largely obviating the need to purchase special devices (although this does not hold true for more technologically advanced mobile learning). However, the 'critical mass' of owners of mobile devices may not translate automatically into use. Amongst English students the use of advanced features of mobile phones, such as email and Internet access shows a relationship with age and the youngest students are the most active, although use of these advanced features is not as common as the ownership of devices enabled with these functions (Jones & Cross, 2009; Jones & Hosein, 2010). Nevertheless in the near future we can expect a variety of mobile devices, including laptops, smart phones, tablets and slates to challenge desktop access. Recent surveys in the US show increasing ownership and use of mobile devices with approximately 50% of students owning such devices and most of this group (80%) using the devices to browse the Web and send email (Smith & Borreson Carruso, 2010).

In parallel, there is evidence of a growing expectation among web users that content is accessible on a mobile device and that mobile interaction is supported, fuelled by the rise in mobile services such as mobile banking (Butcher, 2010). Internal data collected by The Open University show a steady and significant increase over the past couple of years in mobile access to a website containing information and study resources for students. This suggests a learner-led demand for at least one form of mobile learning. Use of mobile technologies will depend on the development and deployment of mobile educational resources by universities as well as growing student access to mobile devices (Sheehan, 2009). A secondary consideration will be the way in which academics and course teams build in requirements for the use of mobile technologies into their courses. Furthermore, it will also depend on the provision of universal services, such as Wikipedia®, Google™ and location aware applications, optimised for mobile use.

Research in the field of mobile learning has changed over the past couple of decades as the early emphasis on design of educational software for portable devices evolved towards socio-technical support for learner mobility (Kukulska-Hulme et al., 2009). This shift was brought about by the proliferation and increasing acceptance of mobile devices as everyday tools supporting life, work, informal learning and leisure, along with developments in technology and infrastructure enabling wireless access to the internet and more diverse channels of social communication including social networks. Mobile access is fuelling the explosion of social media and contributing to the blurring of boundaries between formal and informal learning (Pettit & Kukulska-Hulme, 2007).

The availability of thousands of free and inexpensive 'apps' (small applications for smartphones) is again changing the nature of mobile learning, marking a return to imaginative software design whilst also confirming the importance of users as a key influence on the future direction of mobile learning. Although educators would like to claim that pedagogical considerations shape the design of mobile learning, and indeed in many cases they do, in reality it is difficult to ignore the fact that the mobile marketplace is shaping user expectations and behaviours. There is also a strong push from technology firms forging ahead with new personalized, location-aware and context-aware services that are likely to capture users' imaginations and arguably will meet some of their needs sooner than what can be provided by universities (Educause, 2009).

Mobile learning could remain informal and separate from other forms of networked learning but the argument for its integration into university curricula may be supported by investigations of how young people are adopting personal devices as indispensable tools enabling them to remain in perpetual contact with friends and acquaintances, especially in countries such as Finland and Japan where a mobile culture first became pervasive (Ito, Okabe & Matsuda, 2005; Kasesniemi & Rautiainen, 2002). Currently English university students have not adopted the practices of nomadic workers and are still using mobile technologies in a limited number of quite traditional physical spaces, such as student study bedrooms (Jones & Healing, 2010b). In those university programmes where communication and collaboration are important, the added dimension of mobile interaction may soon be considered essential.

Mobile learning among young people is generally reported as part of formal 'designed learning' projects rather than learner-led activity arising from learners' own requirements (Kukulska-Hulme, Traxler & Pettit, 2007). However, Bradley and Holley (2010) report that "many students are using whatever mobile phone they have for a wide range of learning activities" (p. 238). Mobile phone use has also been researched in the broader context of 'learner voice' case studies that try to elicit learner perspectives on their learning experience including use of technology:

An overwhelming feature that emerged from the case studies was the fact that technologies appeared to be integral to learning for all the students, irrespective of their background, prior IT expertise, learning preferences or subject discipline studied. (Conole, 2008, p.126).

Research with older or mature learners confirms that within more advanced age brackets there are groups of mobile users that can be identified as 'innovators' and 'early adopters' (Rogers, 2003), namely those who are at the forefront of change as evidenced by their active use of social networking and mobile technologies to advance their learning (Kukulska-Hulme & Pettit, 2006; Kukulska-Hulme et al., 2009; Pettit & Kukulska-Hulme, 2007). These groups of individuals are making use of new tools within a particular period of time, ahead of their peers. Beyond social contact, typical uses include accessing fresh content, gathering local information and becoming visible as creators and producers of resources which may be shared with others.

What are the implications for university teachers? Mobile learning challenges teachers to examine how mobility relates to their teaching aims, methods and subject matter. Mobile devices are also extending networked learning into new physical environments and enabling more experimental learning designs in a range of new locations outside the traditional, and even the virtual, classroom. This poses real challenges to educators in terms of:

- Reduced control over the physical location and setting in which learning takes place
- Potential to increase awareness of remote activity in virtual and off-site settings, for example through learner activity logging
- Understanding the possible new learning goals and outcomes offered by mobile learning
- Usability and accessibility issues that continue to be reported on the ground, despite the rhetoric from highly confident or technically-minded users that devices are now 'intuitive' and no longer pose such problems
- Limited access to appropriate devices, reported by teachers (Mifsud & Smørdal, 2006), a situation that is repeated in universities and should be understood in the context of many established users being content with their existing phone – until they consider mobile learning
- Ethical considerations associated with new activity such as learner-generated content created on mobile devices, where spontaneous actions may have unintended consequences for learners, teachers and institutions

In summary, the proliferation of mobile technologies is likely to have a significant impact on design for learning in the medium to long term, however current student expectations are not pushing teachers to work on innovative designs. For some time yet, the use of mobile devices will remain a complementary activity or an alternative way to access course materials and for students to make contact or collaborate with other students. The development of location-aware and context-aware applications is still largely in the realm of research, although the thinking that this generates around the design and use of learning spaces can benefit all who are interested in looking to the future and considering what new choices may present themselves. Mobile learning enables teachers to design for learning beyond the boundaries of their institution, but they will require good advice and examples of how this can be done.

Implications for Design

We have established the broad institutional and external factors affecting choices that university teachers make about their use of networked and mobile technologies for teaching and learning, as well as some specifically human factors that relate to usability, accessibility, ethical issues and feelings of control. We have shown in our case study that the provision of a technological infrastructure at university level has a mediating role with a significant influence on learning practices. The university infrastructure which is intentionally linked to the learning process provides an infrastructure for learning (Guryibe & Lindström,

2009). This infrastructure for learning incorporates a set of design considerations affecting pedagogy and the organization of learning. Externally universal service infrastructures and cloud computing threaten to disrupt the university's organizational boundaries.

We have found that there is no strong imperative from students that would suggest the need to design for a different 'generation'. Nevertheless, teachers need to understand emerging student practices with technology as these give indications of what is becoming common and accepted, and will be particularly relevant to how students may approach learning tasks that have been set. The implications for design are in terms of defining the next generation of designs that take account of infrastructures for learning and student practices with technology but are not driven by these considerations alone. We would argue that learning spaces are becoming a key element of design for learning (Jones & Dirckinck-Holmfeld, 2009). JISC (2009) has produced a valuable guide to the design of physical teaching, learning and social space, to accommodate and make best use of mobile and networked technologies in attractive and flexible ways. In our own work we found during a follow up investigation reported in Jones & Healing (2010b) that the introduction of a new zone on a campus university, specifically designed with wireless access, with comfortable informal seating and 24 hours access, led to an increase in students' use of mobile devices in the following academic year. There are also numerous publications pertaining to the design of virtual space, including in immersive environments such as Second Life®. We would argue that in reality, teachers seldom have the opportunity to design the spaces they would like to teach in, however physical and virtual spaces designed for them in a flexible way can allow teachers to adapt and change what they find in the learning space. This implies a focus on the institutional provision of both physical and virtual learning spaces that make the most of the affordances of new mobile and network technologies. This may involve some additional effort and planning at an institutional level. For teachers, the effort of adaptation could be more acceptable if setting up a learning space were to become a self-evident and valued stage in course and programme design, and individual teaching sessions. This may require a change of attitude and different practices on the part of teachers, learners and institutions.

Spaces only make sense when considered in relation to what is made of them, people's behaviours and appropriation of space, therefore learners' activities and the technologies they make use of are the other key elements. Space can be distinguished from place, the lived-in environment constituted by students and teachers from the available physical and virtual resources (Jones & Dirckinck-Holmfeld, 2009). Students may bring devices with them or access networks and resources within the learning space and beyond it. From this perspective, when designing for learning with mobile and networked technologies, teachers and institutions need to consider the following in an integrated way (see Figure 1):

1. Learning spaces (in the institution and beyond)
    - What are students expected to do for their learning and where can this take place?
    - How is use of learning spaces connected with use of time, e.g. will students return to the space between formal sessions?
    - What are the organizational boundaries and what is permitted or feasible within the institution and beyond?
2. Learners (in formal and informal settings)
    - There is no evidence of a generational step change, but what kinds of changes in learner practices are taking place?
    - How can spaces and technologies be used to elicit feedback from students

Figure 1. Conceptualizing design for mobile and networked learning

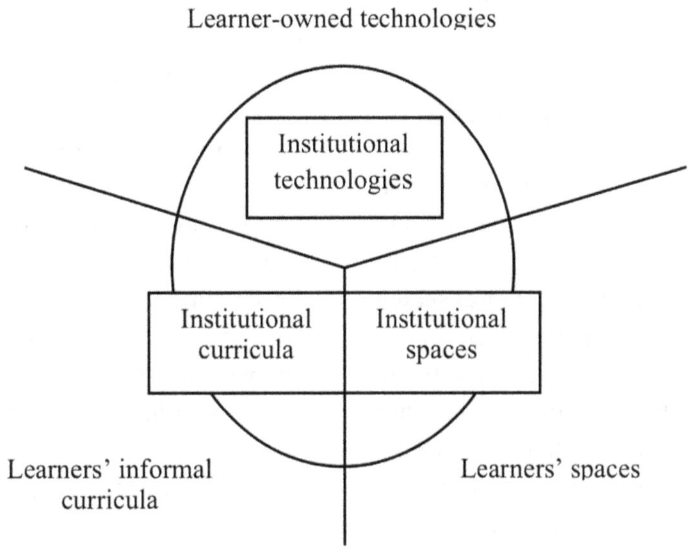

on their learning activity? (e.g. logs of activity, visualisations of learner networks, etc.)
    ◦ What is known about students' experiences and expectations based on their previous use of technology in life and learning?
3. Technologies (institutionally-provided and learner-owned)
    ◦ What level is appropriate for the design of a technological intervention: university, programme, course or class?
    ◦ How flexible and adaptable is the design of the technological environments where learning is expected to take place?
    ◦ Is there any foreseeable conflict between various technologies being proposed in the design, including more traditional tools and media?

It should be understood that pedagogical design will involve several levels of intervention, involving whole institutions and the design of learning infrastructure, through to intermediate levels in terms of the design of curricula and programmes of study in departments and faculties, right down to course teams and individual practitioners who design the tasks and quotidian interactions of particular modules and courses. It also seems important to state that by building continual research on student practices with technology into the practice of teaching, we can create environments where students and teachers are in ongoing dialogue and this in turn has the potential to inform and transform institutional strategy. Thomas (2010) argues that although design of learning space is replacing the previous emphasis on content and outcomes in course design, nevertheless, "… 'the structure of the learning space' cannot be the point of departure in the planning process" (Thomas, 2010, p.509). For him, the important part is planning for an activity that can be described as "an adaptive enterprise", such that the structure of the learning space becomes "a function of the adaptive complex system that it serves" (ibid, p.509). He does, however, acknowledge that this is a daunting requirement. It seems to us that in practical terms, university teachers will want to work with more concrete ways of thinking about design.

FUTURE RESEARCH DIRECTIONS

Students come to university with habits of social engagement mediated by digital networks and they are already familiar with a number of universal services useful in education, such as search engines (e.g. Google™) and Wikipedia®. When they arrive at university students are met by an institutional infrastructure for learning that has been specifically designed to support learning. Because networks and mobile technologies allow students to construct their personal learning environments using a range of services in a variety of spaces we cannot assume that learning will take place only in the buildings and settings that have been designed for that purpose. Many areas of the University will remain the same, such as the lecture theatre, seminar room and library, but they will be used in different ways, and social or recreational areas (café, leisure facility, etc.) are transforming into places for digitally enhanced learning. Universities already struggle with issues around mobile Internet access during classes. Some universities try to block access whilst others encourage it. Research will need to analyze these changes and provide timely advice for educators and educational institutions about the ways that student learning is changing and the kinds of technological provision that the university should be making.

The complex task of design remains one that has to focus on those features of mobile and networked learning environments that can be designed without prescribing the detailed interactions that teachers and learners may undertake in these settings. The university will need great flexibility to accommodate the variety of technology-related demands it will face. The convergence of mobile and networked digital devices, and the changes in the skills required for educational design, mean that there is a constant need to re-think and revise design approaches. From the work we have reported we have identified three key issues for future research.

Contexts for Learning

Mobile devices extend networked learning into new physical environments and enable designs for learning in a range of new locations beyond the classroom. Networked learning took learning beyond known contexts, and mobile technologies take this further by converging mobile telecommunications with wireless and broadband Internet access. These technologies are in one sense an extension of the earlier promise of the Internet and the Web, but education and learning is still largely located in institutions and embedded in practices that are slow to change. These factors may slow the pace, and restrict the scope of changes associated with networked and mobile learning. Research needs to explore both the ways new mobile technologies are being used in the wild and the ways in which the new technological possibilities interplay with institutional and social constraints. For the new technologies to lead to productive outcomes for education and learning we need to know more about the ways learners constitute their own contexts for learning in the new mobile networks.

Space and Place

Fostering a sense of place (Cresswell, 2004) in networked learning environments may be necessary to develop a social and emotional context which is able to sustain learning. Students participating in a networked learning environment are simultaneously situated at a real point in time and space and also displaced from that physical point in a virtual space in the network. Whilst students' learning spaces are never completely disembedded or separated from their off-line activities and spatial locations, they are displaced. The flexibility of virtual spaces requires students to engage in a process of place-making. The adoption of a distinction between designed space and enacted place has theoretical and methodological implications. Firstly, it influences the kinds of interests researchers pursue in their research and secondly, it will affect the methods that are used to understand the students' experience of place within networked and mobile learning environments. The concept of place as distinct from space can improve the design of networked learning environments and it will be important to understand the way students and teachers experience designed spaces and the potentials that exist for them to constitute their own places.

Levels for Design

Research will also need to distinguish between the different levels at which design for learning can be realized. There is a strong tradition of research into classroom activity, the design of resources and materials and the design of various tools and devices. There has been less emphasis on the way intermediate structures can be designed, such as institutional infrastructures for learning, and the overall design of learning spaces. We suggest that the meso level of design may be critical in the deployment of networked and mobile technologies. At its simplest the meso level can be thought of as being intermediate between small scale, local interaction and large-scale policy processes. The meso level can be characterized as the level where bottom-up meets top-down. We think that it is possible to use the distinctions between macro, meso and micro levels in an analytic way which identifies social practice as the locus in which broader social processes are located in small group activity. We think further research on the ways mobile and networked technologies can be designed for use in Higher Education will depend on a strong sense of how the different levels of the educational system interact with the new technologies.

CONCLUSION

Design in mobile and networked learning environments is notoriously difficult because the location, connections and context of the learner are outside of the designer's control (Beetham and Sharpe, 2007). Design cannot be direct and the spaces and activities that are the product of design will be interpreted flexibly by the students and teachers who inhabit the design. Nevertheless design is necessary at various levels. Design needs to take account of:

- The kinds of students that are entering university and how exposure to networked and mobile technologies is changing their experience of learning;
- The infrastructures beyond institutional control and infrastructures for learning that can be designed (Guryibe & Lindström, 2009);
- The specific tools, resources and artifacts used for learning;
- The kinds of tasks and activities that we expect learners to engage in for their learning (Goodyear et al., 2001).

We conclude that design should not be based on a supposed generational gap between teachers and students, nor is there an identifiable generational pressure for change, but there are age-related changes taking place that we ignore at our peril. The younger students are, in advanced industrial economies, the more likely they are to be using social networking, advanced features on their mobile phones, and editing and uploading multimedia files. The older students are, the less likely this is to be the case. There is no singularity or sharp generational divide and there are minorities of students in all age groups that engage in limited or advanced ways with technology. Design has to cope with this variation and include minorities as well as the increasing numbers of younger students who are more accustomed to the new technologies.

The Open University Learning Design Initiative (Conole, 2010) is an example of good practice in fostering a holistic approach to designing for learning, but many institutions will find that their entrenched infrastructures will continue to hamper integrative thinking in design. Furthermore, there is little shared experience of how evolving use of technology in physical and virtual space impacts on design. This is why we have argued that learning spaces should become a new focus of designs for learning, and an important aspect of future research in this area.

Design will take place in an increasingly uncertain policy context in which the boundaries between public and private provision will be subject to change. Firstly, cloud computing is outsourcing institutional provision from the university and secondly, the financial crisis has led some states to begin to withdraw from social support for Higher Education and an increased emphasis on the development of private provision. Within this shifting landscape, the impact of mobile and networked technologies in Higher Education is increasing. Often thinking about mobile technologies has been restricted to small handheld devices connected by broadband mobile and wireless networks. Networked learning in contrast has focused on the distribution of learning via the Internet and Web. Increasingly these two areas of interest converge as devices become hybrid (e.g. iPad, Android tablets) and are able to connect to the Internet and Web seamlessly through both mobile telecommunications and wireless Internet. The challenge will be to design for learning in contexts over which educators have increasingly limited control.

REFERENCES

Bates, T. (2010). *A critique of Tapscott and William's views on university reform.* E-learning and Distance Education Resources website. Retrieved July 22, 2010, from http://www.tonybates.ca/2010/02/14/a-critique-of-tapscott-and-williams-views-on-university-reform/

Bayne, S., & Ross, J. (2007, December). *The digital native and digital immigrant: A dangerous opposition.* Paper presented at the Annual Conference of the Society for Research into Higher Education (SRHE), Brighton 11-13th December 2007. Retrieved July 22, 2010, from http://www.malts.ed.ac.uk/staff/sian/natives_final.pdf

Becta (2006). *Delivering the future for learners: Harnessing technology.* Report of the Harnessing Technology event, 7 November 2006. Retrieved July 22, 2010, from http://foi.becta.org.uk/content_files/corporate/resources/foi/archived_publications/harnessing_technology_event.pdf

Beetham, H., & Sharpe, R. (Eds.). (2007). *Rethinking pedagogy for a digital age: Designing and delivering e-learning.* London, UK: RoutledgeFalmer.

Bennett, S., Maton, K., & Kervin, L. (2008). The digital natives debate: A critical review of the evidence. *British Journal of Educational Technology, 39*(5), 775–786. doi:10.1111/j.1467-8535.2007.00793.x

Bradley, C., & Holley, D. (2010). How students in higher education use their mobile phones for learning. In Montebello, M., Camilleri, V., & Dingli, A. (Eds.), *Proceedings of mLearn 2010* (pp. 232–239). University of Malta.

Bullen, M., Morgan, T., Belfer, K., & Qayyum, A. (2009). The net generation in higher education: Rhetoric and reality. *International Journal of Excellence in E-Learning, 2*(1), 1–13.

Butcher, D. (2010, May 10). Mobile financial services growing quickly but banks missing opportunities. *Mobile Commerce Daily*. Retrieved July 22, 2010, from http://www.mobilecommercedaily.com/ mobile-financial-services-growing -quickly-but-banks-missing-opportunities/

Conole, G. (2008). Listening to the learner voice: The ever changing landscape of technology use for language students. *ReCALL*, *20*(2), 124–140. doi:10.1017/S0958344008000220

Conole, G. (2010, February). *A holistic approach to designing for learning: A vision for the future*. Paper presented at the Annual International CODE Symposium, 18 February 2010, Chiba, Japan.

Cresswell, T. (2004). *Place: A short introduction*. Oxford, UK: Blackwell.

Czerniewicz, L., Williams, K., & Brown, C. (2009). Students make a plan: Understanding student agency in constraining conditions. *ALT-J Research in Learning Technology*, *17*(2), 75–88. doi:10.1080/09687760903033058

Educause. (2009). 7 things you should know about location-aware applications. *Educause, March 2009*. Retrieved June 28, 2010, from http://net.educause.edu/ ir/library/ pdf/ ELI7047.pdf

Goodyear, P., Jones, C., Asensio, M., Hodgson, V., & Steeples, C. (2001). *Effective networked learning in higher education: Notes and guidelines*. Deliverable 9 of the Networked Learning in Higher Education Project, Lancaster University. Retrieved July 22, 2010, from: http://csalt.lancs.ac.uk/ jisc/ Guidelines_final.doc

Guribye, F. (2005). *Infrastructures for learning - Ethnographic inquiries into the social and technical conditions of education and training*. Doctoral thesis, University of Bergen, Norway. Retrieved July 20, 2010, from: http://hdl.handle.net/ 1956/ 859

Guribye, F., & Lindström, B. (2009). Infrastructures for learning and networked tools - The introduction of a new tool in an inter-organisational network. In L. Dirckinck-Holmfeld, C. Jones, & B. Lindström (Eds.), *Analysing networked learning practices in higher education and continuing professional development* (pp. 103-115. Rotterdam, The Netherlands: Sense Publishers, BV.

Hargittai, E. (2010). Digital na(t)ives? Variations in internet skills and uses among members of the "net generation". *Sociological Inquiry*, *80*(1), 92–113. doi:10.1111/j.1475-682X.2009.00317.x

Hermans, H., & Verjans, S. (2009). *Developing a sustainable, student centred VLE: The OUNL-case*. Retrieved May 29, 2009, from http://dspace.ou.nl/ bitstream/ 1820/ 1894/ 1/ Hermans_Verjans_ICDE2009_V4.pdf

Herrington, A., Herrington, J., & Mantei, J. (2009). Design principles for mobile learning. In J. Herrington, A. Herrington, J. Mantei, I. Olney & B. Ferry (Eds.), *New technologies, new pedagogies: Mobile learning in higher education* (129-138). Faculty of Education, University of Wollongong, 2009. Retrieved July 22, 2010, from http://ro.uow.edu.au/

Ito, M., Okabe, D., & Matsuda, M. (2005). *Personal, portable, pedestrian: Mobile phones in Japanese life*. Cambridge, MA: The MIT Press.

JISC. (2009). *Designing spaces for effective learning: A guide to 21st century learning space design*. Retrieved July 20, 2010, from http://www.jisc.ac.uk/ eli_learningspaces.html

Jones, C. (2009). A context for collaboration: The institutional selection of an infrastructure for learning. In C. O'Malley, D. Suthers, P. Reiman & A. Dimitracopoulou (Eds). *Proceedings of the 8th International Conference on Computer Supported Collaborative Learning: CSCL2009: CSCL Practices vol 1* (pp. 292-296). Retrieved June 28, 2010, from http://portal.acm.org/ citation.cfm? id=1600053.1600098

Jones, C., Aoki, K., Ruslan, E., & Schlusmans, K. (2009). A comparison of three open universities and their acceptance of Internet technologies. *M-2009: Proceedings of the 23rd ICDE World Conference on Open Learning and Distance Education including the 2009 EADTU Annual Conference*, 7-10 June 2009, Maastricht NL. Retrieved November 12, 2010, from http://www.ou.nl/ Docs/ Campagnes/ ICDE2009/ Papers/ Final_paper_081jones.pdf

Jones, C., & Cross, S. J. (2009). Is there a net generation coming to university? In H. Damis & L. Creanor (Eds.), *"In dreams begins responsibility"- Choice evidence and change: Proceedings of the 16th Association for Learning Technology Conference* (pp.10-20). Manchester, UK: Nuffield Press. Retrieved November 20, 2010, from http:// eprints.hud.ac.uk/ 7649/ 1/ ALTC_09_proceedings_090806.pdf

Jones, C., & Dirckinck-Holmfeld, L. (2009). Analysing networked learning practices an introduction. In L. Dirckinck-Holmfeld, C. Jones, & B. Lindström (Eds.), *Analysing networked learning practices in higher education and continuing professional development* (pp. 1-27). Rotterdam, The Netherlands: Sense Publishers, BV.

Jones, C., & Healing, G. (2010a). Net generation students: Agency and choice and the new technologies. Special section: Net generation. *Journal of Computer Assisted Learning, 26*(5), 344–356. doi:10.1111/j.1365-2729.2010.00370.x

Jones, C., & Healing, G. (2010b). Networks and locations for student learning. *Learning, Media and Technology, 35*(4). doi:10.1080/17439884.2010.529914

Jones, C., & Hosein, A. (2010). Profiling university students' use of technology: Where is the net generation divide? *The International Journal of Technology Knowledge and Society, 6*(3), 43–58.

Jones, C., Ramanau, R., Cross, S. J., & Healing, G. (2010). Net generation or digital natives: Is there a distinct new generation entering university? *Computers & Education, 54*(3), 722–732. doi:10.1016/j.compedu.2009.09.022

Kasesniemi, E.-L., & Rautiainen, P. (2002). Mobile culture of children and teenagers in Finland. In Katz, J. E., & Aakhus, M. (Eds.), *Perpetual contact: Mobile communication, private talk, public performance* (pp. 170–192). Cambridge, UK: Cambridge University Press.

Kennedy, G. E., Krause, K.-L., Judd, T. S., Churchward, A., & Gray, K. (2008). First year students' experiences with technology: Are they really digital natives? *Australasian Journal of Educational Technology, 24*(1), 108–122.

Koper, R., & Tattersall, C. (Eds.). (2005). *Learning design: A handbook on modeling and delivering networked education and training*. Berlin, Germany: Springer.

Kukulska-Hulme, A., & Pettit, J. (2006, October). *Practitioners as innovators: Emergent practice in personal mobile teaching, learning, work and leisure*. Paper presented at mLearn 2006 conference, Banff, Canada.

Kukulska-Hulme, A., Pettit, J., Bradley, L., Carvalho, A., Herrington, A., Kennedy, D., & Walker, A. (2009). An international survey of mature students' uses of mobile devices in life and learning. In D. Metcalf, A. Hamilton & C. Graffeo (Eds.) *Proceedings of 8th World Conference on Mobile and Contextual Learning (mLearn 2009)* (Short paper, p.143). Florida: University of Central Florida.

Kukulska-Hulme, A., Sharples, M., Milrad, M., Arnedillo-Sánchez, I., & Vavoula, G. (2009). Innovation in mobile learning: A European perspective. *International Journal of Mobile and Blended Learning, 1*(1), 13–35. doi:10.4018/jmbl.2009010102

Kukulska-Hulme, A., & Traxler, J. (2007). Learning design with mobile and wireless technologies. In Beetham, H., & Sharpe, R. (Eds.), *Rethinking pedagogy for a digital age: Designing and delivering e-learning* (pp. 180–192). London, UK: Routledge.

Kukulska-Hulme, A., Traxler, J., & Pettit, J. (2007). Designed and user-generated activity in the mobile age. [from http://www.jld.qut.edu.au/]. *Journal of Learning Design, 2*(1), 52–65. Retrieved July 22, 2010.

Laurillard, D. (2002). *Rethinking university teaching: A conversational framework for the effective use of learning technologies* (2nd ed.). London, UK: RoutledgeFalmer. doi:10.4324/9780203304846

Mayes, T., & De Freitas, S. (2004). *Review of e-learning theories, frameworks and models*. JISC e-Learning Models Desk Study Report. Retrieved July 22, 2010, from http://www.jisc.ac.uk/ uploaded_documents/ Stage 2 Learning Models (Version 1).pdf

McAndrew, P., Goodyear, P., & Dalziel, J. (2006). Patterns, designs and activities: Unifying descriptions of learning structures. *International Journal of Learning Technology, 2*(2–3), 216–242. doi:10.1504/IJLT.2006.010632

Mifsud, L., & Smørdal, O. (2006). Teacher perception of handheld technology: Pedagogical practices. In *Proceedings of IADIS Mobile Learning 2006*. Dublin, Ireland: International Association for Development of the Information Society Press.

Ofcom (2009). *Digital lifestyles: Young adults aged 16-24*. Retrieved June 28, 2010, from http:// www.ofcom.org.uk/ advice/ media_literacy/ medlitpub/ medlitpubrss/ digital_young/

Pedró, F. (2009). *New millennium learners in higher education: Evidence and policy implications*. Paris, France: Centre for Educational Research and Innovation (CERI).

Pettit, J., & Kukulska-Hulme, A. (2007). Going with the grain: Mobile devices in practice. *Australasian Journal of Educational Technology, 23*(1), 17–33.

Prensky, M. (2001a). Digital natives, digital immigrants. *Horizon, 9*(5), 1–6. doi:10.1108/10748120110424816

Prensky, M. (2001b). Digital natives, digital immigrants part II: Do they really think differently? *Horizon, 9*(6), 1–9. doi:10.1108/10748120110424843

Rogers, E. M. (2003). *Diffusion of innovations* (5th ed.). New York, NY: Free Press.

Sclater, N. (2008). *Large-scale open source e-learning systems at the Open University (UK)*. (Research Bulletin Issue 12). Boulder, CO: Centre for Applied Research. Retrieved June 28, 2010, from http://www.educause.edu/ ecar

Selwyn, N. (Ed.). (2008). *Education 2.0? Designing the web for teaching and learning*. TLRP publication.

Selwyn, N., Crook, C., Noss, R., & Laurillard, D. (2008). Education 2.0? Towards an educational web 2.0. In N. Selwyn (Ed.), *Education 2.0? Designing the web for teaching and learning* (pp. 24-26). Institute of Education: TLRP-TEL.

Sharpe, R., & Oliver, M. (2007a). Designing courses for e-learning. In Beetham, H., & Sharpe, R. (Eds.), *Rethinking pedagogy for the digital age: Designing and delivering e-learning* (pp. 41–51). London, UK: RoutledgeFalmer.

Sharpe, R., & Oliver, M. (2007b). Supporting practitioner's design for learning: principles of effective resources and interventions. In Beetham, H., & Sharpe, R. (Eds.), *Rethinking pedagogy for the digital age: Designing and delivering e-learning* (pp. 117–128). London, UK: RoutledgeFalmer.

Sheehan, M. C. (2009). *Spreading the word: Messaging and communications in higher education. (Research study volume 2).* Boulder, CO: EDUCAUSE Center for Applied Research. Retrieved June 28, 2010, from http://www.educause.edu/Resources/ SpreadingtheWordMessagingandCo/168953

Smith, S. D., & Borreson Caruso, J. (2010). *The ECAR study of undergraduate students and Information Technology, 2010*. Research Study, vol. 6. Boulder, CO: EDUCAUSE Center for Applied Research. Retrieved November 14, 2010, from http://www.educause.edu/ ecar

Tapscott, D. (1998). *Growing up digital: The rise of the Net generation*. New York, NY: McGraw-Hill.

Tapscott, D. (2009). *Grown up digital: How the net generation is changing your world*. New York, NY: McGraw-Hill.

Tapscott, D., & Williams, A. (2010). Innovating the 21st century university: It's time. *EDUCAUSE Review, 45*(1), 17–29.

Thomas, H. (2010). Learning spaces, learning environments and the displacement of learning. *British Journal of Educational Technology, 41*(3), 502–511. doi:10.1111/j.1467-8535.2009.00974.x

ADDITIONAL READING

Becta (2008). *Harnessing technology: Next generation learning*. Retrieved June 14, 2011, from http://webarchive.nationalarchives.gov.uk/20101102103654/ publications.becta.org.uk//display.cfm?resID=37348&page=1835

Bennett, S., & Maton, K. (2010). Beyond the 'digital natives' debate: Towards a more nuanced understanding of students' technology experiences. *Journal of Computer Assisted Learning, 26*, 321–331. doi:10.1111/j.1365-2729.2010.00360.x

Brown, J. S. (2006, September/October). New learning environments for the 21st century: Exploring the edge. *Change, 38*(5), 18–24. doi:10.3200/CHNG.38.5.18-24

Buckingham, D., & Willett, R. (Eds.). (2006). *Digital generations: Children, young people and new media*. Mahwah, NJ: Erlbaum.

Castells, M., & Fernández-Ardèvol, M. Qiu, J.L., & Sey, A. (2007). *Mobile communication and society: A global perspective*. Cambridge, MA: MIT Press.

DIUS. (2008). *Informal adult learning: Shaping the way ahead.* January 2008. Consultation document for the period Jan-June 2008. Department for Innovation, Universities and Skills. Retrieved July 22, 2010, from http://www.dius.gov.uk/ publications/ DIUS_adu_lea_bro_an_05%208.pdf

Edwards, P. N. (2003). Infrastructure and modernity: Force, time, and social organization in the history of sociotechnical systems. In Misa, T. J., Brey, P., & Feenberg, A. (Eds.), *Modernity and technology* (pp. 185–225). Cambridge, Mass: MIT Press.

Harrison, S., & Dourish, P. (1996). Re-place-ing space: The roles of space and place in collaborative systems. [New York, NY: ACM.]. *Proceedings of CSCW, 96*, 67–76.

Hemmi, A., Bayne, S., & Land, R. (2009). The appropriation and repurposing of social technologies in higher education. *Journal of Computer Assisted Learning, 25*, 19–30. doi:10.1111/j.1365-2729.2008.00306.x

Herring, S. (2008). Questioning the generational divide: Technological exoticism and adult construction of online youth identity. In Buckingham, D. (Ed.), *Youth, Identity and Digital Media* (pp. 71–92). Cambridge, MA: MIT Press.

Howe, N., & Strauss, W. (1991). *Generations: The history of America's future and the fourth turning: An American prophecy*. Oxford: Oxford University Press.

Howe, N., & Strauss, W. (2000). *Millennials rising: The next greatest generation*. New York: Vintage Books.

Järvelä, S., Näykki, P., Laru, J., & Luokkanen, T. (2007). Structuring and regulating collaborative learning in higher education with wireless networks and mobile tools. *Educational Technology & Society, 10*(4), *71-79*. Retrieved June 30, 2008, from http://www.ifets.info/ journals/ 10_4/8.pdf

Jones, C. (forthcoming). Networked learning environments. In Keppell, M., Souter, K., & Riddle, M. (Eds.), *Physical and virtual learning spaces in higher education: Concepts for the modern learning environment*. Hershey, PA: IGI Global.

Jones, C., Dirckinck-Holmfeld, L., & Lindström, B. (2006). A relational, indirect, meso-level approach to CSCL design in the next decade. *International Journal of Computer-Supported Collaborative Learning, 1*(1), 35–56. doi:10.1007/s11412-006-6841-7

Jones, C., Ferreday, D., & Hodgson, V. (2008). Networked learning a relational approach – weak and strong ties. *Journal of Computer Assisted Learning* special section, *24*(2), 90–102.

Kennedy, D. M. (2008). Digital literacy: What research can tell us about our students. In Tomei, L. A. (Ed.), *The encyclopedia of information technology curriculum integration*. Hershey, PA: Idea Group.

Kennedy, D. M., & Vogel, D. (2009). Improving the flexibility of learning environments: Developing applications for wired and wireless use. In Filipe, J., Cordeiro, J., Encarnação, B., & Pedrosa, V. (Eds.), *Web information systems and technologies II*. London: Springer.

Kennedy, D. M., & Vogel, D. (2009). Integrating pedagogy, infrastructure and tools for mobile learning. In Tanier, D. (Ed.), *The encyclopedia of mobile computing and commerce*. Hershey, PA: Idea Group.

Kukulska-Hulme, A., Evans, D., & Traxler, J. (2005). *Landscape study on the use of mobile and wireless technologies for teaching and learning in the post-16 sector*. JISC-funded project report. Retrieved July 20, 2010, from http://www.jisc.ac.uk/ eli_outcomes.html

Kukulska-Hulme, A., Heppell, S., Jelfs, A., & Nicholson, A. (2005). *Case studies in wireless and mobile learning in the post-16 sector*. JISC-funded project report. Retrieved from http://www.jisc.ac.uk/ eli_oucasestudies.html

Kukulska-Hulme, A., & Traxler, J. (2007). Designing for mobile and wireless learning. In Beetham, H., & Sharpe, R. (Eds.), *Rethinking pedagogy for a digital age: Designing and delivering e-Learning* (180-192). London: Routledge.

Kurti, A., Spikol, D., & Milrad, M. (2008). Bridging outdoors and indoors educational activities in schools with the support of mobile and positioning technologies. *International Journal of Mobile Learning and Organization, 2*(2), 166–186. doi:10.1504/IJMLO.2008.019767

Lakkala, M., Paavola, S., & Hakkarainen, K. (2008). Designing pedagogical infrastructures in university courses for technology-enhanced collaborative inquiry. *Research and Practice in Technology Enhanced Learning, 3*(1), 33–64. doi:10.1142/S1793206808000446

Liljenström, H., & Svedin, U. (Eds.). (2005). *Micro, meso, macro: Addressing complex systems*. London: World Scientific Publishers. doi:10.1142/9789812701404

Markett, C., Arnedillo-Sánchez, I., Weber, S., & Tangney, B. (2006). Using short message service (SMS) to encourage interactivity. *Computers & Education*, *46*(3), 280–293. doi:10.1016/j.compedu.2005.11.014

McAndrew, P., Goodyear, P., & Dalziel, J. (2006). Patterns, designs and activities: Unifying descriptions of learning structures. *International Journal of Learning Technology*, *2*(2/3), 216–242. doi:10.1504/IJLT.2006.010632

Milrad, M., & Jackson, M. (2008). Designing and implementing educational mobile services in university classrooms using smart phones and cellular networks. Special issue of *International Journal of Engineering Education on Mobile Technologies for Engineering Education, 24* (1), 84-91.

Naismith, L. (2007). Using text messaging to support administrative communication in higher education. *Active Learning in Higher Education*, *8*(2), 155–171. doi:10.1177/1469787407078000

Oblinger, D. G., & Oblinger, J. L. (2005). *Educating the net generation*, An Educause e-book publication. Retrieved July 22, 2010, from http://www.educause.edu/ ir/library/ pdf/ pub7101.pdf

Palfrey, J., & Gasser, U. (2008). *Born digital: Understanding the first generation of digital natives*. New York: Basic Books.

Pea, R., & Maldonado, H. (2006). WILD for learning: interacting through new computing devices anytime, anywhere. In Sawyer, K. (Ed.), *Cambridge handbook of the learning sciences* (pp. 427–442). New York: Cambridge University Press.

Prensky, M. (2009). H. sapiens digital: From digital immigrants and digital natives to digital wisdom. *Innovate, 5*(3). Retrieved July 22, 2010, from: http://www.innovateonline.info

Roschelle, J. (2003). Unlocking the learning value of wireless mobile devices. *Journal of Computer Assisted Learning, 19*(3), 260–272. doi:10.1046/j.0266-4909.2003.00028.x

Ryberg, T., & Larsen, M. C. (2008). Networked identities: understanding relationships between weak and strong ties in networked environments. *Journal of Computer Assisted Learning*, *24*(2), 103–115. doi:10.1111/j.1365-2729.2007.00272.x

Salaway, G., & Caruso, J. B. with Nelson, M.R. (2008). *The ECAR Study of Undergraduate Students and Information Technology, 2008 (Research Study, Vol. 8)*. Boulder, CO: EDUCAUSE Center for Applied Research, 2008. Retrieved July 22, 2010, from http://www.educause.edu/ ecar.

Sharples, M., Arnedillo-Sánchez, I., Milrad, M., & Vavoula, G. (2009). Mobile learning: Small devices, Big issues. In Balacheff, N., Ludvigsen, S., de Jong, T., Lazonder, A., Barnes, S., & Montandon, L. (Eds.), *Technology enhanced learning: Principles and products* (pp. 233–249). Heidelberg: Springer.

Spikol, D., Kurti, A., & Milrad, M. (2008). Collaboration in context as a framework for designing innovative mobile learning activities. In Ryu, H., & Parsons, D. (Eds.), *Innovative mobile learning: Techniques and technologies* (pp. 172–196). Hershey, PA: IGI. doi:10.4018/978-1-60566-062-2.ch009

Stead, G. (2005, October). *Moving mobile into the mainstream.* Paper presented at Mlearn 2005, 4th World conference on mLearning. Retrieved July 22, 2010, from http://www.mlearn.org.za/ CD/ papers/ Stead.pdf

Stockwell, G. (2008). Investigating learner preparedness for and usage patterns of mobile learning. *ReCALL*, *20*(3), 253–270. doi:10.1017/S0958344008000232

Straub, E. (2009). Understanding technology adoption: Theory and future directions for informal learning. *Review of Educational Research*, *79*, 625–649. doi:10.3102/0034654308325896

Trinder, K., Guiller, J., Margaryan, A., Littlejohn, A., & Nicol, D. (2008). *Learning from digital natives: bridging formal and informal learning*. HEA Final report, May 2008. Retrieved July 22, 2010, from http://www.heacademy.ac.uk/ projects/ detail/ projectfinder/ projects/ pf2969lr

Vavoula, G. N., Sharples, M., Rudman, P., Lonsdale, P., & Meek, J. (2007). Learning bridges: a role for mobile learning in education. *Educational Technology Magazine*, *47*(3), 33–36.

Walls, S. M., Kucsera, J. V., Walker, J. D., Acee, T. W., McVaugh, N. K., & Robinson, D. H. (2010). Podcasting in education: Are students as ready and eager as we think they are? *Computers & Education*, *54*(2), 371–378. doi:10.1016/j.compedu.2009.08.018

Wellman, B. (2001). Physical place and cyberplace: The rise of the networked individual. In Keeble, L., & Loader, B. (Eds.), *Community informatics: shaping computer-mediated social relations* (pp. 227–252). London: Routledge.

Wellman, B., Quan-Haase, A., Boase, J., Chen, W., Hampton, K., Isla de Diaz, I., et al. (2003). The social affordances of the internet for networked individualism, *JCMC, 8*(3).

Wittel, A. (2001). Towards a network sociality. *Theory, Culture & Society*, *18*(6), 51–76.

KEY TERMS AND DEFINITIONS

Conceptual Tools: In this chapter, the term refers to paper-based analytical instruments that help teachers think through their teaching approach and plan various aspects of teaching.

Digital Natives: People who have grown up with, and become familiar with, digital technology such as computers, the Internet, mobile phones and MP3s. They are usually contrasted with digital immigrants, who were born before the existence of digital technology and have adopted it later on in their lives. Generally used interchangeably with Net Generation and Millennials.

Hybrid Space: The combination of virtual and physical space, for example using geographical coordinates to represent real world events as they happen, on a digital map shared online or through mobile devices.

Infrastructure: Services or facilities which support an operation, which at a high level might include telecommunications, networks, servers, databases, cloud computing. Infrastructures are already in place, ready-to-use, completely transparent and not requiring consideration. They are socio-technical systems, which are reliant on complex organizational practices for maintenance and for making the infrastructure meaningful.

Infrastructure for Learning: A set of resources and arrangements – social, institutional, technical – that are designed to, and/or assigned to, support a learning practice (Guribye 2005).

Neo-Liberal: A market driven approach to economic and social policy that emphasizes the role of private business and minimizes the role of social institutions and the state. It is part of an internationally prevailing ideological paradigm that uses the language of markets, economic efficiency, consumer and individual choice.

Net Generation: Also known as the Millennials, members of an age cohort that have birth dates which fall between the mid 1970s and the early 2000s. It is claimed that this age cohort forms a generation which is defined by its exposure to networked and digital technologies. It is also claimed that they adopt a collaborative or participative approach to learning. Generally used interchangeably with Digital Natives and Millennials.

Social Network: A social structure composed of nodes that can be individuals, groups or larger bodies, connected (tied) together on the basis of interdependencies such as, kinship, common interest, status, acquaintanceship, friendship, financial flows, etc.

Supported Open Learning: The Open University's style of distance learning, enabling students to learn in their own time, at home or wherever they choose, undertaking set activities and assignments using supplied resources with regular and systematic support from a tutor and a community of other learners.

Virtual Learning Environment (VLE): An Internet or Web-based software system designed to support teaching and learning in an educational setting, providing a collection of tools for assessment, communication, the delivery of content, group work and the administration of student groups. Also known as Learning Management System (LMS), Course Management System or Managed Learning Environment.

Section 2
Integrating Arenas Through Designed Learning and Teaching

The second section in this book includes five chapters that in various ways show how educational technologies can be used in order to integrate different arenas related to higher education. It is demonstrated throughout the section how learning and teaching processes can be enhanced through theoretically informed, systematic, and research based design of the educational activities. Also addressed is how different participants or group of participants in higher education can share common spaces for educational purposes.

Chapter 5
Using Online Data for Student Investigations in Biology and Ecology

Nancy M. Trautmann
Cornell Lab of Ornithology, USA

Colleen M. McLinn
Cornell Lab of Ornithology, USA

ABSTRACT

Undergraduate research experiences are difficult to provide in large classes, institutions with no lab or field facilities, and distance-learning courses. This chapter illustrates how to overcome such obstacles and engage undergraduates in environmental and life science investigations using large and rapidly growing online databases including ecological data derived through citizen science and behavioral data available through Cornell University's archive of sound and video. Examples are provided of driving questions and curricular support of undergraduate investigations focusing on two themes central to undergraduate biology: 1) ecology and conservation, and 2) organismal biology and behavior. These database investigations serve one or more of three pedagogical goals: 1) to enable undergraduates to conduct ecological and biological research in any setting, even where fieldwork is impossible, 2) to set the scene for student fieldwork, or 3) to make it possible for students to view their field data within the context of broader temporal and geographic trends.

INTRODUCTION

Large datasets are becoming an increasingly critical component of biological and ecological research, and the resulting web-based tools and resources provide unprecedented opportunities for students to work with data, develop analytical skills, and compare their results with those of peers and professionals across the globe (National Science Foundation Task Force on Cyberlearning, 2008; Porter, 2004). In fields in which professional research relies on use of web-based datasets, cur-

DOI: 10.4018/978-1-61350-080-4.ch005

ricular resources have been developed to scaffold classroom use of these data resources. Examples include the *BioQUEST* curriculum for use in molecular biology and *On the Cutting Edge* for use in geosciences (for more information, see Edelson, 1998; Lombardi, 2007a; Manduca et al., 2010). Organismal biology and ecology have gotten off to a slower start in realizing the classroom potential of online data, but this will likely change rapidly as the field of ecoinformatics gains definition. Automated sensors are assembling a wealth of environmental data (e.g., Lehning et al., 2009), and growing numbers of students and members of the public are collecting and submitting "citizen science" data about organisms they have observed or environmental parameters they have measured. Collectively, these data sources present unprecedented opportunities for research by both professionals and students (e.g., Kelling, Fink, et al., 2009; Kelling, Hochachka, et al., 2009; Lowman, D'Avanzo, & Brewer, 2009; Trautmann, Shirk, Fee, & Krasny, in press).

Engaging students in research promotes deep learning, motivation, career awareness, and recognition of the practice of science (Brewer, 2003; Edelson, 1998; Lombardi, 2007a). Due to rapid advances in cyberinfrastructure, "today's students are entering a scientific workforce in which they are expected to have skills in areas such as data mining, modelling, visualization, and annotation," yet most undergraduate science educators "have limited experience in working with modern e-science resources" (Donovan, 2008, p. 461). Through exploration of data, scenarios, and case studies, even non-science majors can develop the critical-thinking, group work, and problem-solving skills that are highly sought by future employers (Lombardi, 2008). Designing classroom activities that make effective use of online databases and visualization tools to scaffold productive student inquiry is an important challenge for educational designers. Such designs should aim to provide faculty with meaningful examples and rubrics (e.g., Underwood, Smith, Luckin, & Fitzpatrick, 2008), assisting them in addressing 21st century environmental and conservation challenges in their teaching (Brewer, 2003; National Science Foundation Task Force on Cyberlearning, 2008).

Engaging students in research using current scientific data poses a number of challenges, including potentially unwieldy datasets and need for structure to ensure student learning. Such challenges can be overcome using carefully scaffolded educational technologies such as online databases and user-friendly tools for data analysis and visualization. Assessing student learning also can be challenging because intended outcomes typically extend beyond recall of content knowledge to also include development of understandings and skills related to conducting scientific research.

Using examples from our work with faculty teaching environmental and life science courses in diverse settings across the United States, in this chapter we present:

- reasons for engaging undergraduates in investigations using online data,
- several vast and rapidly growing databases of high value in student research related to ecology and animal behavior,
- the learning theory underlying our curriculum development efforts,
- a framework for assessing relevant student learning outcomes, and
- recommendations for future work in this field.

BACKGROUND

Growing efforts to reform undergraduate science education call for engagement of students in scientific processes, including designing investigations and analyzing data. The aim is for students to achieve understanding of how scientific investigations are conducted, how knowledge is tested and advanced, and what types of questions can be addressed through scientific research (DeHaan, 2005; National Research Council, 2002; Ramaley & Haggett, 2005). Traditional undergraduate laboratory exercises do little to meet these goals because students tend to be exposed only to limited aspects of investigation and rarely have the chance to define a problem or design their own experiment (Harker, 1999; Sundberg & Moncada, 1994). Efforts to reform undergraduate science education therefore specify the need to provide opportunities for all students, science majors and non-majors alike, to experience scientific processes through inquiry-based laboratory and field activities that include experimental design and data analysis (Kenny et al., 2001).

Classroom research represents a form of "authentic learning," in which students engage in sustained exploration of complex, real-world problems. Such exploration can motivate students and help them to develop interdisciplinary knowledge and skills, collaboratively construct meaning, and gain experience in making judgments about how to find and evaluate information (Herrington & Herrington, 2006; Lombardi, 2007b; Reeves, Herrington, & Oliver, 2002). In the tradition of situated learning and cognitive apprenticeship, students not only learn to use the tools of the field, but also grapple with cultural definitions of what the field considers to be important questions or acceptable evidence (Brown, Collins, & Duguid, 1989; Lombardi, 2007b). Technology is frequently used in authentic learning environments to build and sustain web-based communities of practice in which students develop competence and higher-order reasoning skills and potentially produce legitimate contributions that may be evaluated by peers or external stakeholders (Lombardi, 2007b). Herrington and Herrington (2006) and Underwood et al. (2008) provide useful examples and recommendations on use of technology in authentic learning and e-science.

Research experiences hold potential not only to build students' understandings about the processes of science but also to enhance their skills as critical, independent thinkers with ability to reason, effectively use information, and distinguish between evidence and opinion (D'Avanzo, 2003). Wenk (2000), for example, found greater growth in intellectual maturity among freshman in a research-based science course compared with those in a more traditional course. Students who read primary literature, formulated their own research question, conducted an experiment, interpreted evidence, and presented and defended their results progressed within a single semester of freshman year to understandings about the nature of scientific knowledge that typically are not reached until students are college seniors or entry-level graduate students.

In large classes, distance-learning courses, and institutions with no lab or field facilities, it is difficult for faculty to provide students with opportunities to conduct their own investigations. One way to overcome such challenges is through use of online data. Rather than collecting their own data in the lab or field, students can conduct authentic investigations using one or more of the vast and rapidly growing collections of data available on the web.

Data Generated through Citizen Science

The term "citizen science" refers to activities that support public collaboration in scientific research, for example, collecting and submitting bird observation data to track population trends over time and geographic setting. The Cornell Lab of Ornithology estimates that 200,000 people per year currently participate in its suite of bird monitoring projects, and scientists use these data to explore current and potential future impacts of environmental change on species distributions, compositions, and extinctions (Dickinson & Bonney, in press; Bonney et al., 2009). For example, eBird (http://ebird.org/) is a citizen science project through which any person, anywhere on earth, can submit records of the birds they have observed. Launched in 2002 by the Cornell Lab of Ornithology and the National Audubon Society, eBird is amassing one of the world's largest and fastest growing biodiversity data resources, currently including over 65 million bird observations submitted by more than 50,000 individuals. The eBird project shares these observations online, making the raw data and various types of analysis and visualization tools accessible for scientific, educational, and recreational use.

Although interested members of the public have been collecting various types of ornithological data since the 18th century, relatively recent efforts to collect and portray the data online have greatly expanded the reach of citizen science and its utility in education. For example, the NestWatch project (http://nestwatch.org/), which aims to track reproductive success for all North American breeding birds, collects information about nest site location, habitat, species, and number of eggs, young, and fledglings. This web-based effort grew out of previous decades during which citizen scientists recorded similar data on paper forms. Once these and other relevant historic data have been entered into NestWatch, the database will contain nearly 400,000 nest records spanning more than 40 years and 500 species – a wealth of information accessible online to anyone interested in exploring trends and factors that influence the breeding success of birds over time and across various North American landscapes. Designers of K-16 educational experiences have begun developing lessons that make use of these resources to teach science content and process skills (e.g., Fee, McLinn, Phillips, Purcell, & Montanez, 2008; Voss & Cooper, 2010).

Another similar yet distinct source of raw data for student investigations is the massive animal sound and video archive maintained by the Macaulay Library at the Cornell Lab of Ornithology (http://macaulaylibrary.org). The largest scientifically annotated collection of its kind, this resource has grown from its beginnings as a tape-based collection of specimens submitted by researchers and trained amateur recordists in the first half of the 20th century to become a digital multimedia resource of great research and educational potential (Gaunt, Nelson, Dantzker, Budney, & Bradbury, 2005). By 2010, the collection had over 100,000 sound specimens and 40,000 videos available online in free streaming format. Users can search for specimens by common name, scientific name, or geographical location. Alternatively, they can browse by taxonomic level or behavioral term such as "forage" or "incubate." For further qualitative and quantitative study, a real-time sound visualization plug-in can be used to display streaming sounds and videos in three formats: 1) as a waveform, 2) as a spectrogram, or 3) as a power spectrum. Full-resolution audio or video files for desktop analysis and additional metadata from recordists and curators can be obtained from the Macaulay Library upon request.

STUDENTS AS INVESTIGATORS

Faculty interested in integrating data-intensive projects into their courses have many options, but some of these reinforce rote learning rather than making use of the potential to engage students in investigations that refine their understanding of selected topics and scientific processes (Songer, 2001). Citizen science, for example, provides a platform for engaging students in relevant, real-life science, and publication of peer-reviewed research incorporating student-collected data demonstrates student ability to participate productively in such endeavors (e.g., Hiemstra, Liston, Pielke, Birkenheuer, & Albers, 2006; Robin, Levine, & Riha, 2005; Verbyla, 2001). However, successful research by professionals using data generated through citizen science does not guarantee meaningful learning for students participating in such projects. Learning outcomes are far richer if students go beyond simply collecting data for use by professional scientists and in addition design and conduct their own investigations using specified data collection protocols. Authentic learning emphasizes the importance of student engagement with questions that have personal meaning or relate to their prior knowledge. One approach is to present students with ill-defined problems that they collaboratively refine into concrete tasks and sub-tasks (Reeves, Herrington, & Oliver, 2002; Stein, Isaacs, & Andrews, 2004).

In this chapter, we focus primarily on student investigations using the outputs of citizen science: the databases and visualization tools produced through various citizen science projects. The following examples illustrate ways in which we and others have responded to the challenge of designing opportunities for student investigations that make use of real-time ecological data and powerful data analysis and visualization tools now available online. The overall goal of such investigations is for students to pose scientific questions and draw evidence-based conclusions using relevant web-accessible data.

Examples of Student-Active Data Investigations

In response to the need for effective curriculum making use of large online datasets, we are working with faculty from a wide range of American institutions to create and implement curriculum resources designed to engage undergraduates in research using data from several rich online collections of data about birds and other organisms. Designed for use in undergraduate biology, ecology, and environmental science courses, these resources support student investigations focusing on two themes central to undergraduate biology: 1) ecology and conservation, and 2) organismal biology and behavior. We invite faculty to review, pilot, and comment on draft resources through a website that provides organized information about various Cornell Lab datasets and associated possibilities for student investigations (http://birds.cornell.edu/orb). Curricular resources outline ways to introduce the databases, spur authentic exploration of relevant scientific questions, and assess the resulting student research reports and learning outcomes.

Each investigation addresses one or more driving questions, such as "What is a species?" or "Why do bird species have such different breeding strategies?" To address overarching questions such as these, students may pose more narrowly defined questions and design investigations using relevant evidence from web-accessible sets of raw data and tools for visualization and analysis. To provide sufficient structure while simultaneously enabling students to direct their own learning, the curricular resources present steps in which students engage, explore, explain, elaborate, and evaluate (Bybee et al., 2006). This "5E" instructional model presents science as a process of discovery (Bybee et al., 1989). Based on the constructivist theory of learning, it views learning as an active process in which students build on their current and prior knowledge to construct new ideas or concepts (Bruner, 1973). The five steps organize activities into a sequence in which students continually build upon what they already have learned (Table 1).

The example investigation outlined in Table 1 addresses the question of why there is such great variety in song types among bird species. Assessment of learning outcomes for this investigation would likely center around understandings about how the form of animal communication relates to function and what constraints might be imposed by internal or external factors such as body size or habitat. Online databases can also be used to support understandings about the nature of science, role of technology, and science process skills. If these outcomes are desired, assessment would focus on the extent to which students have successfully conducted essential steps of scientific research, such as formulating a testable hypothesis, accessing relevant online data, and accurately analyzing and interpreting these data to reach logical conclusions.

Table 1. Phases of a student-active data investigation following the 5E instructional model

Phase	Descriptions of student and instructor activities (adapted from Bybee et al., 2006)	Domain-specific example
Engage	Activate students' prior knowledge and interest, and invite them to learn more	The professor engages the students' interest in the diversity of bird songs by playing audio examples. She invites the students to brainstorm why there might be so many different types of songs among bird species.
Explore	Begin investigating the data, develop a common experience for participants to frame and discuss the problem	The professor raises the question of how to quantify variation in songs, and then presents several examples of parrot sound spectrograms along with a basic diagram to orient students to the axes of the graph. In small groups, the class examines the examples to look for trends.
Explain	Demonstrate understandings, describe and name phenomena, develop goals for further investigation	The professor assigns as reading a recent study of selective forces on the design of parrot vocalizations (Wright & Wilkinson, 2001). As homework, students write a short summary of the researchers' questions, methods, and findings, and they draft ideas for further investigation using the larger set of sounds available online in the Macaulay Library.
Elaborate	Deepen understanding, challenge conceptions, and apply knowledge and skills through additional activities	The class discusses the students' investigation ideas and jointly decides to research the question of how bird song relates to habitat type. Through further discussion, they select methods for identifying habitat type and measuring song complexity. The professor uses example sounds and visualizations to frame a discussion of how to count or time any changes that occur in the direction of the frequency line on a spectrogram. Each student group analyzes a unique part of a large dataset using the agreed-upon methods.
Evaluate	Reflect upon understandings and process with regards to the bigger field of study	Students report the results of their piece of the investigation and interpret these in light of the larger set of results generated by the rest of the class data. They answer discussion questions about how song might be important to birds' survival and reproduction, and generate ideas about how to experimentally determine if the pattern observed was specific to the taxonomic group studied or might apply more generally.

Data-Rich Investigations in Context

Potential benefits of engaging students in data-rich investigations that mirror the professional practice of science include motivation, higher-order thinking, and understanding of science process as well as content (Tosteson, 1997; Windschitl, 2000). Potential costs of such an approach include time spent on relatively open-ended learning, potential technology pitfalls, and complexity of managing individualized student projects. Instructors can maximize the benefits of data-rich classroom activities by delineating intended learning outcomes and selecting the type of activity to meet the targeted learning goals. Such goals may focus on specific science concepts, understanding of the nature of science, or development of skills related to experimental design, data analysis, or critical thinking. Large-scale studies of introductory cell biology and physics courses indicate that replacing lectures and recipe-style laboratory activities with discussion, problem-solving, and data interpretation activities can lead to significant gains in student learning (Hake, 1998; Knight & Wood, 2005). Data-rich investigations also have potential to foster understandings about the nature of science, science as inquiry, and cyber-enabled science (see Manduca & Mogk, 2003; Park Rogers & Abell, 2008; Witzig et al., 2010). According to Brewer:

We have always used real-world ecological issues in conservation biology courses. But now it is possible to explore them in ways that make the experience more authentic. Rather than talking about loss of habitat, students can use the tools themselves, tools that require them to think about how to represent the problem. (2003, p. 658)

In choosing to emphasize depth over breadth of experience, faculty open doors to achieving multiple learning objectives. Over the course of a long-term project, an instructor may choose to direct some aspects in order to familiarize the students with specific concepts or tools while leaving other components open-ended so that students can design their own investigations working individually, in small groups, or collaboratively as a class.

The curricular resources we have designed support database investigations serving three distinct pedagogical goals. One is to enable undergraduates to conduct ecological and biological research in any setting, even where fieldwork is impossible. The remaining two goals enhance rather than replace field studies. Investigations using online datasets can be used to set the scene for student fieldwork or to make it possible for students to view their field data within the context of broader temporal and geographic trends.

Investigation into the question of how bird vocalizations relate to habitat, for example, might start with use of online data to set the scene before students design their field-based studies. Suitable for use in any undergraduate course emphasizing interactions between physics and biology (e.g., introductory biology, animal behavior, or ornithology), this approach might begin with the instructor providing a short overview of how to interpret a spectrogram view of sound and how to search by species or location among the vast collection of recordings in the Macaulay Library (http://macaulaylibrary.org). After perusing research abstracts provided on the project website, students could then decide which habitats and species might be fruitful to investigate and which features of sound to measure (e.g., frequency range, song complexity). Although the Macaulay Library has the world's largest scientifically annotated collection of animal sounds, students wishing to conduct statistically significant hypothesis testing might decide to record and analyze their own audio specimens from specific locations representing various habitat types at their field site.

An environmental studies or conservation biology instructor might structure quite a different lesson around the question, "How do bird populations change over time, and are these changes related to land use?" The instructor might first engage students with a map representing the breeding range of a species, and then ask how they think such maps are derived. After brainstorming ways of doing fieldwork to create such a map, students might learn about and practice the methods of breeding bird survey or atlas projects. (Participants in these projects use spring bird song to listen for the presence of a species, followed with behavioral cues to document probable or confirmed breeding activity for that species in that location, [e.g., http://www.pwrc.usgs.gov/bba/]). Once students have developed a concrete understanding of how breeding range maps are generated and what the data mean, they will be well poised to ask questions about species presence across time or geographic setting, and to investigate possible correlations with factors such as urban development or wildlife management programs.

Manipulating and Visualizing Data

Massive amounts of data are available online, even within single datasets such as the Macaulay Library or eBird. Add to this the data-federation efforts of DataONE, which aims to "transcend domain boundaries and make biological data available from the genome to the ecosystem; make environmental data available from atmospheric, ecological, hydrological, and oceanographic sources; provide secure and long-term preservation and access; and engage scientists, land-managers, policy makers, students, educators, and the public through logical access and intuitive visualizations" (https://dataone.org/). The potential implications are immense for individuals or classes conducting research, as well as for educational resource designers or faculty attempting to scaffold authentic learning.

Compared with "canned" datasets that are used for confirmation-style activities in which students replicate or "discover" a known relationship, real-time or near real-time datasets afford tremendous potential for students to conduct original research of current interest to science. However, massive online datasets may be unwieldy for use by students unless accompanied with user-friendly data analysis and visualization tools. Some citizen science projects consequently provide web-based tools that enable users to visualize patterns or investigate questions of interest. For example, users of the eBird website can call up graphs and maps illustrating seasonal patterns of occurrence of selected bird species at a specified location and year (http://ebird.org). For migratory species, users can view annual arrival and departure dates or all-time records in a given region. Similarly, the NestWatch website makes it easy to query the database and create customized maps, for example color coded to show first egg dates across the range of a selected species in the U.S. and Canada (http://nestwatch.org).

Further data analysis and visualization tools are available through the Science Pipes website (http://sciencepipes.org), making it possible for users to access, analyze, and visualize the huge volume of primary biodiversity data available through the Avian Knowledge Network (http://www.avianknowledge.net/) and selected other sources. Analyses and visualizations in Science Pipes are defined by user-created workflows, termed "pipes." Using a browser-based editor (Figure 1), students create and edit pipes simply by dragging, dropping, and connecting desired workflow components. Because Science Pipes provides tools for original data analyses rather than visualizations of predetermined analyses, it empowers users to conduct open-ended investigations of their own design. Because users never directly manipulate the data on their own computers, large datasets are as simple to use as far smaller ones (see Wilson, Trautmann, MaKinster, & Barker, 2010).

Sound and video recordings constitute another type of online data of use in student investigations. As described previously, Cornell University's Macaulay Library (http://macaulaylibrary.org) offers access to over 140,000 recordings of natural sounds and video files portraying animal behavior, which can be viewed as streaming files with a Flash player. Using RavenViewer audio visualization software, they also can be visualized as continuously drawn waveforms, spectrograms, and power spectra (Figure 2). RavenViewer is a free QuickTime plug-in that provides listeners with a visual means of examining the enormous variation inherent in natural sounds. Without needing to understand how the recordings were obtained or how Fourier transformation produces a spectrogram for each sound, users can easily explore and manipulate their choice of recordings. They can stop the sound, zoom in on selected segments, play in slow motion, or mouse-over to see the sound frequency at any point in a recording. Toggle switches make it easy to explore how various settings change the information display, without needing to be familiar with specialized sound analysis vocabulary. By making sound information explicit, concrete, and visual in a user-friendly way, this type of software opens doors to quantitative understanding and exploration of sounds.

Video files accessible online through Macaulay Library provide a rich source of data for use by students in investigating animal behavior. These scientifically annotated video recordings portray a wide range of organisms and behaviors, offering near limitless potential for undergraduate research, even in settings where field research is not an option. Avoiding the need for specialized recording equipment, animal care and use protocols, and long hours of effort in the field, web-acces-

Figure 1. A simple workflow viewed in the Science Pipes editor (top) and its output (bottom)

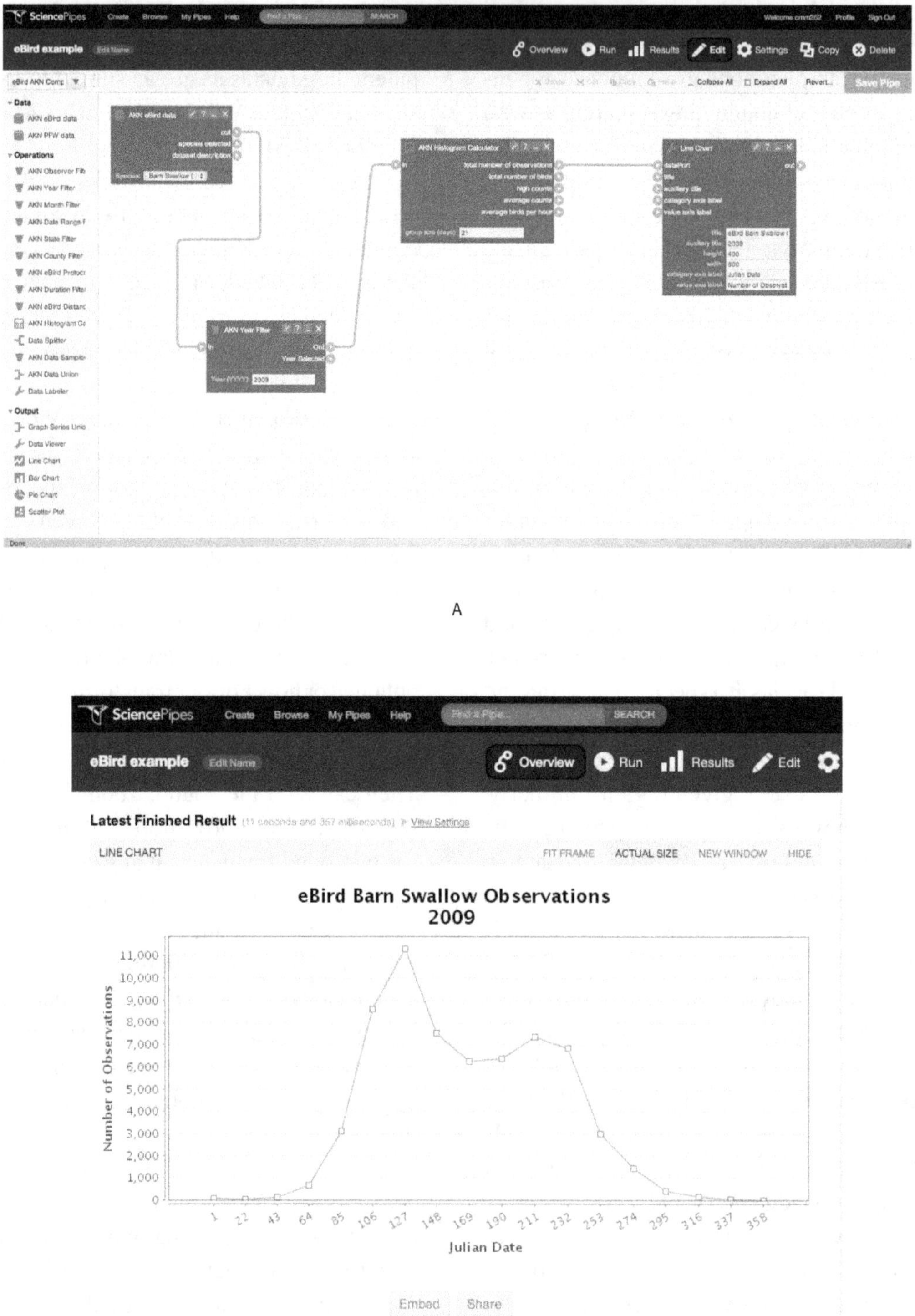

A

B

Figure 2. Screenshot of a RavenViewer window displaying sound information as a waveform (top), spectrogram (middle), and power spectrum (bottom). In the top two graphs, time is depicted on the x-axis. The waveform emphasizes volume or amplitude of the sound, whereas the spectrogram makes it easier to read the frequency. The power spectrum depicts frequency on the x-axis versus amplitude on the y-axis.

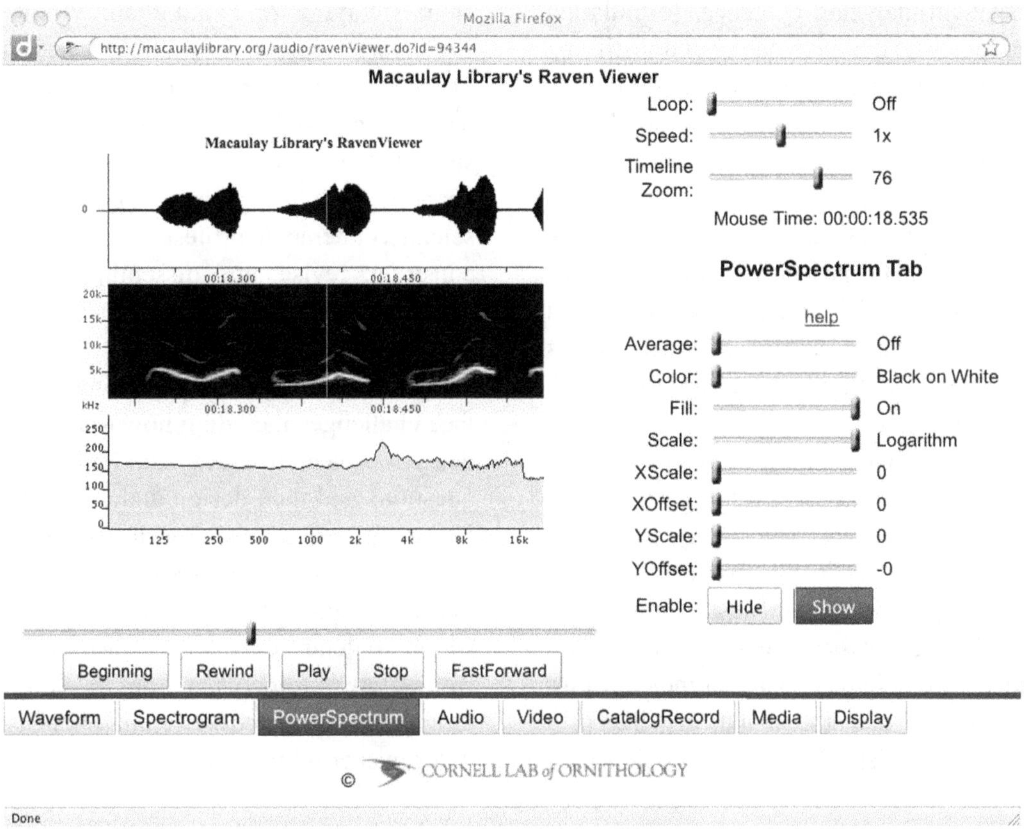

sible sound and video files open up new realms of possibility for student investigations focusing on topics ranging from foraging behavior to parental care. The capability to annotate behaviors directly on streaming videos from the Macaulay Library unfortunately is not currently available. However, if desktop versions of the files are obtained, students can use the free software JWatcher (http://www.jwatcher.ucla.edu/) to conduct quantitative analysis of behaviors.

Another multimedia resource useful for investigating breeding behaviors of birds is CamClickr (http://camclickr.org), an educational game in which citizen scientists can "tag" archived images from nest box cameras with labels indicating the number of eggs and adults present, as well as denote observed behaviors from a pre-defined set of options. One faculty member has used this tool as the foundation of a two-week animal behavior unit in which students learn the difference between observation and inference and become prepared to conduct their own investigations into animal time budgets and behavioral repertoires (Voss & Cooper, 2010).

Structured vs. Open Inquiry

Inquiry-based learning is defined in terms of students addressing scientifically oriented questions through analyzing evidence, formulating explanations, and communicating and justifying their findings in light of possible alternative explanations (National Research Council, 1996). Whether using online data or data collected in the classroom, laboratory, or field setting, approaches to inquiry range from activities that are closely structured by the instructor to open-ended investigations in which students shape their own questions, procedures, and analysis techniques (Table 2; see also National Research Council, 2000, p. 29).

Depending on desired learning objectives, faculty may choose to use a mixture of inquiry levels in their teaching. The highly structured approaches described in the Confirmation and Structured Inquiry columns focus student attention on particular concepts or processes. Opportunities for students to design and conduct their own investigations, on the other hand, are likely to foster deeper understanding of the ways in which scientists study the natural world. Such activities also support development of skills such as making observations and inferences, weighing alternative explanations, and drawing evidence-based conclusions (Drayton & Falk, 2006; Windschitl & Buttemer, 2000; van Zee, 2000). The final steps of communicating and justifying proposed explanations can be highly motivational, inspiring students to achieve deeper levels of learning and enabling them to experience a key way in which scientists interact in professional communities to construct, revise, and disseminate knowledge claims about the natural world (Trautmann, 2009a, 2009b).

Faculty interested in facilitating open inquiry face challenges including how to help their students to select relevant and feasible research questions and then design and conduct suitable investigations. One approach to tackling these challenges is through a stepwise sequence starting with relatively structured experiences in which students learn how to use one or more well-defined protocols in order to learn research techniques and related conceptual understandings. After mastering these techniques and reflecting

Table 2. The range of options in terms of student-generated versus instructor-provided decisions determining each step of the process of designing and conducting an investigation (adapted from Buck, Bretz, & Towns, 2008)

	Type of Activity			
Step in the Investigation Process	**Confirmation (Cookbook Labs)**	**Structured Inquiry**	**Guided Inquiry**	**Open Inquiry (Authentic Research)**
Problem/Question	Provided	Provided	Provided	Student-Generated
Theory/Background	Provided	Provided	Provided	Student-Generated
Procedures/Design	Provided	Provided	Student-Generated	Student-Generated
Results analysis	Provided	Student-Generated	Student-Generated	Student-Generated
Results communication	Provided	Student-Generated	Student-Generated	Student-Generated
Conclusions	Provided	Student-Generated	Student-Generated	Student-Generated

on the types of questions they could be used to address, students are better equipped to design and conduct relevant investigations that are not too far ranging for faculty to feasibly administer.

When students conduct research using online data, use of workflow-style data visualization tools can provide inherent structure to scaffold each step of their investigations. For example, students using Science Pipes select a data source and then specify the types of filtering and analysis they wish to apply. The final step in building each workflow is to specify how to portray the outputs. Faculty face little risk in granting students full control over their investigations using Science Pipes because this inherent structure helps to guide their decision-making process. And it costs nothing but time for students to iteratively repeat the process until they have successfully addressed their question of choice.

Assessment of Learning Outcomes

The National Science Foundation identified four key questions that relate to potential learning outcomes achievable through student investigations using online data:

1. How do learners come to understand science as a process, one that constantly changes as our models and understanding advance?
2. What methods, ideas and tools promote interactive and participatory environments for learning, especially those that take advantage of real (and real-time) scientific data?
3. How can we better understand the potential of new visualization tools for science learning and environmental literacy?
4. What are promising ways of combining environmental science and cyber-learning? (National Science Foundation, 2009, p. 42).

Similarly, a workshop on using data in undergraduate science classrooms in the United States called for rigorous, documented evaluation of the impacts of data-rich experiences on student learning (Manduca & Mogk, 2003). This information would enable faculty to determine how to use data-intensive projects to meet course and departmental learning goals, and ultimately it would lead to enhancement of student learning by informing educators about instructional practices that address students' abilities and needs. In particular, workshop participants noted the need to know if teaching with data increases content and procedural knowledge, improves students' life skills such as critical-thinking ability, and changes their attitudes toward data and science. Looking broadly across projects, workshop participants also highlighted the need to understand what aspects of teaching with data support these learning objectives, under what conditions, and for what types of students. Workshop participants expressed common goals for students in introductory to upper-level classes, because all students need to develop the ability to find, access, manipulate, and interpret data: essential skills for a scientifically literate and capable public as well as for future scientists.

As noted by Brewer (2003):

But just as technological tools in our research are of limited value if we have not identified a question before using them (e.g., Feinsinger 2001), they are of little instructional value if we have not clarified our goals for student learning before bringing them into the classroom... (p. 657)

Effective use of information technology requires faculty to make decisions about the goals of the course that relate to the content, what students should know and be able to do at the end of the course, and how the learning environment will be organized to provide students with the best opportunity to meet the course goals. (p. 657-658)

Faculty who implement student investigations do so to achieve goals ranging from overcoming common scientific misconceptions to achieving insights into experimental design and enhancing critical thinking skills (Ebert-May, Batzli, & Lim, 2003; Ebert-May, Williams, Weber, Hodder, & Luckie, 2004; Hodder, Ebert-May, & Batzli, 2008; Williams, Ebert-May, Luckie, Hodder, & Koptur, 2004). Although content knowledge can be measured through traditional testing, assessment of other types of outcomes may require use of techniques such as pre/post tests of application and analysis skills (Chaplin, 2009), coding for evidence of critical thinking (Hodder et al., 2008), or rubrics to quantify use of evidence and reasoning to back scientific claims (Ruiz-Primo, Li, Tsai, & Schneider, 2010).

RECOMMENDATIONS FOR INSTRUCTIONAL DESIGN

Development of curricular resources in support of data-rich investigation begins with delineation of intended learning outcomes. Applying principles of backward design, such investigations can be highly structured or open-ended depending on desired outcomes (Wiggins & McTighe, 1998). Structured and guided inquiry projects (Table 2) focus on questions that are selected by the instructor or curriculum designer to be relevant to students, address desired science content, and provide multiple directions for inquiry. Following the 5E instructional model outlined in Table 1, the instructional designer formulates an initial question or activity to engage the students in learning about the specified topic using thought-provoking multimedia resources, data sets, or data visualization tools.

Instructional design plays a different role in open inquiry because students engaged in such projects design their own investigations, starting with posing their own questions and progressing through selecting appropriate data sets and analysis techniques. Instructional design in support of such activities should focus on how best to scaffold each step of the research process to enable students to make informed decisions about how to pose a researchable question, select suitable sources of data, and conduct appropriate analyses. Piloting and field testing of draft resources helps to pinpoint areas in which student scaffolding and faculty supports are most needed.

FUTURE RESEARCH DIRECTIONS

Educational research has barely begun to scratch the surface in addressing potential student learning outcomes attributable to undergraduate engagement in research using networked data and analysis tools. Future research is needed to address questions such as these:

- What do faculty aim to achieve through student investigations using online data?
- What attributes of data-driven projects are most effective in achieving desired learning outcomes?
- How can web-based data and accompanying analysis and visualization tools best be designed to support student learning?
- What types of curricular resources and technological tools are needed to scaffold faculty and student implementation of such projects?
- How can student learning outcomes best be assessed and compiled across institutions, faculty, and projects to ascertain what attributes of student investigations are most effective in achieving desired learning outcomes?

It would be useful to create baseline comparisons across various types of projects and implementation strategies, for example to explore the question of whether students who design their own experiments end up with better understandings of the research process compared with those who follow a prescribed series of steps. To facilitate such comparisons, each project would need to be categorized according to inquiry level, ranging from confirmation-style labs to authentic research. Inquiry level could be indexed using a matrix developed by Dolan and Grady (2010) for rating the complexity of scientific reasoning tasks performed by students. Another parameter would be the ways in which students interact with data – whether they work exclusively with web-based data generated by others or supplement this with data they have collected on their own.

Within the discipline of the learning sciences, many interesting studies could be done on computer-supported collaborative learning using online databases and analysis tools. While a few studies have looked at the role played by rich media and student-created artifacts such as visualizations in construction of knowledge and generation of evidence and explanations by secondary students (e.g., Smith & Blankinship, 2000; Zahn, Krauskopf, Pea, & Hesse, 2010), little work has addressed these topics in higher education. In particular, it would be useful to conduct systematic studies to investigate anecdotal reports that working with sound visualization software helps users to develop a scientific understanding of sound waves and the ability to identify bird species by ear (a desired trait for birding enthusiasts as well as undergraduate ornithology students and wildlife professionals). It would be interesting to study how working with real-time spectrograms generated on the fly as in RavenViewer compares to working with static spectrograms or simple images of spectrograms for understanding the representation of sound.

With regard to the generation of workflows and resulting graphical representations of data, a variety of free tools have recently become available for viewing publically available data (e.g., GapMinder, Swivel, Pivot, Google Data Explorer). It remains to be seen which if any will be adopted by professionals as research tools, but these tools may be worth investigating as potential scaffolds for some of the more challenging steps of the scientific process for students. A potential drawback is that despite their ease of use, such tools distance the user from the raw data and how it is represented. Whether this poses a problem for training of scientists and scientifically literate citizens remains to be seen. If this appears to be the case, researchers and education designers could investigate how best to scaffold the tools to the various levels of understanding required by faculty and their students, including both science majors and non-majors.

CONCLUSION

Rapid growth in online data in ecology, organismal biology, and behavior presents unprecedented opportunities for students to conduct original investigations – even under the constraints brought on by large class sizes, lack of access to lab or field facilities, or distance-learning options. Because these massive datasets have become an increasingly critical component of professional science, there is growing need for students to learn how to work with networked data, develop analytical skills, and share their findings with peers and professionals. Such experiences are becoming imperative for *all* students, not only those who are aiming for scientific careers, because of our escalating need for informed citizens who can apply scientifically based reasoning to the issues facing modern society and our global environment. A recent National Science Foundation report entitled *Transitions and Tipping Points in Complex Environmental Systems* identified the power of digital learning in helping students develop holistic perspectives on human dependence on the services provided by healthy ecosystems:

In this digitally connected and socially networked world, people are no longer passive consumers of information. They interact with and contribute to information and co-create solutions in cyberspace. This invites exciting new avenues for learning opportunities that meaningfully connect people to their environment through data and models. It is time to ask how we can best promote environmental literacy by engaging a cyber-connected society for the benefit of environmental science. (2009, p. 9)

Proliferation of online data has been accompanied by development of web-based tools for data analysis and visualization. These tools not only simplify such processes but also make it possible for students and the public to manipulate and explore datasets in ways that would otherwise be unwieldy or impossible. Curricular resources have begun to be developed for use by faculty in engaging undergraduates in a wide range of investigations made possible with networked data, and database manipulation tools continue to be developed and improved. Such efforts are most successful through collaborative efforts involving educators, scientists, and software engineers, as pointed out by Songer:

The design of digital resources that are interactive and engaging, utilize multiple representations of information, and lend to customized and collaborative student-centered learning must begin with an in-depth rethinking of the content and the learning goals as part of the design process, rather than after the design has occurred. Only through discussions with biologists, educators, and software designers might such conversations occur. (2001, http://www.pkal.org/documents/RealizingTheLearningInDigitalLearning.cfm)

With growth in the field of student research using online data comes need for research into impacts on student content knowledge and skills, and possibly also motivation, attitudes, and behavior. Such research will help faculty to determine the value of implementing such projects with their students. It also will help curriculum and educational technology designers to determine ways to design tools, resources, and experiences to maximize the potential for achieving intended learning outcomes. Collectively, these efforts will help to instill in students the skills and scientific habits of mind they will need to be informed citizens in our rapidly changing and increasingly networked world.

REFERENCES

Bonney, R., Ballard, H., Jordan, R., McCallie, E., Phillips, T., Shirk, J., & Wilderman, C. C. (2009). *Public participation in scientific research: Defining the field and assessing its potential for informal science education.* A CAISE inquiry group report. Washington, DC: Center for Advancement of Informal Science Education (CAISE).

Brewer, C. (2003). Computers in the classroom: How information technology can improve conservation education. *Conservation Biology, 17*(3), 657–660. doi:10.1046/j.1523-1739.2003.01739.x

Brown, J. S., Collins, A., & Duguid, P. (1989). Situated cognition and the culture of learning. *Educational Researcher, 18*(1), 32–42.

Bruner, J. (1973). *Going beyond the information given.* New York, NY: Norton.

Buck, L. B., Bretz, S. L., & Towns, M. H. (2008). Characterizing the level of inquiry in the undergraduate laboratory. *Journal of College Science Teaching, 38*(1), 52–58.

Bybee, R. W., Buchwald, C. E., Crissman, S., Heil, D. R., Kuerbis, P. J., Matsumoto, C., & McInerney, J. D. (1989). *Science and technology education for the elementary years: Frameworks for curriculum and instruction.* Retrieved July 12, 2010, from http://eric.ed.gov:80/ ERICWebPortal/ detail?accno=ED314237

Bybee, R. W., Taylor, J. A., Gardner, A., Van Scotter, P., Carlson Powell, J., Westbrook, A., & Landes, N. (2006). *The BSCS 5E instructional model: Origins, effectiveness, and applications (full report).* Colorado Springs, CO: BSCS. Retrieved April 16, 2008, from http://www.bscs.org/ pdf/ 5EFull%20Report.pdf

Chaplin, S. (2009). Assessment of the impact of case studies on student learning gains in an introductory biology course. *Journal of College Science Teaching*, *39*(1), 72–79.

D'Avanzo, C. (2003). Research on learning: Potential for improving college ecology teaching. *Frontiers in Ecology and the Environment*, *1*(10), 533–540. doi:10.2307/3868164

DeHaan, R. L. (2005). The impending revolution in undergraduate science education. *Journal of Science Education and Technology*, *14*(2), 253–269. doi:10.1007/s10956-005-4425-3

Dickinson, J. L., & Bonney, R. B. (Eds.). (in press). *Citizen science: Public collaboration in environmental research*. Ithaca, NY: Cornell University Press.

Dolan, E., & Grady, J. (2010). Recognizing students' scientific reasoning: A tool for categorizing complexity of reasoning during teaching by inquiry. *Journal of Science Teacher Education*, *21*(1), 31–55. doi:10.1007/s10972-009-9154-7

Donovan, S. (2008). Big data: Teaching must evolve to keep up with advances. *Nature*, *455*(7212), 461. doi:10.1038/455461d

Drayton, B., & Falk, J. (2006). Dimensions that shape teacher-scientist collaborations for teacher enhancement. *Science Education*, *90*(4), 734–761. doi:10.1002/sce.20138

Ebert-May, D., Batzli, J., & Lim, H. (2003). Disciplinary research strategies for assessment of learning. *Bioscience*, *53*(12), 1221–1228. doi:10.1641/0006-3568(2003)053[1221:DRSFAO]2.0.CO;2

Ebert-May, D., Williams, K. S., Weber, E. P., Hodder, J., & Luckie, D. (2004). Practicing scientific inquiry: What are the rules? *Frontiers in Ecology and the Environment*, *2*(9), 492–493. doi:10.1890/1540-9295(2004)002[0492:PSIWAT]2.0.CO;2

Edelson, D. C. (1998). Realising authentic science learning through the adaptation of scientific practice. In Fraser, B. J., & Tobin, K. (Eds.), *International handbook of science education* (pp. 317–331). Dordrecht, The Netherlands: Kluwer.

Fee, J. M., McLinn, C. M., Phillips, C. B., Purcell, K., & Montanez, G. (2008). *BirdSleuth: Exploring bird behavior*. Ithaca, NY: Cornell Lab of Ornithology.

Gaunt, S. L., Nelson, D. A., Dantzker, M. S., Budney, G. A., & Bradbury, J. W. (2005). New directions for bioacoustics collections. *The Auk*, *122*(3), 984–987. doi:10.1642/0004-8038(2005)122[0984:NDFBC]2.0.CO;2

Hake, R. R. (1998). Interactive-engagement versus traditional methods: A six-thousand-student survey of mechanics test data for introductory physics courses. *American Journal of Physics*, *66*(1), 64–74. doi:10.1119/1.18809

Harker, A. R. (1999). Full application of the scientific method in an undergraduate teaching laboratory. *Journal of College Science Teaching*, *29*(2), 97–100.

Herrington, A., & Herrington, J. (2006). What is an authentic learning environment? In Herrington, A., & Herrington, J. (Eds.), *Authentic learning in higher education* (pp. 1–13). Hershey, PA: Idea Group Inc.doi:10.4018/9781591405948.ch001

Hiemstra, C., Liston, G. E., Pielke, R. A. Sr, Birkenheuer, D. L., & Albers, S. C. (2006). Comparing local analysis and prediction system (LAPS) assimilations with independent observations. *Weather and Forecasting*, *21*(6), 1024–1042. doi:10.1175/WAF961.1

Hodder, J., Ebert-May, D., & Batzli, J. (2008). Coding to analyze students' critical thinking. *Frontiers in Ecology and the Environment*, *4*(3), 162–163. doi:10.1890/1540-9295(2006)004[0162:CTASCT]2.0.CO;2

Kelling, S., Fink, D., Hochachka, W. M., Iliff, M. J., Sullivan, B. L., Wood, C. L., & Riedewald, M. (2009). Obtaining new insights for biodiversity conservation from broad-scale citizen science data. *Nature Precedings*. Retrieved November 15, 2010, from http://dx.doi.org/ 10.1038/ npre.2009.3967.1

Kelling, S., Hochachka, W. M., Fink, D., Riedewald, M., Caruana, R., Ballard, G., & Hooker, G. (2009). Data-intensive science: A new paradigm for biodiversity studies. *Bioscience*, *59*(7), 613–620. doi:10.1525/bio.2009.59.7.12

Kenny, S. S., Thomas, E., Katkin, W., Lemming, M., Smith, P., Glaser, M., & Gross, W. (2001). *Reinventing undergraduate education: Three years after the Boyer report*. State University of New York at Stony Brook: Boyer Commission on Educating Undergraduates in the Research University.

Knight, J. K., & Wood, W. B. (2005). Teaching more by lecturing less. *Cell Biology Education*, *4*(4), 298–310. doi:10.1187/05-06-0082

Lehning, M., Dawes, N., Bavay, M., Parlange, M., Nath, S., & Zhao, F. (2009). Instrumenting the Earth: Next-generation sensor networks and environmental science. In Hey, T., Tansley, S., & Tolle, K. (Eds.), *The fourth paradigm: Data-intensive scientific discovery* (pp. 45–51). Redmond, WA: Microsoft Research.

Lombardi, M. M. (2007a). *Approaches that work: How authentic learning is transforming education.* Educause Learning Initiative. Retrieved July 7, 2010, from http://net.educause.edu/ ir/ library/ pdf/ ELI3013.pdf

Lombardi, M. M. (2007b). *Authentic learning for the 21st century: An overview.* Educause Learning Initiative. Retrieved July 7, 2010, from http://net.educause.edu/ ir/ library/ pdf/ ELI3009.pdf

Lombardi, M. M. (2008). *Making the grade: The role of assessment in authentic learning.* Educause Learning Initiative. Retrieved July 7, 2010, from http://net.educause.edu/ ir/ library/ pdf/ ELI3019.pdf

Lowman, M., D'Avanzo, C., & Brewer, C. (2009). Ecology: A national ecological network for research and education. *Science*, *323*(5918), 1172–1173. doi:10.1126/science.1166945

Manduca, C. A., & Mogk, D. W. (2003). *Using data in undergraduate classrooms: Report from an interdisciplinary workshop at Carleton College, April 2002*. Retrieved June 29, 2010, from http://serc.carleton.edu/ usingdata/ report.html

Manduca, C. A., Mogk, D. W., Tewksbury, B., Macdonald, R. H., Fox, S. P., & Iverson, E. R. (2010). On the cutting edge: Teaching help for geoscience faculty. *Science*, *327*(5969), 1095–1096. doi:10.1126/science.1183028

National Research Council. (1996). *National science education standards*. Washington, DC: National Academy Press.

National Research Council. (2000). *Inquiry and the national science education standards: A guide for teaching and learning*. Washington, DC: The National Academies Press.

National Research Council. (2002). *BIO 2010: Transforming undergraduate education for future research biologists*. Washington, DC: The National Academies Press.

National Science Foundation. (2009). *Transitions and tipping points in complex environmental systems*. Arlington, VA.

National Science Foundation, Task Force on Cyberlearning. (2008). *Fostering learning in the networked world: The cyberlearning opportunity and challenge*. Arlington, VA.

Park Rogers, M. A., & Abell, S. K. (2008). The design, enactment, and experience of inquiry-based instruction in undergraduate science education: A case study. *Science Education*, *92*(4), 591–607. doi:10.1002/sce.20247

Porter, S. (2004). Scientific data sets: An important tool for student learning. In Cunningham, S., & George, Y. S. (Eds.), *Invention and impact: Building excellence in undergraduate science, technology, engineering and mathematics (STEM) education* (pp. 163–167). Washington, DC: American Association for the Advancement of Science.

Ramaley, J. A., & Haggett, R. R. (2005). Engaged and engaging science: A component of a good liberal education. *Peer Review, Winter*, 8-12.

Reeves, T. C., Herrington, J., & Oliver, R. (2002). Authentic activities and online learning. *Annual Conference Proceedings of Higher Education Research and Development Society of Australasia.* Perth, Australia. Retrieved October 29, 2010, from http://elrond.scam.ecu.edu.au/ oliver/ 2002/ Reeves.pdf

Robin, J., Levine, E., & Riha, S. (2005). Utilizing satellite imagery and GLOBE student data to model soil dynamics. *Ecological Modelling*, *185*(1), 133–145. doi:10.1016/j.ecolmodel.2004.11.022

Ruiz-Primo, M. A., Li, M., Tsai, S.-P., & Schneider, J. (2010). Testing one premise of scientific inquiry in science classrooms: Examining students' scientific explanations and student learning. *Journal of Research in Science Teaching*, *47*(5), 583–608.

Smith, B. K., & Blankinship, E. (2000). Justifying imagery: Multimedia support for learning through explanation. *IBM Systems Journal*, *39*(3&4), 749–766. doi:10.1147/sj.393.0749

Songer, N. B. (2001). *Realizing the learning in digital learning.* Retrieved October 10, 2008, from http://www.pkal.org/ documents/ RealizingTheLearningIn DigitalLearning.cfm

Stein, S. J., Isaacs, G., & Andrews, T. (2004). Incorporating authentic learning experiences within a university course. *Studies in Higher Education*, *9*(2), 239–258. doi:10.1080/0307507042000190813

Sundberg, M. D., & Moncada, G. J. (1994). Creating investigative laboratories for undergraduates. *Bioscience*, *44*(10), 698–704. doi:10.2307/1312513

Tosteson, J. L. (1997). The scientific world view, information technology, and science education: Closing the gap between knowledge-generation and knowledge-consumption. *Science Education*, *6*(4), 273–284.

Trautmann, N. M. (2009a). Designing peer review for pedagogical success: What can we learn from professional science? *Journal of College Science Teaching*, *38*(4), 24–29.

Trautmann, N. M. (2009b). Interactive learning through web-mediated peer review of student science reports. *Educational Technology Research and Development*, *57*(5), 685–704. doi:10.1007/s11423-007-9077-y

Trautmann, N. M., Shirk, J., Fee, J. M., & Krasny, M. (in press). Who poses the question? Using citizen science to help K-12 teachers meet the mandate for inquiry. In Dickinson, J. L., & Bonney, R. (Eds.), *Citizen science: Public collaboration in environmental research.* Ithaca, NY: Cornell University Press.

Underwood, J., Smith, H., Luckin, R., & Fitzpatrick, G. (2008). E-science in the classroom – Towards viability. *Computers & Education*, *50*(2), 535–546. doi:10.1016/j.compedu.2007.07.003

van Zee, E. H. (2000). Analysis of a student-generated inquiry discussion. *International Journal of Science Education*, *22*(2), 115–142. doi:10.1080/095006900289912

Verbyla, D. L. (2001). A test of detecting spring leaf flush within the Alaskan boreal forest using ERS-2 and Radarsat SAR data. *International Journal of Remote Sensing*, *22*(6), 1159–1165. doi:10.1080/01431160010030127

Voss, M. A., & Cooper, C. B. (2010). Using a free online citizen-science project to teach observation and quantification of animal behavior. *The American Biology Teacher*, *72*(7), 437–443. doi:10.1525/abt.2010.72.7.9

Wenk, L. (2000). *Improving science learning: Inquiry-based and traditional first-year college science curricula.* (Unpublished doctoral dissertation). University of Massachusetts, Amherst, MA.

Wiggins, G., & McTighe, J. (1998). *Understanding by design*. Alexandria, VA: Association for Supervision and Curriculum Development.

Williams, K. S., Ebert-May, D., Luckie, D., Hodder, J., & Koptur, S. (2004). Novel assessments: Detecting success in student learning. *Frontiers in Ecology and the Environment*, *2*(8), 444–445. doi:10.1890/1540-9295(2004)002[0444:NADSIS]2.0.CO;2

Wilson, C., & Trautmann, N. M., MaKinster, J. G., & Barker, B. (2010). Science Pipes: A world of data at your fingertips. Exploring biodiversity with online visualization and analysis tools. *Science Teacher (Normal, Ill.)*, *77*(7), 34–39.

Windschitl, M. (2000). Supporting the development of science inquiry skills with special classes of software. *Educational Technology Research and Development*, *48*(2), 81–95. doi:10.1007/BF02313402

Windschitl, M., & Buttemer, H. (2000). What should the inquiry experience be for the learner? *The American Biology Teacher*, *62*(5), 346–350. doi:10.1662/0002-7685(2000)062[0346:WSTIEB]2.0.CO;2

Witzig, S. B., Zhao, N., Abell, S. K., Weaver, J. C., Adams, J. E., & Schmidt, F. J. (2010). Achievable inquiry in the college laboratory: The mini-journal. *Journal of College Science Teaching*, *39*(6), 14–23.

Wright, T. F., & Wilkinson, G. S. (2001). Population genetic structure and vocal dialects in an amazon parrot. *Proceedings of the Royal Society of London: Biological Sciences*, *268*(1467), 609–616. doi:10.1098/rspb.2000.1403

Zahn, C., Krauskopf, K., Pea, R., & Hesse, F. W. (2010). Digital video tools in the classroom: Empirical studies on constructivist learning with audio-visual media in the domain of history. In K. Gomez, L. Lyons, & J. Radinsky (Eds.), *Learning in the disciplines: Proceedings of the 9th International Conference of the Learning Sciences (ICLS 2010) - Volume 1, full papers* (pp. 620-627). Chicago, IL: International Society of the Learning Sciences.

ADDITIONAL READING

Bothun, G. D. (2003). Data driven inquiry: Reforming the teaching of Science 101 through the use of instructional technology. In Kauffman, L. R., & Stocks, J. E. (Eds.), *Reinvigorating the undergraduate experience: Successful models supported by NSF's AIRE/RAIRE program.* Washington, DC: Council on Undergraduate Research.

Bramble, J., & Workman, M. (2007). Data-rich case studies improve students' abilities to interpret graphs in a large non-majors course. *Teaching Issues and Experiments in Ecology, 5*(Research #1). Retrieved October 10, 2008, from http://tiee.ecoed.net/ vol/ v5/ research/ bramble/ abstract.html

Ebert-May, D., Brewer, C., & Allred, S. (1997). Innovation in large lectures: Teaching for active learning. *Bioscience*, *47*(9), 601–607. doi:10.2307/1313166

Griffith, A. B. (2007). Semester-long engagement in science inquiry improves students' understanding of experimental design. *Teaching Issues and Experiments in Ecology, 5*(Research #2). Retrieved October 10, 2008, from http://tiee.ecoed.net/ vol/ v5/ research/ griffith/ abstract.html

Hane, E. N. (2007). Use of an inquiry-based approach to teaching experimental design concepts in a general ecology course. *Teaching Issues and Experiments in Ecology, 5*(Research #3). Retrieved October 10, 2008, from http://tiee.ecoed.net/ vol/ v5/ research/ hane/ abstract.html

Herrington, J., & Kervin, L. (2007). Authentic learning supported by technology: 10 suggestions and cases of integration in classrooms. *Educational Media International*, *44*(3), 219–236. doi:10.1080/09523980701491666

Herrington, J., Oliver, R., & Reeves, T. C. (2003). Patterns of engagement in authentic online learning environments. *Australian Journal of Educational Technology*, *19*(1), 59–71.

Herrington, J., Oliver, R., & Reeves, T. C. (2006). Authentic tasks online: A synergy among learner, task and technology. *Distance Education*, *27*(2), 233–248. doi:10.1080/01587910600789639

Humston, R., & Ortiz-Barney, E. (2007). Evaluating course impact on student environmental values in undergraduate ecology with a novel survey instrument. *Teaching Issues and Experiments in Ecology, 5*(Research #4). Retrieved October 10, 2008, from http://tiee.ecoed.net/ vol/ v5/ research/ humston/ abstract.html

King, P. M., & Kitchener, K. S. (1994). *Developing reflective judgment: Understanding and promoting intellectual growth and critical thinking in adolescents and adults*. San Francisco: Jossey-Bass.

Lopatto, D. (2004). What undergraduate research can tell us about research on learning. *PKAL Volume IV: What works, what matters, what lasts*. Retrieved November 29, 2010, from http:// www.pkal.org/ documents/ Vol4WhatUndergrad ResearchCanTellUs.cfm

McMartin, F., Iverson, E., Wolf, A., Morrill, J., Morgan, G., & Manduca, C. (2008). The use of online digital resources and educational digital libraries in higher education. *International Journal on Digital Libraries*, *9*(1), 65–79. doi:10.1007/ s00799-008-0036-y

Musante, S. (2008). Critical conversations: The 2008 biology education summit. *Bioscience*, *58*(8), 685–689. doi:10.1641/B580804

Nicaise, M., Gibney, T., & Crane, M. (2000). Toward an understanding of authentic learning: Student perceptions of an authentic classroom. *Journal of Science Education and Technology*, *9*(1), 79–94. doi:10.1023/A:1009477008671

Picone, C., Rhode, J., Hyatt, L., & Parshall, T. (2007). Assessing gains in undergraduate students' abilities to analyze graphical data. *Teaching Issues and Experiments in Ecology, 5*(Research #1). Retrieved November 19, 2010, from http://tiee.ecoed.net/ vol/ v5/ research/ picone/ abstract.html

Rettig, J. E., & Smith, G. R. (2009). Class research projects in ecology courses: Methods to "un-can" the experience. *Journal of College Science Teaching, 38*(5), 38–42.

Smith, B. K., & Blankinship, E. (2000). Justifying imagery: Multimedia support for learning through explanation. *IBM Systems Journal, 39*(3&4), 749–766. doi:10.1147/sj.393.0749

Smith, H., Underwood, J., Fitzpatrick, G., & Luckin, R. (2009). Classroom e-science: Exposing the work to make it work. *Journal of Educational Technology & Society, 12*(3), 289–308.

KEY TERMS AND DEFINITIONS

Assessment: The process of monitoring student learning.

Authentic Learning: Learning environments characterized by opportunities for students to actively extend their prior knowledge in order to investigate interdisciplinary, real-world problems.

Biodiversity: The variety of living organisms on Earth, including the number of species and the genetic variation within those species.

Citizen Science: Projects in which the public and/or students partner with scientists in gathering scientific data to address questions of real-world significance.

Ecoinformatics: An interdisciplinary field that focuses on managing and structuring multiple sources of data so that ecological analysis can easily be done.

Inquiry-Based Learning: Activities through which students develop scientific knowledge and skills while conducting processes analogous to those used by scientists in studying the natural world.

Open Inquiry: A relatively unstructured learning approach in which educators act as facilitators to enable students to pose their own questions, design investigations, and analyze and interpret their results.

Ornithology: The scientific study of birds.

Structured Inquiry: A learning approach in which educators guide students by specifying the focus questions, investigation strategies, and/or methods for analysis and interpretation of results.

Taxon: A group of living organisms judged to be a unit. May be used to refer to a species, genus, or other level of organization.

Workflow: A sequence of user-defined steps of operation to be carried out on data or other objects.

Chapter 6
Towards an Activity-Driven Design Method for Online Learning Resources

Trond Eiliv Hauge
University of Oslo, Norway

Jan Arild Dolonen
University of Oslo, Norway

ABSTRACT

In this chapter we focus on the challenges we have encountered in the development of an activity-driven design method for online resources in an education programme for school leaders. The study is part of a follow-up research of the Digital Leadership Project (DLP) at the University of Oslo. The design method is experimental and grounded in Cultural-Historical Activity Theory (CHAT). The study can be seen as a contribution within CHAT in terms of moving from the current use of CHAT as simply a descriptive evaluation tool between analysis and design or design and redesign towards a more developmental model. The study addresses the research problem of interrupting an existing education course design with new technologies and learning objects/resources to try to bridge the gap between different designs for learning. This research contributes to the understanding of how the interplay between cultural artefacts, such as pedagogical ideas, design methods, and technological solutions in a design activity can influence solutions and lead to tensions, which create opportunities for the transformation of the design as a whole.

INTRODUCTION

The process of designing for activities in virtual communities supporting professional learning is consonant with the classical rationale of teachers' planning of everyday teaching: to define, interpret and activate a curriculum object, to make directions for students' work, and to concretise learning tools, activities and timelines of work (Beetham & Sharpe, 2007). In the process of implementation this conceptual design for teaching and learning has to be tested against practices embedded in

DOI: 10.4018/978-1-61350-080-4.ch006

classroom structures and traditions, and the history of the school as an organisation. The purposeful follow-up action of students' learning involves knowing how different institutional levels of design interact and direct learning processes and outcomes (Luckin, 2010; Lemke & Sabelli, 2008; Arnseth & Ludvigsen, 2006).

In this chapter, we present the Digital Leadership Project (DLP) and discuss an activity-theoretical model for designing a set of digital learning resources to be implemented in a study course for school leaders. We describe an inquiry-oriented design process attempting to model technology-enhanced learning activities in between existing structures and practices of learning framed by face-to-face activities and a virtual management system for learning. Specifically, the study addresses the evolutionary process of a design model bridging practices across levels of technology and pedagogy.

The study is highly influenced by a socio-cultural perspective and particularly Cultural Historical Activity Theory (CHAT) (Engeström, 1987, 1999, 2007), and we apply CHAT in two different ways: First and foremost as a lens to analyse how different mediating tools, objectives and social organisation influence designs for learning (cf. approaches by Beetham & Sharpe, 2007; Hauge, Lund, & Vestöl, 2007), which are embedded in a complex social practice. Secondly, we contribute to the CHAT community and design approaches by illustrating how CHAT in this study was used as a developmental model in the actual design phase rather than just as a descriptive evaluation tool between analysis and design or design and redesign (cf. studies by Jonassen, 1999; Mwanza, 2002; Kaptelinin & Nardi, 2006).

With CHAT as an analytical framework we can trace how the actual design team draws on different tools and resources over time when modelling the digital material in the course programme. By analysing what they produce (minutes, sketches, documents, course material), we see how approaches to the design of digital learning resources are transformed and given new meaning by the use of activity theory. Thus, two research questions are formulated for the study:

- What are the mediating tools that influence the design of the digital learning resources in the school leadership programme?
- What characterises the activity-driven design method and its relation to the prevailing designs for learning in the programme?

THEORETICAL ASSUMPTIONS

In conceptualising the making of the DLP resources, we draw on perspectives grounded in Cultural Historical Activity Theory (CHAT) articulated by Engeström (1987, 1999, 2007). Activity theory originates from the socio-cultural and socio–historical theories of Vygotsky (1978), Leont'ev (1978) and others. As the theory is deeply dialectical, contextual and historically oriented towards practices, their objects, mediating artefacts, and social organisation (Cole & Engeström, 1993), it provides a powerful lens through which to describe the complex social practices that arise within such a hybrid learning environment as that presented in the current school leadership programme. For the purpose of this study it is essential that the theory can be applied as an analytical framework for understanding the historical and contextual constraints of the DLP design and as a step-stone for the design modelling.

While activity theory has been used to study information systems design and development (Barab, Schatz, & Scheckler, 2004; Greenhow & Belbas, 2007; Hewitt, 2004; Kuutti, 1996, 1999; Jonassen & Rohrer-Murphy 1999), the research on how it can be used for design purposes is still a field of experimentation. However, in the theory tradition of Leont'ev and Engeström focusing on collective and object–oriented activities in complex environments, the contextual perspective gives a strong framework for sorting out significant forces of interaction and work production (Kaptelinin & Nardi, 2006; Jonassen & Rohrer-Murphy, 1999; Mwanza, 2002). Consequently, we argue that activity theory will give a significant contribution to the design of the DLP resources.

According to Engeström (1999), an activity system is made up of individuals or groups (subjects) acting to accomplish an object of activity. This system thinking recognises a special status of culturally developed artefacts as fundamental mediators of actions, for example the digital learning resources in our study, which relate subjects (students) and the object of activity in a dynamic three-way interaction. However, in the extended version of the activity system, Engeström takes into consideration a set of interrelated collective and regulative forces represented by the community involved (student groups in our case), work distribution (between students/teachers in the current study), and rules at work. The continuous contradictions between the elements of the system are a driving force for change and learning for the actors involved. This extended activity model has to be understood as a collective phenomenon, which moves beyond mere individual activities. It is developmental in nature, object-oriented, and collective, and is based on culturally mediated activities (Engeström, 1999).

The concept of design used in this study is related to this dynamic and collective perspective on human activity framed by the objects of activity, cultural artefacts and contextual interrelations. As the extended activity system has been used as an analytical frame for understanding human activity, it can also be used as a design for change and development. This is an integrated part of the theory of expansive learning particularly expressed in the methodology of Developmental Work Research (DWR), which focuses on analyses of design-redesign practices and the potential for workplace learning (Daniels, Edwards, Engeström, Gallagher, & Ludvigsen, 2010; Engeström, 2007; Sannino, Daniels, & Gutiérrez, 2009). Applied to the actual context of digital learning resource development, we will argue that the DWR approach fits the evolving needs of a revised design for learning in the leadership programme. In fact, what we are creating is a supplementary and virtual *design for learning*, where we are viewing design as an intentional and systematic, but also creative and responsive, approach to situated learning. We acknowledge, as Beethem and Sharpe (2007) argue, that learning never can be wholly designed, only designed *for*, or planned in advance, with an awareness of the contingent nature of learning that demands a constant dialogue with learners in practice (ibid. p. 8). Thus, by the use of activity theory, we argue for a more open pedagogical approach to design than what is found in the field of instructional design that is characterised by its own specific protocols and language (Jochems, van Merrienboer & Koper, 2004).

THE SCHOOL LEADERSHIP COURSE CONTEXT

DLP was designed to serve the growing use of networked learning in the Master programme for school leadership at the University of Oslo. It was run as a pilot project in 2006 - 2008 serving all students in two basic course levels comprising 50 students each, and continued as part of the ordinary programme from 2008. Our research study is grounded on this pilot project. The leadership programme is offered as a blended model of education based on face-to-face seminars, student group work, and a set of learning activities embedded in a virtual learning environment called It's Learning (ITL). The virtual environment also serves as a platform for curriculum information, lesson plans, communication and supervision of students in their work on e-portfolios. Over time ITL has come to play a significant role as a basic management structure for the course activities running in and between joint seminars, student groups and individual students. The programme profile is:

Figure 1. The activity system of the leadership programme

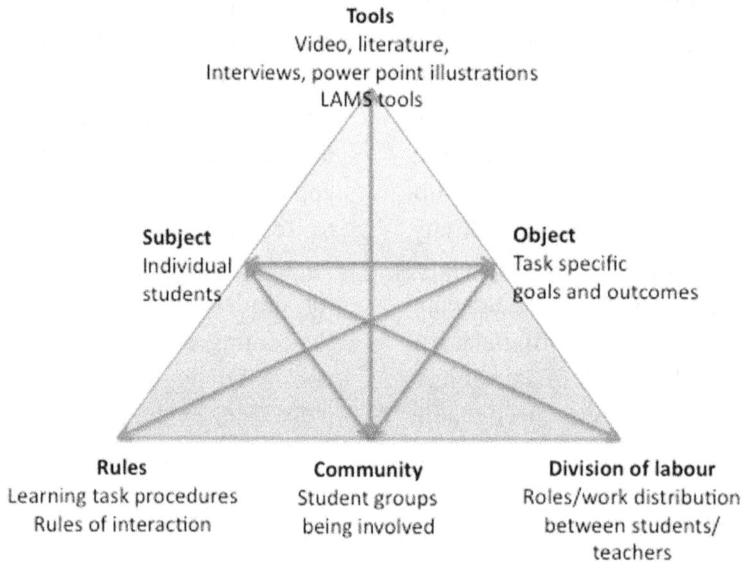

- oriented towards *experiential learning,* which means that the students have to describe and analyse practices and experiences from their own workplace,
- *research–based,* which means that the students have to read and analyse current research literature and theories applied to school leadership and education practices, and
- focused on *leadership for change and development* in the school context.

In Figure 1, the activity-theoretical framework is applied to illustrate the complexities of the course programme exemplified by its main components and their interrelationship. It gives a picture of the prevailing activities and design for learning before the digital learning resources were introduced. The figure shows the interactive system of major study tools in the programme, objects of activity, and how the activities are regulated and intertwined with communal activities and distribution of work between students and teachers.

As an overall assessment, the use of the virtual environment in the programme is pretty close to the mainstream network learning practice in higher education, where written text is the dominant medium for interaction when students and the tutors read, reflect upon and revise electronic texts as described in studies by Goodyear, Banks, Hodgson, & McConell (2004). The tool interactions do not involve the use of voice, video, discussion forums, collaborative spaces for multimedia production or any advanced electronic text development tool, such as wikis. However, when looking at the case study work related to the students' workplace and the e–portfolio system a varied set of tasks and tools were in use, supporting the principles of experiential and workplace learning. For example, the programme has adapted case study principles described by Shulman (2004), Colbert, Trimble and Desberg (1996), approaches in writing to learn programmes (Bazerman, Little, Bethel, Chavkin, Fouquette, & Garufis, 2005; Dysthe, Hertzberg, & Hoel, 2010; Lieberman & Wood, 2003), and student portfolio models (Darling–Hammond & Snyder, 2000; Dysthe & Engelsen, 2003; Zeichner & Wray,

2001). In other words, an advanced set of inquiry-oriented tools for learning is part of the programme and directs activities towards the overall object of enriching the students with deep understandings and competencies in school leadership. However, the existing practices of technology-supported learning are to a great extent only student text productions framed by the ITL platform. DLP can be seen as the next step in utilising more advanced designs and tools, which support the overarching principles of learning in the leadership programme.

THE DLP DESIGN APPROACHES

In this section, we present and discuss available background designs for creating the actual learning resources, the system descriptions of technologies utilised in the process, and the final design model for the resources. The leading design team for the DLP resources comprised two teachers involved in the programme, two researchers of technology and pedagogy, and two external professionals supporting the management of the project. The DLP process documentation by Ottesen and Vennebo (2007) is part of the data material for this study, in addition to minutes, sketches and design documents produced by the design team, and analyses of former digital learning resource designs and participatory observation notes produced by the researchers.

Background Designs for Learning

Three sets of challenges had to be solved by the design team to reach the final solution:

- The implicit model for learning of the leadership programme had to be explicated and discussed as a possible tool for design of the learning resources.
- Current digital learning resources had to be revisited for analyses of design ideas and possible content reuses.
- Available technologies had to be researched with regard to how they could support the learning design requirements and interactive use of multi-media resources.

In approaching the solutions to the first problem the following practice was scrutinised: The course practice is heavily influenced by a widespread and quite influential model for curriculum planning and learning in Norway, (i.e. the relational model for designing teaching and learning) (Bjørndal & Lieberg, 1978; Lyngsnes & Rismark, 2007) which focuses on dimensions such as learners' needs, contexts, curriculum goals, content materials, learning activities and assessment. This way of thinking about curriculum and learning bears similarities to the field of instructional design and technology (Strømnes, Rørvik, & Eilertsen, 1997), but lacks the direction or sequencing of design activities as in Dick and Carey's (2005) instructional design model, and says little about the potential of net–based use of technology. The same holds true for the design models for case study tasks and e-portfolio (cf. Figure 1). Neither of these practices was developed for virtual activities, besides being stored as digital text documents.

In researching the second problem, three former development projects of digital learning resources formed a backdrop for the DLP design discussion: The first one, the *Digital Learning Case* project consists of a variety of short-time video resources embedded in a learning task structure for teacher students (Hauge, 2006a, 2006b). The second one, the *Dilemma* project, is a video application simulating students' project work in school where teachers or student teachers can interactively influence the work process by choosing different pathways to problem-solving. In this last project an activity–theoretical model was applied in analysing the design and the development process (Hauge, Lund, & Vestøl, 2006). While these two projects draw our attention to how video resources could be utilised in sequences of learning activities, they did not offer any integrated net-environment for further utilisation as needed in the DLP project.

The third project, the EU-project CALIBRATE, was designed to integrate e-learning resources (multi-media) in different school subjects from different countries and to make them available for teachers through a common web-portal (Calibrate, 2008). In this project, the researchers related to the design team did a comparative study of eight curricula (Mathematics and Natural Science) from four European countries. A common denominator of these curricula was found in categories linked to Topics, Goals and Activity (TGA) descriptions of the curriculum content (Calibrate, 2006). This classification system was also analysed as a search model for net–based learning resources. When working with the TGA structure in CALIBRATE we discussed its potential as a design tool for creating learning material in the DLP project. However, as the DLP project proceeded the design team realised that this approach was too coarse–grained to fit the needs of goal and activity descriptions at the micro level needed for designing the DLP learning material.

Regarding the third problem, we had to determine the technology environment that would support the interactive learning concept and fit the restricted economy frame of the DLP project. Intensive discussions of user scenarios by the design team showed that neither the Digital Learning Case/Dilemma products nor the Calibrate environment could solve the problem. Furthermore, the ITL system did not support the design of multi–media resources integrated in a deliberate trajectory of student learning. Therefore, the LAMS technology (Learning Activity Management System), a free web–based learning environment developed at McQuarie University, Australia, was chosen to support this last development task.

Figure 2 gives a summary of different features of the technologies/resources that were explored in discussions of actual DLP designs by the design team. Each of the designs was analysed with regard to what they could support in sequencing a set of multi–media resources for learning and how they could be integrated in an interactive virtual learning environment. Gradually, the shortcomings of available designs for learning were clarified when they were analysed as mediating tools in scenarios of digital learning activity systems based on the ground model in Figure 1. The LAMS technology was the winning part in these discussions.

ACTIVITY DESIGN IN LAMS

The Learning Activity Management System (LAMS) uses Java on the server side and JavaScript and Flash on the client side. It is a new generation of educational software that moves e-learning from a content–centric approach to an activity-sequence based approach. The rationale for this move is a focus on learning designs or scripts where the main elements are to include greater focus on context rather than content, activity rather than transfer and absorption, and greater recognition of the role of collaboration rather than just the single learner working alone (Dalziel, 2003, 2007). LAMS has three modules: The first is the authoring tool where teachers or instructional designers can create and preview their designed learning sequence or script through a visual interface, in which each activity in the script is represented by an activity component (grey box), and the transitions from activity to activity are represented by lines connecting the activity components (Figure 3). For each activity in the script the teacher/designer can go into the activity component and give specific instructions on how to complete the task. The grey boxes represent an activity component that can consist of one or many tools. The boxes are dragged from the left pane and dropped in the large right working space. Then, transition lines that sequence the script connect the boxes.

The second module is the learner view where students select the activity from the left-hand pane of the browser window and do their task in a working space on the right side. They complete

Figure 2. Descriptions of designs for learning explored in the study

Technologies/ resources	Design for learning	Support of
Curriculum plan models Case study models E-portfolio	Goal and content oriented models for learning	Existing practices of text production and social learning
Digital learning case	Inquiry-oriented model for learning	Open discussions of video-based cases related to work practices
Dilemma	Interactive and inquiry-based model for learning	Sequenced discussions of video-based work practices in alternative routes of learning
Calibrate	Topic, goal and activity oriented model	Search for classified digital learning resources in education
LAMS	Interactive and activity oriented model for learning	Predefined and sequenced learning tasks in multiple media formats

Figure 3. A script or learning sequence in LAMS authoring mode

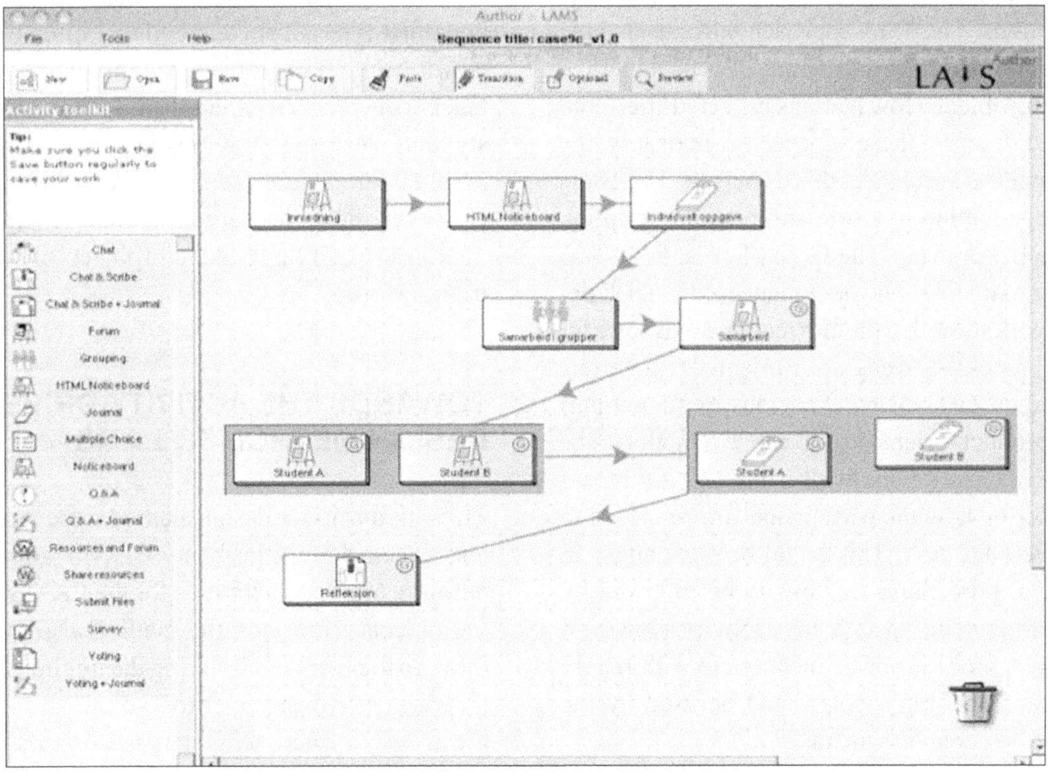

the sequence step-by-step with their progress being shown in the left pane. In this module they also have the possibility to participate in group work. The third module is a monitor view where the teacher can schedule the course for a class and monitor the progress of the class as a whole and each individual student.

Design Conceptions Concretised Through LAMS

The design team had to explicate and translate underlying learning design principles of the leadership programme into sustainable activities in LAMS. The team agreed that the TGA approach should be tried out as a bridging tool in this design work because of the vague descriptive value of the programme model compared to the LAMS activity requirements. The TGA approach implies that a learning resource or object (LO) should be described in terms of Topic, Goal and Activity descriptions. However, the translation work of the TGA approach into the LAMS sequence or script model (understood as LOs) met several difficulties. The TGA approach introduces three important aspects in the making of a curriculum or learning object. However, it says very little about how to describe these aspects. More or less, the designer has to consider this by herself. The Topic directs attention to a title and broad description of the LO domain. The Goal of an activity was harder to decide. The documents of the DLP design work show that the curriculum goals were far more process– and cognitive oriented (e.g. reflect on certain tasks or be conscious of something) than product–oriented (e.g. create a model). The Activity descriptions within the LO are meant to describe how the participants are supposed to complete the task. This could be done either in terms of procedures or steps to be followed by the learner in the specific task activity. However, the TGA procedure was incomplete with regard to how technology tools could be used by the learner in achieving the task.

In addition to the Topic, Goal and Activity considerations, the design team had to discuss examples of curriculum content exposed to the learner. In fact, this was a difficult and tensional issue to solve, because it presupposed a joint understanding of the content matter included for learning, (e.g. videos, literature, case assignments etc). Table 1 shows an example of a TGA description with an additional content description defined as a learning object/sequence in LAMS. The selected script had nine activities, but only the first two of them are shown in the table (translated from Norwegian to English by the authors.)

The work of mapping TGA descriptions into LAMS appeared not to be an easy task for the design team. Like the implicit pedagogical model of the programme, the TGA model did not support any easy or systematic description of tools and activities for the learners. Content descriptions shown in Table 1 turned out to be too vague for a complete mapping of the LAMS sequences, which required explicit descriptions of the resources for learning, such as video support, note taking, individual work, use of discussion forums and other types of student collaboration. In other words, the TGA model did not support the teacher designers in strengthening their script for students' learning activities in a proper way as pointed out by Ottesen and Vennebo (2007). However, the model served an important mediating role in clarifying needs and objects of the DLP design work.

TOWARDS THE ACTIVITY-DRIVEN DESIGN METHOD TO LAMS

The activity-driven design method arose as a direct consequence of the problems described above of defining tools and activities for the LAMS learning objects. However, the method also evolved through the work of clarifying the implicit design for learning in the course programme, and making the underlying activity system more explicit for a

Table 1. An example of a script based on the TGA approach with an additional 'content' column

Topic: ICT, leadership and learning		
Content	**Goal**	**Activity**
The students' everyday experiences from use of ICT in learning.	To make everyday experiences explicit.	Choose two examples from ICT for educational purposes in your school. Describe concretely how ICT is used in your school.
Säljö's chapter in Bråten. Own examples on learning and ICT (cf. Ludvigsen).	To understand how use of ICT in learning gives opportunities but also constrains learning.	i) Read theory by Säljö and Ludvigsen ii) Discuss how use of ICT from the two examples above strengthens the learning process.

redesign which supported the development of the digital learning resources. During this final process it became clear that the TGA model needed to be transformed and concretised regarding the objects of activity and the rules governing the learning activities. The technology tools perspectives also needed to be clarified. Thus, the extended activity system model described in Figure 1 was adopted as a means for further scripting of the LAMS activities. By applying this system model, the design team was able to elaborate the scripts into a richer and more concrete description of the objects of activity, tools use in LAMS and other support technologies, and activity regulations afforded by task procedures, community of learners involved and work distribution between the participants. This elaborated approach helped the designers to specify the learning content for the students (e.g. what concepts the students had to work on based on the course literature, the products expected as outcomes of the activity, and the activity components in LAMS that would support the objects of activity). In this context, the designers also had to articulate the social organisation of learning (e.g. whether the students were going to collaborate or not, and what tools and procedures they should utilise in their work). The design team concluded that the new mapping procedure in LAMS turned out to be far easier to fulfil and less prone to trial and error than the TGA approach (Ottesen & Vennebo, 2007). Table 2 gives an example of a specific curriculum topic transformed into two learning objects for LAMS by the activity-driven design framework. Only two of the seven activities in the script are shown (translated from Norwegian to English by the authors).

Table 2 may be conceived as an actual script for learning objects (LO) implemented in LAMS. The script tells who are going to work on the object, which procedures to follow, which tools and communities that are activated in the work process, and which goals are framing the work. The activity sequence forms the content and structure of the actual learning object.

DISCUSSION

The study can be seen as a contribution within Cultural-Historical Activity Theory (CHAT) in terms of moving from the current use of CHAT simply as a descriptive evaluation tool between analysis and design or design and redesign. For example, Jonassen & Rohrer-Murphy (1999) describe a CHAT inspired framework for analysing needs, tasks, and outcomes that can be applied to design constructivist learning environments. Similarly, Mwanza (2002) argues that the lack of a standard method for applying activity theory to Human Computer Interaction (HCI) has meant that many designers have failed to benefit from the richness of this framework. She developed a method with components such as the 'Eight-Step-Model', the 'Activity Notation Guide' and a technique of 'Generating Research Questions'. However, these components are only used as ethnographic tools

Table 2. An example of a script based on the activity-driven design method

Topic: Leadership and the multicultural education society	
Goals for the topic: The students should learn how to do systematic inquiries of practice and build knowledge about guidance and leadership in education in a multicultural society.	
Activity 1	
Goal	To formulate a problem description for the inquiry.
Object (result)	To understand and describe the role of a problem description in an inquiry.
Who (subject)	Individual students.
Tools	Video or pictures of situations in schools, interviews with headmasters, articles, use of note-tool in LAMS to create problem descriptions.
Procedure	Watch, listen and read. Formulate two or three problem descriptions in the note-tool.
Community	The individual student and peer students.
Activity 2	
Goal	To state the reason for choice of methods in their inquiry.
Object (result)	To understand and describe the relation between problem description and choice of methods.
Who (subject)	Individual students.
Tools	Literature: Postholm and Kvale. Power point about interaction analysis. Multiple-choice inquiry in LAMS.
Procedure	Multiple choice: choose 'right' method in relation to problem description.
Community	Individual work but visual access to peer students.

identifying the organisational needs that can be addressed and transformed. Another approach within HCI is the 'activity-oriented checklist by Kaptelinin and Nardi (2006). Their checklist covers various aspects of how the target technology supports, or is intended to support, human actions (ibid., 270). In this study, however, we argue for an activity-driven design approach that can be used more directly for designing learning resources. The DLP study shows that it is possible to move beyond such a checklist practice and to model learning resources by an activity-driven design method.

The study has addressed the research problem of interrupting an existing education course design by the use of new technologies and a set of new learning resources. Contradictions between different designs for learning occurred similar to what has been described by Barab, MaKinster and Scheckler (2003) and Beetham and Sharpe (2007). The tensions were heavily influenced by different activity perspectives held by the members of the design team (Ottesen & Vennebo, 2006). However, different design preferences were bridged through a continuous dialogue based on experiences with former learning designs (Digital Learning Case, Dilemma) relevant for the DLP project, the existing pedagogical design of the virtual learning environment (ITL), and the prevailing models of learning in the programme. The design contradictions can be looked upon as a necessary means for reaching to the end model of DLP.

FUTURE RESEARCH DIRECTIONS

The DLP experience has shown the usefulness of an activity-driven method for design of online learning resources. However, the method itself evolved through a series of trial and error reflecting different conceptions and preferences in the fields of learning design and school leadership education. The CHAT driven design approach is so far not an obvious option for designers of teaching and learning neither in a face–to–face nor in a virtual setting, and it needs to be further researched and concretised in order to prove the benefits for learning. While the research body is growing with regard to CHAT as an analytical tool for understanding technology-supported practices (cf. Barab, Schatz, & Scheckler, 2003; Hauge & Norenes, 2010; Kaptelinin & Nardi, 2006; Mwanza-Simwami, Engeström, & Amon, 2009), there is still a need for researching design practices based on CHAT and consequences for students' learning.

In our case, the activity method in itself needs to be further explored and refined with regard to how learning resources are described and contextualised in activity theoretical terms, and how it may fit into other virtual environments than LAMS. Further, the study has revealed the necessity to further stimulate and explore discursive practices between partners in the education programme regarding prevailing designs of learning embedded in curricula and management structures of the education programme. This also includes current practices constrained by the virtual learning system ITL. And still, there is a need for researching the use value of the learning resources for the students in the context of the leadership programme. So far, the study may be looked upon as the first step in a developmental cycle of the online learning environment framing the school leadership programme.

CONCLUSION

This study has revealed an activity-driven design method for creating online learning resources in an education programme for school leaders, based on Cultural Historical Activity Theory (Engeström 1987, 1999, 2007). The design method has been developed as part of an evolutionary process between teachers in the programme, technology researchers and project managers, grounded on ideas of experiential and workplace learning and approaches to technology-enhanced learning. The method is experimental and does not follow a ready-made 'tool-kit' in activity theory, simply because such a model does not yet exists (Greenhow & Belbas, 2004; Kaptelinen & Nardi, 2006; Jonassen & Rohrer-Murphy, 1999). Based on this situation we have given a careful description of the design process as well as the resources that have been created.

Activity theory has shown to be a powerful lens for understanding the implicit needs and strategies in the Digital Leadership Project (DLP). The theory has shown to be a strong tool for sorting out significant activities in designing task–specific communications and productions by the learners and how they are related to resources, communities and regulation of work activities. Compared to the implicit pedagogical model in the education programme, the activity-driven design method gave an added value to the scripting of the digital learning resources being implemented in the LAMS (Learning Activity Management System) environment. However, the significant step for reaching to this stage of development was the TGA mapping approach in the EU project CALIBRATE, focusing on a common denominator of curricula in European schools: Topics, Goals and Activities (Calibrate, 2006). This analysis revealed the necessity to go further in explicating how learning activities in a particular education situation are linked to task structures, resources, work regulations, communities and outcomes. The linking of the DLP resources to the LAMS environment necessitated this development as it also stimulated a movement from a content–oriented design approach to a focus on context, activities and collaboration among learners (cf. Dalziel, 2003, 2007).

The study contributes to the understanding of how the interplay between cultural artefacts, such as pedagogical ideas, design methods and technological solutions leads to contradictions in a design activity and creates opportunities for the transformation of the design as a whole (cf. Hauge,

Lund, & Vestøl, 2007; Kaptelinin & Nardi, 2006). In line with Jonassen and Rohrer-Murphy (1999), Greenhow and Belbas (2007), Barab, Schatz and Scheckler (2004) and Lund, Rasmussen and Smørdal (2009), we will argue that activity theory provides an appropriate framework for analysing needs, tasks, activities and outcomes in design of online resources. Our study also shows that activity theory can be used as a mediating means for designing a set of complex learning resources to be used in a technology–rich environment.

ACKNOWLEDGMENT

The Program of Flexible Learning at the University of Oslo 2006 - 2007 supported this research. Special thanks to the members of our design team at the Department of Teacher Education and School Research: Kirsten Sivesind, Eli Ottesen and Kirsten Foshaug Vennebo, and to the students who have spent hours discussing the design ideas at different phases of the project. Thanks to PREflex by Tove Kristiansen and Petrine Djupvik Flaa for supporting the team in critical phases of project management and development of learning resources.

REFERENCES

Arnseth, H. C., & Ludvigsen, S. (2006). Approaching institutional contexts: Systemic versus dialogic research in CSCL. *Computer-Supported Collaborative Learning*, *1*(2), 167–185. doi:10.1007/s11412-006-8874-3

Barab, S., MaKinster, J. G., & Scheckler, R. (2003). Designing system dualities: Charaterizing a web-supported professional development community. *The Information Society*, *19*, 237–256. doi:10.1080/01972240309466

Barab, S., Schatz, S., & Scheckler, R. (2004). Using activity theory to conceptualize online community and using online community to conceptualize activity theory. *Mind, Culture, and Activity*, *11*(1), 25–47. doi:10.1207/s15327884mca1101_3

Bazerman, C., Little, J., Bethel, L., Chavkin, T., Fouquette, D., & Garufis, J. (Eds.). (2005). *Reference guide to writing across the curriculum*. West Lafayette, IN: Parlor Press.

Beetham, H., & Sharpe, R. (Eds.). (2007). *Rethinking pedagogy for a digital age. Designing and delivering e–learning*. London, UK: Routledge.

Bjørndal, B., & Lieberg, S. (1978). *Nye veier i didaktikken (New didactical approaches)*. Oslo, Norway: Universitetsforlaget.

Calibrate. (2006). *Calibrating e-learning in schools*. Report from phase 1 in WP1. Internal report. (EU project no. IST – 028025).

Calibrate. (2008). *Calibrating e-learning in schools*. Project final report. (EU project no. IST-028025). Retrieved June 29, 2010, from http://calibrate.eun.org/ ww/ en/ pub/ calibrate_project/ deliverables.htm

Colbert, J., Trimble, K., & Desberg, P. (1996). *The case for education: Contemporary approaches for using case methods*. Boston, MA: Allyn & Bacon.

Cole, M., & Engeström, Y. (1993). A cultural–historical approach to distributed cognition. In Salomon, G. (Ed.), *Distributed cognitions: Psychological and educational considerations* (pp. 1–46). New York, NY: Cambridge University Press.

Dalziel, J. (2003). Implementing learning design: The learning activity management system (LAMS). In G. Crisp, D. Thiele, I. Scholten, S. Barker & J. Baron (Eds), *Interact, integrate, impact: Proceedings of the 20th Annual Conference of the Australasian Society for Computers in Learning in Tertiary Education* (pp. 7–10). Adelaide, December 2003. Retrieved June 29, 2010, from http://www.ascilite.org.au/ conferences/ adelaide03/ docs/ pdf/ 593.pdf

Dalziel, J. (2007). Building communities of designers. In Beetham, H., & Sharpe, R. (Eds.), *Rethinking pedagogy for a digital age. Designing and delivering e–learning* (pp. 193–206). London, UK: Routledge.

Daniels, H., Edwards, A., Engeström, Y., Gallagher, T., & Ludvigsen, S. R. (Eds.). (2010). *Activity theory in practice. Promoting learning across boundaries and agencies*. London, UK: Routledge.

Darling–Hammond, L., & Snyder, J. (2000). Authentic assessment of teaching in context. *Teaching and Teacher Education, 16*(5-6), 523–545. doi:10.1016/S0742-051X(00)00015-9

Dick, W., Carey, L., & Carey, J. O. (2005). *The systematic design of instruction* (6th ed.). Boston, MA: Allyn & Bacon.

Dysthe, O., & Engelsen, K. S. (Eds.). (2003). *Mapper som pedagogisk redskap. Perspektiver og erfaringer* (Portfolios as tools for learning). Oslo, Norway: Abstrakt forlag

Dysthe, O., Hertzberg, F., & Hoel, T. L. (2010). *Skrive for å lære. Skriving i høyere utdanning* (Writing to learn) (2nd ed.). Oslo, Norway: Abstrakt forlag

Engeström, Y. (1987). *Learning by expanding: An activity-theoretical approach to developmental research.* Helsinki, Finland: Orienta-Konsultit Oy.

Engeström, Y. (1999). Activity theory and individual and social transformation. In Engeström, Y., Miettinen, R., & Punamäki, R. L. (Eds.), *Perspectives on activity theory* (pp. 19–39). Cambridge, UK: Cambridge University Press.

Engeström, Y. (2007). Putting Vygotsky to work. The change laboratory as an application of double stimulation. In Daniels, H., Cole, M., & Wertsch, J. V. (Eds.), *Cambridge companion to Vygotsky* (pp. 363–383). Cambridge, UK: Cambridge University Press.

Goodyear, P., Banks, S., Hodgson, V., & McConell, D. (Eds.). (2004). *Advances in research on networked learning*. Boston, MA: Kluwer Academic Publishers.

Greenhow, C., & Belbas, B. (2007). Using activity-oriented design methods to study collaborative knowledge–building in e–learning courses within higher education. *International Journal of Computer-Supported Collaborative Learning, 2*(4), 363–391. doi:10.1007/s11412-007-9023-3

Hauge, T. E. (2006a). Digital case methodology in collaborative settings. A study of student teachers' co-construction of professional knowledge. In J. Enkenberg, M.-B. Kentz, & O. Hatakka (Eds.). *Emerging practices in educational technology,* (pp. 44–71). Savonlinna Department of Teacher Education, University of Joenssuu.

Hauge, T. E. (2006b). Portfolios and ICT as means of professional learning in teacher education. *Studies in Educational Evaluation, 32*(1), 23–36. doi:10.1016/j.stueduc.2006.01.002

Hauge, T. E., Lund, A., & Vestøl, J. M. (Eds.). (2007). *Undervisning i endring. IKT, aktivitet, design*. (*Teaching in transformation*). Oslo, Norway: Abstrakt forlag.

Hauge, T. E., & Norenes, S. O. (2010). Videopaper as a bridging tool in teacher professional development. In Lindberg, J. O., & Olofsson, A. D. (Eds.), *Online learning communities and teacher professional development: Methods for improved education delivery* (pp. 209–228). Hershey, PA: IGI Global.

Hauge, T. E., Skaar, B., Refseth, Y., Vestøl, J. M., & Hansen, A. S. (2006). Lærerrollen i prosjektarbeid. Kunnskapsutvikling gjennom en multimedial ressurs (The teacher role in project work). *Nordic Journal of Digital Literacy, 1*(2), 108–125.

Hewitt, J. (2004). An exploration of community in a knowledge forum classroom. An activity system analysis. In Barab, S. A., Kling, R., & Gray, J. H. (Eds.), *Designing for virtual communities in the service of learning* (pp. 210–238). Cambridge, UK: Cambridge University Press.

Jochems, W., van Merrienboer, J., & Koper, R. (2004). *Integrated e–learning: Implications for pedagogy, technology and organization*. London, UK: Taylor & Francis.

Jonassen, D., & Rohrer-Murphy, L. (1999). Activity theory as a framework for designing constructivist learning environments. *Educational Technology Research and Development, 47*(1), 61–79. doi:10.1007/BF02299477

Kaptelinin, V., & Nardi, B. A. (2006). *Acting with technology. Activity theory and interaction design*. Cambridge, UK: The MIT Press.

Kuutti, K. (1996). Activity theory as a potential framework for human-computer interaction research. In Nardi, B. A. (Ed.), *Context and consciousness: Activity theory and human–computer interaction* (pp. 17–44). Cambridge, MA: MIT Press.

Kuutti, K. (1999). Activity theory, transformation of work, and information system design. In Engeström, Y., Miettinen, R., & Punamäki, R. L. (Eds.), *Perspectives on activity theory* (pp. 360–376). Cambridge, UK: Cambridge University Press.

LAMS International. (2010). *Learning activity management system* (LAMS). Retrieved July 16, 2010, from http://www.lamsinternational.com/

Lemke, J. L., & Sabelli, N. H. (2008). Complex systems and educational change: Towards a new research agenda. *Educational Philosophy and Theory, 40*(1), 118–129. doi:10.1111/j.1469-5812.2007.00401.x

Leont'ev, A. N. (1978). *Activity, consciousness, and personality*. Englewood Cliffs, NJ: Prentice-Hall.

Liebermann, A., & Wood, D. R. (2003). *Inside the national writing project. Connecting network learning and classroom teaching*. New York, NY: Teachers College Press.

Luckin, R. (2010). *Re-designing learning contexts. Technology-rich, learner–centred ecologies*. London, UK: Routledge.

Lund, A., Rasmussen, I., & Smørdal, O. (2009). Joint designs for working in wikis. In Daniels, H., Edwards, A., Engeström, Y., Gallagher, T., & Ludvigsen, S. R. (Eds.), *Activity theory in practice: Promoting learning across boundaries and agencies* (pp. 207–230). London, UK: Routledge.

Lyngsnes, K., & Rismark, M. (2007). *Didaktisk arbeid (Didactical work)*. Oslo, Norway: Gyldendal Akademisk.

Mwanza, D. (2002). *Towards an activity–oriented design method for HCI research and practice*. PhD thesis. London, UK: The Open University.

Mwanza-Simwami, D., Engeström, Y., & Amon, T. (2009). Methods for evaluating learner activities with new technologies: Guidelines for the Lab@Future Project. *International Journal on E-Learning*, *8*(3), 361–384.

Nardi, B. A. (1996). Activity theory and human–computer interaction. In Nardi, B. A. (Ed.), *Context and consciousness. Activity theory and human–computer interaction* (pp. 7–16). Cambridge, MA: The MIT Press.

Ottesen, E., & Vennebo, K. S. (2007). Developing net–based learning resources for educational leaders. Challenges of design. In S. K. Koch (Ed.). '*Ringer i vann – fem år med Fleksibel læring ved UiO*' (pp. 151-164). Report, University of Oslo. Retrieved June 29, 2010, from http://www.uio.no/ for-ansatte/ organisasjon/ ikt_laring/ fleksibel-laering/ 2007/ pdf/ ottesen_vennebo.pdf.

Sannino, A., Daniels, H., & Gutiérrez, K. D. (Eds.). (2009). *Learning and expanding with activity theory*. Cambridge, UK: Cambridge University Press.

Shulman, L. (2004). *The wisdom of practice. Collected essays of Lee Shulman* (*Vol. 1*). San Fransisco, CA: Jossey-Bass.

Strømnes, Å. L., Rørvik, H., & Eilertsen, T. V. (1997). Didactical thinking and research in Norway during the four last decades. *Scandinavian Journal of Educational Research*, *41*(3), 237–258. doi:10.1080/0031383970410306

Vygotsky, L. S. (1978). *Mind in society: The development of higher psychological processes*. Cambridge, MA: Harvard University Press.

Zeichner, K., & Wray, S. (2001). The teaching portfolio in US teacher education programs: What we know and what we need to know. *Teaching and Teacher Education*, *17*(5), 613–621. doi:10.1016/S0742-051X(01)00017-8

ADDITIONAL READING

Bedny, G. Z., & Meister, D. (1997). *The Russian theory of activity: Current applications to design and learning*. Mahwah, NJ: Lawrence Erlbaum Associates.

Berge, O. (2006). *Reuse of digital learning resources in collaborative learning environments* (PhD thesis). University of Oslo.

Bertelsen, O. W. (1998). *Elements to a theory of design artefacts: A contribution to critical systems development research* (PhD thesis). Aarhus University: DAIMI PB-531.

Cole, M. (1988). Cross-cultural research in the socio-historical tradition. *Human Development*, *31*, 137–151. doi:10.1159/000275803

Cole, M. (1999). Cultural psychology: Some general principles and a concrete example. In Engeström, Y., Miettinen, R., & Punamäki, R.-L. (Eds.), *Perspectives on activity theory* (pp. 87–106). New York: Cambridge University Press.

Davydov, V. V. (1995). The influence of L.S. Vygotski on education. Theory, research, and practice. *Educational Researcher*, *24*(3), 12–21.

de Lange, T. (2010). *Technology and pedagogy: Analysing digital practices in Media Education* (PhD thesis). University of Oslo.

Dobson, M., Burgoyne, D., & Le Blanc, D. (2004). Transforming tensions in learning technology design: Operationalizing activity theory. *Canadian Journal of Learning Technologies*, *30*(1), 20–45.

Ellis, V., Edwards, A., & Smagorinsky, P. (Eds.). (2010). *Cultural-historical perspectives on teacher education and development: Learning teaching. Routledge*. Taylor and Francis.

Flo Jahreie, C. (2010). *Learning to teach. An activity-theoretical study of student teachers' participation trajectories across boundaries* (PhD thesis) University of Oslo.

Il'enkov, E. V. (1977). *Dialectical logic: Essays in its history and theory*. Moscow: Progress.

Jonassen, D. H., & Land, S. M. (Eds.). (2000). *Theoretical foundations of learning environments*. Mahwah, NJ: Erlbaum.

Kaptelinin, V., Kuutti, K., & Bannon, L. J. (1995). Activity Theory: Basic Concepts and Applications. *EWHCI, 1995*, 189–201.

Kaptelinin, V., Nardi, B., & Macaulay, C. (1999). Methods & tools. The activity checklist: a tool for representing the 'space' of context. *Interaction, 6*(4), 27–39. doi:10.1145/306412.306431

Kaufmann, H., & Papp, M. (2006). Learning objects for education with augmented reality. In *Proceedings of EDEN 2006 (European Distance and E-Learning Network) Conference* (pp. 160-165). Vienna 2006.

Ludvigsen, S., Lund, A., Rasmussen, I., & Säljö, R. (Eds.). (2010). *Learning across sites: new tools, infrastructures and practices*. London: Routledge.

Marx, K. (1967). Theses on Feuerbach. In Kamenka, E. (Ed.), *The portable Marx*. New York: Penguin Books. (Original work published 1845)

Mwanza, D. (2001). Where Theory meets Practice: A Case for an activity theory based methodology to guide computer system design. In Michitaka Hirose (Ed.), *Proceedings of INTERACT'2001: Eighth IFIP TC 13 International Conference on Human–Computer Interaction*, Tokyo, Japan, July 9-13, 2001. IOS Press Oxford, UK.

Nardi, B. (Ed.). (1996). *Context and consciousness: Activity theory and human–computer interaction*. Cambridge: MIT Press.

Redmiles, D. F. (2002). Introduction to the special issue on activity theory and the practice of design. *Computer Supported Cooperative Work, 11*(1-2), 1–11. doi:10.1023/A:1015215726353

Robertson, I. (2008). Sustainable e–learning, activity theory and professional development. In R. Atkinson & C. McBeath (Eds.), *Hello! Where are you in the landscape of educational technology? Proceedings ascilite Melbourne 2008*. Retrieved from http://www.ascilite.org.au/ conferences/ melbourne08/ procs/ robertson.pdf

Smørdal, O. (1999). *Work oriented objects - Object oriented modelling of computer mediated cooperative activities: An activity theoretical perspective* (PhD thesis). ISBN 82-7368-206-4. University of Oslo.

Uden, L., Valderas, P., & Pastor, O. (2008). An activity–theory–based model to analyse Web application requirements. *Information Research, 13*(2), paper 340. Retrieved from http://InformationR.net/ ir/ 13-2/ paper340.html

Vygotsky, L. S. (1987). *Thinking and speech*. New York: Plenum.

Wertsch, J. V. (1981). *The Concept of Activity in Soviet Psychology*. Sharpe.

Wertsch, J. V. (1991). *Voices of the mind: A sociocultural approach to mediated action*. Cambridge, MA: Harvard University Press.

Wertsch, J. V. (1998). *Mind as action*. New York: Oxford University Press.

KEY TERMS AND DEFINITIONS

Calibrate (Calibrating e-Learning in Schools): An EU-project (2005–2008) designed to integrate e-learning resources (multi-media) in different school subjects from different European countries and to make them available for teachers through a common web–portal.

CHAT (Cultural-Historical Activity Theory): A theory originated from the socio-cultural and socio–historical theories of Vygotsky (1978), Leont'ev (1978), Engeström (1987, 1999, 2007)

and others. As a theory, it is deeply dialectical, contextual and historically oriented towards practices, their objects, mediating artefacts, and social organisation.

Design Method: An arrangement scheme that structures the development of a product.

Dilemma: A video application simulating students' project work in school where teachers or student teachers can interactively influence the work process by choosing different pathways to problem solving developed at InterMedia, University of Oslo.

DLC (Digital Learning Cases): A set of short–time video resources embedded in a learning task structure for teacher students developed at the Department of Teacher Education and School Research, University of Oslo.

DLP (Digital Leadership Project): A development project designed to stimulate and serve the growing use of online learning in the Master programme for school leadership at the University of Oslo.

ITL (It's Learning): A Norwegian learning management system / online learning environment widely used in Norwegian schools and higher education.

LAMS: Learning Activity Management System: An open source Learning Design system developed at McQuarie University, Australia for designing, managing and delivering sequenced online learning activities. It emphasises collaborative learning activities.

Learning Design: Specifies a pedagogical scenario for how teachers interact with learners, learners interact with each other, and how teachers and learners interact with the tools and resources within an online learning environment.

Learning Resource: An operationalisation of a Learning Design within an online learning environment. It is reusable and may be of any granularity (e.g. a course, a workshop or a lesson). It may specify the sequence of activities, the content (e.g. books, articles, pictures) that will be used in the activities and also services (e.g. forums, chats and wikis) used for communication and collaboration.

Chapter 7
Informed Design of Educational Activities in Online Learning Communities

Urban Carlén
University of Skövde, Sweden

Berner Lindström
University of Gothenburg, Sweden

ABSTRACT

The aim of this chapter is to sketch design implications for organizing online educational activities in higher education that will intentionally engage medical students and professionals in the field together. When using an online forum, which is already embedded in the work practice, participants can build an online learning community (OLC) to discuss specialist subjects. This chapter is based on findings derived from a larger case study about participation in a professional OLC in general medicine. The proposal of an educational activity will complement numerous online activities with a more structured form of learning. As long as participants are challenged in learning about the specialist subject, they will contribute to the collective account. Online participation can be one way to foster students in becoming doctors. Together with qualified professionals, medicine students can create and sustain relationships over their professional careers.

INTRODUCTION

People create relationships and ties in social networks (Haythornthwaite, 2008). At work, building professional networks is an important part of structuring a professional field. Professionals engage together in order to gain advantages both collectively and individually (Beaulieu, Rioux, Rocher, Samson, & Boucher, 2008). Networking is not merely a strategy to stay attractive on the market; it also offers participants opportunities to share knowledge and experiences related to

DOI: 10.4018/978-1-61350-080-4.ch007

what they do at work. In contemporary work life, employees need to continue to educate themselves because of changes at work. Freidson (2001) claims that professional networks are developed over time. People in medicine use an array of networked technologies, from which we can learn how to establish and maintain professional networks. Allan and Lewis (2006) show how the continual change in professional fields pushes people to update themselves more regularly by using the Internet. Online communication can generate forms of continual professional development in the medical practices (Boudioni, McLaren, Woods, & Lemma, 2007; Thompson et al., 2008; Thorley, Turner, Hussey, & Agius, 2009). In medical practices, email lists are frequently used for communicating and collaborating online. This kind of online forum is already embedded in medical professionals' daily work, which makes it an extraordinarily powerful tool for creating continual forms of professional development (Carlén, 2010; Fox & Roberts, 1999; Hew & Hara, 2008; Karagiannis & Vojnović, 2008; Thomas & James, 1999). We argue here that participation in online learning communities (OLCs) can bridge the gap between professional practice and higher education.

During their basic medical education, students build networks with other students. Together they develop strategies and skills for advancing in the professional field. Educational and professional practices, however, do not have to be viewed as separate contexts (Nardi, Whittaker, & Schwarz, 2002; Wenger, 1998). An educational setting can be understood through cultural, ecological, historical, and social aspects, as it exists in a comprehensive context of conditions that refer to the past, present, and future states of these conditions. Lindberg and Olofsson (2005) analyze the intertwined processes of teaching and fostering in teacher training programs through the concept of *edukation*. The concept is founded upon an examination of "how humans are being formed as human among humans" (Lindberg & Olofsson, 2005, p. 10). Medical studies combine educational activities carried out in a professional practice with numerous activities for professionals as they prepare themselves, finally qualify, and take their medical examinations. Learning activities continue in their careers as they make progress as medical practitioners. People need to view learning from the perspective of both the formal and informal structures that challenge them in their daily work. Such a perspective on learning constitutes the intertwined process of how knowledge is constructed within the profession of medicine (Freidson, 1970; McWhinney, 1997). The work of providing themselves with accurate tools and resources is something that all medical practitioners are encouraged to do from the very beginning of their medical education (Beaulieu et al., 2008). Not only do doctors have to deal with the battery of clinical equipment, but they also have to appropriate information and communication technologies (ICT). In these efforts, OLCs may play a part in the profession. Carlén (2010) defines OLCs as groups of individuals who participate in an online environment, using a battery of tools, in order to share common interests. Building OLCs involves the communicative part of using certain tools. The appropriation of new tools generates new terms for the existing terminology. Together they build a knowledge domain in which participants can share knowledge and experiences. For example, McAllister and Moyle (2006) argue that an OLC has the potential to change the culture of medicine from its present state of fragmentation, to one that fosters connections and dialogues between isolated professionals. The professional relationships that are built online become a complementary network of expertise. Thompson et al. (2008) point out that online participation expands the time for knowledge sharing beyond work place activities, blurring the boundaries between work and personal time. Online participation merges into situations in which participants need to figure out what it means to participate online (Fuchs, 2008; Slevin, 2000). Thompson et al. (2008) claims that intertwined boundaries of social and professional networks can be damaging unless people learn how to participate online. For example, medical students have published pictures taken from scenarios in medical training on social networking sites, jeopardizing the integrity of patients. Participants in OLCs face several challenges, which we need to know more about. Designs for learning activities, as situated in the intertwined fields of professional practice and higher education, need to include the engagement of the participants themselves as they learn on how to take part in OLCs. By examining how participants organize themselves in an OLC in general medicine, we intend to generate design implications that incorporate higher education with professional practice.

The aim of this chapter is to sketch design implications for organizing online educational activities that bridge learning in higher education together with continual forms of competence development in professional practice. The informed design will facilitate organizers of higher education in involving professionals in educational activities together with students as they build an OLC for their professional life together. This chapter is influenced by a larger empirical study concerning online participation in a professional OLC in general medicine (Carlén, 2010). In that particular study, general practitioners (GPs) go online by using a rudimentary online forum with the underlying technical structure of an email list managed by a professional association. In this OLC, participants invite newcomers to acquire a voluntary account within an informal setting. Arnseth and Ludvigsen (2006) claim that in such a situation, the distinction between formal and informal learning becomes less important since learning activities tend to overlap. The setting for designing educational activities as a complement to existing ways of learning becomes the focus of this chapter. The goal of this chapter will be to open up collaborations between academia and professional practice, whereby we hope to inspire other professional practices outside the medical profession to consider building an OLC.

BACKGROUND

Taking into account the title of this book, the concept of the informed design of educational technologies needs to be understood in terms of engagement by the participants rather than in terms of deciding what technology contains educational features. The idea in the following section is to explain the concepts of *informed design* and *educational technology* as a transactional approach to understanding teaching and learning as inseparable processes. In this approach, professional practices and higher education become an interlinked arena for learning that integrates several tools and tasks designed for carrying out educational activities. Therefore, educational activities are approached in terms of participation.

Any kind of technology consists of certain affordances. Affordances exist in technical conditions as separated from the participant´s experience, knowledge, culture, and capability to observe and perceive. Technologies are designed to generate specific results for how activities can be carried out by groups of individuals. However, Jones and Dirckinck-Holmfield (2009) suggest that affordances needs to be viewed as relational property, which exists in relationships between artifacts and active agents as they refer to a Gibsonian and ecological stance. These kinds of properties can be viewed as the outcome of design intentions along with changes in teaching and learning. "Designers set tasks, prescriptions for the work the students are expected to do, activity on the other hand is what people actually do. Teachers set the tasks but learners then have to interpret the specifications of the tasks" (Jones & Dirckinck-Holmfeld, 2009, p. 19). *Informed design* is about making intentional changes in how people commonly act together when using specific tools. In line with Jones and Dirckinck-Holmfield, it is not primarily the technology that we aim to re-structure. Rather, we intend to design for learning activities in educational settings that include the relational aspects of technology. Guribye and Lindström (2009) introduce the notion of *infrastructures for learning* that incorporate the technological aspects with the social arrangements of networked learning practices in order to understand and analytically approach the interconnectedness of those conditions under which groups of individuals participate online.

Social practices that appropriate an online forum, challenging us to rethink technology that seems to be universal in its use, result in different ways for organizing activities within the collective. For example, an email list is not especially an educational technology until the participants consider its use for educational means. Understanding education is viewed according to what tools and activities operate in a setting that is deemed to foster learning (Jaldemark, 2010). Activities in higher education are more or less intentional actions performed by students, individually as well as collectively, who engage in various assignments, intending to get credit for what they know and what they do (Carlén & Jobring, 2005). Learning in OLCs can be designed to situate the activities in an educational setting. We want to use the features of the tool as an existing condition, among others, that is already situated in people's lives. When building OLCs, it is the participants themselves who engage in organizing the learning activities, not primarily the teachers. Guribye and Lindström (2009) suggest that certain tasks need to be given the participants in order to prevent participants' merely reading what others discuss. Therefore, informed design includes the perspective of the participants, as they are the ones who negotiate how to communicate and collaborate. We argue that the trend in using tools already situated in students' networks outside academia will have more and more influence on how they learn in higher education. Building professional networks in higher education will foster strategies for later learning by means of continual professional development in which OLCs support collective actions. This approach opens the possibility for designing educational activities that enhance teaching and learning by using rudimentary tools like an email list, but it also makes participation feasible for professionals, who can engage in online higher education based upon their expertise.

APPRENTICESHIP IN HIGHER EDUCATION

One way to understand learning in OLCs is to examine the activities in which actors interact. Theories on Communities of Practice (CoP) provide concepts for analyzing and understanding online participation in social practices. The relationships between practice and community can be understood in three dimensions: *mutual engagement* (what participants want to accomplish together), *joint enterprise* (what participants are there to do), and a *shared repertoire* (what participants know and can do together) (Wenger, 1998). In most educational practices, teachers are expected to be the more competent participants who endeavor to bridge the gap between what is known and what is new for the learners. In *guided participation*, an experienced participant helps another who has less experience to become competent to contribute in specific activities (Rogoff, 1990). Participation in social practices is viewed as an apprenticeship by Lave and Wenger (1991), who exemplify learning as a preparation for participation. The concept of apprenticeship becomes accurate when designing online educational activities for students and qualified professionals in higher education. Apprenticeships do not have to be limited to a strict master-apprentice relation. All people learn something from participating in social practices, even in cases of being the knowledgeable partner. What becomes crucial for understanding learning in an educational setting, viewed from a sociocultural perspective, is the ability to study activities rather than the acquisition of pre-determined tasks. This perspective on learning stretches outside a mere focus on what the participants share in terms of the content. Learning can be understood as how participants engage online collectively, or ways of negotiating how to learn, how to participate, or even how to make up strategies for appropriating tools etc. Learning in work-related practices can be organized in educational structures. Still, most learning organized outside the educational system is referred to as informal learning because of its lack of educational contexts (Gray, 2004). However, this was the main criticism of Lave and Wenger (1991), who created the theories of CoP as a response to this idea, presenting learning as a continual activity in social practices. The challenge for this chapter is to show how learning activities in a professional OLC can influence the design for online higher education, as these two should be viewed as intertwined boundary activities (Jaldemark, 2010).

A Professional Community in General Medicine Goes Online

Below, a case study is briefly presented in order to show how activities can be created that complement existing ways of participating online (cf. Carlén, 2010). The design implications presented in this chapter are influenced by an inductive and exploratory study about GPs who participate online. The objective of that particular study was to understand how an email list, organized and managed by a Swedish professional association of general medicine, functions as an online learning community. The empirical study is characterized by a longitudinal and exploratory examination of the postings considered as online activities, participation structures and positioning, moderating activities, and the affordances of the technology between the years 2000 and 2006. They share knowledge and experiences, coordinate activities, discuss organizational matters, construct professional identities, and negotiate the boundaries of general practice. The online forum functions as a learning arena in its informal setting. This means that most participants engage voluntarily. A moderator started the email list back in 1999 and has now facilitated the activities on a continual basis for over a decade. This is an exceptionally long duration for an OLC, as most of these kinds of learning arenas tend to fail after a while due to their lack of social interaction (Renninger & Shumar, 2002). The long-term sustainability of the OLC makes it a particularly interesting case. Together with a close-knit professional network and connected to the professional association, they have maintained the professional networks as they continually initiate new topics about what happens in general practice.

Today most people in Western networked society regularly use email (Findahl, 2009). Email is embedded in structures for how people educate themselves, carry out their work, and maintain social relations. The professional association in general medicine organizes learning activities by using an online forum mediated through an underlying technical structure described in terms of an email list. It means that the addressee field is always set to the name of the group. A posting sent to the forum reaches all signed-up members, who in turn reply by using their individual email programs. All members have intentionally signed onto the forum. In order to become members, they send a message to the moderator, who adds them to the list of members. After that procedure, they can start posting messages to the forum by themselves. This semi-structured access prevents outsiders from interfering, as no one can read what is discussed unless he or she joins the OLC. However, the design will not include any consideration for online security. Anyone who receives postings is also free to answer in debate or to initiate new topics. As the participants answer previous postings, they create threads, consisting of answers related to the initial posting. The technical affordance consists of a subject field and a related area for body text. These become strategic tools to consider when members participate online (Carlén, 2010; Holt & Graves, 2007; Skovholt & Svennevig, 2006). For example, the text in the subject field conducts the answers in debate as they choose to shift these rubrics to better suit their arguments. Within the body text area, various ways to answer previous messages are revealed through online participation. In the case of an email list, postings constitute clear evidence that the online forum works properly. Several participants must be engaged with various tasks in the educational activity in order to make explicit their continual engagement in the OLC. Some technical affordances become relevant when designing for educational activities in OLC. What makes a tool relevant for educational settings is organizing learning activities, teaching events, lectures and seminars, etc. However, using technologies in education tends to reproduce what is already carried out in campus-based activities (Cuban, 1986). It is the conditions for participation that makes the difference between these settings. The challenge consists in the expectation of what tasks are required from students or teachers within the agenda of the academic culture. Still, we have to understand that online participation differs between the two social practices, even if they both are using a simple email list.

General Practitioners Participate Online

To continue the examination, we present some crucial results and conclusions derived from the study of the OLC in general medicine. Most of the participants who posted were GPs (63.7%). Seventy percent of all participants were males, born in the 1940s/50s (69.9%), who had achieved their medical degrees in the 1970s/80s (69.7%) and were working in larger cities. It was concluded that the professional character described above was rather typical for general practice and for the OLC. One challenge in the design of educational activities is to engage new actors in order to enhance learning through knowledge sharing and experience exchange. Thus, it was shown that specialists in training (who are considered to be younger than the group of participants above), participated separately in a similar online forum, but connected to the professional association as well. One challenge is to prevent such a generational gap among the participants arising from what they share as an interest, not only as topics, but also stemming from who they are in general practice. In order to attract newcomers outside the special group of participants, designing new activities in learning can encourage other actors to engage online. In designing for educational activities, the older generations do not have to be self-appointed teachers who instruct the younger generation in general medicine. Building professional networks needs to involve relationships in which activities are promoted that gain the whole OLC.

In the following section, some findings taken from the empirical study concentrate on the *activities* that indicate the conditions for designing educational activities. Activities are viewed in terms of what is accomplished through member participation. Therefore, the accomplishment of educational activities should stress the incorporation of individual expertise into a collective engagement of dialogues on specific topics and their organization for designing new activities in the OLC. Participants in OLCs accomplish both collective and individual tasks. Four activity types were found: announcements (54.2%), discussion (25.7%), question-answers (12.7%), and stories (7.4%), all of which demonstrate that the email list is actively used for various purposes.

- *Announcement* is a type of activity in which a participant informs the collective about relevant news in the professional practice. This activity is frequent accomplished in the OLC as several events take place outside the online forum (e.g., invitations to conferences), but also within the OLC (e.g., rules for participation).
- *Discussion* is another activity type in which the participants carry out a collective debate about a topic for the collective concern regarding their professional practice or another shared subject. What par-

ticipants accomplish through discussions can be explored through the coordination of the collective action that changes what they do and how they carry out professional work as a coordination of collective actions (e.g., a review of unsatisfactory clinical information produced by the medical industry or media).

- *Question-answer* is an activity type in which a participant initiates an individual problem by asking the collective for support in making satisfied decisions, solving dilemmas at work, or treating patient cases. Such activity is directed to achieving support from the OLC, which differs from the activity type called discussion.
- *Stories* are a means to describe the professional practice in terms of what happens at work through the initiators' perspective of what they experience and want to share. Characteristic of activities like stories is a lack of explicit need for support or comments by the collective (e.g., reflection over the stressful introduction of IT at work). The e-mailing list becomes an arena for sharing experiences, reflections, and ideas about what they observe as participants in the professional practice.

These four activity types have influenced the current work of creating educational activities. It is worth noting that educational activities bridge the informal with the formal forms in the participation structure. Such activity will complement and extend former activities in accomplishing a professional network. In a sense, educational activities can be designed in order to invite new participants in online participation that are not specialized only in the shared interest.

Concerning the management of these activities, the GPs discuss several topics at the same time, running them simultaneously as parallel threads. This means that we can design activities that are not constrained by being limited to one at a time or to a certain sequential order.

The participants create a norm of online participation that requires them to comment on initiated topics. This strategy may mean that some topics are unanswered or ignored. However, investigation showed that only a small number of postings went unanswered, and none of these postings resulted in any unsubscriptions. Rather, this group of participants demanded an answer until they received one, or even re-initiated the topic. In designing activities for an educational setting, collective engagement can be shared in negotiations for how to make participants share knowledge and experiences

Even though the forum is theoretically open for anyone to contribute to the subject of general medicine, GPs contributed in large amount. Participants like medical students, medical practitioners, practitioners in specialist training, and professionals with types of occupational qualifications other than general medicine contributed minimal amounts. The close connection to the professional association of general medicine could explain the huge number of GPs among the participants. Even though the OLC is open for anyone, it is a huge challenge for anyone who does not have full qualifications as a GP to post in the OLC. This participation structure has to be considered when organizing educational activities.

The group of core participants did step in when the moderator was behind in his tasks. It was shown that consistent work in moderating the activities kept them going. The moderator needs to establish various explicit roles that are specifically spelled out for the participants. For example, the moderator has to become an initiator and an interlocutor in a debate, besides moderating in order to generate activities. In the educational design, one challenge for the moderator will be to facilitate the debate that supports the expert or invited guest who is leading a topic and to discuss the rules of participation during the seminars, in parallel with the topic of discussion. In the empirical study, this was found to be crucial to online participation since agreed-upon online behavior requires constant negotiation at the same time that they carry out discussion of the content.

Even when more and more people subscribed to the OLC, it did not increase the number of postings sent by the participants as much as it changed the proportion of existing participants to newcomers. The design concerns the whole OLC rather than small groups of students in order to generate a shared engagement in educational activities.

The participants initiated topics that merely treated related to the subject of general medicine only. No personal and/or private matters were introduced online. Personal matters tend to marginalize the others from participation as they create sub-networks. The strict focus on general medicine challenges the perspective of communities when they socialize more as professionals and less as private characters. In designing for educational activities, this would be one main goal that participants should fulfill themselves.

One issue for further investigation was the idea of using previous threads as material for further learning. Relative to an examination of new topics, some similar topics were found in the Web archive, which indicates that participants do not read former debates when they want to know about specific topics. However, doublets generate a constant form of activity, which has to be viewed as one crucial way to maintain the OLC. In designing for educational activities, the matter of how to adapt the threads within the OLC for further engagement must take into account the collective as these threads generate products of knowledge known as *reifications,* to use a term by Wenger (1998).

Initiators post in threads that have been published by participants, who once posted in a thread that they started. Over 2/3 of the participants were identified as initiators of a new topic. This becomes a challenge in designing for educational activities since it is the expert who initiates the main topic. Students need to become initiators as well. They should initiate aspects of what is discussed in order to lead the examination of a shared topic even further.

One challenge in online participation is to handle the numerous postings in longer threads since they seem to split into several smaller threads that have different subject headings. Participants connect their postings to other postings in several ways, which leaves an opening for designing an educational activity that is planned to be implemented as several smaller threads rather than as one main thread. The participants in the OLC overcome the dispersed structure of threads since they read most of the postings about a topic. Nor does the length of the thread always indicate a healthy ongoing discussion since it has been shown that participants engage in several activities at the same time. A short thread might indicate either that someone has successfully given a precise answer to a question or overlapped with a topic discussed in a parallel thread.

The material presented in the preceding section has design implications for organizing online educational activities that integrate the professional practice into higher education.

DESIGNING FOR EDUCATIONAL ACTIVITIES

In the following section, a number of design implications suggest how an educational activity might be created for online higher education. Design implications have been derived from the four existing activity types in the OLC in general medicine. Designing for educational activities supports participants in accomplishing organized activities that enhance learning about specific topics. A characteristic of an educational activity is to have pre-determined participation structures and tasks that facilitate participants in carrying on a structured discussion. It differs from other activity types in that participants plan the activity in advance within the collective before they start the conversation.

The design implications are presented in four concerns, one for each type of actor — that is, one for the *expert*, a second for *the participants,* and a third for the *moderator,* who acts as a facilitator in debate; finally, a fourth concern deals with the *educational activity*.

- *Division of labor*: In higher education, there is a shared expectation on the part of both teacher and students that the teacher's lecture will grasp the subject of presentation. When higher education and professional practice become intertwined (such as in medicine), educational activities can challenge participating and the rearranging of specified roles. For example, an online educational activity does not have to be presided over specifically by the teacher. When professionals in the medicine field obtain certain knowledge through which they complement each other's expertise, they open the field for a division of labor that also can offer the expert role to any of the students. In such a perspective on distributed knowledge, a division of labor is negotiated in terms of what is executed in lectures, seminars, and examinations on certain topics. The creation of lateral conditions in participation allows actors to shift roles for the sake of the OLC.
- *Planning the educational activity*: The moderator, or in most cases, the teacher of the course, needs to plan what actors should be assigned to lecture or hold seminars online. Belonging to a professional practice, such as a specialist subject in general medicine, is about knowing who the experts are in specific clinical matters. Approaching a specific specialist about a topic or searching for the right person with considerable knowledge will generate possibilities for further planning of the educational activity. The organization of educational activities is not as obvious when going online. Such planning involves the strategy of dividing the topic into pre-determined aspects for initiating ideas as the conversation develops, going from general ideas to the more specific parts of the topic. All aspects of the topic can be viewed as small threads that together build the topic of discussion. It will include several views on the topic as the participants add new information that covers the essentials of the content. In medical practice, the production of "study letters" on relevant clinical issues is an important resource in continual professional development. These letters summarize the updated clinical information addressed by the collective for further distribution. Completed threads summarize the knowledge and the essential aspects that have been discussed. These threads constitute a reification of the activity that helps the participants to share knowledge and to refer to the educational activities through the documents that these threads provide in the OLC.
- *Assigning various tasks within the educational activity*: In the OLC under study, participation is carried out on a voluntary basis, which differs to a large extent from participation in higher education, which is often a mandatory form of engagement. Therefore, participants have to obtain requirements for how they are expected to engage online. These should not specify a total number of postings sent by each person, but should rather be in the form of substantial contributions to the subject in terms of solving the case or of adding relevant information, etc.
- *Rules for participation*: The expectations for how to participate in the OLC include showing good manners and organizing one's written text for others to read and comment on. Most of the rules can be decided before carrying out the learning ac-

tivities. As new incidents occur, the existing rules need to be negotiated to better suit the entire OLC. Continuing negotiation on how to participate will be required for sustainable activity. In fact, the moderator of the educational activity needs to act in parallel with the participants in this matter when carrying out the educational activity. All participants need to share in maintaining the rules in order to carry out the activities. In OLCs, the rules are not merely a matter for the moderator or for the teacher.

- *Using the subject heading*: One way to carry out the educational activity is to use the correct subject heading for the conversations, especially in connection with the smaller threads that examine aspects of the topic, which are carried out in parallel threads. Use of subject headings help to make certain aspects of the topics explicit and help students to stick to the topic, discussing only what is of importance and relevant to these aspects. The main thread that has been initiated by the expert needs to be referred to within the conversation in order to satisfy participants' expectations for the discussion. All those participants who initiate aspects of the topic are required to conduct the discussions in the same way as the original expert who started the thread in order to concentrate on aspects of the topic and avoid irrelevant matters.
- *Placing the posting in the thread:* All who participate need to place their postings into the structure of the ongoing threaded discussion. It is not always correct to insist on a sequential order since the participants post in a dispersed structure, which sometimes means going outside the thread or starting a new thread without actually intending to do so. However, as long as participants continually read the discussions, they will know where to place their postings in the ongoing thread. In addition, the more they engage in the activity, the more they overcome the situation in which others place their postings outside the ongoing thread instead of in sequential order as they attempt to keep up with the discussion anyway. Nonetheless, participants have to use subject headings in order to take a position in a debate. When they point out what statements they have on the topic in the subject heading, they will also encourage others to post who have an opposite opinion on the addressed topic.
- *Considerations for text based conversation*: Inviting experts to initiate topics for educational purposes will enhance the learning activities. Once the initial message is published by the expert, students can post comments and questions on the topic. When they add new information, the moderator steers the focus to what matters for the topic because of what has already been negotiated in the rules. A question-answer activity complements what participants find difficult to understand about the topic. They all gain new knowledge in educational activities as the issues raised by the participants will make the expert understand what people in general find difficult to understand about the specific topic discussed in the OLC.
- *The mission of the expert:* The expert will need support to address certain aspects of the topic. In order to maintain the discussion, selective participants should prepare to initiate aspects of the topic in advance as assigned by the teacher. In a sense, several parallel discussions about the very same topic will complement the initial topic posted by the expert. The expert does not merely engage in his or her own thread, but engages together with other initiators in discussion about aspects of the topic that complement what is known and is considered valuable to know.

- *The mission of students*: It is important to understand that online seminars are not merely about providing accurate information for students to adopt. Online seminars have to challenge what is essential to know about the defined topics. The students need to prepare questions about the subject in advance, which sets the starting point of what they know. The posing of questions helps the experts to know where the seminar needs to begin. The expert has to comment upon the aspects of the topics that are published in the thread.
- *The mission of the moderator*: The moderator is the gatekeeper of the OLC, whose members plan the educational activity with the expert. Together they sketch aspects of the topic to address as initial postings to publish in the OLC. These aspects of topics need to be stressed in the curriculum in order to establish a focus on what is considered valuable to learn and discuss in the course. The introduction of the expert can be carried out by the moderator in order to welcome a guest to the OLC, as was the case in the professional OLC under study. The moderator or participants can invite and suggest experts, based upon what makes this person an expert of the topic. The participants can mirror themselves as part of a professional practice. The moderator coordinates who will involve the participants in discussions. Individuals could be given the task of initiating an aspect of their own or could represent an aspect that has been discussed in each project group in case they work in smaller constellations, which is normally organized for distance courses. The moderator supports the activities in various project groups and also in the common area of the OLC. Such action will prevent participants from merely discussing the topics with project members alone, as they have to contribute for the whole OLC. The moderator will create an overview of the discussions since he or she has to conduct the discussions connected to the course. As the moderator takes the role of being the examiner, he or she grasps the crucial engagement carried out by each individual and group.
- *Affordance of technology*: Since the online forum is based on an asynchronous mode, the participants will be able to communicate whenever they get time by using email. Given this mode and the underlying technical structure of an email list, online participation follows the routines of a daily agenda at work, which in a sense makes it feasible for various actors to engage online. The integration of activities within the OLC into daily work and higher education makes various actors take part along with other students and qualified professionals. The fact that such conditions can be created within the OLC does not make participants interact automatically, since affordances and designed activities are viewed as intertwined participation structures. The affordance of using a rudimentary underlying structure for text-based communication is that it allows all participants to share ideas about the subject with each other without having been divided into groups, in which case they do not know what the other groups are discussing. The educational activities in this chapter are designed with large groups in mind, as the OLC allows them to contribute to the ongoing discussion. No consideration is given to the fact that participants are challenged to write in front of the whole OLC. As people become more and more skilled at communicating in text-based communication, they are also facilitated by the others as together they share knowledge and experiences that are meaningful, even if not always correct from the start. This is the strength of what

OLCs provide when a huge group of participants takes part in distributed forms of learning. As people in OLCs become more and more skilled at conversing online, they can share ways of using text for communication that challenges the way they organize learning.

- *Threads as reification*: The production of threads about topics can be viewed as evidence of knowledge produced in collaboration. How these threads should be used needs to be further investigated. When the threads are finally completed, they could be gathered in an evaluation of the participants' experience to compile these discussions into "study letters" to be use in their forthcoming work. Since these educational activities generate valuable information about specific topics, they can distribute their knowledge to professional practices outside the OLC.

In sum, one characteristic for an educational activity is to use pre-determined topics that the participants intend to execute or solve in discussion, which means they must plan the activity in advance. The sketched educational activity in this section has extended the number of activities in the OLC by proposing a formal structure of what participants can accomplish online. The implications above propose an educational activity that connects various actors from higher education and professional practice to engage together in an OLC. The suggested educational activity does not merely position the expert in the center of attention, but students also can become involved in engagement of relevant topics. The educational activity can be open for engagement among actors, not merely a specific group of competent professionals as was the case in the larger study.

FUTURE RESEARCH DIRECTIONS

All design implications presented in this chapter need to be viewed as proposals for further investigation. This chapter stresses online participation in ways that propose the interlinking of professional practices and higher education in OLCs. As more and more people engage in text-based communication, organizers of higher education and stakeholders of professional associations can collaborate together when building OLCs. Such a strategy facilitates an examination of the transforming of knowledge between networks as some participate in several OLCs. One suggestion for research could be to follow a group of students as they become full participants in the professional practice in a longitudinal approach. How participants appropriate and build OLCs for knowledge sharing in work life needs to be considered as a theme for further research. For example, what happens when younger adults start their working careers as more knowledgeable than previous generations about communicating online? Several research studies have investigated online higher education, but complementary studies are needed about online apprenticeship. For some work practices, this will challenge the form of the apprenticeships themselves since a newcomer to a work practice might have obtained master skills in communicating online that generate new positions and experiences for who is knowledgeable in the OLC. Therefore, a lateral structure when participating has been suggested in this chapter. In a sociocultural tradition, the issue of generational consequences for the transformation of knowledge will reveal how Western network society changes in time because of the tools its members appropriate and use for communication and collaboration (see Säljö, 1999). *Edukation*, which was a concept mentioned by Lindberg and Olofsson (2005), promotes social interactions between various actors, not only between the students and their teachers, but also with professionals in the field, who foster new competent professionals. How social networking sites can support continual professional development has to be further investigated due to the professional relationship that is established in these kinds of online forums. As educational designers learn about how participants engage online, they also intend to design for learning; instead of waiting for interactions to happen, they very much suggest intentional actions to occur. Using design-based research aims to generate a methodological toolkit for those researchers committed to understanding the activities and the development of tools. "One challenging component of doing educational research on design-based interventions is to characterize the complexity, fragility, messiness, and eventual solidity of the design and to do so in a way that will be valuable for others" (Barab & Squire, 2004, p. 4). This approach to research would make it feasible to design an OLC from scratch, as there are educational programs that not yet have organized themselves online. As students and teachers become involved, they become co-participants in the design of the OLC.

CONCLUSION

Understanding change in higher education means that we have to embrace what happens in contemporary work life. When people attend higher education, they have to adopt strategies for their future roles in the work place. Building OLCs is one way for students to learn collaboratively as they create meaning in individual studies. Online educational activities are just one kind of structured activity presented in this chapter. Such activities embrace the concept of apprenticeship that was stressed by Lave and Wenger (1991) as a collaborative form in situated learning. Medical students form professional identities as they endeavor to become full participants in the professional practice (cf. Carlén, 2010). Online participation can be one way to foster students as they assume their professional roles and become doctors (i.e., medical practitioners). In general practice, GPs are challenged by what is still unknown about essential topics in order to cure patients. They discuss the relevant issues of work within the OLC that could motivate students and experts to collaborate in online higher education. The design implications suggest educational activities that are complementary to existing learning activities, which are already structured in ways that make participants gather collective knowledge about shared topics. The design implications have to consider the contributions made by the participants themselves as they are the ones who build the OLC. Such an approach means a change in the participation structures, which requires them to discuss the rules continually in order to maintain an equal attitude for what they do online, no matter whether they are experts or students. Building OLCs is more an educational challenge than an educational technology. As social networking sites become adopted more in the modern work place, those who build OLCs need to consider the conditions at work rather than following the trends on technical platforms. The design implications emphasize online participation, making these principles accurate for various text-based environments. An online forum with the underlying technology of an email list provides an arena for sharing knowledge and experiences, making it applicable for most practices since it does not exclude complementary technologies. Haythornthwaite (2002) found that "the more that pairs communicate, the more media they use for those communications" (p. 183). Building OLCs is constant work to maintain professional relationships, and the work does not stop when the technical platform becomes implemented. Adding online activities to the OLC involves various actors who obtain different kinds of competences.

ACKNOWLEDGMENT

Thanks to the Swedish professional association of general medicine for access to the empirical material for analyzing seven years of postings sent to the OLC. The empirical study is fully explained in a Ph.D. thesis called *A Professional Community Goes Online: A Study of an Online Learning Community in General Medicine* that is included in the research program of LinCS. Accessible online at http://hdl.handle.net/2077/22326

REFERENCES

Allan, B., & Lewis, D. (2006). The impact of membership of a virtual learning community on individual learning careers and professional identity. *British Journal of Educational Technology*, *37*(6), 841–852. doi:10.1111/j.1467-8535.2006.00661.x

Arnseth, H. C., & Ludvigsen, S. (2006). Approaching institutional contexts: Systemic versus dialogic research in CSCL. *International Journal of Computer-Supported Collaborative Learning*, *1*(2), 167–185. doi:10.1007/s11412-006-8874-3

Barab, S. A., & Squire, K. (2004). Design based research: Putting a stake in the ground. *Journal of the Learning Sciences*, *13*(1), 1–14. doi:10.1207/s15327809jls1301_1

Beaulieu, M. D., Rioux, M., Rocher, G., Samson, L., & Boucher, L. (2008). Family practice: Professional identity in transition. A case study of family medicine in Canada. *Social Science & Medicine*, *67*(7), 1153–1163. doi:10.1016/j.socscimed.2008.06.019

Boudioni, M., McLaren, S. M., Woods, L. P., & Lemma, F. (2007). Lifelong learning, its facilitators and barriers in primary care settings: A qualitative study. *Primary Health Care Research and Development*, *8*(2), 157–169. doi:10.1017/S1463423607000187

Carlén, U. (2010). *A professional community goes online - A study of an online learning community in general medicine*. Unpublished doctoral dissertation, University of Gothenburg, Sweden

Carlén, U., & Jobring, O. (2005). The rationale of online learning communities. *International Journal of Web Based Communities*, *1*(3), 272–295. doi:10.1504/IJWBC.2005.006927

Cuban, L. (1986). *Teachers and machines: The classroom use of technology since 1920*. New York, NY: Teachers College Press.

Dewey, J. (1916/1959). *Democracy and education: An introduction to the philosophy of education*. New York, NY: Free Press.

Findahl, O. (2009). *Svenskarna och Internet 2009*. Gävle, Sweden: World Internet Institute.

Fox, N., & Roberts, C. (1999). GPs in cyberspace: The sociology of virtual community. *The Sociological Review*, *47*(4), 643–671. doi:10.1111/1467-954X.00190

Freidson, E. (1970). *Profession of medicine: A study of the sociology of applied knowledge*. New York, NY: Harper & Row.

Freidson, E. (2001). *Professionalism: The third logic*. Oxford, UK: Blackwell.

Fuchs, C. (2008). *Internet and society: Social theory in the information age*. New York, NY: Routledge.

Gray, B. (2004). Informal learning in an online community of practice. *Journal of Distance Education*, *19*(1), 20–35.

Guribye, F., & Lindström, B. (2009). Infrastructures for learning and networked tools: The introduction of a new tool in an inter-organisational network. In Dirckinck-Holmfeld, L., Jones, C., & Lindström, B. (Eds.), *Analysing networked learning practices in higher education and continuing professional development* (pp. 150–162). Rotterdam, The Netherlands: Sense Publishers.

Hara, N., & Hew, K. H. (2007). Knowledge sharing in an online community of health-care professionals. *Information Technology & People*, *20*(3), 235–261. doi:10.1108/09593840710822859

Haythornthwaite, C. (2002). Building social networks via computer networks: Creating and sustaining distributed learning communities. In Renninger, K. A., & Shumar, W. (Eds.), *Building virtual communities: Learning and change in cyberspace* (pp. 159–190). Cambridge, UK: Cambridge University Press. doi:10.1017/CBO9780511606373.011

Haythornthwaite, C. (2008). Learning relations and networks in web-based communities. *International Journal of Web Based Communities*, *4*(2), 140–158. doi:10.1504/IJWBC.2008.017669

Hew, K. F., & Hara, N. (2008). An online listserv for nurse practitioners: A viable venue for continuous nursing professional development? *Nurse Education Today*, *28*(4), 450–457. doi:10.1016/j.nedt.2007.07.009

Holt, T. J., & Graves, D. C. (2007). A qualitative analysis of advance fee fraud e-mail schemes. *International Journal of Cyber Criminology*, *1*(1), 137–154.

Jaldemark, J. (2010). *Participation in a boundless activity*. Unpublished doctoral dissertation, Umeå University, Sweden.

Jones, C., & Dirckinck-Holmfeld, L. (2009). Analysing networked learning practices: An introduction. In Jones, C., Dirckinck-Holmfeld, L., & Lindström, B. (Eds.), *Analysing networked learning practices in higher education and continuing professional development* (pp. 1–27). Rotterdam, The Netherlands: Sense.

Karagiannis, T., & Vojnović, M. (2008). *E-mail information flow in large-scale enterprises*. Technical report: Microsoft Research.

Lave, J. (1988). *Cognition in practice: Mind, mathematics and culture in everyday life*. Cambridge, UK: Cambridge University Press. doi:10.1017/CBO9780511609268

Lave, J., & Wenger, E. (1991). *Situated learning: Legitimate peripheral participation*. Cambridge, MA: Cambridge University Press.

Lindberg, J. O., & Olofsson, A. D. (2005). *Training teachers through technology: A case study of a distance-based teacher training programme*. Unpublished doctoral dissertation, Umeå University, Sweden.

McAllister, M., & Moyle, W. (2006). An online learning community for clinical educators. *Nurse Education in Practice*, *6*(2), 106–111. doi:10.1016/j.nepr.2005.10.002

McWhinney, I. R. (1997). *A textbook of family medicine* (2nd ed.). Oxford, UK: Oxford University Press.

Nardi, B. A., Whittaker, S., & Schwarz, H. (2002). NetWORKers and their activity in intensional networks. *Computer Supported Cooperative Work*, *11*, 205–242. doi:10.1023/A:1015241914483

Renninger, K. A, & Shumar, W. E. (2002). *Building virtual communities: Learning and change in cyberspace*. Cambridge, UK: Cambridge University Press.

Rogoff, B. (1990). *Apprenticeship in thinking: Cognitive development in social context*. New York, NY: Oxford University Press.

Säljö, R. (1999). Learning as the use of tools: A sociocultural perspective on the human-technology link. In Littleton, K., & Light, P. (Eds.), *Learning with computers: analysing productive interaction* (pp. 144–161). New York, NY: Routledge.

Skovholt, K., & Svennevig, J. (2006). E-mail copies in workplace interaction. *Journal of Computer-Mediated Communication*, *12*(1), 42–62. doi:10.1111/j.1083-6101.2006.00314.x

Slevin, J. (2000). *The Internet and society*. Cambridge, UK: Polity.

Thomas, R. E., & James, S. D. (1999). Informal communications networking among health professionals: A study of GP-UK. *Health Informatics Journal*, *5*(2), 74–81. doi:10.1177/146045829900500204

Thompson, L. A., Dawson, K., Ferdig, R. E., Black, E. W., Boyer, J., Coutts, J., & Black, N. P. (2008). The intersection of online social networking with medical professionalism. *Journal of General Internal Medicine*, *23*(7), 954–957. doi:10.1007/s11606-008-0538-8

Thorley, K., Turner, S., Hussey, L., & Agius, R. (2009). Continuing professional development in occupational medicine for general practitioners. *Occupational Medicine*, *59*(5), 324–346. doi:10.1093/occmed/kqp013

Wenger, E. (1998). *Communities of practice: Learning, meaning, and identity*. Cambridge, UK: Cambridge University Press.

ADDITIONAL READING

Anderson, B. (1983/1991). *Imagined communities: reflections on the origin and spread of nationalism*. London: Verso.

Barab, S. A., Kling, R., & Gray, J. (2004). *Designing for virtual communities in the service of learning*. Cambridge, MA: Cambridge University Press.

Bauman, Z. (2001). *Community: Seeking safety in an insecure world*. Oxford: Polity.

Brint, S. (2001). Gemeinschaft revisited: A critique and reconstruction of the community concept. *Sociological Theory*, *19*(1), 1–23. doi:10.1111/0735-2751.00125

Castells, M. (2004). Informationalism, networks, and the network society: A theoretical blueprint. In Castells, M. (Ed.), *The network society: A cross-cultural perspective* (pp. 3–45). Northampton, MA: Edward Elgar.

Guribye, F. (2005). *Infrastructures for learning: Ethnographic inquiries into the social and technical conditions of education and training*. Unpublished doctoral dissertation, University of Bergen, Norway.

Hrastinski, S. (2007). *Participating in synchronous online education*. Unpublished doctoral dissertation, Lund University, Sweden.

James Lin, M.-J., Hung, S.-W., & Chen, C.-J. (2009). Fostering the determinants of knowledge sharing in professional virtual communities. *Computers in Human Behavior*, *25*, 929–939. doi:10.1016/j.chb.2009.03.008

Kienle, A., & Ritterskamp, C. (2007). Facilitating asynchronous discussion in learning communities: The impact of moderation strategies. *Behaviour & Information Technology*, *26*(1), 73–80. doi:10.1080/01449290600811594

Licoppe, C., & Smoreda, Z. (2005). Are social networks technologically embedded? How networks are changing today with changes in communication technology. *Social Networks*, *27*(4), 317–335. doi:10.1016/j.socnet.2004.11.001

Mazzolini, M., & Maddison, S. (2007). When to jump in: The role of the instructor in online discussion forums. *Computers & Education*, *49*(2), 193–213. doi:10.1016/j.compedu.2005.06.011

Perotta, C. (2006). Learning to be a psychologist: the construction of identity in an online forum. *Journal of Computer Assisted Learning*, *22*, 456–466. doi:10.1111/j.1365-2729.2006.00193.x

Stuckey, B., & Smith, J. (2004). Building sustainable communities of practice. In Hildreth, P. M., & Kimble, C. (Eds.), *Knowledge networks: Innovation through communities of practice*. Hershey, PA: Idea Group.

Vavasseur, C., & MacGregor, S. K. (2008). Extending content-based professional development through online communities of practice. *Journal of Research on Technology in Education, 40*(4), 517–536.

Wasko, M., & Faraj, S. (2005). Why should I share? Examining social capital and knowledge contribution in electronic networks of practice. *Management Information Systems Quarterly, 29*(1), 35–57.

Wertsch, J. (1998). *Mind as action*. New York: Oxford University Press.

KEY TERMS AND DEFINITIONS

Continual Professional Development (CPD): Is a synonymous term to continual medical education (CME) that deal with the concern for the improvement and maintenance of scientifically grounded knowledge and skills that include medical, psychological and sociological concern for general practitioners. CPD can be organized as a complement to other forms of learning that embrace all efforts for creating conditions for learning on a regular basis.

General Medicine: A specialist subject that is more often discussed in terms of family medicine. The intricate dilemma of being generalists in a specialist practice is further examined in the Ph.D. thesis *A Professional Community Goes Online: A Study of an Online Learning Community in General Medicine*. In line with the larger empirical study, we use the term *general medicine* in order to discuss this issue in a forthcoming work.

General Practitioner (GP): A general practitioner specializes in general/family medicine.

Semi-Open Access: In order to access the online forum, participants have to first send an e-mail request to the moderator, who then will let them enter the OLC. This kind of structure of online availability do we call semi-open access since it is almost open, but with restrictions for just anyone who "surf the Internet".

Social Networking Site: Defined as a meeting place for group of people who gather to socialize in terms of shared interest and/or activities. Each participant represent themselves on a social network service, similar to a profile on a web page, for building and maintaining social relationships to current and former acquaintances through communication and information by additional services. In comprehensive terms, a social networking site is based on an individual-centered form of participation whereas an OLC is based on a group-centered form of participation. However, this does not reduce social networking sites to be collaborative affairs. In recent times Facebook.com and Academia.edu is considered to be well-known social networking sites. In medicine profession, there are several social networking sites to be found by the reader of this chapter.

Specialist Subject: Is constituted by an educated group of people who share knowledge and experiences that marginalize outsiders from participating due to the lack of terminology, scientific knowledge, practical skills, and discourses etc. in order to contribute to the OLC.

Thread: Is a metaphor for a series of messages or postings that confirm the social interaction among the participants as several postings are technically interlinked into an explicit structure of individual contributions. The construction of threads can be viewed as storylines built collectively around a shared topic. The longer the discussion proceeds, the more it tends to examine the topic in several smaller threads rather than having one longer thread. A thread consists of a series of postings that constitute the activities and that become a tool that reifies what the distributed group of participants know about the initiated topic.

Chapter 8
Boundless Writing:
Applying a Transactional Approach to Design of a Thesis Course in Higher Education

Jimmy Jaldemark
Mid Sweden University, Sweden

ABSTRACT

This chapter discusses the application of a transactional approach to educational design. Its purpose is to describe how such an approach could be applied to a thesis course. To fulfill this purpose the chapter unfolds by indicating that the practice of supervision faces challenges from changes in society. Technology-enhanced participation in supervision is one answer to these challenges. Inspired by scholars such as Bakhtin, Dewey, and Vygotsky the applied transactional approach expands on ideas such as dialogues and educational settings. The implementation of these ideas into the educational design intersects within two principles, group-work, and open and public exchanges of information. The transactional approach is then illustrated with the help of a first-year undergraduate thesis course in the discipline of Education.

INTRODUCTION

A general content of all higher education programs is that they include practices which aim to develop the academic writing of students. The general character of academic writing makes it a phenomenon that is accountable to all practices or situations of educational design in higher education. The design of such practices should include increasing requirements that will help students to become skilled academic writers. This growth in skills could be designed into and examined through tasks throughout their education, for example in

DOI: 10.4018/978-1-61350-080-4.ch008

terms of writing short papers or performing extended thesis-work. Usually thesis-work is located at the end of students' education. The educational design of thesis courses usually involves lectures on research methods and supervision of students work.

In thesis courses supervisors are expected to execute expertise-quality as well as embrace support for the student and help them balance between creativity and criticism (Fraser & Mathews, 1999). In this practice, various pedagogical philosophies are applied (Dysthe, 2002b), particularly with respect to the aim of supervision and what kind of action it should foster. Among other points, this means that the degree of symmetry in the relationship between the supervisor and the student differs. Students could be treated as equal to the supervisor or be placed at various levels of subordination. Furthermore, feedback could include comments from the supervisor as well as from co-students and/or external organizations (e.g., Dysthe, 2002b; Frankland, 1999; Högberg, Eriksson, Bäcklund, & Gustafsson, 1999; Kolmos, Kofoed, & Du, 2008; Parker, 2009; Pearson & Brew, 2002; Wisker, Robinson, & Shacham, 2007).

Design of thesis courses usually embraces models of supervision that include the performance of one-to-one participation between a single student and a teacher (de Beer & Mason, 2009). Such design emphasizes the close geographical relation between the student and the supervisor, in other words one-to-one supervision on campus (Mac Keogh, 2006). Usually, this is the way the practice of supervision is executed in the humanities and social sciences (Dysthe, Samara, & Westrheim, 2006). This design could include supervision as a physically located process at the university or be a distributed process supported by educational technologies, such as e-mail or telephones. Nevertheless, the application of such model in educational design constrains supervision within the limitations offered by the communication between the single student and the single supervisor. However, applying one-to-one models in educational design of thesis courses limits the potential of the single student. At least this is the case if we believe that learning about academic writing occurs both under the guidance of supervisors and together with peers (Vygotsky, 1934/1987). If we develop that idea, the practice of educational design needs to apply thinking that goes beyond the performance of the student-supervisor-dyad.

This chapter shows that transactional approaches to educational design embrace ideas that go beyond the above mentioned dyad. Its purpose is to describe how such an approach could be applied in a thesis course. This approach builds on ideas of how participation within educational settings is inseparable from cultural, ecological, historical, and social aspects of the surrounding environment.

The background section starts with a discussion of how changes in society impact the practice of supervision. The second paragraph in the background starts with a discussion of technology-enhanced participation and ends by linking this idea to the practice of supervision. Thereafter follows the main focus of the chapter, the application of a transactional approach in the practice of supervision. First this section discusses assumptions taken within transactional approaches and how these assumptions differ from interactional approaches. Then follows this chapter's conceptualization of the transactional approach; embracing the two concepts of educational settings and dialogues. Following that section is a case study, an educational setting that illustrates how the design approach unfolds. To give the reader a sense of context and show how the educational design of the thesis course goes beyond the traditional limits of thesis courses this section starts with a description of the program and its first year. This description focuses on aspects of academic writing that are designed into the program. The following section shows how the two design principles, *group work* and *open and public exchange of information* are applied into dialogues in a nine-step working-process in the illustrating educational setting. Finally, future research directions and conclusions bring this chapter to an end.

BACKGROUND

Changes in Society that Impact the Practice of Supervision

Changes in society challenge the practice of supervision as a campus-based one-to-one-process. During recent decades such changes have occurred within the economic, political, and technological spheres. Development in the field of educational technology provides a dynamic that influences the design of higher education. During recent decades we have seen the invention and application of technologies that allows computer-supported many-to-many communication. These technologies supports the production and sharing of files, images, text, videos, and voices and include technologies such as blogs, chat, computer-conferences, desktop video-conferences, twitter, and wikis (Augustsson, 2010; Bassili & Joordens, 2008; Bristol, 2010; Carlén, 2010; Cole, 2009; Hatzipanagos & Warburton, 2009; Hrastinski, 2006; Sim & Hew, 2010). The possibilities allowed by technologies that support participation through Internet challenges educational designs that build on one-to-one models of supervision.

As these educational technologies have emerged, participation through technology-enhanced educational settings has changed from being a peripheral activity on the outskirts of higher education to becoming integrated into the mainstream of higher education. In Swedish higher education the enrolment of students in such settings has risen from being 7% in the early nineties to being approximately 30% of the total enrolled student cohort in the academic year 2008/2009 (Statistics Sweden, 2010; Swedish National Agency for Higher Education & Statistics Sweden, 2010; Utbildningsdepartementet, 1992). Higher enrolment relate to global movements such as changes within the labor-market. This movement emphasizes the importance of life-long learning and includes a rise in enrolment to higher education (Tait & Mills, 1999). This aspect could explain why enrolment to technology-enhanced educational settings has risen. However, the high level of enrolment impacts the funding of higher education and leads to a heavier workload on supervisors (Zhao, 2003). Performing supervision through a one-to-one model might be hard to realize within an era that embraces high student enrolment.

Moreover, in the wake of the emphasis on a policy of life-long learning, many students experience problems completing their thesis within the expected time frame. Commitments in both their working life and family life influences students' ability to perform full-time studies. Together these issues provide incentives for improving the practice of supervision (Dysthe, et al., 2006) and challenge the prevailing one-to-one model of supervision.

Hitherto, few studies discuss aspects of time and space related to the physical separation between students and supervisors. However, while a growing number of students participates in supervision from off-campus locations, design of thesis courses need to pay attention to such participation. This chapter therefore takes up that challenge and discusses the relationship between technology-enhanced participation and supervision. The next section describes various aspects of such participation in the practice of supervision.

Technology-Enhanced Participation in Supervision

Technology-enhanced participation in supervision is receiving growing attention among educational scholars. Two reasons for increasing enrollment are, as mentioned above, society's emphasis on life-long learning, and technological developments. One of the consequences of these reasons for participation is that a higher percentage of "supervisory relationships are likely to be conducted at a distance" (Wisker, et al., 2007, p. 301). However, technology-enhanced participation in the practice of supervision is not easily described as a series of linear relationships. To understand technology-enhanced participation in this practice we need to take a look in the rear-view mirror and discuss ideas that make it possible to describe and interpret the actions of students and teachers, for example the communicative actions within the supervision-process.

The papers of Harasim (1989) and Moore (1989) are two early examples that defines the relationship between educational technology and participation. Thereafter, an extended discussion of this relationship has emerged (e.g., Anderson, 2009; Anderson & Garrison, 1998; Jaldemark, 2010; Laurillard, 2002; Moore & Kearsley, 2005; Paulsen, 2003). The study of Harasim (1989) emphasizes the link between agents, particularly communicative aspects of participation. She concluded that such aspects also marked the difference between participation in different domains of education. She claimed that participation in education performed face-to-face featured one-to-many communication between the teacher and the students; and that distance education comprised of one-to-one communication between teachers and students; and finally, that online education was characterized by many-to-many communication. In her groundbreaking work, she also argued that time was a defining issue between these domains. While face-to-face education depended on participation in synchronous communication, both distance and online education bound communication to asynchronous participation. Face-to face education bound students and teachers to a particular location and to perform communication in a simultaneous fashion. Unlike face-to face education both distance education and online education released agents from the boundaries of location and time. Nevertheless, this triad of distinct and different domains has been blurred during recent decades. Developments within the field of educational technology nowadays also allow technology-enhanced participation in one-to-many and one-to-one modes. Furthermore, educational technologies that have emerged in this development supports both asynchronous and synchronous communication (Jaldemark, 2008).

The discussion of Moore (1989) also comprises three different relationships. However, he focused on the communicative triad between students, teachers and content; the interplay between students and teachers, students and content, and within the group of students. While the ideas of Harasim and Moore were developed in the late 1980s they also reflected the advances within educational technology. The communicative triad of Moore was developed within a distance education framework where applications of computerized technologies still were in their infancy. Harasim's distinction between distance education and online education must also be understood in that context.

The recent decades, have seen development of these early ideas. Paulsen (2003) added a fourth communicative relationship to Harasim (1989), participating one-online. Similar to Moore (1989) this relationship embraces content while the online feature includes interplay with a non-human agent, for example a database or a website. Anderson and Garrison (1998) developed the ideas of Moore by adding three more relationships to the original triad; the interplay within a group of teachers, within content, and between teachers and content.

In a supervision perspective Price and Money (2002) discuss the relationship between educational technology and participation. Similarly to the studies above they reflect over the link between locations and agents. According to their study the practice of supervision embraces three different links, *remote*, *semi-remote* and *traditional*. Participation in remote supervision includes a physical separation between supervisors and students. Therefore all supervision takes place from at least two different locations. In this supervision the communication between students and supervisors is supported by various educational technologies. In the case of more than one supervisor and/or student even three or more locations are possible. Participation in traditional supervision takes place at campus. Here, both students and supervisors are geographically close. Semi-remote supervision is a combination of the two other modes of participation in supervision. Here supervision comprises a combination of meetings on campus and at other sites, for example in a workplace setting or the homes of the students.

To conclude: Studies of technology-enhanced supervision shows that social aspects of supervision, such as the interplay between agents, are important to reach a coherent understanding of the practice of supervision (Parker, 2009). The review above underwrites the view that technology-enhanced participation relates to aspects of content, location, time and other agents. From these ideas, participation in the practice of supervision could be said to be a technology-enhanced communicative exchange of ideas between agents. This exchange embraces the role of cultural, ecological, historical, and social aspects in the surrounding environment. Therefore, content is a fluid phenomenon and inseparable from the communicative exchanges between the agents and the activities where it emerges. The next section shows how transactional approaches to educational design depart from such insights.

THE TRANSACTIONAL APPROACH

Dewey and Bentley (1949/1960) offers a valuable distinction between interactional and transactional approaches to human action. Interactional approaches build on a dualistic world-view where man and the surrounding environment are understood as two separated categories. Human action is understandable without reference to the surrounding environment. Such an approach focuses on a narrow study of human action. Therefore interactional approaches deemphasize cultural, ecological, historical and social aspects of human action. In short, human action is a process of action and reaction without being influenced by environmental and situational aspects.

Transactional approaches on the other hand depart from a world-view where human action is something that cannot be separated from its surrounding (e.g., Altman & Rogoff, 1991; Bakhtin, 1935/1981; Dewey & Bentley, 1949/1960; Vygotsky, 1934/1987). Ontologically this position emphasizes the necessary relationship between man and the environment by regarding that man and the environment as belonging to a dynamic whole. Such an understanding of human beings embraces the inseparability of the actions they perform and the environment in which human action emerges. This whole emphasizes conditions in various settings and the motives of human actions that are influenced by cultural, ecological, historical and social aspects (Jaldemark, 2010, 2011).

The principles and ideas applied in transactional approaches to the design of education should build on this inseparability between human action and the surrounding environment. One way to include environmental aspects of participation in education is to discuss design of education in terms of learning environments (Jonassen & Land, 2000). However, this conceptualization of education is an interactional conceptualization. An ontological analysis of this concept shows that it both separates the agent from the surrounding environment and divides the environment into different environments (Jaldemark, 2010, 2011). Transactional approaches to educational design need concepts that avoid such pitfalls. In the following section such concepts will be unfolded.

Educational Settings

From a transactional approach educational settings are suggested as a concept for design of technology-enhanced participation in higher education. An educational setting is about the circumstances, locations, and time in which education occurs or develops. Therefore, this concept refers to a situation in which education exists and to the totality of its surrounding conditions. By embracing cultural, ecological, historical, and social aspects it relates to past, present, and future states of its condition. Aspects of other settings such as the home setting of the student might intersect with the educational setting. This means that the concept educational setting allows the discussion of educational design in terms of being a complex phenomenon. Participation in an educational setting relates students and supervisor to each other and to actions such as communication as well as to the educational technologies that support their actions (Jaldemark, 2010; Vygotsky, 1978). This collaborative feature of educational settings allows the agents to participate in actions that are above their actual solo-performance level. Moreover, through the collaborative feature of the educational setting students are supposed to learn to independently perform such actions. In other words, in a process of supervision the educational setting of a thesis course should allow a development zone for students to learn about how to perform research (Vygotsky, 1934/1987).

Moreover, using a transactional approach it is possible to discuss the actions performed in educational settings in terms of students and supervisors participation in various dialogues (Bakhtin, 1935/1981; Dysthe, 2002a). This conceptualization is further discussed in the next section.

Dialogues

In the transactional approach of this chapter the relationship between communication, educational settings, and participation in the practice of supervision is essential to educational design (Jaldemark, 2010). Nevertheless, the idea of linking communication to human action has been discussed by scholars for a long time. Dewey (1916) discusses the importance of communication by emphasizing its role in the continuing existence of society. He argued that communication is the way in which agents "come to possess things in common" (Dewey, 1916, p. 5). Furthermore, he argued that to discuss communication as a feature in the design of education there is a need to make a clear distinction of this concept.

Following the transactional approach discussed by among others Dewey and Bentley (1949/1960), Bakhtin (1935/1981, 1953/1986) distinguishes between the concepts communication and language. A word or a sentence is "a unit of *language*, as distinct from the *utterance* as unit of speech communication" (Bakhtin, 1953/1986, p. 73). While the boundaries of words and sentences are determined by language, utterances are framed by changes of the speaking subject; in other words, a switch of speaking agent for example from a student to a supervisor. Moreover "such a change, framing the sentence on both sides, transforms the sentence into an entire utterance" (Bakhtin, 1953/1986, p. 73). Expressed in other words utterances are language in action and relates to the settings in which they occur. Therefore utterances as communicative features relate to participation in educational settings; in this chapter educational settings are where the practice of supervision emerges. In such settings agents performs communication supported by educational technologies. Therefore, communication embraces utterances such as online documents for example a draft of the thesis, study-guides, written entries in blogs, chats or computer-conferences, or spoken utterances from a video-conference, or various other technology-enhanced resources.

Bakhtin (1935/1981, 1953/1986) discussed communication in terms of it being a dialogical process. He argued that human beings are in a constant dialogue with the world, thus listeners and speakers are dependent on each other. Therefore, successful communication assumes that shared meaning is possible. In communication, meanings and utterances are products of social negotiation between agents. Through such negotiation the meaning of each utterance "comes to fruition only in the response" (Bakhtin,

1935/1981, p. 282) from other agents. Therefore, response and understanding condition each other while dialectically merging in a communicative process. In other words, communication is about meaning making. In this sense, meaning making is "a bridge between the speaker and the listener, the writer and the reader" (Dysthe, 2002a, p. 341). This means that communication is inseparable from cultural, ecological, historical, and social aspects of the surrounding environment.

Therefore, within a transactional approach, participation in the practice of supervision is about agents developing a shared meaning in an emerging dialogue; a dialogue that emerges from a dynamic whole inseparable from the surrounding environment. In the next section this process will be illustrated with a thesis course that comprised of technology-enhanced dialogues as well as dialogues performed face-to-face.

THE EDUCATIONAL SETTING OF THE SUPERVISION PROCESS: AN ILLUSTRATIVE THESIS COURSE

The educational setting in this paper is a bachelor program in Behavioral Science given at a Swedish university. The students are enrolled in either a campus-mode or in a blended learning mode; distance students meet on campus 2-3 times each semester. The first and second semesters comprise of studies in the discipline of Education. In the second half of the second semester a period of 10 weeks is allocated to the writing of a thesis. The author of this chapter served multiple roles in this illustrative educational setting. He was the course manager of the first year of the program and therefore responsible for the educational design of both the first and second semester. Moreover, he served as a teacher in some of the courses and was a supervisor in the thesis course. However, the educational design of the first year was not intended to be part of a research project. Later, an evaluation of the thesis course was discussed at a conference (Jaldemark & Lindberg, 2010). Nevertheless, the educational design departed from ideas developed within the author's research (Jaldemark, 2010).

The process of writing a thesis starts long before the final product, the thesis, is completed. We could claim that it starts at the beginning of the thesis course. Nevertheless, from a transactional perspective the boundaries for the process are beyond the thesis course itself. The process of becoming an academic writer starts much earlier than the students' enrolment to higher education. The experiences of students from dialogues around their earlier thinking and writing foster such skills and are present in their thesis writing. However, to demarcate this discussion to higher education this study started the day they enrolled. In this transactional approach, schooling to be a thesis writer starts from the very beginning in the illustrative Behavioral Science program. The practice of supervision followed a plan worked out by the course manager. This plan embraced among others lectures, tasks and assessments. The teachers executed it from the first course throughout the whole year, ending in the second semester's last course, the thesis course. That training aimed at fostering in students the basic skills of academic writing and preparing them for writing a thesis. Therefore, this chapter will start to discuss the preparation phase, then continue with a discussion of the thesis course itself.

However, before presenting the plan for developing the writing-skills of students a few words need to be said about the educational technologies that facilitated the participation of students and teachers. Overall, communication was supposed to occur through the university's own intranet. This system included an assemblage of educational technologies; blogs, chat, computer-conferences, e-mail, individual spaces for saving documents and video-conferences. These technologies were implemented in the plan according to the ideas developed by the course management.

The First Year: An Overview

The first semester started with lectures dealing with issues concerning academic writing. These lectures discussed reference-techniques, such as the APA-standard, and rules to follow if the writer wishes the text to be a part of the academic genre. Training then followed as part of the assessment of the first course. This assessment was two-fold, including a seminar and the writing of a paper. The purpose of the seminar was to train students to compare theoretical views of educational issues. Students were supposed to perform this in smaller groups. The second part of the assessment was a 5-7 pages long individual paper that included training to write summaries of theoretical perspectives and then discuss the consequences of and differences between these perspectives. The students were also required to apply reference-techniques and attach a complete reference list to the paper. To scaffold their writing; the topic and the structure of the paper were given in advance. Later in the first semester the students had new opportunities to develop these skills.

The educational design of the third course of the first semester comprised a structured seven-step working process embracing a blog-posting for each step. In this process students had the opportunity to train several of the skills required in writing a thesis in a Behavioral Science discipline. In the first posting on the blog students wrote about their expectations before a compulsory work-place visit. They also wrote questions that they thought were useful to explore during the visit.

The literature in the course was divided into three different themes, and each of these themes had a blog entry of their own. In these three entries students wrote a short summary and reflection of the literature. At the end of these entries students were supposed to write questions that were generated through the reading of the literature. These questions were supposed to be used later in the working process. The purpose of these early entries was to train the student to do literature reviews and use these reviews of published research to generate interview questions. The two following entries gave further training in methodological skills.

In the fifth entry students composed an interview guide out of the questions generated in the earlier entries. This guide was commented on by a teacher and was supposed to be used during the following work-place visit. Students had visited their chosen work-place at the time of writing the sixth entry and this entry was a reflection on how they experienced the work-place visit. They were supposed to write critically about how they performed their collection of empirical data. This is a skill needed when discussing methodological issues in a thesis. The student chose a narrower theme for the seventh and final entry. This theme was linked to the course content through the working-process. Students then chose what they thought was most interesting to develop further. This entry was expanded into a 5000-word assessment comprising of a research question, a research review, empirical data and a conclusion. In other words, the writing elements included in a thesis. Furthermore, this task included higher requirements in their reference-technique (e.g. using quotations and presenting a complete and proper reference-list).

In the last course of the first semester students carried out a research review. In this task students analyzed theoretical ideas and reflected over the practical consequences of these ideas; skills needed to write both good reviews and a discussion chapter.

The first course of the second semester included discussions on reliability and validity in various data-collection methods, for example when using interviews, observations, or questionnaires in a study. This course also included an opportunity to act as an opponent and to defend academic writing. The second course added a new feature as students were assessed through a research plan that extended their literature review beyond the boundaries of the compulsory literature.

To conclude: As this overview of the first year shows; students were provided with rich opportunities to train many of the necessary skills for writing a thesis. The course management also explicitly expressed these ideas in the study-guides. Building on these experiences the students entered the thesis course.

The Thesis Course: Design Principles and Dialogues

The educational design of the thesis course included a structured working process comprising nine steps; a process that was described in an 18-page study-guide. The theses were written by students in pairs, organized in groups consisting of five to ten pairs led by a supervisor. Each of these groups embraced a particular theses-theme related to the particular competence of the supervisor. The design of the thesis course departed from two interrelated principles that intersect in their emphasis of dialogues between participants. These principles, *group-work* and *open and public exchange of information* are transactional in their character and therefore supports participation in boundless academic writing (Bakhtin, 1935/1981; Lave & Wenger, 1991; Vygotsky, 1934/1987).

Group-work as a principle of educational design emphasizes the idea of students and teachers participating in and developing a learning community. This means that the group has the function of being a major resource in the practice of supervision and in the process of learning to write a thesis. Together, students can produce higher quality than when working alone and through group-dialogues different views can be explored. This principle facilitates the implementation of peer-review-processes into the educational design as well as allowing such processes to occur voluntary within the cohort of students.

Open and public exchange of information is a boundless feature of the educational design of this thesis course. It allows students and supervisors to go beyond the application of one-to-one models in the practice of supervision. The transparency of this principle gives the students rich opportunities to gain insights into how other students and different supervisors handle various aspects of the research process. It is intended to widen their views by offering rich opportunities to develop a deeper understanding of performing research-tasks and report these tasks in a thesis. Moreover, open and public exchanges of information should offer access to more dialogues and provide students with greater amount of advice from their supervisor than one-to-one models could allow. Besides getting advice from their own supervisor, they also have access to advice that is intended for other theses. The consequence is accessibility to advice from all supervisors on every thesis-project. Therefore, this principle multiplies the available resources that students could make use of when working with their research project. From a course management perspective this principle works to reduce the burden of the supervisor and raise the quality of the students' thesis.

These principles were implemented into four different categories of open and public group-dialogues; *emergency dialogues*, *structured dialogues*, *conference dialogues*, and *pair-dialogues*. The emergency dialogues comprises of synchronous sessions. These sessions embraces opportunities for students to discuss issues of an immediate character. Various supervisors were in service in this category of dialogue. Therefore, this dialogue opens up supervision beyond the boundaries of one-to-one models. Boundaries of time are dissolved by saving the sessions in an archive. Asynchronous access to advices is therefore possible. In the illustrating course these sessions lasted 45 minutes and were performed three times a week. Educational technologies such as chat and video-conferences were used in these dialogues.

Students and supervisors were supposed to perform the structured dialogues synchronously. These sessions were closely linked to the working process as the topics were related to different phases in the research process. The performance of these sessions embraced one supervisor and her/his supervision group. In the sessions, students raised problems that they had tried to solve in their work. In the course these sessions included students participating physically on-campus as well as via the telephone. The flexibility of the educational design facilitates students' choice of location and therefore extends the limits of face-to-face models of supervision.

The performance of conference dialogues extended supervision in both time and space. The students submitted the drafts they wanted to be discussed to a computer conference; a conference that was common for all the students in the supervisor-group and also accessible to the other supervisor-groups. Despite the use of educational technology, the idea of these dialogues is similar to the essential idea of traditional supervision-models; discussing drafts of a student's thesis. However, as this process emerged online the dialogue embraced supervisors using functions such as *comments*, and *tracking changes* in the word-processor. Later, the supervisor submitted a response to these drafts. This response was then accessible to the authors and to the rest of the students. The students involved in this dialogue were supposed to learn from the response to their own drafts as well as from supervisors responding to other students' drafts.

The performance of the fourth and last form of dialogues, the pair-dialogues, mainly occurred within the pairs of theses writing. The idea of this dialogue was to facilitate students with opportunities to share ideas and drafts of their thesis. This process of sharing developed within and between the pairs. This meant that peer-reviews of drafts were built into the educational design. In the illustrative course, each pair was allotted a computer conference where they stored drafts of their thesis, shared ideas and resources. Other students were also allowed to download and comment on these documents.

These four categories of dialogues were implemented into the working-process. This process is extensively discussed in the next section.

The Working Process

The thesis course consisted of two modules one of which dealt with issues of research methodology and scientific perspectives, whilst the other consisted of writing the thesis itself. These two modules of the course were integrated into a nine-step working process. The idea behind this integrated solution was to help students to understand the link between the theory of science and the practice of doing research. As discussed elsewhere, this working-process helps to make this link visible (Jaldemark & Lindberg, 2010).

The first step in the working-process was choosing a partner and a theme for the thesis. Here students participated in an election-procedure that occurred during a limited period of time ahead of the start of the thesis course. Each available supervisor had announced a theme related to the particular research they are interested in. Students then ranked the themes after interest and were later allotted one of these themes. Each theme had a limited number of places and the course manager arranged the supervisor-groups following the principle of the date the pairs submitted their theme ranking. Therefore, students were not guaranteed their first choice of theme. Before entering the second step students were informed of the result of this procedure.

The second step included a meeting at the campus. The thesis course, comprising lectures and workshops discussing the research-process, searching in databases, and meetings within the supervisor-groups was introduced at this meeting.

In the third step students compiled a one-page rough draft of a research-plan. It included ideas concerning what research problem the thesis should address, a preliminary purpose and a list of suitable references. This draft was submitted to the supervisors' computer-conference within a week of the on campus meeting. The draft was then discussed within a structured dialogue including the attendance of participants from the whole supervisor-group.

The fourth step embraced students having dialogues with both an examiner and peer-students. These dialogues occurred at the beginning of the fifth week and discussed an expanded draft of the research-plan. In one of these dialogues students from another thesis-pair performed peer-review on the research-plan. In the other dialogue an external supervisor served as an examiner that graded and commented on the research-plan. Their response was based on a draft that should comprise of at least ten pages and include the purpose and the problem of the theses, a review of suitable research, and finally methodological issues such as research approach, sampling, method of data collection, and ethical considerations. Approximately, half of the plan was supposed to deal with methodological issues. Moreover, the examiner also emphasized the use of a proper reference-technique. After the fourth step students considered the research-plan as a rough draft of the thesis. The responses from the peer-review and the assessment were then used in the continuing work of the thesis.

Later in the fifth week, the fifth step was performed. At this stage of the research process students was supposed to be ready to discuss data-collection. Therefore, the supervisor-groups met in a structured dialogue that dealt with these issues, for example the construction of an interview-guide or a questionnaire.

Two weeks later, the third and final structured dialogue was performed. In this step the supervision focused on how to deal with the collected empirical data; for example how to analyze, categorize, and present this data. Students were supposed to prepare written notes that reflected on the collection of data. In a later stage of the thesis, these reflections were useful when discussing the result of the methodological choices. Moreover, the preparation also included the construction of a draft of the analysis subsection of the method chapter.

The seventh step was performed at the beginning of the ninth week. Here the students finalized and submitted a preliminary version of the thesis; a version that consisted of all of the expected chapters of the thesis. This step included the break-up of the relationship between supervisors and students. This meant that students had no more access to advice from their supervisors.

The students that submitted a full version in the preceding step went to the eighth step, the thesis seminar. This step included an online peer-review process between students. This process included aspects of individual character, in terms of assessment of students' performance as opponents and defending their thesis. The course manager appointed two students from different thesis-pairs as opponents for each thesis. In other words, each student had an online written dialogue with a co-student on the preliminary version of the thesis. Using relevant ideas from the dialogues the pairs collaboratively revised and finalized their thesis.

The ninth and final step was the submission of the final version of the thesis. In this step students had a dialogue with an assessing teacher. This teacher assessed the final version of the thesis as well as the written communication performed in the eighth step. This assessment was communicated online to the individual students and comprised a summative aspect in the form of a grade, and a formative aspect embracing a seven-dimension commentary on the single student's efforts.

Scaffolding of the working-process conference dialogues and emergency dialogues was executed on a regular basis. Moreover, students also had access to other resources, such as written instructions, websites, and an online archive comprising general advice on writing a thesis. The latter resource was developed over a longer period and has also been used in other thesis courses.

FUTURE RESEARCH DIRECTIONS

As discussed in the background, the practice of supervision faces challenges from the economic, political, and technological spheres. To meet these challenges complementary ways to design thesis courses are needed. One way to design thesis courses could be to use a transactional approach as a departure point. As shown in this chapter, such an approach to educational design of a thesis course resulted in a rather complex and well-structured design. This approach by the course management embraced cultural, ecological, historical, and social aspects in the process of designing. However, despite building on theoretical ideas developed by influential scholars (e.g., Bakhtin, 1935/1981; Dewey & Bentley, 1949/1960; Vygotsky, 1934/1987), research is needed to widen understanding of the consequences of technology-enhanced participation in supervision through various categories of dialogues. Such research could focus on how these categories could support learning and teaching about research processes, or in other words how technology-enhanced dialogues could facilitate supervision.

Much of the published research concerns rather experienced academic writers that perform research-tasks at the end of their education or at the doctoral level (e.g., Dysthe, 2002b; Pearson, 2005; Wisker, et al., 2007). Particular circumstances, such as being first-year students, novices in academic writing and so on, are appropriate aspects to consider when designing thesis courses. This raises questions such as: What are the particular challenges for first-year thesis-writers? What processes are common for all supervision independently of academic level? How could a transactional approach to designing thesis courses help students understand the research process? How could preceding courses develop the skills needed to perform thesis writing? Such issues have been discussed in this chapter. Nevertheless, from both a design and a research perspective, more attention is needed to these questions.

CONCLUSION

Transactional approaches that underwrite the inseparability between human action and its surrounding environment builds on ideas that were developed during the first half of the 20th century by scholars such as Bakhtin (1935/1981), Dewey and Bentley (1949/1960), and Vygotsky (1934/1987). Nevertheless, reports of applications of such approaches in the design of thesis courses are rarely found. However, as this study shows it is possible to use this approach in the design of such courses.

Transactional approaches to designing thesis courses need to turn away from campus-based models that build on rather unstructured synchronous one-to-one participation. Instead, design of a thesis course could build on the inseparability between students, supervisors, and the features designed into the educational setting. This means complex and structured educational design where participation is intended to occur through a range of suitable educational technologies. The process of design could include considerations of how to apply asynchronous and synchronous communication depending on the purpose of the dialogue. In effect, participation in the practice of supervision could allow an extension of the boundaries regarding time, space, and access. This extension could embrace qualitative responses from both supervisors and other students. Therefore, a transactional approach to the design of a thesis course could optimize opportunities to perform dialogues around problems related to the student's research tasks. This could be a fruitful way to apply a transactional approach to the practice of supervision. It will result in a design that expands the dialogical opportunities by using the idea that students could perform boundless writing when they learn about the process of doing research.

REFERENCES

Altman, I., & Rogoff, B. (1991). World views in Psychology: Trait, interactional, organismic and transactional perspectives. In Stokols, D., & Altman, I. (Eds.), *Handbook of environmental psychology* (*Vol. 1*, pp. 7–40). Malabar, FL: Krieger.

Anderson, T. (Ed.). (2009). *The theory and practice of online learning* (2nd ed.). Athabasca, Canada: Athabasca University Press.

Anderson, T., & Garrison, R. (1998). Learning in a networked world: New roles and responsibilities. In Gibson, C. C. (Ed.), *Distance learners in higher education: Institutional responses for quality outcomes* (pp. 97–112). Madison, WI: Atwood.

Augustsson, G. (2010). Web 2.0, pedagogical support for reflexive and emotional social interaction among Swedish students. *The Internet and Higher Education*, *13*(4), 197–205. doi:10.1016/j.iheduc.2010.05.005

Bakhtin, M. M. (1935/1981). Discourse in the novel. In Holquist, M. (Ed.), *The dialogic imagination: Four essays* (pp. 259–422). Austin, TX: University of Texas Press.

Bakhtin, M. M. (1953/1986). The problem of speech genres. In Emerson, C., & Holquist, M. (Eds.), *Speech genres & other late essays* (pp. 60–102). Austin, TX: University of Texas Press.

Bassili, J. N., & Joordens, S. (2008). Media player tool use, satisfaction with online lectures and examination performance. *Journal of Distance Education*, *22*(2), 93–108.

Bristol, T. J. (2010). Twitter: Consider the possibilities for continuing nursing education. *Journal of Continuing Education in Nursing*, *41*(5), 199–200. doi:10.3928/00220124-20100423-09

Carlén, U. (2010). *A professional community goes online: A study of an online learning community in general medicine.* Göteborgs universitet, Göteborg, Sweden.

Cole, M. (2009). Using wiki technology to support student engagement: Lessons from the trenches. *Computers & Education*, *52*(1), 141–146. doi:10.1016/j.compedu.2008.07.003

de Beer, M., & Mason, R. (2009). Using a blended approach to facilitate postgraduate supervision. *Innovations in Education and Teaching International*, *46*(2), 213–226. doi:10.1080/14703290902843984

Dewey, J. (1916). *Democracy and education: An introduction to the philosophy of education.* New York, NY: Macmillan.

Dewey, J., & Bentley, A. F. (1949/1960). *Knowing and the known.* Boston, MA: Beacon.

Dysthe, O. (2002a). The learning potential of a web-mediated discussion in a university course. *Studies in Higher Education*, *27*(3), 339–352. doi:10.1080/03075070220000716

Dysthe, O. (2002b). Professors as mediators of academic text cultures: An interview study with advisors and Master's degree students in three disciplines in a Norwegian university. *Written Communication*, *19*(4), 493–544. doi:10.1177/074108802238010

Dysthe, O., Samara, A., & Westrheim, K. (2006). Multivoiced supervision of Master's students: A case study of alternative supervision practices in higher education. *Studies in Higher Education*, *31*(3), 299–318. doi:10.1080/03075070600680562

Frankland, M. (1999). The master/apprentice model for the supervision of postgraduate research and a new policy for research education. *Australian Universities'. RE:view*, *42*(1), 8–11.

Fraser, R., & Mathews, A. (1999). An evaluation of the desireable characteristics of a supervisor. *Australian Universities'. RE:view*, *42*(1), 5–7.

Harasim, L. M. (1989). On-line education: A new domain. In Mason, R., & Kaye, A. (Eds.), *Mindweave: Communication, computers and distance education* (pp. 50–62). Oxford, UK: Pergamon.

Hatzipanagos, S., & Warburton, S. (2009). Feedback as dialogue: Exploring the links between formative assessment and social software in distance learning. *Learning, Media and Technology, 34*(1), 45–59. doi:10.1080/17439880902759919

Högberg, M., Eriksson, Å., Bäcklund, I., & Gustafsson, C. (1999). *Mästarprov eller mardröm: Studenters uppfattningar om examination av självständigt arbete*. Stockholm, Sweden: Högskoleverket.

Hrastinski, S. (2006). Introducing an informal synchronous medium in a distance learning course: How is participation affected? *The Internet and Higher Education, 9*(2), 117–131. doi:10.1016/j.iheduc.2006.03.006

Jaldemark, J. (2008). Changes within the practice of higher education: Participating in educational communication through distance settings. *International Journal of Web Based Communities, 4*(2), 173–187. doi:10.1504/IJWBC.2008.017671

Jaldemark, J. (2010). *Participating in a boundless activity: Computer-mediated communication in Swedish higher education*. Umeå, Sweden: Umeå University.

Jaldemark, J. (2011). Critical remarks on conceptualisations of online education. *UFV Research Review, 4*(1), 12–28.

Jaldemark, J., & Lindberg, O. (2010). Enhancing supervision of students dissertations through the use of educational technology. In K. Fernstrom (Ed.), *Readings in technology and education: Proceedings of ICICTE 2010, July 8-10, 2010, Corfu island, Greece* (pp. 146-156). Abbotsford, BC, Canada: University of the Fraser Valley Press.

Jonassen, D. H., & Land, S. M. (2000). *Theoretical foundations of learning environments*. Mahwah, NJ: Erlbaum.

Kolmos, A., Kofoed, L., & Du, X. (2008). PhD students' work conditions and study environment in university- and industry-based PhD programmes. *European Journal of Engineering Education, 33*(5), 539–550. doi:10.1080/03043790802588383

Laurillard, D. (2002). *Rethinking university teaching: A conversational framework for the effective use of learning technologies* (2nd ed.). London, UK: RoutledgeFalmer. doi:10.4324/9780203304846

Lave, J., & Wenger, E. (1991). *Situated learning: Legitimate peripheral participation*. Cambridge, UK: Cambridge University Press.

Mac Keogh, K. (2006, 14-15 December). *Supervising undergraduate research using online and peer supervision.* Paper presented at the 7th International Virtual University Conference, Bratislava, Slovakia.

Moore, M. G. (1989). Editorial: Three types of interaction. *American Journal of Distance Education, 3*(2), 1–6. doi:10.1080/08923648909526659

Moore, M. G., & Kearsley, G. (2005). *Distance education: A systems view* (2nd ed.). Belmont, CA: Wadsworth.

Parker, R. (2009). A learning community approach to doctoral education in the social sciences. *Teaching in Higher Education, 14*(1), 43–54. doi:10.1080/13562510802602533

Paulsen, M. F. (2003). *Online education: Learning management systems: Global e-learning in a Scandinavian perspective*. Bekkestua, Norway: NKI.

Pearson, M. (2005). Framing research on doctoral education in Australia in a global context. *Higher Education Research & Development, 24*(2), 119–134. doi:10.1080/07294360500062870

Pearson, M., & Brew, A. (2002). Research training and supervision development. *Studies in Higher Education*, *27*(2), 135–150. doi:10.1080/03075070220119986c

Price, D., & Money, A. (2002). Alternative models for doctoral mentor organisation and research supervision. *Mentoring & Tutoring: Partnership in Learning*, *10*(2), 127–135. doi:10.1080/1361126022000002446

Sim, J. W. S., & Hew, K. F. (2010). The use of weblogs in higher education settings: A review of empirical research. *Educational Research Review*, *5*(2), 151–163. doi:10.1016/j.edurev.2010.01.001

Statistics Sweden. (2010). *Statistikdatabasen: Utbildning och Forskning*. Retrieved May 31, 2010, from http://www.scb.se

Swedish National Agency for Higher Education, & Statistics Sweden. (2010). *Universitet och högskolor: Studenter och examina på grundnivå och avancerad nivå 2008/09*. Retrieved May 31, 2010, from http://www.scb.se/ statistik/ UF/ UF0205/ 2008L09D/ UF0205_2008L09D_SM_ UF20SM1002.pdf

Tait, A., & Mills, R. (Eds.). (1999). *The convergence of distance and conventional education: Patterns of flexibility for the individual learner*. London, UK: Routledge.

Utbildningsdepartementet. (1992). *Långt borta och mycket nära: En förstudie om svensk distansutbildning*. Stockholm, Sweden: Allmänna förlaget.

Vygotsky, L. S. (1934/1987). Thinking and speech (N. Minick, Trans.). In R. W. Rieber & A. S. Carton (Eds.), *The collected works of L.S. Vygotsky, vol. 1: Problems of general psychology,* (pp. 39-285). New York, NY: Plenum.

Vygotsky, L. S. (1978). *Mind in society: The development of higher psychological processes*. Cambridge, MA: Harvard University Press.

Wisker, G., Robinson, G., & Shacham, M. (2007). Postgraduate research success: Communities of practice involving cohorts, guardian supervisors and online communities. *Innovations in Education and Teaching International*, *44*(3), 301–320. doi:10.1080/14703290701486720

Zhao, F. (2003). Transforming quality in research supervision: A knowledge-management approach. *Quality in Higher Education*, *9*(2), 187–197. doi:10.1080/13538320308149

ADDITIONAL READING

Acker, S., Hill, T., & Black, E. (1994). Thesis supervision in the social sciences: Managed or negotiated? *Higher Education, 28*(4), 483-498.

Anderson, C., Day, K., & McLaughlin, P. (2006). Mastering the dissertation: Lecturers' representations of the purposes and processes of Master's level dissertation supervision. *Studies in Higher Education, 31*(2), 149-168.

Anderson, C., Day, K., & McLaughlin, P. (2008). Student perspectives on the dissertation process in a masters degree concerned with professional practice. *Studies in Continuing Education, 30*(1), 33-49.

Barker, R. G. (1968). *Ecological Psychology*. Stanford, CA: Stanford University Press.

Bates, T. (2005). *Technology, e-learning and distance education* (2nd ed.). London, UK: RoutledgeFalmer.

Carlén, U., & Jobring, O. (2005). The rationale of online learning communities. *International Journal of Web Based Communities*, *1*(3), 272–295. doi:10.1504/IJWBC.2005.006927

Crossouard, B. (2008). Developing alternative models of doctoral supervision with online formative assessment. *Studies in Continuing Education*, *30*(1), 51–67. doi:10.1080/01580370701841549

Daniels, H., Cole, M., & Wertsch, J. V. (Eds.). (2007). *The Cambridge companion to Vygotsky*. New York, NY: Cambridge University Press.

Gibson, J. J. (1986). *The ecological approach to visual perception*. Hillsdale, NJ: Erlbaum.

Grant, B. M. (2005a). Fighting for space in supervision: Fantasies, fairytales, fictions and fallacies. *International Journal of Qualitative Studies in Education, 18*(3), 337–354. doi:10.1080/09518390500082483

Grant, B. M. (2005b). *The pedagogy of graduate supervision: Figuring the relations between supervisors and students*. Auckland, New Zealand: University of Auckland.

Grant, B. M. (2008). Agonistic Struggle: Master—slave dialogues in humanities supervision. *Arts and Humanities in Higher Education, 7*(1), 9–27. doi:10.1177/1474022207084880

Grant, B. M. (2009). Uneasy translations: Taking theories of supervision into teaching. *London Review of Education, 7*(2), 463–472. doi:10.1080/14748460902990385

Greenbank, P., & Penketh, C. (2009). Student autonomy and reflections on researching and writing the undergraduate dissertation. *Journal of Further and Higher Education, 33*(4), 463-472.

Hammick, M., & Acker, S. (1998). Undergraduate research supervision: A gender analysis. *Studies in Higher Education, 23*(3), 335–347. doi:10.1080/03075079812331380296

Heinze, A., & Heinze, B. (2009). Blended e-learning skeleton of conversation: Improving formative assessment in undergraduate dissertation supervision. *British Journal of Educational Technology, 40*(2), 294-305.

Källkvist, M., Gomez, S., Andersson, H., & Lush, D. (2009). Personalised virtual learning spaces to support undergraduates in producing research reports: Two case studies. *The Internet and Higher Education, 12*(1), 25–44. doi:10.1016/j.iheduc.2008.10.004

Ku, H., & Goh, S. (2010). Final year engineering projects in Australia and Europe. *European Journal of Engineering Education, 35*(2), 161–173. doi:10.1080/03043790903497336

Laurillard, D. (2009). The pedagogical challenges to collaborative technologies. *International Journal of Computer-Supported Collaborative Learning, 4*(1), 5–20. doi:10.1007/s11412-008-9056-2

Lee, A., & Green, B. (2009). Supervision as metaphor. *Studies in Higher Education, 34*(6), 615–630. doi:10.1080/03075070802597168

Mainhard, T., van der Rijst, R., van Tartwijk, J., & Wubbels, T. (2009). A model for the supervisor–doctoral student relationship. *Higher Education, 58*(3), 359–373. doi:10.1007/s10734-009-9199-8

Manathunga, C. (2007). Supervision as mentoring: The role of power and boundary crossing. *Studies in Continuing Education, 29*(2), 207–221. doi:10.1080/01580370701424650

Rogoff, B. (1990). *Apprenticeship in thinking: Cognitive development in social context*. New York, NY; Oxford, UK: Oxford University Press.

Rogoff, B. (2003). *The cultural nature of human development*. Oxford, UK: Oxford University Press.

Todd, M., Bannister, P., & Clegg, S. (2004). Independent inquiry and the undergraduate dissertation: Perceptions and experiences of final-year social science students. *Assessment & Evaluation in Higher Education, 29*(3), 335-355.

Todd, M., Smith, K., & Bannister, P. (2006). Supervising a social science undergraduate dissertation: Staff experiences and perceptions. *Teaching in Higher Education, 11*(2), 161-173.

Wenger, E. (1998). *Communities of practice: Learning, meaning, and identity*. Cambridge, UK: Cambridge University Press.

Wertsch, J. V. (1998). *Mind as action*. Oxford, UK: Oxford University Press.

Wertsch, J. V., del Rio, P., & Alvarez, A. (Eds.). (1995). *Sociocultural studies of mind*. Cambridge, UK: Cambridge University Press.

KEY TERMS AND DEFINITIONS

Dialogue: In this chapter communication is discussed in terms of being a dialogical process. In dialogues cultural, ecological, historical, and social aspects bind participants to each other and the surrounding environment.

Educational Settings: An educational setting involves the circumstances, locations, and time in which education occurs or develops.

Environment: In a transactional approach environment is seen as a non-dualistic feature of the world. Therefore this chapter treats it as a concept that is impossible to divide into different environments.

Group Work: A design principle used in the chapter. Here it should emphasize the development of and participation in a learning community.

Interactional Approach: An interactional approach embraces a dualistic world-view. Such approaches depart from the idea that it is possible to understand human action without reference to the surrounding environment. Such approaches could be inspired by ideas developed by, among others, cognitive or constructivist scholars. This chapter offers an alternative to the prevailing interactional approaches, a transactional approach.

Open and Public Exchange of Information: A design principle used in the chapter. This principle should underwrite information as a boundless feature of the educational design. This principle should allow students and supervisors to go beyond the application of one-to-one models in the practice of supervision.

Transactional Approach: A transactional approach embraces a non-dualistic world-view where human action is seen as inseparable from its surrounding environment. This means that to understand human action we need to reference cultural, ecological, historical, and social aspects. Such approaches could be inspired by ideas developed by, among others, pragmatist and sociocultural scholars.

Chapter 9
Authentic Tasks Online:
Two Experiences

Tel Amiel
Universidade Estadual de Campinas (UNICAMP), Brazil

Jan Herrington
Murdoch University, Australia

ABSTRACT

This chapter presents an exploration of the design and methods of two instantiations of authentic learning tasks in online learning environments. The first case employs a service learning orientation involving a distance learning project taught to students in four sites in two countries, while the second case is of a multimedia-based learning environment employing a scenario to engage students in realistic, simulated learning activities. The two approaches are examined through reference to characteristics of authentic tasks. The chapter demonstrates a range of possibilities for the instructor interested in more informed design of technology-based learning environments in higher education, and in particular, the design and creation of authentic learning tasks.

INTRODUCTION

The rise of internet-based education programs has lead to much concern over the quality of the courses offered online. Through learning management systems that model information-based modes of delivery, courses often revert to more transmissive modes (Beetham & Sharpe, 2007). Online learning has strongly perpetuated conventional expository methods of teaching. Many of the pitfalls of online instruction can be attributed to the faulty and somewhat regressive assumption that online courses could be taught following the same principles of face-to-face instruction (cf. Reeves, Herrington, & Oliver, 2004). Simply transferring content and form from one mode of teaching to the other has typically generated online courses where students learn *from* media as opposed to learning *with* them (Reeves, 1998). While learning *from* is not inherently negative, this paradigm has

DOI: 10.4018/978-1-61350-080-4.ch009

had a tendency to produce courses that copy more traditional, expository methods of instruction and presentation to online media.

BACKGROUND

The emphasis on learning *from* media in online classrooms has largely lead to unidirectional content transfer with limited student engagement. Traditional teaching often typifies passive students and fictitious content, scenarios and examples. In many online courses where students read, watch, and listen to a variety of media, they are denied the opportunity to engage with authentic contexts. Learning concepts (especially abstract concepts) is greatly dependent on context and experience (Gagné, 1984; Mezirow, 2000). Inquiry-based models such as those of project-based learning (Han & Bhattacharya, 2001) emphasize context, and focus on student activity and interaction. Providing authentic contexts for engagement in online environments can be quite difficult for teachers, especially when dealing with ill-defined problems. Nevertheless, much work has been done to leverage the potential of online environments in order to create authentic environments paying particular attention to context and audience (Reeves et al., 2004). Among these possibilities is the use of real-world scenarios in order to provide context and setting to meaningful engagement in an online setting.

Some academics contend that for a task to be authentic, it needs to be real. For example, Savery and Duffy (1996) nominated two guiding forces in developing problem-based scenarios: firstly, that the problems must raise the concepts and principles relevant to the content domain, and secondly that the problems must be real. However, research has provided principles to guide the development of realistic and complex learning environments that are not *real* but *cognitively real*, that is, the tasks that are created for students are not real tasks performed in a real workplace setting, but they are 'cognitively real' (Smith, 1986; 1987). Authentic tasks require the creation of real products and artefacts, and are more worthy of the investment of time and effort by students than decontextualised exercises and tasks.

TWO EXPERIENCES

In this chapter, we discuss these two alternatives to enhance the authenticity of the online classroom. First, we review an experiential e-learning model based on service-learning focused on pre-service teachers and multicultural education. Next, we describe a scenario-based model focused on mathematics and pre-service teachers. We finalize the chapter with a comparison of the two approaches based on the characteristics of authentic tasks. Our aim is to demonstrate a range of possibilities for the instructor interested in promoting authenticity in an online environment.

Experiential Learning: E-Service

Within the domain of education, pre-service teachers are usually involved in some form of experiential activity before graduating. The practicum is usually a sustained internship where students assist a more experience teacher to learn about the practice of teaching in an authentic context. This is but one type of experiential learning. It is a long-term and intense experience that occurs parallel to the academic environment. Opportunities such as this exist in other areas of study such as engineering or design, in the form of volunteer work or internships.

Furco (1996) provides a useful set of criteria to define experiential learning models, depending on the emphasis on service and/or learning, and who benefits from the service experience, the student and/or the community. *Volunteer* activities are those where students work for no financial benefit, for example, where students provide some of their time to a community organization such as a community library or a hospital. Here, the community benefits mostly from the time and efforts of the volunteer. An *internship* also places strong focus on service, but the benefit is mostly to the community or organization. For example, students interning at a newspaper agency would likely be assigned to simple, routine tasks in an effort to "get a feel" for the operation. Opportunities such as these occur parallel to academic courses, or after a degree is completed. In these cases, as with the practicum, academic learning is not connected to experiential activities.

An often-underutilized alternative to promoting authentic tasks and assessment is to expand the boundaries of the online classroom, by providing students with offline experiential learning. One possibility is to engage students in service-learning projects with authentic partners and tasks. The service-learning experience can be defined in cooperation with the student, provides tangible outcomes, and assessment can easily be negotiated with the service-learning partner (Densmore, 2000). Simply having an offline experiential activity does not guarantee the authenticity of the project. Defining the authenticity of the engagement is essential, in accordance with the student, course, and community goals.

Service-learning, has been a growing field of educational practice and inquiry. It began as an educational strategy focused on civic education and public service (Kenny & Gallagher, 2002). It is a particularly complex form of experiential learning. In its ideal state service-learning aims at mutuality between the community and students – learning and service are bi-directional. Howard (2003) identifies three essential features:

- service is provided in the community and is based on community needs,
- student academic skills are strengthened, and
- a commitment to civic participation, democratic citizenship, or social responsibility is evident.

Service-learning is a useful correlate to scenario-based environments in that it emphasizes the connection between academic learning *and* action. In the case of service-learning, engagement occurs as part of a structured learning environment. The benefit from engagement is mutual, and community experiences are valued as legitimate and valuable sources of knowledge, which are meant to provide a critical role in the learning process. At the same time, student service must be valuable to, and valued by, the local community. While the field is still young (Kenny & Gallagher, 2002), evidence is mounting towards the multiple positive outcomes of service-learning programs. Well designed programs have been shown to promote academic gains, as well as promoting affective, conative, and behavioral changes towards a more critical stance and commitment to social justice (Astin, Vogelgesang, Ikeda, & Yee, 2000; King, 2004; Kiely, 2005).

In higher education what constitutes a local community can vary. Many courses emphasize engagement for students acting in areas around campus; others act internationally connecting study abroad and service-learning programs. "International service-learning" (Kraft, 2002) opportunities displace the traditional service location to alternative contexts (see for example, Kiely, 2004). There are many benefits but also limitations to a wide adoption of this approach. One need only think of the costs associated with having both students and instructors travel abroad for a substantial amount of time.

An emerging field blending service-learning and distance education has been termed "e-service" (Strait & Sauer, 2004). The incorporation of service-learning programs into distance education can be done in multiple ways. It can be more easily organized in traditional online university courses where the instructor and students are co-located. More interestingly, service-learning can be incorporated to courses with a distributed student group, where learners/instructors are not closely situated. As universities and other institutions engage students from around the globe, service-learning can enrich student experiences by fostering local (from the perspective of the student) engagement, and can enhance coursework by incorporating example originating multiple contexts and cultures into discussions. In order to illustrate this model, we present a particularly complex program integrating service-learning and distance education across two countries and four different locations.

SERVICE AND DISTANCE: AN EXAMPLE

Four universities, two located in Brazil and two in the United States collaborated over a four-year period in an undergraduate exchange program[1]. Each year, for a period of one semester or longer, exchange students traveled abroad and took courses in educational technology and engaged in a service-learning program.

Students worked as partners with a public school teacher in the host country, visiting the school at least twice weekly during their stay. The objective of the program was to prepare pre-service teachers for a multicultural classroom through an authentic experience in a foreign classroom. In order to explore these issues, the students had one, long-term task to accomplish: design and implement a lesson plan in a local public school in partnership with a local school teacher, which would connect public schools across both nations (for further detail on the program and projects, see Amiel, McClendon, & Orey, 2007).

A major exchange, which we report here, involved 26 students simultaneously distributed across two countries and four distant locations. Final projects ranged from creating a student-led, school-based newspaper across four public schools, to fostering a bi-national video-exchange program. These were not simple projects, and students needed a substantial amount of support and scaffolding in order to engage.

Scaffolding and Sharing: Coursework

The course entitled *Multicultural Perspectives on Technology* (MPT) was designed as a seminar, meeting synchronously once weekly. The course was designed to scaffold students in all four locations (Ceará/São Paulo in Brazil and Utah/Georgia in the USA) through issues relating to culture, education, and technology, an intersection of increasing concern and interest (Amiel, 2008). These included concepts that were likely to emerge in interaction with school in another nation: race, religion, gender, nationality, language, disability, and others. The investigation of these topics was meant to provide students with complex, interacting, and systemic view of education and technology, mediated by socio-cultural factors (Amiel & Orey, 2011).

The MPT course was taught in tandem with a course focused on lesson plan design, taught at each institution by local faculty. Students were given guidelines to analyze, and asked to design, develop, implement, and evaluate a lesson plan. Every week a new topic was discussed and students were given time to engage in-group discussion in regards to how the topic would affect the design and implementation of their lesson plan and project. The service-learning experience both fueled discussion and functioned as a "laboratory" to investigate these concepts in the real environment of school.

The weekly meeting of the online course brought together a weeklong field experience by students in all four locations. Students in Brazil (from the USA) could exchange and confront their experiences with the Brazilian partners abroad (in the USA), and vice-versa. It was designed to be more than a forum for discussion and sharing – a sustained moment of mediated reflection on both abstract concepts such as religion and democracy, but also concrete action in their projects and conduct while abroad.

In designing the MPT course, our goal was to maximize the connection between academic learning and successful projects. In order to do so the course was permeated with field/experiential activities, which were intimately connected to both academic objectives *and* the overall service-learning project. These weekly assignments became experiential/field components to the readings and discussions in the online course.

One of the first course activities was focused on critical and multicultural education. Students were asked to devise a questionnaire (examples given) and interview their partner-teacher. The questionnaire aimed at identifying teacher beliefs and practices. Students prepared a report on their activity, including their observations, reflections on the outcomes of the interview, and the implications for their projects. The reports indicated that students created greater bonds with their teachers, had a better sense of teacher beliefs, and prompted them to reflect on how the teacher's perspectives would affect their project.

In order to examine the influence of socio-economic status (SES) on education and technology, undergraduate students visited a private and a public school in their host country, and took notes on human and physical resources. They briefly interviewed students, and questioned teachers and administrators. During the weekly meeting, students discussed these disparities and the potential impact of SES on lesson planning. They then discussed how their investigation would affect their semester-long projects in both countries.

When the course reached the subject of the relationship between religion and schooling, students were asked to visit a religious celebration (congregation, mass, meeting) that they had no familiarity with. In order to identify a celebration to attend, undergraduates were asked to talk to students in their service-learning classroom about their beliefs, and celebrations they attended. Our class was comprised of students of many faiths, including protestant, muslim, mormon, agnostic, and others. Though students were given the option to "opt out" of this assignment, none did so. This activity required no coordination by the professor. Activities such as these were organized to provide students incremental knowledge about their students, their beliefs, and the community at large. They were integrated to the classroom discussion. Once again, the activity promoted the integration of undergraduate students into the school community and was part of a larger, significant task.

As seen in the examples above, authentic tasks can take the form of immediate local action. Though students might be at a distance from the instructor and other students, a large number of experiential opportunities, such as service-learning, can be designed and integrated into an online course.

SCENARIO-BASED IMPLEMENTATION

The second case described in this chapter is a multimedia-based learning environment that uses a scenario of a classroom mathematics teacher exploring alternative assessment (Herrington, Sparrow, Herrington & Oliver, 1997). The program, entitled *Investigating Assessment Strategies in Mathematics Classrooms,* is designed for pre-service mathematics teachers, and it allows them to explore the use and theoretical dimensions of a range of different assessment techniques as an alternative to pencil and paper tests.

McLellan (1996) points out that an authentic context can be represented in a number of ways: the actual work setting, a highly realistic or 'virtual' surrogate of the actual work environment, or an anchoring context such as a video or multimedia program. *Investigating Assessment Strategies* is an example of an anchoring context, and it uses a scenario to anchor the students' activities as they use the program. Carroll (2000) describes scenario-based learning as displaying characteristics elements comprising: a setting, agents or actors, goals and objectives (held by agents), and a plot including actions and events. The scenario in the assessment program can be described as scenario-based learning only at the entry level of the task description, because it includes neither agents nor plot, except through the student's own identification with the teacher's task and the goals of the activity. It does, however, create a realistic place and context for the examination of assessment that is 'cognitively real' (Smith, 1986; 1987; Herrington, Reeves, & Oliver, 2007) rather than physically real.

The assessment program provides pre-service teachers with the experience of observing expert teachers using different types of assessment in classrooms. Students are also able to hear the teachers talk about why and under what conditions they used each particular strategy and to hear school children's comments on how they felt about them. They also have access to informed comment by experts and to the thoughts of other learners with varying degrees of skill. In effect, pre-service teachers using the program are able to investigate assessment strategies by observing experienced teachers in the field demonstrating a range of strategies and techniques, and then reflecting on the most appropriate strategy to use in a particular situation.

Movie files of classroom scenes and interviews are used to provide such opportunities to the students who use the program. Bransford, Vye, Kinzer and Risko (1990) advocated the use of visual elements such as movie clips because they provide a much richer source of information. Gestures and affective elements accompanying the dialogue means that there is much more to notice, and it is possible to find relevant issues which are embedded within the real-life context which might otherwise go unnoticed. Incorporating movie files into the program enables students to experience the classroom almost as if it were first hand, but without any of the inherent problems and dangers. Klein and Hoffman (1993) in a discussion on the development of expertise contended that exposing students to 'manufactured experiences' is one of the best ways to increase the development of perceptual-cognitive skills. They argued that computer technology is able to provide 'low-cost and high-fidelity' experiences that can speed the acquisition of expertise. The two important advantages of using computer-based material are firstly, that the technology allows the learners to sharpen their ability to discriminate by providing them with a number of situations that are similar but subtly different. Secondly, the student is able to practice on a wide variety of situations and configurations, which allows a better development of assessment skills, and to 'quickly size up a situation' (p. 217).

The context of the learning environment needed to be situated in a simulated classroom, and to provide multiple perspectives on assessment, and in so doing, focus strongly on the classroom experience. On this basis, the elements included in the design of the program were 23 different types of assessment appropriate to mathematics, each comprising:

- *Movie clips of teachers using various assessment techniques* within their classrooms with original sound, in order to show an authentic example of particular assessment strategies being used in a real classroom;
- *Movie clips of teachers' comments on the strategies*, to present the teachers' own reflections on the strengths and weaknesses of each approach;
- *Movie clips of children's comments on the strategies* to present their own feelings and thoughts, and whether they liked and disliked each approach;
- *Interviews* with experts in the field to provide theoretical perspectives;
- *Reflections by third year pre-service teachers* to provide practical advice from the perspective of students whose experience is only slightly more advanced than the students who would use the resource;

- *Text descriptions* of each assessment category to provide a simple description of each strategy together with practical advice on its implementation;
- *Teacher and children work samples* to enable students to scrutinize work presented in the scenarios;
- *Problems and investigations* to enable the students to examine the resource within authentic tasks.

The interface of the program simulates the front part of a classroom with the resources located in full view: the movies are accessible on a television, and documents through a clearly labeled filing cabinet; tasks are on the desk. The students access each resource by clicking on the appropriate part of the picture.

Five authentic and complex investigations are provided for students to replicate the kind of task a mathematics teacher might be faced with in real life. The tasks are presented to the student realistically, such as in a memo or letter, rather than simply a list of possible activities, and they include realistic constraints such as deadlines and available resources. For example, one task asks teachers to create a new plan for assessment of mathematics in a school after a parent complains that the sole use of pencil and paper tests is making home life difficult because of the nervousness of the child before each test. Activities assume that students will be working in pairs or small groups, and require them to examine the resource from a variety of perspectives. The investigations can be assigned to students by the teacher to ensure an appropriate representation of topics, or students can choose their own topics. The resource also provides the opportunity for students to design their own investigations. The Cognition and Technology Group at Vanderbilt (1990) contends that such student generation of tasks is beneficial for transfer to other activities.

A teacher's manual provides background on the theoretical framework on which the program was based and also to assist teachers to use the resource in a way most likely to optimize student learning, such as:

- *Length of Time:* Best used over a sustained period of 3-4 weeks rather than for a single session
- *Number of Students:* Students working in pairs or small groups around each computer, rather than individually
- *Teacher Support:* Teacher present during use to provide 'scaffolding' and support, rather than as an independent study activity
- *Setting the Task:* Teacher demonstrates the resource by thinking-aloud as an investigation is modeled. Students then choose an investigation from those provided, or their own choice.

The learning promoted by the assessment program is not the kind that could be packaged and used as a self-contained finished product; it needed to be 'reinvented from location to location' depending on the needs and interests of the learners (Brown & Campione, 1994). Similarly, a diverse array of products result rather than a single correct response to the problem.

A four phase study researching the program and its use with pre-service teachers (Herrington & Oliver, 2000; Herrington, Herrington, & Sparrow, 2000) suggests that the authentic learning model was a successful alternative to the system models frequently used for the development of multimedia programs, and one that enabled students to freely navigate a complex resource. When implemented as recommended, it appeared to provide an effective environment for the acquisition of advanced knowledge. Students used a substantial amount of higher-order thinking, relatively little social and lower order talk, and a moderate amount of procedural talk as they worked with the assessment program. While on their professional practice in schools after using the program, the pre-service teachers used a variety of assessment techniques to assess children's learning, and they were able to speak knowledgably and confidently about the issue of assessment, supporting the view that they had incorporated their learning deeply into their cognitive structures. According to the beliefs of the students themselves, the learning environment appeared to influence the types of strategies they employed and their thinking about assessment as they taught mathematics and other classes during their professional practice.

This case describes the potential of scenario-based complex problems to engage students in a meaningful and realistic way, not by providing experience in real situations and work-place settings, but by giving the opportunity to think and respond as a professional would when faced with realistic problems.

COMPARING TWO ALTERNATIVES

The examples above demonstrate two among many methods that allow for the integration of distance education with local action. We compare and contrast the scenario-based and service-learning models described above using the ten characteristics of authentic tasks developed by Herrington, Oliver and Reeves (2003). Our objective is to expand on the benefits—and also the drawbacks—of these models in order to provide a guide for those interested in enhancing distance education with authentic tasks:

1. *Authentic tasks have real world relevance.* Well-constructed service-learning (SL) programs are oriented towards immediate action within the community. The relationship between what is learned and what is practiced is contextualized in local action, not an envisioned reality. It promotes individualized "relevance" since students apply it to local context. The use of scenarios can provide tasks that would be difficult to spontaneously replicate in the real world – critical incidents, extraneous situations, which might not arise in day-to-day but constitute important skills to acquire.
2. *Authentic tasks are ill-defined, requiring students to define tasks and sub-tasks needed to complete the activity.* By designs, SL implies a negotiation between student and community on what task is to be accomplished. The framework imposed by the learning objectives of the course must be clear but also flexible. The complexity of real-world tasks can be overwhelming and unpredictable, for both the teacher and students. Setting where service takes place must be selected carefully to allow the learner to become a real contributor as opposed to a mere spectator (i.e., internship models). Scenarios define the task based on real-world settings and provide multiple, rich resources and the means to find and select additional resources to investigate the task. Because they provide a representation of reality, they may provide a better scaffold to the complexity of the real-world application.
3. *Authentic tasks comprise complex tasks to be investigated by students over a sustained period of time.* SL programs must be designed to be long term as opposed to simple trials or visits to school. In both SL and scenarios, task planning, support, and scaffolding are necessary to sustain the completion of the task.
4. *Authentic tasks provide the opportunity for students to examine the task from different perspectives, using a variety of resources.* Multiple perspectives are implicit in SL programs through interactions with stakeholders (student, peer, instructor, and community perspectives tend to vary widely). Many events and experiences that will inform task outcome are uncontrollable by the instructor. SL provides the context and perspectives of both scripted and unscripted engagement and the opportunities to reflect on these ex-

periences. Complex scenario-based courses provide resources that are multiple and varied. The scenario might limit the realism of spontaneous associations and interactions. If students are in varied physical locations, the scenarios might not reflect culturally appropriate or meaningful experiences, and producing resources and scenarios for each context may be costly and time-consuming.

5. *Authentic tasks provide the opportunity to collaborate.* Collaboration is implicit in service through student-community relationships – the task simply cannot be accomplished without collaboration. Because action is mostly located in the real world, rather than the virtual environment, group work between students located in different locations is complex and demands great facilitation skills by the instructor. In both SL and scenario design, collaboration occurs in project planning, problem-solving, and sharing concerns and ideas from the field in the virtual environment. With planning, the online environment provides a series of possibilities for synchronous and asynchronous collaborative opportunities across time and place.
6. *Authentic tasks provide the opportunity to reflect.* Though students tend to reflect on their experiences, in SL there is generally a call for meaningful reflection to be fostered by the instructor through activities and discussions related to the task and objectives of the program. Using scenarios, reflection is fostered through a complex authentic task that requires decisions to be made and collaboration, so that students can reflect as a social process, without specific prompts.
7. *Authentic tasks can be integrated and applied across different subject areas and lead beyond domain specific outcomes.* In SL students have to negotiate their activity and participation both in the beginning and at every step during their participation. Scenario designs with complex tasks demand planning for an integrated approach including diverse resources.
8. *Authentic tasks are seamlessly integrated with assessment.* SL has an element of accountability beyond the classroom environment. The student must make a commitment to the instructor and the community (local teacher, for example) based on clear objectives set collaboratively. Expectations must be clear since outcomes can vary significantly and constraints might emerge. Scenario-based assessment provides higher levels of authenticity, as there is always a product that is assessed. This can promote creative (though not unreal) outcomes, which are not constrained by the unpredictable constraints of the real world.
9. *Authentic tasks create polished products valuable in their own right rather than as preparation for something else.* Both learning designs demand a polished final product that is valuable in its own right and demonstrates learning. SL demands a finished product/process to be implemented, however, a product from a scenario may or may not be implemented in a real-world context.
10. *Authentic tasks allow competing solutions and diversity of outcome.* In SL distance students will act in different settings, producing distinct outcomes. This is especially the case when students in the course are from different locations and the contexts of application vary. Because the settings and context vary substantially, there is no accounting for the *exact* outcomes of each student project and success must be measured accordingly. In both, the task must permit flexible outcomes to be judged as equally valid, and the assessment must be designed to account for this.

FUTURE RESEARCH DIRECTIONS

As traditional (and non-traditional) students and institutions incorporate online learning into their educational programs, exploring methods for authentic engagement becomes critical.

The integration of service-learning can provide an opportunity to engage in authentic tasks, enriching the online course itself through the contextual experiences of local engagement. More interestingly, with the rise of open courses (P2PU[2], among others), service-learning can provide an opportunity towards the personalization of learning experiences. This is an opportunity for students and a viable challenge for instructors. The multiplicity and indeterminacy of partnerships and projects can provide an interesting feedback loop to course designers and instructors, who can evaluate their courses based on how well they respond to varied contexts and situations. Instructors can provide students with reasonable autonomy to find service partners of interest. Service and partner-finding guidelines can be provided to students, who in turn are asked to identify and make a commitment to a local partner and project. Similar opportunities and challenges exist for scenario-based models. One can highlight the challenges of designing scenarios for a diverse and distant student base (see Amiel, Squires, & Orey, 2009), but also the opportunities that such diversity provides in terms of solutions and perspectives to the challenges presented by the scenario, many times not envisioned by the instructor (an interesting feedback loop).

This remains a developing field, for both experiential and scenario-based implementations. There is potential to grow as existing/formal and new/informal educational institutions spread their course offerings to an increasingly diverse student population. The multiplicity of variables and contexts will demand research to identify effective and informed "designs" (Amiel & Reeves, 2008) using varied tools, pedagogical methods, and configurations which designers and instructors can use in developing their own tasks.

CONCLUSION

The two models described here are presented as a means to demonstrate the range of possibilities available to those interested in promoting more authentic online learning environments. Whether through a virtual scenario based on real-world cases, or through immediate application through service-learning, students can engage in complex activities in collaboration with their peers. This is by no means a use of the online environment solely to promote more efficient or cost-effective learning. The use of internet-based tools is used in both cases as a tool in the design of a learning environment, providing unique and exciting possibilities. These include the use of multiple realistic scenarios and cases to be investigated by the students, and varied avenues for discussion and reflection for students at transnational distance. The two learning designs described here are by no means the only design alternatives for authentic tasks in online environments, nor are they mutually exclusive. Scenarios could be incorporated into experiential courses, whether they follow a service-learning model, or other methods such as on the job training, or volunteer activities.

The online platform provides exciting new avenues for the development of complex and authentic learning environments. Many educators still attempt to design online courses that closely match the face-to-face experience, ignoring the characteristics and innovative facilities of the new environment. What is needed is a critical analysis of available tools to promote a learning environment, which engages students in complex tasks and meaningful learning activities.

REFERENCES

Amiel, T. (2008). Interculturalidad y TICs: Una relación cíclica. In S. F. d. Amaral, F. G. Gracía & A. M. Rivilla (Eds.), *Aplicaciones educaivas y nuevos lenguajes de las TIC* (pp. 193-206). Campinas, SP: UNICAMP.

Amiel, T., McClendon, J., & Orey, M. (2007). A model for international collaborative development work in schools. *Educational Media International, 44*(2), 167–179. doi:10.1080/09523980701295182

Amiel, T., & Orey, M. (2011). A pedagogical model for abstract concepts: Blending discourse and experience. In Shaughnessy, M. F., & Fulgham, S. (Eds.), *Pedagogical Models: The Discipline of Online Teaching*. Hauppauge, NY: NOVA Publishers.

Amiel, T., & Reeves, T. C. (2008). Design-based research and educational technology: Rethinking technology and the research agenda. *Journal of Educational Technology & Society, 11*(4), 29–40.

Amiel, T., Squires, J., & Orey, M. (2009). Four strategies for designing instruction for diverse cultures. *Educational Technology, 49*(6), 28–34.

Astin, A. W., Vogelgesang, L. J., Ikeda, E. K., & Yee, J. A. (2000). *How service learning affects students*. Los Angeles, CA: University of California.

Beetham, H., & Sharpe, R. (Eds.). (2007). *Rethinking pedagogy for a digital age*. London, UK: Routledge.

Bransford, J. D., Vye, N., Kinzer, C., & Risko, V. (1990). Teaching thinking and content knowledge: Toward an integrated approach. In Jones, B. F., & Idol, L. (Eds.), *Dimensions of thinking and cognitive instruction* (pp. 381–413). Hillsdale, NJ: Lawrence Erlbaum Associates.

Brown, A. L., & Campione, J. C. (1994). Guided discovery in a community of learners. In McGilly, K. (Ed.), *Classroom lessons: Integrating cognitive theory and classroom practice* (pp. 229–270). Cambridge, MA: MIT Press.

Carroll, J. (2000). Five reasons for scenario-based design. *Interacting with Computers, 13*(1), 43–60. doi:10.1016/S0953-5438(00)00023-0

Cognition and Technology Group at Vanderbilt. (1990). Anchored instruction and its relationship to situated cognition. *Educational Researcher, 19*(6), 2–10.

Densmore, K. (2000). Service learning and multicultural education. In O'Grady, C. R. (Ed.), *Integrating service learning and multicultural education in colleges and universities* (pp. 49–58). Mahwah, NJ: Lawrence Earlbaum and Associates.

Furco, A. (1996). *Service-learning: A balanced approach to experiential education. Expanding boundaries: Service and learning* (pp. 2–6). Washington, DC: The Corporation for National Service.

Gagné, R. M. (1984). *The conditions of learning* (4th ed.). New York, NY: Holt, Rinehart, and Winston.

Han, S., & Bhattacharya, K. (2001). *Constructionism, learning by design, and project-based learning*. Retrieved October 15, 2010, from http:// projects.coe.uga.edu/ epltt/

Herrington, A. J., Sparrow, R. L., Herrington, J., & Oliver, R. G. (1997). *Investigating assessment strategies in mathematics classrooms* [Book and CD-ROM]. Perth, Australia: MASTEC, Edith Cowan University.

Herrington, J., Herrington, A., & Sparrow, L. (2000). Learning to assess school mathematics: Context, multimedia and transfer. *Mathematics Teacher Education and Development, 2*, 75–94.

Herrington, J., & Oliver, R. (2000). An instructional design framework for authentic learning environments. *Educational Technology Research and Development*, *48*(3), 23–48. doi:10.1007/BF02319856

Herrington, J., Oliver, R., & Reeves, T. C. (2003). Patterns of engagement in authentic online learning environments. *Australian Journal of Educational Technology*, *19*(1), 59–71.

Herrington, J., Reeves, T. C., & Oliver, R. (2007). Immersive learning technologies: Realism and online authentic learning. *Journal of Computing in Higher Education*, *19*(1), 65–84. doi:10.1007/BF03033421

Herrington, J., Reeves, T. C., & Oliver, R. (2010). *A guide to authentic e-learning*. London, UK & New York, NY: Routledge.

Howard, J. (2003). Service-learning research: Foundational issues. In Billig, S. H., & Waterman, A. S. (Eds.), *Studying service-learning: Innovations in education research methodology* (pp. 1–12). Mahwah, NJ: Lawrence Erlbaum Associates.

Kenny, M. E., & Gallagher, L. A. (2002). Service learning: A history of systems. In Kenny, M. E., Simon, L. A. K., Kiley-Brabeck, K., & Lerner, R. M. (Eds.), *Learning to serve: Promoting civil society through service-learning* (pp. 15–30). Boston, MA: Kluwer.

Kiely, R. (2004). A chameleon with a complex: Searching for transformation in international service-learning. *Michigan Journal of Community Service Learning*, *10*(2), 5–20.

Kiely, R. (2005). A transformative learning model for service-learning: A longitudinal case study. *Michigan Journal of Community Service Learning*, *12*(1), 5–22.

King, J. T. (2004). Service-learning as a site for critical pedagogy: A case of collaboration, caring, and defamiliarization across borders. *Journal of Experiential Education*, *26*(3), 121–137.

Klein, G. A., & Hoffman, R. R. (1993). Seeing the invisible: Perceptual-cognitive aspects of expertise. In Rabinowitz, M. (Ed.), *Cognitive science foundations of instruction* (pp. 203–226). Hillsdale, NJ: Lawrence Erlbaum Associates.

Kraft, R. J. (2002). International service learning. In Kenny, M. E., Simon, L. A. K., Kiley-Brabeck, K., & Lerner, R. M. (Eds.), *Learning to serve: Promoting civil society through service-learning* (pp. 297–314). Boston, MA: Kluwer.

McLellan, H. (Ed.). (1996). *Situated learning perspectives*. Englewood Cliffs, NJ: Educational Technology Publications.

Mezirow, J. (2000). Learning to think like an adult: Core concepts of transformation theory. In Mezirow, J. (Ed.), *Learning as transformation*. San Francisco, CA: Jossey-Bass.

Reeves, T. C. (1998). *The impact of media and technology in schools*. Retrieved October 10, 2010, from http://it.coe.uga.edu/ ~treeves/ edit6900/ BertelsmannReeves98.pdf

Reeves, T. C., Herrington, J., & Oliver, R. (2004). A development research agenda for online collaborative learning. *Educational Technology Research and Development*, *52*(4), 53–63. doi:10.1007/BF02504718

Savery, J. R., & Duffy, T. M. (1996). Problem based learning: An instructional model and its constructivist framework. In Wilson, B. G. (Ed.), *Constructivist learning environments: Case studies in instructional design* (pp. 135–148). Englewood Cliffs, NJ: Educational Technology Publications.

Smith, P. E. (1986). *Instructional simulation: Research, theory and a case study*. ERIC Document Reproduction No. (ED 267 793).

Smith, P. E. (1987). Simulating the classroom with media and computers. *Simulation & Games, 18*(3), 395–413. doi:10.1177/104687818701800306

Strait, J., & Sauer, T. (2004). Constructing experiential learning for online courses: The birth of e-service. *EDUCAUSE Quarterly, 27*(1).

ADDITIONAL READING

Annette, J. (2002). Service learning in an international context. *Frontiers: The Interdisciplinary Journal of Study Abroad, VIII*. Retrieved from http://www.frontiersjournal.com/ issues/ vol8/ vol8-01_annette.htm

Bingle, R. G. (2003). Enhancing theory-based research on service-learning. In Billig, S. H., & Eyler, J. (Eds.), *Deconstructing service-learning: Research exploring context, participation, and impacts* (pp. 3–21). Greenwich, CT: Information Age.

Brown, J. S., Collins, A., & Duguid, P. (1989). Situated cognition and the culture of learning. *Educational Researcher, 18*(1), 32–42.

Choi, J., & Hannafin, M. (1995). Situated cognition and learning environments: Roles, structures and implications for design. *Educational Technology Research and Development, 43*(2), 53–69. doi:10.1007/BF02300472

Densmore, K. (2000). Service learning and multicultural education. In O'Grady, C. R. (Ed.), *Integrating service learning and multicultural education in colleges and universities* (pp. 49–58). Mahwah, NJ: Lawrence Earlbaum and Associates.

Eyler, J., & Giles, D. (1999). *Where's the learning in service-learning?* San Francisco: Jossey-Bass.

Grusky, S. (2000). International service learning: A critical guide from an impassionate advocate. *The American Behavioral Scientist, 43*(5), 858–867. doi:10.1177/00027640021955513

Guthrie, K. L., & McCracken, H. (2010). Teaching and learning social justice through online service-learning courses. *The International Review of Research in Open and Distance Education, 11*(3).

Herrington, A., & Herrington, J. (2007). What is an authentic learning environment? In Tomei, L. A. (Ed.), *Online and distance learning: Concepts, methodologies, tools, and applications* (pp. 68–76). Hershey, PA: Information Science Reference. doi:10.4018/978-1-59904-935-9.ch008

Herrington, J., & Oliver, R. (2000). An instructional design framework for authentic learning environments. *Educational Technology Research and Development, 48*(3), 23–48. doi:10.1007/BF02319856

Kahne, J., & Westheimer, J. (1996). In the service of what? The politics of service learning. *Phi Delta Kappan, May*, 317-323.

Lave, J., & Wenger, E. (1991). *Situated learning: Legitimate peripheral participation*. Cambridge: Cambridge University Press.

Lombardi, M. M. (2007). Approaches that work: How authentic learning is transforming higher education. *ELI Report No 5. Boulder, CO: EDUCAUSE Learning Initiative*.

Lombardi, M. M. (2007). Authentic learning for the 21st century: An overview. *ELI Report No. 1. Boulder, CO: EDUCAUSE Learning Initiative*.

Lowery, D., May, D. L., Duchane, K. A., Coulter-Kern, R., De'Bryant, Morris, P. V., Pomery, J. G., Bellner, M. (2006). A logic model of service-learning: Tensions and issues for further consideration. *Michigan Journal of Community Service Learning* (Spring), 47-60.

McLellan, H. (Ed.). (1996). *Situated learning perspectives*. Englewood Cliffs, NJ: Educational Technology Publications.

Newmann, F. M., & Wehlage, G. (1993). Five standards of authentic instruction. *Educational Leadership*, *50*(7), 8–12.

Petraglia, J. (1998). *Reality by design: The rhetoric and technology of authenticity in education*. Mahwah, NJ: Lawrence Erlbaum Associates.

Porter, M., & Monard, K. (2001). Ayni in the global village: Building relationship of reciprocity through international service-learning. *Michigan Journal of Community Service Learning*, *8*(1), 5–17.

Rhoads, R. A., & Howard, J. (1998). *Academic service learning: a pedagogy of action and reflection*. San Francisco: Jossey-Bass Publishers.

Wilson, J. R., & Schwier, R. A. (2009). Authenticity in the process of learning about instructional design. *Canadian Journal of Learning and Technology*, *35*(2). Retrieved from http://www.cjlt.ca/ index.php/ cjlt/ article/ view/ 520/ 253.

Woo, Y., Herrington, J., Agostinho, S., & Reeves, T. C. (2007). Implementing authentic tasks in web-based learning environments. *EDUCAUSE Quarterly*, *30*(3), 36–43.

KEY TERMS AND DEFINITIONS

Authentic Task: A realistic, but not necessary real, learning activity that requires thinking and acting in ways required in real-world tasks.

Authentic Learning Environment: A learning setting that provides students with tasks, resources and supports to enable the creation of realistic, collaborative and polished products.

e-Service: A blend of service-learning and distance-learning programs, allowing non co-located learners to participate in local (to the learner) service-learning opportunities.

International Service-Learning: Service-learning opportunities which extend beyond the national borders (for the learner).

Service-Learning: Experiential approaches to education with a balance between service activities and learning opportunities where both the learner and the community benefit from the proposed task or project.

Scenario: A contextualized description of a problem in a realistic setting that requires exploration of a solution.

Scaffolding: In an educational sense, the metacognitive support provided by the teacher, students, professionals and others, together with relevant resources, to assist the learning process.

ENDNOTES

1 This project is sponsored in part by the Fund for the Improvement of Postsecondary Education (FIPSE), U.S. Department of Education and the Coordenação de Aperfeiçoamento de Pessoal de Nível Superior (CAPES) in Brazil.

2 P2PU is an example in the open education movement, describing itself as "an online community of open study groups for short university-level courses." See http://www.p2pu.org

Section 3
Emerging Educational Technologies

The last ten years has seen an increase of available educational technologies, technologies becoming more and more advanced and offering greater possibilities for innovative educational activities than ever before. In this section, some of these emerging educational technologies and practices are presented. Throughout the included chapters it is stressed that teaching and learning in higher education but must be supported by informed design and use of available technologies.

Chapter 10
Designing for Learning in Computer-Assisted Health Care Simulations

Lars O. Häll
Umeå University, Sweden

Tor Söderström
Umeå University, Sweden

ABSTRACT

This chapter is about designing for learning in educational computer-assisted simulations (ECAS) in health care education (HCE). This is an area in need of an informed educational framework for analysis and design, on a research level as well as on a practice level. Drawing upon the works of Luckin (2008, 2010), an Ecology of Resources framework is proposed, which, informed by experiences from the research field (Gaba, 2004; Issenberg et al., 2005), can support researchers as well as practitioners in analyzing and designing health care simulations. Using this framework, we will discuss original empirical data from two studies from the Learning Radiology in Simulated Environments project, and more specifically how changes in design, or adjustments to the Ecology of Resources, impact the simulation process. Data include video-recorded observations of collaborative simulation training, a student questionnaire directly after training and later follow-up interviews. We will illustrate the usefulness of the framework and point out some challenges and suggestions for future development and research.

INTRODUCTION

This chapter will address a challenge central to the research field of learning in educational computer-assisted simulations (ECAS) in higher education: the need for an informed educational framework for analysis and design. In order to further enhance teaching and learning with ECAS in health care education (HCE), such a framework is needed as a complement to the often empirically strong but theoretically limited research which currently seems to be dominating health care research on this topic.

DOI: 10.4018/978-1-61350-080-4.ch010

We will propose Luckin's *Ecology of Resources* model of learner context (Luckin, 2008, 2010) as one possible framework, but we note that when applying this model to the field of health care ECAS, there are relevant experiences from this field that can be used to inform it. We will primarily draw upon the empirical research review work of Issenberg *et al.* (2005) as well as Gaba's (2004) conceptualization of health care simulation applications. This will lead us to focus on the resources, decided by features as well as uses of simulator technology, that are available to learners in a given ECAS training and on the interactions between resources and simulation process and outcomes.

In addition to sketching out this informed framework for analysis and design of health care ECAS, we will apply it to two studies performed within the Learning Radiology in Simulated Environments project and present a modest contribution of original empirical data. Using the framework, we will illustrate how changes in design, or in the Ecology of Resources, impact aspects of the simulation process, and how adjustments can be made to the ecology to enhance teaching and learning.

We begin by introducing, through the background section, the topic of ECAS in health care education and the limitations of current research, followed by an introduction to the research and development project within which the chapter's empirical data were produced. The next section, informing analysis and design of health care simulation, introduces Luckin's Ecology of Resources model, tunes it to the health care ECAS field through Gaba (2004) and Issenberg *et al.* (2005), and applies the tuned model to our own studies. The methodical issues related to the empirical data are dealt with in the methodical concerns section and the empirical results are presented in Learning radiology—Empirical findings. We finish off by discussing the usefulness of the framework and future research directions.

BACKGROUND

Health care education seems to be in transition and to be facing new challenges in terms of design for learning. It has been stated that medical education, or parts of it, should and is undergoing a paradigm shift from an educational model focused on learning through clinical practice to a model focusing more on documented expertise before clinical practice (Aggarwal & Darzi, 2006; Debas *et al.,* 2005; Luengo *et al.*, 2009). A central cause is decreased opportunities for clinical training on patients, a tendency which is also true for nurse education (Tanner, 2004). Reasons include, but are not limited to, changes in practitioner mobility, altered patient expectations, the Bologna Accord and new forms of governance of training (Luengo *et al.,* 2009, s.105). With decreasing opportunities for students to gain clinical experience from training on actual patients, educational computer-assisted simulation alternatives are spreading (Issenberg *et al.*, 2005; Nehring, 2009). These tools are designed to allow students to develop, and educators to evaluate, competence, proficiency or expertise on tasks (such as radiological diagnosis or intravenous catheter placement) prior to performance on actual patients (Aggarwal & Darzi, 2006). This type of training is characterized by model-based imitation of clinical practice.

Simulations are, generally speaking "the technique of imitating the behaviour of some situation and process...by means of a suitably analogous situation or apparatus" (Simulation, n.d.). Simulations will have some framework in the shape of a spatial and temporal context, starting positions, aims, means, agents and time where the agents have more or less influence over the process. Educational simulations have the overarching aim of developing participants' competence in relation to what is imitated. Computer-assisted simulations will require more or less direct interaction with computer software. Within the field of health care education, there is a wide range of simulations applied within a wide range of subject domains, varying on a range of dimensions including technology (e.g., PC and mannequin), type of competence (e.g., cognitive, communicative and psycho-motor), participants (e.g., number and profession) etc. (Bradley, 2006; Gaba, 2004; Lane *et al.*, 2001; Nehring, 2009).

New educational tools have a tendency to produce high expectations regarding their intrinsic contribution to learning (Cuban, 2001; Dillenbourg *et al.*, 2009), or in other words, 'hype'. Even though the research community on ECAS seems to be cautiously positive about its general potential, research has shown that the specifics of the technology and how it is used affect the outcome of learning. Studies on ECAS outside the health care education niche have shown that minor, informed design revisions and additions to the tools can change its impact on process and learning (e.g., Chandler & Chaille, 1993; Chang *et al.*, 2008; Hulshof & de Jong, 2006; Swaak *et al.*, 2008; Trey & Samia, 2008; Windschitl & Andre, 1998). Studies have also indicated that ECAS are effective in some cases and less in others and that they are impacted by contextual and educational conditions such as the quality of the introductions (Winberg & Hedman, 2008), participant experiences (Tao & Gunstone, 1999), group characteristics (Schoenecker *et al.*, 1997) etc. However, even though the impact of designable *features and uses* of health care simulations, such as educational feedback, are discussed within the health care research literature (Issenberg *et al.*, 2005), it seems to be quite rare that the impact of these features and uses actually is at the center of the empirical attention in previous research, which instead often relies on measuring the impact of simulation training on competence or comparing it to 'conventional alternatives' (e.g., Agazio *et al.*, 2002; Ahlberg *et al.*, 2002; Ashurst *et al.*, 1996; Kothari *et al.*, 2002; O'toole *et al.*, 1999).

A significant contribution to the field of learning through educational simulations can be made by focusing research not on comparing different media but instead on developing and tuning techniques for their application. As has been stated by researchers on technology-enhanced learning, we need to investigate *under which designable conditions a certain technique is beneficial for learning* (Dillenbourg *et al.*, 2009). However, it is important that designability does not ignore the specifics of the technology itself. To inform design of simulation learning, we need to focus on understanding how *interactions between technology features and technology uses impact simulation outcomes*. Such a focus will be illustrated in this chapter. In order to achieve this, we will draw upon two studies on ECAS training within health care education. By comparing the features and uses of these simulation trainings, we will discuss how the interaction between features and uses impacts process and outcomes. After introducing the research and development project from which the empirical data is drawn, we will suggest a theoretically informed framework which can support this discussion and which can function as a framework for analysis and design of learning in ECAS in health care education.

Learning Radiology in Simulated Environments

Within the Learning Radiology in Simulated Environments (LRiSE) project, a joint, three-year research and development project including education and health care researchers from the universities of Umeå and Stanford, several studies were performed on learning with a screen-based radiological virtual reality (VR) simulation (Häll *et al.*, 2009; Häll *et al.*, in press; Nilsson, 2007; Nilsson *et al.*, 2006; Söderström *et al.*, 2008). Radiological examination is an example of the general health care education development tendency described above, where training on patients is reduced due to the risks associated with excessive exposure to x-ray radiation and simulation has been put forward as an alternative.

Educators using this simulation will want to design the conditions of its application to enhance its contribution to students' learning without losing sight of the practical reality of their educational practice with its limited resources. We have performed empirical studies of students' learning about principles of radiological examinations under different educational designs—initially, in a more experimental context and later as an integral part of a part of a university program course. It was during the latter integration of the simulation into the curriculum that the design issues discussed in this chapter were raised. In this chapter, we will draw upon original data from two such studies.

The basic scenario is common for both studies: we let students work collaboratively with the simulation during one session, we observe the collaboration using a digital video (DV) camera and we let students comment on the experience in survey and follow-up interviews.

The Radiology Simulator

The simulator used in both studies drawn upon here is basically a standard PC equipped with simulation software, illustrated in Figures 1-3. It has two monitors, one representing a three-dimensional anatomical model, X-ray tube and film, and the other representing two-dimensional X-ray images. The control peripherals used for interaction include a standard keyboard and mouse as well as a special pen-like mouse device and a roller-ball mouse.

Using the simulator, the students can perform real-time radiographic examinations of a patient's jaw (Figure 1) or cervical spine (Figure 2 and Figure 3), which is one of the examinations studied and practiced in respective courses. It allows the user to position the three-dimensional model of the patient, the X-ray tube and the film. X-ray images can then be 'exposed' at will by students and immediately presented by the simulator as geometrically correct radiographs rendered from the positions of the models. Exercises have been developed for the simulator including replication of standard views and replication of incorrect views. It is also possible to view the two-dimensional X-ray image change in real-time as the model is manipulated and experiment in an improvised manner.

Same Technology, Different Design

Even though the same simulator or *feature/tools*, albeit with different part of the body modeled, was used in both studies, the *uses* were varied.

Both LRiSE studies were concerned with learning radiological diagnosis through simulation. The first case, the dentistry jaw case, was a bit more experimental, with simulation being a voluntary extra-curricular activity in connection with a course on oral and maxillofacial radiology. Also, the triad-groups in which the students worked were created by teachers by drawing lots. A total of 18 students participated in a one-hour, teacher-led simulation session. The original research aim was to evaluate the impact of simulation training. The second case, the nurse spine case, was more practice-oriented, with simulation being integrated into the curriculum and participation being obligatory. The overall research aim was to support the 12 students' learning during a clinical training course. In addition to curriculum integration, a few things distinguish the nurse case from the dentistry case. In order to support collaboration, we enabled students to choose partners with whom to work (instead of randomization) during the obligatory training session, reduced group size to two and removed the teacher supervision from the session. We also increased the duration of the simulation, from one hour to two hours, and

Figure 1. Illustration of a Dentistry student working with the radiological VR simulator, jaw model

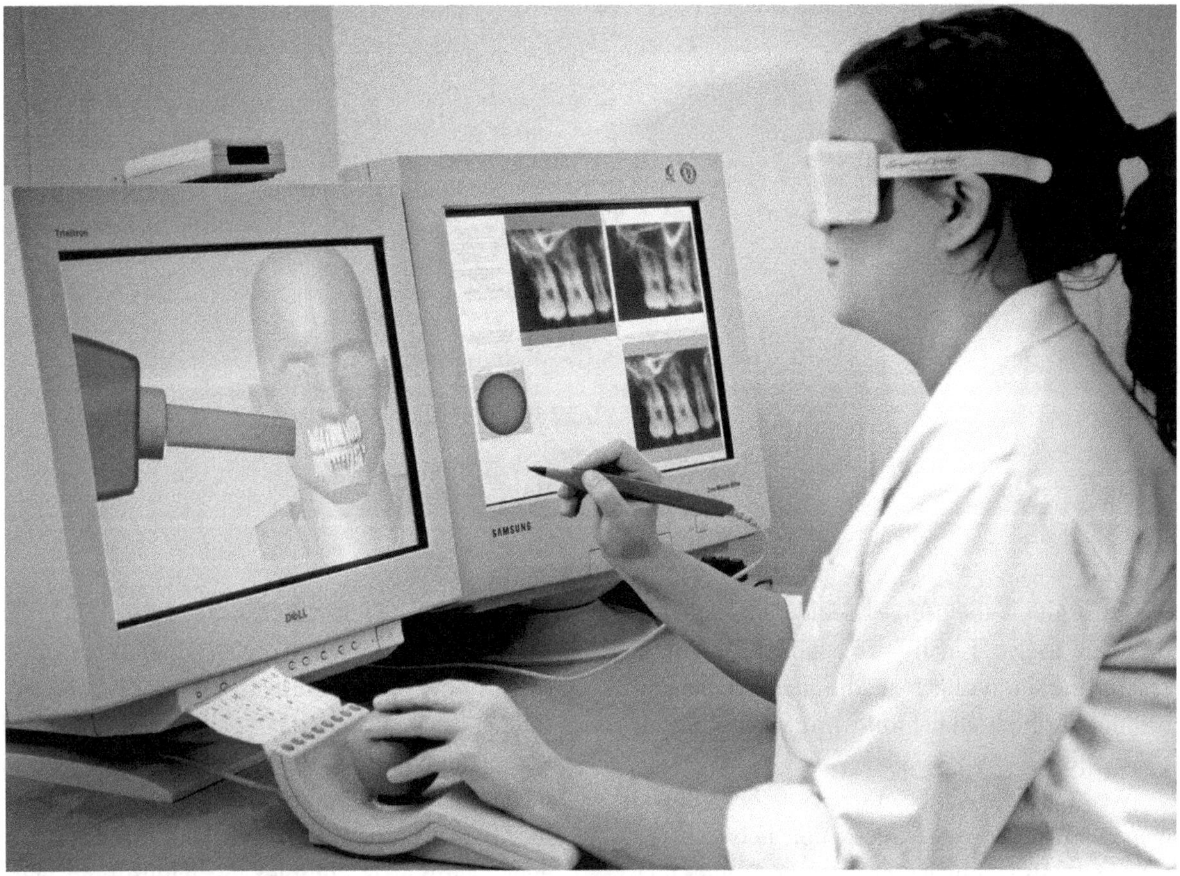

Figure 2. Photo of the VR simulator screens, spine model

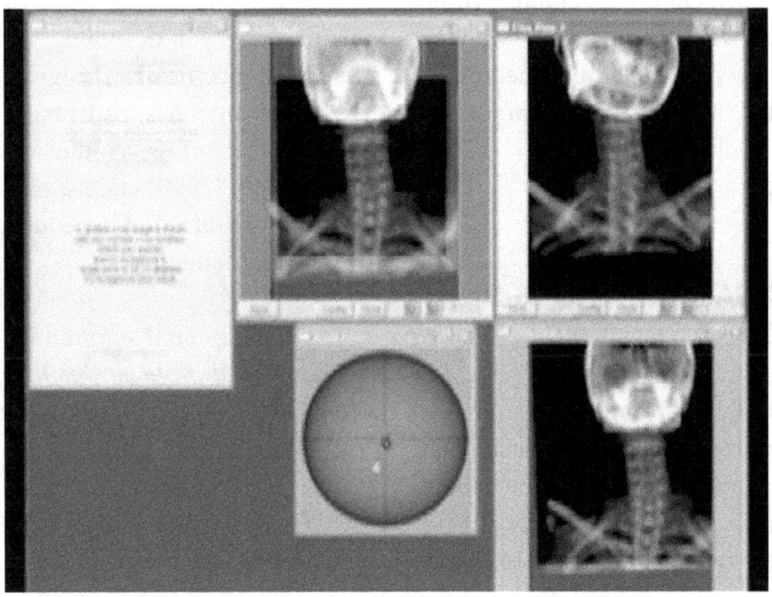

Figure 3. Photo of the VR simulator screens, spine model

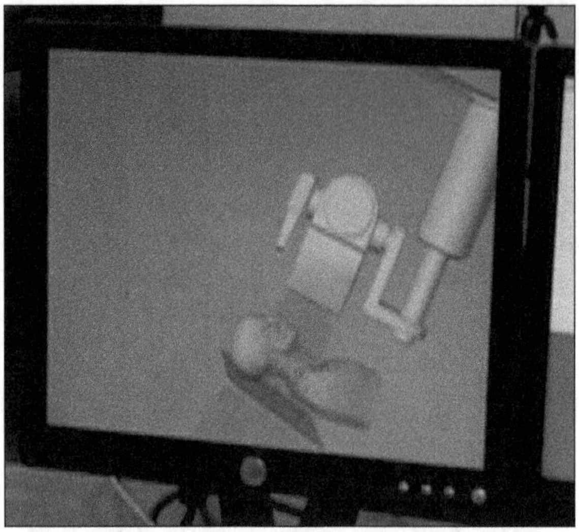

we let students themselves decide how much of this time to use. Finally, we enabled students to reserve the simulation for additional, independent training throughout the following weeks of clinical training.

We will discuss the impact of these design changes, and how the interaction between features and uses impact process and outcomes, in the remainder of the chapter. However, we want to inform this discussion by drawing upon educational theory and empirical findings within the field of learning with ECAS. In the following section, we will thus introduce the theoretical works of Luckin (2008, 2010) and simulation learning research works of Issenberg *et al.* (2005) and Gaba (2004).

INFORMING ANALYSIS AND DESIGN OF HEALTH CARE SIMULATION

Design issues can be approached in numerous ways, all with limits and benefits. Educational design is, from an overall point of view, about how to support learning in a particular case. It is a structural planned and reflexive attempt to enable learning. Goodyear (2005) talks about 'the set of practices involved in constructing representation of how to support learning' (p. 82); Wenger (1998) defines design as 'a systematic, planned and reflexive colonisation of time and space in the service of undertaking' (p. 228), undertaking in this context being support for learning. However, learning is complex by nature, and even though previous educational research on specific issues in other contexts or with other technologies does constitute a powerful resource, we need a framework for designing computer simulation training specifically. Design of computer-assisted training often has, as Cuban (2001) notes, a focus on technology as 'the activity creating tool'. Jaldemark (2010) claims, on the contrary, that in design of education the educational problem has to be highlighted.

To get an optimal solution we need focus on the educational problem. Such a problem might be how to secure high-level participation among the students. (p. 71)

Consequently, design issues need, as already mentioned, to consider contextual and educational conditions in which the interaction between the learner and her environment is in focus.

An Ecology of Resources Perspective

The Ecology of Resources model will be used as theoretical framework to map out the complexity of the design of ECAS training with respect to the complex nature of the learner's context (Luckin, 2008, 2010). The learners' context is the interactions between the learner and a set of interrelated resource elements that are not tied to a physical or virtual location. Context is something that belongs to an individual and that is created through his or her interactions in the world (Luckin, 2010). From an educational design perspective, then, different types of resources with which the learner interacts need to be identified and understood to enable opportunities for learning.

The model is focussed on the resource elements with which the learner simultaneously interacts (Figure 4). The resources available to the learner are called the zone of available assistance (ZAA). The ZAA forms the boundaries of the zone of proximal adjustment where productive activity could happen. However, whether the activity can be regarded as productive is based on the quality of the negotiation between the learner and, in Luckin's words, a more able partner (MAP).

The MAP is responsible for working with the learner to ensure that an optimal subset of resources from the ZAA is pulled together, so that the learner's interactions with this subset of resources form a ZPA centred on the needs of the learner (Luckin, 2010).

The quality is based on how well the need of the learner is met and on which scaffolding makes an important contribution. The Ecology of Resources model has its theoretical underpinning in Vygotsky's cultural theory and the tutorial assis-

Figure 4. The resource elements and their filters (Luckin, 2010, p. 94)

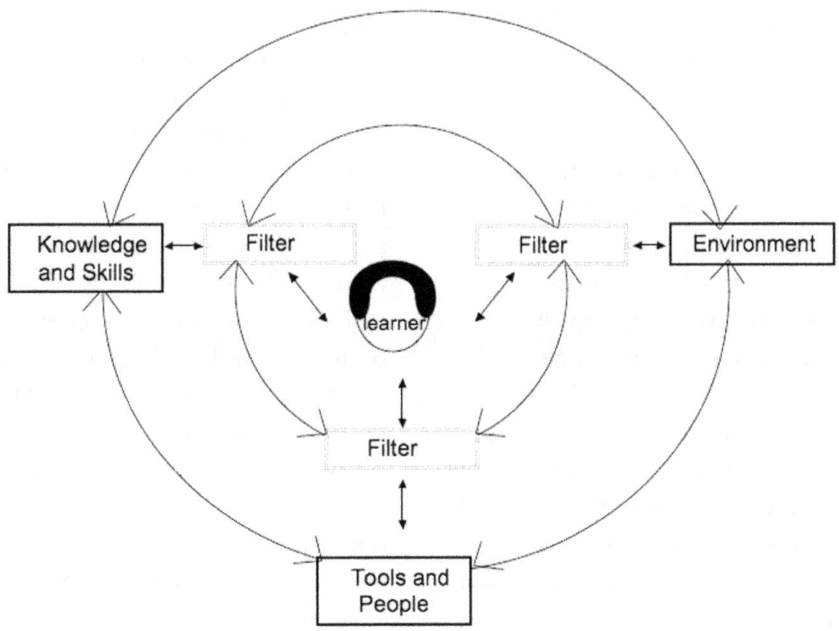

tance called scaffolding, which in Luckin's terms is the relation between more able partners and the learner's construction of a narrative that makes sense of the meanings distributed amongst these resources (Luckin, 2010; cf. Vygotsky, 1991).

Figure 4 illustrates that the learner interacts simultaneously with different resources. Luckin (2010) claims that all of the resources are interrelated and mutually involved in the learner's interaction with the resources that forms his or her context. Interaction on a general level implies interplay, a communicative process where groups or individuals by their actions have mutual influence on each other (Goffman, 1959; Mercer *et al.*, 2005) which Luckin also emphasizes: 'each element has an influence upon, and is influenced by, the element to which it is linked' (2010, p. 94).

One of the resource categories in the model is the knowledge and skills to be learned (e.g., principles of radiology). A second category of resource is tools and people. It includes but is not limited to artifacts such as a simulator and in formal education other people such as teachers and peer students. The last category in the model is environment, which includes the location and surrounding environment with which the learner interacts. In our case, the arguments will be based on students' interaction with a computer simulation in which both teachers and peer students are involved.

These resources are, however, filtered by elements like curriculum, organization and administration, which regulates the ways a learner interacts with a resource. The knowledge resources that subject domains such as radiology constitute are filtered by scope and content of specific curricula. The tools and people resource is filtered by specific opportunities and constraints for example social relationships and access to technology entail. The environment resource is filtered by organizational factors such as opening hours, timetables etc. Luckin suggests that available resources are often filtered by the actions of others, which means that the learner's interactions are filtered, for instance, by the teacher's instructions and underlying pedagogy. A resource can be the object of interaction as well as a filtering tool for interaction.

Luckin's framework focuses our attention on key resources and filters in the learner's context and to the interaction between them. While some elements are quite static from a teacher's point of view, such as the simulator technology, other elements are more readily adjustable, such as teacher-led instruction and feedback. It is the educator's task to adjust the Ecology of Resources where possible in order to best support learners. Luckin's intention, however, has been to create a general framework for design, and as such it needs to be adapted to specific areas of application, such as health care simulation. This is where field-specific research is important.

Adapting the EoR Framework to Health Care ECAS

Health care researchers have previously made some groundwork in trying to understand what is unique and important for health care simulation as an educational technique. Gaba and Issenberg are prominent examples. They help us specify the content of Luckin's general framework with field-specific knowledge. This is illustrated in Table 1, and will soon be elaborated. It should be noted that while Gaba's (2004) contribution is that of an field-expert conceptualizing important simulation application dimensions, Issenberg *et al.* (2005) build upon a systematic review of empirical simulation research. For the purpose of informing Luckin's framework for design, however, they are complementary.

Beginning with the EoR resource Skills and Knowledge, filtered by the curriculum, Gaba (2004) points to five important aspects of simulation application. (1) First, he lists the purpose and aims of the simulation activity (i.e., what the educator wants to achieve by having students

Table 1. Adaptation of Luckin's EoR to health care simulation using Gaba (2004) and Issenberg et al. (2005)

EoR resource	EoR filter	Gaba (2004) simulation application dimensions	Issenberg *et al.* (2005) features and uses for effective learning
Skills and Knowledge	Curric.	(1) The purpose and aims of the simulation activity (2) The health care domain in which the simulation is applied (3) The type of knowledge, skill, attitudes, or behaviour addressed in simulation	(a) Repetitive practice. (b) Curriculum integration. (c) Individualized learning. (d) Defined outcomes or benchmarks.
Tools and...	Admin.	(4) The technology applicable or required for simulations (5) The extent of direct participation in simulation (6) The feedback method accompanying simulation	(a) Repetitive practice. (e) Range of difficulty level. (f) Capture clinical variation. (c) Individualized learning. (d) Defined outcomes or benchmarks. (g) Simulator validity.
...People	Admin.	(7) The unit of participation in the simulation (8) The experience level of simulation participants (9) The health care disciplines of personnel participating in the simulation	(h) Multiple learning strategies.
Environment	Org.	(10) The site of simulation participation	(i) Controlled environment.

engage in simulation). Variations include training, instance assessment, rehearsal and research. In the LRiSE studies, the aims are training students in applying radiology, which is the subject domain, and in patient diagnosis, aims that are present in the curriculum. (2) Second is the health care domain in which the simulation is applied—for instance, imaging, primary care, psychiatry, ward-based, and procedural and dynamic high hazard domains. In our case, the domain is imaging dental and spinal radiology. (3) The third aspect is the type of knowledge, skill, attitudes or behaviour addressed in the simulator. Variations include conceptual understanding, technical skills, decision making, teamwork and attitudes. In our case, it is conceptual understanding of radiology for patient diagnosis in relation to the jaw or spine.

Issenberg *et al.* (2005) highlight that (a) the learner should engage in repetitive practice with the intent of improving his or her skills. A simulator as well as the curriculum can contribute to enabling this. In the LRiSE studies, with a single primary training session, this is somewhat supported by the simulator's ability to produce random variations of specific tasks, making repetition support conceptual understanding. (b) Second, there should be recognition of the importance of curriculum integration (i.e., that simulation is not an extra-ordinary or extra-curricular activity but instead integrated into the core of the curriculum). (c) Also, there should be support for individualized learning (i.e., making learners active participants and allowing them to break down tasks into their components). Our simulator supports this somewhat by enabling students to choose to practice on specific tasks involved in radiological examinations. (d) In addition, learners need defined outcomes and benchmarks for performances (i.e., attainable goals of improvement). In our study, the simulator provides formative and summative feedback as visual comparisons between student solutions and ideal solutions, accompanied by numerical information about distances between the two. This gives the feedback limited merit as a benchmark.

In Luckin's model, Tools and People are presented as one integrated resource. It is separated here to ease the presentation. With regards to the

EoR resource Tools, Gaba (2004) points to three important elements. (4) First is the technology applicable or required for simulations, with variations including verbal role playing, standardised patients, physical/virtual part-task trainers, screen-based patients, site replicas, mannequin or full VR. In the LRiSE studies a screen-based VR simulator is used. (5) Second is the extent of direct participation in the simulation, varying between remote viewing with/without interaction, hands-on participation and immersive participation. In the LRiSE studies, it is on-site and hands-on and/or observational participation for those currently not manoeuvring the simulator. (6) Third is the feedback method accompanying the simulation, varying between zero, automatic simulator critique in real time or delayed, direct or delayed instructor critique and video-based post-hoc debriefing, individually or in group. In the LRiSE studies, feedback is primarily provided by the simulator in relation to performance on specific tasks, but for the dentists the present teacher can also give feedback. Issenberg *et al.* (2005) add another six points, some of which have already appeared under the Skills and Knowledge resource and thus will not be repeated. (e) First, they note that simulators should support a range of difficulty levels in order to let learners begin at a basic level and progress to higher difficulty levels. In the LRiSE studies, the differences in difficulty levels between tasks are somewhat limited. (f) Second, simulators need to capture clinical variation and be valid representations of a complex practice (i.e., the range of patients and conditions as well as simulator fidelity is important). In the LRiSE studies, the model is based on actual scans, but of only one adult male with conform anatomy and a set of ailments, which does entail limits in this respect.

With regards to the People resource, Gaba (year) highlights three dimensions of simulation application. (7) First, the unit of participation varies between individual, crew, team, work unit and organisation. In the LRiSE studies, the simulator is developed for single-user application, but it has some support for small groups through its visual nature. (8) Second, the experience level of simulation participants varies between primary/secondary school, college/university, initial professional education, residency and continuing education. In the LRiSE studies, the participants are in their initial professional education. (9) Third, the health care disciplines of personnel participating in the simulation have variations including imaging, technicians, nurses, physicians, managers and regulators. In the LRiSE studies, which deal with radiology, this would be imaging. (h)Issenberg *et al.* (2005) highlight with regards to this resource the value of support for multiple learning strategies (i.e., support for adapting the simulator for large groups, small groups with/without instructor, and individual independent learning). In the LRiSE studies, the simulator does enable students to train independently or with teacher support, individually or in small groups.

Finally, the last resource highlighted by Luckin is the Environment. (10)Gaba (2004) points to the different sites of simulation participation, which vary between home/office multimedia, school/library multimedia, dedicated laboratories with physical or VR part-task trainers, replica of clinical environments and actual in situ simulation. In the LRiSE studies, the screen-based VR simulator falls under school/library multimedia. (i)Issenberg *et al.* (2005) highlight the value of situating simulation training in controlled environments where learners can make mistakes without consequences and teachers can focus on learners instead of patients.

When applying Luckin's framework to the analysis and design of ECAS in health care education, using Gaba (2004) and Issenberg *et al.* (2005) in this way helps us focus attention on resources that emerge as important within this field; it makes us more informed. However, it still leaves us with gaps of information. How, for instance, can educators adjust the Ecology of Resources to support a group of learners when the simulator's unit of participation is innately one? If it is not viable to have a teacher present during training sessions, how do we adjust the Ecology of Resources to compensate for this? These gaps in information can either be filled with the experienced educator's personal experience, or with more specific research on these design issues. The framework thus supports practitioners as well as researchers. Further adaptation of the framework to specific health care education simulation Ecology of Resources will be a future challenge for practitioners and researchers.

The central design changes made between the two LRiSE studies, previously presented, are related to the Tools and People. More specifically, the presence of a teacher during the training sessions and group size and creation was varied. This means that we are in a sense exploring the simulator's support for 'multiple learning strategies', and how this is related to other ecology resources, to the simulation process and the outcomes. What happens when we remove the teacher or change group creation and size? How can we adjust the Ecology of Resources to compensate for potential drawbacks?

In this chapter's modest empirical contribution, we will explore some of these interactions by illuminating the empirical questions presented below.

When using a screen-based simulator such as the radiology simulator, does teacher presence impact:

a. the portion of time spent solving technical issues
b. the portion of time spent discussing non-task-related issues
c. experiences of a sufficiency of instructions
d. experiences of simulation feedback sufficiency
e. experiences of engagement with the simulation

Furthermore, the interactions between the filters of tool and people/group size and creation will be delimited by concentrating on the relation between group creation and size and:

a. distribution of group member access to the simulation
b. perceptions of distribution of control over the simulation
c. perceptions of distribution of control over the verbal space
d. the inclusiveness of verbal activity

We want to repeat that this is a modest contribution of empirical data, and that we are dealing with a limited portion of the potential. We encourage studies that can be done under the framework that we are proposing.

METHODICAL CONCERNS RELATED TO THE CHAPTER'S EMPIRICAL DATA

We use observations of training sessions in order to describe differences in peer interaction during simulation, and we use survey and interviews to describe changes in peer appreciation of simulation. Key aspects of the simulation cases have already been presented, and what follows here is additional information regarding methodological considerations.

Observation of Simulation Training Using Video-Recordings

To enable analysis and comparisons of the simulation process, as expressed in peer interaction, the simulation sessions were recorded using a DV camera, a familiar method among researchers on health care education (Hindmarsh, 2010; Koschmann *et al.*, in press; Rystedt & Lindwall, 2004). The camera was placed so that the upper half part of the students was visible while the computer screen was not. Analysis of the video-recorded simulation sessions was supported by an observational schemata developed during the dentistry study and reused for the nurse study. It was developed through two phases.

In phase one, three questions were posed to a number of randomly chosen video-recorded training sessions: 1) What are the participants talking about? 2) How are they talking about it? 3) How do they relate to each other and to the learning environment as a whole? From the detailed descriptions generated by these questions, thematic categories of group interaction were inferred. With regard to the first question, statements such as 'We need to turn the head downward' or 'Up, more, up' grounded the category of 'action-proposals', which is a sort of suggestion for solutions which are lacking causal arguments. Other content categories were 'interpretations', 'functionality/technical issues', and 'social/off-task'. With regard to the second question, we noted, for instance, terminology and logical coherence. With regard to the third question, we noted who was operating the simulator, who was speaking, whether the talk was monologue-ish or inclusive. When we were unable to create more categories (i.e., we had reached saturation) phase one ended. In this chapter, we have primarily been focusing on basic data, both qualitative (such as which member is operating the simulator) and quantitative (such as time spent talking about different content).

In phase two, all video data was split into one-minute time segments and coded with the previously abstracted themes. This means that every minute of simulation is one observational unit, with a dominant content and shape. In our descriptive presentations of the observations, these time-segments are our empirical unit of observation. This allowed us to conduct a highly structured analysis based on an understanding that was influenced by the current set of data.

All coding of the training sessions was performed by one of the researchers. In order to produce a measure of the coding stability (Krippendorff, 2004), one of the sessions was re-coded, by the same researcher, and compared with the original for each category described above. The percent agreement between original coding and re-coding was 97% for content, 92% for terminology and 98% for manoeuvre, verbal space and verbal activity, respectively.

Survey of Participant Experiences of Simulation Training

As a means to gather background information, experiences of participation and perspectives on simulation training, we let participants fill out a questionnaire directly after training. We developed the survey ourselves, based on our perspective on learning. It focused on perceptions of their interactions with the tasks, the group and the tool in relation to learning. It also inquired into students' ideals and prior experiences to enable understandings of how interactions may be filtered.

Answers were given either by grading statements on a five-point scale or choosing one 'best fit' alternative, in most cases with the possibility of open-ended commenting. Since the data set was rather extensive, it has not been translated or enclosed in this document.

Complementing Interviews

As a complement to the quantitatively focused surveys, we later performed follow-up interviews with participants, half of the dentistry group (9) and all but one in the nurse group (11). The aim was to better understand the experience of participating in simulation training, and to get a better understanding of students' perspectives of certain issues. With open-ended questions, themes included training impact on learning, collaborating in groups, simulation tasks, realism and functionality, teacher presence and need for additional training. All interviews were performed individually with an effective time usage of 30–50 minutes. In the dentistry case, video-recordings of the respondents' training session were played on a laptop computer to support recall because they were performed months later. All interviews were recorded on tape. A qualitative approach was adopted in the analysis focusing on inferring categories of responses, sometimes referred to as *meaning concentration* (Kvale & Brinkmann, 2009). We posed specific questions to each transcript, extracted the responses related to it and inferred categories of ideas from these responses. Quotes of student responses have been translated from Swedish into English.

LEARNING RADIOLOGY: EMPIRICAL FINDINGS

This section presents the chapter's modest empirical contribution. It is focused on how the simulation process is filtered or perceived to be filtered through the ecology of resource, or the features and uses of the simulation. We present comparisons of simulation training from two different studies, Dentistry and Nursing. The comparisons are made at the level of specific design choices regarding teacher presence and group creation and size.

Adjusting the Teacher Resource

While Dentistry groups have a teacher present during their training session, Nurse groups work independently. How does this *use*-related design aspect filter peer interaction and appreciation when simulator *features* are kept constant? How does this impact simulation training? The following questions are posed to the video-, survey- and interview data regarding teacher presence:

a. Does teacher presence impact the portion of time spent solving technical issues?

- Yes. It is almost doubled without teacher present. To answer this question, we measured how large a portion of the total time segments was dominated by talk about simulation functionality and compared the mean ratio for the two studies. This number was 5.1% for the Dentistry groups (n= 336 minutes) and 9.1% for the Nurse groups (n=596). This is illustrated in Figure 5.

b. Does teacher presence impact time spent discussing non-task-related issues?

-No. It is very low for both groups. To answer this question, we measured how large a portion of the total time segments was dominated by social talk, which was the only non-task-related content category found in the observations. This number was 2.1% for Dentistry groups (n= 336 minutes) and 1.5% for Nurse groups (n=596). This is illustrated in Figure 5.

c. Does teacher presence impact experiences of sufficiency of prior instructions?

-Yes. Without at teacher present, there is a greater need for high-quality instructions. To answer this question, we asked the participants, through the survey, whether they thought that the simulation tasks 'included/were preceded by sufficient instructions'. A clear majority, 88%, of Dentistry participants (n=17) agreed with this statement while significantly less, 42%, of Nurse students (n=12) agreed.

d. Does teacher presence impact experiences of simulation feedback sufficiency?

-No. Equal amounts in both studies report sufficiency of simulation feedback. To answer this question, we asked the participants, through the survey, whether they thought that the simulation 'gave feedback that led us forward' and whether it 'explained what went wrong' when the task didn't turn out as expected. Agreement ratio for these questions was 79% vs. 75% and 58% vs. 50% for Dentistry (n=18) and Nurse groups (n=12) respectively.

Figure 5. Illustration of the portion of time groups spends talking about non-task, social and technical issues

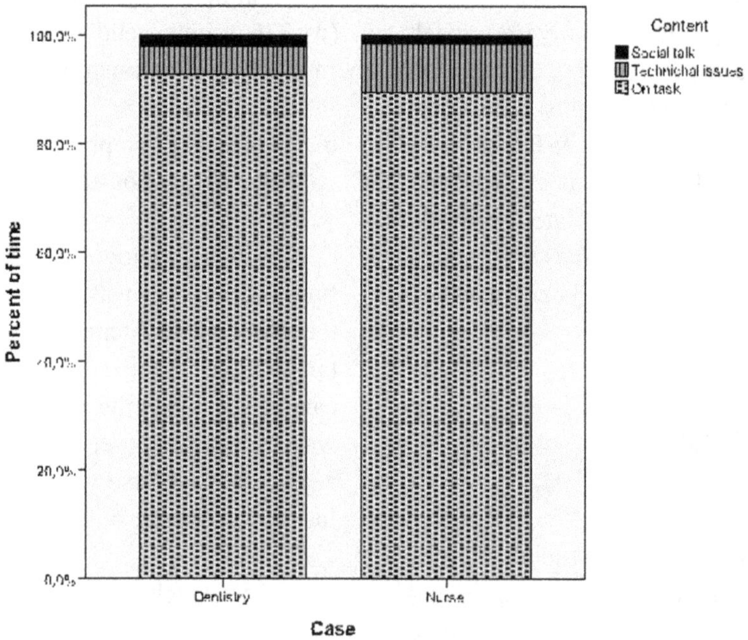

e. Does teacher presence impact experiences of engagement with the simulation tasks?

-No. Equal amount report experiences of meaning and motivation. To answer this question we asked the participants, through the survey, whether they thought that the simulation tasks 'felt meaningful and engaging'. Agreement ratio was 83% for Dentistry groups (n=18) as well as for Nurse groups (n=12).

f. Does teacher presence impact experiences of need for a present teacher?

-Yes. Students seem to adapt to the conditions for their training. We asked participants, through the survey, whether they thought teacher presence could be substituted with nothing but written instructions. None of the Dentistry students thought this would be possible (n=18), while 42% of the Nurse students thought that it would (n=12).

When we returned to this question in the interviews with the Nurse and Dentistry students, it was clear that the primary reason they see for having a teacher present would be for technical support, and a secondary reason would be for conceptual support when they get stuck on some task. Nurse students also see benefits for learning in not having a teacher present during training. This seems to be related to two factors: a) the fear of making mistakes, which is reduced when there is no expert there to watch your every move; and b) the usefulness of making and correcting mistakes. One of the participants stated that having a teacher present could be useful 'for introduction right at the beginning, to get started with the program. Otherwise you progress by trying, and you learn more from making mistakes and correcting them yourself than by having someone showing you what to do'. A female arguing along the same lines added that 'it was quite good to work independently, because then you are not afraid of embarrassing yourself'.

Adjusting the Peer Resource: Group Creation and Size

While groups in Dentistry were created randomly with three students in each, groups in Nurse were dyads created by students themselves. How does this *use*-related design aspect filter peer interaction and appreciation when simulator *features* are kept constant? These questions were posed to the video-, survey- and interview data regarding group creation and size:

a. Does group creation and size impact distribution of group member access to the simulation?

-Yes. Distribution is much more equal in Nurse groups. One indicator of peer inclusion in simulation activities is to what extent participants are given access to the simulator (i.e., time spent actually hands-on operating the simulator). This was noted for each member during observations. It turns out that there are big variations between groups and between populations regarding the differences in access for group members. We have compared the most active and least active operators in each group, in each case, based on the portion of total simulation time that they are the active operators. For Dentistry groups, the difference varies from a small 13% difference to a complete 100% difference (i.e., in some groups one member operates the simulator at all times). The mean difference in operation time for members in Dentistry groups is 48%. Access to the simulator is, in other words, rather unequally distributed. For Nurse groups, however, the difference varies between 7% and 30% with a mean of 14%. This illustrates that access to the simulation tends to be significantly more equal in the Nurse groups. This difference in participants' access to the simulator, between cases, is illustrated in Figure 6.

b. Does group creation and size impact perceptions of distribution of control over the simulation?

-Yes. Nurse students perceive the control as being more equally distributed. To answer this question, we asked students, through the survey, if participants perceived that 'no one operated the simulator more than the others'. 68% of Dentistry students (n=18) agreed with this, and 92% of Nurse students (n=12).

c. Does group creation and size impact the inclusiveness of verbal activity?

-Yes. A greater portion of utterances are inclusive in Nurse groups as compared to Dentistry groups. To answer this question, we noted, during the observations, for each time segment whether the verbal activity was characterized by monologue (i.e., someone talking without showing interest in or allowing for actual exchange with the other participants), or if it was characterized by being inclusive. We then produced a mean for each case showing that Nurse students had 90% (n=613) inclusive utterances while Dentistry students had 65%, (n=364). This difference in peer inclusion, between cases, is illustrated in Figure 7a.

d. Does group creation and size impact perceived distribution of control over the verbal space?

-Yes. More students in Nurse groups perceive the distribution as equal. To answer this question, we asked students, through the survey, if they perceived that 'everyone talked approximately an equal amount'. 44.4% of Dentistry students (n=18) agreed with this, and 75% of Nurse students (n=12). This difference in perceived peer inclusion, between cases, is illustrated in Figure 7b.

Figure 6. Illustration of how access to the simulator is distributed between participants during training, in the Dentistry and in the Nurse case

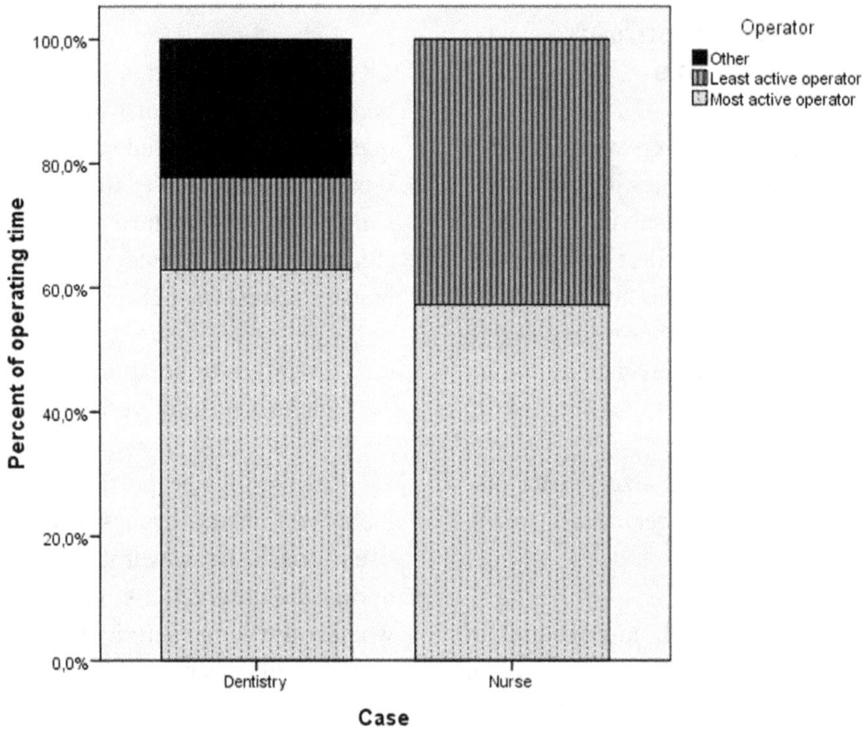

DISCUSSION

In this section, our empirical contribution will be used to discuss how changes in design, or in the Ecology of Resources, impact aspects of the simulation process, and how adjustments can be made to the ecology to enhance teaching and learning.

Thoughts about the Empirical Contribution

When applying the framework on our own studies, it was obvious that it supported the gathering and structuring of available information, as well as pointing to areas of uncertainty in need of empirical support. Our empirical studies make a modest contribution to the investigation a few of these areas (i.e., how some use-related design aspects filter peer interaction and appreciation when simulator features are kept constant). Or in other words, they inform educational design choices by giving insight into how adjustment of conditions such as group characteristics and teacher presence filters the students' interaction and consequently influences outcomes of simulation training.

Adjusting the Teacher Resource

One of the filters adjusted between our two studies was the people-filter—more specifically; the presence of a teacher was varied. This design issue stems from the interrelation of limited teacher resources and the potential need of a teacher present during training. A teacher present during every training session can become costly when for each session the number of participants in

Figure 7. a) Illustration of the observed verbal inclusion in the Dentistry and in the Nurse study. b) Illustration of the perceived distribution of verbal space in the Dentistry and in the Nurse study

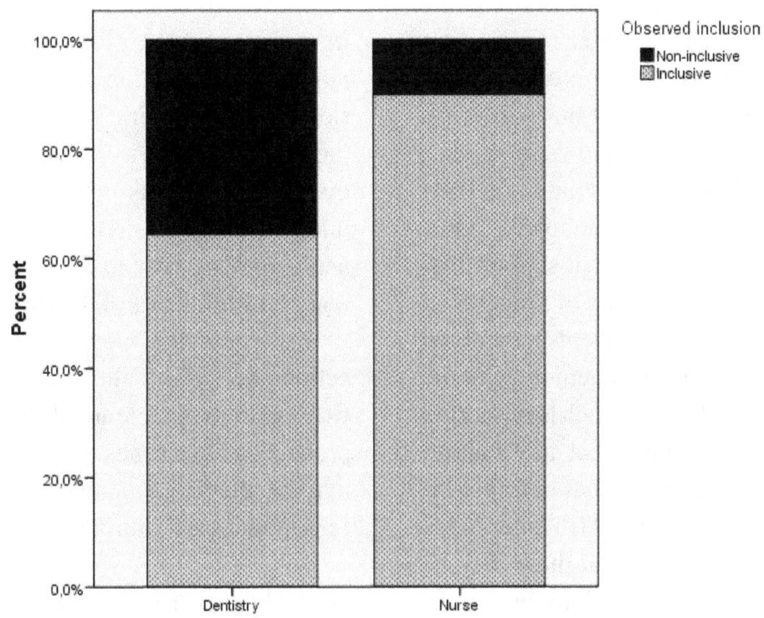

A

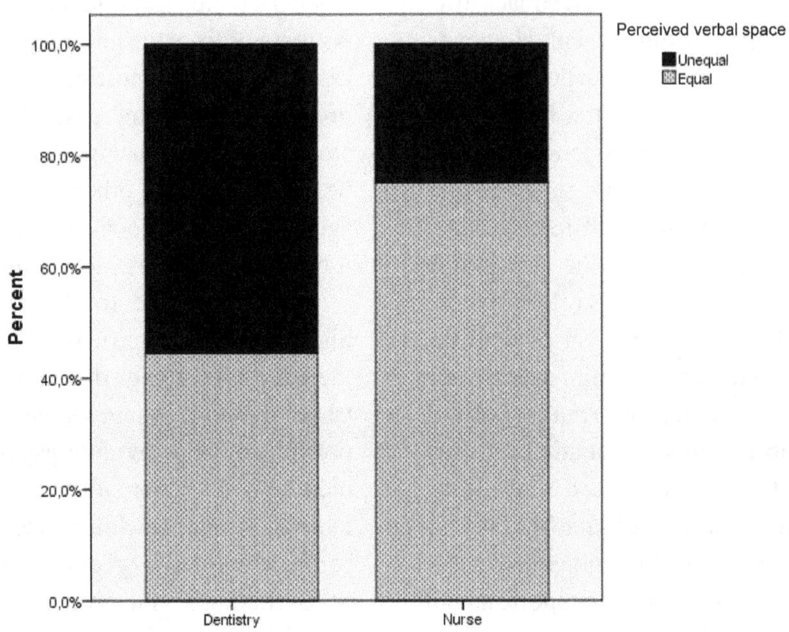

B

each session decreases, the duration increases and when the number of sessions increase.

Results indicated that the teacher is a valuable resource when the students' experience in relation to the simulator with its specific features is lacking. This is made apparent by the fact that the Nurse students spend almost double the time solving technical issues and that more Nurse students ask for better instructions for the simulator tasks. It is also as a resource for technical support that the teacher is considered valuable by students in the interviews. However, the students' perceived experience of, for example, engagement with the simulation seem not to change, which is supported by the observation that time spent idly talking about social, non-task-related issues does not increase without a teacher present. Also, interviews with Nurse students indicated that there may be benefits in not having a teacher looking over a student's shoulder, in that it reduces the fear of making potentially productive errors.

In principle, a teacher should not need to be available during training. Sufficient introductions and instruction prior to training and feedback after training should work as a supplement. However, in the case investigated here, teacher non-presence needs to be counteracted with better instructions and introductions prior to the session so as not to reduce the quality of the session.

But we also see that the need for a teacher is depending on the tool itself: the scaffolding capacity of the tool. The teacher's role as a more able partner, in Luckin's terms, varies with the context-specific simulation domain issues Gaba (2004) and Issenberg *et al.* (2005) put forward. If the tool itself enables a good negotiation between the learner and the tool in a good scaffolding process, the need for a teacher in a MAP sense decreases. The results from the studies also show that the students wanted technical support and not to negotiate the tasks to be solved. But the teacher in her role as a MAP can help the students work with the tool in a productive way. With reference to the aspects highlighted by empirical studies from the field (Table 1), there are a few things that a teacher can do to support students in their interaction with the tool, such as understanding the aim of the simulation and its relation to the curriculum as a meaningful context in order to make the simulation activity meaningful; giving students ownership and making them active participants; understanding the tool; evaluating performance and clarifying how to improve (feedback); realizing the limitations of the simulation validity etc.

In other words, we have indicated some interactions between features and uses, between the filters of tools, people and skills, and the simulation process and outcomes. Rough indications as they may be, they are valuable for teachers designing for simulation training under these conditions.

Adjusting the Peer Resource

Another adjustment was made to the people-filter, and that was to the group creation and group size—more specifically, the impact of changing from teacher-created triads to peer-created dyads. This issue stems from the interrelation between limited resources and supporting learning in groups. If group size can be increased in each training session without increasing duration, resources may be redistributed to other aspects of the training, such as introductions and feedback. However, it can also make interaction more complicated.

With reference to the simulation aspects highlighted by empirical studies from the field, there are a few things that may impact this design issue: the aim, where assessment of individual proficiency or individual psychomotor development may be better suited for smaller groups or individual training while conceptual development, can be supported by peer interaction and dialogue of conflicting perspectives; the technology, where the visibility of the simulation space impact if multiple users can have some ownership over the activity simultaneously; feedback, for the same reasons; repeatability, with low repeatability being problematic for larger groups if the students need to take turns operating it; site of participation, where a desktop simulation, for instance, will set physical limits to group size; subjects, where prior experience of each other as well of the subject probably will influence collaboration; and of course the unit of participation, if it is defined.

Results indicate that in peer-constructed dyads, access to the simulation tend to be much better distributed than in the randomized triad counterparts. This is also manifested in the participants' experiences of the simulation, as they are aware of the differences in access. The group size also has an impact on the characteristics of the verbal activity, with the dyads encouraging inclusion to a higher degree. This is also manifested in the participants' experience, as they perceive, for instance, differences in the distribution of verbal space, with the dyads generating a better distribution. For those who consider active and tool-related participation as a fundament of the learning process, these are interesting relations.

Given the features of the radiology simulator in this study and the results indicating support for the peer-created dyads, changes in group size and creation need to be complemented with other adjustments as well if not to risk affecting simulation outcomes negatively.

This is another example of interactions between features and uses, between the filters of tools and people, and the simulation process and outcomes.

Aside from the empirical contribution being quite small, there are also other limitations. One of them is that it is difficult to draw absolute relations between specific filters due to our making several adjustments to the filters at the same time. Ideally, we would be able to make one adjustment at a time and record the effects. When working with training sessions given once a year, and with practical and ethical limitations, this would take quite some time. Another aspect that would enhance our data is empirical data on proficiency development, such as can be gained from a pre test – post test method. This too, however, is better suited for experimental settings and not for conducting research in practice where additional tests can be regarded as too intrusive.

FUTURE RESEARCH DIRECTIONS

With this chapter, we have tried to contribute to addressing one of the central challenges in the research field of ECAS in health care education: the need for an informed educational framework for analysis and design of simulation training. We have proposed Luckin's Ecology of Resources as such a framework for educational design informed by experiences from the field of ECAS in health care education, focusing on the resources available in the learners' ecology and interactions between them in order to understand what impacts the simulation process and outcomes and thereby inform teaching and learning. These filters include characteristics of the applied tools, participating individuals such as teachers and peers, skills and knowledge to be developed and the learning environment.

We do believe that a framework such as this can be beneficial. In principle, it can help educators structure and objectify important aspects of simulation learning sessions and support their design of simulation learning. For instance, it gives attention to the learners' interaction with the tool and its scaffolding opportunities, which give consequences for possible design choices related to the role of teachers and peers in educational computer-assisted health care simulations.

However, more work can be done in adapting it to health care ECAS in general and to divisions of simulation applications. On the ground level, one of the continuous challenges will be to integrate more of the empirical work that already has been done, that is currently being done and that will need to be done. We have chosen to build upon the works of Gaba (2004) and Issenberg *et al.* (2005), which we consider as two key texts within the field. Future developments will synthesize more key works, which could include McGahies *et al.'s* (2010) recent review of simulation-based medical education as well as more particular works such as Cook & Triola's (2009) on virtual patients.

In addition to establishing key resources, the interactions between them, the simulation process and the outcomes need to be researched in order to support adjustments to the Ecology of Resources. This is, in our view, an area in particular need of research, and one to which the chapter's modest empirical investigation is intended to contribute.

For those who are interested in engaging further with the theoretical foundation of the Ecology of Resource framework, Luckin does herself provide a discussion of some important concerns, regarding, among other things, the issue of multiple ecologies emerging due to multiple participants and the tension between embodied and distributed cognition (Luckin, 2010).

CONCLUSION

The research field of ECAS in health care education is in need of an informed educational framework for analysis and design of simulation training. Luckin's Ecology of Resources framework (2008, 2010) appears to be one productive alternative for practitioners as well as researchers. Further conceptual and research efforts are needed to adapt the framework to the general field of ECAS in health care education and to its particular subdivisions. If this venture is successful, it will clearly enhance teaching and learning with health care ECAS.

REFERENCES

Agazio, J. B., Pavlides, C. C., Lasome, C. E., Flaherty, N. J., & Torrance, R. J. (2002). Evaluation of a virtual reality simulator in sustainment training. *Military Medicine, 167*(11), 893–897.

Aggarwal, R., & Darzi, A. (2006). Technical-skills training in the 21st century. *The New England Journal of Medicine, 355*(25), 2695–2696. doi:10.1056/NEJMe068179

Ahlberg, G., Heikkinen, T., Iselius, L., Leijonmarck, C. E., Rutqvist, J., & Arvidsson, D. (2002). Does training in a virtual reality simulator improve surgical performance? *Surgical Endoscopy, 16*, 126–129. doi:10.1007/s00464-001-9025-6

Ashurst, N., Rout, C. C., Rocke, D. A., & Gouws, E. (1996). Use of a mechanical simulator for training in applying cricoid pressure. *British Journal of Anaesthesia, 77*(4), 468–472.

Balacheff, N., Ludvigsen, S., de Jong, T., Lazonder, A., & Barnes, S. (Eds.). (2009). *Technology enhanced learning: Principles and products*. Berlin, Germany: Springer.

Bradley, P. (2006). The history of simulation in medical education and possible future directions. *Medical Education, 40*, 254–262. doi:10.1111/j.1365-2929.2006.02394.x

Chandler, T. N., & Chaille, C. (1993). Process highlighters in a computer-simulation—Facilitation of theory-oriented problemsolving. *Journal of Educational Computing Research, 9*(2), 237–263. doi:10.2190/3GGG-K9CC-19XC-9G0W

Chang, K.-E., Chen, Y.-L., Lin, H.-Y., & Sung, Y.-T. (2008). Effects of learning support in simulation-based physics learning. *Computers & Education, 51*(4), 1486–1498. doi:10.1016/j.compedu.2008.01.007

Cook, D. A., & Triola, M. M. (2009). Virtual patients: A critical literature review and proposed next steps. *Medical Education, 43*, 303–311. doi:10.1111/j.1365-2923.2008.03286.x

Cuban, L. (2001). *Oversold and underused: Computers in the classroom*. Cambridge, MA: Harvard University Press.

Debas, H. T., Bass, B. L., Brennan, M. R., Flynn, T. C., Folse, R., & Freischlag, J. A. (2005). American Surgical Association Blue Ribbon Committee report on surgical education: 2004. *Annals of Surgery, 241*, 1–8.

Dillenbourg, P., Järvelä, S., & Fischer, F. (2009). The evolution of research on computer-supported collaborative learning. In Balacheff, N., Ludvigsen, S., de Jong, T., Lazonder, A., & Barnes, S. (Eds.), *Technology enhanced learning* (pp. 3–19). Berlin, Germany: Springer. doi:10.1007/978-1-4020-9827-7_1

Engum, S. A., Jeffries, P., & Fisher, L. (2003). Intravenous catheter training system: Computer-based education versus traditional learning methods. *American Journal of Surgery, 186*, 67–74. doi:10.1016/S0002-9610(03)00109-0

Fritz, P. Z., Gray, T., & Flanagan, B. (2008). Review of mannequin-based high-fidelity simulation in emergency medicine. *Emergency Medicine Australasia, 20*, 1–9. doi:10.1111/j.1742-6723.2007.01022.x

Gaba, D. M. (2004). The future vision of simulation in health care. *Quality & Safety in Health Care, 13*(Supplement 1), 2–10. doi:10.1136/qshc.2004.009878

Goffman, E. (1959). *The presentation of self in everyday life*. New York, NY: Anchor Books.

Goodyear, P. (2005). Educational design and networked learning: Patterns, pattern languages and design practice. *Australasian Journal of Educational Technology, 21*(1), 82–101.

Häll, L.-O., Söderström, T., Nilsson, T., & Ahlqvist, J. (2009). Integrating computer based simulation training into curriculum – Complicated and time consuming? In K. Fernstrom & J. Tsolakidis (Eds.), *Proceedings of the International Conference of Information Communication Technologies in Education* Corfu, Greece, 9–11 July, 2009.

Häll, L. O., Söderström, T., Nilsson, T., & Ahlqvist, J. (in press). Collaborative learning with screen-based simulation in health care education: An empirical study of collaborative patterns and proficiency development. *Journal of Computer Assisted Learning*.

Hindmarsh, J. (2010). Peripherality, participation and communities of practice: Examining the patient in dental training. In Llewellyn, N., & Hindmarsh, J. (Eds.), *Organisation, interaction and practice* (pp. 218–240). Cambridge, UK: University Press. doi:10.1017/CBO9780511676512.011

Hulshof, C. D., & de Jong, T. (2006). Using just-in-time information to support scientific discovery learning in a computer-based simulation. *Interactive Learning Environments, 14*(1), 79–94. doi:10.1080/10494820600769171

Issenberg, S. B., McGaghie, W. C., Petrusa, E. R. I., Lee, G. D., & Scalese, R. J. (2005). Features and uses of high-fidelity medical simulations that lead to effective learning: A BEME systematic review. *Medical Teacher, 27*, 10–28. doi:10.1080/01421590500046924

Jaldemark, J. (2010). *Participation in boundless activity: Computer mediated communication in Swedish higher education*. Doctoral dissertation, Umeå University, Umeå.

Koschmann, T., LeBaron, C., Goodwin, C., & Feltovich, P. (2010). Can you see the cystic artery yet? A simple matter of trust. *Journal of Pragmatics*. doi:.doi:10.1016/j.pragma.2009.09.009

Kothari, S. N., Kaplan, B. J., Demaria, E. J., Broderick, T. J., & Merrell, R. C. (2002). Training in laparoscopic suturing skills using a new computer-based virtual reality simulator (MIST-VR) provides results comparable to those with an established pelvic trainer system. *Journal of Laparoendoscopic & Advanced Surgical Techniques. Part A.*, *12*(3), 167–173. doi:10.1089/10926420260188056

Krippendorff, K. (2004). *Content analysis. An introduction to its methodology*. Thousand Oaks, CA: Sage.

Kvale, S., & Brinkmann, S. (2009). *Den kvalitativa forskningsintervjun* [The qualitative research interview]. Lund, Sweden: Studentlitteratur.

Lane, J. L., Slavin, S., & Ziv, A. (2001). Simulation in medical education: A review. *Simulation & Gaming*, *32*(3), 297–314. doi:10.1177/104687810103200302

Luckin, R. (1998). *ECOLAB: Explorations in the zone of proximal development* (DPhil Thesis: CSRP Technical Report 486): School of Cognitive and Computing Sciences, University of Sussex.

Luckin, R. (2006). Understanding learning contexts as ecologies of resources: From the zone of proximal development to learner generated contexts. In T. Reeves & S. Yamashita (Eds.), *Proceedings of World Conference on E-learning in Corporate, Government, Healthcare, and Higher Education* 2006 (pp. 2195–2202). Chesapeake, VA: AACE.

Luckin, R. (2008). The learner centric ecology of resources: A framework for using technology to scaffold learning. *Computers & Education, 50*, 449–462. doi:10.1016/j.compedu.2007.09.018

Luckin, R. (2010). *Re-designing learning contexts. Technology-rich, learner centred ecologies*. London, UK: Routledge.

Luengo, V., Aboulafia, A., Blavier, A., Shorten, G., Vadcard, L., & Zottmann, J. (2009). Novel technology for learning in medicine. In Balacheff, N., Ludvigsen, S., de Jong, T., Lazonder, A., & Barnes, S. (Eds.), *Technology enhanced learning* (pp. 105–120). Berlin, Germany: Springer. doi:10.1007/978-1-4020-9827-7_7

McGaghie, W. C., Issenberg, S. B., Petrusa, E. R., & Scalese, R. J. (2010). A critical review of simulation-based medical education research: 2003-2009. *Medical Education*, *44*(1), 50–63. doi:10.1111/j.1365-2923.2009.03547.x

Mercer, N., Littleton, K., & Wegerif, R. (2004). Methods for studying the processes of interaction and collaborative activity in computer-based educational activities. *Technology, Pedagogy and Education*, *13*(2), 193–209. doi:10.1080/14759390400200180

Nehring, W. M., & Lashley, F. R. (2009). Nursing simulation: A review of the past 40 years. *Simulation & Gaming*, *40*(4), 528–551. doi:10.1177/1046878109332282

Nilsson, T., Söderström, T., Häll, L.-O., & Ahlqvist, J. (2006). Collaborative learning efficiency in simulator-based and conventional radiology training. *Paper presented at the 10th European Congress of DentoMaxilloFacial Radiology*, Leuven, Belgium, 31st May to 3rd June, 2006.

Nilsson, T. A. (2007). *Simulation supported training in oral radiology. Methods and impact in interpretative skill.* Doctoral dissertation, Umeå University, Umeå.

O'toole, R. V., Playter, R. R., Krummel, T. M., Blank, W. C., Cornelius, N. H., & Roberts, W. R. (1999). Measuring and developing suturing technique with a virtual reality surgical simulator. *Journal of the American College of Surgeons*, *189*(1), 114–128.

Rystedt, H., & Lindwall, O. (2004). The interactive construction of learning foci in simulation-based learning environments: A case study of an anaesthesia course. *PsychNology Journal*, *2*(2), 165–188.

Schoenecker, T. S., Martell, K. D., & Michlitsch, J. F. (1997). Diversity, performance, and satisfaction in student group projects: An empirical study. *Research in Higher Education*, *38*(4), 479–495. doi:10.1023/A:1024966627400

Simulation (n.d.). In *Oxford English Dictionary.* Retrieved from http://dictionary.oed.com

Söderström, T., Häll, L.-O., Nilsson, T., & Ahlqvist, J. (2008). How does computer based simulator training impact on group interaction and proficiency development? In *Proceedings of the International Conference of Information Communication Technologies in Education*, Corfu, Greece, 10–12 July, 2008.

Swaak, J., Van Joolingen, W. R., & De Jong, T. (1998). Supporting simulation-based learning: The effects of model progression and assignments on definitional and intuitive knowledge. [REMOVED HYPERLINK FIELD]. *Learning and Instruction*, *8*(3), 235–252. doi:10.1016/S0959-4752(98)00018-8

Tao, P. K., & Gunstone, R. F. (1999). Conceptual change in science through collaborative learning at the computer. *International Journal of Science Education*, *21*(1), 39–57. doi:10.1080/095006999290822

Trey, L., & Khan, S. (2008). How science students can learn about unobservable phenomena using computer-based analogies. *Computers & Education*, *51*(2), 519–529. doi:10.1016/j.compedu.2007.05.019

Vygotsky, L. S. (1978). *Mind in society: The development of higher psychological processes*. Cambridge, MA: Harvard University Press.

Vygotsky, L. S. (2001). *Tänkande och språk* [Thought and language]. Gothenburg, Sweden: Daidalos.

Wenger, E. (1998). *Communities of practice: Learning, meaning, and identity*. New York, NY: Cambridge University Press.

Winberg, T. M., & Hedman, L. (2008). Student attitudes toward learning, level of pre-knowledge and instruction type in a computer-simulation: Effects on flow experiences and perceived learning outcomes. *Instructional Science*, *36*(4), 269–287. doi:10.1007/s11251-007-9030-9

Windschitl, M., & Andre, T. (1998). Using computer simulations to enhance conceptual change: The roles of constructivist instruction and student epistemological beliefs. *Journal of Research in Science Teaching*, *35*(2), 145–160. doi:10.1002/(SICI)1098-2736(199802)35:2<145::AID-TEA5>3.0.CO;2-S

ADDITIONAL READING

Alessi, S. M. (1988). Fidelity in the design of instructional simulations. *Journal of Computer-Based Instruction*, *15*(2), 40–47.

Bandali, K., Parker, K., Mummery, M., & Preece, M. (2008). Skills integration in a simulated and interprofessional environment: an innovative undergraduate applied health curriculum. *Journal of Interprofessional Care*, *22*(2), 179–189. doi:10.1080/13561820701753969

Choi, W. (1997). Designing effective scenarios for computer-based instructional simulations: classification of essential features. *Educational Technology*, *5*(11), 13–21.

Corbett, N. A., & Beveridge, P. (1982). Simulation as a tool for learning. *Topics in Clinical Nursing*, *4*(3), 58–67.

de Jong, T., Martin, E., Zamarro, J. M., Esquembre, F., Swaak, J., & van Joolingen, W. R. (1999). The integration of computer simulation and learning support: An example from the physics domain of collisions. *Journal of Research in Science Teaching, 36*(5), 597–615. doi:10.1002/(SICI)1098-2736(199905)36:5<597::AID-TEA6>3.0.CO;2-6

Decker, S. (2007). Integrating guided reflection into simulated learning experiences. In Jeffries, P. R. (Ed.), *Simulation in nursing education: From conceptualization to evaluation* (pp. 73–85). New York: National League for Nursing.

Dooling, S. L. (1986). Designing computer simulations for staff nurse education. *Journal of Medical Systems, 10*(2), 139–149. doi:10.1007/BF00993120

Ellaway, R. H., Kneebone, R., Lachapelle, K., & Topps, D. (2009). Practica continua: Connecting and combining simulation modalities for integrated teaching, learning and assessment. *Medical Teacher, 31*(8), 725–731. doi:10.1080/01421590903124716

Elliott, S., & Gordon, J. A. (1998). Integration of self-directed computerized patient simulations into the internal medicine ambulatory clerkship. *Academic Medicine, 73*(5), 611. doi:10.1097/00001888-199805000-00086

Greenberg, R. (2004). Technology-Enhanced Simulation: Looking ahead to 2020. In Loyd, G. E., Lake, C. L., & Greenberg, R. B. (Eds.), *Practical health care simulations* (pp. 275–280). Philadelphia: Elsevier Mosby.

Issenberg, S. B. (2006). The scope of simulation-based healthcare education. *Simulation in Healthcare, 1*(4), 203–208. doi:10.1097/01.SIH.0000246607.36504.5a

Jaakkola, T., & Nurmi, S. (2008). Fostering elementary school students' understanding of simple electricity by combining simulation and laboratory activities. *Journal of Computer Assisted Learning, 24*(4), 271–283. doi:10.1111/j.1365-2729.2007.00259.x

Jeffries, P. R., & Rizzolo, M. A. (2006). *Designing and implementing models for the innovative use of simulation to teach nursing care of ill adults and children: A national, multi-site, multi-method study*. New York: National League for Nursing.

Jeffries, P. R., & Rogers, K. J. (2007). Theoretical framework for simulation design. In Jeffries, P. R. (Ed.), *Simulation in nursing education: From conceptualization to evaluation* (pp. 20–33). New York: National League for Nursing.

Krummel, T. M. (1998). Surgical simulation and virtual reality: the coming revolution. *Annals of Surgery, 228*(5), 635–637. doi:10.1097/00000658-199811000-00002

Loyd, G. E., Lake, C. L., & Greenberg, R. B. (Eds.). (2004). *Practical Health Care Simulations*. Philadelphia: Elsevier Mosby.

Meakim, C., & Wahl, S. (2007). Creating an environment for simulation in a school of nursing. *Clinical Simulation in Nursing Education, 3*(1), e11–e13. doi:10.1016/j.ecns.2009.05.033

Nebel, D., Farbom, C., Le, D. H., & Attstrom, R. (2004). Simulation of patient encounters using a virtual patient in periodontology instruction of dental students: design, usability, and learning effect in history-taking skills. *European Journal of Dental Education, 8*(3), 111–119. doi:10.1111/j.1600-0579.2004.00339.x

Ravert, P. (2002). An integrative review of computer-based simulation in the education process. *Computers, Informatics, Nursing, 20*(3), 203–208. doi:10.1097/00024665-200209000-00013

Reznek, M. A. (2004). Current status of simulation in education and research. In Loyd, G. E., Lake, C. L., & Greenberg, R. B. (Eds.), *Practical health care simulations* (pp. 27–49). Philadelphia: Elsevier Mosby.

Rieber, L. P., Smith, M., AlGhafry, S., Strickland, B., Chu, G., & Spahi, F. (1996). The role of meaning in interpreting graphical and textual feedback during a computer-based simulation. *Computers & Education, 27*(1), 45–58. doi:10.1016/0360-1315(96)00005-X

Ronen, M., & Eliahu, M. (2000). Simulation – A bridge between theory and reality: The case of electric circuits. *Journal of Computer Assisted Learning, 16*(1), 14–26. doi:10.1046/j.1365-2729.2000.00112.x

Rosen, K. R. (2004). The history of medical simulation. In Loyd, G. E., Lake, C. L., & Greenberg, R. B. (Eds.), *Practical health care simulations* (pp. 275–280). Philadelphia: Elsevier Mosby.

Rystedt, H., & Lindstrom, B. (2001). Introducing simulation technologies in nurse education: A nursing practice perspective. *Nurse Education in Practice, 1*(3), 134–141. doi:10.1054/nepr.2001.0022

Veenman, M. V. J., & Elshout, J. J. (1995). Differential effects of instructional support on learning in simulation environments. *Instructional Science, 22*(5), 363–383. doi:10.1007/BF00891961

Waldner, M. H., & Olson, J. K. (2007). Taking the patient to the classroom: Applying theoretical frameworks to simulation in nursing education. *International Journal of Nursing Education Scholarship, 4*(1), 1–14. doi:10.2202/1548-923X.1317

Zhang, J. W., Chen, Q., Sun, Y. Q., & Reid, D. J. (2004). Triple scheme of learning support design for scientific discovery learning based on computer simulation: experimental research. *Journal of Computer Assisted Learning, 20*(4), 269–282. doi:10.1111/j.1365-2729.2004.00062.x

Ziv, A., Wolpe, P. R., Small, S. D., & Glick, S. (2003). Simulation-based medical education: an ethical imperative. *Academic Medicine, 78*(8), 783–788. doi:10.1097/00001888-200308000-00006

KEY TERMS AND DEFINITIONS

ECAS: Educational Computer-Assisted Simulation: a generic term we use for simulations developed and used for educational purposes and that are supported by computer software. Sometimes used in conjunction with HCE, resulting in HCECAS.

Ecology of Resources: "...A set of inter-related resource elements, including people and objects, the interactions between which provide a particular context." (Luckin 2008, p.451) "It is grounded in an interpretation of Vygotsky's Zone of Proximal Development, is concerned with learning and considers the resources with which an individual interacts as potential forms of assistance that can help that individual to learn. These forms of assistance are categorized as being to do with Knowledge and Skills, Tools and People and the Environment (Luckin 2010, s.159).

Filter: A term used in this chapter to specifically refer to the Filter elements of Luckin's (2010) model. These serve a mediating, filtering, purpose between learner and resources.

HCE: Health Care Education: a generic term we use for educational training, including programs, for health care professions such as medicine, dentistry, nursing, pharmacy etc.

LRiSE: Learning Radiology in Simulated Environments: a joint, three-year research and development project including education and health care researchers from the universities of Umeå and Stanford, in which several studies were performed on learning with a screen-based radiological VR simulation. The chapter's empirical contribution rests upon data from this project.

Resource: A term used in this chapter to specifically refer to the Resource elements of Luckin's (2010) model. The primary categories or domains of resources in this model are Knowledge & Skills, Tools & People and Environment.

Simulation: A term used in this chapter to refer to technologically supported techniques for imitating situations and/or processes. We have a specific interest in computer-supported simulations developed and used for educational purposes within health care education.

Chapter 11
The Impact of Instructional Simulation Use on Teaching and Learning:
A Case Study

Michael C. Johnson
Brigham Young University, USA

Charles R. Graham
Brigham Young University, USA

Su-Ling Hsueh
Brigham Young University, USA

ABSTRACT

As simulation usage becomes more prevalent in education, it is important to analyze how teaching and learning is impacted by its use. We present here a case study of a specific computer-based instructional simulation, the Virtual Audiometer, and instructor and student perspectives regarding the simulation use's effects on teaching and learning. Specifically, findings are described within a model of five areas in which technology can effect education: visualization, authentic engagement, quality and quantity of practice and feedback, interaction and collaboration, and reflection. Although room for improvement was identified, data showed that in this specific case, the computer-based instructional simulation improved teaching and learning experiences in all five areas. An understanding of how simulations impact teaching and learning can help inform design of both the simulations produced for higher education and the implementation of these simulations within a course.

INTRODUCTION

Many consider simulations as potentially powerful educational tools (Aldrich, 2002; de Jong & van Joolingen, 1998; Lee, 1999; Winer & Vázquez-Abad, 1981) or reported successful use of simulations in education (Cameron, 2003; Henderson, Kleme & Eshet, 2000; Lieberth & Martin, 2005; Windschitl & Andre, 1998). However, there have been conflicting reports about the effectiveness of simulations (Aldrich, 2002; de Jong & van Joolingen, 1998; Lee, 1999; Winer & Vázquez-Abad,

DOI: 10.4018/978-1-61350-080-4.ch011

1981). While simulations hold great potential, there are several reasons reported for the discrepancy between the potential of simulations and the research results, for example, lack of instructional supports (Zhang, Chen, Sun, & Reid, 2004), poor implementation or integration problems (Weston, 2005), or mode of use—with some researchers claiming possible differences between the use of simulations for practice and the use of simulations to present instruction (Lee, 1999).

Although simulations often require instructional augmentation to truly facilitate learning (Gibbons, McConkie, Seo, & Wiley, 2002), West and Graham (2005) and Roschelle, Pea, Hoadley, Gordin, and Means (2000) argued that technologies such as computer–based simulations have the potential to be catalysts for more efficient and/or more profound student learning. Little research has been done, however, to show how simulations affect the dynamics of teaching and learning, especially from the perspectives of the instructor and students. As a research team, we set out to answer one question: how does simulation usage change what teachers and students do and how do those changes facilitate the learning process? An understanding of how instructors and learners use simulations holds the potential of helping inform the design and implementation of simulations in other contexts.

BACKGROUND

To provide a background for the study, the definition of computer-based instructional simulations and the strengths and limitations of their use in education are discussed.

Definition of Computer-Based Instructional Simulations

There are many types of simulations; in this chapter we focus on computer-based instructional simulations (CBIS). A CBIS is a computer program that allows learners to actively explore a domain by manipulating input variables of a model of the domain (de Jong, 1991; Lee, 1999). Other researchers further differentiate between simulations and educational or instructional simulations (Gibbons et al., 2009; Lee, 1999; Winer & Vázquez-Abad, 1981) because they do not deem that all simulations are instructional. Gibbons et al. (2009) stated that for a simulation to be considered instructional, it needs to have the following characteristics:

1. The simulation contains one or more dynamic models of physical or conceptual systems. (These might include cause effect systems, human performance models, or environmental models.)
2. The model engages the learner in interactions that result in model state changes. (In other words, the model reflects the effects of the users actions on the system.)
3. The model state changes occur according to a non-linear logic. (Simulations may be based on mathematical models, decision trees, or other appropriate means of expressing the model complexities.)
4. The model experience is supplemented by one or more designed augmenting instructional function. (For example, instruction either within or external to the simulation helps direct student activities, attention, and provide just in time information, etc.)
5. The simulation is employed in the pursuit of one or more instructional goals.

It is not requisite that the "augmenting instructional functions" be embedded into the simulation. A teacher, instructor, tutor, or other individual may serve these functions. Thus how the simulation is implemented becomes even more important if it is to have a positive effect on students' learning.

Advantages and Strength of CBIS

Simulations have often been compared with other instructional methods in order to identify their comparative instructional effectiveness and impact upon the learning approach. We've summarized below the strengths and limitations of computer-based instructional simulation (CBIS) reported in the research literature.

Improves Teaching Aims and Methods

Traditional classroom lecturing often focuses more on factual (declarative) knowledge than on procedural (applied) knowledge. By using well-designed CBIS for teaching, instructors may more easily avoid becoming simply didactic knowledge providers (Orrill, 2001). In addition, students' understanding of content knowledge can be improved (Ncube, 2010; Yeh, 2004).

When using CBIS for practice, instructors can concentrate on clarifying important concepts, exploring new methods of teaching, and attending to individual students' needs in class activities, because students have already practiced necessary skills and knowledge using CBIS (Lenderman & Niess, 1999; Baillie & Percoco, 2000). Although computer-based instructional simulation might reduce the explicit amount of factual knowledge presented, conceptual learning can be enhanced. Use of simulations may also help promote interaction and communication and facilitating teamwork and collaborative learning (Kuriger, Wan, Mirehei, Tamma, & Chen, 2010; Ncube, 2010). Similarly, simulations can also help provide students much needed feedback on performance (Kuriger et al., 2010).

Improves Learning and Practice

Computer-based instructional simulations could benefit learning by offering practical experience in visualizing conceptual and other kinds of knowledge (White, Kahriman, Luberice, & Idleh, 2010; Gordon & Gordon, 2009; de Jong & Njoo, 1992). Well-designed and implemented CBISs may allow for trial-by-error practice (Baillie & Percoco, 2000), thus promoting experimentation (Rawson, Dispensa, Goldstein, Nicholson, & Vidal, 2009) and permitting students and faculty to learn from their errors (Smith-Stoner, 2009). The dynamic and evolving systems of CBIS may potentially help students comprehend complicated phenomena (Turkle, 2004) and otherwise correct students' misconceptions and improve their understanding (Liu, Lin & Kinshuk, 2010). In addition, CBIS hold the potential for enhancing learners' skill levels (Boyd & Jackson, 2004). As Rawson, et al. (2009) suggested, simulations can afford realistic and engaging practice.

Computer-based instructional simulations can provide nearly unlimited opportunities for practice. For example, surgeons can practice operational skills and overcome obstacles before performing actual operations. In one study, it was reported that surgical residents improved skills by 30-40 percent after five days of practice with a CBIS (Mangan, 2000). The virtual reality of CBIS is a powerful technique to train students with better skills to prevent errors (Kneebone, 2003). For instance, medical errors resulting from deployment of unfamiliar skills caused the deaths of an estimated 44,000 people per year (Mangan, 2000). If students have more opportunities to practice their skills on different and specific cases through the use of CBIS, these types of avoidable deaths and critical incidents may be decreased or avoided.

Motivates Students

Reigeluth and Schwartz (1989) found that CBIS might provide effective and highly motivational instruction. Well-designed simulations provide suitable material for individual work and for group collaboration settings. By working effectively with group members, students may became more active learners and thus improve their learning (Yarger, Thomas, Boysen & Pease, 2003). Students revealed that the simulation was not only interesting while working with team members, but it provided real-world and hands-on experience to be applied in future situations (Mitchell, 2004).

Researchers have reported that computer-based instructional simulation enhanced motivation and learning interest (Hariri, Rawn, Srivastava, et al., 2004). In some fields, familiarity with CBIS programs may be important as the student seeks for employment (Baillie and Percoco, 2000). Baillie and Percoco (2000) indicated CBIS helped improve students' retention of the lesson; however, no retention testing has been conducted to verify this evidence in the literature review.

Saves Operational Cost and Time

Use of CBIS may allow learners to practice basic skills with collected data before receiving instruction from teachers or trainers (Mangan, 2000; Lederman & Neiss, 1999) and practice with virtual cases may help students practice foundational skills and knowledge. Teachers and trainers can build from important foundational concepts and values without wasting class time on explaining or scaffolding fundamental knowledge and skills.

Computer-based instructional simulation may also help reduce the cost of human objects in experiments and create real-world like experience for learners at any time and place (West & Graham, 2005). For example, using CBIS in medical training may reduce institutional costs (time, money, resources) of seeking patients for examinations. Or using CBIS in psychology experiments can alleviate the need for students to buy experimental animals or set up experimental environments.

Increase Safety

The virtual reality of simulation protects students' safety in experimental settings (Ncube, 2010). For example, a flight simulator provides students realistic practice without risk of injury to the students or others. In a virtual chemistry lab, students are free from possible chemical dangers (West & Graham, 2005). With medical simulations, no lives are potentially harmed in virtual operations (Mangan, 2000). Simulation allows learners to practice skills and knowledge in safe environments, and eliminate the need for experimental participants.

Barriers and Limitations of CBIS

There are two primary categories of barriers and limitations of the CBIS usage described in the literature, which we report below.

Capital Costs and Time Constraints

Gibbons et al. (2002) stated, "Cost is one of the strongest constraints on instructional simulation design given the current status of design and development tools" (p. 9). One of the main barriers to simulation use is adequate funding to purchase or develop professional CBIS programs (Baillie & Percoco, 2000). Generally speaking, the capital cost of CBIS is higher than other technologically instructional methods. Even though common flight simulation program can be purchased online at the price of $65.00 (USD), most specific and professional simulations tailored for specific needs can impose costs of thousands of dollars. It is common to see that the high price of CBIS discourages instructors even though they would like to integrate simulations into their teaching. Some instructors feel that they lack the time to train students to use CBIS; students feel overwhelmed with so much information (Baillie & Percoco, 2000). Moizer, Lean, Towler and Abbey (2009) also report the lack of resources as one of the primary obstacles to simulation usage in higher education.

Technical Barriers and Other Barriers

Teachers are not confident with technical support and think that appropriate software and hardware is difficult to obtain (Baillie & Percoco, 2000;

Moizer, et al., 2009). Teachers are not always computer experts; therefore, they leave students to discover appropriate CBIS usage by relying upon the instructional menu. Some teachers naturally resist using computer-related materials (Baillie & Percoco, 2000).

Moizer, et al. (2009) described other issues that instructors and institutions may see as risks associated with simulations, which thus serve as barriers to simulation usage. One of these is the loss of instructor control over student learning. Another barrier they mentioned is student resistance or negative reaction to using simulations. Another barrier that the authors mention is the suitability of simulations for the kinds of learning outcomes the teacher is hoping to accomplish. In other words, instructors may worry that the simulation is too complex or overly simplistic or that the skills or knowledge desired are not facilitated through using the simulation. Similarly, Rawson, et al. (2009) also reported the lack of feedback in some simulations as a concern, as it has been shown to lead students to draw faulty conclusions regarding the system they are learning about. Finally, poor implementation can make the use of the simulation less effective in helping students learn (Ioannidou et al., 2010; Weston, 2005).

METHODOLOGY

To describe the effects of simulations on teaching and learning, we took a case study approach to provide rich descriptions of how the use of a simulation affected teaching and learning in a particular case. We chose one course where a simulation, the Virtual Audiometer, was used extensively as part of the curriculum in a course in the Department of Communication Disorders at Brigham Young University. The course focused on hearing loss and an introduction to audiometric testing procedures.

Procedure

We used a variety of methods to collect data. We interviewed the faculty initially, then asked follow-up questions on a variety of occasions over the course of the study. We observed 20 different students complete their homework assignments using the Virtual Audiometer on two different assignments. We observed classroom instruction on nine occasions over the course of the semester of the study, including demonstration of new procedures using the Virtual Audiometer. At the end of semester, we surveyed the students on their impressions of the use of the Virtual Audiometer both as an instructional tool and as a practice tool for homework assignments. Table 1 summarizes the variety of data types that were collected as part of the case.

To analyze the data, the team used a constant comparison methodology. As we collected data, we met together to discuss new findings and look for trends. We met together several times throughout the duration of the study to discuss the cases and implications of what we were finding in our data. We also triangulated data from the various sources of data we collected to assure that our data was reliable and our conclusions were as

Table 1. Data collection methods

Method	Description
Faculty Interviews	1 principle interview plus several brief follow-up interviews over the course of the semester
Classroom observations	9 classroom observations at various times throughout the semester
Student Observations	20 student observations across two different assignments
Student Surveys	44 students surveyed

valid as possible. To further enhance validity, we also conducted member checks by running findings past the instructors in the cases and validating our findings with other faculty members in the department of Instructional Psychology and Technology at Brigham Young University.

Theoretical Framework

As a research team we saw themes emerging from the data that were an overlap between the perspectives of Roschelle, et al. (2000) on characteristics of an effective learning experience and West and Graham (2005) on ways that technology can enhance teaching and learning. We also noticed that as we analyzed the data that the ways students were learning and the professor was teaching with the simulation seemed to fall under the areas discussed in those articles. So we combined these similar views to create a framework upon which to further analyze the usage of the Virtual Audiometer simulation. This combined framework is described below:

1. Visualization: The use of technology should help illustrate visually to the students the theory behind the technique (West & Graham, 2005). This appears to be true with simulations (Gordon & Gordon, 2009; de Jong & Njoo, 1992).
2. Authentic Engagement: Students should be actively engaged in the learning process rather than passive receivers of knowledge (Roschelle et al., 2000), and engagement is more meaningful if it is authentic (i.e., similar to real-life experiences) (West & Graham, 2005).
3. Quality and Quantity of Practice and Feedback: Technology can be used to provide more and higher quality practice opportunities (Roschelle et. al., 2000; West & Graham, 2005; also see Kneebone, 2003; Mangan, 2000).
4. Interaction and Collaboration: Technology can be used to provide students the opportunity to interact with each other or with the instructor (West & Graham, 2005). Xu and Yang (2010) found similar results with simulation usage: "Our results suggest that social interaction and psychological safety had a positive impact on knowledge development in student groups, and that this synergistic knowledge development enabled students to form complex mental models" (p. 223).
5. Reflection: The use of technology should "support meaningful student reflection" (West & Graham, 2005, pg. 3). This includes students spending time making meaning of their experiences, taking their actual or simulated experiences and relating them to general principles (Swan, 2005). This could also include understanding the results of the procedures. Schön (1987) discussed at least two types of reflection: "reflection-on-action," which is when people reflect back on actions they have taken in the past, and "reflection-in-action," which is when people reflect on their actions as they are making decisions while acting or performing. We believe that technology holds the potential to act as a catalyst for, facilitate, and enhance both types of reflection.

CASE DESCRIPTION

In this chapter we explore how the use of a simulation, the Virtual Audiometer, changed how the instructor taught and how students learned in an undergraduate course on the administration of hearing tests (see Figure 1). In a course on audiometric testing in the department of Communication Disorders (formerly the department of Audiology and Speech Language Pathology), the professor, Dr. David A. McPherson, uses a simulation called the Virtual Audiometer (created by Dr. McPherson and Dr. Richard Harris

Figure 1. The Virtual Audiometer allows instructors and students to conduct hearing tests on virtual patients

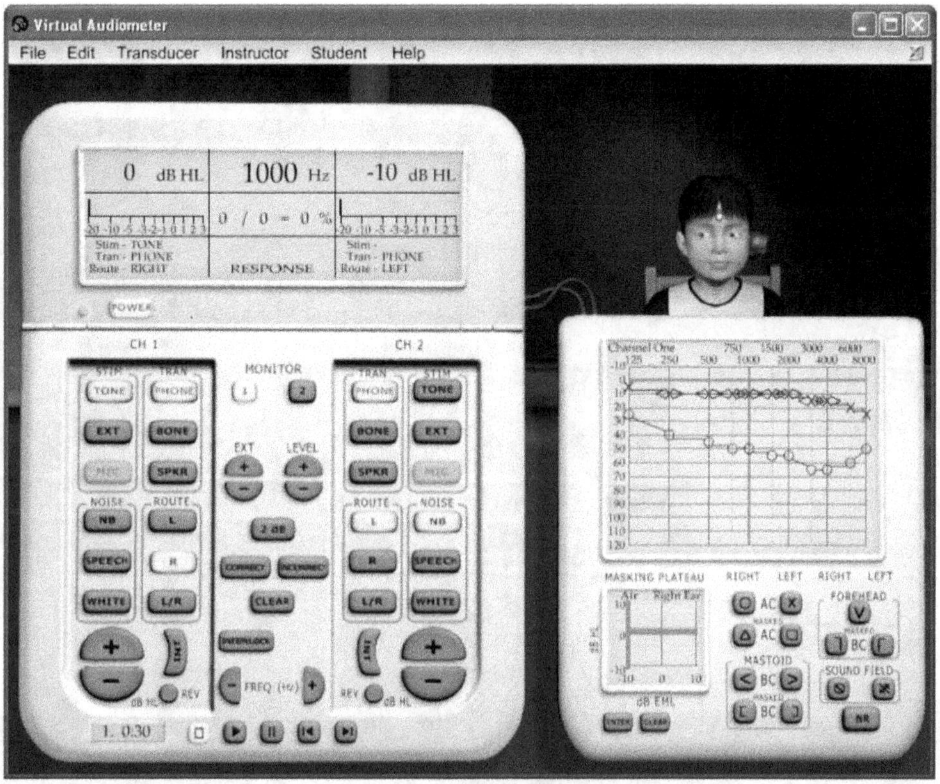

in cooperation with Brigham Young University's Center for Teaching and Learning).

The Virtual Audiometer allows for a variety of audiometric testing procedures using a variety of patient profiles – simulated geriatric, adult, teen and child patients (both male and female). Using these 8 characters, faculty can use the Profile Maker portion of the tool to create a nearly infinite set of cases by changing the settings on relevant variables (Figure 2). As users conduct testing, they record their findings in an electronic audiogram.

When a student completes an assignment, the work is submitted through email in the form of a flat data file that includes the original patient profile and a capture of the student's testing results. The faculty member can then view this file in the Session Viewer tool and the tool will highlight areas where the test results obtained by the student are out of line with the patient's profile. This allows the professor to see where students are on or off target so they can provide students with feedback (either individually or collectively; see Figure 3 and Figure 4).

The instructor used the simulation in the course in a couple of ways. First, the instructor used the simulation to demonstrate new procedures to the class. After providing a lecture and discussion of key course concepts, the instructor illustrated these concepts by demonstrating related audiometric testing procedures using the Virtual Audiometer. Second, the students were asked to conduct hearing tests on a variety of virtual patients in order to practice the new procedures they were learning and better understand other course concepts.

Figure 2. The Virtual Audiometer has a variety of characters for faculty to use to build virtual patients with all types of hearing losses

Figure 3. The Virtual Audiometer Profile Maker allows instructors to edit existing virtual patient profiles or create new profiles

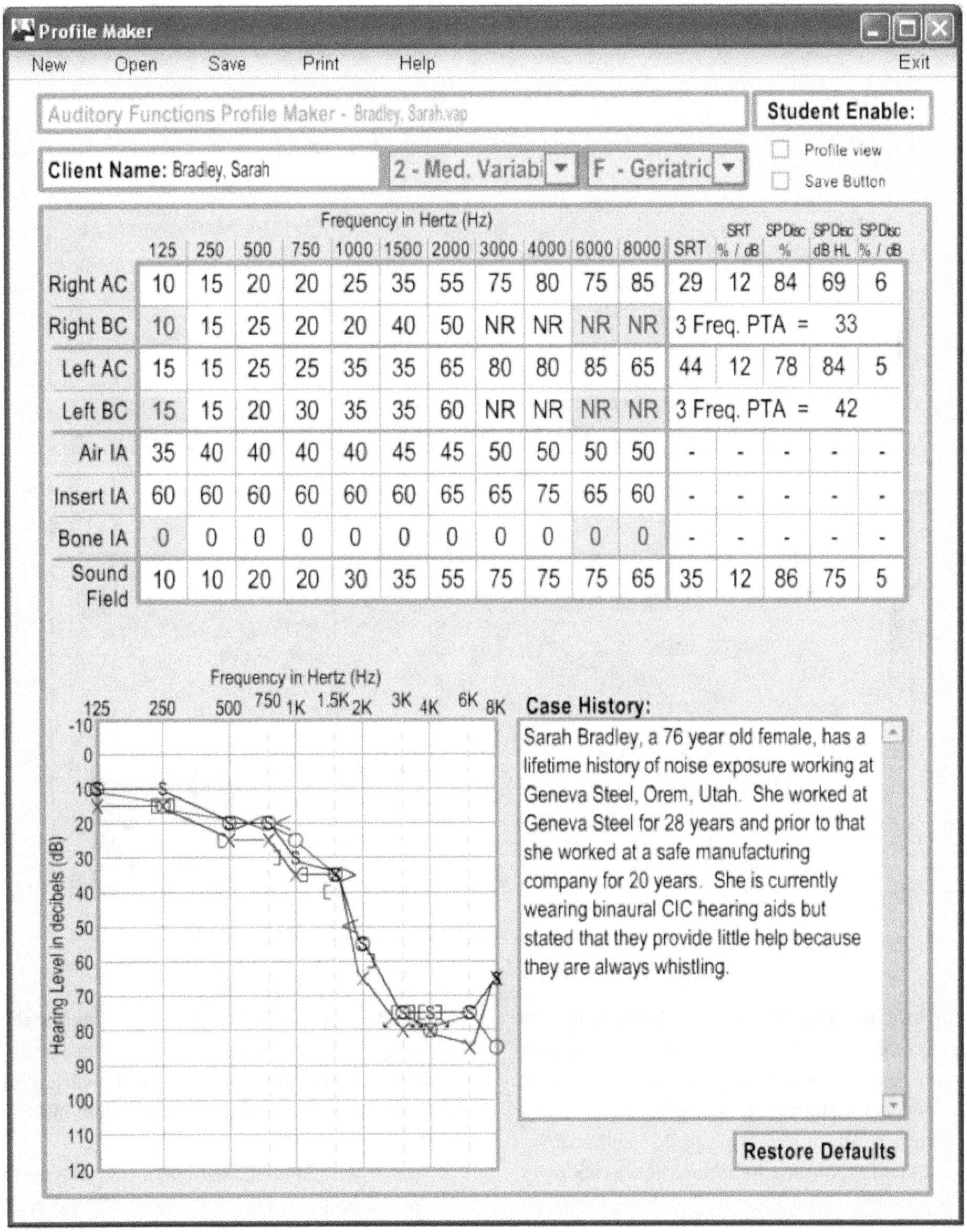

Figure 4. The Virtual Audiometer Session Viewer allows instructors to compare the test results students recorded against the original virtual patient profile

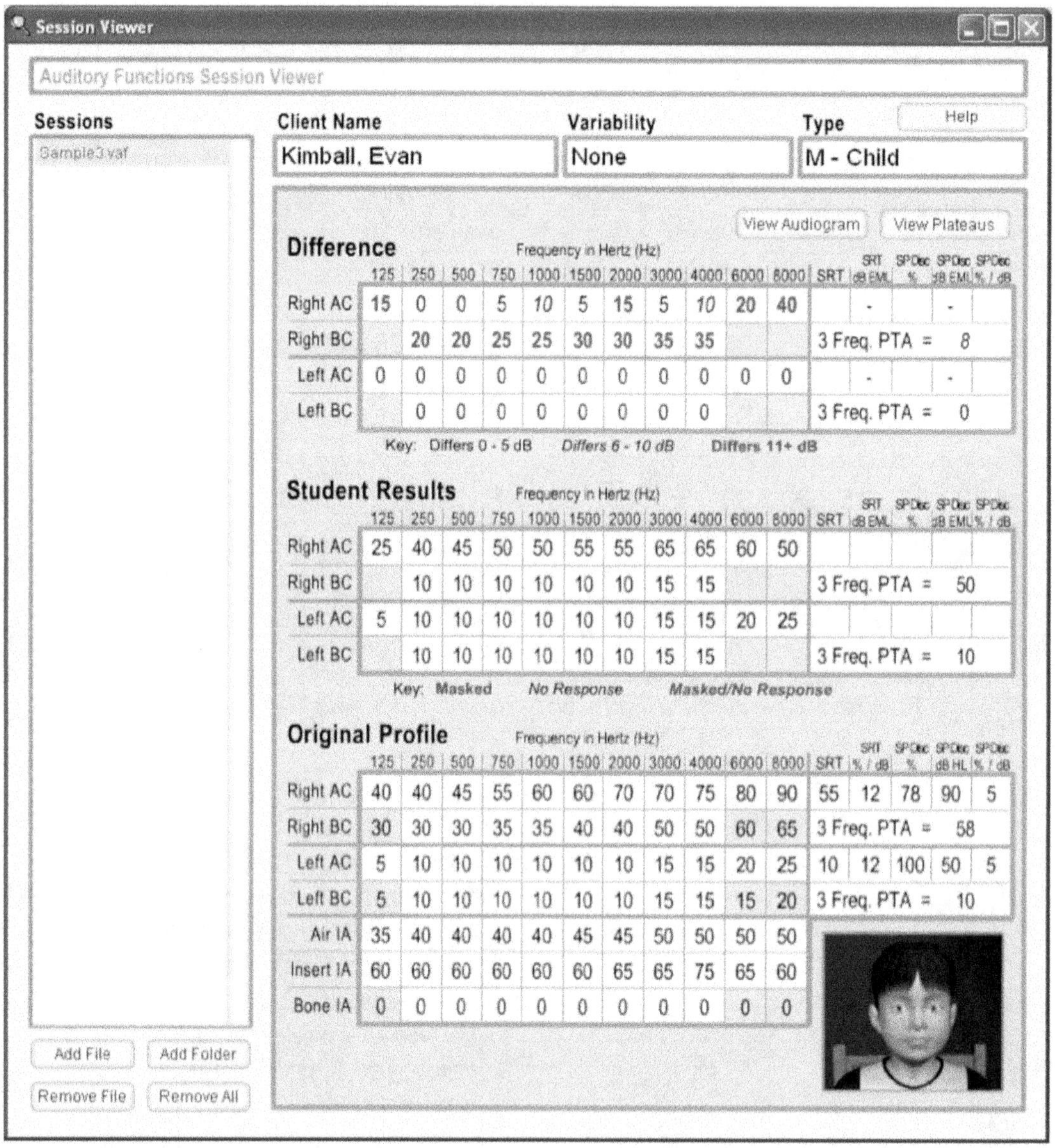

Prior to using the Virtual Audiometer, the professor used a portable audiometer to demonstrate testing skills in class. It was very difficult, however, for students to see what the professor was doing. The professor also used a video camera so students could see the actions he was taking on the portable audiometer unit, but he reported that the use of the video camera was difficult and not as effective as he desired. Using the portable units required the professor to either test students in the class or bring other individuals in for his demonstrations, so this approach limited the variety of patients/cases the instructor could demonstrate to the students.

Out of class, students also conducted tests using the portable units. The students would test each other and try to simulate hearing loss by wearing earplugs. The use of the portable units allowed students to get hands-on practice. However, due to cost and logistics, access to the portable units was limited. Thus, practice opportunities were also limited.

According to the professor, the Virtual Audiometer simulation was developed to alleviate many of the challenges they faced trying to use the portable audiometric testing units. The simulation also dealt with many of the barriers and limitations to simulation use described in the literature. Although the creation of the Virtual Audiometer has taken the time the two professors and university resources, relative to purchase of additional portable audiometers, the Virtual Audiometer is nearly infinitely more scalable. The cost for students is also fairly reasonable ($39.00 USD). Training students on the use of the simulation has been simplified by the instructor's use of the simulation in class to demonstrate. Technical barriers to usage have been few since the instructor and his colleague were involved in the design and production of the tool. Also, due to the instructors' involvement in design, they feel that the simulation has been useful in helping students achieve the learning outcomes of the course. There has also been little resistance on the part of the students to using the tool because it has afforded them more practice. One limitation reported with the implementation of the Virtual Audiometer is the lack of feedback on their performance, The design of the simulation does not give students feedback on whether they are performing the hearing tests correctly or not.

FINDINGS

As we analyzed the data we collected, we found that the use of the Virtual Audiometer simulation functioned as a catalyst for enhancing all five characteristics of the framework described earlier. In some situations, though, we found that some modifications to implementation or design of the simulation could further enhance these characteristics. Below, we discuss how the simulation affected teaching and learning within the context of this framework.

Visualization

A major portion of the students reported that one of the main advantages of the Virtual Audiometer was that it helped them to visualize course content. The students reported that use of the Virtual Audiometer enhanced their ability to visualize concepts in at least three ways.

First, the Virtual Audiometer was shown in class via projector, which allowed students to see exactly what the professor was doing. Students were able to see what actions the professor was taking (i.e., the buttons the professor was pressing, settings on the audiometer, etc.) and how the patient would respond without having to look in multiple locations. One student commented, "We were able to see what buttons he was pushing and what frequencies he was testing.. .. A wonderful way to present to a class this size."

Second, the instructor could select cases that were specifically useful to get across a particular concept. In other words, he could much more easily target the cases to match the concept he was trying to teach. One student reported, "Using Virtual Audiometer helps to see how specific hearing losses look." This was helpful not only for in-class demonstrations, but for the selection of cases for student practice.

Students reported that due to the use of the simulation for out-of-class assignments, they could "see" the underlying concepts. Specifically, several students reported that seeing the procedure performed in class, performing the procedure themselves, seeing the virtual patient respond, and creating and seeing the audiogram (the record the students make of the patient's responses) helped enhance their learning.

Third, the professor helped create a new interface for recording the resulting audiogram. The students perceived a benefit from seeing an audiogram built before their eyes. One student reported that "without [the Virtual Audiometer] we wouldn't have been able to visualize how the procedures worked.. .. If we were just shown pictures of completed audiograms it wouldn't have been as effective."

Authentic Engagement

Even though prima facie use of actual equipment might be considered a more authentic form of engagement, as our team reviewed what was occurring in the class, a more important consideration became evident. The more authentic cases demonstrated in class and used for practice out of class with the Virtual Audiometer seem more important to the students' understanding of the underlying concepts of hearing tests than to be able to physically touch the equipment. Using real equipment is potentially beneficial, but instructor and student responses alike indicate that the variety and targeting of cases made possible through the use of the Virtual Audiometer does more to help students learn to perform hearing tests and to think like professional audiologists than using authentic equipment alone. Anecdotally, the realism of the Virtual Audiometer seems to be sufficient to help students learn how to use real audiometers. However, to more definitively answer the question of transfer of procedural skills, we would need to conduct additional research.

With the ability to do more demonstrations in class, the professor was able to solicit input from the students on how he should proceed during demonstrations as well as discuss the meaning of what he was doing and the results of the test. This seemed to get students actively involved. During classroom observations, few students were engaged in other activities; most appeared to be following along closely with the demonstrations and participated through offering suggestions for next steps and discussing what kinds of hearing pathologies the virtual patient might be experiencing.

Another aspect that students reported enjoying was that demonstrations often led the professor to share anecdotes from his professional practice. One student, for example, mentioned that the professor's use of the Virtual Audiometer in class "helped me get an idea of how audiometry is done. He would explain what is done clinically. I enjoyed hearing about a couple of experiences [he had] doing audiometry."

Previous to implementing the Virtual Audiometer, the professor used to assign students to test each other on portable audiometers. In one sense, students were authentically engaged because they were using real equipment with real people. However, they often could not test for specific types of hearing loss (except, perhaps, by chance). And because students would attempt to imitate hearing loss by wear earplugs when they were being tested, these practice test experiences were actually a bit contrived.

On the other hand, with the Virtual Audiometer, the instructor could select or create specific cases that helped illustrate the principles and procedures currently being learned in class. Also, the Virtual Audiometer had different cases that students could use for practice. So for the purpose of teaching and learning the procedures and the underlying concepts, the Virtual Audiometer appears to have helped provide a more authentic and engaging experience.

Quality and Quantity of Practice and Feedback

Previous to using the Virtual Audiometer, students had difficulty following what was going on in class demonstrations and it was consequently difficult for the professor to include students in the process. Thus, the opportunities for guided practice as a group were limited.

After implementing the Virtual Audiometer, however, students were better able to see each action and follow the procedure the professor was using to complete hearing tests. The professor could also allow students to provide input as to what steps he should take. In this way, he provided students with review of previously learned material and guided practice opportunities with new procedures. For many students this practice helped them be able to more confidently complete their own assignments. One student reported that "example practices in class were helpful." However, many students commented that they would like even more opportunities to participate in the in-class demonstrations.

Prior to using the Virtual Audiometer, students tested each other, but it was difficult to really assess how well the students were doing without the professor testing each student patient then comparing his results with the results the students obtained. This practice could have provided some opportunity for variety because students could then test several other students. However, the opportunity for students to test a variety of cases would then be highly unlikely and left to chance. Additionally, the limited number of portable audiometers and the coordination of student schedules made extra practice opportunities logistically difficult.

With the Virtual Audiometer, the professor was able to create known profiles for all the virtual patients. The creation of these virtual patients allowed for a higher quality of student practice. It also permitted easier assessment of student learning because the professor could then compare student results against known profiles. The Virtual Audiometer came with a built-in utility that allowed the professor to quickly compare student results to patient profiles and showed where student responses were beyond an acceptable error threshold. The professor would look for problem trends and offer correction to the class when there appeared to be errors or misconceptions. Even though students were being assessed, many students mentioned that they would have liked more direct confirmatory and corrective feedback.

Another advantage of the Virtual Audiometer, that facilitated a higher quantity of practice opportunities, was that students could use the simulation anytime or anywhere they had a computer with the application loaded. Rather than being limited by a few portable units, students could use their own computers or visit any computer lab on campus to practice procedures.

Interaction and Collaboration

Prior to using the Virtual Audiometer, it was difficult to get students involved in in-class demonstrations. Students did work with each other out of class, though, on the couple of occasions that they were able to do practice tests.

Because use of the Virtual Audiometer allowed the professor to more easily demonstrate procedures in class, it freed him to invite students to participate in the demonstration process. He would often ask students to provide input on what steps he should take next and occasionally they would discuss the rationale for how they should proceed (especially on steps where there were discrepancies among class members as to what should happen next). This served to get students discussing the procedures and asking questions about what they were seeing the professor do and why he was doing it.

On our survey, some students reported wanting to be even more involved in the in-class demonstrations. So, even though the simulation does permit more interaction and collaboration in class, some efforts could be made to further enhance this in-class interaction.

As a tool for student assignments, the typical use of the Virtual Audiometer did not promote as much interaction and collaboration among the students as the use of the portable audiometer units. We found an interesting exception, however, while observing a pair of students who did use the Virtual Audiometer collaboratively. These two students would begin the procedure individually, then at certain points (for example after finishing air conduction at a particular frequency) they would stop and compare their responses. If their answers were different, they would try to figure out who made an error. If they were the same, then they moved on. During the observation they also discussed factors that weighed in to how they should proceed at key decision points.

Even though these students still came away with some questions as to whether they were completing procedures correctly, they were able to provide some preliminary validation for each other and provide some assistance during practice. If this type of collaboration were allowed and encouraged, the simulation could be a catalyst for meaningful student collaboration and interaction outside of class.

Reflection

Prior to using the Virtual Audiometer, there was a greater focus on teaching facts and procedures. However, because the simulation allowed the professor to more easily demonstrate procedures, more time was available to discuss implications of the actions he was taking and to model reflective practice. As the professor worked through new procedures with students, he spent some time modeling reflection-in-action during the procedure and some reflection-on-action as they discussed the results of the test (Schön, 1987). As the professor learns to use the simulation more efficiently (e.g. not reviewing the entire process every time a new aspect of the process is introduced), even more class time could be freed up to meaningfully discuss actions and results.

There is some evidence that the use of the Virtual Audiometer helped students think about what they were learning at a higher level (i.e., starting to reflect-in-action). One day after taking a few questions, the professor commented to his teaching assistant that they didn't used to get questions of that nature. He later commented that students used to be more concerned with the mechanics of what he was doing and now he is getting more questions dealing with why he is doing what he is doing and what the results mean.

Prior to using the Virtual Audiometer, there is no record of students doing reflection as part of their out-of-class practice. According to the professor, more time was spent just trying to learn the procedures. Although the assignments with the Virtual Audiometer did not specifically call for reflection, at least some students reported having spent time attempting to analyze the cases of the virtual patients they were testing. The professor could further encourage students to reflect by making it part of homework assignments. Use of the Virtual Audiometer further enhanced opportunities for reflection because students were now having a higher number of more authentic experiences upon which to reflect.

FUTURE RESEARCH DIRECTIONS

Simulations that are used within an instructional context facilitate a different kind of learner-content interaction than more traditional materials. Gibbons (2009) emphasized this difference when describing the non-linear nature of the logic that drives a simulation. Sophisticated simulations, like the Virtual Audiometer, model the real-world because there are so many possible ways to interact with the simulation. The traditional design paradigm has sought to reduce variability in the learner-content interaction. For example, interaction with the content is often scripted and optimized for a particular way of experiencing the content. On the other hand, interaction with human agents is not always as structured and predictable. Moore (2007) positioned this as a tension between "dialog" and "structure" in his theory of transactional distance. Human interaction tends to be "constructive" in that it is synergistic and builds on earlier contributions. A potentially fruitful direction for future research would be to explore the nature of the learner-content interaction when an instructional simulation is being used.

In additional to learner-content interaction, Moore (1989) identified learner-learner and learner-instructor interaction as major categories of interaction in any learning environment. The case study presented in this chapter just touched lightly on how the use of an instructional simulation impacted the learner-learner and learner-instructor interactions in a course. The affordances manifest in different simulations will make possible and even encourage or discourage certain kinds of interaction with others. An in-depth analysis of what features of a simulation enable learner-learner and learner-instructor interaction around the content could be valuable to simulation designers. Additionally, an understanding of how instructors integrate the use of simulations into their face-to-face and out-of-classroom experiences could provide valuate guidelines to those considering the use of instructional simulations.

CONCLUSION

We found that in the case reviewed in this chapter, the use of an instructional simulation helped to enhance the teaching and learning environment in the five ways suggested by the framework we utilized (Roschelle, et al., 2000; West & Graham, 2005): (a) improved visualization through in-class demonstrations and hands-on practice, (b) enhanced authentic feedback through the actions of the simulated patients, (c) enhanced quality and increased quantity of practice and feedback over the use of the portable audiometers, (d) increased amount and quality of interaction and collaboration, and (e) increased and enhanced reflection as students tried to make sense of what the virtual patients' pathology was rather than just focusing on learning procedural knowledge.

Even though the simulation facilitated more student feedback than they would have had without the simulation, we found that some students wanted even more feedback than was being provided. The professor would respond to general trends and errors he saw in the assignments, but students wanted more specific and personal feedback on the quality and correctness of the steps they were taking. The design of the simulation did not facilitate that type of feedback. There was also minimal interaction and collaboration between students on out-of-class assignments, although some students took the initiative to work together.

Simulations like the Virtual Audiometer, have potential for enhancing both face-to-face instructional learning environments as well as online learning environments. It is likely that instructional simulations like the Virtual Audiometer, will be increasingly used in blended learning contexts where the simulation acts as a bridge between in-class and online practice. Therefore, it is imperative that we learn both what makes a good simulation and how to integrate simulations effectively into instruction.

REFERENCES

Aldrich, C. (2002). *A field guide to educational simulations*. Retrieved July 15, 2010, from http://www.simulearn.net/ pdf/ astd.pdf

Baillie, C., & Percoco, G. (2000). A study of present use and usefulness of computer-based learning at a technical university. *European Journal of Engineering Education*, *25*, 33–43. doi:10.1080/030437900308625

Boyd, A., & Jackson, M. (2004). An effective model for rapid skills acquisition through a simulation-based integrated learning environment. *Educational Computing Research*, *30*, 1–21. doi:10.2190/E8CN-91GX-R6WA-Y05N

Cameron, B. (2003). The effectiveness of simulation in a hybrid and online networking course. *TechTrends*, *47*(5), 18–21. doi:10.1007/BF02763200 de Jong, T. (1991). Learning and instruction with computer simulations. *Education and Computing, 6*(3-4), 217–229. doi:10.1016/0167-9287(91)80002-F

de Jong, T., & Njoo, M. (1992). Learning and instruction with computer simulation: Learning processes involved. In Corte, E. d., Linn, M. C., Mandl, H., & Verschaffel, L. (Eds.), *Computer-based learning environments and problem solving* (pp. 411–427).

de Jong, T., & van Joolingen, W. R. (1998). Scientific discovery learning with computer simulations of conceptual domains. *Review of Educational Research, 68*(2), 179–201.

Gibbons, A. McConkie, Seo, K., & Wiley, D. (2009). Simulation approach to instruction. In C. R. Reigeluth & A. A. Carr-Chellmean (Eds.), *Instructional-design theories and models*, vol III (pp. 167-197). New York, NY: Routledge.

Gibbons, A. S., McConkie, M., Seo, K., & Wiley, D. (2002). *Theory for the design of instructional simulations and microworlds*. Unpublished manuscript, Utah State University, Logan, UT.

Gordon, S. P., & Gordon, F. S. (2009). Visualizing and understanding probability and statistics: Graphical simulations using Excel. *PRIMUS (Terre Haute, Ind.), 19*(4), 346–369. doi:10.1080/10511970701882891

Hariri, S., Rawn, C., Srivastava, S., Youngblood, P., & Ladd, A. (2004). Evaluation of a surgical simulator for learning clinical anatomy. *Medical Education, 38*(8), 896–902. doi:10.1111/j.1365-2929.2004.01897.x

Henderson, L., Klemes, J., & Eshet, Y. (2000). Just playing a game? Educational simulation software and cognitive outcomes. *Journal of Educational Computing Research, 22*(1), 105–129. doi:10.2190/EPJT-AHYQ-1LAJ-U8WK

Ioannidou, A., Repening, A., Webb, D., Keyser, D., Luhn, L., & Daetwyler, C. (2010). Mr. Vetro: A collective simulation for teaching health science. *International Journal of Computer-Supported Collaborative Learning, 5*(2), 141–166. doi:10.1007/s11412-010-9082-8

Kneebone, K. (2003). Simulation in surgical training: Educational and practical implications. *Medical Education, 37*, 267–277. doi:10.1046/j.1365-2923.2003.01440.x

Kuriger, G. W., Wan, H., Mirehei, S. M., Tamma, S., & Chen, F. F. (2010). A web-based lean simulation game for office operations: Training the other side of a lean enterprise. *Simulation & Gaming, 41*(4), 487–510. doi:10.1177/1046878109334945

Lederman, N., & Niess, M. (1999). Is it live or is it Memorex? *School Science and Mathematics, 99*, 357–359. doi:10.1111/j.1949-8594.1999.tb17495.x

Lee, J. (1999). Effectiveness of computer-based instructional simulation: A meta analysis. *International Journal of Instructional Media, 26*, 71–85.

Liu, L., & Kinshuk. (2010). The application of simulation-assisted learning statistics (SALS) for correcting misconceptions and improving understanding of correlation. *Journal of Computer Assisted Learning, 26*, 143–158. doi:10.1111/j.1365-2729.2009.00330.x

Mangan, R. (2000). Teaching surgery without a patient. *The Chronicle of Higher Education, 46*, 49–53.

Mitchell, R. (2004). Combining cases and computer simulations in strategic management courses. *Education for Business, 79*, 198–204. doi:10.3200/JOEB.79.4.198-204

Moizer, J., Lean, J., Towler, M., & Abbey, C. (2009). Simulations and games: Overcoming the barriers to their use in higher education. *Active Learning in Higher Education, 10*(3), 207–224. doi:10.1177/1469787409343188

Moore, M. G. (1989). Editorial: Three types of interaction. *American Journal of Distance Education, 3*(2), 1–7. doi:10.1080/08923648909526659

Moore, M. G. (2007). The theory of transactional distance. In Moore, M. G. (Ed.), *Handbook of distance education* (2nd ed., pp. 89–105). Mahwah, NJ: Lawrence Erlbaum.

Ncube, L. B. (2010). A simulation of lean manufacturing: The lean Lemonade Tycoon 2. *Simulation & Gaming, 41*(4), 568–586. doi:10.1177/1046878109334336

Orrill, C. (2001). Building technology-based, learner-centered classrooms: The evolution of a professional development framework. *Educational Technology Research and Development, 49*, 15–34. doi:10.1007/BF02504504

Rawson, R. E., Dispensa, M. E., Goldstein, R. E., Nicholson, K. W., & Vidal, N. K. (2009). A simulation for teaching the basic and clinical science of fluid therapy. *Advances in Physiology Education, 33*, 202–208. doi:10.1152/advan.90211.2008

Reigeluth, C., & Schwartz, E. (1989). An instructional theory for the design of computer-based simulations. *Computer-Based Instruction, 16*, 1–10.

Roschelle, J. M., Pea, R. D., Hoadley, C. M., Gordin, D. N., & Means, B. (2000). Changing how and what children learn in school with computer-based technologies. *The Future of Children, 10*(2), 76–101. doi:10.2307/1602690

Schön, D. A. (1987). *Educating the reflective practitioner*. San Francisco, CA: Jossey-Bass.

Smith-Stoner, M. (2009). Expanding access to learning. *Nurse Educator, 34*(6), 266–270. doi:10.1097/NNE.0b013e3181bc7424

Swan, R. (2005, December). *Design structures for intrinsic motivation*. Paper presented at the Interservice/Industry Training, Simulation, and Education Conference (I/ITSEC), Orlando, FL.

Turkle, S. (2004). How computers change the way we think. *The Chronicle of Higher Education, 50*, 26–28.

West, R., & Graham, C. (2005). Five powerful ways technology can enhance teaching and learning in higher education. *Educational Technology, 45*(3), 20–27.

Weston, T. J. (2005). Why faculty did—and did not—integrate instructional software in their undergraduate classrooms. *Innovative Higher Education, 30*(2), 99–115. doi:10.1007/s10755-005-5013-4

White, B., Kahriman, A., Luberice, L., & Idleh, F. (2010). Evaluation of software for introducing protein structure: Visualization and simulation. *Biochemistry and Molecular Biology Education, 38*(5), 284–289. doi:10.1002/bmb.20410

Windschitl, M., & Andre, T. (1998). Using computer simulations to enhance conceptual change: The roles of constructivist instruction and student epistemological beliefs. *Journal of Research in Science Teaching, 35*(2), 145–160. doi:10.1002/(SICI)1098-2736(199802)35:2<145::AID-TEA5>3.0.CO;2-S

Winer, L.R., & Vázquez-Abad, J. (1981). Towards a theoretical framework for educational simulations. *Simulations/Games for Learning, 11*(3), 114-119.

Xu, Y., & Yang, Y. (2010). Student learning in business simulation: An empirical investigation. *Journal of Education for Business, 85*, 223–228. doi:10.1080/08832320903449469

Yarger, D., Thomas, R., Boysen, P., & Pease, L. (2003). Simulation as learning tools. *Bulletin of the American Meteorological Society, 84*, 1489–1490. doi:10.1175/BAMS-84-11-1489

Yeh, Y. (2004). Nurturing reflective teaching during critical-thinking instruction in a computer simulation program. *Computers & Education, 42*, 181–194. doi:10.1016/S0360-1315(03)00071-X

Zhang, J., Chen, Q., Sun, Y., & Reid, D. J. (2004). Triple scheme of learning support design for scientific discovery learning based on computer simulation: experimental research. *Journal of Computer Assisted Learning, 20*(4), 269–282. doi:10.1111/j.1365-2729.2004.00062.x

ADDITIONAL READING

Aldrich, C. (2003). *Simulations and the future of learning: An innovative (and perhaps revolutionary) approach to e-learning*. San Francisco: Pfeiffer.

Aldrich, C. (2005). *Learning by doing*. San Francisco, CA: Pfeiffer.

Cruickshank, B., & Olander, J. (2002). Can problem-based instruction stimulate thinking? *Journal of College Science Teaching, 31*, 374–377.

de Jong, T., & van Joolingen, W. R. (2007). Model-facilitated learning. In J. M. Spector, M. D. Merrill, J. Van Merrienboer, & M. P. Driscoll (Eds.), *Handbook of research for educational communications and technology* (3rd ed., pp. 457-468; 36). New York: Lawrence Erlbaum.

Gibbons, A. McConkie, Seo, K., & Wiley, D. (2009). Simulation approach to instruction. In C. R. Reigeluth & A. A. Carr-Chellmen (Eds.), *Instructional-design theories and models*, vol III (pp. 167-197). New York: Routledge.

Gibbons, A. S. (2001). Model-centered instruction. *Journal of Structural Learning and Intelligent Systems, 14*(4), 511–540.

Green, K. (2001). Campus Computing, 2001: The 12th National Survey of Computing and Information Technology in American Higher Education. *Campus Computing,* 1-38.

Green, K. (2004). Tech budgets get some relief cautious support for open source application. *Campus Computing,* 1-7.

Grossen, B. (1991). The fundamental skills of higher order thinking. *Journal of Learning Disabilities, 24*, 343–352. doi:10.1177/002221949102400603

Lieberth, A. K., & Martin, D. R. (2005). The instructional effectiveness of a web-based audiometry simulator. *Journal of the American Academy of Audiology, 16*(2), 79–84. doi:10.3766/jaaa.16.2.3

Pogrow, S., & Buchana, B. (1985). Higher-order thinking for compensatory students. *Educational Leadership, 45*, 40–43.

Rieber, L. P. (2004). Microworlds. In D. H. Jonassen (Ed.), *Handbook of research on educational communications and technology* (2nd ed., pp. 355-395; 22). Mahwah, N.J.: Lawrence Erlbaum.

Romme, G. (2004). Perceptions of the value of microworld simulation: Research note. *Simulation & Gaming, 35*, 427–436. doi:10.1177/1046878103261916

Tsai, Y. (1997). Social conflict and social cooperation: Simulating "the tragedy of the commons.". *Simulation & Gaming, 24*, 356–362. doi:10.1177/1046878193243007

Weller, J. (2004). Simulation in undergraduate medical education: Bridging the gap between theory and practice. *Medical Education, 38*, 32–38. doi:10.1111/j.1365-2923.2004.01739.x

Wynder, M. (2003). Facilitating creativity in management accounting: a computerized business simulation. *Accounting Education*, *13*, 231–250. doi:10.1080/0963928041000167 6639

Zohar, A., & Dori, Y. (2003). Higher order thinking skills and low-achieving students: Are they mutually exclusive. *Journal of the Learning Sciences*, *12*, 145–181. doi:10.1207/S15327809JLS1202_1

KEY TERMS AND DEFINITIONS

Audiometer: An instrument for gauging and recording acuity of hearing

Audiometry: The testing of hearing using an audiometer

Computer-Based Instructional Simulation (CBIS): A computer program that allows learners to actively explore a domain by manipulating input variables of a model of the domain and that includes appropriate instructional augmentation

Reflection-*In*-Action: When people reflect on their actions as they are making decisions while acting or performing

Reflection-*On*-Action: When people reflect back on actions they have take in the past

Virtual Audiometer: A specific CBIS used to demonstrate audiometric procedures to students that also allows students to test virtual patients with the virtual audiometer. The simulation includes tools like the Profile Maker and Session Viewer, which allow the instructor to create infinite, specific virtual patients for students to practice on while data is collected about student accuracy.

Chapter 12
3D Virtual Worlds in Higher Education

Lucia Rapanotti
The Open University, UK

Shailey Minocha
The Open University, UK

Leonor Barroca
The Open University, UK

Maged N. Kamel Boulos
University of Plymouth, UK

David R. Morse
The Open University, UK

ABSTRACT

3D virtual worlds are becoming widespread due to cheaper powerful computers, high-speed broadband connections and efforts towards their tighter integration with current 2D Web environments. Besides traditional gaming and entertainment applications, some serious propositions are starting to emerge for their use, particularly in education, where they are perceived as enablers of active learning, learning by doing, and knowledge construction through social interaction. However, there is still little understanding of how 3D virtual worlds can be designed and deployed effectively in the education domain, and many challenges remain. This chapter makes a contribution towards such an understanding by reporting on three notable case studies at the authors' own institutions, which have pioneered the use of Second Life, a 3D virtual world, in higher education.

INTRODUCTION

3D virtual worlds, such as Second Life[1,2], appear to offer new opportunities for educators to teach in immersive and creative spaces. While reliable data on their actual uptake is still lacking and is, in fact, difficult to obtain due to the fast pace of change in this sector, a flavour of the widespread interest in education can be gained by looking at the snapshots and lists published online, for instance, at the Virtual Environments home[3], the Second Life in Education home[4], the Virtual Worlds Watch

DOI: 10.4018/978-1-61350-080-4.ch012

network[5] or the Jokadia Virtual Worlds wiki[6], as well as the growing number of books recently published on the subject (see, e.g., Wankel & Kingsley, 2009; Annetta, Folta & Klesath, 2010; Molka-Danielsen & Destchmann, 2009). From such data, it transpires that a vast number of higher education institutions, particularly in the US and UK, have a presence in virtual worlds, especially in Second Life.

While firm evidence on the pedagogical effectiveness of virtual worlds remains somewhere in the future, there are indications from a growing body of work that there are advantages to their adoption in education, including their ability to evoke a strong sense of presence even in remote participants (Witmer & Singer, 1998; De Lucia, Francese, Passero & Tortora, 2009), to increase their social awareness and communication (Capin, Noser, D. Thalmann, Pandzic, & N. Thalmann, 1997), to support closely coupled collaboration (Heldal, Schroeder, Steed, Axelsson, & Spante, 2005; Otto, Roberts, & Wolff, 2006) at a distance, and to enable constructivist and situated learning (Bronack, Riedl & Tashner, 2006; Hollins & Robbins, 2008).

Due to the dearth of authoritative pedagogical frameworks or widely recognised design good practices for adopting 3D virtual worlds, educators face a range of both pedagogical and learning space design challenges that can directly affect learning outcomes and the learner's experience. While not claiming to provide all the answers, this chapter will attempt to disentangle some of the issues, based on current practice and experience with 3D virtual worlds at the authors' own institutions, in the hope of contributing to the ongoing discourse on the matter. After an initial review of the use of 3D virtual worlds in education, and some related pedagogical theories, the chapter will discuss three representative case studies on the use of Second Life.

Specifically:

- the first case study will concern a Second Life environment developed as part of an innovative post-graduate research programme recently launched by The Open University (Rapanotti, Barroca, Vargas-Vera & Reeves, 2010; Barroca, Rapanotti, Petre &Vargas-Vera, 2010);
- the second case study will discuss the experiences of introducing Second Life in a part-time and distance learning undergraduate course at The Open University to support socialisation and team working in small group projects amongst globally distributed students (Minocha & Morse, 2010);
- the third case study will focus on the University of Plymouth 'Sexual Health' Public Education and Outreach SIM in Second Life (Kamel Boulos & Toth-Cohen, 2009).

The key themes in our case studies are socialisation, the building of online communities and meaningful interaction mediated by 3D virtual worlds. The case studies will address characteristics of 3D virtual worlds as learning environments and how their affordances and pedagogy have influenced their design and the development of learning activities; it will also include a discussion of any specific research questions addressed and the outcome of any evaluation carried out. The chapter will also reflect on the future of 3D virtual worlds.

RELATED WORK

With the increase in social software tools deployed in education (such as blogs, wikis, podcasts, social networking sites, social bookmarking sites, 3D virtual worlds or massively multiplayer online role-playing games) a new pedagogy is starting to emerge. According to Dawley (2009) social software tools afford new forms of knowledge construction, which not only impact the way individuals interact and learn, but also affects the thinking process itself, with virtual worlds providing particular affordances for new forms of online communication and knowledge representation. The underlying theory of learning through social software tools has also been considered by Dalsgaard (2006) who argues that such technology supports a social constructivist approach to learning: this emphasises the socially and culturally situated context of cognition in which the process of acquiring knowledge occurs in shared endeavours (Duffy & Cunningham, 1996), as opposed to cognitive constructivism, which focuses on individuals making intellectual sense of the materials on their own (Felix, 2005). Social constructivism, with its emphasis on learner's personal meaning, and situated and contextual learning, complements and contrasts more traditional educational schools of thought, such as behaviourism or cognitivism (Ertmer & Newby, 1993) in which the responsibility rests with the educator to deliver knowledge, while the learner passively receives it (Felix, 2005).

Triggered by technological advances, we are witnessing a change in the learner's profile. Students born in the 1980s and 1990s, sometimes referred to as the 'Net Generation' or 'Generation Y,' have grown up with information technology: adapting to changing technology and finding information online is second nature to them, but they often lack the skills to analyse and synthesise such information, or to think critically, creatively and collaboratively (Carpenter, Wetheridge, Smith, Goodman & Struijvé, 2010). At the same time, there is a growing need for retraining in the workplace, with more mature workers re-entering education. As a consequence we are witnessing a shift in focus from delivery to interactive education: educators conversing with the students instead of broadcasting, empowering students to learn through discovery and collaboration rather than just absorbing the facts (Tapscott, 2009), placing responsibility on learners to interact actively with materials (Molka-Danielsen & Deutschmann, 2009) rather than passively receive knowledge, emphasising collaboration rather than competition, and knowledge construction rather than instruction (Elliot, 2009). This shift is often accompanied by a move away from traditional classroom-based instructional approaches and learning spaces towards more informal constructivist ones (see, e.g., (Oblinger, 2006) or (Lynch, Carbone, Arnott & Jamieson, 2002), which reports on a move from a traditional classroom setting to a 'studio' setting for teaching information technology). In the online learning domain, this move is being facilitated by tools such as discussion fora, social networks and institutional virtual learning environments, which enable conversational interactions between individuals or groups, from real-time instant messaging to asynchronous collaborative teamwork (Minocha, 2009). According to Hollins and Robbins (2008) virtual worlds provide yet another opportunity for educators to engage students while challenging the conventions of the classroom.

In this landscape, 3D virtual worlds open new possibilities for informal online learning when compared to 2D learning environments. In an avatar-based 3D virtual world, such as Second Life, the user's avatar and its appearance add new dimensions to the user's online identity, and immersion enriches human perceptions through embodiment. According to Stary (2001), immersion allows users not just to interact with the software as separate entities, but to become part of the artificial world, directly manipulating artificial objects as active participants rather than passive consumers of visual information: through their avatars they can navigate (fly, walk, sit, teleport) the 3D space, encounter other avatars and communicate with them through gestures, voice or text, and instant messaging. These communication and interaction mechanisms create a sense of presence and place in the 3D virtual world (Witmer & Singer, 1998; De Lucia, Francese, Passero & Tortora, 2009), which is more similar to face-to-face (offline) situations in the real world than interactions in a 2D virtual environment such as Facebook®[7], or even through video conferencing. This particular affordance is greatly helped by the very high plasticity and programmability of the latest generations of 3D virtual worlds (Kamel Boulos, Ramloll, Jones & Toth-Cohen, 2008). Virtuality and simulation also play an important role in synthetic knowledge acquisition (Peschl & Riegler, 2001) (i.e., acquisition of knowledge which allows us to predict and anticipate situations or events, situated cognition) (Dieterle & Clarke, 2008) and situated learning (Dede, 2009). Bronack, Riedl and Tashner (2006) observe that because of their characteristics (i.e., sense of presence, immediacy, movement, artefacts and communication means unavailable in other tools) 3D virtual worlds are particularly suited to support social constructivism, particularly for distance learners who have fewer opportunities to mix with their tutors and peers in real-life.

Second Life is currently the most widely adopted virtual word in education, being used in a range of disciplines, from arts and music, literature and mathematics, architectural design and modelling, to psychology and language learning, to name a few (collections of case studies can be found in Wankel, 2009; Wankel & Kingsley, 2009; Rufer-Bach, 2009; Annetta, Folta & Klesath, 2010; Molka-Danielesen & Deutschmann, 2009). Although Second Life can facilitate traditional educator-led learning, so far the focus of educators using Second Life has been more towards activities and spaces which may be difficult, unsafe or resource-intensive in real life, such as holding virtual team meetings and conferences with geographically distributed participants, role playing, training and simulations (e.g., in healthcare or crime investigation); it has also been used for 3D data visualisations (e.g., weather data) and 3D modelling (e.g., DNA and RNA models of genetics).

CASE STUDY: BUILDING VIRTUAL RESEARCH COMMUNITIES

The Context

The Open University (OU), UK, is a market leader in higher education at a distance, with over two hundred thousand distance learners worldwide. Although the majority of those learners are studying towards degrees at undergraduate and postgraduate[8] levels, the OU also offers a selection of research degrees, including Masters of Philosophy (MPhil) and Doctor of Philosophy (PhD), and has a (relatively smaller) population of research students. At the latest published count, in 2008/09, the OU had 627 full-time residential research students, and 676 part-time research students at a distance. OU part-time research students work mainly from home, but are also required to participate in some activities on campus, and meet with their supervisors face-to-face from time to time.

In the last decade, the UK has seen a dramatic change in the nature of research degrees, particularly at doctoral level. What was in essence a form of research apprenticeship forged around the student-supervisor relation has been challenged in recent years by the rise of new research degree offerings (e.g., doctorate by publication or practice based), the establishment of external quality benchmarks and quality assurance processes, and an emphasis on explicit research skills recognition and training (Park, 2005). Also, increased importance is now placed on the quality of the research environment and the integration of research students within global research communities. Such a shift has raised significant challenges for HE institutions, particularly when it comes to their provision to remote research students. It is in response to such challenges that our project was set up.

The Project

The OU Computing Department has currently a population of just over 30 part-time distance research students from as far as the US, South Africa, Japan and the Philippines. At the beginning of 2008, a project was set up, led by the first and third authors (of this chapter), aimed at investigating how to: enhance and further develop our provision to research students; promote a wider use of technology to support distant research students; foster distributed communities around specific research areas; and extend our reach to international markets.

One of the outcomes of that project is a Masters level research award, the Virtual MPhil[9]: launched as a pilot in October 2009, it aims to provide an online MPhil experience comparable to that of residential full time students, but with no face-to-face requirements. The Virtual MPhil has led to a novel infrastructure of processes, practices and technology to support the student-supervisor dialogue remotely, foster online research communities, and develop and track research skills. The project ethos was to deliver innovation, support and guidance in a rapidly changing landscape, whilst allowing for flexibility and individual user's choice. The technological infrastructure provided is comprehensive, spanning a variety of online technologies, from asynchronous to synchronous to immersive. In introducing technology into our research degrees, considerations were given to how each type of technology could support comparable functions, without necessarily requiring a forced duplication from the full-time, face-to-face to the remote online model, and how it could foster a community spirit and a sense of belonging for distance research students. Among the innovations was the development of a virtual campus called deep|think in Second Life. An in depth account of how research students are supported on the Virtual MPhil as a whole can be found in (Barroca, Rapanotti, Petre & Vargas-Vera, 2010).

In this section we focus primarily on the deep|think campus and its role within the programme. The main research questions behind the project in general, and the virtual campus design and deployment in particular, were:

- how to provide remote students an online research experience comparable to our full-time resident students;
- how to design a fit-for-purpose virtual environment to meet the needs of a globally distributed online research community.

The Deep|Think Campus

As well as being geographically distributed around the world, our part-time students are usually in full-time employment, often working as IT professionals. As a consequence they have very limited opportunities to participate in face-to-face sessions or to benefit from daily exchanges with peers and senior researchers, often making them feel more isolated and less integrated in our research community than our residential students. deep|think was designed as a space in which distance students can experience, albeit virtually, some of the interactions which enrich the daily life of our residential research students. Technically, deep|think is a large Second Life development, made of two simulations (SIMs) which have been modelled into five distinct, but interconnected small islands, each with a well-defined function: a *welcome island* to welcome visitors and for orientation purposes; a *study island* with meeting spaces, common rooms and exhibition facilities; a *library island* for access to a variety of resources for study and research (a recreation space, the *Beach Bar*, is provided nearby for relaxation and fun activities (e.g., chatting, playing pool or listening to music and dancing); a *sandbox*, for 'rezzing' (i.e., making 3D objects appear within the virtual world) objects and scripting activities; and a *central island* with a main auditorium and related smaller theatres for large events, such as conferences, workshops and lectures. A recurrent theme in the design is lightness and openness, with land, sky and water used imaginatively to create a variety of social and collaborative spaces (see Figure 1). A detailed description of the campus can be found in (Rapanotti, Barroca, Vargas-Vera & Reeves, 2010).

The Student Experience

Induction and In-World Skills

All our new research students go through a programme of induction into the university and their degree, in order to gain an understanding of what doing a degree entails, to become familiar with the OU and its structures, and to introduce students to each other, to their supervisors, and to the broader research community. Two residential induction sessions are run every year (in autumn and spring), each organised as a two-day intensive programme of workshops and events. On the Virtual MPhil induction is conducted online using a variety of technologies (including Moodle, podcasts, video conferencing and Second Life) and delivery modes (i.e., synchronously, asynchronously, individually and in groups).

The induction resources and activities related to deep|think aim to introduce the virtual space to new students, develop their digital literacy in the medium and function as an ice-breaker among peers and with academics. We have created an introductory podcast, accompanied by additional links to resources, to help new students set up their Second Life account, overcome some initial technological hurdles and locate deep|think in Second Life. Students are invited to review these materials in their own time prior to accessing the virtual space for the first time. Students and their supervisors are then invited to a tour of deep|think, led by us, for a brief introduction of the facilities and to the basics of inworld interaction.

As part of the design of deep|think, we have included spaces and functionalities to support further engagement both on an individual and group basis. In particular, on arrival, users are teleported to the welcome island, the entry point for the community. As well as a 3D model map and text panels with general information to visitors, we have designed a garden tour, called the *path*

Figure 1. Spaces on deep|think. From top-left, clockwise: the main auditorium; a 'sky pod' (a small meeting room suspended in the sky); the Beach Bar; the sandbox; the students' common room; an underwater theatre.

to enlightenment, which visitors can take for an interactive introduction to Second Life and various deep|think features, including: teleportation maps and points for fast point-to-point travel around the islands; reflection post-boxes, to send anonymous reflections on using deep|think; and notecard givers, ubiquitous on deep|think, used for induction, training and general user help. Orientation areas like ours are fairly common in Second Life and are found to be particularly useful to novice users. The path to enlightenment is one of the locations we take visitors during the induction tour.

For further engagement and inworld skill development we have also designed an interactive tutorial, called Mary's Quest, that students can take individually or in groups, in their own time. Mary is a fictional student avatar, protagonist of a machinima introductory video (available from the Virtual MPhil home) about deep|think; Mary's Quest takes visitors around key locations on deep|think and teaches them how to make good use of tools and facilities. Quests are widely used in virtual settings to keep learners interested and motivated. For example quests and challenges have been used in game settings to teach users network security across a broad range of scenarios (Boit, Eirund, Geimer, Mendonca Ott & Sethmann, 2008). As visitors proceed through their challenges, they learn new skills and become more competent users. Mary's Quest is used to develop our members' inworld skills: the quest locations paint a picture of Mary's growing familiarity with deep|think, discovering spaces useful to her study, such as where to participate in public events, to get together with her peers, to show off her work, to find online resources and to socialise and have fun. Some 'breadcrumbs' of Mary's use of the islands are scattered around for visitors to discover, adding an element of fun to the experience. The sandbox challenge is particularly taxing, taking newcomers through the basics of scripting and sculpting in the 3D environment.

Community

Residential students are fully integrated into the research community and have a variety of opportunities for both informal and formal research dialogues, above their normal interactions with supervisors. These include traditional mechanisms, such as research groups, research seminars and an annual research student conference, but also less common practices such as regular workshops to discuss research skills or self-help student groups.

For our part-time students, a set of social spaces has been designed on deep|think to provide a choice of appropriate environments for formal and informal activities for both students and supervisors. Events such as conferences and workshops are supported by a large auditorium which can host up to 180 avatars at any one time, with video stream capabilities and slide presentation screens. For smaller groups or supervisory sections, a selection of meeting spaces are available, from little pods in the sky to underwater theatres, in a variety of styles and arrangements to suit different tastes and needs. An exhibition centre provides facilities for poster displays, which can be used by students and academics to make their research work visible to the wider community. The deep|think library allow access to OU library licensed and free content: designed as an open-air garden, it includes four *explore and playback zones*, each supporting browsing of a variety of materials. Some spaces are customisable by users, like our staff and students rooms; others are mainly for socialising, like our Beach Bar.

It should be noted that matching design to function and meaning was one of the drivers for the design of deep|think (as well as the overall technological infrastructure of the Virtual MPhil). However, it was not our intention to prescribe how users should use the space for their own particular needs. Instead, we wanted to provide the lower layers of functional access, skills and practices that underpin the 'creative appropriation' by the users to determine their own environments and contexts for research, in accordance with Sharpe, Beetham & McGill (2009)'s pyramid model for effective e-learners. We will return to this point in our reflection at the end of this section.

Data Collection

The first and third authors (of this chapter) have established a long-term programme of evaluation for the Virtual MPhil to test: the comparability of the experience between distance online and residential face-to-face students; and the design fitness of our virtual environment to meet the needs of a globally distributed online research community.

The evaluation programme comprises three major stages: Stage 1, prior to the October (2009) pilot start and now completed, was aimed at informing the design and development of our infrastructure; Stage 2, currently running, covers the first year of the pilot, aiming at extensive user testing and fine-tuning of the infrastructure; Stage 3, started in October 2010, aims at continuous monitoring and improvement of the programme and its infrastructure, hopefully leading to a set of guidelines and codified practices for the effective match between technology and function in the context of distributed research communities.

The overall evaluation approach is that of collecting snapshots from diverse communities of stakeholders, on diverse aspects of the programme and its infrastructure, at critical times during the degree.

During Stage 1, primary data were collected via surveys distributed to academics and research students both within and outside the OU, structured feedback forms from participants in organised tours of deep|think, and free-form comments from occasional visitors of the islands. These were complemented by secondary evidence from the literature, educational virtual worlds, online communities and mailing lists, as well as direct inspection of existing Second Life educational worlds. Our primary aim was to collect a body of evidence as to current usage and attitudes towards the use of Second Life in higher education, particularly for research supervision and communities, as well as guidance for, and initial feedback on, our design of the islands. The supervisors we surveyed had on average 8 years of online supervision experience, using a variety of tools and spending over 70% of their supervisory time online.

During Stage 2, currently running, we have started to collect primary data from our own students, supervisors and researchers, both through surveys and interviews, and through our established processes of induction and students' progress monitoring. We have also instrumented deep|think with a variety of sensors to collect statistics on the use of the space, which complement our evaluation mailboxes where visitors can leave their comments should they wish to do so. Also, while our welcome island is public and can be visited by anyone with a Second Life account, the remaining islands require registration, so we can monitor how many users register to access the islands. The number of deep|think registered users has grown steadily from 33 in October 2009 to 126 at the beginning of October 2010, and currently deep|think is visited on average by 80 to 100 distinct avatars every month.

Reflections

Mirroring findings in the literature, our data indicate that among the factors which make Second Life appealing for education are the possibility of creating a bespoke immersive learning experience, the strong sense of presence it evokes even in remote participants, a more personal experience than with other more traditional communication technologies, the fact that it is free and universal (up to a point) and that it can support large groups. On the other hand, we found that the main barriers include the need for high specification machines and bandwidth, a steep initial learning curve, variable performance and reliability of the software, and the fact that interaction through avatars is not to everybody's taste.

One notable result from our Stage 1 evaluation is that the supervisors we surveyed provided an overwhelming positive feedback on the use of virtual worlds for supervision, with half of them claiming that a blend of current technology can support all aspects of supervising students online. The feedback from students, however, was more mixed, with a split between those who favoured the use of virtual worlds and those who preferred other more conventional communication technologies.

Feedback from tours of deep|think, both in Stage 1 and 2, was unanimously positive as to the design of the islands that were perceived as pleasant, open, welcoming, colourful, inviting, and well-signposted. The variety of immersive spaces provided was also seen favourably as an enabler to a wide range of learning and teaching activities, student collaboration and socialisation.

Similar to students surveyed in Stage 1, our students were also split into those who expressed a preference for deep|think as a platform for meeting and sharing over more traditional synchronous conferencing systems we offer (i.e., Elluminate Live! and Skype), and those who thought that the latter provided all the functions they needed, in a more efficient manner and with much less initial learning and effort required. Some also stated that they had no inclination to be part of a virtual world, again reinforcing our previous findings that such a paradigm is still seen as unusual and not to everybody's taste. In fact, we have noticed a much greater emotional response to the use of Second Life compared to more conventional technology, particularly in relation to the use of avatars as a proxy for interaction.

Technical problems were also experienced by some of our students, detracting from their overall experience: for instance some of them, those with lower machine specs or limited internet bandwidth, experienced poor performance of the Second Life software, with their avatars not been rendered properly by the environment (e.g., appearing as a cloud of vapour, which happens under low bandwidth conditions) or not been responsive to movements; the voice chat facility in Second Life also exhibited poor reliability at times.

We have also been monitoring the patterns of use of deep|think. From what we have observed so far, after taking part in our tours and exhibiting some initial curiosity, it appears that only a small minority of our users continue to make regular use of deep|think. The more persistent users tend to be those who are already well integrated within the Second Life community, or those who have a particular interest in the technology for research or scholarship purposes. For instance, students engaged in evaluating the design of virtual worlds or in developing immersive learning environments tend to meet their supervisors on deep|think or other Second Life locations.

A larger constituency of uses appear to be interested in participating in formal, structured events, should these be made available to them. For instance, some of our groups have started to run scheduled formal meetings using the deep|think sky pods, where the ambience and facilities mirror those of a small meeting room in real life. Others have run public lectures for an invited audience. Such events seem to generate a good level of attendance.

We have also noticed that often it takes time and repeated exposure to Second Life for users to start to appreciate the potential of the medium. We have examples of users who over a period of a few months have completely reversed their position on the use of Second Life, from one of skepticism, if not plain hostility, to one of enthusiastic engagement.

As a result of our observations, we are now rethinking our original approach to community engagement, striving for more active ways of engaging users. In particular, we are designing a structured programme of events for the upcoming academic year, including a series of formal lectures and workshops, which is more closely coupled with similar events we run using other synchronous technology. Conscious of the reservations expressed by potential users, we have also widen access to deep|think, allowing larger constituencies of students and academics to make use of their space.

CASE STUDY: SUPPORTING DISTRIBUTED TEAM-WORKING

The Context

Software development teams are increasingly working collaboratively at a distance and across multiple time zones. This creates challenges in communication, building shared values and trust, coordinating activities, and distance can slow group communication and consensus making (Cummings & Kiesler, 2007). In response to these trends, social software tools such as wikis, blogs, and 3D virtual worlds such as Second Life are being integrated into communication and collaboration processes to enhance the productivity and effectiveness of virtual teams (e.g. Farrell, 2006; Decker, Ras, Rech, Jaubert & Rieth, 2007; Rufer-Bach, 2009).

In order to prepare students for these changes in software engineering practice, there is a need to use technology in software engineering education to simulate authentic structures and work practices. Use of collaborative and discourse tools will provide students with the experience of communicating and negotiating with diverse stakeholders with different views and backgrounds, and also enable the development of transferable skills for working with community tools in the computing industry (Minocha, Petre & Roberts, 2008). Furthermore, team working is a skill that continues to be in demand by employers (see, for example the report published by e-Skills UK, the Sector Skills Agency for ICT and Computing (Ratcliffe, 2009)). This requirement has long been recognised by professional computing institutions such as the British Computer Society and the Association of Computing Machinery. The subject benchmark statement for Computing in the UK states that students should have "the ability to work as a member of a development team, recognising the different roles within a team and different ways of organising teams" (QAA, 2007).

In response to these requirements for software engineering practice, a course called 'Team working in distributed environments' (course code: M253[10]) was launched in 2005. M253 is a six-month long, second level part-time distance-education course in the Computing curriculum at the OU. The course is presented twice per year and has 150-250 students on each presentation. While studying the course, students, typically in teams of four to six students per team, work at a distance on a software requirements gathering and analysis scenario. Example scenarios include: requirements analysis and design of prototype websites for a holiday lettings agency, a gardening club, or a travel agency that offers specialist tailor-made holidays. Each student team is assigned a tutor, who: has the role of a team mentor (not a manager); moderates discussions in the forum if required; monitors progress; resolves any student problems, and assesses the assignments and provides feedback on them. Further information on the design of the course can be found in Oldfield & Morse (2005, 2007).

Technologies on the Course

When the course was first launched in 2005, each student team was assigned an online discussion forum for asynchronous communication and for sharing documents. It was suggested that teams could chose other synchronous or asynchronous technologies for team communication. Students have been using online conferencing tools such as FlashMeeting[11], Skype[12] and instant messaging tools (e.g. Yahoo Messenger[13]). In 2007, each team was given a wiki as a collaborative working space for team-related materials such as meeting agendas and notes, decisions, list of tasks, and so on. In 2008, the course team decided to introduce a 3D virtual world to a volunteer set of M253 students and tutors to support synchronous communications and team working. The course team felt synchronous avatar-based communication and real-time collaboration in Second Life would help student teams in the following ways:

- enhance socialisation within teams;
- support team building and facilitate team meetings better than other synchronous technologies which the students have access to, such as Skype and instant messaging.

Perceived Lack of Socialisation in 2D Environments

Socialisation encompasses the social act of coming together for a common purpose, for example, when students familiarise themselves with one other and learn the norms, roles, rules and codes of conduct of the team. Socialisation activities could involve students sharing their personal interests such as photography, travelling, etc. in their first few blog posts or discussing their reasons for taking up the course in the discussion forum. As a result of this shared experience, participants are able to gain an awareness of one another, relate to one another (Wegerif, 1998) and establish a connection. Although blogs, wikis and forums can support socialisation, their asynchronous nature can affect students' perceptions of social presence and the effectiveness of collaboration. Our empirical research on the pedagogical role and effectiveness of wikis (Minocha & Thomas, 2007) and blogs (Kerawalla, Minocha, Kirkup & Conole, 2008; Minocha & Roberts, 2008) in distance education has shown that inadequate socialisation at the start of the collaborative activity was a key obstacle to conducting group projects or activities at a distance. A 3D virtual world such as Second Life that supports synchronous interactions via avatars with voice, text and gestures may facilitate socialisation, an antecedent for effective online collaboration (Minocha & Roberts, 2008). The sense of presence and sense of place that a 3D virtual world gives makes learning, and indeed socialising a more 'human' experience than many other 2D technology-enabled learning environments.

Our overall research purpose in introducing Second Life in M253 has been to investigate the pedagogical effectiveness of a 3D virtual world in supporting working in a distributed team. This led us to formulate Research question 1.

Research Question 1

Does a 3D virtual world such as Second Life facilitate socialisation and team working amongst students working on a team project at a distance?

Our students, as part of their OU studies or at their workplaces use a number of other collaboration and communication technologies - Skype and instant messaging being two popular tools. In our informal discussions with students, we noted that they often compared their Second Life experiences to tools that they were already familiar with, which led us to formulate Research question 2.

Research Question 2

How does Second Life compare to other collaboration tools such as instant messaging or Skype?

We were interested in finding out the obstacles (if any) that students face in their interactions with Second Life so that we could improve our induction and training procedures. This led to Research question 3.

Research Question 3

What are the difficulties that students experience in becoming acquainted with and working in Second Life?

In the next section, we describe the process of training M253 students to use Second Life. We will then present the research methodology for eliciting students' experiences in Second Life. Finally, based on our empirically grounded data, we will draw conclusions about the effectiveness of Second Life in supporting team working at a distance.

Introducing Second Life on M253

The course team was interested in evaluating the effectiveness of Second Life on M253 before using it on the course more widely, with the second and last authors (of this chapter) leading the evaluation. Volunteer students are recruited for the Second Life trial at the start of every presentation; typically, 18-24 students are recruited in each presentation, corresponding to 3-4 teams. The course team provided Second Life training to four M253 tutors when Second Life was first introduced on the course, and the volunteer students are allocated to these tutors because some training and induction is required before users can feel comfortable interacting with Second Life.

Developing Students' Second Life Skills

Based on our experience since 2008, we have identified two key areas of training and skills development in Second Life: (a) using the Second Life software; and (b) communication and group-working skills.

The Second Life website[14] has resources that explain how to download the software and create an account, including the steps necessary to create an avatar. The website also has a quick start guide which introduces new users to the Second Life user interface, how to change an avatar's appearance, how to walk and fly, and how to communicate within Second Life using instant messaging, text chat and voice. We send the URLs of these resources, along with our own user guide, to the students so that they can install the software, become familiar with the interface and learn about avatar-based interactions. We have found that taking students through the Second Life user interface features again when they come inworld for the first session is helpful. Before the first session, we (the course team and the tutor(s), who act as trainers or facilitators) enquire of the students' avatar names and send them details of the meeting venue. We then 'friend' the avatars: this enables us to know when the students come into Second Life and teleport them to the meeting location if the students find it difficult to reach it themselves.

During the first session, we run a tutorial on the main OU island[15] where we introduce Second Life user interface features to the students and give them an opportunity to ask questions. In this session we also ask the students to 'friend' one another as a way to learn this Second Life feature and also as a means of socialisation (i.e., getting to know one another). We provide the students with a guide to the etiquette and norms for interaction and collaboration inworld. Figure 2 shows a tutorial in progress using a slide presenter within Second Life.

In Second Life there are many interesting educational islands[16]. We take students on tours to some of these islands, so that students are exposed to the potential of 3D virtual worlds in education and learn to navigate (fly, walk, teleport) and communicate (group chat in text and voice). The tours also facilitate socialisation. In our first couple of sessions we give students notecards with landmarks of meeting locations in deep|think and take them on a tour of deep|think. Our chosen locations are a mix of formal (chairs and tables) and informal (bean bags on the floor or in a tree house or underground) locations so as to give some variety to the students. Figure 3 shows one of the meeting locations in deep|think – the sky pods. The design of the pods is such that communication in one pod cannot be heard in another pod: two breakout discussions are in progress in Figure 3.

After these induction sessions, the tutor continues to provide support with regard to interacting in Second Life, if required, to the students

Figure 2. An induction tutorial in progress Picture courtesy of the Five points island, Georgia State University, USA

Figure 3. Meeting pods in deep|think

when they start meeting inworld for their teamwork. The tutor does not participate in their team meetings (as per the course design) but informs the students that he or she will be available in Second Life during the meeting times so that the students can send him or her a message if they need help.

Data Collection

At the start of the course, we send the research information sheet and a consent form to the students by email. The information sheet has the following details: the research team contact details, the motivation for the research, how the research will be carried out and how much time it will involve, who has access to the data collected, and how the data will be stored and handled. In the consent form, we explain that participants are agreeing to be audio and video recorded, how their anonymity would be maintained, and that they have the right to withdraw at any point during the study without any impact on the course or their assessment. We also encourage students to contact us if they have any questions prior to giving their consent to participate in the research. The ethical guidelines of the British Educational Research Association (BERA)[17] were followed in the preparation of the research materials, including all interview protocols, which were submitted to the OU's Ethics Committee[18] for review and approval.

The empirical investigations, guided by the research questions, involved: conducting group-interviews (see Figure 4) within the first month of the course, thus starting to elicit early and collective feedback from the students about their experiences with the Second Life software, how we (the tutor and research team) can support them better and the extent to which Second Life is supporting their teamwork; interviews with individual students by email mid-way through the course to allow the students to think and report on their experiences with Second Life (guided by open-

Figure 4. Group interview with the students. Picture courtesy of the University of Worcester Island, UK.

ended questions); and semi-structured interviews with individual students in Second Life once the course has ended to enable students to reflect on their personal experiences and perceptions of Second Life. The questions in the semi-structured interviews focus on how Second Life contributed to their team meetings; how it compares to other collaboration and synchronous communication technologies that the students may have used at work or on other courses; their choice of spaces within Second Life for meetings, and any recommendations they might have for the course team and researchers to consider when enhancing the student experience in Second Life.

We have analysed the data collected over the last two presentations of the course: May 2009 - October 2009 and November 2009 - April 2010, involving 24 and 20 students, respectively. An inductive analysis (after Braun & Clarke, 2006; Thomas, 2006) of the data was undertaken to identify themes, sub-themes, and any causal or other relationships between themes, using the research questions as guidance. The inductive approach is not as strong as some other approaches in the area of theory or model development (e.g. grounded theory, discourse analysis), but it provides a simple and efficient way of analysing qualitative data for deriving findings linked to focused evaluation questions (Thomas, 2006).

Reflections

Our investigations have shown that students felt a sense of fun, engagement and commitment to other team members because they perceive a Second Life meeting to be similar to a face-to-face meeting. The students explained that the sense of presence and being in the same place within Second Life helped to generate team spirit, with the added advantage that their real life identities were hidden. The avatar-based interactions can give a sense of anonymity, of hiding real-life characteristics such as physical appearance, physical disabilities, or ethnicity, which was preferred by students. With regard to teamwork, Second Life gives a face-to-face style interaction so students feel that their decision-making is faster and easier in Second Life than in asynchronous technologies (e.g. a discussion forum) or in audio-conferencing systems such as Skype. The students felt that the face-to-face style encounter in Second Life and the synchronicity of interaction gave them a sense of accountability to other team members.

Even though a 3D virtual world may provide a face-to-face environment, the expressiveness of current avatars is limited (Meadows, 2008). The avatars can be moved next to each other to talk but often stare blankly into space, inert and unengaged. In current 3D worlds such as Second Life there is a limited set of emotional cues, facial expressions and gestures in Second Life that made it a rather impersonal experience for some students. This minimal set of user interface controls and their lack of transparency (the controls can be difficult to interpret and interact with), has a potential to convey 'false' behaviour or 'no response' which may be unintended. An important focus of future research is, therefore, how to make avatars more expressive – able to make appropriate eye contact, smile, accurately show interest or boredom, and so on (Donath, 2008).

Students described the difficulties they experienced in becoming acquainted with and working in Second Life. The initial induction and training can appear onerous or time consuming to some students because they feel that they have to spend two to three hours just getting started on using the technology. Students felt that it took them a while to get used to the Second Life interface in spite of our initial induction and training. Students found that sometimes there was a lag while using Second Life or the software crashed. These problems could also be caused by an unstable or poor network connection at the student's end. Other difficulties in using Second Life include that the application is resource hungry and not all PCs or laptops have the graphics card required. Running Second Life requires a high-specification graphics card and a minimum of 4 gigabytes of random access memory (RAM). That said, it is possible that this problem will diminish once older computers have become obsolete. Some students who do not have a headset, prefer not to use voice (perhaps because of their 'foreign' accent), or are unable to use voice in Second Life may not enjoy the meetings as much as they would if they were using voice. There were regular occasions where students joined the meeting, but did not have any sound. This happened to three out of the four members of a team. Generally this was resolved by a reboot, but this typically delayed the meeting by 5-10 minutes and caused dissatisfaction among other team members. Without voice communication, Second Life becomes an instant messaging platform and the multimodal capability of Second Life is not exploited.

The multiple modalities of Second Life can support users with special needs; for example, use of instant messaging and chat instead of audio for users with hearing problems. Virtual Ability, Inc.[19] is a non-profit corporation based in Colorado, USA whose aim is to enable people with a wide range of disabilities by providing a supportive environment for them to enter and thrive in online virtual worlds like Second Life. Their island in Second Life has been designed to make it accessible to users who may have a range of disabilities (mental or physical) in real life.

In the DELVE project (Design of Learning Spaces in 3D Virtual Environments[20]), we have investigated the relationship between the designs of learning activities and the designs of learning spaces in Second Life. One of our findings was that for distance education students, photo-realistic or artistically realistic representations of their institutions may help to engender a sense of ownership and belonging to the institution (Minocha & Reeves, 2010). This outcome from the DELVE project was re-affirmed by M253 students who preferred using the learning spaces in our university's islands even though we had suggested quieter places on other islands where we felt students would not be interrupted. Students were distracted by noises (e.g. sounds of water flowing or the sound of the wind), interrupted by visitors, and had concerns about privacy.

It takes time to gain a feeling of engagement, a sense of presence and mutual awareness in Second Life. Therefore, it is only towards the end of the course that students get a 'good' feel for the technology and begin to realise how Second Life has supported their tasks on the course. As Second Life or other 3D virtual worlds are integrated into other courses within the OU, this initial set up time will not be required. Then, it will seem natural for students beginning this course, or any other course utilising Second Life, to use Second Life for meetings.

We have found that some students in the last two presentations of the course have formed their own self-help study groups and continued to meet with one another on a regular basis in Second Life after the end of the course. In addition to participating in regular meetings in Second Life related to their courses, students are also participating in events and activities organised on the OU's islands in Second Life (e.g. lecture series, quizzes, parties, Christmas pantomime). This illustrates the role that Second Life can play in community building, specifically in distance education or amongst part-time students where students may have limited opportunities to meet face-to-face.

Although our empirical investigations have been carried out in Second Life, it is hoped that the results will be applicable to other avatar-based and configurable virtual worlds. The research described in this case study could enhance uptake of virtual worlds by organisations facing the challenges of facilitating socialisation, employee engagement, team building and knowledge sharing in a distributed workforce (for one such recent initiative, please see nteams[21]), particularly in overcoming the limitations of asynchronous communication and collaboration technologies such as e-mail, wikis, blogs, and discussion forums (Minocha, Petre & Roberts, 2008).

CASE STUDY: THE UNIVERSITY OF PLYMOUTH (UOP) SEXUAL HEALTH SIM

Overview

Designed to provide education about sexually transmitted infections (STIs), prevention of unintended pregnancy, and promotion of equalitarian sexual relationships, the University of Plymouth Sexual Health SIM in Second Life[22] (Kamel Boulos & Toth-Cohen, 2009) provided a wide variety of educational experiences, including opportunities to test knowledge of sexual health through quizzes and games, Web resources integrated within the virtual context, and live in-world seminars on sexual health topics. A mini-evaluation of the project was conducted in 2007/2008. Primary methods of evaluation consisted of a survey (n=135) and traffic statistics on the virtual programme. Evaluation results indicated that the Sexual Health SIM was positively viewed by its audience and fostered the development of a vibrant virtual community.

Detailed Description of the UoP Sexual Health SIM Experience

The UOP Sexual Health SIM in Second Life provided its sexual health education in a relaxing, playful setting alongside the (virtual) ocean, with giant flowers and soaring butterflies. Visitors to the SIM were offered a wide range of 3D scripted objects and games to explore and interact with, including a virtual condom-dispensing machine offering free (virtual) male condoms and practical information. They could also chat with the resident pseudo-intelligent chatterbot, 'Alice', to find out simple facts about contraception and STIs. An interactive kiosk provided an atlas illustrating sexually transmitted infections (STIs) and ways to prevent them, and enabled visitors to listen to associated voice narration or access related Web media such as a PowerPoint quiz game or Web page. An interactive 3D Earth globe offered access to current STIs/HIV/AIDS statistics and information from 53 European region countries. Visitors could also access a selection of premier international Web-based and in-world resources from leading organisations, including, among others, the World Health Organization, the National Health Service (NHS) in England, the Society of Obstetricians and Gynaecologists of Canada, and from the USA, the Centers for Disease Control and Prevention, RESOLVE—the National Infertility Association, HealthInfo Island,[23] and Ohio State University (3-D tour of the testis). Media formats included streaming video/audio, podcasts, in-world custom search engines retrieving quality sexual health results from the UK Intute database[24] and Healia[25], and a newsstand that refreshed every 10 minutes to display the top two sexual health headlines on Yahoo! News. There was even an 'AIDS-related Kaposi Sarcoma Experience' clothing dispenser. People wearing the clothing were able to see and experience on their own avatar how Kaposi Sarcoma lesions look and feel in AIDS patients (Figure 5 - for a discussion of the wider educational potential of the concept, see Huang, Kamel Boulos & Dellavalle, 2008). The SIM also afforded opportunities to test knowledge of sexual health by participating in quiz games and other fun experiences.

Designing a proper 3D online world service in Second Life presents a social community fostering challenge. The task is not (just) that of '3D development and scripting' but of building long lasting 'community scaffolds'. 3D virtual worlds are part of the social Web movement, which is all about people, vibrant online communities and persistent social networks. To maximise their social experience, visitors to the UOP Sexual Health SIM were able to join at no cost a public Group inworld (called 'Sexual Health SIM'), which facilitated opportunities for communication and social networking. Also overlooking the ocean was an open air seminar space where people could participate in live inworld voice-enabled sexual health events and seminars; watch slide shows,

Figure 5. An avatar wearing the 'AIDS-related Kaposi Sarcoma Experience' skin in Second Life created using Adobe Photoshop and similar tools. The skin shown in this picture was prepared by Second Life user: Bailey Yifu for the UOP Sexual Health SIM and employs the principles of captology.

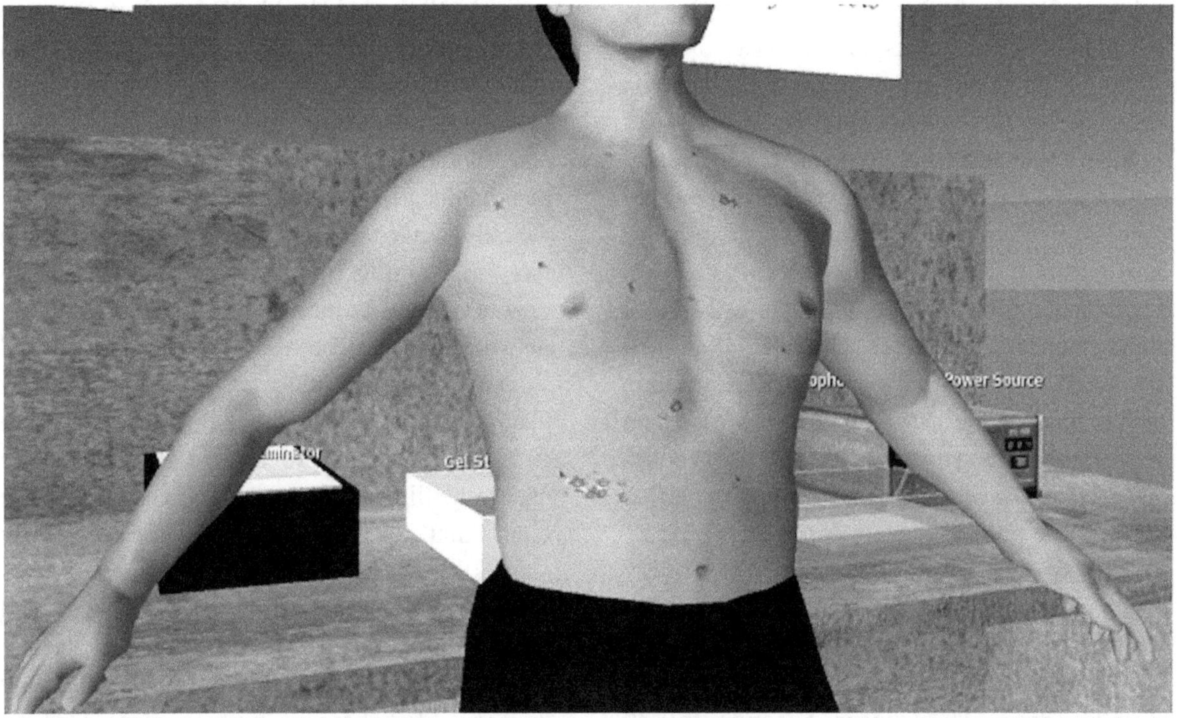

videos and presentations by sexual health experts on a variety of subjects; and engage in lively and lengthy discussions about them. The UOP Sexual Health SIM organised inworld seminars on a range of topics, including domestic violence; STIs, contraception and family planning; female sexuality; sexual purity and healthy relationships from a Christian Orthodox perspective; and 'sex and disability'.

People were always able to contact SIM personnel and other community members in-world, and even transport to a skybox where they could have informal discussions together in a more private setting.

Before leaving the SIM, visitors were invited to provide feedback about the overall experience and specific features of the SIM via a questionnaire that was fully administered in-world and automatically e-mailed to SIM personnel. We also collected statistics on overall usage of the SIM, including logging of avatars' attendance at our live events, as well as 24/7 monitoring of traffic to our SIM. We had an advanced visitor counter installed in our land for this purpose that was able to track repeat, as well as unique/new visitors, and provide us with useful statistics and daily reports via e-mail, including visitors per day, peak visitors (peak concurrency), and total visitor-minutes spent on our land (owner's minutes/visits were not counted or monitored). The latter statistic ('total time visiting') served as a rough measure of visitors' interest in, and perceived utility of, our SIM, besides directly corresponding to the official Linden Lab daily traffic figures for our parcel. The SIM received more than 4000 unique visitors between July 2007 and June 2008. Repeat visitors figures for the same period were much higher.

Evaluation results (questionnaire and SIM traffic) indicated that the Sexual Health SIM was positively viewed by its audience and are detailed in Kamel Boulos & Toth-Cohen (2009). Briefly, more than 200 people responded to two or more of the six closed-ended survey questions between mid-July 2007 and mid-May 2008. We chose to include in our results the responses of 135 avatars, those completing all of the six closed-ended questions. 96% of these were visiting the SIM for the first time. At the time they took the survey, respondents' time in Second Life ranged from 0 days to >3 years. 39% of the respondents had been in Second Life for 30 days or less. (The date/time each avatar took the questionnaire is recorded with her/his answers; an avatar's Second Life account creation date or birthday can be found in her/his Second Life public profile.)

25% of respondents rated the SIM as very useful, 56% as fairly useful, and 19%, not useful. The largest percentage of respondents rating the SIM as very useful was resident of Second Life from 0-30 days. 44% of those in Second Life 0-30 days rated the SIM as very useful, which is a good result. Younger avatars still developing their SL skills are usually more sensitive to any usability issues or non-straightforward presentations of in-world material and activities, which could affect their perceived usefulness of the SIM, compared to more senior Second Life residents.

39% of respondents reported they had "learned something new" during their visit, and 54% planned to return. 16% reported that what they had learned at the SIM would definitely change their behaviour, 36% said possibly, and 30% said it would not change their current behaviour at all. (Current behaviour can be either healthy, and hence no need to change it, or non-healthy.) 59% stated they would recommend the SIM to a friend.

Unique Challenges and Strategies to Address Them

In the UOP Sexual Health SIM project, we were not targeting a finite and well-defined, formal student group or programme of study. This meant that it was much more difficult to target, recruit and maintain a stable audience for our sexual health education programme in Second Life, but we believe we have successfully managed to do this job, judging from our project's evaluation results (Kamel Boulos & Toth-Cohen, 2009).

Moreover, unlike when dealing with formal students who are usually pre-motivated (at least to some extent, as evidenced by the fact they are enrolled in a formal programme of study and are usually willing to complete their course/achieve a pass mark or better), this was not necessarily always the case with our audience (the general public). Our task was much more difficult: we wanted people not just to acquire some new knowledge, but also to change their attitudes and ultimately their real-life behaviour (with no relapse), where applicable. The latter is particularly difficult to achieve (and to measure); for example, it is easy to tell people about the dangers of smoking (every pack of cigarettes has a 'smoking kills' label these days), but it is much more difficult to make someone quit smoking (and not revert back again to their smoking habit after some time). To help us address this educational challenge, the UOP Sexual Health SIM experience team employed principles of captology[26] and marketing/advertising psychology in designing many of the SIM's objects (e.g., the Kaposi Sarcoma skin shown in Figure 5 and our virtual condoms dispenser). Some commentators criticised our approach in developing the latter by arguing that one cannot use a Second Life virtual condom in real-life sex.

In answering them, we used the examples of the various radio receivers that are used by the Coca-Cola Company in marketing their carbonated soft drinks and come in the form of a Coke can, bottle or cup[27]. One cannot drink from such radio cans, bottles and cups, but it is the message that matters in both our virtual condoms and the Coca-Cola radio cases ('remember to use a condom'; 'drink Coca-Cola')!

We also fostered a vibrant community and support network around our SIM to help us achieve our goals and maximise the impact of our inworld sexual health education. In particular, we fostered strong mutual links with related presences and communities in Second Life. We helped some of them develop and promote their in-world STIs/HIV/AIDS-related activities, delivered presentations about the UOP Sexual Health SIM at their events, installed promotional displays about our SIM on their parcels, and even mirrored parts of our in-world content in a showroom donated by the 'Second Life HIV/AIDS Network Headquarters'. Driven by the motto 'knowledge is the enemy of (sexually transmitted) disease', the ultimate goal of the UOP Sexual Health SIM has always been to help people make their own well-informed sexual health choices by offering them quality information about all options, without imposing any particular direction or method on them.

TECHNOLOGICAL FUTURE OF 3D VIRTUAL WORLDS

The fourth author has discussed the future of 3D virtual worlds in great detail in a number of recent publications (Huang, Kamel Boulos & Dellavalle, 2008; Kamel Boulos & Burden, 2007; Kamel Boulos, Hetherington &Wheeler, 2007; Kamel Boulos, Ramloll, Jones & Toth-Cohen, 2008; Toro-Troconis & Kamel Boulos, 2009). Non-gaming 3D virtual worlds are part of the future 3D Internet, though of course not in their current (2010) form, which can be compared to the Web in the early 1990s in terms of technology, and is still also largely proprietary, rather than based on open standards.

The 3D Internet or next-generation 3D high-definition media-rich Web is expected to become a reality in the next decade, and will also fully support mobile devices, which are rapidly developing in many exciting ways (e.g., projector phones[28] and becoming the primary mode of Web access for many users today). In the not so distant future, we will need to develop friendly versions of our 3D Web presences and virtual worlds that can run on iPhone/smart phones and small MIDs (Mobile Internet Devices), possibly by taking advantage of new cloud computing technologies for server-side processing of all the intensive graphics that are involved in rendering these complex worlds: once processed on the server, the output can then be streamed to the iPhone/smart phone much like any Internet video stream.[29]- These advances will make virtual worlds available on mobile low-powered devices, thus supporting the growing trend of ubiquitous m-learning (mobile learning `anywhere') in higher education. This will be particularly useful for mature, part-time learners (learners `on the move'), and will also mean that students will no longer need or be limited to expensive high-end desktop computers to make proper use of virtual worlds.

True 3D will be the next step after HD (High Definition) media: current isometric 3D presentations on flat screens are only pseudo-3D and lack realism and immersiveness. Technologies for proper stereoscopic 3D (S3D) visualisation (Kamel Boulos & Robinson, 2009), which can result in much more immersive 3D virtual worlds experiences, are currently being perfected and are at the same time becoming much more affordable, including a number of auto-stereoscopic solutions and solutions for mobile devices.[30] Moreover, NUIs (Natural User Interfaces) and augmented reality are promising more natural and usable modes of interaction with the 3D Internet (e.g., multi-touch displays), Microsoft's Project Natal,[31]

Layar,[32] etc. Stereoscopic 3-D support, augmented reality and virtuality, virtual globes integration, and other graphical and interaction modalities will increase the realism and immersiveness of virtual worlds, making them even more suited to certain types of scientific, high-fidelity architectural, geographic and other simulations, as well as in various clinical/telemedical, emergency preparedness and military training scenarios, among other applications that could benefit from a more faithful `like real' reproduction of real life scenes and activities in virtual worlds environments. In-world interactive simulations and training scenarios are important in `learning by doing' and experiential learning.

Proper integration of 3D virtual worlds into the flat Web is also on the horizon with 3D virtual worlds and interfaces becoming seamlessly integrated into the flat Web, complementing current embedding of the flat Web into virtual worlds as, for example, in the Second Life Shared Media Viewer 2 released in 2010.

The European Commission and other consortia and groups are looking very seriously and heavily investing heavily into this future 3D Internet vision.[33] Moreover, non-traditional virtual worlds companies have expressed much interest in the concept; for example, a 'developer/evangelist' at Microsoft recently declared "I have zero interest in gaming. The future is a simplified 3D world on your desktop",[34] while a 3D desktop patent was filed by Apple in December 2008.[35] The emerging 3-D virtual worlds standards and other usability, accessibility and reliability developments will make virtual worlds more affordable, more mainstream, more viable as an investment option for higher education institutions, more practical for routine use by both students and educators in higher education, and much easier to integrate into existing virtual learning environments and Web applications.

OVERALL REFLECTIONS

From our experiences, it follows that a notable advantage of a 3D virtual world like Second Life is the possibility of creating a bespoke immersive learning experience and a safe environment to facilitate remote interactions. With judicious design, it is possible to create an environment which can accommodate a wide range of educational activities and learning styles, and offer a more personal experience than more conventional communication technologies, like video conferencing or online fora, particularly when limited user customisation is allowed. However, care must be taken to make the environment pleasant and welcoming to users, and issues of accessibility, efficiency and ease of use should be given proper consideration.

There is some evidence that 3D virtual worlds evoke a much stronger sense of presence in some remote participants compared to more traditional communication technologies, particularly when participants are involved in collaborative activities or group work. Some perceive the 3D immersive experience as very close to its face-to-face real world counterpart, with team members developing real commitment to one another. Indeed influencing behaviour and the transfer of skills from the virtual to the real world was a common challenge in all our case studies.

Particularly noticeable is the ability of virtual worlds to foster communities. It is often the case that contacts in Second Life are not just 'once-only', though they can definitely be so if a user chooses to limit him/herself to only one-time encounters. On the other hand, we have observed that it is sometimes difficult to get a community started, particularly in the context of informal learning, where learners are not enrolled on a formal programme of study or the use of the technology is not linked to coursework or assessment.

The relative immaturity of 3D virtual world technology is cause for some concern. From a technical viewpoint, its requirements for high computer specifications and bandwidth have a negative effect on its accessibility, and variable performance and reliability of the software may detract from the quality of the overall experience. Newcomers often face a steep learning curve and may require specific induction and training, which could be onerous and time consuming both to set up and to take part in. Interacting though avatars is still perceived as unusual by some, and often associated with gaming, rather than serious endeavours, making some users resistant even to approach the technology. However, these barriers are likely to be overcome as the technology matures and becomes more stable, and as 3D virtual worlds become more widespread as a paradigm for online interaction.

FUTURE RESEARCH DIRECTIONS

Current research on 3D virtual worlds only provides a fragmented picture of their potential and challenges for education, so that many lines of enquiry remain open for further investigation. Notwithstanding the difficulties in setting a future research agenda in such a rapidly changing technological landscape, this chapter has highlighted some areas where further research would be beneficial.

One such area is to provide a better understanding of the pedagogical affordances of 3D virtual worlds, in particular with reference to online communication and knowledge representation, and their relation to social cognition, and situated and informal learning. Few authors have started to engage with this topic; for instance: Bronack, Riedl and Tashner (2006) discuss the application of a pedagogical framework based on principles of social constructivism to the development of a virtual word for distance education; Hollins and Robbins, (2008) identify five affordances for learning common to virtual worlds, including Second Life; along similar lines, Lim (2009) identifies six dimensions of learning afforded by Second Life, which may help in the design of educational environments.

Also in need of further exploration is the establishment of frameworks, guidelines and practices for the design of educational 3D virtual worlds, with particular attention to issues of usability and accessibility. Research which has started to address these issues includes: a study on the impact of design affordance on constructivist learning in virtual worlds (Dickey, 2003); techniques to help manage the learner's cognitive load through the application of multimedia principles to virtual world design (Nelson & Erlandson, 2008); interaction design and usability design principles emerging from current virtual worlds design practices (Minocha & Reeves, 2010); and a catalogue of design concerns for the engineering of virtual worlds located within an emergent theory of design (Rapanotti & Hall, 2010).

Another possible line of enquiry is to gain a better understanding of the dynamics of virtual world communities. It has been acknowledge that many of the communities formed around Second Life tend to become tightly-knit with time, with people getting to know each other better and more personally through their digital identities (and sometimes also by their real identities). Some Second Life groups feel like a real family; bonds are real and so are losses.[36] The relationships may even extend to real life: that is why 3D virtual worlds are sometimes also referred to in the literature as 3D real-virtual worlds, since they are and can be a very real part of our real lives (Sivan, 2008).

CONCLUSION

This chapter has made a contribution towards a better understanding of how 3D virtual worlds can be deployed in education, by offering a balanced view of the potential and challenges of current 3D virtual world technology based on the authors' direct experiences of Second Life educational projects, and a critical assessment of what has been reported in the literature.

The chapter has also provided an indication of the many ways virtual worlds are being developed and are likely to shape education in the near future, as well as some of the key research challenges that still remain. On balance, there are strong indications that 3D virtual worlds are here to stay and will influence education in many different ways in the years to come.

ACKNOWLEDGMENT

Many thanks go to academic colleagues at The Open University, UK who have contributed to the Virtual MPhil programme, particularly Maria Vargas-Vera, Ahmad Reeves, Graham Roberts, Darrel Ince and Jon Hall. The research on the M253 case study was supported by JISC[37] and a Teaching Fellowship from the Centre for Open Learning in Mathematics, Science, Computing and Technology, one of the Centres for Excellence in Teaching and Learning at The Open University, UK. We would like to thank our colleagues Mike Innes, Ian Cooke and Derek Richardson who helped set up the volunteer M253 student groups, and express our sincere gratitude to the students and tutors who participated in the M253 study. We would also like to thank Chris Swaine and Susan Easton (of the former Education UK Island) for providing a generous Second Life land grant, which made possible the realisation of the University of Plymouth Sexual Health SIM project.

REFERENCES

Annetta, L. A., Folta, E., & Klesath, M. (2010). *V-Learning: Distance education in the 21st century through 3D virtual learning environments*. New York, NY: Springer.

Barroca, L., Rapanotti, L., Petre, M., & Vargas-Vera, M. (2010). *Supporting research degrees online*. In International Conference of Education, Research and Innovation (ICERI 2010), Madrid, Spain, 15-17 November.

Beynon, W. (2005). Computational support for realism in virtual environments. In *11th International Conference on Human-Computer Interaction (HCI 2005)* (pp. 22-27). Las Vegas, USA, July.

Boit, A., Eirund, H., Geimer, T., Mendonca, J., Ott, A., & Sethmann, R. (2008). *NetS-X-The network security experience*. In 7th European Conference on i-Warfare (ECIW 2008), Plymouth, UK, June 30- July 01.

Braun, V., & Clarke, V. (2006). Using thematic analysis in psychology. *Qualitative Research in Psychology*, *3*(2), 77–101. doi:10.1191/1478088706qp063oa

Bronack, S., Riedl, R., & Tashner, J. (2006). Learning in the zone: A social constructivist framework for distance education in a 3-dimensional virtual world. *Interactive Learning Environments*, *14*(3), 219–232. doi:10.1080/10494820600909157

Capin, T., Noser, H., Thalmann, D., Sunday Pandzic, I., & Thalmann, N. (1997). Virtual human representation and communication in vlnet. [March-April.]. *Computer Graphics and Applications*, *17*(3), 42–53. doi:10.1109/38.574680

Carpenter, J., Wetheridge, L., Smith, N., Goodman, M., & Struijvé, O. (2010). *Researchers of tomorrow. A three year (BL/JISC) study tracking the research behaviour of Generation Y doctoral students*. Annual Report, June. Retrieved November 26, 2010, from http://explorationforchange.net/attachments/056_RoT%20Year%201%20report%20final%20100622.pdf

Cook, D. A. (2009). The failure of e-learning research to inform educational practice, and what we can do about it. *Medical Teacher, 31*(2), 158–162. doi:10.1080/01421590802691393

Cummings, J. N., & Kiesler, S. (2007). Co-ordination costs and project outcomes in multi-university collaborations. *Research Policy, 36*, 1620–1634. doi:10.1016/j.respol.2007.09.001

Dalsgaard, C. (2006). Social software: E-learning beyond learning management systems. *European Journal of Open, Distance and E-Learning*, September. Retrieved November 26, 2010, from http://www.eurodl.org/materials/contrib/2006/Christian_Dalsgaard.htm

Dawley, L. (2009). Social network knowledge construction: Emerging virtual world pedagogy. *Horizon, 17*(2), 109–121. doi:10.1108/10748120910965494

De Lucia, A., Francese, R., Passero, I., & Tortora, G. (2009). Development and evaluation of a virtual campus on second life: The case of second DMI. *Computers & Education, 53*(1), 220–233. doi:10.1016/j.compedu.2008.08.001

Debenhan, M. (2007). Epistolary interviews online: A novel addition to the researcher's palette. *JISC TechDis*, February. Retrieved November 26, 2010, from http://www.techdis.ac.uk/index.php?p=3_7_31_1

Decker, B., Ras, E., & Rech, E., J., Jaubert, P. & Rieth, M. (2007). Wiki-based stakeholder participation in requirements engineering. [March/April.]. *IEEE Software, 24*(2), 28–35. doi:10.1109/MS.2007.60

Dede, C. (2009). Immersive interfaces for engagement and learning. *Science, 323*(5910), 66–69. doi:10.1126/science.1167311

Dickey, M. D. (2003). Teaching in 3D: Pedagogical affordances and constraints of 3d virtual worlds for synchronous distance learning. *Distance Education, 24*(1), 105–121. doi:10.1080/01587910303047

Dieterle, E., & Clarke, J. (2008). Multi-user virtual environments for teaching and learning. In Pagani, M. (Ed.), *Encyclopedia of multimedia technology and networking* (2nd ed.). Hershey, PA: Idea Group, Inc.doi:10.4018/978-1-60566-014-1.ch139

Donath, J. (2008). Giving avatars remote control. The HBR list: Breakthrough ideas for 2008. *Harvard Business Review, 86*(2), 31.

Duffy, T. M., & Cunningham, D. J. (1996). Constructivism: Implications for the design and delivery of instruction. In Jonassen, D. H. (Ed.), *Handbook of research for educational communications and technology* (pp. 170–198). New York, NY: Simon & Schuster Macmillan.

Elliot, B. (2009). *E-pedagogy: Does e-learning require a new approach to teaching and learning?* Scottish Qualifications Agency.

Ertmer, P. A., & Newby, T. J. (1993). Behaviorism, cognitivism, constructivism: Comparing critical features from an instructional design perspective. *Performance Improvement Quarterly, 6*(4), 50–70. doi:10.1111/j.1937-8327.1993.tb00605.x

Farrell, K. (2006). *Wikis, blogs and other community tools in the enterprise*. IBM, March. Retrieved November 26, 2010, from http://www.ibm.com/developerworks/library/wa-wikiapps.html

Felix, U. (2005). E-learning pedagogy in the third millennium: The need for combining social and cognitive. *ReCALL, 17*(1), 85–100. doi:10.1017/S0958344005000716

Harry, D., & Donath, J. (2008). *Information spaces. Building meeting rooms in virtual environments*. In CHI 2008 (pp. 3741-3746). Florence, Italy, April 05-10.

Heldal, I., Schroeder, R., Steed, A., Axelsson, A. S., & Spante, M. (2005). *Immersiveness and symmetry in copresent scenarios*. In IEEE [Bonn, Germany: IEEE Computer Press.]. *Virtual Reality (Waltham Cross)*, (March): 12–16.

Hollins, P., & Robbins, S. (2008). *Educational affordances of multi user virtual environments (MUVE)*. In Researching Learning in Virtual Environments (ReLIVE 08) (pp. 172–180). Milton Keynes, UK, November 20-21.

Huang, S. T., Kamel Boulos, M. N., & Dellavalle, R. P. (2008). Scientific discourse 2.0. Will your next poster session be in Second Life ®? *EMBO Reports, 9*(6), 496–499. doi:10.1038/embor.2008.86

Kamel Boulos, M. N. (2009). *Novel emergency/public health situation rooms and more using 4-D GIS*. In ISPRS WG IV/4 International Workshop on Virtual Changing Globe for Visualisation & Analysis (VCGVA2009). Wuhan University, Wuhan, Hubei, China, 27-28 October, ISPRS Archives.

Kamel Boulos, M. N., & Burden, D. (2007). Web GIS in practice V: 3-D interactive and real-time mapping in Second Life. *International Journal of Health Geographics, 6*(51).

Kamel Boulos, M. N., Hetherington, L., & Wheeler, S. (2007). Second Life: An overview of the potential of 3-D virtual worlds in medical and health education. *Health Information and Libraries Journal, 24*(4), 233–245. doi:10.1111/j.1471-1842.2007.00733.x

Kamel Boulos, M. N., & Maramba, I. (2009). Pitfalls in 3-D virtual worlds health project evaluations: The trap of drug-trial-style media comparative studies. *Journal of Virtual Worlds Research, 2*(2), 4–6.

Kamel Boulos, M. N., Ramloll, R., Jones, R., & Toth-Cohen, S. (2008). Web 3D for public, environmental and occupational health: Early examples from Second Life®. *International Journal of Environmental Research and Public Health, 5*(4), 290–317. doi:10.3390/ijerph5040290

Kamel Boulos, M. N., & Robinson, L. R. (2009). Web GIS in practice VII: Stereoscopic 3-D solutions for online maps and virtual globes. *International Journal of Health Geographics, 8*(59).

Kamel Boulos, M. N., Scotch, M., Cheung, K.-H., & Burden, D. (2008). Web GIS in practice VI: A demo "playlist" of geo-mashups for public health neogeographers. *International Journal of Health Geographics, 7*(38).

Kamel Boulos, M. N., & Toth-Cohen, S. (2009). The University of Plymouth sexual health SIM experience in Second Life®: Evaluation and reflections after one year. *Health Information and Libraries Journal, 26*(4), 279–288. doi:10.1111/j.1471-1842.2008.00831.x

Kemp, J., & Livingstone, D. (2006). *Putting a Second Life "metaverse" skin on learning management systems*. In First Second Life Education Workshop at the Second Life Community Convention (SLCC) (pp. 13-18). San Francisco, USA, August 20.

Kerawalla, L. J., Minocha, S., Kirkup, G., & Conole, G. (2008). Characterising the different blogging behaviours of students on an online distance learning course. *Learning, Media and Technology, 33*(1), 21–33. doi:10.1080/17439880701868838

Lim, K. Y. T. (2009). The six learnings of Second Life: A framework for designing curricular interventions in-world. *Journal of Virtual Worlds Research, 2*(1), 4–11.

Lynch, K., Carbone, A., Arnott, D., & Jamieson, P. (2002). *A studio-based approach to teaching Information Technology*. In Seventh World Conference on Computers in Education (WCCW2001). Copenhagen, Denmark, July 29–August 3, Australian Computer Society.

Meadows, M. S. (2008). *I, avatar: The culture and consequences of having a Second Life*. California: New Riders.

Minocha, S. (2009). *A study of the effective use of social software to support student learning and engagement*. JISC Final Report, University of Bristol, UK, January. Retrieved November 26, 2010, from http://www.jisc.ac.uk/whatwedo/projects/socialsoftware08

Minocha, S., & Morse, D. R. (2010). Supporting distributed team working in 3D virtual worlds: A case study in Second Life. *Interactive Technology and Smart Education, 7*(4), 200–219. doi:10.1108/17415651011096021

Minocha, S., Petre, M., & Roberts, D. (2008). Using wikis to simulate distributed requirements development in a software engineering course. *International Journal of Engineering Education, 24*(4), 689–704.

Minocha, S., & Reeves, A. J. (2010). Interaction design and usability of learning spaces in 3D multi-user virtual worlds. *IFIP Advances in Information and Communication Technology, 316*, 157–167. doi:10.1007/978-3-642-11762-6_13

Minocha, S., & Roberts, D. (2008). Laying the groundwork for socialisation and knowledge construction within 3D virtual worlds. *ALT-J: Research in Learning Technology, 16*(3), 181–196. doi:10.1080/09687760802526699

Minocha, S., & Thomas, P. G. (2007). Collaborative learning in a wiki environment: Experiences from a software engineering course. *New Review of Hypermedia and Multimedia, 13*(2), 187–209. doi:10.1080/13614560701712667

Molka-Danielsen, J., & Destchmann, M. (Eds.). (2009). *Learning and teaching in the virtual world of Second Life*. Trondheim, Norway: Tapir Academic Press.

Nelson, B. C., & Erlandson, B. E. (2008). Managing cognitive load in educational multi-user virtual environments: Reflection on design practice. *Educational Technology Research and Development, 56*(5/6), 619–641. doi:10.1007/s11423-007-9082-1

Norman, G. (2003). RCT = results confounded and trivial: The perils of grand educational experiments. *Medical Education, 37*, 582–584. doi:10.1046/j.1365-2923.2003.01586.x

Oblinger, D. (2006). *Learning spaces*. EDUCAUSE E-Book. Retrieved November 28, 2010, from http://www.educause.edu/LearningSpaces

Oldfield, S. J., & Morse, D. R. (2005). *Truly virtual teams: (Team) work-in-progress*. In 6th Higher Education Academy Subject Network for Information and Computer Science Conference. York, UK, August.

Oldfield, S. J., & Morse, D. R. (2007). Exploiting connectedness in the informatics curriculum. *Italics, 6*(3), 27–46.

Otto, O., Roberts, D., & Wolff, R. (2006). *A review of effective closely-coupled collaboration using immersive CVEs*. In ACM International Conference on Virtual Reality Continuum and Its Application (VRCIA), June 14-17. Hong Kong: ACM Press.

Park, C. (2005). New variant PhD: The changing nature of the doctorate in the UK. *Journal of Higher Education Policy and Management, 27*(2), 189–207. doi:10.1080/13600800500120068

Peschl, M. F., & Riegler, A. (2001). Virtual science: Virtuality and knowledge acquisition in science and cognition. In Riegler, A., Peschl, M. F., Edlinger, K., Fleck, G., & Feigl, W. (Eds.), *Virtual reality: Cognitive foundations, technological issues & philosophical implications* (pp. 9–32). Frankfurt am Main, Germany: Peter Lang.

QAA. (2007). *QAA subject benchmark statements*. Retrieved November 26, 2010, from http://www.qaa.ac.uk/academicinfrastructure/benchmark/default.asp

Rapanotti, L., Barroca, L., Vargas-Vera, M., & Reeves, A. J. (2010). deep|think: A Second Life environment for part-time research students at a distance. In *10th IEEE International Conference on Advanced Learning Technologies (ICALT)*. Sousse, Tunisia, July 5-7.

Rapanotti, L., & Hall, J. G. (2010). Design concerns in the engineering of virtual worlds for learning. *Behaviour & Information Technology*, in press. Retrieved November 26, 2010, from http://www.informaworld.com/smpp/content~db=all~content=a922852732~frm=titlelink

Ratcliffe, M. (2009). *Researching graduate employment in IT*. e-Skills, UK. Retrieved November 26, 2010, from http://www.e-skills.com/public/File/Catalyst/090611Experian-final.pdf

Rufer-Bach, K. (2009). *The Second Life grid: The official guide to communication, collaboration and community engagement*. Indiana, US: Wiley Publishing Inc.

Sharpe, R., Beetham, H., & McGill, L. (2009). *Frameworks for developing digitally literate learners*. In 16th International Conference of the Association for Learning Technology (Alt-C 2009). Manchester, UK, 8-10 September.

Sivan, Y. (2008). 3D3C real virtual worlds defined: The immense potential of merging 3D, community, creation, and commerce. *Journal of Virtual Worlds Research, 1*(1), 1–31.

Stary, C. (2001). Exploring the concept of virtuality: Technological approaches and implications from tele-education. In Riegler, A., Peschl, M. F., Edlinger, K., Fleck, G., & Feigl, W. (Eds.), *Virtual reality: Cognitive foundations, technological issues & philosophical implications* (pp. 113–128). Frankfurt am Main, Germany: Peter Lang.

Tapscott, D. (2009). *Grown up digital: How net generation is changing your world*. New York, NY: McGraw Hill.

Thomas, D. R. (2006). A general inductive approach for analyzing qualitative evaluation data. *The American Journal of Evaluation, 27*, 237–246. doi:10.1177/1098214005283748

Toro-Troconis, M., & Kamel Boulos, N. M. (2009). Musings on the state of 3-D virtual worlds for health and healthcare in 2009. *Journal of Virtual Worlds Research, 2*(2), 4–15.

Wankel, C., & Kingsley, J. (2009). *Higher education in virtual worlds: Teaching and learning in Second Life*. Emerald Group Publishing Limited.

Wegerif, R. (1998). The social dimension of asynchronous learning networks. *Journal of Asynchronous Learning Networks, 2*(1), 34–49.

Witmer, B., & Singer, M. (1998). Measuring presence in virtual environments: A presence questionnaire. *Presence (Cambridge, Mass.), 7*(3), 225–240. doi:10.1162/105474698565686

KEY TERMS AND DEFINITIONS

Avatar: A computer user's representation in a virtual world.

Chatterbot (a.k.a. chat bot): A computer program designed to simulate an intelligent conversation with humans. In 3D virtual worlds, chatterbots usually take the form of avatars.

Inworld: Being logged onto a 3D virtual world.

Landmark: A Second Life® precise location which can be stored and used to teleport from other locations.

Machinima: A computer 3D animation generated via a real-time graphics engine.

Notecard: An item of text and/or embedded textures, images, etc. that can be stored, retrieved and transferred between avatars.

Parcel: A unit of virtual land in Second Life®.

Rezzing: Making 3D virtual objects appear in a virtual world.

Scripting: Writing software using a scripting language.

Sculpting: Creating 3D objects in a virtual world.

SIM: Short for simulator or simulation; it is the term commonly used to indicate a Second Life® virtual region or the simulator process on the server host machine which supports that region.

Teleportation: The direct transfer of an avatar from one location to another within a virtual world.

Virtual world: A computer-based simulated environment in which users can interact with each other and form online communities. Most current virtual worlds are 3D avatar-based virtual environments.

ENDNOTES

1 All the URLs in the chapter were last accessed on 26 November 2010.
2 http://secondlife.com/
3 http://www.virtualenvironments.info
4 http://sleducation.wikispaces.com/
5 http://virtualworldwatch.net/
6 http://wiki.jokaydia.com/page/Main_Page
7 http://www.facebook.com/
8 Equivalent to 'graduate' in North American countries.
9 http://www.virtualmphil.open.ac.uk/
10 http://www3.open.ac.uk/study/undergraduate/course/m253.htm
11 http://flashmeeting.open.ac.uk/home.html
12 http://www.skype.com/
13 http://uk.messenger.yahoo.com/
14 http://secondlife.com/
15 http://slurl.com/secondlife/Open%20University/97/45/25
16 http://secondlife.iste.wikispaces.net/SL-Tours
17 http://www.bera.ac.uk/files/2008/09/ethica1.pdf
18 http://www.open.ac.uk/research/ethics/index.shtml
19 http://virtualability.org/default.aspx
20 http://tinyurl.com/3g937f
21 http://www.nteams.com/ and a YouTube video at http://www.youtube.com/watch?v=qLvL2bRG4M0
22 http://healthcybermap.org/slsexualhealth/
23 http://slurl.com/secondlife/Healthinfo%20Island/
24 http://www.intute.ac.uk/
25 http://www.healia.com/
26 http://captology.stanford.edu/
27 http://www.google.com/images?hl=en&q=coca-cola%20radios
28 http://www.youtube.com/watch?v=DjbHd9t6n8s
29 See, for example, http://www.spectrum.ieee.org/mar09/7892 and http://www.onlive.com/
30 See, for example, http://spectrum.ieee.org/semiconductors/devices/sharp-offers-3d-viewing-without-glasses and http://news.bbc.co.uk/1/hi/technology/10323971.stm
31 http://www.xbox.com/en-US/live/project-natal/

32 http://www.layar.com/

33 See: International Organization for Standardization (ISO)--Draft requirements for the 'MPEG-V for 3-D Virtual Worlds' emerging standard (May 2008): http://www.virtualworldsnews.com/files/w9902_draft_requirements_for_mpegv.doc; Input for the Future Internet research programme (March 2008)--3-D Internet is now a strategic European Commission objective: ftp://ftp.cordis.europa.eu/pub/fp7/ict/docs/netmedia/UCM-Position-paper.pdf; The European Commission FP7 Work Programme 2009-2010 Draft version 01-07-08--Look for 'Objective ICT-2009.1.5: Networked Media and 3D Internet' on p.20: http://ict.euforskning.no/file.axd?file=ICT+WP+2009-10+01-07-08.doc; European Future Internet Portal: http://www.future-internet.eu/ and EU Future Media & 3D Internet Task Force (FM3DI-TF): http://www.futuremediainternet.eu/

34 http://secondlife.reuters.com/stories/2008/07/18/microsoft-eyes-integration-between-opensim-and-windows-live-id/

35 http://news.cnet.com/8301-13579_3-10121240-37.html

36 The Sojourner is offline (UOP Sexual Health SIM blogpost - 26 May 2008): http://slsexualhealth.wordpress.com/2008/05/26/the-sojourner-is-offline/

37 http://www.jisc.ac.uk

Chapter 13
Debating Across Borders

Mats Deutschmann
Umeå University, Sweden

ABSTRACT

Internationally, virtual world environments such as Second Life® (SL) have become accepted as platforms for innovative educational activities at many universities in recent years. One such activity includes innovative ways of students coming in contact with other students in so-called telecollaborations. The present case study explores the initial stages in an Action Research process, namely the design and initial implementation of a telecollaborative language learning activity between four universities in Second Life under the EU-funded Avalon project. The chapter describes how theoretical frameworks including the Ecology of Language Learning (van Lier, 2004), the Five Stage Model of Computer Supported Collaborative Learning (Salmon, 2004) and Activity Theory (Leont'ev, 1978) were used in order to address different aspects of the design of the course. Based on questionnaire responses from students and observations, the chapter then goes on to evaluate the relative success/failure of the first course trial. Finally, the chapter discusses the implications of the lessons learnt from this pilot project on further developments of the course concept in the action research process, and goes on to discuss implications of the findings for the use of virtual worlds in more mainstream educational settings.

INTRODUCTION

The Internet, and more specifically, social software such as virtual worlds have greatly contributed to global communication over the last decades. In language learning, in particular, this development presents new exciting possibilities (Kern, 2000; 2006; Thorne, 2000; 2008; Kramsch & Thorne, 2002; Warschauer, 1998; 1999; 2006). Increased access to digital technologies has meant that online tools such as e-mail, online discussion forums, blogs, wikis, and more recently virtual 3D world platforms such as Second Life®, are increasingly being used in education to bring

DOI: 10.4018/978-1-61350-080-4.ch013

students together. 3D worlds, in particular, offer spaces where genuine communicative acts can take place at a distance, simulating real world activity, but with the advantage that they allow learners from different geographical locations to meet in meaningful authentic communication using the target language in an immersive common space (Deutschmann & Panichi, 2009a; Deutschmann et al., 2009; Stevens, 2006; Nardi, 2006).

One of the traditional challenges in language education has been to provide meaningful contexts for authentic communication. Various approaches to overcoming this problem have led foreign language educators to design and implement pedagogic strategies incorporating internet based communicative activities, such as the use of virtual tandem language exchanges using chat, message boards, discussion forums, blogs and more recently audio-visually synchronous environments such as virtual worlds (see Campbell, 2003 and Dieu, 2004, for example). In bringing together learners from different language backgrounds, on-line environments, such as SL, increase the scope for cross-cultural interaction to the extent that the target language becomes the only viable option for meaningful communication. If, in addition, tasks are designed in such a way that the information needed is contained in the knowledge capital of the student group so that the students themselves become the source of the course content, two of the potential problems related to second language learning situations are addressed: motivation for using the foreign language and subject relevance. Virtual worlds in language education can thus go towards answering needs claims made by researchers such as Warschauer (1997:487) who "demands" that students be given the opportunity to "conduct actively 'meaningful tasks and solve meaningful problems in an environment that reflects their own personal interests as well as the multiple purposes to which their knowledge will be put in the future'". However, conducting this type of international collaboration within the framework of set curricula and timetables can be challenging. In addition, there are technological challenges that arise, particularly when dealing with openly accessible tools located outside the institutional systems and fire-walls.

In this study, the first stages of an Action Research process to develop a telecollaborative language learning activity between four universities under the EU-funded project *Avalon* (Access to Virtual and Action Learning live ONline) will be described. Action Research, a "framework for thinking systematically about what happens in social situations, implementing action for change and monitoring and evaluating the effects of the action with a view to continuing development" (Hudson, Owen & van Veen, 2006:581), has been used extensively as a method for designing, developing and evaluating social situations such as collaborative learning activities, and is the key method of design used under the Avalon framework. This chapter will describe how different theories and models have been used as tools in the initial stages of design of a telecollaborative course (*Avalon Debating*) in order to enhance the language learning outcomes and to foresee and solve potential problems that may arise during the course activity. These theories include the Ecology of Language Learning (van Lier, 2004), the Five Stage Model of CSCL (Salmon, 2004) and Activity Theory (Leont'ev, 1978). The chapter will also evaluate the second stage of the Action Research process, namely the first implementation, in order to estimate the relative success/failure of the design and the reasons for this. Finally, the last part of the chapter will critically discuss the use of innovative technology for this type of set-up in light of the findings. What were the advantages and problems encountered and how can those be addressed, and most importantly, what were the real learning outcomes? Here institutional goals will be viewed against the goals of the designers of the course and the problems arising when these do not match will be pointed to. The chapter will also evaluate the implications of collaborative learning in virtual worlds for university language education at large.

BACKGROUND

AVALON (Access to Virtual and Action Learning live Online) is an ongoing 2-year multilateral project funded under *Key Activity 3* (ICT) of the EU *EACEA Life Long Learning Programme* (LLP). Key Activity 3 focuses on the development of innovative ICT-based content, services, pedagogies and practice embedded into long-term educational strategies and distributed via innovative methods and learning environments. The 26 participating European partners include 10 state funded universities and 16 other public and private organisations operating in the following areas: language education, teacher training, intercultural training, language testing and certification, online education, publishing, business communication and networking, design of 3D environments and language learning in Second Life® (hereafter referred to as SL). The project is a transversal programme, which targets language learners from the Leonardo da Vinci, Erasmus and Gruntdvig communities.

The overall aims of the project include:

- the creation case studies which will include field-tested communicative scenarios and the guidance on how utilise them;
- the provision of the necessary skills for language teaching professionals to work in these new online environments through a targeted training course;
- promotion of general awareness in mainstream educational contexts of the potential of these environments.

As mentioned, the AVALON project as a whole uses a framework of Action Research for the development of language learning scenarios in virtual worlds. Most course concepts under the project undergo at least three iterations. Each iteration consists of a design stage and an implementation stage followed by an evaluation stage, during which the course design is modified based on the findings of the previous iteration. The modified course concept then goes through a second iteration and so on (see Figure 1 below).

As such we are thus constantly observing, documenting and reflecting over the processes taking place under the project. In addition to direct observation and reflection, data is also collected using surveys, which include open ended questions to the students to learn about their opinions about the effectiveness of mediating environment.

Several of the case studies conducted under the project so far have included telecollborative elements. Telecollaboration refers to the use of different types of Internet communication tools in order to support social interaction, dialogue, debate, and intercultural exchange between internationally-dispersed learners in parallel language classes (O' Dowd, 2006; Belz, 2003). Arguably, the best telecollaborative projects are those that are: 1. based on common interests of the student groups involved, and 2. fully integrated

Figure 1. The moments of Action Research (from Hudson, Owen & van Veen, 2006)

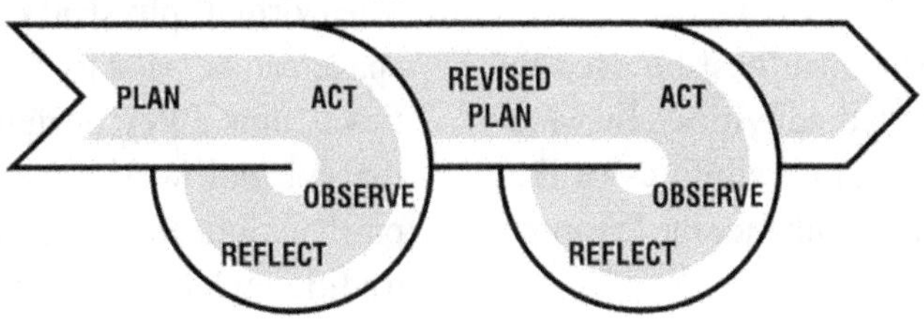

into the curriculum and not just extra-curricular activities (Dooly, 2008). These prerequisites often represent a challenge since curricula, educational structures, as well as academic cultures often differ greatly from country to country, and even from university to university within the same country. Such differences may well create problems in telecollaborative projects and should as far as possible be taken into account in the early design stage in order to avoid problems during the actual collaborative events. In addition, although free communication based on common interests may develop students' language skills, it is hard to evaluate and examine, thus potentially affecting motivational aspects.

APPLYING THEORY IN THE DESIGN PROCESS

One of the early challenges in a design process such as the one represented under the Avalon Action Research framework was making informed decisions that addressed the link between the intended learning outcomes and the actual activities of a learning event. In addition, the technical possibilities and limitations of the tool needed to be worked into this formula. Questions that arose during this planning stage included:

- What are the intended learning outcomes?
- Who are the learners?
- How are the learning outcomes best achieved under the given resource constraints (time for example)?
- What specific activities need to be included in the design?
- How can the environment best be used to allow for the intended activities? In what ways can the technical possibilities of the environment be used to enhance the learning activities?
- What are the limitations of the learning environment, and what technical 'risks' can be foreseen?
- How are students motivated to partake in the intended activities?
- What are the main threats that may affect this motivation?

This list of questions is by no means comprehensive but illustrates just some of the type of problems that had to be addressed. In order to do so, we needed tools (lenses that would help us see the issues at hand clearly, and which would give us models to help us address these).

It was decided early during the project that the courses under the Avalon project be based on socio-cultural models of learning, where authentic communication in the target language and collaboration with peers from various parts of the world were central to the activities, and where the use of the affordances of the environment would enhance this process. In addition, courses should also pay attention to the acquisition of new specific knowledge (content acquisition) that fitted existing curricula among the partner institutions. As such, the theories and models we used in our designs had to answer to this view of learning.

Addressing the Language Learning Activities: Ecology of Language Learning

In the Avalon project the environment (i.e. the 3D virtual world of SL), and more specifically the learning environment that we have built on Avalon Island, is central to the learning designs. The (virtual) physical *environment* and how this space can be used to enhance the planned activities is thus a key design issue. We would argue that virtual world learning environments are partly unique in this respect, and differ from more traditional VLEs (virtual learning environments) in relation to design. Just as with any other VLE, we have to consider the affordances the environment offers in terms of tools and how these can be used effectively to support the intended learning outcomes. In addition, however, we have to take the three dimensional space into account in the design. What atmosphere do we want to convey in our learning landscape? Do we build traditional environments based on existing reference frameworks associated with learning (class rooms, lecture halls, etc), or do we construct new types of environments? How should we position different activities in our learning environment spatially? And most importantly, how will the physical environment affect the learning experience? These are just some examples of design issues that had to be considered.

Current literature in the field (e.g. Lim, 2009; Molka-Danielsen & Deutschmann, 2009; Molka-Danielsen et al., 2010; Panichi et al., 2010) indicates that designs for learning in virtual world environments need to take into consideration the effects of both of these aspects of the environment on the learning processes (i.e. the available tools and the physical 3d design, as well as their respective interaction and interdependency). With this in mind, we needed a language learning theory where the *environment* was included as an important component.

Ecology of Language Learning

Ecology of Language Learning emphasizes the emergence of linguistic development through learners' interactions with their environment - spatial, social, cultural, educational, and so on - bringing to light commonalities between primary language development and second-language learning. Language ecology may be defined as the study of interactions between any given language and its environment: "The true environment of a language is the society that uses it as one of its codes. Language exists only in the minds of its users, and it only functions in relating these users to one another and to nature, i.e. their social and natural environment" (Haugen, 1972:325).

According to this model, all language learning is situated in an environment and, as such, is contextualised. The environment offers different *affordances*, possibilities for learning. Thus, to be able to evaluate the potential for learning, the affordances of the environment must be taken into account. In an ecological approach to learning, however, the environment and its affordances are not limited to a static framework. The agents that inhabit the space also constitute an integral part of the environment. What this means is that a human agent him- or herself can constitute an affordance of the environment in question. In a biological context (where the term ecology originally comes from), this could mean, for example, that for a dung fly, the most essential affordance of the savannah landscape is in fact not the wide open spaces or the grass that grows there, but the elephants that inhabit the landscape, and more specifically the dung that they produce, which in turn is the pre-requisite for the dung fly's reproductive cycle. In an ecological approach to language learning, the concepts of environment and affordances are thus complex and potentially involve a number of interactional relationships including: subject-learner, mode of transmission-learner, physical environment-learner, teacher-learner, learner-learner, group-learner, group-teacher, etc. This means that the potential outcomes of the learning processes are as variable as the infinite possibilities of these interactions, and will differ from person to person and from occasion to occasion. The outcomes of these interactions then go on to feed into yet further interactions between elements in the environment in a continual process of change. In this sense the system is dynamic and interdependent, and variables cannot be isolated. The focus in the ecological approach to language learning is thus process oriented. The nature of the interaction between learners and all the aspects of the environment (including other learners) decide where you end up, the result.

The consequence of this view of language is that every learning event is unique and although the initial learning framework can be made stable, the actual processes that then take place are impossible to replicate since the environment by definition changes every time a new agent enters it. In an ecological approach to design, the role of the designer is thus not to dictate the exact learning outcomes of a learning event, but rather to maximise its learning potential by making the affordances available to the learners.

ADDRESSING THE SOCIAL PROCESSES IN THE STUDENT GROUP: THE FIVE STAGE MODEL OF CSCL

In our courses, participants would be joining the courses from different institutional settings and many would initially be unfamiliar with SL. Since one of our basic design prerequisites included group collaborations, another central aspect of interest in the course design that we needed to address was that of group processes, and how we as teachers could support these in order to maximise the learning outcomes. We needed a model that would help us predict the stages of development that the group would go through and how these would affect the learning outcomes. For this purpose Salmon's Five Stage Model was of great help.

Salmon's Five Stage Model (2004) envisages the group processes in CSCL (computer supported collaborative learning) as five stages of development. The first stage, the *Access and Motivation* stage, involves the participants engaging in trying to access the system. During this stage extensive support is needed to minimise technical anxiety and to make sure that participants are made aware of the tools available in the system. The second stage in the model is the *Online Socialisation* stage during which the participants familiarise themselves with each other and their learning environment. During this stage it is important to work socialisation tasks into the design and to allow time for these. A collaborative approach to learning is dependent on this stage and its importance should not be underestimated. The third stage in Salmon's model is the *Information Exchange* stage, where participants begin to explore the range of information available to them and the interaction at this stage concerns the content and the sharing of information. During the fourth stage, the *Knowledge Construction* stage, participants start to become involved in active interaction and knowledge construction, responding and reacting to each other's input. The final stage in Salmon's model is the *Development* stage, where learners become more responsible for their own learning, need less support from the e-moderator and start exploring their own learning needs outside the course structure independently. For a summary of the model see Figure 2 below.

Although the model was developed for more traditional VLEs, it does provide a useful model for group processes as a course proceeds. This helps when designing courses such as the ones developed under the Avalon project. For example, the model brought our attention to the importance of initial technical initiation and made us more aware of the importance of building in social activities into the designs.

ADDRESSING THE PROBLEMS OF MOTIVATION AND COMPLEX SYSTEMS: ACTIVITY THEORY

Many of the course concepts developed under the Avalon framework are particularly complex since they involve collaborations between different institutional systems, all of which have different routines and goals. In addition, the project utilises complex technology, which more often than not is new to learners, educators and technicians. There are thus many factors that lie outside the immediate course setting that can influence the activities in the actual course. We thus needed a theoretical framework that would help us become aware of these factors to help us anticipate problems and work solutions into the design. Activity Theory

Figure 2. Salmon's Five Stage Model (2004: 29)

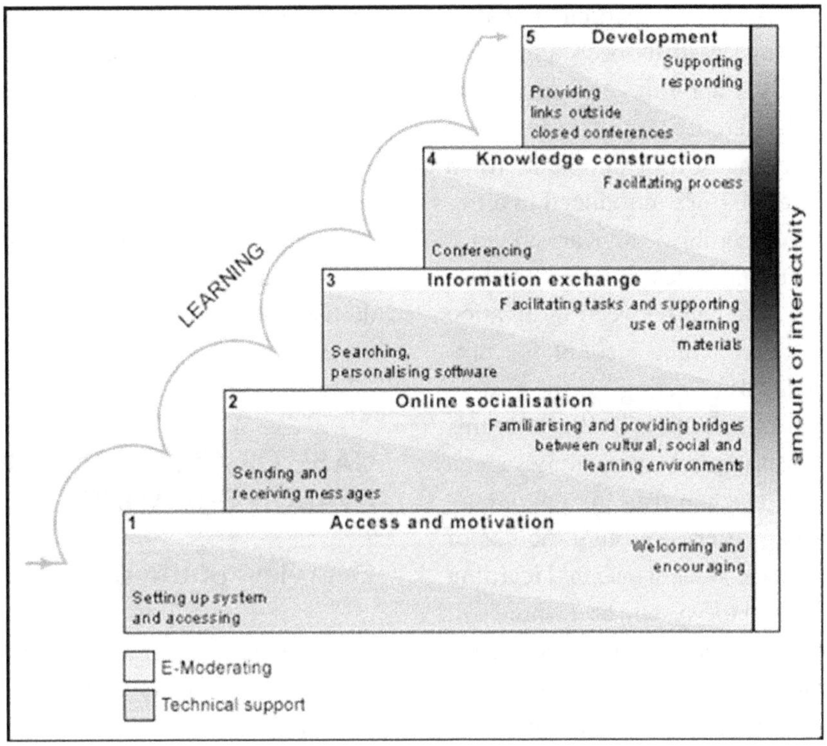

is one such framework for examining complex systems holistically.

Activity theory, originally developed by Leont'ev (1978), uses the concept that any activity is essentially motive driven. Thus, in order to understand an individual's actions we have to have a clear idea of the motives driving him/her. In addition, there are various factors that may influence (negatively and positively) an individual's activities towards a goal and the model tries to provide a framework for making these visible. The theory has recently been developed by researchers such as Engström (1987, 1999, 2001) and the notion of 'community' has been added to the two original interacting units in the model, namely the individual and the object. This addition thus makes the theory more applicable to systems rather than just a being a theory that explains individual action. Using this framework, we envisage the interactions between the parts of a social system as a whole as being motive driven.

With influence from Human-Computer Interaction Theory (Nardi, 1996), the theory has been further modified to include variables such as rules (i.e. the conventions and guidelines for activities within the system). In its present form Activity Theory is primarily used to describe activity in complex socio-technical systems and is often described as consisting of six interacting parts (Bryant et al., 2005): *Object* being the objective of the system as a whole, *subject* representing the persons engaged in the activity, *community* representing the greater social context (i.e. all people involved directly or indirectly), *mediating artefacts and/or tools* representing the tools and/or concepts used by the subjects to accomplish the task, *division of labour* representing the balance of activities between the participants including such concepts as formal and informal hierarchies, and finally *rules* representing the formal and informal guidelines and codes for the activities in the system. The activity theory framework is summarised below in Figure 3. The text in brackets refers to what each part refers to in this particular study.

The theory has successfully been applied to anticipate and analyse activities in educational systems, often with reference to systems undergoing paradigmatic changes, for example as when innovations such as ICT are introduced to a traditional educational setting (see Karasavvidis, 2009, for example). It provides an analytic framework for bridging "the gap between motivation and action" and a "coherent account for processes at various levels of acting" in the system (Kaptelinin & Nardi, 2006:62). To illustrate this with two simple examples, firstly envisage a situation where a teacher tries to encourage changes in learning patterns through the use of collaborative methods, student oriented learning and ICT. If the *rules* of the system as a whole still reward detailed individual surface knowledge through its examination and evaluation structures, chances are that the anticipated changes in learning patterns will not take place. In a second example, envisage a course structure where the *mediating artefact* is the problem. If students are unable to access the system because of bandwidth issues, for example, no amount of pedagogic design will help to realise the outcomes. Hence if we want to change action, or even understand action, we have to be aware of the objectives in the system motivating them, and the factors that may hinder members from participating in the activity. Activity Theory helps to identify such variables.

CASE OF STUDY: DESIGNING AVALON DEBATING

Overview of the Course Concept

The course concept arose from a perceived need to include further spoken elements into distance and Internet courses on academic proficiency (such as 'academic writing' and 'composition classes')

Figure 3. General framework of Activity Theory as applied in this study

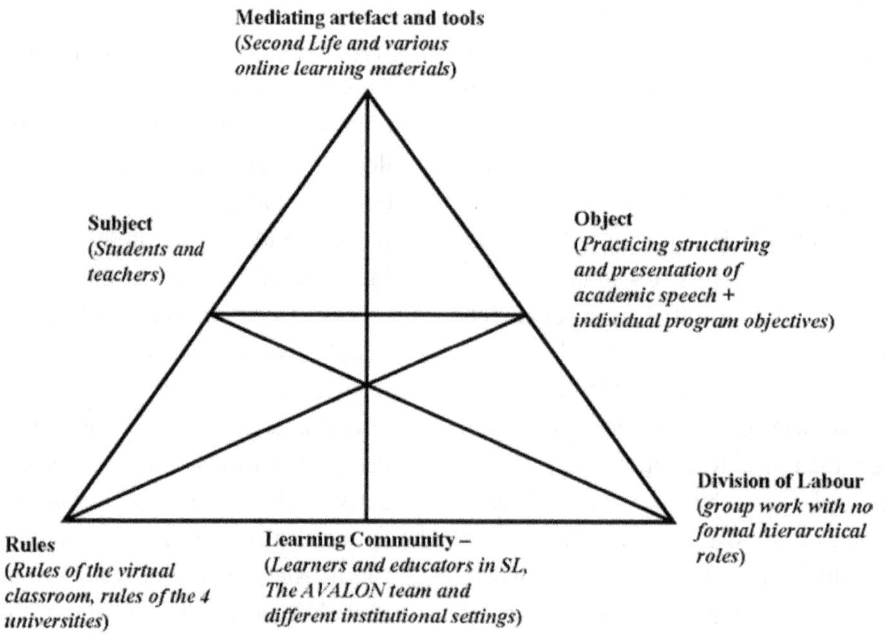

in English. We also wanted to give the students a chance to use their English skills in an authentic setting where they would be communicating with peers who did not speak their native tongue. The course design thus constituted telecollaborations between different universities under the Avalon framework, resulting in mixed student groups from different academic and national backgrounds. The target audience for this particular course was university students who were reasonably proficient in English (B2-C1) but needed to develop their English communication and presentation skills for academic purposes. Since the focus lay on academic presentation, we also envisaged the course to be a viable option for native speaking university students. The course addresses two distinct types of professional discourse:

- The discourse of collaboration where the students have to negotiate their ideas and come up with a common end product.
- The discourse of public, formal presentation of academic content.

Central to the course idea is a collaborative exercise based on the principle of the competitive public debate. The idea is that the students should learn the basic principles of rhetoric and public speaking, while at the same time partaking in an engaging activity. Students from different language backgrounds are thus brought together in SL, where they have to group themselves into mixed teams in order to prepare their presentations for or against a particular topic in a final competitive debate. The course consists of five distinct phases:

1. Technical initiation where the students get to know the VLE.
2. Social initiation where the students get to know each other and group themselves into mixed nationality groups;
3. A theoretical background phase during which the students are introduced to some of the basic principles of public speaking;
4. A collaborative research phase where students work in smaller groups in order to prepare their arguments for or against a particular topic;
5. A public presentation phase, where the students partake in a public competitive debate and where they are judged by their peers and an expert panel.

The course is relatively short, maximum ten weeks, and all the actual course activities take place in SL. In addition, there is a course homepage that contains links to instructions on how to get started in SL. On the homepage it is also possible to see the course structure: timetable, objectives, session outlines and links to resources such as YouTube clips about debating.

The sections below will discuss how the different theories mentioned in Part 2 were applied to the design of different aspects of the course.

APPLICATIONS OF ECOLOGY OF LANGUAGE LEARNING IN THE DESIGN

The Ecology of Language Learning was central as a starting point for the design of the language learning activities in the course. Accordingly, our ambition was to maximise the affordances of the environment (i.e. to make maximum use of the possibilities of the course environment for language learning). Note that in accordance with the theory, the 'environment' here includes the physical environment of SL, as well as the social/psychological environment (including the framework activities, the other course participants, the teachers etc).

Firstly the tasks were designed according to a collaborative model, where students had to build the content and structure of their presentations together in dialogue and negotiation with each other. This meant that one of the most important affordances of the environment would be the fellow students, motivating authentic communication in order to solve the problem at hand. Similarly, the theory motivated us to be careful not to "over-design" the course activities. It was important that we left freedom in the design for the students to contribute with their own ideas and knowledge, so that the interplay between participants and the communication resulting from this was not predetermined. Accordingly, we did not decide on the debating topics prior to the course and we did not designate specific roles to the group members. We wanted to leave the specifics up to the participants and did not attempt to steer them in any direction as regards to the structure or content of their presentations or how they were supposed to conduct their collaborations. Also, based on previous experiences of course design in SL (Deutschmann et al. 2009), we knew that too detailed controlling of roles and activities could have a demotivating effect on learners. We also tried to maximise the affordances offered by the members of each collaborative team by mixing groups so that each constellation consisted of students from different universities (and countries) who could contribute with different reference frameworks, and so that there would be a dynamic intercultural social setting where students not only had to solve the task at hand, but also had get to know each other and learn to communicate and collaborate with peers from different cultural backgrounds using the target language. Because the groups were competing against each other, we argue that the social dimension was further strengthened as in-group bonding took place. Note here, that the idea of other members of the language learning event constituting affordances of the environment ties in very closely to the idea of *learning community*, under the Activity Theory framework.

The affordances of the *learning community* in its broader sense were also exploited in the research phase, when students were preparing arguments for or against the topics. Since the topics were related to new media issues, we encouraged the students to explore other areas of SL and interview avatars that they met. For example, we gave a group working on the topic of online education the coordinates of *Edunation* island, which houses an active community of online educators working in SL.

Ecology of Language Learning also made us pay attention to the VLE in our design. For example, we encouraged learners to make full use of the voice transmission, text chat as well as the instant messaging tools so that both the spoken and the written modes were addressed. The affordances of 3D space could also be exploited: We decided to allocate different groups headquarters on the island which were far enough apart so that they could not hear what was being discussed in the other groups; a physical affordance of SL is the fact that the software simulates real life sound behaviour in terms of volume and distance, so that avatars can hear each other more loudly when close and more faintly when far apart, and not at all when very far apart. Similarly, the affordances of SL were also used in order to strengthen the pedagogic design of the task during the final competitive debate. We used a formal lecture room setting for the final debate, and students were encouraged to 'dress up' in order to add to the 'grandeur' of the occasion. In addition, the polling tool used for voting, gave a very visual representation of the evaluation. This gadget worked in such a fashion that coloured bars represented each group and the group that received the most votes could observe their bar rising above the other groups' as the audience voted (see Figure 4).

Overall, as previously pointed out in Part 2, the theory helped us to become aware of the fact that "the role of the designer is not to dictate the exact learning outcomes of a learning event, but rather to maximise its learning potential by making the affordances available to the learners."

Figure 4. The final debate in Avalon Debating

APPLICATIONS OF THE FIVE STAGE MODEL IN THE DESIGN

With the help of the Five Stage Model we tried to take account of the expected group process progressions in the design. Accordingly, we designed for the different stages in the course, starting with the *Access and Motivation* stage.

Access and Motivation: Technical Initiation

Using a virtual world for learning activities can be quite a novel experience for many students. Many are unfamiliar with the concept of virtual worlds and others have pre-conceived ideas of this type of environment. In pre-course surveys for example, we have found that some students associate virtual worlds with gaming and other leisure activities, and thus find it hard to take the environment seriously in a learning context. Relating this to the Activity Theory framework, this may mean that motivation is affected prior to the course as a result of attitudes towards the *mediating artefact* (again note how the different theories feed into each other). Technical initiation in the case of SL does thus not only entail teaching the students about the technicalities of the environment, but also involves motivating its use in order to challenge potential misconceptions. Therefore, and in accordance with the Five Stage Model, it was decided at an early stage that we should pay close attention to technical initiation in the course framework. This decision also built on former experiences in SL (Deutschmann & Panichi, 2009b) where we had found that insufficient attention to technical initiation had led to frustration and high drop-out rates.

It was thus decided that participants were required to try out SL (establish avatars, and test basic communicative tools) prior to the course start. This process was to be initiated through other means of communication such as email, instructions on the course homepage as well as one-to-one synchronous guidance face-to-face or via telephone or Skype®. The one-to-one coaching would also give us a chance to motivate the use of the virtual world for educational purposes and discuss any potential misgivings. At the end of the technical initiation, each participant should thus have an avatar and should have mastered the basic skills of moving and communicating in-world prior to the course start.

Coaching each student through the functionalities of the VLE is obviously a time consuming business and in later Avalon courses we have started using a "buddy" system whereby more experienced students who are familiar with SL help their less experienced peers to get to know the environment. This also means that the students have an opportunity to discuss the use of the environment for learning with someone who has already undergone the experience.

Social Initiation

Creating a social context for the learning activities in this course was of key importance. From an Ecology of Language Learning point of view, one of the key affordances available for each learner in the environment were the other students and we thus needed to create prerequisites for them to get know each other. The Five Stage Model points to the importance of socialisation in Stage 2 of the developmental progression and almost the entire first session was thus dedicated to socialisation. During this session time was set aside for presentation activities and the formation of groups. Socialisation was also something that went on over the entire span of the course.

Information Exchange

After the initial processes of technical and social initiation the factual information on debating followed – how to structure a speech, how to create cohesion in the presentation, how to produce an interesting introduction etc. This activity could theoretically have been placed later in the course, after the students had gathered factual information, but according to the Five Stage Model it made sense to place the activity at this point. Students would thus be given more time to get to know each other and the environment before starting working independently on their presentations. The information on the structuring of a public speech was primarily given in the form of Youtube videos, which were streamed into SL while the students watched. After each film students were also encouraged to ask questions and discuss what they had seen.

Knowledge Construction

During the rest of the course the students would work in groups structuring their debates. The first of these meetings would be timetabled and teachers would be there to help out, whereas the organisation of later sessions was left in the hands of the students (times and places etc). This way we gradually left more responsibility and freedom to the students as they became more familiar with the environment, each other and the tasks at hand. Worth mentioning here is also the fact that we encouraged the students to go to other parts of SL where they could engage with the SL community at large. For example, we would give them the contact names of other partners in the Avalon network that they could speak to.

Development

Our ultimate ambition with the course was that students should continue visiting SL and engage with each other and the community after the course. Unlike other VLEs, which tend to be isolated environments in the form of password controlled learning management systems, SL does offer learners the possibility to pursue their learning interests in the environment after a course has finished. If we take language learning as an example, there are many islands that are dedicated to language learning activities. For example, it is possible to attend language workshops and conferences such as the SLanguages conference, which is given under the *Edunation* island framework. There is also the possibility to find tandem partners with whom to practice the target language. In fact, part of the Avalon project is dedicated to building up an active language learning community which goes beyond the actual course frameworks. As we shall see later in Section 4, at least some of the students intended to keep visiting SL after the end of the course.

APPLICATIONS OF ACTIVITY THEORY IN THE DESIGN

Central to the design of *Avalon Debating* was the telecollaboration. When designing such activity it is important to be able to take several systematic factors into account in the design. Each partner will have its own agenda and reason for joining the activity, and it is important to be aware of these. It is also important to be aware of differences in the learning cultures of the different institutions. For example, students may be more or less familiar with working autonomously and the forms of examination may vary vastly from university to university. In addition, the technical pre-requisites for the different student groups may be very different. Activity Theory provided us with a framework for pin pointing different variables that could affect the course activities. According to Engström (2001, p.133) using the Activity Theory framework to course design involves asking four central questions, namely: 1.Who are the learners? 2. Why do they learn and make the effort? 3. What do they learn, what are the contents and outcomes of learning? and 4. How do they learn?

In the first iteration of the course, the student group, who were recruited using the AVALON network of teachers and researchers, consisted of twelve students from four universities: five from Manchester University, England; three from Mid Sweden University, Sweden; one from the University of Pisa, Italy, and three from the University of Central Missouri, USA. When designing the course we discussed it with teachers from all the partner universities in order to get a clear idea of the students and the sort of programmes they were attending.

The Manchester students were teacher trainees and were attending the course as part of an elective on on-line learning. From these students' point of view, the main interest in the course lay in partaking in an on-line learning event of this nature in order to gain experience and ideas for their future professional lives. More specifically, the students also had the choice to use the experiences from the course when writing their special papers, which constituted a large part of the program. In addition, all the Manchester students were international exchange students and, as such, were also interested in the course from a language learning perspective. The motivation for the Manchester students thus went beyond the purely instrumental (i.e. making up credits in a course); it fed directly into their professional interests as potential future online teachers.

The Swedish participants were all students on an Internet English language program. They had been recruited on a voluntary basis and *Avalon Debating* replaced a regular five-week course unit that involved academic presentation and oral proficiency. As such, the Swedish students' motivation for joining the course thus consisted of practicing oral academic discourse in an authentic setting with native speakers. Having said this, however, it is important to note that many of the students on this type of course are very instrumentally motivated. Internet courses often represent an alternative to unemployment and are taken in lack of a better option, in order to achieve credits so that student loans can be granted. Of course, there are other types of learner profiles partaking in this type of course too. One important group is adult learners who are trying to improve their qualifications while at the same time working full time. This adult group typically consists of women (very often single mothers), who because of professional and family commitments are unable to attend ordinary campus courses. The point to be made here is that the completion of courses and the registering of formal academic credits often constitute a strong objective among this group. There are good practical reasons for this: in the Swedish system student grants and loans are suspended if credits are not achieved.

The Italian student was attending a PhD program and her motivation for participating in Debating in SL was to improve her oral proficiency. An acceptable level of English is a prerequisite for any PhD student within the Italian system. Without good skills in English, a student will not be granted his/her certificate. Language support is often provided outside the ordinary program curriculum by so-called university based *language centres*. It is also these centres that test and evaluate the language skills of the students. The courses run under the language centres can be fairly loosely structured and the main emphasis is on communicative proficiency. As such, teachers are fairly free to decide on activities that work towards this general aim.

The students from Central Missouri were attending an electorate composition class on the theme of *Cyber Culture* and were offered extra credits in their ordinary course if attending *Avalon Debating*. In addition, they were encouraged to use the debating topics as starting points for their future compulsory compositions, but did not have to do so if they did not want to. The course activities under *Avalon Debating* were thus entirely attended on a voluntary basis.

The institutional settings of the four groups differed greatly too. The Manchester students and the students from University of Central Missouri were all campus based, and had access to technical support. The Swedish students were working from their homes with no technical support, as was the Italian student.

Bearing the central issue of Activity Theory in mind, namely motivation, we wanted to create course content that was relevant to all of them. When designing the course, the different motivational starting points thus had to be worked into the design. With questions 1, 2 and 3 of Engströms model in mind, and based on the different prerequisites of the different student groups the objectives of the Debating in SL course were worked out and listed on the course homepage. These were:

- **Technical/tools:** Learning to use virtual worlds for learning, both as a tool for communication and a source of information.
- **Social:** To get to know friends from other countries and being able to collaborate with them in an online environment towards a common goal.
- **Academic:** The focus here is on presenting ideas in a convincing manner, looking at issues such as structure, cohesion, presentation techniques etc.

The first of these learning objectives was designed to appeal to the Manchester and Missouri students' academic interests in particular. Both of these groups had an interest in the digital medium itself and the Manchester students, in particular, also had an interest in how the actual learning processes were affected by the medium. For the Swedish students this objective also made sense since they were attending an Internet course and *Avalon Debating* represented a new way of approaching e-learning.

The social objective was mainly included as a way of addressing the fourth question in Engtröm's list, namely "How they learn?" This also fits in closely with Ecology of Language Learning and the Five Stage Model, and as such it was important to include this in the overall explicit objectives.

The academic objective was included primarily with the Swedish and Central Missouri students in mind. Both of these students groups were actually studying courses that involved academic presentation. In order to accommodate the Manchester students' (and central Missouri students') subject interests, the topics chosen for the debate all dealt with matters related to various aspects of Internet culture, subjects which were also of general interest for all the students involved. In summary then, the learning activities in the course were designed bearing the different academic objectives of the student's groups in mind, and thus fits into an Activity Theory model where motivation and objectives are key issues.

Another key issue related to motivation is the reward system that is built into the system. Working reward systems into the design that fed into the student's individual programmes was tricky. There was no meaningful common way of formally accrediting the students as a group, and instead individual solutions had to be worked out. As described above, these included giving the students the option to use the experience of the course as the basis for a special project (Manchester students); replacing an ordinary course module with the debating course and grading it as any ordinary course (but adding a written task to the primarily oral task in the course in order to meet the regular course criteria) as was the case for the Swedish students; giving students extra credits thus enabling them to improve the grades on the ordinary courses (the students form University of central Missouri) or using the course as one activity in a learning process leading towards improved proficiency (Italian student). The overall framework is summarised in Figure 5.

In Figure 5 above note how the examination/ formal rewards (large arrows) within the respective student group differ. In other words the activity, though common for all the students involved, serves different purposes depending on what programmes they were attending. Also note how the special areas of interest (areas of overlap)

Figure 5. Avalon Debating in relation to the student groups' academic programmes

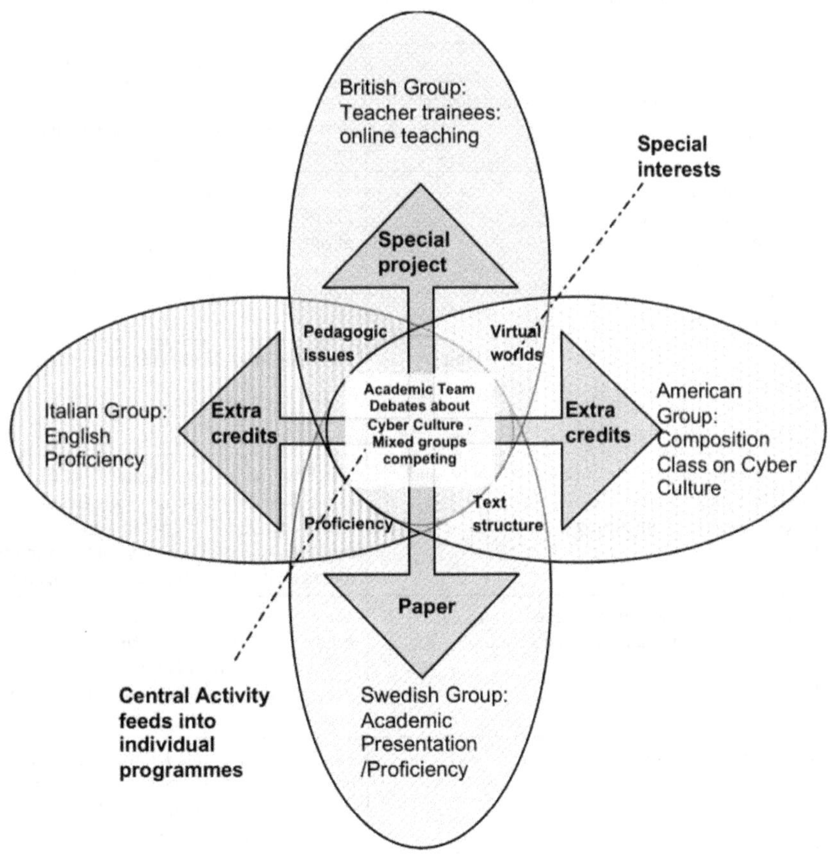

differ for each student group, but how the central activity (the debate) is still something that is of relevance to all (but for different reasons).

SUMMARY OF HOW THE THEORIES CONTRIBUTED TO THE DESIGN

There were of course internal reward models worked into the design of *Avalon Debating* which were common for all the students. One such feature was the final debate, which was a competitive event where the groups would compete against each other. Other less formal reward systems included the social design of the course, where students were reliant on each other as s group in order to accomplish the task. An overview of the sessions can be seen in Table 1.

EVALUATING THE FIRST ITERATION OF THE COURSE

The first iteration of *Avalon Debating* was run in March-May 2009. Twelve students attended the course which lasted approximately eight weeks. Obviously it is difficult to draw any firm conclusions on the basis of such a small number of students, but it is important to remember that the course was only one of a number of different course trials under the Avalon the project. Although no significant quantitative data could be extracted from the course iteration it was still valuable in providing us with qualitative feed-back on the course design. The results below are based on two data sets: firstly, observations and reflections, as well as informal feed-back that we received during the course, and secondly, the

Table 1. Overview of sessions held under Avalon Debating

Sessions in SL	Activities	Theoretical influences in Design
Technical Initiation	• Conducted on a one to one basis face to face or via Skype®.	*The Five Stage Model* (Access and Motivation stage) *Activity Theory* (pointing to the mediating artefact as an important factor in the design)
Session 1: **Introduction**	• Checking tools • Introducing each other • Course outline • Splitting into groups • Socialising in smaller groups • Deciding on topics	*The Five Stage Model* (Social Initiation) *Ecology of Language* Learning (stressing the importance of other participants as affordances) *Activity Theory* (instrumental in deciding on topics together with students)
Session 2: **Overview -Debating techniques**	Short lecture on debating and presentation techniques • Demonstration videos • Discussions on videos	*The Five Stage Model* (Information Exchange)
Session 3: **Preparation of Presentation**	• Data gathering at different locations in SL and over the Internet • Group work on organising presentation	*The Five Stage Model* (Knowledge Construction) *Ecology of Language Learning* (working in groups where each member contributes) *Activity Theory* (making use of the community at large; topics related to each group's special areas of interest)
Session 4-5 **Preparation of Presentation 2 (Time and location decided by the group)**	• Data gathering at different locations in SL • Group work on organising presentation	*The Five Stage Model* (Knowledge Construction) *Ecology of Language Learning* (working in groups where each member contributes) *Activity Theory* (making use of the community at large; topics related to each group's special areas of interest)
Session 6 **Final Debate**	• Presentations groups 1-4 • Voting • Reflection and Evaluation	*Ecology of Language Learning* (making use of the physical space to support the language learning event) *Activity Theory* (making use of the community at large; topics related to each group's special areas of interest)

results of a post-course feed-back questionnaire (see Appendix 1) that all students completed.

OBSERVATIONS, REFLECTIONS AND INFORMAL FEEDBACK

Based on observations and reflections from the teachers on the course we could conclude that the course had worked well on the whole. There were for example, no drop-outs, something which we had experienced as problematic in previous SL courses (see Deutschmann et al. 2009). The learning goals seemed to be relevant to all students, who seemed engaged in the topics and the process of organising their contributions for the final competitive debates. On a more problematic note, the design of the social context was tricky, and this was especially obvious in the early parts of the course. The initial grouping of students, for example, had been expected to to be an easy process taking minimal effort, but instead it turned out to be very messy and took time from the initial socializing process. We had underestimated the problems involved in organizing 12 SL beginners spatially and socially. The students were confused as to who was working with whom (they could not relate to the names of the avatars as some people referred to themselves using their real names), and they had problems understanding where their headquarters were. At the end of a fairly long procedure a few students did still not know what teams they were working with, where their headquarters were, and what topic they were debating. This of course meant that valuable time was taken from socialising and just getting used to the environment. In future runs of the course, we thus allocate more time for socialisation and just getting used to the environment in initial sessions, when no other activity is planned. We had catered for socialisation but underestimated its importance. We also found that sound issues were a common problem, for example, poor quality sound, distortion and feed-back, inability to activate sound etc. Most of these issues could, however, be dealt with by adjusting settings. Again, longer time to get used to the technicalities of the environment would probably have helped here. As an illustration, it is noteworthy that there were no sound problems during the final debate at the end of the course, after students had spent considerable time in the environment.

Results from End-of-Course Feedback Questionnaire

The questionnaire was offered to all the students and all twelve students answered it. The survey consisted of nine sections addressing different aspects of the course, the first of which was personal details (not included below). Below the answers from each section of the questionnaire are discussed in turn.

What Did You Learn?

The second question on the feed-back survey, "*What do you think you learnt during the course?*", was an open ended question where we wanted the learners to reflect over what they had learnt in general terms without leading questions. As expected, the answers here were quite diverse but it is interesting to note that all the answers could be related to the general learning goals that we had set up for the course (see above), namely learning goals related to the technical tool (to learn how to use SL for communication and information), social learning goals (to get to know and collaborate with students from other countries), and academic learning goals (to present ideas in a structured and convincing manner). Also note that many students included more than one thing in their description resulting in a total that exceeds twelve. The answers are summarised below:

- Things learnt related to the learning goal "technical tools": Six students mentioned that they had learnt new things about the technical environment (SL). Some comments were very positive: "*When firstly joining, I did not know how to even change my avatar's clothes, but now I could handle more affordances of second life. It's really exciting*!", while other were more neutral "*I learnt how to use SL in order to coordinate learning with students from other countries*." One student was more sceptical in relation to the environment but still acknowledged that he/she had gained new useful insights: "*I learnt to be patient! Sounds bugs and visual bugs were frequent but after a while you sort of just went with it*."

- Things learnt related to the social learning goal: Five students explicitly mentioned that they had learnt how to collaborate online with students from other cultures. Comments here included: "*I learnt to collaborate with other participants, for sure*.", "*I learnt a lot about online socializing in general*" and "*I learnt about cultures*".
- Things learnt related to the academic learning goals "rhetoric": Seven students referred to the fact that they had gained new knowledge on how to structure a speech and how to improve their presentation techniques. Some of these comments were very positive, for example, "*I learnt quite a lot from the course especially about the ways to make your speech a blast, it was really exciting!*"

There was a slight difference in what the students answered depending on what institution they came from. The Manchester students, for example, all emphasised the social and technical learning goals, while the academic learning goals seemed to be of greater importance to the other student groups. This would make sense, given that the teacher trainees probably were more interested in the activities and how the learning environment supported these than the other students, who probably had a more academic focus in their studies. Note, however, that this is highly speculative due to the limited number of participants.

SL as an Environment for Communication

In the third part of the survey we wanted to find out more about how SL worked as a communicative environment. Firstly we wanted to know if the students felt more or less comfortable communicating in SL than they would in a face-to-face situation. In answer to the question "*Has the Second Life course made you feel more/less/no difference comfortable communicating in English*?", four of the students maintained that it had made them feel more comfortable, one had felt less comfortable and seven claimed that it had made no difference. In response to the question "*Did you encounter any problems in communicating with your group, and if so how did you solve them*?" only one student claimed it had been problematic. The student in question had asked the speakers to use the chat to clarify what they meant. In response to the final question on this theme namely, "*Did Second Life pose any special problems/opportunities when communicating in English? If so, what and why*?" two students claimed that it offered special affordances since they could use voice, while one pointed to technical problems interfering with communication. The other respondents simply answered "*no*" to this question. The overall impression was that SL had worked well as a communicative environment, although there was little indication that the environment was in any way "extra ordinary" in this respect. Again, it is hard to draw any conclusions from such a limited number of answers.

How Engaging Was SL as a Tool?

In the fourth section of the questionnaire we wanted to find out to what extent the students used SL as an environment outside the actual scheduled lessons. On average, students spent two hours a week in SL outside scheduled lessons on activities that were related to the course, and one hour on activities that were not related to the course. The span here was great however, especially in relation to activities that were not related to the course. One student, for example, spent six hours in SL on leisure activities while many did not spend any leisure time in SL. Here it is practically impossible to draw any conclusions since time spent in-world will depend on a number of variables including work load. In fact, some pointed out that they would have liked to spend more time but were too busy. In the last question on this theme, "*How did your group maintain contact and meet outside scheduled class sessions*?", we wanted to see which channels of communication the students were using during their collaborative work outside scheduled time. All students listed e-mails as a way of keeping in touch, which is probably explained by the need for an easy asynchronous means of communication. Many were in different time zones and it was probably inconvenient to meet synchronously at times. When it came to synchronous communication, three listed MSN®, three used Skype® and six used SL. It seems then that at least half of the students opted for other means of synchronous communication in addition to SL.

Social Aspects: Group Work

In section five we wanted to enquire about group processes and find out whether the collaborative design had worked. The first question asked how many hours a week the students worked as a group outside scheduled class time. On average the students seemed to have worked approximately two hours a week outside scheduled time. The groups differed greatly though. One group maintained they worked approximately five hours, while one did not meet at all. In response to the next question "*Did you feel part of your group? Why?*", all students but one answered "*yes*". Motivations here included praise of the other team members. One student commented specifically on the environment and how it helped in-group bonding: "*Yes, after several meetings with my group, we feel the attachment as a group. And we even hanged out there in second life and learnt new tricks (like flying vertically which I still cannot do!)*". As mentioned above, one student did not feel any group membership and motivated this with the comment, "*The group was absent. No collaboration, the other members displayed indifference to the group's work.*" In response to the question "*Did you socialise with anyone from the course outside scheduled time*?" five students answered "*yes*", which was encouraging. In response to the next question in this section, "*Do you think you will keep in touch after the course*?", two answered "*yes*", five answered "*maybe*" or "*probably*", three answered "*probably not*", one answered "*no*" and the final student gave a long answer as follows: "*That would be fine by me! But I have a feeling we won't keep in touch. Don't ask me why... I do have a theory however. We never actually talked much about "personal" issues, it was just work related, and therefore I guess it's hard to really establish a "bond" to the others.*" This was a clear indication that in spite of our efforts we should perhaps have spent even more time on socialising in the design. In response to the final question in this section, "*If so, what tool do you think you will use for this?*", four listed SL. Other common tools mentioned were e-mail, Skype® and MSN®. On the whole the answers of this section were encouraging. Students on the whole did seem to feel some sense of group belonging and many wanted to continue meeting after the course. Based on this limited sample, it is hard to evaluate to what extent the environment of SL contributed to group bonding but there are at least some indications that it did. It is, however, also clear that students seem to use SL in combination with other synchronous tools, but we do not know what motivates this.

Technical Aspects

Section six of the questionnaire addressed technical aspects of the environment. In response to the first question "*What technical problems (if any) did you encounter during the course*?" the most common problem seemed to be audio issues; six students listed this variable. Four students also listed the "*crashing*" of SL on their computers as a problem. In the next question "*Did you manage solve them and how*? ", we wanted to assess the seriousness of the issues. Here only one student answered "*no*". The rest seemed to have been able to solve the issues and "*rebooting*" seemed to be the most common strategy. One student's problem was obviously related to inexperience of the environment as the solution to the audio problem was "*just found the right button eventually*". It is clear from the answers that the students experience SL to be a relatively unstable environment, especially when it comes to audio. This may be a result of hardware and bandwidth issues, but definitely poses a problem when, as in oral proficiency classes, the entire task design is dependent on audio.

The Students' View of SL as a Learning Environment

In section seven of the questionnaire we wanted to explore the students' thoughts of the environment as a place for learning. This section consisted of one question only, "*In your opinion, do you think that SL is an appropriate environment for learning? Why? Why not*?", and it was encouraging to see that all twelve students answered "*yes*" to this question. Motivations included comments such as: "*Apart from a few technical difficulties (which we all have to accept with an open mind, I guess) I found the environment motivating and engaging.*", "*I think it is a great tool for distance education. It provides access for some that may not otherwise have any way to attend school.*", "*It's fun while you do schoolwork.*", "*freedom of expressing*", and "*It offers a lot of authentic and real life simulation activities.*" Others were more reserved in their praise but still expressed positive attitudes as to the potential of the environment: "*Kinks need to be worked out. It is creative and can be used in many fantastic ways and the saying the "sky's the limit" truly applies here.*" and "*Yes, I do think so. In spite of all the technical hurdles and challenges, SL can be an exciting place for learning especially language in that with our avatar we can do what is impossible in the real life and we can expect the unexpected. SL helps to set free our imagination and to enjoy the learning to the maximum level.*" One student also commented on problems with the course design in relation to the environment:

"I guess it can be, if students are given more time to explore and maneuver around in-world so to speak. Then there will be more opportunities to discover errors and problems and a bigger chance of solving them. For example voice chat and bad connections, 'cause stuff like that is really annoying when we are about to start a lecture or presentation. If those issues could be solved then SL would be a completely marvelous tool for online education! Maybe you guys should arrange some informal meetings and 'happenings' for future students? That could be a good way of getting to know the people behind the avatars and also... yeah that's right, to discover potential errors and bugs!:) Such 'events' should of course be optional for the individual students, but you should stress the importance of them participating."

Again it seems that there is a need for even more effort to be been spent on technical and social initiation.

Affective Aspects of the Environment

In section eight, we wanted to capture some of the feelings that students held towards environment and the learning experience. We tried to do this by giving the students a list of adjectives/ descriptive phrases where they could choose as many as they liked to describe how they felt. Of the 14 descriptions listed, six were positive, six were negative and two were neutral/indifferent. The most common descriptions chosen by the students were positive: The words *comfortable*, *curios*, *motivated* and *satisfied (the learning environment lived up to your expectation)* were all chosen by six respondents, and four listed the adjectives *excited* and *happy*. The most common negative description was *frustrated*, which was chosen by four students. *Anxious* was chosen by two students, *disappointed* and *sceptical* scored one each, while no student chose the adjectives *scared* and *confused* to describe their experience. Of the neutral descriptions listed, *hard to say* scored two, and *indifferent* one. The results mirrored the findings from the previous section: on the whole the students were positive to the environment but seemed to have some misgivings, primarily related to technical aspects.

General Thoughts on the Course and Future Use of SL

The final section of the questionnaire addressed general feed-back on the course structure. We wanted to know what had worked and what had not. In addition we wanted to find out if the students would be using SL in the future. Comments on what worked well with the course included the collaborative work, mentioned by six students with comments such as: "*The collaboration part. Groups of three feels like a really great way of organizing things. Not too difficult to coordinate.*" Three students also expressed appreciation of the organization of the course (information structure etc), as one student put it: "*There were also clear and precise instructions concerning what we were supposed to do. The framework of the course, so to speak, feels very pedagogical.*" It seems that combining the in-world activities with a clear instructional framework on a homepage outside the environment was a successful strategy. Three students mentioned the communicative/social aspect of the course as a success with comment such as: "*meeting people*" and "*Being able to talk to others, not just through forums but actually speaking*!". Four students appreciated the academic learning aspects of the course (i.e. the information on how to structure and present ideas). One student found that the course gave her /him new insights on how to use virtual worlds for teaching and finally, one student appreciated the fact there was such good turn-up to all the sessions.

On the question of what worked less well with the course, eight students mentioned technical hitches. One student also found it confusing to meet in large groups in SL and finally one student found the time differences between the European and American students to be problematic.

Finally, in response to the question "Do you think you will use Second Life in the future and if so for what?", three answered "*no*" and one "*I don't think so*". Of the remaining eight positive answers, four said they would use for teaching in the future, two said they would use it to practice their English skills, one student wanted to try the environment for music performances, and one would just use it "*for fun*". Again it was encouraging to see how many of the students seemed to appreciate the possibilities the environment offered for their future learning needs. In addition, half of the students had already joined groups within SL that had nothing to do with the course itself. We felt that this case was demonstrative of a good integration of nodes within the active learning system.

In summary, the student questionnaires confirmed some of the reflections of the teachers. The course concept worked well on the whole but even more attention could have been paid to technical and social initiation. In spite of the technical problems associated with SL, we were pleased to see how positive the students were towards the environment and how many seemed to be motivated to stay on in SL to pursue further learning. From this we may speculate that SL supports the final stage "Development", in the Five Stage Model, but again, it is hard to draw any conclusions from the limited sample.

DISCUSSION: LESSONS LEARNT

In the study above we have used three theoretical frameworks and models for the design of the course activities in *Avalon Debating*, namely the Ecology of Language Learning, The Five Stage Model and Activity Theory. The Ecology of Language Learning was used to design the learning activities in such a fashion that the students themselves contributed to the content and essentially 'made the course'. What we as course designers did was to provide the basic framework and the prerequisites for the learning events to take place, but the content (subject matters) and group processes were decided by the students themselves. The overall ambition was thus to provide a language learning event based on authentic communication and the student centred interests, and where the environment and ongoing processes could decide exactly where the course ended up. Based on the evaluations and reflections, we would argue that we at least partly achieved our aims, and that the theoretical framework thus helped us in the design.

Similarly, the Five Stage Model helped us to focus on the progression of group processes during a collaborative course of this nature, but here we probably underestimated the importance of the initial stages. Arguably, we are not alone in this shortcoming. It is easy to focus on the learning goals, and the importance of social processes is often neglected. In our case, the insights from the first run of the course led us to change the course concept in future iterations to include extra sessions at the start, where the students could socialise without having any other extra demands on them. Although we have not evaluated these iterations at this point in time, our initial gut feeling is that the students get to know each other even better, and that this helps in creating a better learning environment. In response to the course evaluations, the "Access and Motivation" or the technical initiation stage has been further improved to include more detailed aspects such as adjusting sound levels etc.

The strength of Activity Theory in the design of the course was that it takes a number of factors into account in order to explain failures and successes, including technical, formal and social structures. The framework helped us to take many of these factors into consideration early in the planning stages, and the end result was satisfactory. One key factor explaining this relative success of the course was the fact that we had tried to accommodate for the different objectives of the four student groups. This was clear from the student evaluations, where the achievements of different learning goals were listed among the students depending on the institutional setting they came from. Not having adapted the course to the different learning profiles of the student groups, would have probably led to a course which we as educators might have wanted, but perhaps not the students. On previous occasions this has been our experience when designing courses and the result has often been that students simply drop out (see Deutschmann et al. 2009, for example). On this course occasion, no one dropped out and attendance was excellent. The theory also takes the technical framework into account, and with SL it seems clear that this is a key issue. On the one hand, SL as an environment was perceived very positively by the students and probably helped motivating them. On the other hand, based on the Activity Theory framework, paying close attention to the technicalities of the environment in our evaluation helped us to see its shortcomings. From this we learnt that we need to pay extra close attention to the technical matters in future iterations. We need to make sure that students have the correct hardware such as headphones and adequate computers, and that they need added skills on how to control settings in SL. By turning up or down individual sound, for example, many distortion and feed-back issues can be solved, but students need to know how to do this at an early stage. It is not just enough to get them to activate their voice and hope for the best.

The design and first iteration of *Avalon Debating* have demonstrated the usefulness of using theoretical models in the very practical process of designing a course. The models have helped us to focus on different key issues, which would otherwise probably have gone us by. The study also demonstrates the Action Research process in course design. Using theories is primary in the design, but the intended outcomes also have to be evaluated by testing them in real life, and even if we design for certain aspects (such as social initiation) it is not always the case that this is the outcome in real life. Evaluating the student responses on these matters have thus given us further important input into the design process, and has helped us to enhance the learning outcomes.

Using the Activity Theory model when placing the models developed under Avalon Debating in a greater language educational context, we can foresee some basic problems. In *Avalon Debating* we deemed the course a relative success because students participated actively, were engaged and did not drop out. Although these outcomes probably also mean that students improved their communicative skills, it is unlikely that 'engagement' in itself is an acceptable outcome in most university institutions of today. In an increasingly competitive world of academia, educational systems instead strive for concrete 'results', or rather standard indicators, which can easily be compared and used to rank students, teachers, departments and universities.

From an ecological approach to language learning this creates several problems. Traditional ways of testing and grading students in language courses are highly individual, while an ecological approach to language learning is based on a communicative social approach. Communication, by definition, involves interaction. Minimally, you need at least one speaker and one interlocutor, and what decides the making of successful communication is as much dependent on the speaker as the listener. Applying these principles in more complex, intercultural contexts as we have done, means that the 'best' student is not necessarily the one with complex vocabulary and perfect British received pronunciation, but perhaps someone who is alert to differences in communicative skills and who can adapt his/her language accordingly. These types of language proficiency skills are harder to evaluate using traditional exam methods, and indeed it is questionable if they can be evaluated at all (or even should be) by anyone else than the persons that are partaking in the actual speech event.

This illustrates a basic dilemma for language educators, namely the provision of relevant rewards that mirror the significance and the nature of the subject at hand. Real communication requires complex and adaptable language skills, but at the same time we are required to evaluate and standardise these skills in an efficient fashion that our institutions and students deem fair and reliable. These two requirements do not always match. At the same time it is important that the form of examination is relevant since, for many students, *rewards* in the form of exam results and formal grades are an important factor affecting motivation. A basic problem with our course model was thus that we did not develop systematic methods for testing the learning outcomes. We were process rather than result oriented.

If we, in accordance with Activity Theory, believe that action is motive driven and that motives are determined by rewards, looking at existing reward models becomes essential if we want to initiate change in language education. If we take an ecological approach to language learning, traditional reward models are in many cases immaterial to the subject at hand and there is a general need to move from models based on traditional reinforcement theories to more socio-culturally based theories. Consequently, there are calls for new ways of conceptualizing and exploring motivation as an ongoing changing complex of processes where the notions of self and identity are included (Ushioda, 2001 and Syed, 2001). Further, Wang (2008) states that it is necessary to account for self-concept, which also includes a cultural dimension in the motivation models. In turn, developing models for evaluation that include factors such as these is of outmost importance and a real challenge, but a necessary one if our institutions are to provide relevant language skills for today's global society.

FUTURE RESEARCH DIRECTIONS

The evaluation of *Avalon Debating* left many questions that merit further attention. Firstly, much more research on virtual worlds and language learning is needed in order to give us better empirical basis for any claims made. Aspects such as the importance of technical and social initiation, for example, need to be tested in controlled settings in order to evaluate their importance. Further there are several issues related to the impact of the technical environment on communication and language learning that need to be explored. In our course development, for example, we used SL because of its affordances which included the 3D space as well as synchronous channels for oral and written communication. While the students were very positive to the environment it still turned out that half of them chose to use other tools (MSN® and Skype®) when they were communicating synchronously outside course sessions. Why? It would thus be interesting to further explore when and why different tools are chosen and what the advantages of each device may be, so that future course designs can take this into account leading to more informed choices when designing language learning environments.

Another point that merits further exploration is if, and how, the students continued to use the learning community of SL for their own development once the course was over. This type of research would give interesting insights into aspects of life-long learning and motivation.

We also feel that there is further need to explore the technical possibilities and limitations of SL to make better use of the possibilities of the environment in future courses. There is also room for more innovative models of design where aspects such as identity in relation to language learning can be investigated using the affordances of the avatar (whose gender and appearance you can change quite easily). One such project, *Identifying Identity*, is currently being undertaken by the author, where voice morphing and gender changes will give learners the opportunity to enter avatars of the opposite sex in order to become more aware of issues related to language and gender.

Finally, there is an urgent need for research which explores how learning activities based on the Ecology of Language Learning and other socio-constructivist learning theories can be examined in a way that is acceptable to our institutions.

CONCLUSION

In this chapter we have used Ecology of Language Learning, the Five Stage Model and Activity Theory to design and analyze the activities of *Avalon Debating*, a language proficiency course in SL. The evaluations of the first iteration of the course show that 3D virtual worlds offer good potentials for language education, but that there are still technical issues related to voice that cause interference in the environment. To be used effectively, we also need to pay careful attention to matters such as social and technical initiation. Further research is also needed in order to evaluate the impact of the environment on communication and language learning in general. The overall conclusion is that innovative environments such as virtual worlds have great potential to enhance both teaching and learning practice using methods based on collaboration and active participation, but that in order for this to gain maximum impact, we need to gain a better understanding of how we can use these environments effectively, and we may also have to review traditional forms of examination so that they better reflect new learning practices.

REFERENCES

Belz, J. A. (2003). Linguistic perspectives on the development of intercultural competence in telecollaboration. *Language Learning & Technology, 7*(2), 68–117.

Bryant, S., Forte, A., & Bruckman, A. (2005). Becoming Wikipedian: Transformation of participation in a collaborative online encyclopedia. *Proceedings of GROUP International Conference on Supporting Group Work* (pp. 1-10).

Campbell, A. P. (2003). Weblogs for use with ESL classes. *The Internet TESL Journal, 9*(2).

Deutschmann, M., & Panichi, L. (2009a). Instructional design, teacher practice and learner autonomy. In J. Molka-Danielsen & M. Deutschmann (Eds.), *Learning and teaching in the virtual world of Second Life* (pp. 27-44). Trondheim, Norway: Tapir akademisk forlag.

Deutschmann, M., & Panichi, L. (2009b). Talking into empty space? - Signalling involvement in a virtual language classroom in Second Life. *ALA Journal, 18*(3-4), 310–328.

Deutschmann, M., Panichi, L., & Molka-Danielsson, J. (2009). Designing oral participation in Second Life – A comparative study of two language proficiency courses. *ReCALL, 21*(2), 70–90. doi:10.1017/S0958344009000196

Dieu, B. (2004). Blogs for language learning. *Essential Teacher, 1*(4), 26–30.

Dooly, M. (2008). *Telecollaborative language learning: A guidebook to moderating intercultural collaboration online*. Bern, Switzerland: Peter Lang.

Engström, Y. (1987). *Learning by expanding: An activity-theoretical approach to developmental research*. Helsinki, Finland: Orienta-Konsultit.

Engström, Y. (1999). Activity theory and transformation. In Engeström, Y., Miettinen, R., & Punama¨ki, R.-L. (Eds.), *Perspectives on activity theory* (pp. 19–38). Cambridge, UK: Cambridge University Press.

Engström, Y. (2001). Expansive learning at work: Toward an activity theoretical reconceptualization. *Journal of Education and Work, 14*(1), 133–156.

Haugen, E. (1972). *The ecology of language*. Stanford, CA: Stanford University Press.

Hudson, B., Owen, D., & van Veen, K. (2006). Working on educational research methods with Master's students in an international online learning community. *British Journal of Educational Technology, 37*(4), 577–603. doi:10.1111/j.1467-8535.2005.00553.x

Kaptelinin, V., & Nardi, B. (2006). *Acting with technology: Activity theory and interaction design* (p. 62). Cambridge, MA: The MIT Press.

Karasavvidis, I. (2009). Activity theory as a conceptual framework for understanding teacher approaches to Information and Communication Technologies. *Computers & Education Archive, 53*(2), 436–444. doi:10.1016/j.compedu.2009.03.003

Kern, R. (2000). *Literacy and language teaching*. Oxford, UK: Oxford University Press.

Kern, R. (2006). Perspectives on technology in learning and teaching languages. *TESOL Quarterly, 40*(1), 183–210. doi:10.2307/40264516

Kramsch, C., & Thorne, S. L. (2002). Foreign language learning as global communicative practice. In Block, D., & Cameron, D. (Eds.), *Globalization and language teaching* (pp. 83–100). London, UK: Routledge.

Molka-Danielsen, J., & Deutschmann, M. (Eds.). (2009). *Learning and teaching in the virtual world of Second Life*. Trondheim, Norway: Tapir Akademisk Forlag.

Molka-Danielsen, J., Deutschmann, M., & Panichi, L. (2010). Designing transient learning spaces in Second Life for language learning. *Designs for Learning, 2*(2), 22–33.

Nardi, B. A. (Ed.). (1996). *Context and consciousness: Activity theory and human-computer interaction*. Cambridge, MA: MIT Press.

Nardi, H. (2006). Strangers and friends: Collaborative play in World of Warcraft. *Proceedings of the 2006 20th Anniversary Conference on Computer Supported Cooperative Work.*

O'Dowd, R. (2006). *Telecollaboration and the development of intercultural communicative competence*. München, Germany: Langenscheidt-Longman.

Panichi, L., Deutschmann, M., & Molka-Danielsson, J. (2010). Virtual worlds, language learning and intercultural exchange. In F. Helm & S. Guth (Eds). *Telecollaboration 2.0 for language and intercultural learning* (pp. 165-195). Bern, Switzerland: Peter Lang publishers.

Salmon, G. (2004). *E-moderating: The key to teaching and learning online*. London, UK: Taylor & Francis.

Stevens, V. (2006) Second Life in education and language learning. *TESL-EJ, 10*(3).

Syed, Z. (2001). Notions of self in foreign language learning: A qualitative analysis. In Dörnyei, Z., & Schmidt, R. (Eds.), *Motivation and second language acquisition* (pp. 127–148). Honolulu, HI: University of Hawaii Press.

Thorne, S. L. (2000). Beyond bounded activity systems: Heterogeneous cultures in instructional uses of persistent conversation. *The Proceedings of the Thirty-Third Hawaii International Conference on Systems Science.* New York, NY: IEEE Press.

Thorne, S. L. (2008). Transcultural communication in open internet environments and massively multiplayer online games. In Magnan, S. (Ed.), *Mediating discourse online* (pp. 305–327). Amsterdam, The Netherlands: John Benjamins.

Ushioda, E. (2001). Language learning at university: Exploring the role of motivational thinking. In Dörnyei, Z., & Schmidt, R. (Eds.), *Motivation and second language acquisition* (pp. 93–125). Honolulu, HI: University of Hawaii Press.

van Lier, L. (2004). *The ecology and semiotics of language learning: A sociocultural perspective*. London, UK: Kluwer Academic Publishers. doi:10.1007/1-4020-7912-5

Wang, F. (2008). Motivation and English achievement: An exploratory and confirmatory factor analysis of a new measure for Chinese students of English learning. *North American Journal of Psychology, 10*(3), 633–646.

Warschauer, M. (1997). Computer-mediated collaborative learning: Theory and practice. *Modern Language Journal, 81*(4), 470–481. doi:10.2307/328890

Warschauer, M. (1998). Online learning in sociocultural context. *Anthropology & Education Quarterly, 29*(1), 68–88. doi:10.1525/aeq.1998.29.1.68

Warschauer, M. (1999). *Electronic literacies. Language, culture, and power in online education*. Mahwah, NJ: Lawrence Erlbaum.

Warschauer, M. (2006). *Laptops and literacy*. New York, NY: Teachers College Press.

KEY TERMS AND DEFINITIONS

Action Learning: A cyclic pedagogic method developed by Revans (1980) consisting of four stages: to explore, plan, act and reflect on a learning task.

Activity Theory: A cultural historical framework introduced by Leont'ev (1978) and further developed by Engström (1987, 1999, 2001) to examine interactions of a social system with a particular objective.

Affordances: The possibilities an environment offers. This can be different depending on who the subject is; water does not offer the same affordances to a human as it does to a fish.

Division of Labor in Activity Theory: These are the responsibilities and roles of persons that are part of a social system that may affect the achievement of goals of that system, for example IT center support personnel.

Mediating artefacts in Activity Theory: Are elements of the social system that help to facilitate the (learning) activity.

Objects in Activity Theory: These are the primary goals of the social system.

Rules in Activity Theory: These are the rules of the social system of study, such as rules of the course or rules of the university.

Second Life™: Is a trademark and name of the 3D multi user virtual environment or platform developed by Linden Lab. Through motional use of member characters called "avatar" the platform supports social meetings and among other, educational activities.

Subjects in Activity Theory: These are the primary actors seeking to achieve the goals of the social system, such as teachers and teaching assistants.

Telecollaboration: The use of different types of Internet communication tools in order to support social interaction, dialogue, debate, and intercultural exchange between internationally dispersed learners in parallel language classes.

APPENDIX 1: POST COURSE QUESTIONNAIRE

1. Some general information about you
    a. What is your avatar name?
    b. What Second Life course activity have you just finished?
    c. When did your course end (date)?
2. What do you think you learnt during the course?
3. Some questions related to your language learning and communication (please answer n/a if not applicable to you)
    a. Has this Second Life course made you feel more/less/no difference comfortable communicating in English?
    b. If you are not a native speaker of English, how would you describe your English now? Basic, satisfactory, good, excellent.
    c. Did you encounter any problems in communicating with your group? How did you solve them?
    d. Did Second Life pose any special problems/opportunities when communicating in English? If so, what and why?
4. Questions related to the technical tools you used during the course
    a. How many hours a week did you spend in Second Life for course related work outside the scheduled time (1,5 hours)?
    b. How many hours a week did you spend in Second Life for activities which were NOT related to this specific course
    c. How did your group maintain contact and meet outside scheduled class sessions (SL, e-mail, skype, etc)?
    d. During the course we used three asynchronous tools to communicate information about the course: a course web page, a blog and e-mail send-outs. Which tool did you primarily consult?
5. Some questions related to how you worked as a group.
    a. How many hours did you spend working with your group outside scheduled class time?
    b. Did you feel part of your group? Why?
    c. Did you socialise with anyone from the course outside scheduled time?
    d. Do you think you will keep in touch after the course?
    e. If so, what tool do you think you will use for this?
6. Technical Aspects
    a. What technical problems (if any) did you encounter during the course?
    b. Did you manage solve them and how? (For example, "someone from the group helped me")
7. In your opinion, do you think that SL is an appropriate environment for learning? Why? Why not?
8. Try to describe how you feel about the learning experience in Second Life. Mark the adjectives that best describe your feelings (you can choose as many descriptive adjectives below as you like).
    a. Excited
    b. Happy
    c. Scared
    d. Confused
    e. Comfortable
    f. Indifferent

g. Anxious
h. Frustrated
i. Curios
j. Motivated
k. Sceptical
l. Satisfied (the environment lived up to your expectations)
m. Disappointed
n. Hard to say

9. What you thought about the course and if you will use Second Life after this course.
    a. What do you think worked well with the course and why?
    b. What do you think worked less well and why (also, feel free to suggest any changes here)?
    c. Do you think you will use Second Life in the future and if so for what?

Chapter 14
Designing Learning Ecosystems for Mobile Social Media

Jari Multisilta
University of Helsinki, Finland

ABSTRACT

Social media has gained interest not only in entertainment applications, but also with learning and business applications; however, there are not many research frameworks available for designing learning activities for learning ecosystems based on mobile social media. In this chapter, a framework for designing and analyzing learning activities in learning ecosystems that are based on mobile and social media is presented. The framework is based on Activity Theory (AT) and Experiential Learning Theory (ELT). In the chapter the existing research on e-learning, mobile learning, and multimodal learning are discussed and reviewed. The research on learning ecosystems based on mobile social media is also positioned to this multi-scientific research field. Finally, two examples of using the framework for designing, learning, and analyzing learning activities in mobile social media learning ecosystems are presented.

INTRODUCTION

Social media applications have gained popularity because of services like Blogger, Facebook, Flickr, Twitter and YouTube. The idea behind social media is that users are actively contributing to the services, for example sending their blog notes, images or videos to the service, creating tags and doing other types of social activities, for example commenting on and rating blogs, images and videos others have posted. Many social media applications are designed for entertainment purposes through the creation of unique individual experiences for the user. An interesting question is: Can mobile social media be applied to learning?

Social media applications can, at the very least, be seen as a way to support the learning process. Wikis and blogs are already used for doing col-

DOI: 10.4018/978-1-61350-080-4.ch014

laborative learning activities in the classroom; moreover, many social media applications have been designed for desktop or laptop usage. It would be useful if there is support for designing social media applications for learning outside the classroom. Some social media applications have a mobile client or can be used with a browser in the mobile device. For example, using a mobile phone bundled with social media client software, users can post to their blogs or Flickr accounts. In the future, social media services will be designed based upon the needs of the mobile users. The mobility aspect in social media is emphasized also because of new type tablet computers, such as Apple's iPad.

Social media services for learning applications can be designed using existing programming paradigms and tools, such as a client-server model, Ajax programming, user-centered design models, participatory design, and guidelines for creating usable web pages; however, it is believed that the design process as well as the designed system can be improved by designing learning activities with a theoretical and conceptual framework. Tynjälä and Häkkinen (2005) argue that "a major problem related to learning in virtual environments is that, in group work, certain phases of problem-solving may be so difficult that the productive sharing and elaboration of knowledge through electronic tools is almost impossible" (p. 327). Although the usability and usefulness of ICT systems and tools is a difficult, multifaceted problem, it is believed that it can be at least partly solved by using appropriate design methods and tools.

There has been a lot of discussion on learning theories for eLearning, web-based learning, and mobile learning (Mwanza-Simwami, 2007; Naismith, Lonsdale, Vavoula, & Sharples, 2004; Nichols, 2003; Oliver & Pelletier, 2006; Sharples, Taylor, & Vavoula, 2005; Trifonova & Ronchetti, 2003). One of the main questions in this discussion has been the need of a separate theory of learning for web-based or mobile learning. In this chapter the discussion is extended to learning with mobile social media and the need of learning theories for learning ecosystems based on mobile social media.

Nichols (2003) claims that "literature in eLearning is practice-based and is typically presented in a descriptive format" (p. 1). Research is focusing on reporting experiments, but with a lack of unified concepts and theory. This would mean that practitioners do not use learning theories when they are designing eLearning environments and eLearning activities. It is argued, that the use of a learning theory as a model, or framework helps the practitioners to analyze and design learning activities in learning ecosystems based on mobile social media.

According to Mwanza (2007) learning with mobile devices is still a new research area and more work is needed in order to understand the benefits and effects of using technology to support learning. From this point of view, discussing the characteristics of learning with technology and building theoretical concepts and frameworks for supporting the design and implementation of pedagogically meaningful applications for learning with mobile social media is justified.

Currently, there are not any research frameworks available for studying learning ecosystems based on mobile social media. In this chapter, a social media design framework that could be used for designing learning activities for next generation mobile social media services is presented. The model is based on Activity Theory (AT) and Experiential Learning Theory (ELT). Related frameworks based on the AT, namely the SEA Framework (Multisilta, 2008) and the framework for analyzing mobile learning according to Sharples et al. (2005) is also discussed. Activity Theory has been widely accepted for designing user interfaces (Barthelmess & Anderson, 2002; Fjeld, Lauche, Bichel, Voorhorst, Krueger, & Rauterberg, 2002; Kaptelinin & Nardi, 2006; Oliver & Pelletier, 2006), pedagogical applications (Kukulska-Hulme, Traxler, & Pettit, 2007; Uden, 2007) and mobile learning (Sharples, Taylor, & Vavoula, 2007); however, AT has not yet been used to explain collaborative learning activities in mobile social media. Experiential Learning Theory describes the learning process with concepts the researcher believes support learning with social media. Social media is, in any case, about sharing experiences and an impulse to learn and share can be, for example, an unexpected event or unknown problem outside classroom. The aim of this chapter is to combine these theoretical frameworks to design a new framework that could be used in designing mobile social media-based learning applications and activities. Finally, the design framework is applied to design a learning activity for learning outside the classroom and to analyze and evaluate the experience of a learning activity.

THEORETICAL BACKGROUND

In this section Activity Theory (AT), Experiential Learning Theory (ELT) and related AT based models are discussed as a theoretical background for the study. The role of user experience and *felt experience* in designing learning activities is also discussed. First, the concepts of mobile social media, mobile learning and multimodal learning are presented. These concepts create a basis for discussing learning ecosystems based on mobile social media.

Mobile Social Media

Mobile social media is a relatively new phenomenon that was born with the emerging technological developments of the Internet and mobile devices and the change in the way of people consider the Internet as a social network (Lugano, 2010). Based on Lerman (2008), social media applications support users in creating content, annotating content with tags, evaluating content, and creating social networks with other users sharing similar interests. In social media, users are seen as being both content consumers and producers. Social media applications are based on the Web 2.0 that was first defined by Tim O'Reilly (O'Reilly, 2005; O'Reilly, 2007). In Web 2.0 the network is seen as a platform for all connected devices, which use networked applications on that platform. The platform delivers the software as a continually updated service. Platforms and applications are constantly improving all the time because people consume and remix data from multiple sources as well as provide their own data and services in a form that allows remixing by others (O'Reilly, 2007). In comparison to Web 1.0, Web 2.0 is based on the architecture of participation and it delivers rich user experiences.

Wikipedia is a well-known example of Web 2.0 application that consists of community created articles that anyone can edit. In Wikipedia Web 2.0 is defined to be "a perceived ongoing transition of the World Wide Web from a collection of web-sites to a full-fledged computing platform serving web applications to end users." This definition summarizes O'Reilly's original ideas of Web 2.0.

The concepts of Web 2.0 and social media are intertwined so that social media applications are based on Web 2.0. Before defining mobile social media in detail, characteristics of social media are discussed. Typical features of social media include tags, rating systems and recommendation systems. Social media applications support the sharing of the tags for particular resources with other users (Marlow, Naaman, Boyd, & Davis, 2006). A tag is also a link to other resources using the same tag (Marlow et al., 2006). Tags in a social media application form a folksonomy, which is a non-hierarchical taxonomy created by the users (Marlow et al., 2006).

Heyes, Brereton and Viller (2008) define mobile social software to be a system that can be used with a wide range of mobile devices and aims to support socializing, and take advantage of social information or social networks. They also argue that such a system should be useful, easy to access and easy to use if they are going to compete with existing desktop and laptop software. In his PhD thesis, Lugano (2010) develops a model for Mobile Social Software (MoSoSo) that can be described as "a class of mobile applications whose scope is to support informal mobile social networking" (p. 123). Important building blocks of MoSoSo are user profile, mobile social network and social algorithms. According to Lugano, MoSoSo is often associated with a dedicated mobile application and not a general service (Lugano, 2010, p. 125). Although standalone mobile applications have often a limited set of features they also support the idea that MoSoSo is associated to a well-defined activity (Lugano, 2010). This kind of trend can clearly be seen in many mobile applications available for example from AppStore, Android Market or Nokia Ovi. Many mobile applications implement an activity that is also available using a web browser, but the mobile application is easier to use on a small screen than a web page designed for laptop or desktop screens.

The usefulness of mobile social software could be related to features available only in mobile platforms. Clearly, mobility itself adds new features to social media. Also, the ability to add contextual information, such as location or other sensor based data, when accessing a social media service with a mobile device could improve the value of a social media service or provide a new dimension to the service. For example, the activity of uploading a video to a sharing service from an event with a mobile device can happen from the place where the video was taken. In this sense, mobile social media can also be described as context-aware (Gay, 2009). In the context-aware computing the relationship between context and activities is emphasized.

To summarize, it can be said that social media is a combination of people, technologies, and practices that enables users to share their experiences with other users as well as build shared meaning among communities. The experiences are mediated by technologies as a form of content, for example my real experience is reflected as a set of images. Mobility adds the freedom of time and place – a user can share her experiences from wherever there is reasonable network access. In addition, mobile social media may support the automatic gathering of context information, for example by adding geotags to images or videos.

Mobile Learning

The early definition for mobile learning approached it from e-learning tradition and simply defined mobile learning as e-learning on a mobile device (Trifonova & Ronchetti, 2003). A more appropriate way to define mobile learning might be to try to examine how it differs from traditional learning. In mobile learning, learners can continually be on the move (Sharples, Taylor, & Vavoula, 2005). Learners are not just moving from one place to another, but they also move from one context to another and from one technology to another. Based on Sharples et al. (2005), some aspects of informal and workplace learning are fundamentally mobile, even without mobile learning technologies as such. Sharples, Taylor and Vavoula (2007) define mobile learning as "the processes of coming to know through conversations across multiple contexts amongst people and personal interactive technologies" (p. 4). The focus in this definition is the communicative interaction between the learner and technology. In their definition Sharples at al. does not make a difference between people and technology but instead consider it as a dynamic communicational system (Sharples et al., 2007). With this system, communication is seen as sharing of understanding and not only as sharing of messages (Pask, 1975; Sharples et al., 2007).

It is widely accepted that mobile learning should be learner-centered, knowledge-centered, assessment-centered, and community-centered (Sharples et al., 2005). These elements of effective learning suggest a close relation to social media that clearly is user-centered, knowledge-centered and community-centered. Assessment in social media could be represented by peer-review based commenting, voting and reputation systems.

Perry, O'Hara, Sellen, Brown, and Harper (2001) have studied mobile work and mobility and they define four key factors in mobile work: planning, working in "dead time," accessing remote technological and informational resources, and monitoring the activities of remote colleagues. They did not study mobile learning, but the factors of mobile work and mobility can be easily seen to describe also mobile learning activities. Vavoula (2005) studied everyday adult learning; his research indicates that "51% of the reported learning episodes took place at home or in the learner's own office at the workplace (i.e. in the learner's usual environment). The rest occurred in the workplace outside the office (21%), outdoors (5%), in a friend's house (2%), or at places of leisure (6%). Other locations reported (14%) included places of worship, the doctor's surgery, cafes, hobby stores, and cars. Interestingly, only 1% of the self-reported learning occurred on transport [...]." (Sharples et al., 2005, p. 1) It can be said that learning ecosystems based on mobile social media are also characterized by just-in-time learning.

Sharples et al. (2005) explains that computer technology and learning are both ubiquitous. The concept of mobile learning is closely related to ubiquitous learning and context-aware ubiquitous learning. Context-aware ubiquitous learning system integrates authentic learning environments and digital (virtual) learning environments, hence, as a result, enables the learning system to more actively interact with the learners. This is possible because of current mobile devices and sensors, such as Radio-frequency identification (RFID). (Chu, Hwang, Shi, Lee, & Chien, 2009; Hou, Ogata, Miyata, & Yano, 2009). It can be said that learning in a workplace or outside the classroom on a field trip can be ubiquitous.

Multimodal Learning

Multimodal learning refers to a learning process, where the learner utilizes two or more different modalities (i.e. means of communication during the process) (Anastopoulou, Sharples, & Baber, 2003). It is claimed that multimodal learning environments can facilitate learning processes because learners are different, and by adapting to their styles, learning improves. Learning with technology often involves multimodal communication. It has been argued that learning occurs in a greater context using visual communication, and not only language (Jewitt, 2006).

Multimodal information processing has been studied from many perspectives. For example, Ketamo and Multisilta use multimodal information processing in developing adaptive multimedia learning materials for learning geometry (Ketamo & Multisilta, 2003). The Dual Coding Theory is one of the most tested theories on multimodal information processing (Clark & Paivio, 1991). According to the Dual Coding Theory information is processed in two channels, verbal and visual (Mayer & Sims, 1994). These channels process information in the short-term memory by combining the observations of the channels. Finally the information is processed in the long-term memory. The knowledge or conceptual structures in long-term memory are evaluated and rebuilt according to the information received and combined in different channels. (Ketamo & Multisilta, 2003)

Learning ecosystems that build on social media and video are clearly multimodal. Learners sharing their experiences with video are using at the very least pictorial and audio modality.

Mobile Learning Activities

What kinds of classifications are there for learning activities in ecosystems that are based on mobile social media? This kind of classification of activities could be useful when designing the learning ecosystems. Naismith, Lonsdale, Vavoula, and Sharples (2004) identified five major types of learning activities in mobile learning and classify them under pedagogical paradigms. The researcher argues that the classification can also be used for learning ecosystems based on mobile social media.

The identified activities are (Naismith, Lonsdale, Vavoula, & Sharples, 2004):

1. Behaviourist: activities that promote learning as a change in learners' observable actions.
2. Constructivist: activities in which learners actively construct new ideas or concepts based on both their previous and current knowledge.
3. Situated: activities that promote learning within an authentic context and culture.
4. Collaborative: activities that promote learning through social interaction.
5. Informal and lifelong: activities that support learning outside a dedicated learning environment and formal curriculum.

In this chapter, the focus is in situated-activities and collaborative-activities that clearly characterize experiential and mobile learning in higher education.

Rogers and Price (2009) identified four types of activities where mobile learning could be applied: a) physical exercise games, b) participatory simulations, c) field trips and visits, and d) content creation. It is claimed that mobile learning activities (i.e. learning activities outside the classroom) are mostly related to information access and content sharing.

In this chapter, Experiential Learning Theory (ELT) and Activity Theory (AT) have been selected as theoretical frameworks, which are used to explain learning in ecosystems based on mobile social media. These learning theories were selected because they explain learning as an active process and, hence, can be used to explain mobile learning from a constructivist, situated, collaborative, and informal point of view; moreover, other combinations of theoretical frameworks may also be used successfully in describing mobile learning as can be seen, for example, in Naismith et al. (2004) and Rogers and Price (2009).

Experiential Learning Theory (ELT)

Based on Dewey (1938) an experience is characterized by two principles, which are continuity and interaction. The continuity defines that our experiences are a continuum in which each experience will influence to our future experiences. Interaction refers to the current situation and its influence on one's experience. The fact that the experience affects to the mind and continuum of experiences can be described as learning; conversely, Dewey (1938) points out that not all experiences support learning.

Felt experience is one's interpretation of the experience (McCarthy & Wright, 2004). For example, I can express my experience by telling others about it, drawing, taking a photo etc. The use of technology as a means of sharing our experiences with our family, friends, or communities is called a *shared felt experience*.

According to McCarthy and Wright (2004), interacting with technology involves us emotionally, intellectually, and physically. In case of social media, the interaction with technology is related. For example, a shared learning experience with technology. In this case, the role of technology is to mediate the experience to the learning community. In other words interaction in social media can also be shared understanding.

Technology is mediating our learning experiences to others while being an experience in itself. Based on Kolb (1984), the experiential learning theory defines learning as "the process whereby knowledge is created through the transformation of experience. Knowledge results from the combination of grasping and transforming experience" (p. 41).

The Experiential Learning Theory presents the learning process as a circle (Figure 1). The process can be divided into four stages: concrete experience (CE), reflective observation (RO), abstract conceptualization (AC), and active experimentation (AE). The learning process can begin from any stage.

Figure 1. Experiential Learning Theory (Adapted from Kolb, [1984])

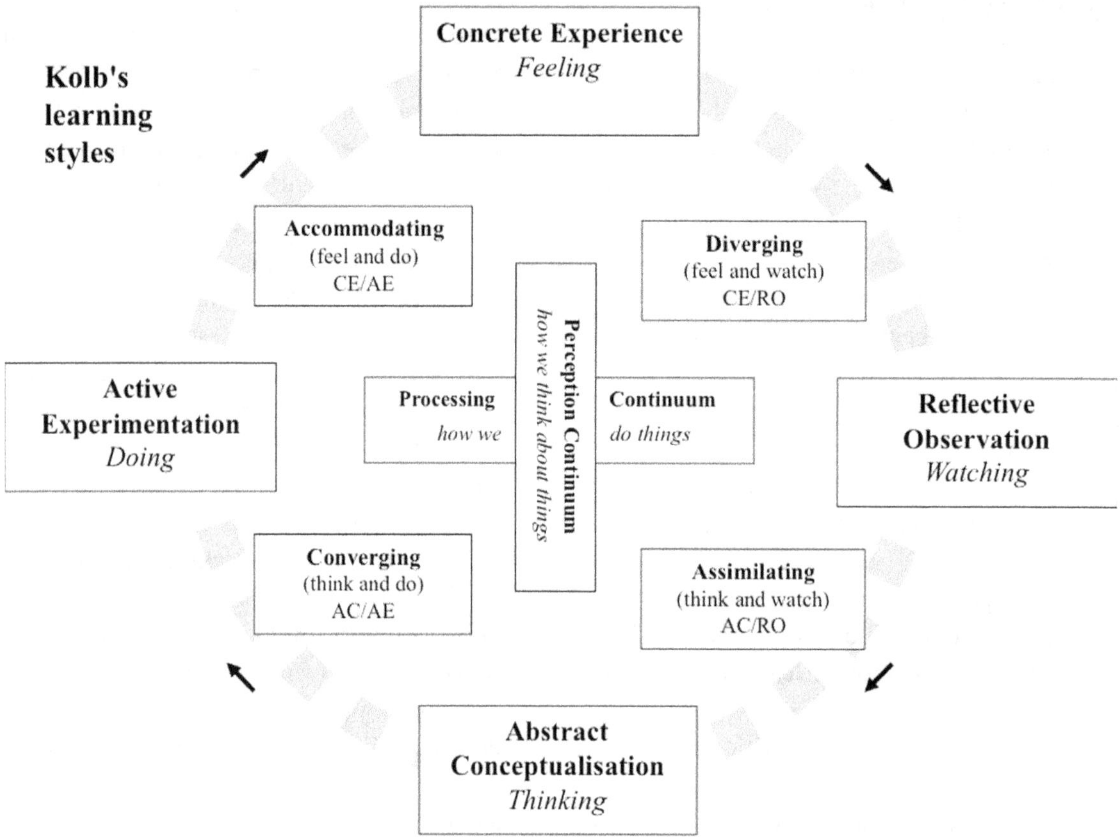

Within the learning stages, there are four learning styles. They represent a learning style by combining the learning abilities from the circle to a specific learning style and are based on both research and clinical observation of the patterns of Kolb's Learning Style Inventory scores (Kolb, Boyatzis, & Mainemelis, 2001).

1. Diverging learning style according to Coffield, Moseley, Hall, and Ecclestone (2004), emphasizes concrete experience and reflective observation. It is also imaginative and aware of meanings and values; it views concrete situations from many perspectives and adapts by observation rather than by action. It can also be described as feeling-oriented.
2. Assimilating learning style emphasizes reflective observations and abstract conceptualization. Understanding a wide range of information and putting it into concise, logical form is natural for people in this learning style (Kolb et al., 2000).
3. Converging learning style is a combination of abstract conceptualization and active experimentation. Based on Kolb et al. (2001), people with a converging learning style are best at finding practical uses for ideas and theories.
4. Accommodating learning style emphasizes active experimentation and concrete experience. In this style, hands-on experiences and acting based on feelings, rather than on logical analysis, is dominant (Kolb et al., 2001).

In Experiential Learning Theory, learning "is a process involving the resolution of dialectical conflicts between opposing modes of dealing with the world (i.e. action and reflection, concreteness and abstraction)" (Coffield et al., 2000, p. 63). The learning styles people adapt may change over time and may also depend on the learning situation. In addition to the four basic learning styles, there are second order and third order learning styles. Second order learning styles combine two of the first order styles and the third order learning style combines all of the four basic styles into a holistic model. (Kolb, Boyatzis, & Mainemelis, 2001, p. 243).

Activity Theory (AT)

Activity Theory is based on Vygotsky's cultural-historical psychology (Engeström, 1987; Engeström, Miettinen, & Punamäki, 1999; Kaptelinin & Nardi, 2006; Oliver & Pelletier, 2006) and it focuses on understanding human activity and work practices (Uden, 2007). There is a lot of research related to Activity Theory in learning and software design. For example Barthelmess and Andersson (2002) discussed the role of Activity Theory in software development and Fjeld et al. (2002) applied Activity Theory to groupware design. Activity Theory has also been applied to learning from digital games (Oliver & Pelletier, 2006), to interaction design (Kaptelinin & Nardi, 2006; Kuutti, 1996; Nardi, 1996) to mobile learning (Uden, 2007) as well as for designing constructivist learning environments (Jonassen & Rohrer-Murphy, 1999).

The central idea in Activity Theory (AT) is that all human actions are called activities. An activity involves an object that is to be transferred to the output of the activity. In the AT, a subject performs the activity using a tool. A tool can be a physical tool or an abstract tool, such as computer software, which they mediate the activity, between the subject and the object. The interaction can be mediated, which can be abstract, concrete, or both as well as the interaction between the subject, object, and community.

Engeström extended the original AT by adding community to the model (Figure 2). Rules mediate the activity between the community and the subject. The activity may be collaborative (i.e. several subjects jointly do an activity using tools and dividing the work between each subject). The object can be, for example, a problem to be solved.

In general, tools, rules, and division of work mediate the relationship between subject, community and object. Tools, rules and division of work are artifacts that are used to achieve the outcome. Artifacts are not necessarily a fixed set of tools or things, but they can evolve over time. (Engeström, Miettinen, & Punamäki, 1999; Kaptelinin & Nardi, 2006)

Activities take place in a specific context, that is characterized by a network of different parameters or elements that influence each other (Engeström, 1987; Uden, 2007). Activity can furthermore be divided into actions and an action into operations. In general, activities are based on high-level goals (for example, documenting a work process with images and video clips). Activities involve more practical goals (using a mobile phone to record a video) and operations are routine or automatic (launching a video application, pressing a record button). For example, rules can describe the procedure of documenting the learning process using mobile devices, images, video clips, and sharing services.

In Activity Theory, an important issue is that contradictions can occur between a subject, object, and community. Thus, a subject and the community can try to solve the contradiction using a tool, division of labour, and rules. Given the potential for contradictions, the activity system can change and thus will eventually lead to learning.

Figure 2. Engeström's view of Activity Theory describing activity as a collective phenomenon (Adapted from Engeström [1987] and Engeström, Miettinen, & Punamäki [1999])

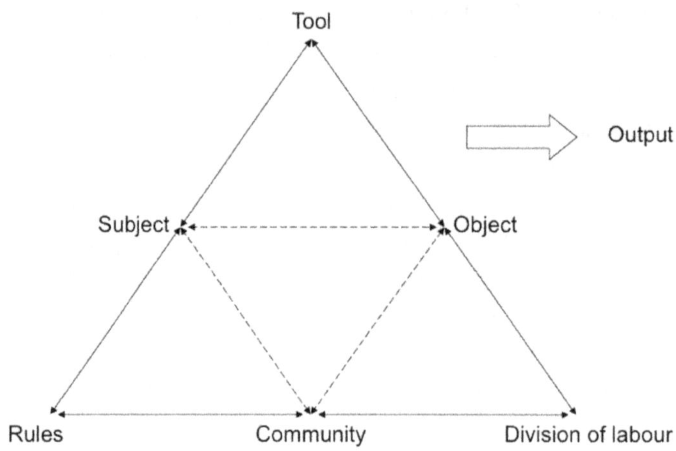

Other AT-Based Frameworks

Sharples, Taylor and Vavoula (2005) present an application of Activity Theory for analyzing the activity system of mobile learning. They divide the activity system into two layers, technological and semiotic layers. The semiotic layer describes learning as a semiotic system in which the learner's actions are mediated by cultural tools and signs. The technological layer represents learning with technology. Sharples et al. (2005) emphasize that the layers are in dynamic interaction and both are needed in analyzing mobile learning. Sharples et al. (2005) have also slightly changed the naming of the nodes representing rules, community and division of labour as in Engeström's AT model (Figure 3).

The Shared Activities and Experiences (SEA) framework originates from the need to describe sharing and experiences in social media in theoretical terms (Multisilta, 2008). It is based on Activity Theory, Mobile Web 2.0 Ecosystem (Jaokar, 2006), and the idea of considering the user experience or the *shared felt experience* as a central design rule. The SEA framework has been used in designing user experiences and user activities for mobile social media services (Multisilta, 2008; Kiili, Multisilta, Suominen, & Ketamo, 2009).

In Activity Theory, an important issue is that contradictions can occur in the system. Hence, providing solutions to these contradictions will eventually lead to learning. In the SEA framework, the contradiction is replaced by a more general expression, namely the point of inspiration (or experience). The point of inspiration provides the subject with the initiation of an activity. In learning applications, contradiction is one type of point of inspiration.

The user experience is considered to be a subset in the SEA. In general, user experience (UX) describes the overall experience a user has when using a technology (McCarthy & Wright, 2004). A user's point of inspiration may also not be an experience as such, but it can be, for example, a remixing session of videos recorded by others. So, the SEA framework characterizes certain types of activity systems, but not all kinds of activity systems.

In the SEA framework, there are two modified AT model triangles representing two separate users (Figure 4). This is to emphasize that users are going to share experiences with other users by sharing some of the components of the system

Figure 3. A framework for analyzing mobile learning according to Sharples et al. (2005)

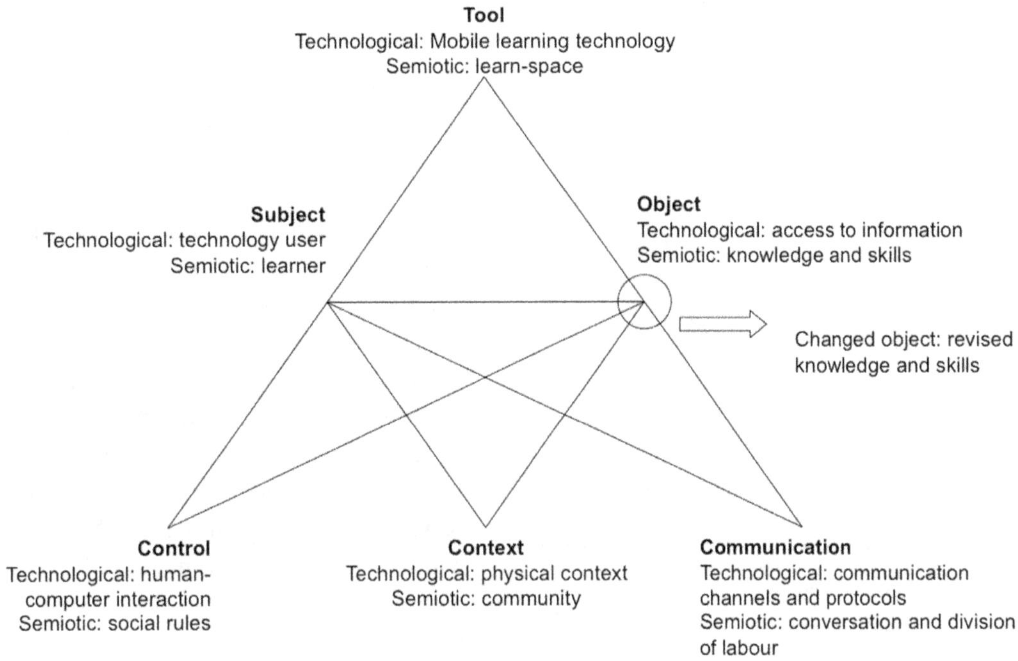

with other users; however, users may have different tools and objects in their activity system.

Subjects are sharing the community, rules and division of labour (although they can be in different communities working under different rules). They are using the same system operating under the same rules and they can divide their activities using available tools, for example by rating images, and thus expressing the general opinion of the group.

EXPERIENTIAL LEARNING ACTIVITIES IN HIGHER EDUCATION

In this section it is discussed how AT, SEA and ELT can be used to analyze learning activities in ecosystems based on social mobile media in higher education. First, an example of a student (subject) who is doing her learning experiment out of the classroom is studied. In this example, the student has limited support from other students or teacher. For example, a student could be doing fieldwork on an archeological site, observing a natural phenomenon away from the classroom or doing a practise work at a hospital.

During the activity there is a need to quickly find out a solution to a problem the student has not encountered before. This is the point of inspiration or the concrete experience (CE) she has. The concrete experience leads to an activity of trying to solve the problem. Trying out different known solutions and ways of working does not provide the solution. This part of the process may require the student to do several iterations of Kolb's active experimentation - concrete experience (reflective observation) abstract conceptualization circle. If the student finds a solution, (i.e. learns a new solution to a previously unknown problem or challenge), she documents her way of working. For example, using her mobile phone camera and recording a video where she explains the problem and the solution. She then shares the solution (i.e. her learning experience and understanding of if)

Figure 4. Shared Experience and Activities (SEA) framework

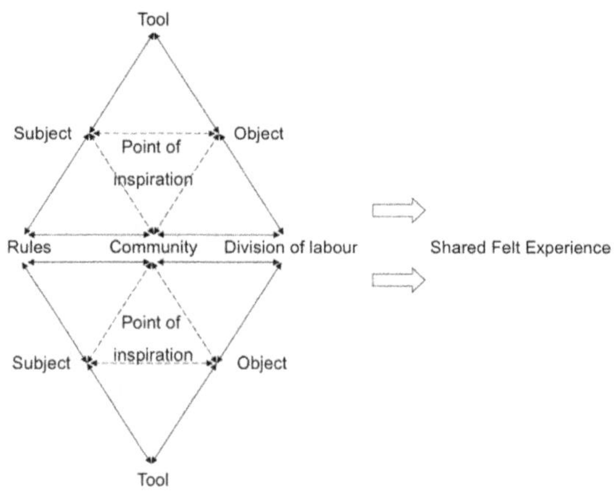

with the learning community by uploading the video to the video database.

It may be that the student cannot solve the problem by herself, and then she would use the support systems from her learning community. The local community (the students nearby) could provide some help, but most likely the student would have to contact the teacher or other students who are away. A searchable solution database in the learning ecosystem, where others have recorded the solutions to the problems they have solved, could help the student to solve the problem. In addition, the student can contact the co-learners who can help her by calling or by sending a text or a video message. The solution video database could include a rating system (i.e. the learner can rate how well the video supported her problem solving).

The learners can add tags to the recorded videos and a mobile device can automatically add geo-tags to the videos so they can be searched, based on keywords (tags) and location. For example, the system could automatically suggest videos in which the contextual tags match the current context of the student. Another student may have been studying with the same problem, and at the same location, and documented her work by recording a video there whereby the video could be suggested to the student when she accesses the video database.

The mobile social media learning ecosystem described above was piloted by Kiili, Multisilta, Suominen and Ketamo (2009). They focus on the use of social mobile video in teaching HCI in higher education. They report results of a pilot study in which a social video application, MoViE, was used to teach basic HCI concepts to 12 students. Based on Kiili et al. (2009) the social and creative aspects of videos make learning more engaging and authentic. The MoViE has been developed to address the collaborative and creative demands of learning and it enables several novel ways to utilize videos in educational purposes (Multisilta & Mäenpää, 2008; Multisilta & Suominen, 2009; Multisilta, Perttula, Suominen, & Koivisto, 2010). The results indicated that video blogging can be a effective method in HCI education, but some of the students need support and more strict tagging rules to get the best out of this kind instructional method (Kiili et al., 2009). Furthermore, blogging turned out to be a much more of an effective methodology with respect to evaluating a students' level of understanding verse the traditional paper-pencil tests.

DESIGNING AND ANALYZING LEARNING ACTIVITIES

In this section two examples of designing and analyzing learning activities using Activity Theory, SEA framework and Experiential Learning Theory are presented. The design case is presented in the form of a table in Table 1 and the analyzing case in Table 2.

In the first case the aim is to design a video sharing service that supports students in sharing short video clips from their outside the classroom learning activities. The videos are stored in the system and can be accessed based on the user, date, the keywords the user has given (tags), or location. The system can be used instead of taking

Table 1. An example of the learning activity design in SEA

Activity	Action	Operation	Point of inspiration	Felt experience and meaning
Observe the visibility of product X in your neighborhoods, report it to the community.	Observe the store near you. Shoot a video to demonstrate what you saw.	Launch recording application	Experience of the visibility of product X.	Passion to share your "proofs" Joy of creating a recording Diverging with Kolb's model.
		Press record button		
	Upload video to a social media service	Connect the phone to WLAN/3G	Share your video clips with a community. Gaining points.	Joy from sharing the experience. Joy from the reward.
		Open service from browser		
		Select clip from phone directory		
		Press upload		
	Tag the video	Select a tag	Help users to find your clip easily	Assimilating Kolb's theory.
		Write a description		
	Watch and comment on videos others have produced	Select clips from service	Create added value for the community	Converging in Kolb's theory. Creativity, deepening the learning experience
		Write a message.		

written notes, for example, in field trips or on work practice periods (on-the-job learning).

The design example in Table 1 is related to students studying marketing concepts. They are trying to learn how to improve the effectiveness of certain products in a dealer shop. The aim is to visit a shop, record a video using a mobile phone describing the marketing efforts in the shop and share this video with other students. The video actually represents the person's felt experience of the marketing activities in the shop. The video is uploaded to the sharing service automatically from the phone. The recording software automatically adds several tags (such as the gps location) to the video. By sharing videos from shops all over the city or the country and then analyzing the content of the videos, the students could help create a more effective and efficient sales campaign. The video sharing activity is part of a larger support system where the salespeople and students collaborate. In this system they collect activity points every time they share a video, or comment on videos sent by others. The commenting can be done by writing comments to the video author, or by responding with another video.

The activity design process starts by defining, or recognizing the points of inspiration for users (ie. students and salespeople). This is the motivation for users to use the service. The next step is to describe the components of activity system (subject, object, tools, community, rules, and division of labour) and activities needed for creation of an experience. The activities are divided into actions and operations. In conjunction with this, the designer should analyze and anticipate the experience the service is targeting for. For example, in our outdoor learning pilot study, which is described later, the meaning of the experience was to let users document their collaboration and provide a tool for them to go back to the actual problem solving situation and reflect on the learning experience.

The co-creation and collaboration aspect is important when designing learning ecosystems based on mobile social media. The designer should analyse the collaboration aspect at every

Table 2. Classification of the content of the videos according to Kolb's learning styles (RO Reflective Observation, AC Abstract Conceptualization, AE Active Experimentation, and CE Concrete Experience) and the SEA framework

Theme	Freq	Kolb's learning style	SEA framework
Solving activity	52	CE, RO	Community
Test clips	27	CE	Tool
Discussion of the problem/planning the solution	20	AC	Point of inspiration
Team member or coach giving orders to the team	19	AE	Division of labour, communication
Team member suggesting a possible solution	13	AC	Rules, communication
Question posed to the team	13	RO, AC	Rules, communication
Dividing the work	10	AE, CE	Division of the labour
Debriefing, analyzing the solution	10	AC	Shared felt experience
Team success	9	CE	Shared felt experience
Verbal support to other team members	8	CE	Shared felt experience
Clips not from the activities	5	-	
Surprise, hesitation	4	CE	Shared felt experience
Celebration of success: "we are good"	2	CE	Achieving the goal. Shared felt experience
Cameraman commenting	2	RO	Rules, communication
Understanding, bright idea	1	AC	Shared felt experience
Discussing other than activity-related issues	1	-	Shared felt experience (not activity related)
Unsuccess / failure	1	CE	Shared felt experience
Team members ignoring a comment from a team member	1	CE, RO	Communication

step. In this case, the collaboration is related to the analyzing phase, where students and salespeople use the videos to create meaning and shared understanding of the marketing interventions seen in the video clips.

The design framework presented in this chapter can also be used in analyzing learning activities. This is demonstrated by analyzing outdoor learning activities in continuing education for a group of 34 persons from a small town in central Finland. They represented housekeepers, chefs and cooks doing practical work in small teams. The aim of the learning activities was to train for group work activities by playing outdoor games and solving practical puzzles in small teams.

The training day was organized by a training company on their farm in the countryside not far from the town itself. Before the outdoor activities, the participants were tested using a simple learning style test. The test consisted of five statements each contains four possible answers. Each of the options represented one of Kolb's learning styles. The participants were asked to rank the options from 1 to 4 based on their own reaction to the situation described in the statement. There were 27 complete forms. Seven participants understood the filling of the form incorrectly. For example, some

Figure 5. The classification of learning styles among participants

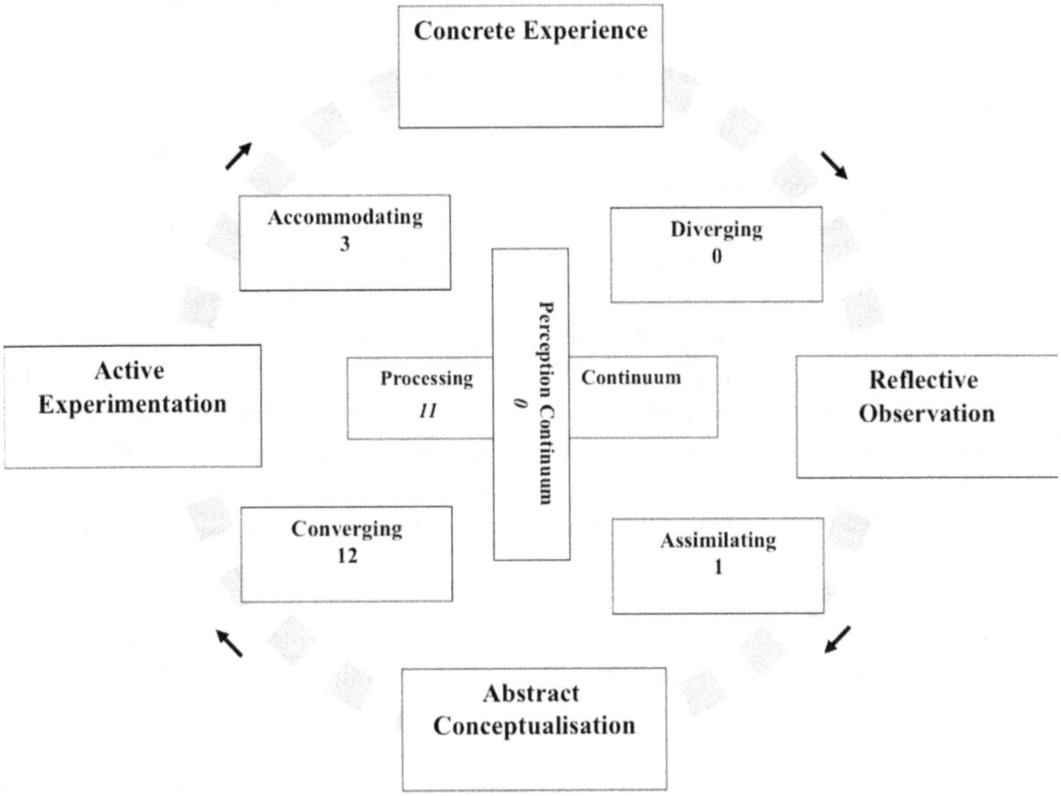

participants had ranked only one or two options in a statement, not all of them. These incorrectly returned forms were not analyzed at all.

The forms were analyzed by computing the ranks of each learning style in a form. The participants were positioned in Kolb's learning styles circle according to the top two ranks they got on the test (Figure 5). Interestingly, most of the participants represented the Active Experimentation learning style. The most important combinations were Active Experimentation with Reflective Observation and Active Experimentation with Abstract Conceptualization.

During the training the participants were divided into four groups. Each group had its own coach where each group did four different gaming and puzzle-solving activities. Each activity was observed for 20 minutes. In each group, there was a person whose role was to record video clips of the group's activity. The recording device was a Nokia 5800 XpressMusic mobile phone. Before a group activities started, the persons responsible were showed how to use the camera functionality in the Nokia phone, and then they were asked to record a short video clip whenever they felt it there was a significant contribution being made.

The video clips were later uploaded to the Nokia Ovi service, and the participants received accounts for the service so that they could view the clips. Overall, the groups produced 124 video clips. The clips were watched and, based on the content of the clip; they were classified into 18 themes (see Table 2). The themes are related both to the Kolb's learning styles and the SEA framework concepts.

Based on the view counts on the Ovi service, only a few participants watched the videos afterwards; however, the coaches watched the videos and told that they got valuable feedback from the activities by watching the videos afterwards.

The most popular topic for videos was the actual solving activity; however, it was found that those videos were not very informative because they only show the actual doing; conversely, the more interesting videos were those who where participants discuss the problem, planning the solution, and giving orders to others or ask questions.

Table 2 is an example how Kolb's ELT and SEA can be used in evaluating learning activities. The evaluation process starts by defining individual learning styles of the participants. After the initial phase, a learning intervention is implemented among the test group and the group activities are observed or constructed from the output (such as the videos in the previous example) of the group. The activities were then analyzed by classifying them according to Kolb's learning styles and to SEA framework elements. The results were collected and are summarized in a table format. Finally, the participants were interviewed and observed while they were reviewing and watching the videos in the video sharing site. Based on this information, the relation between the actual *felt learning experiences* and the observed experiences can be determined. This will lead to improvements in designing future learning activities and learning ecosystems based on mobile social media.

FUTURE RESEARCH DIRECTIONS

Technology is developing rapidly and new devices, services, and concepts appear almost every week. Still, the rapid adoption of social media services suggest that social media is here to stay. More research is needed to study how people experience sharing and always-on lifestyle. In the experiments presented in this chapter, it has been realized that mobile devices are still difficult to use for example in producing texts, such as tags to video clips. This is why there is a need to support learning activities on mobile devices by developing semi-automatic tagging systems to learning ecosystems based on mobile social media.

The researcher beliefs that video as a medium will have a major role in learning in the near future. This is why video production tools, concepts and applications in learning should be studied carefully. In addition to videos and mobile devices, future devices will be developed to produce and utilize sensor data. Currently, mobile devices include gps, compass and accelerometers that can produce contextual data for applications. This kind of contextual data can also enrich future mobile learning applications.

Although learning as a mental process does not change, emerging technologies will allow us to more efficiently utilize our thought processes, and as a result, force us to reevaluate, and redesign various learning paradigms. Hence, every time we have a new technology researchers should reflect on existing frameworks to test and evaluate these technologies and there suitability for learning applications. Thus, new theoretical frameworks for learning ecosystems based on mobile social media are still needed and more research should be focused on this area.

CONCLUSION

In this paper a framework for designing and analyzing learning activities for social media services that is based on Activity Theory and Experiential Learning Theory was presented. The framework has a strong emphasis on sharing experiences using social media; consequently, this is not a complete design model as such, but it is intended to be used in conjunction with other available design methods.

The framework can be used to analyze and design learning experiments involving, for example, mobile video sharing services. First, the framework can be used in designing learning activities based on sharing experiences with mobile social media. An important design issue is how to support the point of inspiration for sharing the learning experience with others. The point of inspiration can act as a strong motivation to share learning experiences. For example, a student might want to share her learning experiences among other students because she wants to earn professional status in her class. Sharing valuable information with others could promote credibility and professionalism among the co-learners. The framework can also be used in evaluating learning activities. The evaluation data could provide important information on how people learn with mobile social tools.

Two examples on how to use the theoretical framework were presented. First, the concept of a mobile video sharing service for outside the classroom learning was presented. In this example, the researchers designed an example of a mobile learning activity for product visibility observation. Second, results from a continuing education learning activity that was documented using mobile phones and the Nokia Ovi service were presented. The learning activity was evaluated using the theoretical framework developed in this chapter. Based on the analysis, researchers can find out how the actual *felt learning experience* is related to the experiences observed using the framework. Finally, this will lead to improvements in designing future learning activities and learning ecosystems that are based on mobile social media.

ACKNOWLEDGMENT

The author would like to acknowledge the Academy of Finland for a Researcher Mobility Grant for 2008 and 2009.

REFERENCES

Anastopoulou, S., Sharples, M., & Baber, C. (2003). Multimodality and learning: Linking science to everyday activities. In *Proceedings Of HCII 2003, Vol. 2* (pp. 576-580). Crete, Greece: Lawrence Erlbaum Associates, Inc. Retrieved November 17, 2010, from http://portal.cetadl.bham.ac.uk/ Lists/Publications/ Attachments/ 64/ multimodality.pdf

Barthelmess, P., & Anderson, K. M. (2002). A view of software development environments based on activity theory. [CSCW]. *Computer Supported Cooperative Work, 11*(1-2), 13–37. doi:10.1023/A:1015299228170

Chu, H.-C., Hwang, G.-J., Shi, Y.-R., Lee, C.-I., & Chien, W.-W. (2009). A conceptual map-oriented mindtool for conducting collaborative ubiquitous learning activities. In S. C. Kong, H. Ogata, H. C. Arnseth, C. K. K. Chan, T. Hirashima, F. Klett, … S. J. H. Yang (Eds.), *Proceedings of the 17th International Conference on Computers in Education* (pp. 559-563). Hong Kong: Asia-Pacific Society for Computers in Education.

Clark, J. M., & Paivio, A. (1991). Dual coding theory and education. *Educational Psychology Review, 3*(3), 149–170. doi:10.1007/BF01320076

Coffield, F., Moseley, D., Hall, E., & Ecclestone, K. (2004). *Learning styles and pedagogy in post-16 learning. A systematic and critical review*. London, UK: Learning and Skills Research Centre.

Dewey, J. (1938). *Experience and education.* New York, NY: Macmillan. Retrieved October 15, 2010, from http://gyanpedia.in/ tft/ Resources/ books/ dewey2.pdf

Engeström, Y. (1987). *Learning by expanding: An activity-theoretical approach to developmental research.* Helsinki, Finland: Orienta-Konsultit.

Engeström, Y., Miettinen, R., & Punamäki, R.-L. (Eds.). (1999). *Perspectives on activity theory*. New York, NY: Cambridge University Press.

Fjeld, M., Lauche, K., Bichel, M., Voorhorst, F., Krueger, H., & Rauterberg, M. (2002). Physical and virtual tools: Activity theory applied to the design of groupware. *Computer Supported Cooperative Work, 11*, 153–180. doi:10.1023/A:1015269228596

Gay, G. (2009). *Context-aware mobile computing. Affordances of space, social awareness, and social influence. Synthesis lectures on human-centered informatics # 4*. Morgan & Claypool.

Girgensohn, A., & Lee, A. (2002). Making web sites be places for social interaction. In *Proceedings of the 2002 ACM Conference on Computer Supported Cooperative Work* (pp. 136-145). New York, NY: ACM.

Herrington, A., Herrington, J., & Mantei, J. (2009). Design principles for mobile learning. In J. Herrington, A. Herrington, J. Mantei, I. Olney, & B. Ferry, (Eds.), *New technologies, new pedagogies: Mobile learning in higher education*. Faculty of Education, University of Wollongong. Retrieved July 15, 2010, from http://ro.uow.edu.au/ edupapers/ 88

Heyer, C., Brereton, M., & Viller, S. (2008). Cross-channel mobile social software: An empirical study. In *Proceeding of the Twenty-Sixth Annual SIGCHI Conference on Human Factors in Computing Systems* (pp. 1525-1534). New York, NY: ACM.

Hiltunen, M., Laukka, M., & Luomala, J. (2002). *Mobile user experience*. Finland: IT Press.

Hou, B., Ogata, H., Miyata, M., & Yano, Y. (2009). JAMIOLAS 3.0: Supporting Japanese mimicry and onomatopoeia learning using sensor data. In S. C. Kong, H. Ogata, H. C. Arnseth, C. K. K. Chan, T. Hirashima, F. Klett, … S. J. H. Yang (Eds.), *Proceedings of the 17th International Conference on Computers in Education* (pp. 593-597). Hong Kong: Asia-Pacific Society for Computers in Education.

International Organization for Standardization. (1999). *ISO 13407. Human-centered design processes for interactive systems*. Geneve, Switzerland: International Organization for Standardization.

Itin, C. M. (1999). Reasserting the philosophy of experiential education as a vehicle for change in the 21st century. *Journal of Experiential Education, 22*(2), 91–98.

Jaokar, A. (2006). *What is Mobile Web 2.0?* Wireless Business & Technology. Retrieved July 15, 2010, from http://wbt.sys-con.com/ read/ 251673.htm

Jewitt, C. (2006). *Technology, literacy and learning: A multimodal approach. Milton Park, Abingdon*. Oxon, UK: Routledge.

Jonassen, D. H., & Rohrer-Murphy, L. (1999). Activity theory as a framework for designing constructivist learning environments. *Educational Technology Research and Development, 47*(1), 61–79. doi:10.1007/BF02299477

Kaptelinin, V., & Nardi, B. A. (2006). *Acting with technology. Activity theory and interaction design*. Cambridge, MA & London, England: The MIT Press.

Ketamo, H., & Multisilta, J. (2003). Towards adaptive learning materials: Speed of interaction and relative number of mistakes as indicators of learning results. *Education and Information Technologies, 8*(1), 55–66. doi:10.1023/A:1023978325223

Kiili, K., Multisilta, J., Suominen, M., & Ketamo, H. (2009). Learning experiences on mobile social media. In S. C. Kong, H. Ogata, H. C. Arnseth, C. K. K. Chan, T. Hirashima, F. Klett, ... S. J. H. Yang (Eds.), *Proceedings of the 17th International Conference on Computers in Education* (pp. 535-542). Hong Kong: Asia-Pacific Society for Computers in Education.

Kolb, D. A. (1984). *Experiential learning: Experience as the source of learning and development*. New Jersey, USA: Prentice-Hall.

Kolb, D. A., Boyatzis, R. E., & Mainemelis, C. (2001). Experiential learning theory: Previous research and new directions. In Sternberg, R. J., & Zhang, L. F. (Eds.), *Perspectives on cognitive, learning, and thinking styles*. Mahwah, NJ: Lawrence Erlbaum.

Kong, S. C., Ogata, H., Arnseth, H. C., Chan, C. K. K., Hirashima, T., & Klett, F. ... Yang, S. J. H. (Eds.), (2009). *Proceedings of the 17th International Conference on Computers in Education*. Hong Kong: Asia-Pacific Society for Computers in Education.

Kukulska-Hulme, A., Traxler, J., & Pettit, J. (2007). Designed and user-generated activity in the mobile age. *Journal of Learning Design*, *2*(1), 52–65.

Kuutti, K. (1996). Activity theory as a potential framework for human-computer interaction research. In Nardi, B. A. (Ed.), *Context and consciousness. Activity theory and human-computer interaction*. Cambridge, MA: Massachusetts Institute of Technology.

Lerman, K. (2008). *Social browsing & information filtering in social media*. Retrieved December 15, 2009, from http://arxiv.org/ abs/ 0710.5697

Lugano, G. (2010). *Digital community design. Exploring the role of mobile social software in the process of digital convergence. Jyväskylä Studies in Computing, 114*. Jyväskylä, Finland: University of Jyväskylä.

Marlow, C., Naaman, M., Boyd, D., & Davis, M. (2006). HT06, tagging paper, taxonomy, Flickr, academic article, to read. *Proceedings of the Seventeenth Conference on Hypertext and Hypermedia* (pp. 31-40). New York, NY: ACM.

Mayer, R. E., & Sims, V. K. (1994). For whom is a picture worth a thousand words? Extension of a dual-coding theory of multimedia learning. *Journal of Educational Psychology*, *86*(3), 389–401. doi:10.1037/0022-0663.86.3.389

McCarthy, J., & Wright, P. (2004). *Technology as experience*. Cambridge, MA & London, England: The MIT Press.

Multisilta, J. (2008). Designing for mobile social media. In A. Karahasanović, & A. Følstad (Eds.), *Proceedings of The NordiCHI'08 Workshops New Approaches to Requirements Elicitation & How Can HCI Improve Social Media Development*? (pp. 72-79). Trondheim, Norway: Tapir.

Multisilta, J., & Mäenpää, M. (2008). Mobile video stories. In *Proceedings of the 3rd International Conference on Digital Interactive Media in Entertainment and Arts, 349* (pp. 401-406). New York, NY: ACM.

Multisilta, J., Perttula, A., Suominen, M., & Koivisto, A. (2010). Mobile video sharing: Documentation tools for working communities. In *Proceedings of the 8th International Interactive Conference on Interactive TV & Video* (pp. 31-38). New York, NY: ACM.

Multisilta, J., & Suominen, M. (2009). MoViE: Mobile video experience. In A. Lugmayr, H. Franssila, O. Sotamaa, & J. Vanhala (Eds.). *Proceedings of 13th International Academic MindTrek Conference: Everyday Life in the Ubiquitous Era*. New York, NY: ACM.

Mwanza, D. (2002). *Towards an activity-oriented design method for HCI research and practice*. PhD Thesis. United Kingdom: The Open University.

Mwanza-Simwami, D. (2007). Concepts and methods for investigating learner activities with mobile devices: An activity theory perspective. In Arnedillo-Sánchez, I., Sharples, M., & Vavoula, G. (Eds.), *Beyond mobile learning workshop* (pp. 24–25). Trinity College Dublin Press.

Naismith, L., Lonsdale, P., Vavoula, G., & Sharples, M. (2004). *Literature review in mobile technologies and learning. NESTA Futurelab Series, Report 11*. Bristol, UK: NESTA Futurelab.

Nardi, B. A. (Ed.). (1996). *Context and consciousness. Activity theory and human-computer interaction*. Cambridge, MA: Massachusetts Institute of Technology.

Nichols, M. (2003). A theory for e-learning. *Educational Technology & Society*, 6(2), 1-10. Retrieved October 22, 2010, from http://www.ifets.info/ journals/ 6_2/1.pdf

O'Reilly, T. (2005). *What is web 2.0? Design patterns and business models for the next generation of software.* Retrieved December 15, 2009, from http://www.oreillynet.com/ pub/a/ oreilly/ tim/ news/ 2005/09 /30/ what-is-web-20.html

O'Reilly, T. (2007). What is web 2.0? Design patterns and business models for the next generation of software. *Communications & Strategies, 65*(First Quarter), 17-37. Retrieved October 21, 2010, from http://ssrn.com/ abstract=1008839

Oliver, M., & Pelletier, C. (2006). Activity theory and learning from digital games: Developing an analytical methodology. In Buckingham, D., & Willett, R. (Eds.), *Digital generations. Children, young people, and new media*. Mahwah, NJ & London, UK: Lawrence Erlbaum Associates, Publishers.

Pacey, A. (1999). *Meaning in technology*. Cambridge, MA & London, England: The MIT Press.

Pask, G. (1975). Minds and media in education and entertainment: Some theoretical comments illustrated by the design and operation of a system for exteriorizing and manipulating individual theses. In Trappl, R., & Pask, G. (Eds.), *Progress in cybernetics and systems research. IV* (pp. 38–50). Washington, DC & London, UK: Hemisphere Publishing Corporation.

Perry, M., O'Hara, K., Sellen, A., Brown, B., & Harper, R. (2001). Dealing with mobility: Understanding access anytime, anywhere. *ACM Transactions on Computer-Human Interaction, 8*(4), 323–347. doi:10.1145/504704.504707

Rogers, Y., & Price, S. (2009). How mobile technologies are changing the way children learn. In Druin, A. (Ed.), *Mobile technology for children* (pp. 3–22). Boston, MA: Morgan Kaufmann. doi:10.1016/B978-0-12-374900-0.00001-6

Sharples, M., Taylor, J., & Vavoula, G. (2005). Towards a theory of mobile learning. In *Proceedings of mLearn 2005 Conference*, Cape Town, South Africa, 2005. Retrieved December 15, 2009, from http://www.mlearn.org.za/ CD/ papers/ Sharples-%20Theory %20of%20Mobile.pdf

Sharples, M., Taylor, J., & Vavoula, G. (2007). A theory of learning for the mobile age. In Andrews, R., & Haythornthwaite, C. (Eds.), *The Sage handbook of e-learning research* (pp. 221–247). London, UK: Sage.

Trifonova, A., & Ronchetti, M. (2003). Where is mobile learning going? In A. Rossett (Ed.), *Proceedings of World Conference on E-learning in Corporate, Government, Healthcare, & Higher Education* (pp. 1794-1801). Chesapeake, VA: AACE.

Tuomi, P., & Multisilta, J. (2010). MoViE: Experiences and attitudes—Learning with a mobile social video application. *Digital Culture & Education, 2*(2), 165-189. Retrieved October 21, 2010, from http://www.digitalcultureandeducation.com/

Tynjälä, P., & Häkkinen, P. (2005). E-learning at work: Theoretical underpinnings and pedagogical challenges. *Journal of Workplace Learning, 17*(5/6), 318–336. doi:10.1108/13665620510606742

Uden, L. (2007). Activity theory for designing mobile learning. *International Journal of Mobile Learning and Organisation, 1*(1), 81–102. doi:10.1504/IJMLO.2007.011190

Vavoula, G. N. (2005). *D4.4: A study of mobile learning practices: Internal report of MOBIlearn project.* Retrieved July 15, 2010, from http://www.mobilearn.org/ download/ results/ public_deliverables/ MOBIlearn_D4.4_Final.pdf

ADDITIONAL READING

Cobcroft, R. S., Towers, S. J., Smith, J. E., & Bruns, A. (2006). Mobile learning in review: Opportunities and challenges for learners, teachers, and institutions. In: *Online Learning and Teaching (OLT) Conference 2006,* 26 September 2006, Queensland University of Technology, Brisbane.

Coffield, F., Moseley, D., Hall, E., & Ecclestone, K. (2004). *Learning styles and pedagogy in post-16 learning: A systematic and critical review.* Learning and Skills Research Centre. London, UK. Retrieved November 17, 2010, from http://www.lsneducation.org.uk/ research/ reports/

Coiro, J., Knobel, M., Lankshear, C., & Leu, D. (Eds.). (2008). *The handbook of research on new literacies.* New York: Lawrence Erlbaum Publishers.

Commission of the European Communities. (2009). *Europe's digital competitiveness report. Main achievements of the i2010 strategy 2005-2009.* COM(2009) 390, Brussels. Retrieved November 17, 2010, from http://ec.europa.eu/ information_society/ eeurope/ i2010/ docs/ annual_report/20 09/ com_2009_390_en.pdf

Conole, G., & Fill, K. (2005). A learning design toolkit to create pedagogically effective learning activities. *Journal of Interactive Media in Education, 8,* 1-16. Retrieved November 17, 2010, from jime.open.ac.uk/ 2005/08

Garcia-Lorenzo, L. (2010). Framing uncertainty: Narratives, change and digital technologies. *Social Sciences Information. Information Sur les Sciences Sociales, 49*(3), 329–350. doi:10.1177/0539018410370730

Hollan, J. D., & Hutchins, E. L. (2009). Opportunities and challenges for augmented environments: A distributed cognition perspective. In Lahlou, S. (Ed.), *Designing user-friendly augmented work environments: From meeting rooms to digital collaborative spaces* (pp. 269–289). London: Springer. doi:10.1007/978-1-84800-098-8_9

Kaptelinin, V., Kuutti, K., & Bannon, L. (1995). Activity theory: Basic concepts and applications. In B. Blumenthal, J. Gornostaev & C. Unger (Eds.), *Fifth International Conference, EWHCI'95, Selected papers* (pp. 189-201). Berlin: Springer.

Kukulska-Hulme, A., & Traxler, J. (Eds.). (2005). *Mobile learning: A handbook for educators and trainers.* New York: Taylor & Francis Inc.

Kuutti, K. (1996). Activity theory as a potential framework for human-computer interaction. In Nardi, B. A. (Ed.), *Context and Consciousness: Activity Theory and Human-Computer Interaction*. Cambridge, MA: MIT Press.

Lahlou, S. (2010). Digitization and transmission of human experience. *Social Sciences Information. Information Sur les Sciences Sociales*, *49*(3), 291–327. doi:10.1177/0539018410372020

Leont'ev, A. N. (1978). *Activity, consciousness, and personality*. Englewood Cliffs, NJ: Prentice-Hall.

Lewis, S., Pea, R., & Rosen, J. (2010). Beyond participation to co-creation of meaning: Mobile social media in generative learning communities. *Social Sciences Information. Information Sur les Sciences Sociales*, *49*(3), 351–369. doi:10.1177/0539018410370726

Pea, R. D. (2006). Video-as-data and digital video manipulation techniques for transforming learning sciences research, education and other cultural practices. In J. Weiss, J Hunsinger & P. Trifonas (Eds.), *International handbook of virtual learning environments* (pp. 1321-1394). AA Dordrecht, The Netherlands: Springer.

Shannon, C. E., & Weaver, W. (1949). *The mathematical theory of communication*. Urbana: University of Illinois Press.

Sharples, M., Arnedillo-Sánchez, I., Milrad, M., & Vavoula, G. (2009). Mobile learning. Small devices, big issues. In Ludvigsen, S., Balacheff, N., de Jong, T., Lazonder, A., & Barnes, S. (Eds.), *Technology-enhanced learning: Principles and products*. Dordrecht: Springer.

Sharples, M., Corlett, D., & Westmancott, O. (2002). The design and implementation of a mobile learning resource. *Personal and Ubiquitous Computing*, *6*, 220–234. doi:10.1007/s007790200021

Simanowski, R., Schäfer, J., & Gendolla, P. (Eds.). (2009). *Reading moving letters: Digital literature in research and teaching: A handbook*. Bielefeld: Transcript Verlag.

Wagner, E. D. (2005). Enabling mobile learning. *EDUCAUSE Review*, *40*(3), 41–52.

KEY TERMS AND DEFINITIONS

Activity Theory: The Activity Theory is based on Vygotsky's cultural-historical psychology and a concept of artifact-mediated and object-oriented action, and further developed by Engeström. It describes learning activities as an interactive system of subject, community, object, rules, division of labour and tools.

Experiential Learning Theory: The experiential learning theory defines learning as the process of four stages and their interplay: concrete experience, reflective observation, abstract conceptualization, and active experimentation.

Learning Ecosystem: A system of interacting individuals and groups with an shared aim to learn using different supporting systems, such as learning environments, learning devices and tools.

Mobile Social Media: Social media applications and services that can be used with mobile devices and aim to support socializing. Mobile Social Media take advantage of social information, social networks and contextual data, such as location.

Multimodal Learning: Multimodal learning refers to a learning process, where the learner utilizes two or more different modalities (i.e. means of communication during the process).

Shared Felt Experience: The use of technology as a means of sharing our experiences with our family, friends or communities is called a *shared felt experience*.

Social Media: Social media is a collection of web-based of technologies that support users in creating and sharing content, annotating content with tags, evaluating content, and creating social networks with other users sharing similar interests. In social media, users are seen as being both content consumers and producers. Tags, rating systems and recommendation systems are typical features of social media.

Chapter 15
Mobile Learning in Higher Education

Rui Zeng
University of Texas Health Science Center at Houston, USA

Eunice Luyegu
Franklin University, USA

ABSTRACT

In recent years, there has been an explosion in the growth of mobile learning across all sectors of education. Keen interest in mobile learning has led to a proliferation of views, perspectives, and diverse activities underpinned by different learning theories. This chapter focuses on various dimensions of mobile learning, including definitions, theoretical dimensions, mobile learning applications in higher education, and future research directions. Mobile learning is still an emerging and immature field. The chapter provides broad definitions and discussions of mobile learning drawing upon existing work. By exploring the experiences and views of various researchers, the chapter reveals the opportunities and challenges involved with mobile learning.

INTRODUCTION

With the proliferation of mobile computing technology, mobile learning (m-learning) has begun to offer stunning new technical capabilities in education (DiGiano et al., 2003). Mobile learning is "the exploitation of ubiquitous handheld technologies, together with wireless and mobile phone networks to facilitate, support, and enhance and extend the reach of teaching and learning" (Brown, 2010, p. 28). Compared to other types of learning activities, mobile learning starts from the assumption that learners are continually on the move, from physical locations to topics; mobile learners are usually the ones who initiate learning activities and self-control their educational processes and outcomes; and they may "engage with their surroundings to create impromptu sites of learning" (Sharples, Taylor, & Vavoula, 2005, p. 3). Younger generations who have grown up

DOI: 10.4018/978-1-61350-080-4.ch015

using portable video game devices and wireless technology are attracted to this innovative way of learning and communication (Yi, Liao, Huang, & Hwang, 2009). Researchers and instructors are interested in the technical design and the development of mobile technologies (Peng, Su, Chou, & Tsai, 2009) and have implemented various studies to probe this new genre of learning.

We have seen growing visibility and significance of mobile learning: technological mobile learning innovations are deployed in academic settings to demonstrate technical feasibility and pedagogic possibility (Taylor & Evans, 2005); mobile technologies are used as flexible replacements for static desktop technologies used in conventional e-learning (DiGiano et al., 2003; Chen, Kao, & Sheu, 2003); and mobile learning technologies are enhanced with informal, personalized, situated learning (Clough, Jones, McAndrew, & Scanlon, 2008). However, relatively little is known about the big picture of how higher education institutions make use of mobile devices to support teaching and learning, nor are well summarized theories and principles for mobile learning available for instructors and practitioners in the field.

The objectives of this chapter are to show how mobile learning can transform the delivery of education in higher education as well as to introduce sound mobile learning theories. Specifically, the chapter will present the current status of mobile learning in higher education, explore what mobile learning is, provide theoretical information on mobile learning, introduce the latest research on mobile learning and various examples of how mobile learning is used in higher education, outline the challenges faced when designing and implementing mobile learning, and give future research directions.

DEFINITIONS OF MOBILE LEARNING

The explosive growth of mobile devices that support personal communication are accelerating the transition away from desktop web-based application and are transforming social notions of discourse and knowledge. Today's mobile devices have strong computing capabilities with high-frequency central processing unit (CPU). Wrist-worn devices, mobile phones, handheld computers, web pads, pen tablet computers, laptop computers, and so forth have been widely used in mobile learning (Sharples & Beale, 2003). These devices put convenient multimedia service applications into practice with friendly human computer interfaces and operation modes. Through a variety of network connection techniques, the devices can also access abundant network resources. These devices have been deployed as learning tools in both formal and informal learning contexts and have been used from small-scale, short terms trails to larger, more sustained and blended deployment (Traxler, 2009).

In spite of the enthusiasm with mobile learning, the concept of mobile learning is still emerging and unclear (Brodt & Verburg, 2007). Definitions of mobile learning have emerged from different perspectives. Some emphasize the relationship between mobile learning and e-learning, claiming that it is the combination of e-learning and mobile computing (Holzinger, Nischelwitzer, & Meisenberger, 2005). Others believe that it is a "special type of e-learning, bound by a number of special properties and the capability of devices, bandwidth, and other characteristics of the network technologies being used" (Stone, 2004, p. 146). Yet still, others claim that it is e-learning carried out by means of mobile devices such as PDAs (Personal Digital Assistants) and digital cell phones (Rosenthal, 2003), and that it is e-learning using mobile devices and wireless transmission (Milrad, 2003).

Some researchers define mobile learning purely in terms of its technologies and hardware, that is, it is learning that takes place with the help of portable electronic tools (Quinn, 2000); it involves using mobile devices such as smart phones and PDAs to facilitate the learning process

(Mahamad, Ibraham, Foad, & Taib, 2008); and it is the provision of education and training on PDAs/palmtops/handhelds, smart phones, and mobile phones (Keegan, 2005). Some define it, not in terms of technologies and hardware, but in terms of modalities: it provides a new range of interaction paradigms – it has pervasive and ubiquitous nature, small size, and provides different interaction modalities than conventional e-learning methods (e.g., touch screens) (Ardito, Buono, Costabile, Lanzilotti, & Piccinno, 2009).

Some researchers look at the underlying learner experience and try to distinguish mobile learning from other forms of e-learning. For example, in Koole's Rational Analysis of Mobile Education (FRAME) model (2005, 2009; Koole & Ally, 2006), she describes m-learning as a process resulting from the convergence of mobile technologies, human learning capacities, and social interaction. Barbosa and Geyer (2005) noted that mobile learning increases a learner's capability to physically move their own learning environment as they move. From the literature review, the following words can be identified from various studies to describe mobile learning: "personal, spontaneous, opportunistic, informal, pervasive, situated, private, and context-aware", which is contrasted with characteristics of conventional e-learning: "structured, media-rich, broadband, interactive, intelligent, and usable" (Traxler, 2009, p. 14).

THEORETICAL DIMENSIONS OF MOBILE LEARNING

Naismith, Lonsdale, Vavoula, and Sharples (2004) reveal six broad theory-based categories of mobile learning activities through an extensive literature review in mobile technologies and learning. The six categories include behaviorist, constructivist, situated, collaborative, informal and lifelong, and learning and teaching support.

As its name indicates, behaviorist m-learning activities promote learning as a change in learners' observable behavior—an external change we can observe. Examples of such m-learning activities include instructors using text messages to collect students' responses to questions posed by instructors, and students using mobile devices to take multiple choice quizzes and receiving immediate feedback. In Wang, Shen, Novak, and Pan's (2009) study, students used short text messages to send their feedback to the instructor, take polls, and take quizzes. The instructor also had the option to give students feedback using text messaging. Similar classroom response systems have been used in several other studies (Ward, Reeves, & Health, 2003; Wood, 2004; Woods & Chiu, 2003) and covered various disciplines including biology, chemistry, language learning, physics, and so forth.

In constructivist m-learning activities, learners actively construct knowledge and ideas based upon both previous and current knowledge. Constructivists portray learning as an active, contextualized process of constructing knowledge rather than acquiring it (Ormrod, 2007). In Lonsdale, Baber, and Sharples' (2004) study, the researchers designed a participatory simulation—a kind of learning game in which players play an active role in the simulation of a system or process—using mobile phones. Students were engaged in an interactive role-playing game based on the water cycle. Text messages that guided the students through their roles in the simulation were triggered by learners' physical position in the game. Klopfer and Squire's (2002; 2008) PDA based environmental detectives are another example of using m-learning for knowledge construction and skill development. Students participated in a real-time simulation based on a local watershed. Facing an environmental disaster, they needed to implement different strategies to solve the problem. The PDAs used in the study provided students with the scenario and virtual world data.

Situated m-learning activities provide learning in realistic contexts while at the same time offer access to supporting materials (Naismith, Lonsdale, Vavoula, & Sharples, 2004). Situated m-learning is learning that occurs in the same context in which it is applied. Principles of situated learning include presenting knowledge in an authentic context, and learning requires social interaction and collaboration (Lave, 1988). The pervasive and ubiquitous nature of mobile devices makes them perfectly suitable for these kinds of learning activities. Examples of such m-learning activities include field trips of learning about fish biodiversity (Pfeiffer, Gemballa, Jarodzka, Scheiter, & Gerjets, 2009), history and cultural content (Wu, Chang, Chang, Yen, & Heh, 2010), and plant identification (Yang & Lin, 2010). In the first study, Pfeiffer and his colleagues used mobile devices to support knowledge acquisition in a field trip. Students who used mobile devices to review dynamic visualizations for learning biodiversity exceeded those who viewed static learning materials. In the second study, Wu and his colleagues combined a mobile treasure hunting learning situation with a field trip for learning history and cultural content. The researchers found that most students liked the learning experience and provided positive feedback which led the researchers to believe such mobile learning models can work well for learning in field trips. Students in Yang and Lin's study used PDAs to investigate plants that matched assigned clues. The students then worked together sharing information and discussing assigned tasks. The results of the study showed that students gained knowledge through mobile learning activities. It is important to note that situated learning and constructivism are compatible and are mutually supportive.

Collaborative m-learning activities are defined by Naismith et al. (2004) as activities that promote learning through social interaction. Collaboration involves the mutual commitment of group members to coordinate their efforts in order to solve a problem (Roschelle & Teasley, 1991). Collaborative learning supported by computer technology (i.e., Computer Supported Collaborative Learning [CSCL]), provides collaborative group members with different environments and mediation techniques for social interaction and learning support (Silverman, 1995). With the popularization of mobile devices, a new term Mobile Computer Supported Collaborative Learning (MCSCL) has emerged. As the name suggests, mobile devices have become another tool for supporting CSCL. Mobile technologies can be used to facilitate and enhance interactions and collaborations among learners. Mobile devices can communicate with other similar devices thus enabling learners to share data, messages, and files. Learners can also communicate through shared data network. Nguyen, Guggisberg, and Burkhart (2006), in their paper, introduced CoMobile, a system they designed to support collaborative learning through interactive multimedia forums. PuzzleView is another MCSCL tool designed to support collaborative learning (Deng, Chang, Hu, & Chan, 2005). Using this system, students can, in real time, view teammates' annotations and information on their Tablet PCs. Besides these applications, mobile devices are also used in dissemination activities, collaboration, and analysis of results (Cortez, et al., 2004).

Informal and lifelong m-learning is another theory-based category of mobile learning summarized by Naismith et al. (2004). Informal m-learning is based on the notion that learning can happen anytime anywhere. According to Rossett and Hoffman (2007), "informal learning tends to be authentic, typically happening beyond the control of the people who manage training programs, outside the limits of classrooms and environments established to deliver formal instruction at a distance" (p.167). In other words, learning can happen in various situations (e.g., when you are watching TV, reading newspaper, surfing the Internet, and so on). Mobile learning technologies enable embedding learning into everyday life. With a portable device, patients can watch audio-visual materials during their course of treatment (Wood, Keen, Bassu, & Robertshaw, 2003); children can play mobile games while learning in the process (Spikol & Milrad, 2008); and people in rural areas can also have opportunities to access abundant information.

Learning and teaching support category refers to activities that assist in the coordination of learners and resources. The value of any online environment is limited by how accessible it is to students and the level of student engagement (Armatas, Holt, & Rice, 2005). If students cannot or do not have access to the online environment, they may miss important announcements or information their instructors deliver. With mobile technologies, however, instructors can push information (i.e., due dates of assignments, class announcements, exam date, and so on), to students' mobile devices. Examples in this category of mobile learning consist of information retrieval (e.g., e-books, timetables) with PDAs (Kim, Mims, & Holmes, 2006) and short messaging delivery through mobile devices (e.g., appointments information, feedback, room changes, and study tips) (Riordan & Traxler, 2003).

Aside from the categories identified by Naismith, Lonsdale, Vavoula, and Sharples (2004), Connectivism, a new learning theory, has caught people's attention in recent years, and has been adopted by some researchers as a theory for new technologies including mobile learning. Both social constructivism and Connectivism emphasize the importance of social context to learning (Low & O'Connel, 2006). According to Connectivism, learning is a process of connecting specialized nodes or information sources, and it may reside in non-human appliances. Currency (e.g., up-to-date knowledge) is the intent of all connectivist learning activities, and choosing what to learn and the meaning of incoming information (i.e., decision-making) is a learning process (Siemens, 2004).

Siemens (2005) introduced Learning Development Cycle (LDC) as a meta-learning design model that can be used to address different domains of learning and can be used for designing new tools and processes such as blogs, wikis, and social mobile networks. He argues that learning networks and ecologies are developing as informal learning approaches and are different from the traditional course delivery mechanism, thus instructional designers need to embrace Internet-era design. Siemens considers learning as an activity that occurs within an ecology and pointed out that the task of instructional designers is to design the ecology—create the right environment for continued learning. In his paper *Learning Development Cycle: Bridging Learning Design and Modern Knowledge Needs*, Siemens introduced LDC which attends to four broad learning domains: transmission, emergence, acquisition, and accretion and is composed of the following five stages:

- Scope and object of learning design
- Creation of learning resources
- User experience
- Meta-evaluation to determine effectiveness and accuracy of design process and assumptions
- Formative and summative evaluation of project and learner experience (p. 23).

In addition to Connectivism, activity theory, a social and cultural psychological theory, has also been used for designing mobile learning environments and for analyzing conceptual frameworks for mobile CSCL (Zurita & Nussbaum, 2007). Engestrom (1987) extended Vygotsky's idea that human beings' interactions with their environment are mediated through the use of tools and signs, to an activity theory model which include the following components:

- Tools (by what means are the subjects performing this activity?)

- Subject (who are involved in a common goal and carrying out this activity?)
- Object (why is this activity taking place?)
- Rules (are there any individual or group norms, rules, and roles governing the performance of this activity?)
- Community (what is the environment in which this activity is carried out?)
- Division of labor (who is responsible for what, when carrying out this activity and how they are organized?)
- Outcome (what is the desired outcome from carrying out this activity?) (as cited in Zurita & Nussbaum, 2007).

Furthermore, Sharples, Taylor, and Vavoula (2005) have offered a framework for theorizing mobile learning based upon Engestrom's activity theory model. They suggest that a theory of mobile learning should be tested against a list of criteria:

- Is it significantly different from current theories of classroom, workplace, or lifelong learning?
- Does it account for the mobility of learners?
- Does it cover both formal and informal learning?
- Does it theorize learning as a constructive and social process?
- Does it analyze learning as a personal and situated activity mediated by technology? (p. 4).

To sum up, the confluence of the advances in theory and the affordances of mobile technology have created abundant opportunities for educators in higher education. Mobile devices can be used for more than just information delivery and retrieval in education. Mobile learning demands new educational approaches of delivery and facilitation (Corbeil & Valdes-Corbeil, 2007); integrating it into the curriculum demands a change in teaching approaches and strategies (Crow, Santos, LeBaron, McFadden, & Osborne, 2010).

MOBILE LEARNING IN HIGHER EDUCATION

Alexander (2004) describes mobile learning in higher education as "going nomadic." By saying nomadic, he means that "the wireless, mobile, student-owned learning impulse cuts across our institutional sectors, silos, and expertise-propagation structures" (p. 34). Alexander introduced a story in his paper that was discussed in several other papers and websites around that time. The story is about a Texas law professor, upset by the level of distraction caused by using mobile devices, brought a ladder to class, climbed up it, and unplugged a ceiling-mounted wireless access point so that students could not have wireless connectivity in his classroom. That, however, was the situation six years ago. Today, professors and administrators in higher education have, at least gradually, embraced mobile learning. After witnessing an increase in the use of mobile devices in different areas of society, higher education educators have been trying to exploit the potential of mobile technologies for education. From a large number of case studies documenting trials and pilots in the public domain, Kukulska-Hulme and Traxler (2007) summarized some emerging categories of mobile learning, including technology-driven mobile learning, miniature but portable e-learning, connected classroom learning, informal, personalized, situated mobile learning, mobile training/performance support, and remote/rural/development mobile learning. We feel mobile learning in higher education can fall into any of these categories except the last one. Thus, we use these categories to organize our discussion of mobile learning in higher education.

Connected Classroom Learning

Litchfield, Dyson, Lawrence, and Zmijewska (2007), in their literature review, summarized mobile learning projects and reported that the majority of m-learning projects have been focused on improving interactivity in the classroom or on ubiquitous learning—increasing students' access to learning materials anytime anywhere. At Abilene Christian University in Texas, Central Michigan University, and some other universities, students have been using mobile devices to listen to podcast lectures from their professors and take quizzes (Ash, 2010). These activities fall into connected classroom learning category (Kukulska-Hulme & Traxler, 2007).

Technology-Driven Mobile Learning

At Boise State University, mobile technologies have been used for teaching mobile learning. Instructors from the instructional technology program at Boise State University recently introduced a graduate level course titled *Mobile Learning: Devices, Applications & Pedagogy*. Students can use mobile devices to visit the mobile Moodle course management system and participate in class activities. This trial can be categorized as technology-driven mobile learning as defined by Kukulska-Hulme and Traxler (2007), because mobile devices are used to demonstrate technical feasibility and pedagogic possibility in this case.

Miniature but Portable E-Learning

To address higher education's mobile learning needs, commercial learning management system—Blackboard—launched their mobile platform Blackboard Mobile Learn. Open source course management system Moodle also has its mobile offerings. Both bring two-way teaching and learning to mobile devices and create an interactive mobile learning experience for students and teachers on the go. Mobile and wireless technologies in this case, are used to re-enact approaches and solutions used in conventional e-learning as miniature but portable e-learning (Kukulska-Hulme & Traxler, 2007).

Informal, Personalized, Situated Mobile Learning

In healthcare education, mobile learning has been widely used for training. The typical education training of a physician or nurse includes about two years of learning biomedical facts and concepts, followed by several years in which the students learn by doing in a didactic mode (Iyengar & Zeng, 2010). Usually, students need to follow experienced senior staff from bedside to bedside, observing procedures, and performing them under close supervision for a sufficient period of time. Mobile devices have been widely used in healthcare, for example using short message services to provide support for healthcare students during practice placements (Young et al., 2010); using m-learning for clinical expertise remote access and real time clinical support (Ferenchick, Fetters, & Carse, 2008; Garrett & Jackson, 2006; Hareva, Okada, Kitawaki, & Oka, 2009); using m-learning to improve healthcare in rural areas (Zimic et al., 2009); and using portable human patient simulation in acute care medicine (Kobayashi et al., 2008). These learning methods are location sensitive and are deployed to deliver educational experiences that would be otherwise difficult, thus fall into Kukulska-Hulme and Traxler's (2007) informal, personalized, situated mobile learning category.

Campus Wide Mobile Initiatives

Kukulska-Hulme and Traxler (2007) predict that "mobile education, however innovative, technically feasible, and pedagogically sound, may have no chance of sustained, wide-scale institutional deployment in higher education in the foreseeable future, at a distance or on site" (p. 20). We, however, still witness universities' attempt to set up mobile campuses. One example of such a trial is Abilene Christian University in Texas. The university gave students mobile devices and then had professors integrate the machines and their tools into the way courses are taught, and measured changes in student perceptions. In this university's 2008-2009 mobile-learning report, 89% of students and 87% of faculty polled called the program successful. In Armatas, Holt, and Rice's (2005) paper, they shared their thoughts on how to integrate mobile technologies with the current e-learning environment in which universities have made major investments. They concluded that university administrators are willing to provide students with a motivating and engaging virtual learning environment, but they also need to consider the heavy investment schools need to make in technology and infrastructure support. There needs to be a balanced and sustainable use of e-learning system that can pull students into the learning environment and mobile learning solutions that can push information to students.

We end this section by introducing a set of research-informed guidelines to address pedagogical methodologies along with practical concerns such as cost, usability, technical, and institutional support. In other words, the guidelines can be used to direct using mobile technologies and to provide policy initiatives. The guidelines were proposed by O'Malley, et al. (2003) and summarized by Naismith et al. (2004). They include:

- Investigate a cost model for infrastructure, technology, and service.
- Study the requirements of all those involved in the use of technology (learners, teachers, content creators) to ensure it is usable and acceptable.
- Assess that the technology is suited to the learning task and examine advantages and disadvantages of each technology before making a decision on which one to use.
- Assign the necessary roles for initiating and thereafter supporting mobile learning.
- Develop procedures and strategies for the management of equipment when it is provided by the institution.
- Provide training and (ongoing) technical support to the teachers to enable them to use mobile technologies to enhance current and to enable new instructional activities.
- Consider the use of mobile technologies for student administration tasks.
- Consider the use of mobile technologies to support collaborative and group learning.
- Discover and adopt suitable applications that match the needs of your specific classroom and map directly to your curriculum needs.
- Ensure security and privacy for the end users (p. 34).

FUTURE RESEARCH DIRECTIONS

Opportunities and challenges are emerging for learners, instructors, and higher education institutions from the increasing availability of mobile devices and associated infrastructure. There is significant research on mobile learning, but gaps still exist. Most research on mobile learning is still in an exploratory phase with many learning and teaching issues still to be investigated (Litchfield, Dyson, Lawrence, & Zmijewska, 2007).

Principles and Strategies for Mobile Learning Design

Mobile learning's current use appears to be predominantly within a didactic, teacher-centered paradigm (i.e., content delivery through mobile devices) (Herrington & Herrington, 2008). To provide effective learning with mobile technologies, we need to choose sound design approaches, select the right content, and follow theoretically grounded guidelines. In recent years, some educators have used mobile devices to experiment with situated learning and collaborative learning. Researchers have also begun to use models such as Learning Design Cycle and activity theory model to guide mobile learning analysis and design. Siemens (2005) noted that we are currently still in the beginning stages of social and technological alternations, and new design approaches are needed for serving learners. Further design and development research is needed to refine sound instructional strategies and pedagogical approaches that suit mobile learning.

Effective Mobile Learning Evaluation Methods

The field of mobile learning is currently characterized by pilots and trials intending to test mobile technologies in various learning contexts. The quality of these projects, including evaluation methodology and reporting, is the key for the sustained deployment of mobile learning. The evaluations at the moment, however, are based on tacit foundations of common-sense view of learning (Traxler & Kukulska-Hulme, 2005). There is a need for theoretical justification to support the selection of any given evaluation methods which can assure the credibility of outcomes of mobile learning projects. Further research is needed to develop a systematic and comprehensive evaluation framework.

Mobile Learning for Different Disciplines

Mobile learning has been widely used in language learning and healthcare. Researchers from the fields of chemistry, biology, physics, and so forth have also begun to dip their toes in the water. Different instructors and disciplines will have different conceptions of teaching (Kember, 1997), thus more research is needed in this area to test the general principles and teaching strategies that best suit students and to generate effective and practical case studies and examples that can benefit future practitioners.

Mobile Supported Fieldwork

Fieldwork provides students with opportunities to implement classroom theory into real life situations. Mobile learning has been used by a few educators, especially those in healthcare, to support and train students when they begin their practice. It is important, however, for educators in other fields, too, to examine the feasibility of this mobile learning method. Moreover, applicable m-learning and teaching strategies about the conduct of fieldwork with mobile devices should be investigated.

Strategies for Low Cost Mobile Learning

A major barrier of adopting mobile learning into universities is the cost. Although mobile devices are popular nowadays, not every student owns a cell phone with a data plan. The sustained educational practices or long-term institutional commitment most of the time has failed due to the cost. To overcome this barrier, both technology research and educational research are needed. Since students use different kinds of mobile devices, new technical protocols and techniques of "one-fits-all" mobile interface design need to be investigated; strategies on learning activities suitable for use with various mobile devices should also be examined.

CONCLUSION

Mobile technologies have grown in such rapid pace that they have now overtaken the boom of personal computers in today's professional and social contexts (Attewell, 2005). The trend has also resulted in escalating transformations of the educational world. Yet, mobile learning is still an emerging and immature field. The pedagogical use of mobile devices is not widespread in higher education (Herrington & Herrington, 2008).

Mobile learning is not just about learning using portable devices, but learning across contexts. How can we enhance mobile learning experiences? How can learning in mobile environments be effectively measured? What is the impact of mobile devices on classroom teaching? These and many more questions urgently need investigation. Rather than providing answers to all of the above questions, this chapter has sought to provide broad definitions and discussions of mobile learning drawing upon much existing work. By exploring the experiences and views of various researchers, the chapter reveals the opportunities and challenges involved with mobile learning.

REFERENCES

Alexander, B. (2004). Going nomadic: Mobile learning in higher education. *EDUCAUSE Review*, *39*(5), 28–35.

Ally, M. (Ed.). (2009). *Mobile learning: Transforming the delivery of education and training*. Edmonton, AB: Athabasca University Press.

Ardito, C., Buono, P., Costabile, M. F., Lanzilotti, R., & Piccinno, A. (2009). Enabling interactive exploration of cultural heritage: An experience of designing systems for mobile devices. *Know Techn Pol*, *22*, 79–86. doi:10.1007/s12130-009-9079-7

Armatas, C., Holt, D., & Rice, M. (2005, December). *Balancing the possibilities for mobile technologies in higher education*. Paper presented at the 22nd ASCILITE Conference, Brisbane.

Ash, K. (2010). Full speed ahead in higher ed. *Technology Counts*, *29*(26), 30–31.

Attewell, J. (2005). *From research and development to mobile learning: Tools for education and training providers and their learners*. Retrieved from http://mlearning.noe-kaleidoscope.org/ public/ mlearn2005/ www.mlearn.org.za/ CD/ papers/ Attewell.pdf

Barbosa, D. N. F., & Geyer, C. F. R. (2005, May). *Pervasive personal pedagogical agent: A mobile agent shall always be with a learner*. Paper presented at IADIS International Conference Mobile Learning, Malta.

Brodt, T., & Verburg, R. (2007). Managing mobile work – Insights from European practice. *New Technology, Work and Employment*, *22*(1), 52–65. doi:10.1111/j.1468-005X.2007.00183.x

Brown, J. (2010). Can you hear me now? *T+D*, *64*(2), 28-30.

Chen, C. M., & Hsu, S. H. (2008). Personalized intelligent mobile learning system for supporting effective English learning. *Journal of Educational Technology & Society*, *11*(3), 153–180.

Chen, Y. S., Kao, T. C., & Sheu, J. P. (2003). A mobile learning system for scaffolding bird watching learning. *Journal of Computer Assisted Learning*, *19*, 347–359. doi:10.1046/j.0266-4909.2003.00036.x

Clough, G., Jones, A. C., McAndrew, P., & Scanlon, E. (2008). Informal learning with PDAs and smartphones. *Journal of Computer Assisted Learning*, *24*, 359–371. doi:10.1111/j.1365-2729.2007.00268.x

Corbeil, J. R., & Valdes-Corbeil, M. E. (2007). Are you ready for mobile learning? Frequent use of mobile devices does not mean that students or instructors are ready for mobile learning and teaching. *EDUCAUSE Quarterly*, *2*, 51–58.

Cortez, C., Nussbaum, M., Santelices, R., Rodriguez, P., Zurita, G., Correa, C., & Cautivo, R. (2004, March). *Teaching science with mobile computer supported collaborative learning (MCSCL).* Paper presented at the 2nd International Workshop on Wireless and Mobile Technologies in Education, Jungli, Taiwan.

Crow, R., Santos, I. M., LeBaron, J., McFadden, A. T., & Osborne, C. F. (2010). Switching gears: Moving from e-learning to m-learning. *MERLOT Journal of Online Learning and Teaching, 6*(1), 268–278.

Deng, Y., Chang, S., Hu, M., & Chan, T. (2005, July). *PuzzleView activities: Encouraging participation in mobile computer support collaborative learning.* Paper presented at the 5th IEEE International Conference on Advanced Learning Technologies, Kaohsiung, Taiwan.

DiGiano, C., Yarnall, L., Patton, C., Roschelle, J., Tatar, D., & Manley, M. (2003). Conceptual tools for planning for the wireless classroom. *Journal of Computer Assisted Learning, 19*, 284–297. doi:10.1046/j.0266-4909.2003.00030.x

Engestrom, Y. (1987). Comment on Blackler et al activity theory and the social construction of knowledge: A story of four umpires. *Organization—The Interdisciplinary Journal of Organisation. Theory and Society Studies, 7*(2), 301–310.

Ferenchick, G., Fetters, M., & Carse, A. M. (2008). Just in time: Technology to disseminate curriculum and manage educational requirements with mobile technology. *Teaching and Learning in Medicine, 20*(1), 44–52. doi:10.1080/10401330701542669

Garrett, B. M., & Jackson, C. (2006). A mobile clinical e-portfolio for nursing and medical students, using wireless personal digital assistants (PDAs). *Nurse Education in Practice, 6*(6), 339–346. doi:10.1016/j.nepr.2006.07.015

Hareva, D. H., Okada, H., Kitawaki, T., & Oka, H. (2009). Supportive intervention using a mobile phone in behavior modification. *Acta Medica Okayama, 63*(2), 113–120.

Herrington, A., & Herrington, J. (2008). *Authentic mobile learning in higher education*. Retrieved from http://www.aare.edu.au/ 07pap/ her07131.pdf

Holzinger, A., Nischelwitzer, A., & Meisenberger, M. (2005). Lifelong-learning support by m-learning: Example scenarios. *eLearn, 11*, 2.

Iyengar, M. S., & Zeng, R. (2010). *Mobile learning for biomedicine*. Unpublished manuscript, School of Biomedical Informatics, The University of Texas Health Science Center at Houston, Houston, Texas.

Keegan, D. (2002). *The future of learning: From e-learning to m-learning.* Retrieved from http:// www.eric.ed.gov.proxy.lib.wayne.edu/ PDFS/ ED472435.pdf

Kember, D. (1997). Reconceptualization of research into university academics' conceptions. *Learning and Instruction, 7*(3), 255–275. doi:10.1016/S0959-4752(96)00028-X

Kim, S. H., Mims, C., & Holmes, K. P. (2006). An introduction to current trends and benefits of mobile wireless technology use in higher education. *AACE Journal, 14*(1), 77–100.

Klopfer, E., & Squire, K. (2008). Environmental detectives—The development of an augmented reality platform for environmental simulations. *Educational Technology Research and Development, 56*(2), 203–228. doi:10.1007/s11423-007-9037-6

Klopfer, E., Squire, K., & Jenkins, H. (2002, August). *Environmental detectives: PDAs as a window into a virtual simulated world.* Paper presented at the 1st IEEE International Workshop on Wireless and Mobile Technologies in Education, Växjö, Sweden

Kobayashi, L., Patterson, M. D., Overly, F. L., Shapiro, M. J., Williams, K. A., & Jay, G. D. (2008). Educational and research implications of portable human patient simulation in acute care medicine. *Academic Emergency Medicine, 15*(11), 1166–1174. doi:10.1111/j.1553-2712.2008.00179.x

Koole, M. L., & Ally, M. (2006, April). *Framework for the rational analysis of mobile education (FRAME) model: Revising the ABCs of educational practices.* Paper presented at the International Conference on Networking, International Conference on Systems, and International Conference on Mobile Communications and Learning Technologies, Morne, Mauritius.

Koole, M. L. (2005). *The framework for the rational analysis of mobile education (FRAME) model: An evaluation of mobile devices for distance education.* Alberta: Athabasca University.

Koole, M. L. (2009). A model for framing mobile learning. In Ally, M. (Ed.), *Mobile learning: Transforming the delivery of education and training* (pp. 25–47). Athabasca, AB: Athabasca University Press.

Kukulska-Hulme, A., & Traxler, J. (Eds.). (2005). *Mobile learning: A handbook for educators and trainers.* New York, NY: Taylor & Francis, Inc.

Kukulska-Hulme, A., & Traxler, J. (2007). Learning design with mobile and wireless technologies. In Beetham, H., & Sharpe, R. (Eds.), *Rethinking pedagogy for the digital age* (pp. 180–192). London, UK: Routledge.

Lave, J. (1988). *Cognition in practice: Mind, mathematics, and culture in everyday life.* Cambridge, UK: Cambridge University Press. doi:10.1017/CBO9780511609268

Leigh, E., & Spindler, L. (2004). Simulations and games as chaordic learning contexts. *Simulation & Gaming, 34*(1), 53–69. doi:10.1177/1046878103252886

Litchfield, A., Dyson, L. E., Lawrence, E., & Zmijewska, A. (2007). *Directions for m-learning research to enhance active learning.* Retrieved from http://www.ascilite.org.au/ conferences/ singapore07/ procs/ litchfield.pdf

Lonsdale, P., Baber, C., & Sharples, M. (2004). Engaging learners with everyday technology: A participatory simulation using mobile phones. In Brewster, S., & Dunlop, M. (Eds.), *Mobile human-computer interaction – MobileHCI 2004* (pp. 461–465). Heidelberg, Germany: Springer. doi:10.1007/978-3-540-28637-0_57

Mahamad, S., Ibrahim, M. N., Foad, M. I., & Taib, S. M. (2008). Open source implementation of m-learning for primary school in Malaysia. *International journal of social sciences, 3*(4), 309-313.

Mayadas, A. F., Bourne, J., & Bacsich, P. (2009). Online education today. *Science, 323*, 85–89. doi:10.1126/science.1168874

Milrad, L. (2003). Mobile learning: Challenges, perspectives, and reality. In Nyiri, K. (Ed.), *Mobile learning: Essays on philosophy, psychology and education* (pp. 151–164). Vienna, Austria: Passagen Verlag.

Naismith, L., Lonsdale, P., Vavoula, G., & Sharples, M. (2004). *Literature review in mobile technologies and learning.* Bristol, UK: Nesta Futurelab.

Nguyen, D. P., Guggisberg, M., & Burkhart, H. (2006, July). *CoMobile: Collaborative learning with mobile devices.* Paper presented at the 6th International Conference on Advanced Learning Technologies, Kerkrade.

O'Malley, C., Vavoula, G., Glew, J. P., Taylor, J., Sharples, M., & Lefrere, P. … Waycott, J. (2005). *Mobilearn WP4: Pedagogical methodologies and paradigms.* Retrieved from http://www.mobilearn.org/ download/ results/ public_deliverables/ MOBIlearn_D4.1_Final.pdf

Ormrod, J. E. (2007). *Human learning* (5th ed.). Upper Saddle River, NJ: Pearson Education, Inc.

Peng, H., Su, Y., Chou, C., & Tsai, C. (2009). Ubiquitous knowledge construction: Mobile learning redefined and a conceptual framework. *Innovations in Education and Teaching International, 46*(2), 171–183. doi:10.1080/14703290902843828

Persico, D., Pozzi, F., & Sarti, L. (2010). Monitoring collaborative activities in computer supported collaborative learning. *Distance Education, 31*(1), 5–22. doi:10.1080/01587911003724603

Pfeiffer, V. D. I., Gemballa, S., Jarodzka, H., Scheiter, K., & Gerjets, P. (2009). Situated learning in the mobile age: Mobile devices on a field trip to the sea. *ALT-J, 17*(3), 187–199. doi:10.1080/09687760903247666

Quinn, C. (2000, Fall). M-learning: Mobile, wireless, in-your-pocket learning. *LiNE Zine.* Retrieved from http://www.linezine.com/ 2.1/ features/ cqmmwiyp.htm

Riordan, B., & Traxler, J. (2003, August). *Supporting computing students at risk using blended technologies.* Paper presented at the 4th Annual LTSN-ICS Conference, Galway, Ireland.

Roschelle, J., & Teasley, S. D. (1991). The construction of shared knowledge in collaborative problem solving. In O'Malley, C. (Ed.), *Computer supported collaborative learning* (pp. 67–97). Berlin, Germany: Springer.

Rosenthal, K. (2003). Touch vs. tech: Valuing nursing specific PDA software. *Nursing Management, 34*(7), 58. doi:10.1097/00006247-200307000-00017

Rossett, A., & Hoffman, B. (2007). Informal learning. In Reiser, R. A., & Dempsey, J. V. (Eds.), *Trends and issues in instructional design and technology* (pp. 166–127). Columbus, OH: Pearson Merrill Prentice Hall.

Sharples, M., & Beale, R. (2003). A technical review of mobile computational devices. *Journal of Computer Assisted Learning, 19*(3), 392–395. doi:10.1046/j.0266-4909.2003.00040.x

Sharples, M., Taylor, J., & Vavoula, G. (2005). *Towards a theory of mobile learning*. Retrieved from http://www.eee.bham.ac.uk/ sharplem/ Papers/ Towards%20a%20theory%20of%20 mobile%20learning.pdf

Siemens, G. (2004). *Connectivism: A learning theory for the digital age*. Retrieved from http:// www.elearnspace.org/ Articles/ connectivism.htm

Siemens, G. (2005). *Learning development cycle: Bridging learning design and modern knowledge needs*. Retrieved from http://www.elearnspace. org/ Articles/ ldc.htm

Silverman, B. (1995). Computer supported collaborative learning (CSCL). *Computers & Education, 25*(3), 81–91. doi:10.1016/0360-1315(95)00059-3

Spikol, D., & Milrad, M. (2008, March). *Combining physical activities and mobile games to promote novel learning practices.* Paper presented at the 5th IEEE International Conference on Wireless, Mobile, and Ubiquitous Technology in Education, Beijing, China.

Stone, A. (2004). Designing scalable, effective mobile learning for multiple technologies. In Attwell, J., & Savill-Smith, C. (Eds.), *Learning with mobile devices* (pp. 145–153). London, UK: Learning and Skills Development Agency.

Taylor, J., & Evans, D. (2005). Pulling together: Keeping track of pedagogy, design and evaluation through the development of scenarios—A case study. *Learning, Media and Technology, 30*(2), 131–145. doi:10.1080/17439880500093588

Traxler, J. (2009). Current state of mobile learning. In Ally, M. (Ed.), *Mobile learning: Transforming the delivery of education and training* (pp. 9–24). Edmonton, AB: Athabasca University Press.

Traxler, J., & Kukulsa-Hulme, A. (2005, October). *Evaluating mobile learning: Reflections on current practice.* Paper presented at the 4th World Conference on Mobile Learning, Capte Town, South Africa.

Wang, M., Shen, R., Novak, D., & Pan, X. (2009). The impact of mobile learning on students' learning behaviours and performance: Report from a large blended classroom. *British Journal of Educational Technology, 40*(4), 673–695. doi:10.1111/j.1467-8535.2008.00846.x

Ward, C. R., Reeves, J. H., & Health, B. P. (2003). *Encouraging active student participation in chemistry classes with a Web-based, instant feedback, student response system.* Retrieved from http://www.files.chem.vt.edu/ confchem/ 2003/ a/ ward/ ConfChem_SRS.htm

Wood, J., Keen, A., Basu, N., & Robertshaw, S. (2003, June). *The development of mobile applications for patient education.* Paper presented at the 2003 Conference on Designing for User Experiences, San Francisco, CA.

Wood, W. B. (2004). Clickers: A teaching gimmick that works. *Developmental Cell, 7*, 796–798.

Woods, H. A., & Chiu, C. (2003). *Wireless response technology in college classrooms.* Retrieved from http://www.mhhe.com/ cps/ docs/ CPSWP_WoodsChiu.pdf

Wu, S., Chang, A., Chang, M., Yen, Y., & Heh, J. (2010, April). *Learning history and cultural contents via mobile treasure hunting in five-harbor district of Tainan, Taiwan.* Paper presented at the 6th IEEE International Conference on Wireless, Mobile and Ubiquitous Technologies in Education, Kaohsiung, Taiwan.

Yang, J., & Lin, Y. (2010). Development and evaluation of an interactive mobile learning environment with shared display groupware. *Journal of Educational Technology & Society, 13*(1), 195–207.

Yi, C., Liao, P., Huang, C., & Hwang, I. (2010). Acceptance of mobile learning: A respecification and validation of Information System success. *International Journal of Psychological and Behavioral Science, 2*(1), 55–59.

Young, P., Moore, E., Griffiths, G., Raine, R., Stewart, R., Cownie, M., & Frutos-Perez, M. (2010). Help is just a text away: The use of short message service texting to provide an additional means of support for health care students during practice placements. *Nurse Education Today, 30*(2), 118–123. doi:10.1016/j.nedt.2009.06.010

Zimic, M., Coronel, J., Gilman, R. H., Luna, C. G., Curioso, W. H., & Moore, D. A. (2009). Can the power of mobile phones be used to improve tuberculosis diagnosis in developing countries? *Transactions of the Royal Society of Tropical Medicine and Hygiene, 103*(6), 638–640. doi:10.1016/j.trstmh.2008.10.015

Zurita, G., & Nussbaum, M. (2007). A conceptual framework based on activity theory for mobile CSCL. *British Journal of Educational Technology, 38*(2), 211–235. doi:10.1111/j.1467-8535.2006.00580.x

ADDITIONAL READING

Ally, M. (Ed.). (2009). *Mobile learning: Transforming the delivery of education and training.* Edmonton, AB: Athabasca University Press.

Attwell, J., & Savill-Smith, C. (Eds.). (2004). *Learning with mobile devices.* London: Learning and Skills development Agency.

Beetham, H., & Sharpe, R. (Eds.). (2007). *Rethinking pedagogy for the digital age*. London: Routledge.

Herrington, A., & Herrington, J. (2008). *Authentic mobile learning in higher education*. Retrieved from http://www.aare.edu.au/ 07pap/ her07131.pdf

Khan, B. (2007). *Flexible learning for an information society*. Hershey, PA: ISP.

Kukulska-hulme, A., & Traxler, J. (Eds.). (2005). *Mobile learning: A handbook for educators and trainers*. New York, NY: Taylor & Francis, Inc.

Litchfield, A., Dyson, L. E., Lawrence, E., & Zmijewska, A. (2007). *Directions for m-learning research to enhance active learning.* Retrieved from http://www.ascilite.org.au/ conferences/ singapore07/ procs/ litchfield.pdf

Naismith, L., Lonsdale, P., Vavoula, G., & Sharples, M. (2004). *Literature review in mobile technologies and learning*. Bristol, UK: Nesta Futurelab.

Nyiri, K. (Ed.). (2003). *Mobile learning: essays on philosophy, psychology and education*. Vienna, Austria: Passagen Verlag.

Ryu, H., & Parsons, D. (2009). *Innovative mobile learning: techniques and technologies*. Hershey, PA: Information Service Reference.

Sharples, M. (Ed.). (2006). *Big issues in mobile learning: Report of a workshop by the Kaleidoscope network of excellence mobile learning initiative*. Retrieved from http://telearn.noe-kaleidoscope.org/ warehouse/ Sharples-2006.pdf

Vavoula, G., Pachler, N., & Kukulska-Hulme, A. (Eds.). (2009). *Researching mobile learning: Frameworks, tools and research designs*. New York: Peter Lang.

KEY TERMS AND DEFINITIONS

Behaviorist m-Learning: The process of promoting learning through changing learners' observable behaviors using mobile technologies (e.g., text messaging).

Collaborative m-Learning: The process of enhancing learning through data sharing, message exchanging, file transferring, shared data network, and other technologies supported by mobile devices.

Connectivism: A social and cultural psychological theory that emphasizes the importance of social context to learning.

Constructivist m-Learning: The process of actively constructing knowledge and ideas based upon previous and current knowledge using mobile technologies as a facilitation tool.

Informal m-Learning: Learning that is impromptu and happens anytime, anywhere with mobile technologies.

Mobile Learning: The process of constructing knowledge through self-initiated learning, social interaction, and impromptu learning using mobile technologies.

Situated m-Learning: The process of learning in realistic contexts while using mobile devices to support knowledge acquisition and on-site information access.

Chapter 16
Designing for Active Learning:
Putting Learning into Context with Mobile Devices

Carl Smith
London Metropolitan University, UK

Claire Bradley
London Metropolitan University, UK

John Cook
London Metropolitan University, UK

Simon Pratt-Adams
Anglia Ruskin University, UK

ABSTRACT

This chapter will focus on the design, implementation, and evaluation of a recent location based, context aware system for urban education students, trainee teachers, and language learning students. We first describe the detailed design of a case iteration centered on urban education and then move on to briefly describe how the design was iteratively adapted using evolutionary prototyping for language learning. Evaluation results are presented which detail the range of learning outcomes achieved from the point of view of the students. We then discuss future work that incorporates social media and augmented reality. The chapter concludes by discussing the active learning that our design appears to encourage. A major conclusion is that there is much to commend the Zone of Proximal Development context sensitive design as a catalyst for active learning.

DOI: 10.4018/978-1-61350-080-4.ch016

INTRODUCTION

In this chapter we will focus on the design, implementation and evaluation of recent location based, context aware systems for urban education students, trainee teachers and language learning students which is part of the CONTSENS project (http://www.ericsson.com/ericsson/corpinfo/programs/using_wireless_technologies_for_context_sensitive_education_and_training/). One aim of Design Research or Design-Based research (Design-Based Research Collective, 2002) is to identify and model technology-mediated, social learning and behaviours in order to design tools that support and promote the practices under investigation. For example, Cook (2002) has proposed a Design Research approach which revolves around evolutionary prototyping. What this means in simple terms is that we need to consider repeated cycles of: empirical work, theory/model development and tool/artifact refinement. These particular aspects are typically conceived as overlapping activities and phases (rather than as sequenced 'steps'); it is thus an evolutionary Design Research approach to analyzing the role of theory/models, empirical work and technology in learning.

The aim of this project was to provide a catalyst for active learning in context. Specifically, the goal was to provide a contextualised, social, cultural and historical account of urban education, focusing on systems and beliefs and reflecting on continuity and change in urban settings so that activities contribute to the construction of the surrounding discourses. In terms of our Design Research approach, which revolves around evolutionary prototyping, there is evidence to support our claim that there is a generality to our design and active learning. Specifically, the Urban Tour (described below) has been repurposed for language learning and tested successfully with a new set of learners.

This chapter is structured as follows. We first provide an account of the design based research focus which motivates our work alongside the theoretical and conceptual perspectives. Second, we describe the detailed design of a case Iteration centered on urban education which was also iteratively adapted using evolutionary prototyping for language learning. Evaluation results for both iterations of the case study are presented. We then discuss future work and conclude by discussing the active learning that our design appears to encourage and relate these preliminary findings back to our conceptual orientation.

BACKGROUND

Design Based Research: Evolutionary Prototyping

At the core of this research is the design of mixed reality scenarios to explore the relationship between contextual factors and knowledge formation. "The skill of writing is to provide a context in which other people can think" (Schlossberg, 1977). The dynamic creation of context using print has now radically evolved under the influence of mediums such as augmented and mixed reality. These new mediums provide information which is "inherently about who you are, where you are, what you are doing, and what is around you". (Shute, 2009) Context is central and being able to adapt and manipulate the elements of the context has never been easier and more accessible.

An example of this is how the physical use of space can be altered to reflect the subject content under review. For instance the context of one subject (language learning) can be transferred to another (urban education) through a rapid reconfiguration in the attachment of required information within the augmented space. However whilst learning in these new forms of augmented spaces represents a paradigm shift for education it also provides a new set of design challenges for the educational technologist. All aspects of the user's context (physical, technical and social) should take an increasing role in the design. Design-based research was introduced with the expectation that researchers would systematically adjust various aspects of the designed context so that each adjustment could be tested and fed back into the next iteration of the intervention (Plomp, 2007). Mixed reality scenarios allow for this infinite adjustment in the contextual design and form the basis of this research.

Theoretical and Conceptual Perspectives

Society experienced technologically and socially driven transformations during the industrialisation of the first third of the 20th Century; it was against this background that Lev Vygotsky defined the characteristics of human development as a development which is based on the instrumental conditioning of reflexes or as the extension of the body by tools for mastering nature (Vygotsky 1978/1930, p. 19 ff.). The "higher psychological processes", as Vygotsky termed them, result from a relation "between human beings and their environment, both physical and social" (p. 19). Vygotsky considered "social interactions" to be those like 'to speak' as the transformation of practical activities such as 'to use a tool'. The leading processes are that of internalization and that of the instrumental use of a tool; this happens where "An operation that initially represents an external activity is reconstructed and begins to occur internally" (Vygotsky 1978/1930, p 56-57). Further, the social situation of the external activity, like the conditions for the use of tools, is internalized: "An interpersonal process is transformed into an intrapersonal one" (Vygotsky 1978/1930, p 57). These processes of internalization depend on the children's development (Vygotsky was concerned primarily with child development): "The transformation of an interpersonal process into an intrapersonal one is the result of a long series of developmental events" (Vygotsky 1978/1930, p 57).

Vygotsky then went on to propose the Zone of Proximal Development as follows:

"It is the distance between the actual developmental level as determined by independent problem solving and the level of potential problem solving as determined through problem solving under adult guidance or in collaboration with more capable peers ... The zone of proximal development defines the functions that have not yet matured but are in the process of maturation, functions that will mature tomorrow but are currently in embryonic state. These functions could be termed the "buds" or "flowers" of development rather than the "fruits" of development. The actual development level characterizes mental development retrospectively, while the zone of proximal development characterizes mental development prospectively." (Vygotsky, 1978/1930, p. 86, my bold)

In this work we agree with Vygotsky's view that development is a socially negotiated and appropriative process involving the internalization of cultural products. Vygotsky (1978/1930) went on to further refine the Zone of Proximal Development:

"It is the distance between the actual developmental level as determined by independent problem solving and the level of potential problem solving as determined through problem solving under adult guidance or in collaboration with more capable peers." (Vygotsky, 1978/1930, p. 86).

In summary, Vygotsky (1978/1930, p. 90) proposed "that an essential feature of learning is that it creates the zone of proximal development; that is, learning awakens a variety of internal developmental processes that are able to operate only when the child is interacting with people in his environment and in cooperation with his peers. Once these processes are internalized, they become part of the child's independent developmental achievement." The implication of Vygotsky's line of argument on internalization and child development was, and continues to be, important in terms of learning from childhood onwards: it is not the learning object that is ruling the learning, but the student's development, i.e. the phases within a student's development, the so-called "zones of proximal development", in which the student is susceptible to internalizing learning objects. As can be seen from the above quote, this process relies on interaction with people using tools to mediate learning. However, one further notion that needs conceptual elaboration given our interest in mobile learning is the situation and situations in which the learning takes place. For us the situations are now 'in the hand', i.e. at the disposal of learners through their use of mobile/cell phones. Consequently, the concept of *situated learning* comes into play.

Lave and Wenger (1991), the main proponents of situated learning, emphasise the situated character of meaning-making. Situated learning theory (SLT) focuses on the notion of practice and social practices in order to overcome the limitations inherent in cognitive and/or structuralist accounts of learning. Lave and Wenger (1991), according to Arnseth (pp. 294 f.) see learning as constituted in the lived in-world, i.e. the world as it is experienced in social practice, and as participation in a community with practice shaping and constitution knowledge and knowing and with learners gradually able to master procedures for talking and acting through participation. Also SLT, which emerged at the beginning 1990s, examined cultural practices of learning of the day, such as apprenticeship. Due to the historic context at the time, SLT critically questioned pervasive school-based learning at that time. It was not conceptualised as a critique of cultural practices and products of cultural practices that is now possible with ubiquitous mobile devices that give access to cultural resources. For us, cultural practices constituted by fluid context generation with and through mobile devices have since emerged and become prevalent (for detail see Pachler, Bachmair & Cook, 2010).

In our studies below we focus on cultural practices that are constantly negotiated and re-negotiated. For us, this approach raises questions about applicability of the apprenticeship model in relation to learning with mobile devices in so far as apprenticeship focuses on a certain historically developed repertoire of practices, whose meaning and significance is produced and reproduced in situ (Arnseth 2008, p. 297). Rather, we emphasise the ever evolving and changing nature of these cultural practices. SLT, for us, places too much emphasis on social reproduction (Arnseth 2008, p. 299) and too little on interconnections and temporal emergence, i.e. 'how meanings and functions of actions and objects emerge in and through practical activity' (p. 300). Our view of SLT is thus augmented by Vygotskian notions: the student is susceptible to internalizing learning objects in a process that relies on interaction with people using tools (like mobile phones) to mediate learning and meaning-making more generally.

Initial Design Decisions

The outcomes of a previous NOF project 'The Cistercians in Yorkshire' (http://www.nof-digitise.org/search/showrecord/?id=142) formed the basis of the initial design for the case study used in this chapter. The Cistercians in Yorkshire project was designed to train archaeologists via the detailed use of virtual reconstructions of five Cistercians Abbeys. The central hypothesis behind the design of the resource was that the user can learn a great deal more about a specific building or style of architecture if they are able to interact with the material in ways that is not possible, either on site, or via traditional print media. A comprehensive database of visualisations contained (but did not prescribe) the entire set of reasoning that led from the design of the 2D plans to the 3D reconstructions. Inheritance and the innate structural hierarchy of the reconstructions were utilized to allow the visual disaggregation of a design into its original elements. These underlying designs provided the learner with the ability to drill down through the final presentation of the model (the front end to the whole data set) into all the component objects and any architectural element within the model to automatically load any linked information. These objects could then be extracted from their hierarchical structures, manipulated, measured and reconfigured according to the user's unique research query.

For example each Cistercian Abbey can be represented as a collection of their constituent architectural mouldings. A significant amount of the architectural style is imbedded in the structure of these mouldings along with invaluable information about their origins. The user is able to search and transform these 2D mouldings into their final 3D forms in order to examine how (for instance) the Gothic style of architecture compares and potentially relates to the Romanesque style. Questions relating to the levels of certainty, the actual construction process carried out by the master masons, the evolution of the structures at multiple levels, and their related influences could also be tackled. The capacity for users to have this 'active hand' in the construction of their own 'take on things' via visualisations which can be dynamically generated and transformed on the fly, in situ, and 'saved' has already been shown to contribute towards the successful construction of contextual learning (Smith, 2009)

However technology itself does not determine practice (Boyd, 2009). Since technology mediates everyday life, its adoption has to do more with the social setting and cannot be understood separately from the contexts in which learners are situated. Therefore, a careful understanding of the larger context can lead to radical improvements in the design of learning activities and educational opportunities. The core aim of this research was to evolve this initial design within a socially situated context.

Another important factor in the initial design decisions lies in the difference between declarative and procedural designs. The procedural mode of guidance can be described as a linear sequence of instructions. The more precise we make a procedural representation, the more prescriptive it becomes. A declarative approach is more concerned with the many different ways that something can be achieved. "It describes the structure of a knowledge base (a map for example) rather than specifying a set of instructions for action. The creative activation of this knowledge base is at the disposal of the user because a declarative approach offers alternative options for action." (Boyle, 2002)

STUDY

The Urban Education tour is based on a small area known as Eden Grove close to London Metropolitan University (North Campus), and it explores how schools from 1850 to the present day are signifiers of both urban change and continuity of educational policy and practice. The theoretical perspective was to allow collaborating learners to interact: with each other, with the mobile phones and with the physical environment in order to generate their own context for development within a Zone of Proximal Development.

Iteration 1: Design of Urban Education Tour

The tour was developed using the initial design outlined above in conjunction with a complex interplay between mobile learning technologies, iconic physical infrastructures and educational discourses. The aim was to visualise urban education through various collective images and representations (cf: Durkheim's notion of the social imaginaire). This was intended to enable researchers in both formal and informal learning contexts, when combined with the real, to examine past and present representations of urban form, and relate these to a contemporary Iteration of urban education (Pratt-Adams, Maguire & Burn, 2010). The overall intention was to create a digital 'technoscape' (Appadurai, 1996; Urry, 2006) to represent urban land, space, and subjects using a combination of social and cultural scripts. These included oral histories, local historical stories, and material elements that detail changes in the urban form, such as old photographs of pupils, school buildings and historical maps. The aim was for the researcher to move through the re-constructed landscape and thus "perform that landscape" (Sheller & Urry 2006, p. 9)

The tour supports the University's continuing mission of connecting with the local community and bridging the gap between formal and informal learning as a continuum of activities (Cook, Pachler & Bradley, 2008). This is the geographical area from which many of the students are drawn. It is an area steeped in social and cultural heritage, as "Cities are very much the crucibles of cultural juxtaposition, fusion, hybridization and syncretism" (Sheller & Urry 2006, p. 14).

A tutor (the fourth author of this chapter, now moved to another institution) had developed the original tour and was closely involved in the creation of the mobile tour. The development and production process involved the following elements:

- Initial field work and documentation of the site
- Capture and digitisation of oral histories, Pathe news clips and local historical stories.
- Capture and digitisation of material elements that detail changes in the urban form, such as photographs depicting the evolution of school buildings and historical maps
- MEDIASCAPE production (see below) to support the underlying pedagogy of the tour

Implementation

The project used a combination of smart phones: HTC Advantage and HTC Diamond (running the Mediascape authoring environment on the Windows Mobile operating system). Mediascapes or Mscapes are a form of media which overlays digital sight, sounds and interactions onto the physical world to create immersive and interactive experiences. The cameras on the smart phones were used to allow students to produce video podcasts of themselves and take photos. This instant capture of report writing and note making in situ was designed to promote real time reflection. Images captured with the phones were automatically geospatially tagged with their location information using GPS. These smart phones are also capable of instant upload of data to sites like Flickr. Finally QTVR (quicktime VR) movies of the interiors of the structures under investigation can be viewed and manipulated in real time on location (as access to the interiors was not available during the fieldwork).

Users running the Mscape player on a mobile device can move through the physical world and trigger digital media with GPS via an invisible interactive map. (Figure 1) shows the authoring environment where the zones are initially set up on a map which has been geo-referenced to the physical site. Content (Figure 2) is triggered using scripted behaviours (predefined logic applied to the media delivery).

The training starts with minimal instruction for the user. The intention is that whilst the technology (GPS) is working behind the scenes the content is very much at the forefront in order to minimise any technical concerns. The users can see themselves positioned on the map (Figure 3) and as they walk along the tour their position is updated until they enter into a training zone. Once they have entered a zone, audio and textual instructions are automatically triggered to the mobile device (Figure 4).

Figure 1. Mscape

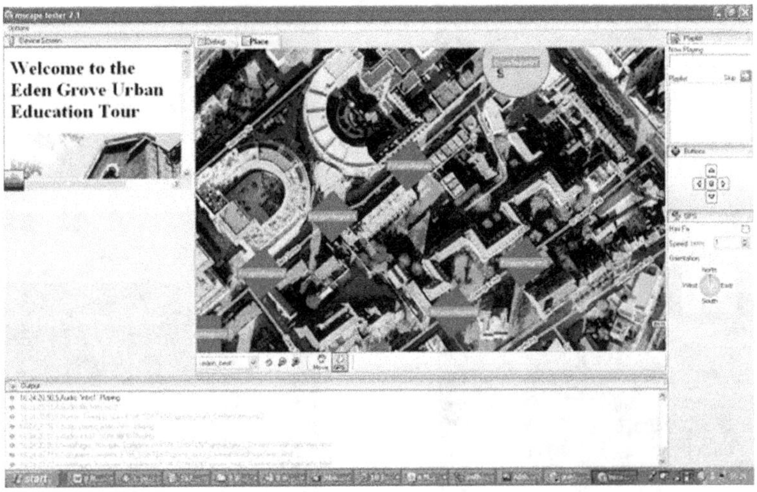

Figure 2. Zones

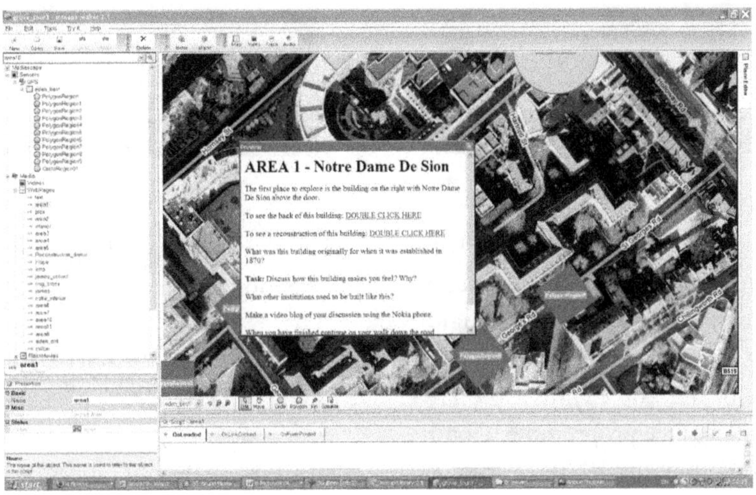

Learning Tasks

Some examples of the varied learning activities involved in the application include a section where the user is asked to examine both the physical architecture and the virtual architecture in the same physical location. The virtual architecture in this instance includes areas which were not available to view on the day of the tour and visualizations of the building as it was in the late 19th century. The user is then asked to examine what the building was originally used for when it was established in 1870. The user also has the opportunity to listen to the oral history of a former pupil at the school and adopt their point of view whilst in the same physical space where the events took place. *The user can reinvest the insight gained back into the context and augment the space.*

In another section the user is asked to look at a newsreel of a religious procession from the 1930s that was filmed in Eden Grove (Figure 5 and Figure 6) whilst they are standing in the same location where the film was shot. The students can reflect on the significance of religion (in this case Roman Catholicism) on the locale and its influence on schooling.

Figure 3.

Figure 4.

In the 1920s this area was known as the Ring Cross Estate (Figure 7) and was in the second highest criterion for overcrowding and squalor, with people living in some of the worst slums. During the middle of the 20th Century, the area was part of a slum clearance programme. Conditions improved throughout the 1970s (Figure 8). The user is shown these street scenes and asked to approximate by physically sketching out how much of the area in the archive footage still remains and how much of it has been redesigned. The student is encouraged to reflect on the impact of the social conditions on educational standards.

The final section exposes the user to the differing architectural styles of the buildings. The user is introduced to a traditional Victorian 3-decker (Figure 9) style school design (where the hall is located at the centre with classrooms coming off a central point) and asked to compare it to the more recent open style designs (Figure 10) where each classroom is given some access to the playground. The central activity is to examine what the architecture suggests about the educational approaches of the time.

Iteration 2: Design of Language Learning Tours

The aim of this iteration of the design was the realisation from the previous instances shown above that the way information is spatially represented directly impacts on our cognition. “In the everyday world, humans organise and manipulate objects in space to facilitate thinking. We are constantly organising and reorganising space to enhance performance” (Kirsch, 1995). All forms of media use some level of spatial arrangement to organise information.

Computer-assisted language learning (CALL) has embraced virtual learning environments such as Second Life but using actual physical structures as a means of scaffolding language learning has not yet been explored. The method of loci was adopted by ancient orators in order to remember and

Figure 5.

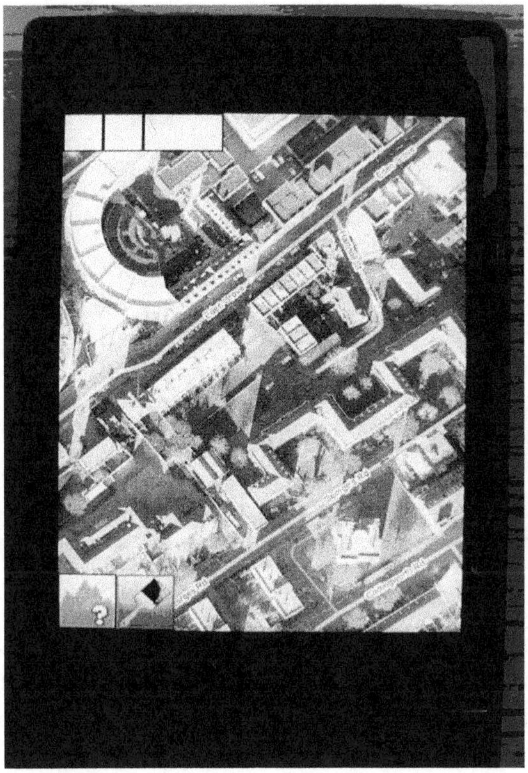

Figure 6.

Figure 7. Ring Cross Estate (1920s)

Figure 8. Ring Cross Estate (1970s)

Figure 9. The Three Decker

organise speeches using a combination of visual memory and location (Yates, 92). "The problem of seeing and retaining complex information is older than print.... The principle ancient mnemonic device was called 'The Method of Loci' and places its emphasis on memorability (via intelligibility and transparency) through visual structures such as concept maps. It is very much concerned with the acquisition of new knowledge. It plays upon methods that we use informally, and it is a tradition that survives today .....Visualization was in itself an important method of theory building. It may have been more important than text." (Wong &. Storkerson, 1996)

So would our pre-existing spatial design act as a catalyst and activate the abilities of language learners if carried out in situ? The tour was translated into four languages: German (Figure 11), Spanish, Italian and French but the content remained exactly the same. The users were tested in the classroom using this content as text only and then in situ using our design.

Although we accept that our description above is brief, we point out that reusing another iteration of our design here for language learning was very easy and quick to achieve, something that we see as a pointer to the generality of our approach. In the future research section we will explore ideas for extending the Language Learning design.

Figure 10. The Open Plan

Figure 11. German version of Urban Tour

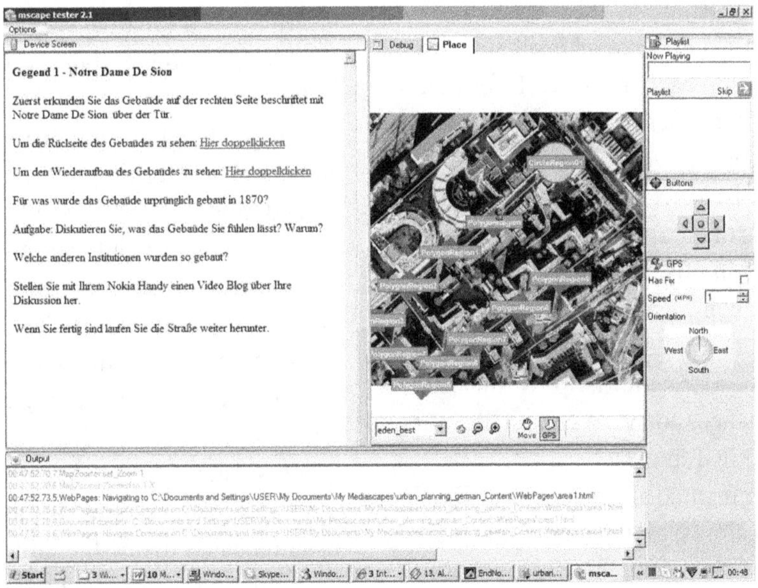

EVALUATION

All the tours (urban education and each of the language tours) have been used and evaluated with representative learners. Some of the evaluation data from the two studies follows.

Iteration 1: Urban Education Evaluation

The urban education tour was taken by three separate groups of students, facilitated by one or more of the project team members (Figure 12). In each group the students divided themselves into smaller groups (pairs or threes, depending on how many students there were). Each group had a GPS enabled smart phone with the tour pre-loaded, and one or more Nokia N95 phones to take photos, videos and record interviews for the tasks. After the tour was completed (after approximately an hour) the students returned to the university, and completed a questionnaire. Afterwards, we engaged the students in an informal group interview. 22 students were involved in total. The tutor who had developed the original tour and been closely involved in the creation of the mobile tour was also interviewed to ascertain if his aims of the tour had been met, his views on how the trials went and to get his perception of how the tour was received by the students. Some of the evaluation data gathered from both the students and the tutor will be presented.

Responses to the quantitative questions in the questionnaire are presented in Table 1 and Table 2 below. The mean 'average score' is obtained by allocating a score for each answer: 1 for 'extremely useful', 2 for 'useful', 3 for 'uncertain' and so on. The lower the average score, the more positive the rating is. Thus the tables below the % figure represents the proportion of the population that responded in this category.

The qualitative comments made in the questionnaire throw more light on responses made in the quantitative questions and help to illustrate the learners' experiences and views about the tour (some are included in Table 3).

All students commented about what they liked about the tour, and almost all the comments were positive. Not all of the comments are quoted in this chapter because of space constraints, but 7 students said it was 'interesting', 4 that it was 'informative', 4 said it was 'very good' and 3 'useful'. Many of the comments related to the content of the tour: "Very informing"; "It gave a better insight into the buildings we looked at, as it had pictures from the past as well as inside images of the buildings"; it "allowed you to travel into the past whilst still in the present, your very own tardis"; I "know more history about the local area"; "brought alive area". Other comments were that it was "very interesting because it was interactive"; "it was good to experience the locations as well as the visual/audio info. from the mobile"; it provided "a creative way of learning".

Figure 12. Students taking the Urban Education Mobile Tour

All the students thought the tour was useful in learning the subject (41% extremely useful). The majority, 91%, thought that the mobile device enhanced the learning experience: 50% 'strongly agreed' and only 9% were 'uncertain' (2 users). All gave a comment to show how they felt about the learning experience, and 19 thought that the mobile device enhanced the learning experience.

Some of the comments show that the mobile tour provided more than a guide to the area, and with the additional information and media files (photos, maps, videos, etc.) it enabled participants to see the area and the buildings in the past, and in some cases inside the buildings.

A number of comments show that the location and context aware technologies enhanced the learning experience because the information to learn from was provided in situ and it was provided to them easily, in a format that was easy to assimilate. Comments included: "the information given was underlined by the 'experience' of the area and therefore given context in both past and present"; "I think it was good to have interesting information while you were on site. So you could see the differences of then and now." Some students

Table 1. Usefulness of the tour in learning about the subject matter

	Extremely useful	Useful	Uncertain	Not useful	Extremely un-useful	Average score
How would you rate the tour's usefulness in learning the subject?	41%	59%	0%	0%	0%	1.59
	100% positive		**0%**	**0%**		

Table 2. Other quantitative question results

	Strongly agree	Agree	Uncertain	Disagree	Strongly disagree	Average score
The mobile device enhanced the learning experience	50%	41%	9%	0%	0%	1.59
	91% positive		9%	0% negative		
The mobile learning experience was fun	73%	27%	0%	0%	0%	1.27
	100% positive		0%	0% negative		
It was easy to use the equipment	14%	59%	27%	0%	0%	2.14
	73% positive		0%	0% negative		
It was easy to navigate through content	9%	82%	9%	0%	0%	2.00
	91% positive		9%	0% negative		
I would take another mobile learning course if it was relevant to my learning needs	68%	32%	0%	0%	0%	1.32
	100% positive		0%	0% negative		
I would recommend mobile learning as a method of Iteration to others	45.5%	45.5%	9%	0%	0%	1.64
	91% positive		9%	0% negative		

Table 3. Qualitative comments from the questionnaire

Q: What did you think of the mobile learning course you have just experienced?
It gave a better insight into the buildings we looked at, as it had pictures from the past as well as inside images of the buildings.
It was very good and allowed you to travel into the past whilst still in the present, your very own tardis.
Very useful, providing a creative way of learning. An interactive example of future technologies to display new learning opportunities for staff and students.
Brought alive area and things I wasn't aware of.
Very interesting because it was interactive. It was good to experience the locations as well as the visual/audio info. from the mobile.

Q: In what ways did it (or did not) enhance the learning experience?
It gave a wider perspective for learning, it wasn't just standing looking at buildings, it gave you more information from the past with narration and images and guides your thinking and triggers thought.
It made use of actual reality and history. It made me aware of the differences between past and present.
The information given was underlined by the 'experience' of the area and therefore given context in both past and present.

Q: The course used location-based technologies to provide relevant learning materials to your phone. How did you find this?
The info. offered was very useful as it gave further insight into what we were learning and gave us images that we wouldn't have been able to see.
Very useful in terms of contextualising the info.

Q: What did you like most about the mobile learning course?
You can tour at your own pace.
Interaction between technical device and learning "in situ" the history of education in the urban area.
A different way of learning.
Brought history alive with combination of walking and videos etc. like having own guide to area and subject.
That it got you moving, looking and learning. That we were outside.

said that the mobile tour was triggering their own thoughts and encouraging them to think more for themselves about the area: it "got me thinking about things more"; "it guides your thinking and triggers thought".

In the group interviews several comments were made that the mobile tour promoted "active learning" and that they were less passive than they would have been on a tutor-led tour. In the first group, talking about the difference between the two tours, one student said, "I felt like I was more passive, like I was just taking in information, and with this one I felt like I was, it was triggering my own thoughts and I was getting to think for myself about the area and the buildings".

Another student went on to say that doing the mobile tour was "active learning". This was described as, "we were active because there was the task, there was the whole going back to, take a picture, video that, try and get an overview of the whole area … and by doing this you're actually physically getting into the whole context of what it is that you're learning, your mind is open to what it is you're supposed to be doing". Another agreed, saying, "you don't lose concentration".

Students in group 2 also made comments about being able to concentrate more and stay focused on the mobile tour. One said, "Easier to concentrate as well, because there were so many things to look at".

One student in group 3 talked about the mobile tour being a "learning experience", and because of that she will remember more: "you tend to remember more through experience than actually reading from a book …this was, a learning experience, 9 out of 10 times you're more likely to remember that in your memory than actually something you've read in a book or heard … *it's something you experience, so you're experiencing the whole process of what the place, where the place is, and then learning the history"*.

Group 2 made some comments about working in pairs to complete the tour. One said, "I think working in pairs makes you have a discussion rather than just answering"

In the interviews, several students said that because the information and the tasks were 'pushed' to the phone, "It made it easier than trying to find the information every time you got somewhere"; "you didn't have to know when to look for what, it just came up".

For one user, using the tour became an experience: "The GPS was telling us, the instructions were to look at certain things, *so you're encouraged to look*, you're following instructions but at the same time it's becoming an experience which is something that you will take back and interpret it to your own ways."

In response to the question 'what did you like most about the mobile learning course', "The interaction between the technical device and learning 'in situ' the history of education in the urban area."; "you can tour at your own pace", which supports approaches for learning beyond the classroom/ lecturer room and personalized learning.

A good indication that the students had a positive experience and felt that they learned from the tour is that they all agreed that they would take another mobile learning course (68% answered 'strongly agree'). All except 2 would recommend mobile learning as a method of Iteration to others (45.5% answered 'strongly agree').

The tutor, who was interviewed after the tours had taken place, believes that there are lots of benefits to the Urban Education mobile tour and that it can provide more effective learning experiences and opportunities to utilise new and different pedagogies. Points made include that students move from being passive to active learners, they can take more control over their learning, and they can be engaged in more productive pedagogical approaches, such as small group work and investigative problem-based learning. The mobile tour can be more focused, but at the same time provide a multi-tasked and multimedia experience that allows students to get below the surface of the tasks. He also feels that the mobile technologies employed excited and intrigued the students, and helped them to become more engaged in the tour.

Iteration 2: Language Learning Evaluation

9 international students used the software in the same location as that used for the Urban Education tour. Their command of English ranged from that of the beginner to intermediate. They carried out the tour in much the same way, except that all 9 students completed the tour individually. Afterwards they each completed the same questionnaire (it was not possible to engage them in a discussion afterwards because of time constraints).

The results to the quantitative questions follow below in Table 4 and Table 5.

Qualitative comments made in the questionnaire provide more depth on their views. Some of the comments made are in Table 6. Note that fewer students evaluated the language learning package, and their comments on the whole are much briefer, which has resulted in less qualitative comments than for the Urban Education Tour.

89% rated it as being useful for learning the subject. 100% thought the mobile device enhanced the learning experience, and the comments made by 7 of them illustrate their views. 2 users made comments that it provided them with "situated learning": "Situated learning."; "Situating your learning experience." 2 others said that it made it more concrete and real: "More concrete."; "Made it more real". Comments from the other 3 suggest that they found it to be a new and interesting way to learn languages: "Better than a course book for languages."; "It was an excellent new approach to learning languages."; "It allowed me to learn English in interesting way.". They all agreed that the mobile learning experience was fun (33.33% answered 'strongly agree).

On the use of the location-based technologies, all the users indicated that the learning materials provided to the phone were useful and relevant. 2 users said it was "very useful." Responses to the question were brief (and hence not included in Table 6), but one said it was a "new experience", another "unusual", and one said "this works very well".

Responses about the features of the tour and its content were also very positive. In response to the question 'what did you like most about the mobile learning course', 2 comments related to the fact that they liked the "novelty" factor of it, and 2 suggested that they liked the interaction of working with others. Other comments made were: "Not in classroom - outside"; "Different way of learning."; "Being embodied whilst learning."; "Being active."

The usability and design of the course was also very well received. They all found the equipment easy to use and easy to navigate through the content. On the design, they all made positive comments; 2 thought it was "well designed", 2 "excellent" and 2 "good".

An indication that they all had a positive learning experience, is that all of them agreed that they would take another mobile learning course (44% strongly agreed) and that they would recommend mobile learning as a method of Iteration to others (33% strongly agreed).

In conclusion, the reaction from the students towards the languages tour has been very positive. The use of the context sensitive technologies clearly made a difference to the experience of learning a language. The learning experience was enhanced for two users because it provided "situated learning", whilst another liked "being active" and three others commented about the fact that they were outside of the classroom, learning in a group and interacting with other people. For others the learning experience was enhanced because it was "more concrete" and "made it more real". One liked "being embodied whilst learning". For two users it was the "novelty" factor that they liked. Some commented about the approach to learning languages, saying "Very new way of learning. I enjoyed it a lot"; "It was an excellent new approach to learning languages"; "Better

Table 4. Usefulness of the tour in learning about the subject matter

	Extremely useful %	Useful %	Uncertain %	Not useful %	Extremely un-useful %	Average score
How would you rate the tour's usefulness in learning the subject?	33.33	55.56	11.11	0	0	1.78
	89% positive		11%	0% negative		

Table 5. Other quantitative question results

	Strongly agree %	Agree %	Uncertain %	Disagree %	Strongly disagree %	Average score
The mobile device enhanced the learning experience	66.67	33.33	0	0	0	1.33
	100% positive		0%	0% negative		
The mobile learning experience was fun	33.33	66.67	0	0	0	1.67
	100% positive		0%	0% negative		
It was easy to use the equipment	44.44	55.56	0	0	0	1.56
	100% positive		0%	0% negative		
It was easy to navigate through content	66.67	33.33	0	0	0	1.33
	100% positive		0%	0% negative		
I would take another mobile learning course if it was relevant to my learning needs	44.44	55.56	0	0	0	1.56
	100% positive		0%	0% negative		
I would recommend mobile learning as a method of Iteration to others	33.33	66.67	0	0	0	1.67
	100% positive		0%	0% negative		

Table 6. A selection of qualitative comments from questionnaire

Q: What did you think of the mobile learning course you have just experienced?
Good course.
Great.
Very new way of learning. I enjoyed it a lot.

Q: In what ways did it (or did not) enhance the learning experience?
Better than a course book for languages.
Situated learning.
It was an excellent new approach to learning languages.
More concrete.
It allowed me to learn English in interesting way.

Q: What did you like most about the mobile learning course?
Went out with group.
Different way of learning
Being embodied whilst learning.
The interaction of other people
Novelty factor.
Being active.

than a course book for languages"; "It allowed me to learn English in interesting way". As one student commented, "the information given was underlined by the 'experience' of the area and therefore given context in both past and present". Another student commented that "it was triggering my own thoughts and I was getting to think for myself about the area and the buildings." "By relating the language learning to physical structures it made the learning more memorable."

FUTURE RESEARCH DIRECTIONS

Following the interventions described above, and following our Design Research method described in the Introduction, we have taken into account comments made in the evaluations for improvements to our designs and hence for future work. Consequently, the next stage of development is discussed below as we start to consider how we can further develop the tours.

Social Media

A potential way of extending the urban education project is to incorporate the dynamic use of real time social data. We become part of a larger social identity through passing around ideas. We spread ideas around through dialogue and other forms of interaction. They become 'contagious patterns of cultural information that pass from meme to meme which in turn have the ability to change the actions of a group' (Dawkins, 1976). A meme is a basic unit of cultural ideas, social semiotic symbols or practices, which can be transmitted from one mind to another via texts or speech, etc.

Learning interventions can now harness the power and potential utility of the wider social network. If we can spread ideas bi-directionally through these cultural networks in real time then we can harness instant feedback and reuse. This will help create what can be termed mobile meme machines (http://mememachine.com/). Application Program Interfaces (APIs) exist for Twitter and Facebook which will make it easy to talk to Augmented Reality (AR) browsers in real time. Students should be able to share and critique their ideas on urban or school design both in situ and in reflection. Metadata could then potentially be gathered in real time via these social networks and used to capture the meaning and sense-making process in learning. All kinds of annotations, classifications, discussions, usage information, and references can then be added as an extra layer on top of the content information. This metadata can be used to enable users to find all kinds of new media for instruction and learning (and potentially keep their Zone of Proximal Development on display). Metadata in this sense is closely related and can be fed into the core processes of learning as reflection, guidance, and feedback (Specht, 2009).

During the urban planning studies students learnt that the physical design of any educational institution has a direct impact on the delivery of the education that takes place within that context. Learning space design shapes our behavior and influences our thinking. As a result, a way of extending that understanding is to get the learner to participate in the design of that context in order to control how their learning environment operates.

The idea of this application of the system is for urban designers working in pairs to use simple open source 3D software (i.e Google sketch up http://sketchup.google.com/ or blender http://www.blender.org/) to create basic additions or revisions to current school designs (in the form of 3D sketches). This is a useful way to give students the opportunity to highlight the areas of their institutions that in their opinion lead to negative effects on their learning.

In order to test the validity of the findings a virtual version of the application will be created which will be used by individuals only. This will involve individuals using the recently available Google Earth API (http://code.google.com/apis/earth/). In essence, instead of placing their 3D models and annotations into real space they will enter them into virtual space, via the AR application. This data will then be compared to examine how significant the world as a platform is in this scenario.

Augmented Reality

Another way of extending the project is to build an Augmented Reality (AR) version of the tour. AR specifically generates composite views using the real scene viewed by the user and a virtual scene generated by the computer. The key aspect of AR is that the virtual elements enhance the person's perception of the world by supplying relevant information that is not contained in the real world.

AR is more powerful than VR as its influence is bi directional. "If we consider AR as a visualisation technique, the relationship of real and virtual objects is one of focus and context: Either we want to provide additional virtual context to an important object in the real world or we want the user to focus on a virtual object embedded in a real context" (Kalkofen, Mendez, & Schmalstieg, 2009). The learner in an AR environment can locate points of interest (POI) which have been pre-embedded into the scene or they can place (and eventually activate) their own POI into the scene in real-time.

The construction of psychological and physical space is one of the constituent parts in the generation of context. MAR (Mobile Augmented Reality) systems have been referred to as "intelligence amplifying systems to enhance human cognitive activities, such as attention, planning, and decision making" (Brooks, 1995).

AR crucially provides both the direct primary experience (the real world scene) and the mediated representation (the digital augmentation). As a result Augmented Reality (AR) provides significant support for real time situated learning. Practice and theory can now feed off each other in the same space. A good example of this is an engineer working on an engine whilst wearing glasses that provide a digital overlay showing the potential areas which could be responsible for a known problem. The theory informs the practice in the same space.

Extending the Language Learning Project

A lot of virtual media is often accused of isolating learners from reality but augmented-reality has the opportunity to draw learners further into reality by amplifying the already existing authentic context. The inherent high resolution nature of real life must be taken advantage of in order to enhance learning. Language is fundamentally about the local context. As a result the classroom is arguably not the most efficient environment for enhancing and assessing language performance. Through acquiring a language in context you acquire a culture. Authentic cultural language should directly mesh with authentic cultural situations.

As highlighted by Vygotsky's Zone of Proximal Development (ZPD), maintaining successful immersion in language learning depends on working at a level just above the comprehensible level of the student. An average teacher has many students with differing levels of ability in their language skills, and as a result, personalized immersion instruction is almost impossible to apply.

Augmented Reality in this context provides an excellent vehicle for immersive and dynamic language learning. Adding extra information onto the surrounding environment is the core function of Augmented Reality. A language learner is supplied with the ability to acquire a language whilst being augmented within their authentic environments. Learners can see local people having conversations in the target language and real objects being labeled dynamically. Preference settings could easily tailor the method to the individual level of ability ensuring the learners remain within their ZPD.

CONCLUSION

Taking into account our conceptual perspective outlined above, the following questions now arise:

1. Are the students susceptible to internalizing cultural resources in a process that relies on interaction with people using tools (like mobile phones) to mediate learning?
2. Do meanings and the functions of actions and objects emerge in and through practice?

The two questions, derived from our conceptual position are clearly related and any answer to them can only be preliminary given the small scale nature of our case studies. In terms of question 1 we believe there are indications that the learners were becoming more reflexive as a result of the Urban Tour (Iteration 1). As we pointed out above, the benefit of the location-based technology was that it prompted the students to look at the buildings relevant to the learning context on the route which they may otherwise have missed, making it more interesting. One student commented: "It was quite interesting because there was information coming, when it was working, the information that was coming through it was giving us like a background of where we were and what it's about and making us look at things that maybe I wouldn't have looked at if I was just walking past it. Like I wouldn't have noticed that cross on that church school … I wouldn't have noticed that if I was just walking down the street …". In this sense we can say that the mobile tour appears to be acting as part of what Vygotsky calls the 'more capable peer' and was assisting the learners as they move through stages of development in the Zone of Proximal Development. The answer to question 2 is suggestive at this point. Group 2 in the Urban Tour (Study 1) made some comments about working in pairs to complete the tour. One said, "I think working in pairs makes you have a discussion rather than just answering".

Consequently, we tentatively conclude that there is much to commend the ZPD situated cultural practice design acting as a catalyst for active learning. For example, by drawing on the evaluation of iteration 1, we can say that the benefits from the student perspective concluded that: 91% of participants thought the mobile device enhanced the learning experience. The learning content provided was easy to assimilate, allowing more time to concentrate on the tasks. It allowed instant reflection in situ. The mobile tour promoted "active learning": the appearance of content on the devices prompted them to engage with the tour (the approach emphasised making learning relevant to them as 'lived complexities'). They were less passive than they would have been on an equivalent tutor-led tour because they were not "merely taking in information", as they were interacting with the content on the mobile devices, the physical environment and other students. The mobile tour triggered their own thoughts and thus encouraged them to think more reflectively about the area.

We have less rich data for the second iteration of the case study but the benefits according to the students concluded that: 100% thought the mobile device enhanced the learning experience. The learning experience was enhanced because it was "situated" in the physical environment, and therefore it was "more concrete". One learner liked "being embodied whilst learning". For one learner the richness of the approach to language learning enhanced the learning experience, saying it was "better than a course book for languages", which implies that such an approach can not only provide a better learning experience, but also lead to richer learning. The approach to language learning was cited by several learners as being "new", "different" and "interesting" and some liked the "novelty" factor.

Whilst different issues have emerged from each of the studies, one aspect that is common to both of the studies is that our design has fostered active learning, which has occurred through a combination of factors. As the content was pushed to the mobile devices it engaged the learners in the learning activity, and encouraged them to interact with the material and learning content on the devices, the physical environment and the other students in their group act as communities of practice (Lave & Wenger 1998). The tasks then made them think and reflect on what they were looking at and being asked to do (a finding from Iteration 1). Another common aspect is that the whole learning experience was "more concrete" and "real" because it took place in situ, and was directly related to the learning context.

We will end the chapter by highlighting the generality of this pedagogical approach in terms of supporting learner mobility that engages learners in discourse about the changing nature of urban education and to acknowledge the fluidity, hybridity and change that characterise urban spaces. Indeed, we note that in terms of our Design Research approach, which revolves around evolutionary prototyping, there is evidence to support our claim that there is a *generality to our design for active learning*. The Urban Tour described in this chapter has been repurposed for language learning and tested successfully with a new set of learners. Specifically, we claim that some of the transferable skills and outcomes of the project are as follows:

1. Critical understanding of a range of cultures and social situations and the ability to apply these to real world issues. These real world issues could include inner city, urban, community; schooling of working class children, past/present lived urban experiences, movement of peoples in/out of locales.
2. Awareness of a wide range of issues that have implications for a range of professional contexts including teacher education, teacher workforce and other work in/with schools, educational research, urban design professionals, planning and regeneration, community development.
3. Use of audio-visual and technical materials to support team/collaborative learning, academic dialogue as well as learner autonomy and reflexivity in the communication of complex ideas and completion of tasks.
4. Making the links between theoretical analysis and practical contexts - can relate this to understanding and use of praxis. Praxis in this context means firstly 'shared practice' - when communities of practice bring together learners and practitioners to develop and share useful learning insights. Secondly it is also the process of putting theoretical knowledge into practice - so in this case this would include applying theories of urban education/urban studies with the real, lived context of the Eden Grove working class community.
5. Application of higher order cognitive and intellectual skills: exploring issues in depth and over time.
6. Carrying out research and investigate the subject within a conceptual framework, pose and answer questions and construct arguments. In essence this combines the use of historical descriptions, visual/digital materials and mobile technologies and student-led research activities to explore, examine and explain the community from the past in order to understand and engage with the present, as urban space and society becomes made and remade.
7. Develop general Iteration skills, problem solving skills and communication skills.

In this chapter we have attempted to capture, interpret and understand specific transformations in urban spaces. We have found that these transformations can be made both visible and tangible through augmenting the space around the user: "Traditionally architecture was place-bound, linked to a condition of experience. Today, mediated environments challenge the givens of classical time, the time of experience [...] Architecture can no longer be bound by the static conditions of space and place, here and there" (Duarte, 2009). We conclude that during these studies we successfully used design based research to tailor the use of technology in a number of contexts. These designs were used to intensify the appreciation of space as a social by-product and that this approach has led to a discernable improvement in active learning.

REFERENCES

Appadurai, A. (1996). *Modernity at large: Cultural dimensions of globalisation*. Minneapolis, MN: University of Minnesota Press.

Arnseth, H. C. (2008). Activity theory and situated learning theory: Contrasting views of educational practice. *Pedagogy, Culture & Society*, *16*(3), 289–302. doi:10.1080/14681360802346663

Boyd, D. M. (2009). *Taken out of context: American teen sociality in networked publics*. PhD thesis. University of California, Berkeley

Boyle, T. (2002). Towards a theoretical base for educational multimedia design. *Journal of Interactive Multimedia in Education, 2002*(2), 1-16.

Brooks, F. (1995). *The mythical man-month: Essays on software engineering*. Addison-Wesley Professional.

Cook, J. (2002). The role of dialogue in computer-based learning and observing learning: An evolutionary approach to theory. *Journal of Interactive Media in Education*, (5): 1–29.

Cook, J., Pachler, N., & Bradley, C. (2008). Bridging the gap? Mobile phones at the interface between informal and formal learning. *Journal of the Research Centre for Educational Technology*, *4*(1), 3–18.

Dawkins, R. (1976). *The selfish gene*. Oxford, UK: Oxford University Press.

Design-Based Research Collective. (2002). Design-based research: An emerging paradigm for educational inquiry. *Educational Researcher*, *32*(1), 5–8.

Duarte, F., & Firmino, R. J. (2009). Infiltrated city, augmented space: Information and communication technologies, and representations of contemporary spatialities. *The Journal of Architecture*, *14*(5), 545–565. doi:10.1080/13602360903187493

Durkheim, E. (1895). *The rules of sociological method* (8th edition, trans. Sarah A. Solovay and John M. Mueller, ed. George E. G. Catlin, 1938, 1964 edition). Glencoe, IL: The Free Press.

Kalkofen, D., Mendez, E., & Schmalstieg, D. (2007). Interactive focus and context visualization for augmented reality. In *Proceedings International Symposium on Mixed and Augmented Reality* (pp. 191-200). Nara, Japan.

Kirsh, D. (1995). The intelligent use of space. *Artificial Intelligence*, *73*(1-2), 31–68. doi:10.1016/0004-3702(94)00017-U

Lave, J., & Wenger, E. (1991). *Situated learning: Legitimate peripheral participation*. Cambridge, UK: Cambridge University Press.

Lave, J., & Wenger, E. (1998). *Communities of practice: Learning, meaning and identity*. Cambridge, UK: Cambridge University Press.

Pachler, N., Bachmair, B., & Cook, J. (2010). *Mobile learning: Structures, agency, practices*. New York, NY: Springer.

Plomp, T., & Nieveen, N. (2007). Introduction to education design research. *Proceedings of the Seminar conducted at the East China Normal University*, Shanghai.

Pratt-Adams, S., Maguire, M., & Burn, E. (2010). *Changing urban education*. London, UK: Continuum.

Schlossberg, E. (1977). For my father. In Brockman, J. (Ed.), *About Bateson: Essays on Gregory Bateson* (pp. 143–167). New York, NY: Dutton.

Sheller, M., & Urry, J. (Eds.). (2006). *Mobile technologies of the city*. London, UK: Routledge.

Shute, T. (2009). *Do well by doing good*. Retrieved from http://www.ugotrade.com/2009/04/04/do-well-by-doing-good-talkingexperience-and-design-in-a-mobile-world-with-nathan-freitas-and-david-oliver

Smith, C. (2009). *The unit of construction + the multiple point of view = The evolution of form*. Electronic Visualisation and the Arts Conference (EVA). British Computer Society. London

Specht, M. (2009). *Learning in a technology enhanced world: Context in ubiquitous learning support. Inaugural Address. September, 11, 2009*. Heerlen, The Netherlands: Open University of the Netherlands.

Urry, J. (2007). *Mobilities*. Cambridge, UK: Polity Press.

Vygotsky, L. (1978). *Mind in society. The development of higher psychological processes* (Cole, M., Eds.). Cambridge, MA: Harvard University Press. (Original work published 1930)

Wong, J., & Storkerson, P. (1996). Hypertext and the art of memory. *Visible Language, 31*(2), 126–157.

Yates, F. (1992). *The art of memory*. London, UK: Pimlico.

ADDITIONAL READING

Cartman J., & Ting R. *Strategic mobile design. Creating engaging experiences*. Berkeley, CA: NewRiders.

Fling, B. (2009). *Mobile design and development: Practical concepts and techniques for creating mobile sites and web 'apps'*. O'Reilly Media Inc. USA. Comprehensive history of the mobile phone market, as well as guidelines, standards and techniques for developing mobile products.

Jones, M., & Marsden, G. (2006). *Mobile interaction design*. Chichester, UK: Wiley & Sons Ltd.

Smith, C., Cook, J., & Pratt-Adams, S. (2009). *Context sensitive mobile learning: Designing a 'technoscape' for urban planners*. Mobile Learning, Barcelona, 26-28 February.

KEY TERMS AND DEFINITIONS

Active Learning: An approach that links the conscious and unconscious processes of activities conceptualized as thinking and learning

Augmented Reality: The generation of composite views using the real scenes viewed by the user and the virtual scene generated by the computer

Cloud Computing: For mobile devices are an on-demand solution where resource data doesn't reside on a mobile device but instead is hosted on a server and accessed via the internet. An example is *Second Life* which is streamed to mobile devices. It contrasts with an 'apps' solution where apps run locally on a mobile device.

Context Aware System: Context-aware computing refers to a general class of mobile systems that can sense their physical environment, i.e., their context of use, and adapt their behavior accordingly.http://en.wikipedia.org/wiki/Context-aware_pervasive_systems, accessed 23 July 2010.

GPS: (Global Positioning System): Uses a network of satellites to indicate the users' position on a GPS receiver. Many mobile devices (e.g. Smartphone's) are fitted with a GPS receiver.

Laptop: Many describe them as portable, not mobile. They have most of the typical components of a desktop computer.

Mobile Devices Types: A wide range of handheld devices, many telephony and networked. PDA (Personal Digital Assistant) from information management to networked, and phone functions

Mobile OS: A mobile operating system, also known as a Mobile OS. It is the operating system that controls a mobile device. Common mobile device OS: Symbian OS, RIM Blackberry, Apple iPhone, Windows Phone or Mobile, Google Android, Palm OS, Mobile Linux,

Netbooks: Small, lightweight laptop computers for general computing and to access the internet

Smartbook: Smartphone and netbook features with all-day battery life, 3G and/or WiFi

Smartphones: combine mobile phone and handheld computer, include iPhone and Nokia models

Tablet Computers: A notebook computer that has an LCD screen and QWERTY keyboard. MID (Mobile Internet Device) multimedia-capable mobile device providing wireless Internet access. They fill a size and function niche between smartphones and Tablet PCs.

Urban Education: Recognizes the complexities of the urban setting, urban lives and educational contexts in the face of new and emerging social and cultural relationships. The Iteration of urban education links urban education theory with issues of policy and critical urban pedagogy and practice.

Zone of Proximal Development: It is the distance between the actual developmental level as determined by independent problem solving and the level of potential problem solving as determined through problem solving under adult guidance or in collaboration with more capable peers … The zone of proximal development defines the functions that have not yet matured but are in the process of maturation, functions that will mature tomorrow but are currently in embryonic state. These functions could be termed the "buds" or "flowers" of development rather than the "fruits" of development. The actual development level characterizes mental development retrospectively, while the zone of proximal development characterizes mental development prospectively.

Section 4
Informed Design Models and Educational Technology

Over the years, research and practices related to instructional design and educational technology design have often been demonstrated through the use of different kind of models. In this section, five chapters provide innovative and challenging design models to enhance teaching and learning in higher education in theoretically informed ways.

Chapter 17
Fostering NCL in Higher Education:
New Approaches for Integrating Educational Technology Instructional Design into Teachers' Practice

Serena Alvino
Institute for Educational Technologies, National Research Council, Italy

Guglielmo Trentin
Institute for Educational Technologies, National Research Council, Italy

ABSTRACT

Networked Collaborative Learning (NCL) is undeniably a double-edged sword. On the one hand it can yield high-quality learning and enhance both teachers' and learners' satisfaction. On the other hand, however, it requires careful planning and specific skills for the design and management of online learning activities. This is one of the main reasons for the limited adoption of NCL in a number of educational contexts. The focus of this chapter is a specific proposal aimed to foster the wide diffusion of Educational Technology (ET) and NCL in higher education (HE). In this perspective the chapter analyses the main barriers that limit the diffusion of Network-Based Educational Technology (NBET) approaches, in particular NCL, and then, in order to overcome them, presents an innovative approach to faculty training in Educational Technology Instructional Design. This approach is founded on multidimensional scaffolding, which supports teachers to integrate rules, heuristics, and best practices for design of active and collaborative online learning into their everyday activity.

DOI: 10.4018/978-1-61350-080-4.ch017

INTRODUCTION

Although learning is indeed an "individual" process of growth and transformation of personal knowledge, it is however advisable for it not to remain an "isolated" process, even when it is managed online. Over 20 years ago, in his work entitled "Megatrends," John Naisbitt (1984) claimed that one of the keys to the success of distance learning was the combination of "high-tech" with "high-touch," (i.e. of the sophisms of technology with contact between people, in our specific case between educators, course students, experts etc).

Technology itself is seldom the real obstacle to educational innovation centred on Educational Technology (ET). As pointed out by the AECT[1], since *Educational Technology* can be considered as "the study and ethical practice of facilitating learning and improving performance by creating, using, and managing appropriate technological processes and resources" (Januszewski & Molenda, 2008), it doesn't relate only to technology as a "tool," but also and mainly to theories, methods and practices facilitating learning through specific technology-based resources and processes. In fact, the main problems concerning ET-centred innovation are almost always related to achieving better understanding of the role of the human component within the technology-based processes, and of the potential and limitations of network-mediated interaction in the improvement of distance learning processes (Naisbitt, 1984).

On the one hand, if we analyse the most common uses of Information and Communication Technology (ICT) in higher education, it is not difficult to realise that students often find themselves assuming a passive role within a learning process which is mainly guided by the educational material prepared by the teacher (Collins & Van der Wende, 2002; Kirkwood, 2009).

On the other hand, social constructivism (Vygotsky, 1978; Gunawardena et al., 1995) has brought to light the importance of interaction–among learners and between teachers and learners–in attaining specific learning goals. More generally, it has revealed the impact that these interactions can have on cognitive and metacognitive processes, on the motivation to learn, on self-esteem and on the development of social belonging (Bronfenbrenner, 1979).

Several research studies and experiences (Bruffee, 1999; Collazos, et al., 2004; Kreijns & Kirschner, 2004) have shown that collaborative learning experiences normally enhance the development and the employment of high-level thinking skills (Brown, & Palincsar, 1989). These premises can be easily extended to Networked Collaborative Learning (NCL), whose pedagogical dimension is based on social constructivism (Daradoumis & Marquès, 2000; Felder & Brent, 2001).

In this sense, the term NCL does not merely indicate that the education process is supported by a computer network, but also (and more significantly) that the process is underpinned by, and conducted through, a network of inter-relationships among all the actors of the process: learners, teachers, tutors, experts (Trentin, 2010). These inter-relationships are intrinsic to collaboration within a community pursuing a common learning goal. So the network should be seen primarily as a social network, and not merely as a computer network for distance communication between individuals.

The NCL approach has various important implications (Koschmann, 1996; Fink, 1999).

- *educational implications*: emphasis on "learning by doing," students involvement in a collaborative knowledge building, and a change in teacher's role from "authority and knowledge holder" into "guide and facilitator";
- *a new vision of the "information" concept*: the information itself is inert matter, lacking that dense network of logical and communicative connections which can transform it into significant group knowledge;
- *a new focus of the learning process*: the subject is placed at the centre of the learning

process; information must be understood and interpreted before being assimilated, and thus it must be situated, or derived by a process of individual participation in socially-structured practices.

While NCL is certainly not the only option open to a teacher looking to adopt ICT in HE (Adam & Warren, 2008), it nonetheless offers enormous potential for innovating teaching approaches (Daradoumis & Marquès, 2000). One way it does this is by leveraging the technologies and forms of communication that students are now accustomed to using in their daily lives (Culligan, 2003).

However, it calls for careful planning, and can only be introduced with suitable preparation and training, especially in the design and management of online learning activities.

This takes us to the wider issue of professional development for academic staff, something that plays a critical role in the pedagogical sustainability of NCL (Seufert & Euler, 2003; Attwell, 2005; Briggs, 2005; Trentin, 2010). The role of the *e-teacher* cannot be improvised; it should form an integral part of the teacher's overall professional growth. This does not simply mean acquiring sufficient know-how to introduce technology in support of habitual teaching practices (Kirkwood, 2009). Rather, it means totally rethinking and revising those practices (Felder & Brent, 2001; Bates, 2003). This is probably the reason why approaches focusing on NCL are less commonly applied (Zemsky & Massy, 2004).

In this sense, the focus of this chapter is, on the one hand to understand the causes that limit the diffusion of NCL approaches in higher education and, on the other hand, to propose possible solutions to foster a wider use of the same approaches. Consequently the main objectives of this chapter are:

- to analyse the stages through which university teachers progressively master Network-Based Educational Technology (NBET) (i.e. the specific area of ET which focuses on the educational use of network technology);
- to identify the main causes of the poor exploitation of NCL potentialities in higher education
- to describe new approaches to Educational Technologies Instructional Design which are able to improve and enhance teachers' skills in designing effective NCL activities and courses.

BACKGROUND

The examination of processes that have characterised the progressive approach of faculty teachers to ICT instructional use, highlights at least four recurrent stages (Zemsky & Massy, 2004; Trentin, 2008):

Enhancements to traditional course configurations: It envisages the use, within a traditional learning/teaching process, of fresh types of materials (in digital format) made available by the teacher on the faculty's website or found directly by the student on the Internet. The approach therefore introduces no significant changes to the traditional teaching method (Creighton & Buchanan, 2001; Sauter, 2003).

Use of new course management tools: It envisages the use of specific software systems (LMS[2], CMS[3], etc.) to facilitate both teacher/student interaction from a distance (one-to-one or group) and more effective, structured organisation and distribution of teaching material (Attwell, 2007).

Use of learning objects: In this stage, the objective is to make the learning activities as rich and motivating as possible using traditional tools for the development of educational materials (Longmire, 2000; Shamsuar, 2008). For example, there are multimedia materials, tele-lessons by video streaming, interactive simulations etc.

New course configurations: Of the four stages, this is clearly the one which, more than the others, aims to make substantial changes to the way of teaching with the support of ICT. Teachers are therefore required to reassess their teaching methods and to reap the maximum benefit from the use of new technologies and help facilitate their students' learning process. This process is based on active learning (Fink,1999; Briggs, 2005) and the combination of diverse modes of interaction among students, teachers, tutors etc., carried out either face-to-face or from a distance, synchronous or asynchronous (Salomon, 2002; 2004). Clearly this is not irrespective of the availability of both teachers and students to assume a different way of behaving reciprocally from what happens in a normal classroom situation.

As can be imagined, the four stages correspond to different time phases for their respective introduction.

The *Enhancements to traditional course configurations* is definitely the fastest development stage and lies in the initial phases of the innovation process. Also the stage introducing the *Course Management Systems* evolves fairly rapidly, but not so much in terms of the number of teachers adopting NBET than in terms of the student-teacher ratio involved in courses and programmes employing course management software.

These two initial stages generally complement and reinforce each other reciprocally (Zemsky & Massy, 2004). However, neither of them is based on the introduction of *learning objects* nor on the development of *new course configurations*. On the whole, they introduce a limited adoption of ICT mainly based on: (a) the use of digital resources to present contents (e.g. PowerPoint), (b) the almost unconditioned adoption of the teaching-style underpinning CMS, (c) the use of automated tests and, (d) sporadically, the organization of theme forum discussions related to the course content. At best, they also envisage importing and using simple learning objects.

New courses configurations are rarely developed and often don't exploit the wide possibilities offered by new educational technologies to promote user-centred, personalized and flexible learning processes (Klobas & Renzi, 2003; Elliot, 2008).

This trend reflects the various ways network-based Educational Technology is used in higher education (Howell et al., 2004). In particular, the taxonomy of Figure 1 presents an overview[4], where the various NBET approaches have been grouped into six macro-categories (Trentin, 2006; 2008) and arranged according to the level of complexity.

Informative use: this is the simplest and most immediate way to use the Web, based on the network channel for sending information to students (information about the course, dates of exams, office hours etc.)

Distributive use: according to this approach the Web is considered as a one-directional channel for supplying students with any digital material which can be electronically delivered: slides used in the lessons, handouts, articles and book chapters, exercises, texts of previous exams, self-assessment tests, etc.; generally however materials not specially designed for distance learning activities (hence not planned and developed *ad hoc*).

Interactive use: this is the way of using the Web which fosters the various forms of personal interaction:

- "one-to-one" teacher/student, used for requests for information, questions and answers about specific topics of the course, for providing individual corrections of assignments etc.
- "one-to-many," typical of the tele-lessons delivered in synchronous mode with the possibility of dialoguing with the teacher using synchronous and/or asynchronous return channels;
- "many-to-may," almost always based on asynchronous interactions using forums, computer conferencing systems, e-groups etc. to conduct collaborative types of activity, one- to two-week workshops etc.

Figure 1. A possible taxonomy of the main NBET approaches in higher education (Trentin, 2008)

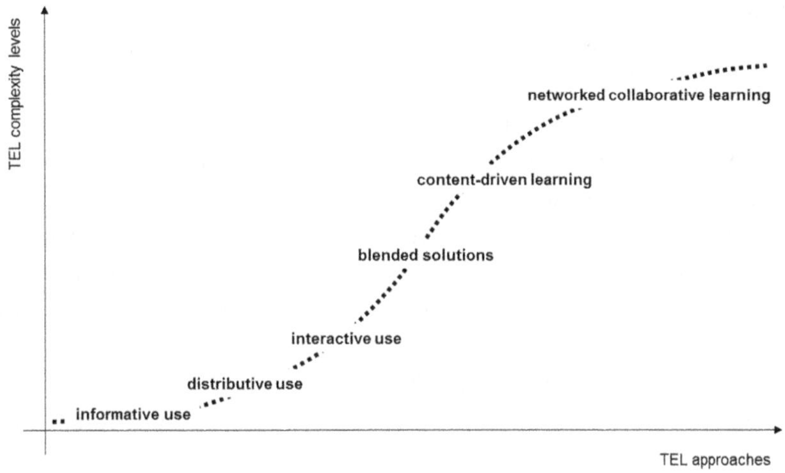

Blended solutions: solutions which use an alternation of classroom and distance activities, where the latter are not optional, but are an integral part of the course (Davies & Fill, 2007; MacDonald, 2008). This type of approach is often used to reduce the number of face-to-face lessons in order, for example, to help working students or those living far from the university site.

Content-driven e-learning: This approach envisages web-based courses (or parts of them) mostly based on pedagogically-structured educational resources. In this case it is not therefore a question of putting onto the web materials which are already available to the teacher in various forms (see *distributive use*), but of developing specific materials, designing and creating them according to Distance Education methodologies (Garrison, 2003): thus, teaching materials which, besides being vehicles of disciplinary content, are also able to offer the student a didactic guide to their use, with exercise and self-assessment environments and learning itineraries which are customised to suit the users' varying needs, etc.

Networked Collaborative Learning (NCL): NCL approaches fall under the wider paradigm of Computer-Supported Collaborative Learning (CSCL), (i.e. "an emerging branch of the learning sciences concerned with studying how people can learn together with the help of computers") (Stahl et al., 2006, p.1). CSCL is founded on collaborative learning, as mutual engagement of participants in a coordinated effort to pursue a specific learning goal (Stahl et al., 2006). In other words, while educational resources play a key role in "content-driven" learning to guide the students towards the declared educational goal, NCL educational processes are directly managed by the teacher and are based on the integration between individual and collaborative study (Daradoumis & Marquès, 2000; Trentin, 2010).

NCL can be considered as a specific approach to NBET, which requires the presence of various general conditions in order to be effectively applied; among them we can identify (Felder & Brent, 2001; Palloff & Pratt, 2005):

- the teacher's willingness to redesign the course, making even quite considerable modifications to the version conceived for face-to-face teaching (Paulson, 2002);

- the specific ability of teachers (or tutors) to design learning activities based on online interaction and to organise and manage online learning groups (Klobas et al., 2008);
- the pertinence of the collaborative strategy to the declared educational goals;
- classes with low numbers of students;
- the availability of adequate network services supporting group communication, distance interactions among all participants (students, teachers, tutors, etc.), and structuring of a virtual space, in terms of areas, actors and relative rules;
- students who are able to access frequently the virtual space.

The lack of these essential conditions is often the main cause of the restricted use of NCL in higher education.

At the same time, this low diffusion constitutes a sort of paradox, since the social dimension is a key element in higher education, where there is a strong need for direct teacher/learner contact and where the teachers should adopt a variety of strategies, especially interactive ones, to support learning.

A FOCUS ON HOW TO INTEGRATE NBET IN UNIVERSITY TEACHERS' PRACTICE

One of the most critical aspects linked to the diffusion of NCL approaches is teachers' acquisition of at least the basic skills of Educational Technology Instructional Design (i.e. knowledge and awareness of the main theories, principles, and best practices to design learning processes based on specific educational models and strategies [deriving from the main learning theories] and enhanced by the integration of specific technologies, such as ICT).

In fact, university teachers are essentially experts in a given disciplinary/content domain and they often lack pedagogical skills and know-how. What can be realistically asked of them is to (Young, 2002; Zeminsky & Massy, 2004):

1. make available their knowledge on a specific content domain, together with the methods to teach them;
2. invest a reasonable amount of time in acquiring elementary instructional design skills;
3. acquire familiarity with the typical dynamics of an educational process based on online interaction, and with the methods for conducting it.

In this perspective, a number of faculty training initiatives have been undertaken over the years (De Vries et al., 1995; Grant, 2004) aimed at the sharing of methodological and technological best practices for Educational Technology Instructional Design and targeting those teachers who are interested in innovating their teaching, with particular attention to the social dimension of learning.

Some successful experiences (Trentin, 2006; Klobas et al, 2008; Palloff & Pratt, 2010) have demonstrated that, in order to guarantee a high follow-up rate for faculty training processes, the training stage must be organized around project/problem-based strategies, with one-to-one assistance of the teachers in their first experience of planning online teaching activities. This assistance is fundamental when adopting NCL approaches, since they require constant adaptation of the learning path to the ongoing interaction and collaboration processes.

However, if on the one hand "personalised" faculty training guarantees high follow-up rates, on the other hand it introduces costs which can be afforded only with the support of regional, national or international funding; this is the reason why these initiatives are rarely set up (Trentin, 2006).

The problem is thus how to diffuse NCL best practices at affordable costs, while assuring constant support to the teachers who try to integrate these practices in their courses.

In the following sections, this chapter will present an innovative approach to Educational Technology Instructional Design teacher training, based on a multidimensional scaffolding which fosters teachers to integrate the rules, heuristics and best practices for easily and effectively designing active and collaborative online learning in their everyday activity.

AN INNOVATIVE APPROACH TO TEACHER TRAINING IN EDUCATIONAL TECHNOLOGY INSTRUCTIONAL DESIGN

Over the last twenty years, a number of Instructional Design (ID) models have been proposed and adopted to formalise the design process. ID is defined by Reigeluth *et al.* (2003) as "that branch of knowledge concerned with theory and practice related to instructional strategies and systematic procedures for developing and implementing those strategies" (p.574). Since educational scenarios are often poorly structured and influenced by a number of variables, the main assumption behind ID principles and procedures is that there is no generally effective formula to be applied every time and everywhere, but that the best options must be chosen each time for specific contexts and situations and for particular learning objectives and contents. Thus, the role of models in ID is to provide teachers and designers with conceptual tools fostering the modelling, structuring and management of a learning process. ID models may support the sharing of best practices and thus the training of novices; they also allow meta-analysis and evaluation of the design process itself.

Recently, several authors (Silber, 2007; Jonassen, 2008) have criticised the conventional linear and procedural ID models (Clark, 1995), as well as other recursive and spiral-based models (Tripp & Bichelmeyer, 1990), arguing that ID as practised by expert designers is not a procedure, but a problem-solving process. To tackle design problems experts refer to a mental "template" which is able to capture both declarative knowledge and context-related heuristics (Foshay et al., 2003).

Other critics argue that ID is an iterative process of decision-making and model-building (Jonassen, 2008). The principal role of a designer is to make decisions which help bridge the gap between ideas and reality. These decisions are taken all along the ID process, which proceeds through a progressive contextualization and introduction of constraints, guided by those heuristics and good practices which are held to be effective for a particular problematic situation (Alvino et al., 2009).

According to these premises, one of the first steps for fostering the integration of Educational Technology (especially NBET) ID into teachers' practice should be the sharing and interiorization of heuristics and good practices. Normally teachers develop a meaningful tacit knowledge based on mental schemata that are progressively enriched by everyday experience. Unfortunately, there is not a widespread inclination to make this knowledge explicit and share it, especially in the field of Computer Supported Collaborative Learning (CSCL), and particularly in Networked Collaborative Learning (NCL), where computer-mediated interactions among learners are promoted as a key factor for improving learning, but where good practices in how to structure these interactions have so far been little shared by experts (Koschmann, 1996). But if no generally effective formula is given, novices and unskilled teachers should be able to refer to models and resources which can guide or scaffold them during the design process. In view of this, recent national and international initiatives aimed at promoting the sharing of models of expert designers' heuristics and best practices, as well as learning materials, take on a key role for both informal learning experiences and formal teacher training.

The Sharing of Reusable Learning Resources and Models

In last few years, a number of studies and initiatives have been carried out to support the modelling, formalisation and sharing of ID good practices.

In particular, a number of models and standards have been studied and proposed for the devising of a common semantic and technical way of sharing learning materials (Wiley, 2001; ADL, 2004), and for the making explicit and formalising of design models (Dillenbourg & Hong, 2008).

Current trends in the e-learning field show the benefits arising from investment in the creation, sharing and reuse of *Learning Objects* (LOs) (i.e. "any digital resource that can be reused to support learning") (Wiley, 2001, p.7). According to Wiley's general definition, LOs are digital resources which can be generated with purposes which may be either educational (such as tutorials, self-learning units and modules, but also case studies, webquests, simulations, etc.) or not (such as scientific papers, digital book chapters, glossaries, FAQ lists, etc), and which a teacher can use to enrich and integrate the learning process he/she is designing. Thus, LOs are a specific educational technology which (more or less explicitly) embodies ID strategies (transmissive, active, collaborative, etc.) and techniques (tutorial, multimedia fruition, problem-solving, simulation, etc) (Wiley, 2001), which can be applied to a specific educational context, normally with a small effort of adaptation. So, LOs can be considered precious "items in the teacher's toolbox" which can be used to enrich a module or a course, taking advantage of the experience of other teachers.

But teachers often do not need to search for new learning materials; they rather need for a scaffold when structuring a learning experience integrating Educational Technologies and NBET in particular. So they often search for models which can be adapted and contextualized to their own scenarios, especially in NCL settings, since varying the approaches to structuring students' interactions and to group composition can be very important for successful collaborative learning.

An important bridge has recently been created between collaborative learning and traditional ID methods with *Computer Supported Collaborative Learning scripts* (Dillenbourg & Hong, 2008). CSCL scripts computationally specify, sequence, and distribute the roles and activities involved in a computer-supported collaborative learning situation, thus providing a certain degree of scaffolding for fostering learners' engagement in potentially more effective interactions (Weinberger et al., 2008). Successful collaborative learning normally depends upon effective interaction amongst learners. When they are left to their own devices, they rarely engage in productive interactions. Collaboration scripts aim to foster collaborative learning by shaping the way in which learners interact with one another. These models specify a sequence of learning activities and learners' roles, based on the use of NBET, thus triggering engagement in social and cognitive activities that would otherwise occur rarely or not at all (Kobbe *et al*, 2007).

Recently a distinction has been introduced between *micro-scripts* and *macro-scripts* (Dillenbourg & Hong, 2008, p.7):

- *Micro-scripts* are "dialogue models, mostly argumentation models, which are embedded in the environment and which students are expected to adopt and progressively internalize."
- *Macro-scripts* are "pedagogical models (i.e. they model a sequence of activities to be performed by groups)."

The main difference between them is in the granularity (dimension) of the prescribed actions. For instance a micro-script may automatically prompt a student to respond to post, while a macro-script may model a brainstorming activity in a group.

Macro-scripts can also assume three main levels of abstraction: (a) the *schema level*, which is the most abstract one, presents the solution to a general recurrent educational problem; (b) the *instance level* presents a particular instantiation of the general problem, characterised by specific contents, roles, tools, services and particular target users; (c) the *session level* is the formalized representation of a concrete educational session (Dillenbourg & Hong, 2008).

In this framework, we can place models such as (Alvino, 2008):

- *pedagogical design patterns* (i.e. design-oriented schemas), which embed particular strategies or techniques in order to make good practices transferable; they are not instantiated in a particular knowledge domain or oriented to specific targets, but provide solutions to typical educational problems; although formulated in plain language, they observe particular structural templates, thus they can be considered as a particular type of schema-level macro-scripts;
- *lesson plans*, which represent in plain natural language the instantiation of the solution to a general educational problem in a specific knowledge domain and for a specific target, in terms of objectives, strategies, resources, and so on; these models can be considered as a particular type of instance-level macro-scripts;
- *EML Units of Learning,* which model the flow and structure of modules or entire courses by using formal languages (EML – Educational Modelling Languages; for instance the IMS-LD specification (IMS, 2003)), on the basis of their embedded methods, proposed activities, the roles involved, services and resources; like *lesson plans*, these models can be considered as a particular type of instance-level macro-scripts, but they differ from the former in being automatically interpretable by computers.

Macro-scripts in particular have shown a very interesting potential in providing a scaffold for teachers designing collaborative learning experiences based on NBET. Several types of research initiatives have tackled this challenge by investigating: the identification of templates for devising a common way of formalising and sharing these resources (e.g. *Pedagogical Pattern Project, TELL project*); the creation of communities in which CSCL scripts are shared and exchanged; the definition of CSCL script design processes based on the reuse of patterns, exemplars, and other script components (Alvino et al, 2009); and the development of CSCL script authoring tools based on practitioner-friendly abstractions and graphic representations (Hernández-Leo et al, 2006).

Both LOs and CSCL scripts could provide teachers with a fundamental scaffold. Despite this, very few teachers are aware of the potential of reusing LOs and scripts, and many of them do not know how to search, find and integrate these resources into their learning initiatives.

In order to tackle this problem, a first fundamental step is *to support the sharing of LOs and design models in open and free repositories*. In this perspective, a number of national and international initiatives have been carried out to set up repositories of LOs (such as *Merlot, Ariadne Knowledge Pool*, the *GEM Catalog,* etc.), pedagogical design patterns (such as *The Pedagogical Pattern Project*), lesson plans (such as *Curriki, EDSITEment, Education World*)[5], and other scripts.

Accessing these systems teachers can concretely identify LO which fit their needs and reuse them by downloading a file or simply annotating their location (URL). Subscribing to the communities underpinning these repositories, teachers can also share the resources they authored, although filtered by an evaluation process of their quality.

Furthermore, local initiatives supporting the sharing of educational resources and design models are more and more widespread; local, targeted and customized repositories are normally developed to fulfil the specific needs of determinate educational institutions, such as Universities or training centres, or specific professionals, or particular content domains and topics. Like the international initiatives, normally the repository is underpinned by a community, which can be both virtual and presencial.

In any case, sharing educational materials is not a straightforward task for teachers, but requires them to invest their time in searching for resources which fit their needs, and to prepare new contributions in easily re-usable and adaptable form. *Teachers' motivation to share and reuse LOs and CSCL scripts should be fostered* though easy-to-use systems which allow retrieval of high-quality and effective resources. An early example in this direction is the *Merlot project repository*, which promotes teachers' confidence in availing themselves of the repository by offering a quality guarantee, at least to a certain extent, for the LOs that can be retrieved; it also adds value to these LOs by including user comments and proposals for assignments. In this way, repositories of educational resources for TEL could turn into a basis for the formation of teachers' learning communities.

The possibility to express and formulate their actual needs through the retrieval system, so as to find the most adequate resources for each situation, is a fundamental condition to motivate teachers to share and reuse digital educational resources. Unfortunately, most of the international metadata standards used to describe LOs (see for example *Dublin Core Metadata Element Set Version* 1.1 (DCMI, 2003) or the *Learning Object Metadata* standard (IEEE, 2002)) are unable to give a clear pedagogical picture of them or to describe design models adequately. In addition, it is a hard challenge to devise metadata models which can be successfully employed by a wide variety of user communities, as these are usually characterised by different languages, backgrounds, motivations and objectives. To overcome this limitation, recent studies analyse the problem from the perspective of educational practice, proposing metadata application profiles which include pedagogical descriptors which are able to describe NBET dimensions and which can be selected according to the orientation and the objectives of specific user communities (e.g., GEM http://thegateway.org/, EDNA - http://www.edna.edu.au/). The POEM (*Pedagogy Oriented Educational Metadata*) model, for instance, has been progressively moulded on the needs of a variety of teachers' communities involved in its validation process; it aims to capture the main educational characteristics of both LOs and scripts, such as CSCL macro-scripts, including learning strategies, suggested activities, contextual information, etc.(Alvino et al., 2008).

A Multidimensional Scaffolding Supporting Teachers to Build a Personal ID Mental Model

Providing novices and unskilled teachers with examples of best practices and reusable learning materials is a fundamental step towards enriching their expertise. Unfortunately, this step is often not sufficient to foster the integration of these heuristics into everyday practice. In fact, teachers often do not know for instance how to integrate LOs and scripts into the learning experiences they are designing. Whereas expert designers tackle educational design problems on the basis of a well-known and shared set of principles and heuristics that form their mental model (Silber, 2007), novices or unskilled teachers who have not yet developed the same mental structure cannot act likewise, unless supported by a scaffold. Thus, initially they need to refer to a simplified and structured model in order to approach the design problem.

Teacher training in the field of ID should take these premises into account. *Teachers should be fostered to build a personal ID mental model* by providing them with *a scaffolding that progressively fades out* once the mental model is more structured. This should be a "multidimensional" scaffolding characterized by:

- *basic general ID models*, which provide a clear structure for the main steps and decisions of an ID process, especially in the field of NCL;
- *reusable educational resources and models*, such as LOs and CSCL scripts, that teachers can retrieve on the Web and reuse to design individual or collaborative activities or entire courses;
- *heuristics and best practices* concerning (a) how to progressively introduce recursivity into the basic general ID models and (b) how to integrate reusable resources into an ID process (especially if based on NBET)

According to this approach, teachers should primarily build their own ID mental model on *a clear structure of the main steps of an ID process*. To this end, traditional models such as ADDIE[6] (Clark, 1995) turn out to be very useful, since they can be considered as phase models of problem-solving, which try to represent what an expert designer knows schematically, procedurally, and in an outlined form (Jonassen, 2008). Although we could identify at least 13 versions of the ADDIE model, each of them is characterized by a "cascade" sequence of design steps and by the fact that the output of each design phase is the input of the following one. Using these models as a reference in ID teacher training could help to clearly outline the main elements, constraints and decisions which characterize each phase and which are necessary to develop the subsequent steps. In particular, when designing a NBET-based NCL experience, it is fundamental to identify and take into account some initial constraints, such as (Alvino et al, 2009): (a) economic and financial constraints, (b) user-profiling constraints, (c) context-related constraints, and (d) technological constraints. In addition, the teacher or the designer has to take some decisions on a number of fundamental topics, such as (Trentin, 2001; Alvino, 2009):

- definition of the aims of the learning process and structuring of the learning objectives;
- definition and structuring of the learning content;
- definition of the learning strategies and techniques (and possible reuse of schema-level CSCL scripts, such as pedagogical design patterns);
- definition of the learning activities (and possible reuse of instance-level CSCL scripts, such as lesson plans) and of the learning groups (in terms of number, dimension and composition).
- definition of the required learning resources: identification of already-available resources, development of new ones, reuse of LOs retrieved on the Web;
- definition of monitoring and evaluation aims, criteria and indicators;
- definition of course schedule and other detailed design elements;
- identification of the communication needs and of the interaction channels and rules;
- definition and structuring of tools and areas characterizing the Learning Management System (LMS) (or other systems and tools supporting the networked learning process).

When an expert designer tackles ID as a problem-solving process, he/she normally does not analyse these topics exactly in this order; firstly he/she focuses on some decisions and then refines the design through an iterative and recursive process. This can be done because expert designers are well aware of the reciprocal conditioning of the different design elements. Thus the "cascade" structure could provide a first fundamental scaffold for novices, since it acts as an "ordinate checklist" which reminds them of the fundamental steps they should not neglect.

Once this basic structure has been embedded in unskilled teachers' mental ID model, they could be provided with *heuristics and best practices about how to introduce recursivity into the linear-cascade model*, progressively approaching a problem-solving perspective.

A first step could be to identify a *two-layered design process* characterized by a *macro-design phase* and a *micro-design phase* (Trentin, 2001). The linear-cascade model is split into two main partially-overlapping ID phases (see Figure 2). In the "macro" phase, aims, objectives, contents, learning strategies and evaluation criteria are generally defined and outlined. In the following "micro" phase there is an iterative process of revision and/or integration of what has been defined in the macro-design; each decisional topic being reviewed and defined in greater detail; subsequently, learning techniques, activities, groups and resources are defined, together with the characteristics of the monitoring process, the schedule, etc. Parallel to the two-layered process, interaction and communication issues are tackled and technological decisions taken.

This model has revealed its effectiveness in a number of faculty courses and teacher training curricula (Trentin, 2006; Klobas et al., 2008).

Once they are skilled in managing this two-layered ID process, teachers could try to carry out more iterative processes of revision. To this end, they should be provided with *further rules and heuristics to effectively manage the constraints which characterize the ID of a NCL process based on NBET.*

In fact, in a NCL process we can identify three main types of constraint (Alvino et al., 2009): 1) *initial*: technical, financial and contextual constraints characterizing the specific learning context); 2) *structural*: constraints deriving from choices and decisions taken during the design process which condition posterior choices (i.e. objectives, contents, etc.); 3) *heuristic*: constraints related to the application of the heuristics and good practices for effectively structuring the learning

Figure 2. A comparison of three ID models: the ADDIE model, the two-layered design model and the Recursive Constraints Analysis model

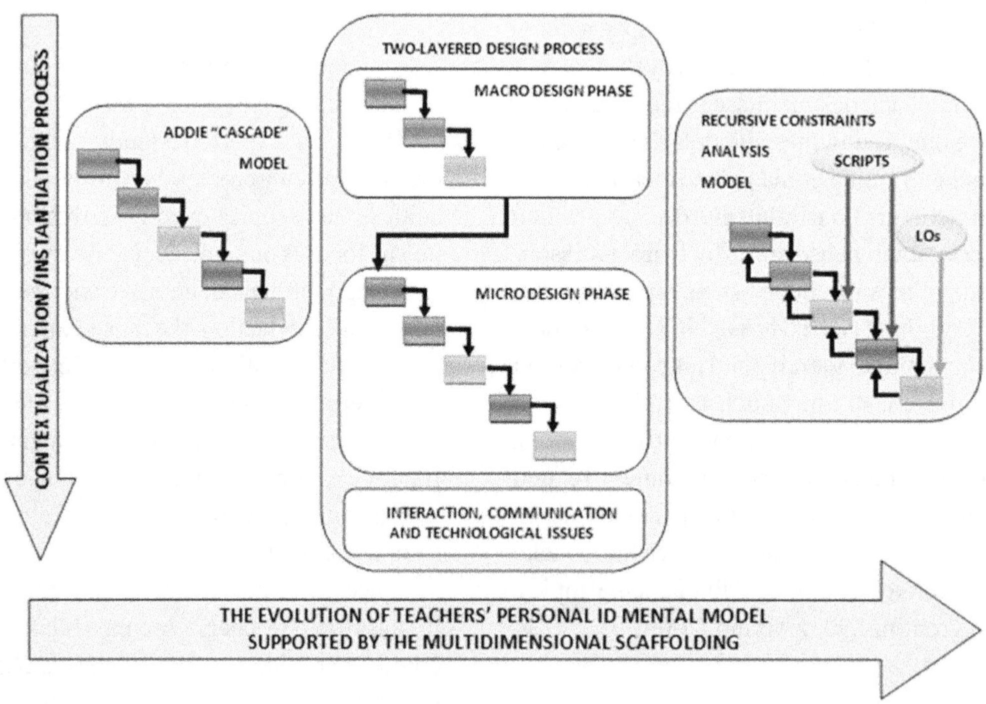

community, organizing collaborative activities and modelling the learning environment. According to the *Recursive Constraints Analysis model* (Alvino, 2008), each decision taken during the ID process and concerning the above mentioned topics: (a) should take into account the initial, structural and heuristic constraints introduced before that step and (b) might introduce new structural and heuristic constraints which will condition subsequent choices. If previous structural and heuristic constraints conflict with the new decisions, some changes could be introduced into the design without modifying the general framework. In this way, to obtain a coherent instructional design, *teachers need to assume a permanent attitude of iterative review* (see Figure. 2). *These rules are especially true when teachers want to integrate LOs and CSCL scripts into the ID process*. In fact, these resources are normally characterized by structural and heuristic constraints which have to be taken into account when integrating them into a specific ID process. As stressed before, LOs and CSCL scripts can be integrated at different steps of the ID process, when defining learning strategies, techniques, activities and materials. For instance teachers should be aware that specific collaborative activities require specific tools (such as forum, wiki, etc.) and specific group configurations, or *social structures*, in terms of number, dimension, composition and participants' tasks (Persico & Sarti, 2005; Alvino et al., 2009).

All the heuristics and good practices characterizing the scaffolding described above should be supplied to teachers gradually, so they can be integrated step-by-step into their mental ID model.

FUTURE RESEARCH DIRECTIONS

The multidimensional scaffold presented in this work is a conceptual framework which is useful for guiding teacher trainers in their task of supplying the necessary support to novices and unskilled teachers as they build their own mental ID model, especially when involved in the design of processes based on NBET. Although the joint effect of theory and practice, together with effective educational resources and individual and collaborative activities (such as case-study, designing and meta-analysis) could successfully support teachers, new research directions are currently showing potential advances in the ID field related to *Computer-Aided Instructional Design (CAID)*.

In particular, new research lines are investigating the possibility of embedding the above- mentioned innovative ID models and best practices in a new generation of software which are able to support unskilled teachers in the process of designing a material, an activity or a course. These systems would provide a further important scaffold, guiding the user through the different phases of the design process, by means of a user-friendly interface.

Currently, new research lines focused, for instance, on the formalization of CSCL scripts, are systematically translated into practice only by initiatives which implement *Learning Design*-based (IMS, 2003) authoring tools and platforms (such as *Recourse Learning Design Editor* or *LAMS - Learning Activity Management System*). The LD theories aim to structure the learning process by modelling reusable Units of Learning which are represented by means of formal languages (*EML - Educational Modelling Languages*) and are thus interpretable also by automatic agents. (Koper, 2001). Unfortunately, the Learning Design standard (IMS-LD) (IMS, 2003) has shown important limitations when modelling collaborative processes based on NBET, since in the current version of IMS-LD there is no way to directly represent groups as "entities"; this limitation leads to some difficulties in modelling collaborative learning processes, since these involve, among other things, the definition of groups or the structuring of the flow of collaborative learning activities (Miao et al., 2005).

Other initiatives aimed at improving and integrating the IMS-LD have demonstrated that macro-scripts, when embedded in the interface of CAID design tools (see e.g. *COLLAGE* (Hernandez-Leo et al., 2006))[7], could provide a useful support in the design process (Hernández-Leo et al., 2006).

In addition, current trends are showing the effective role of *diagram-based graphical representation of ID best practices and CSCL scripts* in CAID tools. In fact, formalisms such as UML diagrams, conceptual maps, flowcharts, decision trees, etc. are widely used in education to represent and clarify complex relationships or flows characterizing educational processes based on NBET. For instance, Alvino et al. (2009) provided evidence for the useful support offered by a new formalism for modelling and visualizing social structures involved in a CSCL activity, called *Social Structure Representation* (SSRs). SSRs are diagrams whose aim is to complement existing CSCL scripts with hints and best practices concerning the design of collaborative groups' social structures (in terms of number of groups, dimension, composition, etc.) for a particular learning environment (including resources, tools and services). Similarly to this proposal for the use of SSRs, there are other research initiatives (Paquette, 2005; Persico & Sarti, 2005) which deal with visual artefacts for supporting educational modelling and instructional design tasks.

Future research should take into account the potential of embedding Educational Technology ID models and CSCL scripts in CAID systems. Via a user-friendly interface, these best practices could underpin the design process performed by the teacher, even fostering the interiorization of those practices. During the ID process, innovative systems could dynamically show (for instance through formalisms such as SSRs) all the implications of the teacher's decisions on the educational process in terms of (structural and heuristic) constraints, thus supporting a highly-aware authoring process. Lessons resulting from the instantiation of CSCL scripts could be stored in a repository (integrated into the CAID system) and shared as well the LOs they suggest to use, thus favouring the generation of a teacher community.

CONCLUSION

The introduction of NBET into higher education is a long process which is strongly conditioned by many variables, such as, for instance, the actual skills of faculty members in the educational uses of ICT and in the related instructional design approaches. Furthermore, teachers' initial experiences of using NBET are generally awkward, thus it would be useful to provide them with support in their choice of methods, in accordance with the learning objectives.

For this reason, the chapter highlights two key conditions for fostering the process of spreading NBET, and especially NCL, in higher education:

- the setting up of *ad hoc* faculty training courses aimed at introducing Educational Technology Instructional Design to teachers and at laying the foundations for regular use of these methodologies;
- providing teachers with a direct and an indirect scaffolding when involved in their first experiences as instructional designers of NCL activities and courses based on NBET.

Teachers should be made aware that their role will change when adopting NBET approaches. In fact, although teachers continue to play a central role in TEL, their role inevitably tends to change from a traditional teacher to a facilitator of the learning process: this figure is expected to provide learners with both a direct support, concerning contents, methodologies and coordinating issues, and an indirect scaffold based on a set of resources, practices, models and tools made available to them. This change can be observed particularly when NCL approaches are adopted; in fact, NCL activities cannot draw on the same criteria which underpin face-to-face collaborative learning. In this perspective, academic teachers need to master NBET methods and interiorize heuristics aimed to exploit those dynamics that make computer mediated communication (CMC) an effective learning strategy.

Once outlined the main issues and dynamics which have conditioned the rare and limited adoption of NCL methodologies in higher education, this chapter has proposed an innovative solution to Educational Technology ID teacher training, aimed at fostering their wider diffusion. This approach requires the teacher trainer to manage direct and indirect support and to propose theory and practice in a flexible way, gradually introducing elements of complexity and variability and progressively fading out the scaffolding. To provide the described multidimensional scaffolding, teacher trainers should be expert instructional designers who master NBET methods and best practices for the design of CSCL and NCL experiences, as well as the know-how to use the main resources, models and tools which could support unskilled teachers in the design process. In addition, NBET methods, CSCL and NCL should be learnt first-hand, so faculty training should include active and collaborative online activities, such as case study, problem-solving, learning-by-designing, etc. Setting up effective faculty training courses therefore requires particular attention both in choosing the teaching staff, and in defining the learning and communication management tools.

Important support in carrying out these initiatives could come from CAID systems. The chapter outlines a number of research lines investigating different ways of providing unskilled teachers with a computer-based scaffolding which is able to guide them throughout the ID process. Some of these research lines continue to comply with the IMS-LD standard, trying to improve and integrate it, others try to overcome its limitations. These research directions, especially those dealing with diagram-based or visual artefact-based graphic representation of ID best practices, could effectively enhance the integration of Educational Technology Instructional Design into teachers' practice, and consequently integration of NBET and NCL into higher education.

REFERENCES

Adam, P., & Warren, L. (2008). A strategy for educational technology in higher education. *Journal of Computer Assisted Learning, 10*(1), 50–54.

ADL - Advanced Distributed Learning Initiative. (2004). *SCORM 2004 – v. 1.3*. Retrieved July 10, 2010, from http://www.adlnet.gov/downloads/205.cfm

Alvino, S. (2008). *Computer supported collaborative learning e riusabilità: Un approccio all'integrazione di risorse riusabili in processi di apprendimento collaborativo* [CSCL and reusability: an approach to the integration of reusable resources in collaborative learning processes]. Unpublished doctoral thesis, University of Genoa, Genoa, Italy.

Alvino S., Asensio-Perez J. I., Dimitriadis Y., & Hernandez-Leo, D. (2009). Supporting the reuse of effective CSCL learning designs through social structures representations. *Distance Education - Special Issue on Learning Design, 30*(2), 239–258.

Alvino, S., Forcheri, P., Ierardi, M. G., & Sarti, L. (2008). Describing learning features of reusable resources: A proposal. *International Journal of Social Science, 2*(3), 156–162.

Attwell, G. (2005). *E-learning and sustainability. EdTechPost: Technology for learning, thinking and collaborating.* Retrieved June 30, 2010, from: http://www.ossite.org/Members/GrahamAttwell/sustainibility/attach/sustainibility4.doc

Attwell, G. (2007). The personal learning environments: The future of eLearning? *eLearning Papers, 2*(1). Retrieved June 30, 2010, from http://www.elearningeuropa.info/files/media/media11561.pdf

Bates, T. (2003). *Higher education and e-learning: Integration or change?* Presentation. University of British Columbia. Retrieved April 30, 2010 from http://bates.cstudies.ubc.ca/

Briggs, S. (2005). Changing roles and competencies in academics. *Active Learning in Higher Education, 6*, 256–268. doi:10.1177/1469787405057753

Bronfenbrenner, U. (1979). *The ecology of human development*. Cambridge, MA: Harvard University Press.

Brown, A., & Palincsar, A. (1989). Guided cooperative learning and individual knowledge acquisition. In Resnick, L. B. (Ed.), *Knowing, learning, and instruction* (pp. 393–451). Hillsdale, NJ: Lawrence Erlbaum.

Bruffee, K. A. (1999). *Collaborative learning: Higher education, interdependence, and the authority of knowledge*. Baltimore, MD: Johns Hopkins University Press.

Clark, D. (1995). *Introduction to instructional system design. Performance, learning, leadership, & knowledge*. Retrieved June 13, 2010, from http://www.nwlink.com/~donclark/hrd/sat1.html

Collazos, C., Guerrero, L., Pino, J., & Ochoa, S. (2004). A method for evaluating computer-supported collaborative learning processes. *International Journal of Computer Applications in Technology, 19*, 151–161. doi:10.1504/IJCAT.2004.004044

Collins, B., & Van der Wende, M. (2002). *Models of technology and change in higher education: An international comparative survey on the current and future use of ICT in higher education. Technical Report*. Enschede, The Netherlands: University of Twente, Center for Higher Education Policy Studies.

Creighton, J. V., & Buchanan, P. (2001). Toward the e-campus: Using the Internet to strengthen, rather than replace, the campus experience. *EDUCAUSE Review, 36*, 12–13.

Culligan, M. (2003). Digital natives in the classroom. In B. Hoffman (Ed.), *Encyclopedia of educational technology*. Retrieved October 28, 2010, from http://www.etc.edu.cn/eet/eet/articles/learnstrategy/

Daradoumis, T., & Marquès, J. M. (2000). A methodological approach to networked collaborative learning: Design and pedagogy issues. In M. Asensio, J. Foster, V. Hodgson, & D. McConnell (Eds.), *Proceedings of the 2000 International Conference on Innovative Approaches to Lifelong Learning and Higher Education through the Internet*, (pp. 72 – 77). Lancaster, England.

Davies, H. C., & Fill, K. (2007). *Embedded blended learning in university's teaching culture: Experiences and reflections*. Retrieved October 28, 2010, from http://eprints.ecs.soton.ac.uk/14600/

DCMI - Dublin Core Metadata Initiative. (2003). *Dublin core metadata element set, version 1.1: Reference description*. Retrieved January 30, 2010, from http://www.dublincore.org/documents/dces/

De Vries, L., Naidu, S., Jegede, O., & Collis, B. (1995). On-line professional staff development: An evaluation study. *Distance Education, 16*(1), 157–173. doi:10.1080/0158791950160112

Dillenbourg, P., & Hong, F. (2008). The mechanics of macro scripts. *International Journal of Computer-Supported Collaborative Learning, 3*(1). March, 2008. New York, NY: Springer. Retrieved January 03, 2010, from http://www.springerlink.com/content/9q14234gx52x1784/

Elliot, B. (2008). *E-pedagogy: Does e-learning require a new approach to teaching and learning?* Retrieved March 28, 2010, from http://d.scribd.com/docs/22rc8wz72z067xrb1fpk.pdf

Felder, R., & Brent, E. (2001). Effective strategies for cooperative learning. *Journal of Cooperation and Collaboration in College Teaching, 10*(2), 66–75.

Fink, L. D. (1999). *Active learning. Oklahoma instructional development program*. Retrieved January 30, 2010, from http://honolulu.hawaii.edu/intranet/committees/FacDevCom/guidebk/teachtip/active.htm

Foshay, W. R., Silber, K. S., & Stelnicki, M. B. (2003). *Writing training that works*. San Francisco, CA: Pfeiffer/Jossey-Bass.

Garrison, D. R. (2003). Self-directed learning and distance education. In Moore, M. G., & Anderson, W. G. (Eds.), *Handbook of distance education* (pp. 113–127). New Jersey: Lawrence Erlbaum Associates, Inc., Publishers.

Grant, M. M. (2004). Learning to teach with the web: Factors influencing teacher education faculty. *The Internet and Higher Education, 7*, 329–341. doi:10.1016/j.iheduc.2004.09.005

Gunawardena, C. N. (1995). Social presence theory and implications for interaction and collaborative learning in computer conference. *International Journal of Educational Telecommunications, 1*(2/3), 147–166.

Hernández-Leo, D., Villasclaras-Fernández, E. D., Asensio-Pérez, J. I., Dimitriadis, Y., Jorrín-Abellán, I. M., Ruiz-Requies, I., & Rubia-Avi, B. (2006). COLLAGE: A collaborative learning design editor based on patterns. *Journal of Educational Technology & Society, 9*(1), 58–71.

Howell, S. L., Williams, P. B., Lindsay, N. K., & Laws, R. D. (2004). Trends affecting distance education and distance learning. *Online Journal of Distance Learning Administration*. Retrieved March 28, 2010, from: http://www.teenet.net/thirtytwotrends.htm

IEEE - Learning Technology Standards Observatory. (2002). *Learning object metadata*. Retrieved June 13, 2010, from http://ltsc.ieee.org/wg12/files/LOM_1484_12_1_v1_Final_Draft.pdf

IMS. (2003). *Learning design v 1.0 final specification*. Retrieved June 22, 2010, from http://www.imsglobal.org/learningdesign/index.cfm

Januszewski, A., & Molenda, M. (Eds.). (2008). *Educational technology: A definition with commentary*. New York, NY: Lawrence Erlbaum Associates.

Jonassen, D. H. (2008). Instructional design as design problem solving: An iterative process. *Educational Technology, 48*(3), 21–26.

Kirkwood, A. (2009). E-learning: You don't always get what you hope for. *Technology, Pedagogy and Education, 18*(2), 107–121. doi:10.1080/14759390902992576

Klobas, J., Renzi, S., & Trentin, G. (2008). Approaching TEL in university teaching: Trends and faculty training need. In M. Kendall & B. Samways (Eds.), *Proceedings of the WCC 2008*, Milan 8-10 September, (pp. 145-148). New York, NY: Springer.

Kobbe, L., Weinberger, A., Dillenbourg, P., Harrer, A., Hämäläinen, R., & Fischer, F. (2007). Specifying computer-supported collaboration scripts. *International Journal of Computer-Supported Collaborative Learning, 2*(2-3), 211–224. doi:10.1007/s11412-007-9014-4

Koper, E. J. R. (2001). *Modelling units of study from a pedagogical perspective: The pedagogical metamodel behind EML*. Heerlen, The Netherlands: Open Universiteit Nederland. Retrieved June 01, 2010, from http://eml.ou.nl/introduction/docs/ped-metamodel.pdf

Koschmann, T. D. (1996). *CSCL: Theory and practice of an emerging paradigm*. New Jersey: Lawrence Erlbaum Associates.

Kreijns, K., & Kirschner, P. A. (2004). Determining sociability, social space, and social presence in (a)synchronous collaborative teams. *Cyberpsychology & Behavior*, *7*(2), 155–172. doi:10.1089/109493104323024429

LAMS. (2010). *Learning Activity Management System website*. Retrieved from http://www.lamsinternational.com/

Longmire, W. (2000). *A primer on learning objects*. Retrieved October 28, 2010, from http://www.astd.org/LC/2000/0300_longmire.htm

MacDonald, J. (2008). *Blended learning and online tutoring*. Aldershot, UK: Gower.

Miao, Y., Hoeksema, K., Hoppe, H. U., & Harrer, A. (2005). CSCL scripts: Modelling features and potential use. In T. Koschmann, D. Suthers & T. W. Chan (Eds.), *Proceedings of the Computer Supported Collaborative Learning 2005: The Next 10 Years!* (pp. 423-432). Mahwah, NJ: Lawrence Erlbaum.

Naisbitt, J. (1984). *Megatrends: ten new directions changing our lives*. New York, NY: Warner Books.

Palloff, R. M., & Pratt, K. (2005). *Collaborating online: Learning together in community*. San Francisco, CA: Jossey-Bass.

Palloff, R. M., & Pratt, K. (2010). Faculty training and mentoring at a distance: Learning together in the virtual community. In Luppicini, R., & Haghi, A. K. (Eds.), *Cases on digital technology in higher education* (pp. 111–125). Hershey, PA: IGI Global. doi:10.4018/978-1-61520-869-2.ch008

Paquette, G., Léonard, M., Ludgren-Cayrol, K., Mihaila, S., & Gareau, D. (2005). Learning design based on graphical modelling. *Educational Technology & Society, 9*(1), 97-112. Retrieved January 13, 2010, from http://ares.licef.teluq.uqam.ca/Portals/29/docs/pub/ingenierie/Graphic%20Knowledgebased%20V2.pdf

Paulson, K. (2002). Reconfiguring faculty roles for virtual settings. *The Journal of Higher Education, 73*, 123–140. doi:10.1353/jhe.2002.0010

Pedagogical Pattern Project. (2010). *Pedagogical pattern website*. Retrieved from http://www.pedagogicalpattern.org

Persico, D., & Sarti, L. (1995). Social structures for online learning: A design perspective. *Proceedings of Conference on Methods and Technologies for Learning*, (pp. 51-60). Palermo, Italia.

Recourse Learning Design Editor. (2010). *Recourse learning design editor website*. Retrieved from http://tencompetence-project.bolton.ac.uk/ldauthor/index.html

(1999). InReigeluth, C. M. (Ed.). Instructional design theories and models: *Vol. 2. A new paradigm for instructional design theory*. Mahwah, NJ: Lawrence Erlbaum Associates.

Reigeluth, C. M., Molenda, M., & Nelson, L. M. (2003). Instructional design. In Nadel, L. (Ed.), *Encyclopedia of cognitive sciences* (*Vol. 2*, pp. 574–578). UK: Nature Publishing Group.

Salmon, G. (2002). *E-tivities: The key to active online learning*. London, UK: Kogan Page.

Salmon, G. (2004). *E-moderating: The key to teaching and learning online*. London, UK: Kogan Page.

Sauter, V. L. (2003). Web design studio: A preliminary experiment in facilitating faculty use of the web. In Aggarwal, A. K. (Ed.), *Web-based education: Learning from experience* (pp. 131–154). Hershey, PA: Information Science Publishing. doi:10.4018/9781591401025.ch009

Seufert, S., & Euler, D. (2003). Sustainability of e-learning innovations: Findings of expert interviews. Retrieved January 13, 2010, from http://www.scil.ch/publications/docs/2003-06-seufert-euler-sustainability-elearning.pdf

Shamsuar, N. (2008). *Multimedia in computer-aided learning application: Usage and effectiveness*. Saarbrücken, Germany: VDM.

Silber, K. H. (2007). A principle-based model of instructional design: A new way of thinking about and teaching ID. *Educational Technology, 47*(5), 5–19.

Stahl, G., Koschmann, T., & Suthers, D. (2006). Computer-supported collaborative learning: An historical perspective. In Sawyer, R. K. (Ed.), *Cambridge handbook of the learning sciences* (pp. 409–426). Cambridge, UK: Cambridge University Press.

TELL. (2010). *Project website*. Retrieved from http://cosy.ted.unipi.gr/tell/

Trentin, G. (2001). Designing online courses. In Maddux, C. D., & LaMont Johnson, D. (Eds.), *The web in higher education: Assessing the impact and fulfilling the potential* (pp. 47–66). London & Oxford, UK: The Haworth Press Inc.

Trentin, G. (2006). The Xanadu project: Training faculty in the use of ICT for university teaching. *International Journal of Computer Assisted Learning, 22*, 82–196.

Trentin, G. (2008). Technology enhanced learning and university teaching: Different approaches for different purposes. *International Journal on E-Learning, 7*(1), 117–132.

Trentin, G. (2010). *Network collaborative learning: Social interaction and active learning*. Oxford, UK: Chandos Publishing Limited.

Tripp, S., & Bichelmeyer, B. (1990). Rapid prototyping: An alternative instructional design strategy. *Educational Technology Research and Development, 38*(1), 31–44. doi:10.1007/BF02298246

VandenBos, G., Knapp, S., & Doe, J. (2001). Role of reference elements in the selection of resources by psychology undergraduates. [from http://jbr.org/articles.html]. *Journal of Bibliographic Research, 5*, 117–123. Retrieved October 13, 2001.

Vygotsky, L. S. (1978). *Mind and society: The development of higher psychological processes*. Cambridge, MA: Harvard University Press.

Weinberger, A., Collar, I., Dimitriadis, Y., Mäkitalo-Siegl, K., & Fischer, F. (2008). Computer-supported collaboration scripts: Theory and practice of scripting CSCL. Perspectives of educational psychology and computer science. In Balacheff, N., Ludvigsen, S., Jong, T. d., Lazonder, A., Barnes, S., & Montandon, L. (Eds.), *Technology-enhanced learning. Principles and products* (pp. 155–174). Springer Verlag.

Wiley, D. A. (2001). *The instructional use of learning objects*. Retrieved July 10, 2010, from http://reusability.org/read/

Young, J. R. (2002). Hybrid teaching seeks to end the divide between traditional and online instruction. *The Chronicle of Higher Education, 48*(28), A33-A34. Retrieved May 30, 2010, from http://chronicle.com/free/v48/i28/28a03301.htm

Zemsky, R., & Massy, W. F. (2004). *Thwarted innovation: What happened to e-learning and why*. Final Report for The Weatherstation Project of the Learning Alliance at University of Pennsylvania. Retrieved June 01, 2010, from http://www.csudh.edu/dearhabermas/WeatherStation_Report.pdf

ADDITIONAL READING

Dillenbourg, P. (2002). Over-scripting CSCL: The risks of blending collaborative learning with instructional design. In P. A. Kirschner (Ed), *Three worlds of CSCL. Can we support CSCL,* (pp 61-91). Heerlen: Open Universiteit Nederland.

Gustafson, K. L., & Branch, R. (2002). *Survey of instructional design models* (4th ed.). Syracuse, NY: ERIC.

Littlejohn, A. (Ed.). (2004). *Reusing online resources*. London: Kogan Page.

Rowland, G. (1992). What do instructional designers actually do? An initial investigation of expert practice. *Performance Improvement Quarterly, 5*(2), 65–86. doi:10.1111/j.1937-8327.1992.tb00546.x

KEY TERMS AND DEFINITIONS

Computer Supported Collaborative Learning (CSCL): An emerging branch of the learning sciences concerned with studying how people can learn together with the help of computers. CSCL is based on the concept of collaborative learning as the mutual engagement of participants in a coordinated effort to pursue a specific learning goal.

CSCL Script: A CSCL script computationally specifies, sequences, and distributes the roles and activities involved in a computer-supported collaborative learning situation, thus providing a certain degree of scaffolding for fostering learners' engagement in more potentially effective interactions. Collaboration scripts aim to foster collaborative learning in shaping the way in which learners interact with one another, thus triggering engagement in social and cognitive activities that would otherwise occur rarely or not at all.

Educational Technology: The study and ethical practice of facilitating learning and improving performance by creating, using, and managing appropriate technological processes and resources.

Educational Technology Instructional Design: A branch of theoretical and practical knowledge which identifies the main theories, principles and best practices to design learning processes based on specific educational models and strategies (deriving from the main learning theories) and enhanced by the integration of specific technologies, such as ICT.

Instructional Design (ID): Instructional Design is a branch of theoretical and practical knowledge which identifies and models the rules governing the choice of the most suitable learning methods for the pursuit of specific educational goals, taking into account the context-related variables and limitations.

Learning Object (LO): Any digital resource that can be reused to support learning, and integrated by a teacher into the learning process he/she is designing so as to enrich it; learning objects can be generated with explicit educational purposes, such as tutorials, self-learning units and modules, but also as case studies, web quests, simulations, etc., or not; in the second case they are normally integrated in the learning process as reference resources, such as scientific papers, digital book chapters, glossaries, FAQ lists, etc.

Network-Based Educational Technology (NBET): The specific area of ET which focuses on the educational use of network technology.

Networked Collaborative Learning (NCL): A learning approach supported by a computer network and (above all) underpinned by a network of inter-relationships that link up the learners along the educational process. These inter-relationships help the members of a learning community to collaborate together in pursuit of a specific learning goal. So the network should be considered primarily as a network of individuals rather than merely a computer network for distance communication between the same individuals.

Scaffolding: The concept of scaffolding derives from constructivist theories and is closely bound up with the supposed need of learners to have recourse to external human, technical and organisational support systems in order to exercise and expand their inner potential. These support systems may develop on both the intellectual, social and affective planes, and may derive either from the direct action of the teacher or an indirect action. The latter consists in the setting up, preparation and continual integration into the learning environment of learning and support tools and resources which facilitate the learning process.

ENDNOTES

1. Association for Educational Communications and Technology.
2. Learning Management System.
3. Content Management System / Course Management System.
4. The overview is the result of various studies carried out in several Italian university between 1999 and 2006
5. The URL of the main repositories cited in this section are: Merlot http://www.merlot.org; Ariadne Knowledge Pool: http://ariadne.cs.kuleuven.be/silo2006/NewFederatedQuery.do; the GEM Catalog http://www.thegateway.org/browse; The Pedagogical Pattern Project: http://www.pedagogicalpatterns.org/; Curriki: http://www.curriki.org; EDSITEment: http://edsitement.neh.gov/; Education World: http://www.education-world.com/a_lesson/index.shtml
6. ADDIE is an acronym deriving from the main phases of the model itself: Analysis, Design, Development, Implementation, Evaluation
7. . Collage, a high-level IMS-LD compliant authoring tool that is specialized for CSCL Collage helps teachers in the process of creating their own potentially effective collaborative Learning Designs by reusing and customizing patterns, according to the requirements of a particular learning situation. These patterns, called Collaborative Learning Flow Patterns (CLFPs), represent best practices that are repetitively used by practitioners when structuring the flow of (collaborative) learning activities.

Chapter 18
Social Network Informed Design for Learning with Educational Technology

Caroline Haythornthwaite
University of British Columbia, Canada

Maarten de Laat
Open Universiteit Nederland, The Netherlands

ABSTRACT

This chapter discusses and illustrates how knowledge of social networks can be used to inform social and technical design for learning and teaching in higher education. The chapter introduces the social network perspective and how this can be used to explore learning. It shows how a relational approach can be used to explore the basis of learning ties, uncover social roles and positions, and form a basis for a network's social capital. This is followed by a discussion of current research directions illustrating how this approach can be applied in education. This research indicates how knowledge of informal learning networks can facilitate informed design for learning, teaching, and professional development.

INTRODUCTION

This chapter describes features of social networks that can be tapped to improve social and technical design for learning, teaching and professional development in higher education. By *social networks* we mean the configurations of connectivity that exist when people interact with each other by communicating, sharing resources, and working, learning or playing together, supported through face-to-face interaction as well as through the use of educational, and information and communication technology. Each interaction defines a connection between people, known as a social network tie. These ties vary in strength from weak to strong according to the range and types of activities people engage in and the importance, reciprocity and longevity of the connection. The

DOI: 10.4018/978-1-61350-080-4.ch018

patterns of connectivity described by the full network of ties help inform design of social and/or technical support for learning, knowledge acquisition, trust, collaboration and community.

While a substantial body of literature exists on social networks, particularly in relation to analytic techniques of social network analysis, fewer studies and reviews address learning (De Laat, 2006). This chapter focuses on how learning can be explored and examined from a social network perspective, leading to network informed design for learning, including the use of educational technology. By informed design we mean the design of meaningful collaborations, based on social network configurations that support learning, teaching and professional development. The first half of the chapter presents background on a social network perspective on learning. This is followed by a presentation of current research directions on how social network analysis can be used to study and design informal learning networks among teachers.

A SOCIAL NETWORK PERSPECTIVE ON LEARNING

There are two features that distinguish the social network approach to the study of social phenomena. The first is that the unit of analysis is the interaction between actors, rather than an aggregate of actor behavior; and the second is that attention is given to the network structures that emerge from interactions among actors. Social network *relations* (i.e., interactions, transactions, communications, collaborations, etc.), are the basis for *ties* between *actors* in a *network* (Wasserman & Faust, 1994). The principles of social network analysis derive from graph theory, which looks at patterns of relational connections between nodes in a graph. The nodes in a social network graph are the actors, who can be individuals or collective units such as teams or organizations. In learning and education settings, the actors may be teachers connected to each other within a school; teachers and students in a class; schools connected as part of a district school system; departmental connections across a university; or universities connected through inter-university course sharing. In contemporary settings, these connections are as likely to be accomplished through technology as they are through face-to-face contact.

The network approach draws our attention to the way patterns of interaction provide an environment for exchange of resources (Wasserman & Faust, 1994). Such resources include tangible goods and services, and intangibles such as communication, social support, information, knowledge and learning. From a design perspective, data on social network patterns can be used to provide an understanding what kinds of information, objects, communications, etc. are exchanged among network actors, and how the flow of these exchanges supports overall goals. Systems can be designed to facilitate such flows, and to correct or adjust existing flows.

Of equal importance are the overall structures that networks exhibit. Observing or using statistical techniques to analyze patterns of interaction reveals such structures (Scott & Carrington, 2010). One well-used measure of network structure is density, the extent to which all members of a network are connected to each other. Research has shown that members of dense networks are likely to be in frequent contact, and thus quickly become aware of new resources that enter the network. Network structures also show how some parts of the network may be densely connected, while other areas are only sparsely connected. Cliques, clusters or components show dense subset of network members who are likely to have access to similar resources. By contrast, isolates or isolated cliques may be found with no connection to other parts of the network, and thus off the main route for resources more generally available to others.

Research in social network analysis provides a rich history of studies, concepts and analytical techniques for considering patterns of network connections. While it is beyond the scope of this chapter to review such literature, the following are a few useful concepts that are becoming familiar in social science: central or peripheral actors; network stars, brokers, and isolates; strong and weak ties; network density; actor centrality; network centralization; cohesion; and structural holes. (For more in-depth coverage of social network analysis, see Wasserman & Faust, 1994; Wellman & Berkowitz, 1997; Monge & Contractor, 2003; Watts, 2004; Borgatti, Mehra, Brass & Labianca, 2009; Scott & Carrington, 2010).

Relational Approach to Learning

Key to a social network approach is the attention to relations. A *relational approach* emphasizes the interaction between people, whether for commerce, work, play, or learning. Data on what interactions happen between people can be gathered in a number of ways. Traditionally, data were collected by asking participants about who they interact with using questionnaires, surveys, interviews, or observation. Increasingly, automated ways of collecting network data from online interaction are being used (De Laat, 2006). This includes studies of communication via email, online discussion, blogs commentaries, or twitter streams, as well as hyperlink analyses of connectivity across sites (for a review, see Gruzd & Haythornthwaite, 2011). Work from the related area of bibliometrics examines records of publication and co-citation to find networks of interconnected authors and information resources.

In learning settings, we can examine *who interacts with whom* to gain a sense of general contact among learners (see De Laat, Lally, Lipponen & Simons, 2007 for an overview). But, we can also delve more deeply into the *content, direction*, and *strength* of these interactions, asking:

- *Who learns from whom*? Does learning happen only in one direction (e.g., from the teacher to the student)? Asking more generally about learning can reveal that perhaps students learn as much from each other as from the teacher as would be desirable in a collaborative learning setting.
- *What do they learn from each other*? Are different people important sources or explainers of different kinds of information and learning? While a teacher may provide support for learning subject matter, perhaps fellow students are active in helping learn about how to write well, or how to use technology.
- *What kinds of interactions happen between people who learn together*? Along with the expected discussion of the learning material, how much resource sharing or social support is happening? How do these relations co-occur (e.g., do people who spend more time socializing together also learn more often from each other)?
- *Which direction do resources flow?* Is information or knowledge 'transferred' from one person to another in only one direction, or does learning flow both ways? Are learning tasks set by an authority or set collaboratively by the group as a whole?
- *How frequently do learning interactions happen? How important are these interactions to the people involved, or to the recipient of the learning?* Frequent interaction suggests a stronger need or desire to engage in the activity, suggesting the relation is of importance to those involved. The kind of interaction can matter too, such as whether someone is giving or receiving support for a minor or major emotional need.

These relations are the underpinning first of the ties between individuals and then of the network as a whole. Pairs may be strongly tied (i.e., engaged in many different kinds of relations, interacting frequently, and/or in relations that are of high personal significance). Others may be weakly tie (i.e., engaging occasionally with partial commitment to the activities of the network). While some strong tie connections are necessary to keep a network active and alive, networks with a committed core can sustain a small to large weak tie contingent. In technology enhance learning settings, these weak ties are represented in lurkers and/or occasional contributors to online lists and communities. Some of these weakly committed people are novices, watching and learning how to behave in this community (De Laat, Lally, Lipponen & Simons, 2006). Others may remain only partly engaged as they mix time in one community with time in many others. This latter set of network members has been made famous by Granovetter (1973) in his discussion of the 'strength of weak ties'. Those who travel in multiple social circles are able to bring information from one circle to another, thereby increasing the range of information and opportunities, and potential learning that becomes available to members of the focal network.

Network Social Capital

If we go a bit further in considering the collective knowledge and access to resources that is held in a network, and that network members can access, we begin to distinguish networks that are resource rich from those that are resource poor. Networks that are rich in *social capital* hold within their membership the social means to respond to need - economic, social, informational (Lin, 2001). This has been referred to by Putnam (2000) as "bonding social capital." Networks that are poor in social capital do not hold such resources and hence cannot rely of others in the network to be able to help when needed. Such networks must rely on "bridging social capital." Network structures for each of these kinds of capital will be different: the former with strong internal bonds, good lines of communication and resource sharing; the latter with connections to outside groups through bridging connections and broker roles.

Learning networks, and networks that aim to be at the forefront of new ideas and techniques, require attention to both kinds of capital. Groups that are good at monitoring the outside environment, and include the expertise to evaluate it, demonstrate an "absorptive capacity" for integrating innovations into current practice (Cohen & Levinthal, 1990). In learning settings, creating the "safe space" (Bruffee, 1993) for exposure of ignorance on the way to learning requires the kind of strong ties and trust associated with bonding social capital. These kinds of ties are also necessary for sustaining the trust needed to achieve joint goals (e.g., depending on a division of labor to meet assignment deadlines for school or work, and trusting others' research, opinions and work effort) (Cook, Snijders, Buskins & Cheshire, 2009). However, for exposure to new ideas, learners need contact with weak ties who have access to new and different kinds of information and experience. In learning settings and elsewhere, a balance of attention to strong and weak tie network connections is needed, one that perhaps changes over time as requirements at the search phase of a project give way to consolidation for a report or action stage. For education, stimulating collaborative learning with the support of technology design can come into play not only in how open or closed a network needs to be, but also when it should be open to new input and when it needs to be closed for task completion (see also, Haythornthwaite, 2002b; 2010).

Relations and Design

We can take two views about using relational information for the design of meaningful collaborations to support learning, teaching and professional development configurations in learning and education. One way to view relations is to take what is perceived to be an important connection between actors and look at how this plays out in the network of interest. For example, we might determine that the relation of interest is 'collaborative work', and ask participants "who have you collaborated with on classwork" (as done by in studies of intra-class interaction by

Haythornthwaite, 2001, 2002a, or by analyzing reply-chain relationships in online discussions by networked communities, De Laat, 2006). Or, we might consider it sufficient to ask "who do you learn from," perhaps about a particular topic, and thus map the learning connections among students and/ or teachers of the network (Haythornthwaite, 2006; see below).

A second way to view relations is to take an existing connection and uncover what underpins this connection. For example, what relations underpin a successful technology enhanced learning community, co-authoring relationship, or collaborative work relationship? Participants in such partnerships can be asked what they do with each other. For example, in a study of collaborative research groups Haythornthwaite (2006) found nine kinds of relations associated with learning. Members of three interdisciplinary groups were first asked to name the five to eight people with whom they worked most closely. They were then asked *who* did they learn from, and *what* sorts of things did they learn from each of these people. Analysis of the responses revealed four major learning categories relating to knowledge exchange and learning activities:

- Fact or field knowledge: learning about a field, gaining information and knowledge possessed by another about a topic;
- Process: how to do something, look at a problem, use a technique, work with others;
- Method (how to use a particular method, research ethics);
- Joint Research (collaborative, joint work on research projects, writing together, data collection, analysis).

And five less frequent and less prevalent kinds of learning:

- Technology (how to use a particular computer technology [e.g., software]; technical aspects of using a computer system [e.g., databases]);
- Idea generation (brainstorming, idea sharing, common language building, common identity building);
- Socialization (how to behave in and navigate the work or academic worlds, the "politics" of science and grant funding);
- Networking (providing contacts to talk to, passing on students, gatekeeping);
- Administration (working on project-related administrative tasks).

Taking these as social network relations, the research further suggested that certain people were involved with the exchange of different kinds of information, suggesting certain routes for information within the network. In this case, knowledge bridges between disciplines within teams were found to form around a combination of type of information and role within the team: senior personnel were more likely to exchange fact or field knowledge with each other; and methodologists were more likely to learn about methods from each other.

While specifics of what people 'learn' from others can be expected to differ across settings, the results of this study are presented here to show the range of activities people identify when asked about learning. This includes practices we might not consider within that category - joint research, socialization - and yet become part of the overall learning tie between people. Discovering such relations provides input for design of systems and practices that pay attention to the need for this kind of network interaction.

While the study above looked inside the network for the type and extent of interaction, if we consider only the learning going on within a class, work group, or online learning community, we may miss more ramifying effects resulting from this learning. For example, in studies of "community-embedded learners" (i.e., online learners who engage through the e-learning environment but are also embedded in their own geographically-local communities), Kazmer (2007) found five major knowledge transfer routes:

- From local community to online classmates and the online learning community
- From the online course to the learner's workplace;
- From the online course to the learner's home community
- From one local community to another through contacts in the e-learning community
- From one educational institution to another through contact in the e-learning community

These kind of result suggests that different social designs for learning configurations may have differential outcomes depending on the constitution of the network. The online/offline combination in this example extended the network of the learning class well beyond the (geographical) borders of the institution operating the course. Moreover, the direction of knowledge flow can be unexpected. When students are embedded in different local communities and workplaces, they bring into the class examples from more varied backgrounds, enhancing the learning experience of all class participants. The network of connections and information flow is thus quite different from what might be found in a more traditional, face-to-face setting.

Examples of where the boundaries between formal and informal learning get blurred were found in studies conducted for the Learner Experiences Project (LXP; funded by JISC, a UK-based advisory body stimulating the use of ICT in higher education). This study investigated how students fit technology into their day-to-day learning activities (Conole, De Laat, Dillon & Darby, 2006). The LXP project collected 85 audio logs (voice messages delivered by phone rather then written diaries) by 20 students from four different universities and subject areas on how they used technology to support their learning. Twelve students' audio logs were followed up with semi-structured interviews to help contextualize and extend the findings from the audio logs. The LXP study showed that students were fluent with many technologies and applications, including computers, mobile phones, email, skype, SMS, VLE, social networking sites. Moreover, their use of these new 'smart' and adaptive technologies showed they were used to design and maintain new forms of collaborations with their peers, suggesting a shift towards Salomon's (1993) notion of 'distributed cognition' and shared enterprise assisted by educational technology. Using these communication technologies, students tapped into a broad range of social network relations that helped them with the learning task at hand in a real-time, just-in-time manner.

Roles and Positions

Network patterns also reveal how particular actors take on certain roles within the network as a whole. These roles are sometimes novel ones such as 'hacker' or 'wizard', and sometimes more traditional ones such as 'parent'. Different types of *roles and positions* are identified by the pattern of relations associated with the individual and their interactions with others. Network roles we are familiar with include the 'network star' who can be identified because they appear centrally in the network as people who give information or other resources to many others; 'gatekeepers' who bring information from outside the network into the network; and the 'technological guru' who is everyone's resource for questions about the use of technologies (Wasserman & Faust, 1994).

Recent work in e-learning communities is beginning to reveal new learning roles (see Strijbos & De Laat, 2010 for a review on online role behavior). Haythornthwaite, Bruce, Andrews, Kazmer, Montague & Preston (2007; Preston, 2008) describes three roles that have emerged in *Mirandanet*, an international online teacher professional development community for the promotion of technology in education: e-facilitators, braiders, and accomplished fellows. Members take on these roles as they become more involved with the online community. *E-facilitators* emerge who help to shape the argument, provide summaries and influence the direction of the discussion. *Braiders* take the online community discussions and reinterpret these in different styles and for different audiences; and *Accomplished Fellows* set up working parties to explore a subject in more depth. These roles each have relational connections to others (e.g. e-facilitators both receive ideas and influence the direction of discussion; braiders act as bridges to other communities, disseminating knowledge from one community to another; and accomplished fellows act in an entrepreneurial fashion to gather people and resources into a new learning collaboration). Elsewhere, in a distance education community, Montague (2006; Haythornthwaite et al, 2007) describes the emerging role of *learner-leaders* in online classes. Much like the new roles in Mirandanet, students emerge as leaders in the learning process both inside and outside the online environment (see also De Laat, Lally, Lipponen & Simons, 2006). Montague emphasizes how students take on a leadership role, letting their learning 'rub off on others' or even 'light a fire' outside the online environment.

LEARNING AND NETWORKS

A social network approach invites several ways of approaching technology enhanced design for social learning configurations. First, we can approach *learning as a relation* that connects people: a student learns from a teacher; a teacher instructs students; and novices learn collaboratively from each other. It can be a directed relation, with a child learning from a parent, a novice from an expert, or an apprentice from a master craftsman. It can also be a technology-based relation (e.g., information exchange via databases, knowledge exchange via listservs, and communication via a number of computing applications). While our focus here is on learning settings, the wider learning happening on the Internet suggests other aspects of learning, as individuals not only actively search for information online, but also contribute information (e.g., through social media). Such technology enhanced e-learners may also join communities where, regardless of their age or experience, they engage in setting the learning goals of the community (for more on this, see Gee, 2005; De Laat, 2006; Jenkins, 2006; Haythornthwaite & Andrews, 2011).

Second, we may think of *learning as the characterization of a tie*. Communities of inquiry, research teams, and study groups come together with the express purpose of learning from each other and/or together (Wenger, 1998; Barab and Roth, 2006). Learning is in that sense the essence of the tie. Similarly, learning is the tie that connects network of class members, collaborative learners, peer-to-peer learners, distributed learners, online learners, communities of interest, peer productions, scholarly communities, and academic disciplines. While different kinds of relations and relationships may develop – from learning to socializing, from classmate to good friend – the initial and characterizing view of these collectives is that they are learning collectives. For some, joining a learning collective attaches them to a "latent tie structure" (Haythornthwaite, 2002a, 2005). This structure puts the individual learner in a position where they may be able to make closer connections, thus activating a "latent tie" into an active tie (e.g., when strangers in a class begin to interact with each other around class material, discussions, and projects). Technology can be a major enabler of latent ties, for example by supporting lurkers in online communities who learn who could be contacted if a particular kind of question arises.

Third, we may see the *learning characterization as an outcome of relations*. For example, the kinds of relations, roles, etc. that lead a set of individuals to recognize that they belong to a functioning group or community include things like: *relations* that include social as well as instrumental exchanges, trust, generalized reciprocity, and social support; *roles* that support altruistic provision of information, acceptance of delayed return on social or informational 'investment', and specialized duties; *outcomes* that sustain personal and collective reputation and reward; and *network* attention to group members, group goals, and survival of the group (McGrath, 1984; McLaughlin, Osborne & Smith, 1995; Wellman, 1997, 1999). To characterize a community as a "learning community" it may be sufficient to add that the focus of the group is toward a learning outcome, however defined. However, given the controversy and multiple definitions associated with the idea of community (e.g., can you have 'virtual' community?), we do not hold out any expectation that characterizing a group or community as a 'learning group' or a 'learning community' will be any simpler than it has been for the more general definition of 'community'. Of interest for further research and for design is what network structures lead to the interpretation that the community is a learning community, and how to augment this outcome through technology support (e.g., see the work on collaboratories, Bos, Zimmerman, Olson, Yew, Yerkie, Dahl & Olson, 2007).

Fourth, we can use the definition or discovery of *learning relations as input for design*. Certainly this is the basis for development of educational technology systems that are labeled as virtual learning environments (VLE), learning management and/or course management systems (LMS, CMS). At their simplest, these systems provide facilities for the execution of instrumental relations: submission of assignments, return of evaluations, posting of questions, answers, and general announcements. In more elaborate and more sophisticated designs, systems build in more general interaction support (e.g., through discussion lists, wikis, data sharing facilities, live chat sessions, profile pages, and arena for social discussions [see De Laat & Lally, 2005 for example]). Increasingly, mobile devices are gaining attention as sites of distributed and technology-enhanced learning (Pachler, Bachmair & Cook, 2009). Design is both social and technical, sometimes to enhance interpersonal relations to compensate for the lack of face-to-face contact, and sometimes to take advantage of new ways of achieving work and learning, such as creating joint products through wikis (Haythornthwaite & Andrews, 2011).

Finally, we can think of *learning as the network outcome of relations* (i.e., as the net result of data gathering, discussion, argumentation, synthesis, application, and generation of ideas, information, and knowledge). The capital this network holds ranges from the joint understanding of a subject area, to the agreed and understood practices of how to be this learning group. It includes the human capital of each individual within the network, but, perhaps more to the point for the network, it includes the synergies between people and their knowledge as mobilized and mobilizable within the network (Lin, 2001; Haythornthwaite, 2010). It is social, organizational, sociotechnical, and cultural capital (Bordieu, 1986; Putnam, 2000; Lin, 2001; Orlikowski, 2002; Resnick, 2002). It is a group's competence in joint technology use (DeSanctis & Poole, 1994), and its transactive memory (Wegner, 1987; Contractor, Zink & Chan, 1998; Hollingshead, Fulk & Monge, 2002; Monge & Contractor, 2003; Kazmer, 2006); and it is a community's knowledge of its history, and a society's ability to support its citizens.

With this background on the social network perspective and how this perspective can used to inform technology enhanced design for learning, we now turn to a discussion of current research directions.

INFORMAL LEARNING NETWORKS

At the Ruud de Moor Centre at the Open University of the Netherlands, research has been underway looking into informal learning networks in the educational workplace and how these influence teacher professional development. The aim is to use the findings first to understand current patterns of interaction, and then to use this information in concert with network members goals to design social and technological means of ameliorating perceived omissions in network connectivity.

The research follows 32 projects each year in the educational sector, focusing on teacher professional development. Informal learning by these teachers tends to deal with tacit knowledge, embedded in day-to-day practice. It involves spontaneous learning activities that are mostly 'off the radar' of human resource departments and management staff. As a practice that is often invisible, and confined to relatively small networks or communities, informal learning is the "invisible work" of professional practice (Timmermans, Bowker & Star, 1998; Star & Strauss, 1999).

Interviews with school leaders revealed that most have little or no awareness of what teachers learn spontaneously in their day-to-day practice, nor how to stimulate or reward this. Some even expressed the opinion that teachers are not knowledge workers or professionals at all (De Laat, 2008a). While the literature on workplace learning does not support this view, without empirical evidence it has been hard to counteract this impression. Thus, research was undertaken to explore learning networks, with a particular focus on understanding how teachers build and maintain a web of social relations in support of their professional development (De Laat, 2008b). The following sections present findings from studies carried out under this program using social network analyses techniques to describe and understand how teachers engage in social learning. Findings from these studies form the basis for the informed design of technology enhanced social network configurations supporting teacher professional development.

Figure 1.

Multi-Method Framework for Examining Learning Networks

Social network analysis helps to understand how people design and maintain a social network to assist their learning. One of the more important research questions that emerges from our research program is: What constitutes a learning tie? When is a connection perceived as a learning relationship and what is its quality (Haythornthwaite & de Laat, 2010)? In addressing these kinds of questions, the Ruud de Moor Centre research group started by interviewing teachers about their social networks using a multi-method framework, shown in Figure 1 (see De Laat, 2006 for a detailed description).

This framework combines social network analysis (SNA) to find out 'who is talking to whom', with content analysis (CA) to find out 'what they are talking about', and with contextual analysis (CxA) to bring in the context of the organization and to find out 'why they are talking as they do'. The aim is to paint a more complete picture of networked learning processes in a

Figure 2.

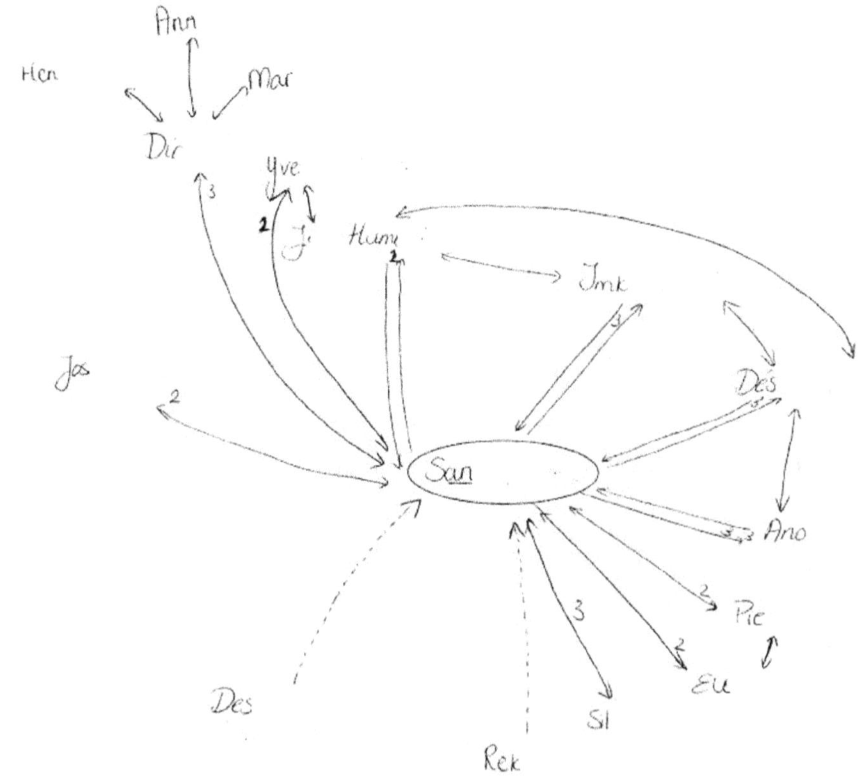

naturalistic setting (Erlandson, Harris, Skipper & Allen, 1993). This approach holds promise for contributing to the design of better pedagogical frameworks that more effectively support informal learning in various social configurations.

Contact Maps

In the process of using this multi-method approach we developed an interview method using *contact cards* (see Figure 2). During the interview, participants are invited to visualize their egocentric network, including their connections to others and the connections among these others. They are asked to draw these contact diagrams as a way to describe who they engage with during particular occasions for learning. Such meaningful (online) collaborations with colleagues and other professionals in the field are important ways in which teachers learn to solve their work-related problems, and improve their work and classroom practice (Lieberman & Wood, 2002; Dresner & Worly, 2006). In order to visualize these networks, it is necessary to address a problem of sufficient meaningfulness to the teacher's daily practice but one that is also sufficiently challenging that they need to reflect on it with others. The resulting contact cards act both as a research tool and as a source for designing and extending social networks in the schools.

Figure 2 shows the contact card for a teacher reflecting on her social learning network, and thinking about how and when certain 'critical learning friends' were used for her professional development. In this data set the topic was about creating continuing learning trajectories for indi-

Figure 3.

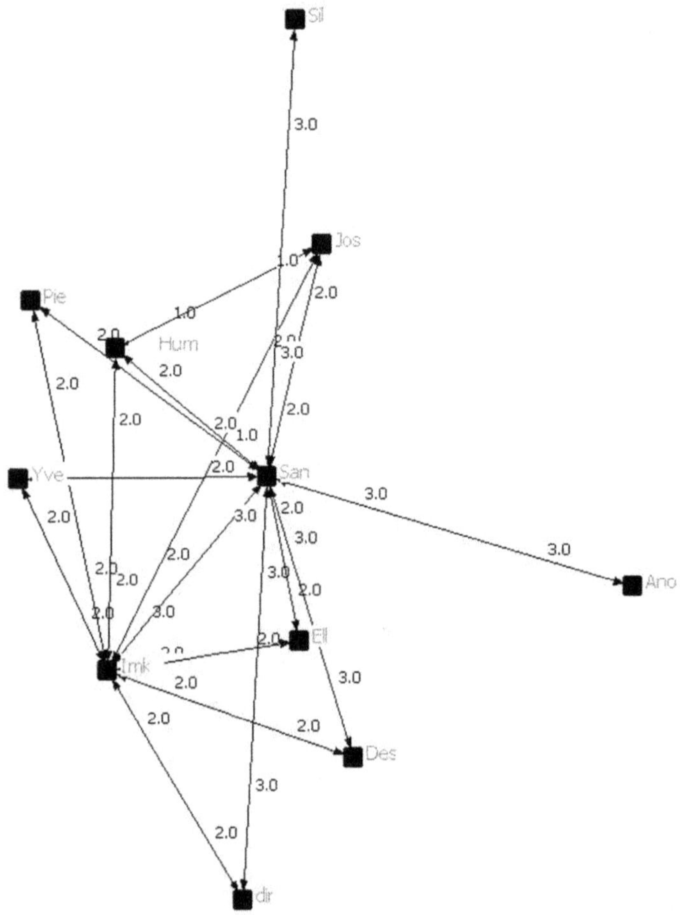

vidual students in her class. This is a difficult topic, and as can be seen the teacher ('San', positioned in the center of the figure) is not dealing with the problem on her own. She engages with a range of people to discuss and reflect on how to realize learning trajectories in her classroom. (All names show are pseudonyms.)

After the contact card is created with the teacher during the interview, the data is transferred to a social network analysis package for further analysis and more advanced network visualizations (see Figure 3; data analysis and visualizations are created using the UCINET social network analysis package; Borgatti, Everett & Freeman, 2002).

An advantage of this process is that we can ask the teacher at a later time to provide updates to this network. To do so, she adds nodes to the diagram, and in the background we can measure network dynamics to see if there are significant changes. These visualizations have proven to be an aid for the teachers to further design, develop and reflect on their own networks.

From Individual Teacher Networks (Ego Networks) to School Wide Networks (Whole Networks)

After developing contact cards with several (preferably all) teachers in a school it is possible

Figure 4.

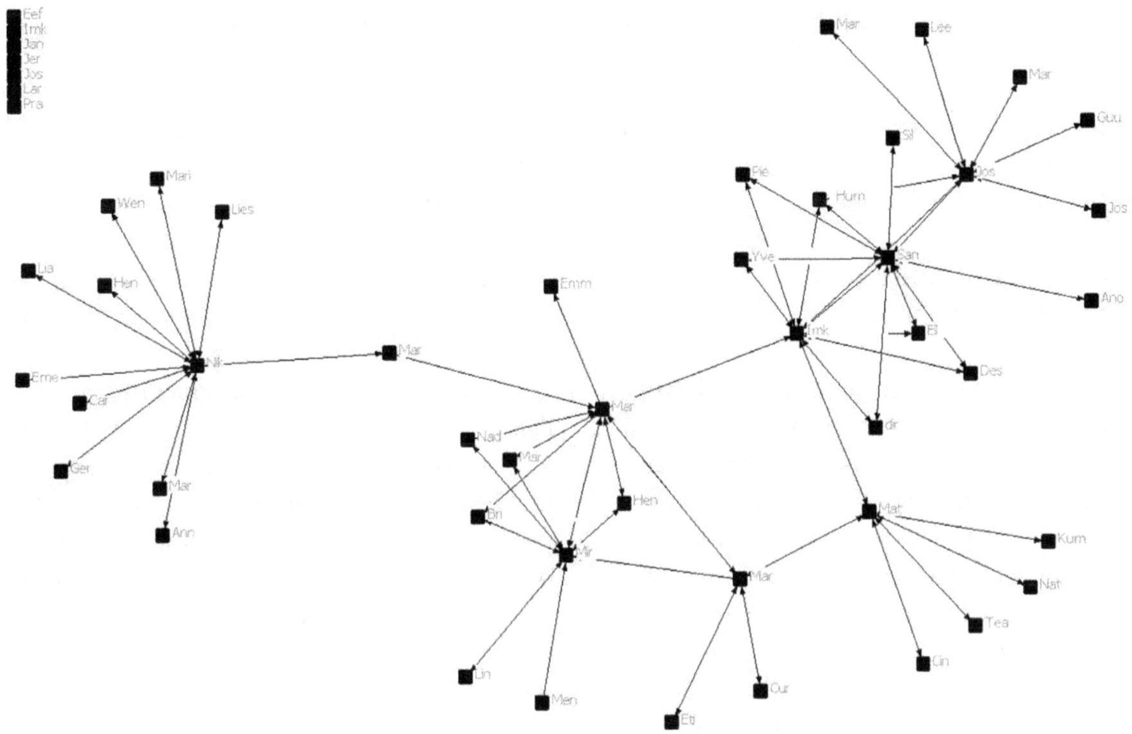

to build a collective network that reveals a social learning network structure within the entire school (see Figure 4).

In our projects we have found that drawing these networks stimulates other teachers to join in and produce contact cards of their own, making it possible to build up to the whole network configuration. This can also facilitates the design of social learning configurations that support teacher professional development. The advantage of using social network software is that it supports the shift from ego-networks (those centered on an individual) to whole-networks (those consisting of connections among all actors) relatively easily. This way we can illustrate the way the learning activities portrayed in ego-networks (that only a relatively small number of teachers is aware of) connect into a school-wide social learning structure.

This visible evidence of the network, in both its connections and the content of connections, is important for laying the groundwork for new participants. When presenting a visualization of the whole network, teachers can see not only 'who talks to whom', but also 'what they are talking about'. This makes it easier for other teachers to join new networks when they encounter particular work-related issues or if they wish to learn more about topics that interest them. In our research experiments with designing (online) social networks among teachers in and between schools, we find that working with these visualizations stimulates a networking attitude amongst teachers in the school towards learning. They become aware that they are not alone in their classroom and that professional development is also an social activity; one that is spontaneous and deeply connected to day-to-day challenges in the workplace (De Laat 2008a).

Another advantage of these visualizations is that they serve as very concrete artifacts for the teachers to help them reflect on how they act as networked learners. In the next section we explore this further by using social network analysis as a tool for reflecting on how teachers see themselves acting as a networked learner.

Contact Maps: Activities, Strategies, and Values

In this section we present how social network analysis can be used as a tool for reflecting on networked learning strategies and competencies. Here we focus on the strategies teachers develop, what their networked learning attitude is, and the value this holds for them. In our research program we explore teachers' self-image of themselves as networked learners. We conduct interviews where our focus is on networked learning literacy (i.e., skills and competencies in learning with and/ or from others), how this facilitates meaningful networked learning activities aimed at designing social learning configurations, and the personal value this has for the teacher. The focus is not so much on the social connections teachers have, but rather on the teachers themselves. Through introspection we aim to find out how the teacher sees him or herself as a networked learner and how literate is he or she when acting as a networked learner.

Each interview begins with a conversation about what a teacher thinks networked learning is and what this means for him or her. We aim to keep this conversation as grounded as possible in local processes (e.g., by referring to concrete everyday examples in the workplace). This exploration serves as a base for talking about networked learning activities and strategies. We focus on the skills and competencies the teacher relies on while engaging in these networked learning activities, exploring why these are seen as learning activities, what the activity produces, and why is it perceived to be of value. During the interviews the concepts mentioned are written down and the teacher draws lines to show where concepts are connected.

The result is a concept network showing which skills are used for which learning activities and the value this holds for the teacher. In Figure 5, the circular nodes refer to skills and competencies used by the teacher when engaging in networked learning activities (square nodes). The triangular nodes show the value these networked learning activities have for the teacher.

Studying these network structures in more detail (Figures 6 and 7) shows that, for this teacher, strategies for learning something new (aimed at exchanging information, changing self perceptions and get new ideas) involves being open, vulnerable and sensitive, and has value when meeting new people to learn from. Thus, this teacher is conscious about using weak ties (Granovetter, 1973) (i.e., when it comes to learning something new, she finds it best to reach out to new people for alternative perspectives and 'refreshing' dialogues).

The teacher is also aware that personal interest in a particular issue or item involves activities aimed at 'give and take'. In order to be successful, the teacher realizes (and demonstrates in the concept map) the need to be open, caring and able to communicate her needs in order to get what she is after (see Figure 7).

This teacher appears to have well developed ideas about which networking attitude is best used in which circumstances. This shows how such professionals can be quite aware of the information landscape and network to which they belong. It shows a high degree of understanding not only of their work needs, but of the processes needed to operate within this setting. What is shown are aspects of the transactive memory that sustains group functioning. Another way to look at this is that the ideas presented are theories of social learning used by a teacher when engaging in day-to-day informal professional development in the workplace. Theories that are tested in the day to

Figure 5.

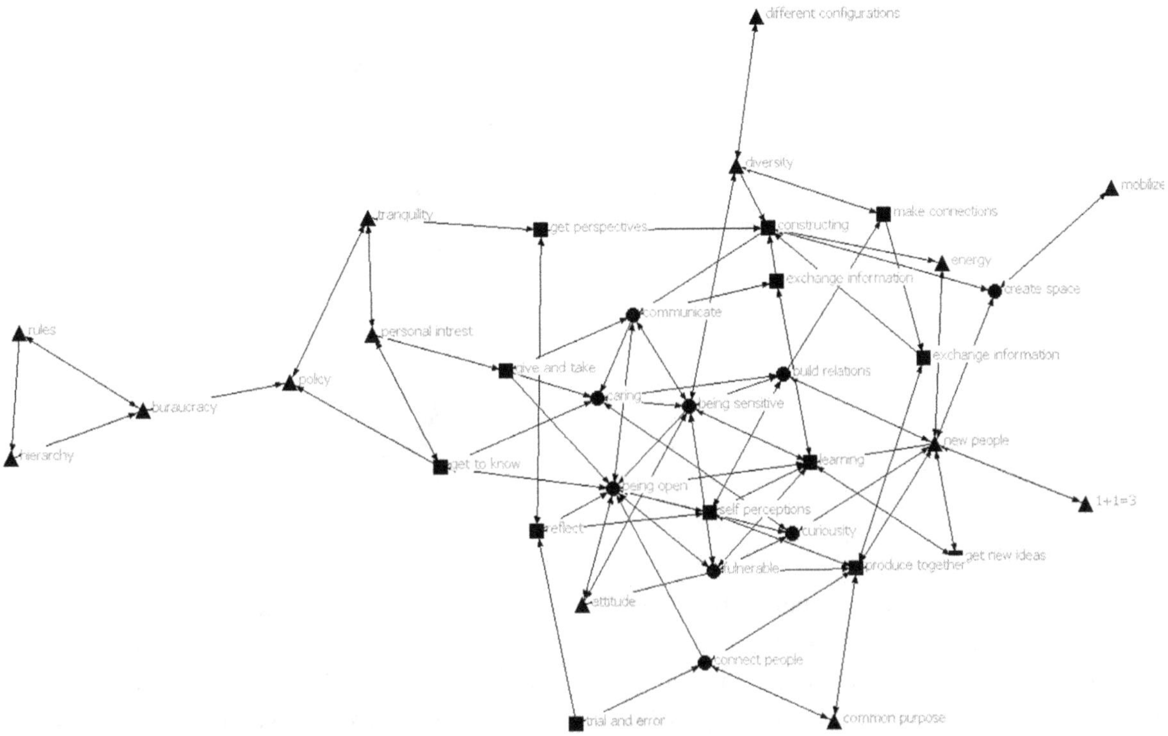

Figure 6.

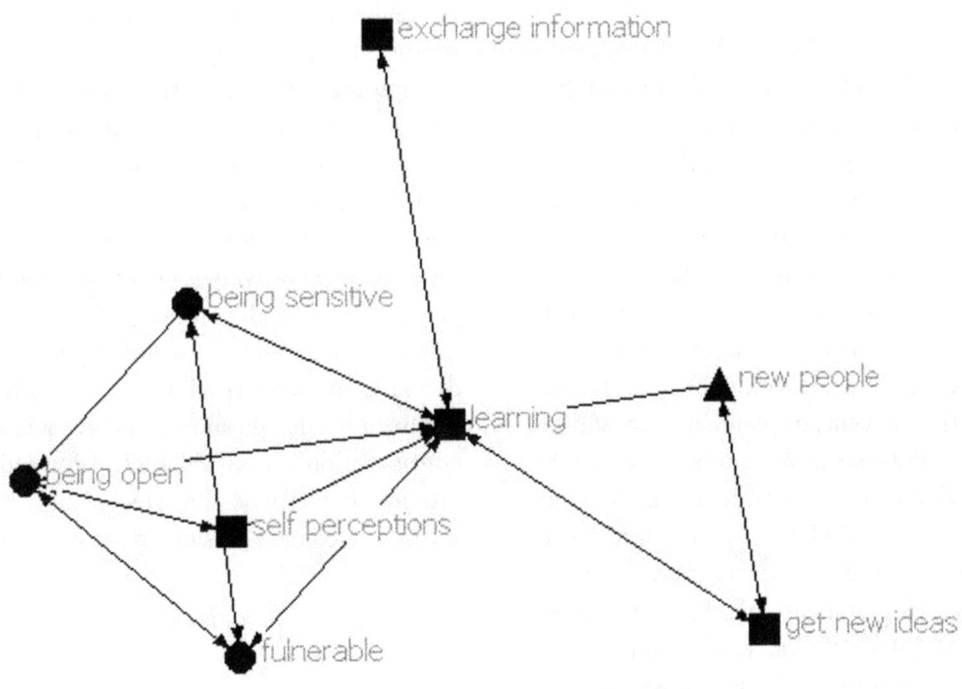

Figure 7.

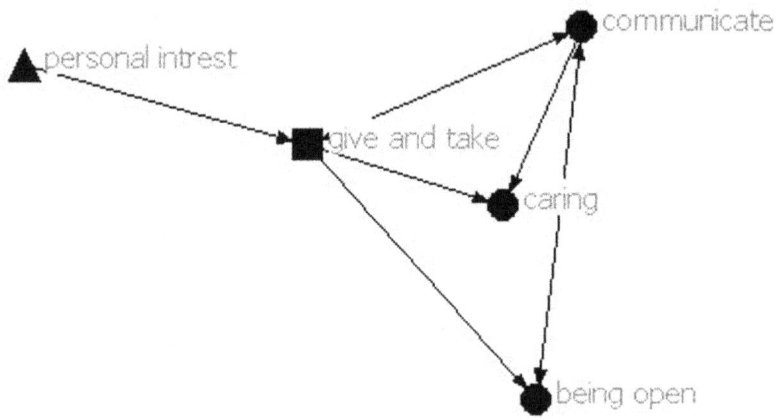

day search for information in their network and in concert with emerging ideas of who they are within their learning area (for similar ideas along this line, see Cook & Brown, 1999; Engeström, 2009).

Summary

The methods presented above hold promise for providing both useful and usable information about networks for research purposes as well as research-based interventions and informed design of teacher professional development in school organizations. By repeatedly applying these social network methods, it is possible to visualize network dynamics over time and explore what causes them to change. This allows assessment of the effects on the network structures of such things as critical events or planned interventions aimed at designing social networks. For example, you might find that after a professional development activity, networks have become more dense, perhaps indicating a significant increase in the flow of knowledge and products among network members; or that isolates or isolated cliques have become connected and/or integrated with the network. Social network measures may reveal how particular individuals are emerging as key players in the professional development network, such as knowledge brokers who reaching out to more peripheral members in the network, or acting as a bridge to connect peripheral actors to central activities. These features can show strengths and/or weaknesses in the network that need supporting or attending to by school officials. By conducting these measures repeatedly a researcher, administrator or teacher can follow the dynamics and growth of the entire network structure in the school organization. In this way you can follow how members travel towards or away from the core activities as well as how new members start participating in the networked learning. Such information provides research input about group dynamics as well as administrative information for the future design and support of social network configurations. Further, such information also provides input for design of technical systems that can be implemented to support networked learning.

FUTURE RESEARCH DIRECTIONS

A number of opportunities are available for future research. These include integration of network data gathering and analysis into learning software (learning management systems/virtual learning system) so that patterns of interactions among learners and teacher can be captured and provided as feedback to participants. At RdMC we are currently developing a networked learning "App" for mobile devices, initially designed for teachers to visualize and manage social networks. Real-time presentation of such networks has the potential to make visible the group dynamics that are currently obscured. There is a need for a research agenda in education that puts emphasis on large scale and long term networked learning interactions. This way we can learn more about the behavioral aspects of successful networked learning strategies, competences and values as well as the nature of ties and how ties evolve through these interactions. Educational design and practice can then be informed by evidence of actual interaction.

Examining learning networks need not be confined to educational settings. Other groups (in business, research, and service) can also be examined using the same principles, providing insight into knowledge and learning practices across settings. Networks are not limited by organizational boundaries and it is important to study how formal, informal and non-formal network ties interconnect and benefit teaching and learning, and bridge between different constituencies such as between businesses and higher education.

Network patterns can also extend to include, or focus on, non-human actors. For example, the use of reading materials can be integrated into the examination of a learning network. A network of 'who is reading what' can provide information on the breadth or depth of knowledge being accumulated across the network and in cliques within the network. Bibliometric studies of use of resources (e.g., in the reference lists of participant's papers or referred to in discussions) can provide an understanding of the knowledge being mobilized within a network. A network study can also reveal what resources are of importance, whether it is a central human actor, a peripheral actor such as a gatekeeper, or a primary resource such as an employee handbook.

CONCLUSION

This chapter has addressed the way the social network approach, and studies informed by a social network perspective, can be used to understand and design for learning. Areas for exploration include the kinds of relations that constitute a learning tie and thus support the activity of learning; the network roles that emerge and directly support learning and knowledge aggregation, synthesis and distribution; the interconnections between focal and distant networks that show transfer points between communities or social worlds; and the relational basis and network structures of groups, communities and organization that support learning in the service of social capital.

We believe the combination of social network data collection, with social network statistics and visualizations of connections, content and contextual information provides a rich view of learning networks. Overall, we believe this rich combination of data, combined with the ability to follow processes over time, can serve to increase our understanding of networked learning research issues such as what constitutes a learning tie, how learning ties activated and supported, and what kinds of learning outcomes and forms of network capital are produced for the enterprise as a whole. Beyond the appeal of the data for researchers, we believe the inclusion of the feedback process described in this chapter, and the way teacher and student networks can be used to design whole school networks in education and beyond, provides valuable and visible information about the extent and perceived value of collaborative learning.

Finally, we believe that technology designed to enhance learning and learning experiences need to attend to the fundamentals of social networks in order to provide appropriate support for learning networks and networked learning.

REFERENCES

Barab, S. A., & Roth, W. M. (2006). Intentionally-bound systems and curricular based ecosystems: An ecological perspective on knowing. *Educational Researcher, 35*(5), 3–13. doi:10.3102/0013189X035005003

Bordieu, P. (1986). The forms of capital. In Richardson, J. G. (Ed.), *Handbook of theory and research for the sociology of education* (pp. 241–258). Westport, CT: Greenwood Press.

Borgatti, S. P., Everett, M. G., & Freeman, L. C. (2002). *UCInet for Windows: Software for social network analysis*. Harvard Analytic Technologies.

Borgatti, S. T., Mehra, A., Brass, D., & Labianca, G. (2009). Network analysis in the social sciences. *Science, 323*, 892–895. doi:10.1126/science.1165821

Bos, N., Zimmerman, A., Olson, J., Yew, J., Yerkie, J., Dahl, E., & Olson, G. (2007). From shared databases to communities of practice: A taxonomy of collaboratories. *Journal of Computer-Mediated Communication, 12*(2), 16. Retrieved from http://jcmc.indiana.edu/vol12/issue2/bos.html. doi:10.1111/j.1083-6101.2007.00343.x

Bruffee, K. A. (1993). *Collaborative learning: Higher education, interdependence, and the authority of knowledge*. Baltimore, MD: John Hopkins University Press.

Cohen, W. M., & Levinthal, D. A. (1990). Absorptive capacity: A new perspective on learning and innovation. *Administrative Science Quarterly, 35*, 128–152. doi:10.2307/2393553

Conole, G., De Laat, M., Dillon, T., & Darby, J. (2006). *JISC LXP: Student experiences of technologies final report*. Retrieved January 19, 2007, from http://www.jisc.ac.uk/media/documents/programmes/elearning_pedagogy/lxp%20project%20final%20report%20dec%2006.pdf

Contractor, N., Zink, D., & Chan, M. (1998). IKNOW: A tool to assist and study the creation, maintenance, and dissolution of knowledge networks. In Toru, I. (Ed.), *Community computing and support systems. Lecture Notes in Computer Science, 1519* (pp. 201–217). Berlin, Germany: Springer-Verlag.

Cook, K. S., Snijders, C., Buskins, V., & Cheshire, C. (Eds.). (2009). *E-Trust: Forming relationships in the online world*. New York, NY: Russell Sage Foundation.

Cook, S. D. N., & Brown, J. S. (1999). Bridging epistemologies: The generative dance between organizational knowledge and organizational knowing. *Organization Science, 10*(4), 381–400. doi:10.1287/orsc.10.4.381

De Laat, M. F. (2006). *Networked learning*. Apeldoorn, The Netherlands: Politie Academie.

De Laat, M. F. (2008a). *Netwerkleren, een haalbaarheidsstudie naar de kansen voor netwerkleren als vorm van professionalisering voor leraren [Networked learning: A feasibility study on networked learning for teacher professional development*]. Heerlen, The Netherlands: RdMC.

De Laat, M. F. (2008b). *Onderzoeksprogramma Netwerkleren [Networked Learning: A Research Programme]*. Heerlen, The Netherlands: RdMC.

De Laat, M. F., & Lally, V. (2005). Investigating group structure in CSCL: Some new approaches. *Information Systems Frontiers, 7*(1), 13–25. doi:10.1007/s10796-005-5335-x

De Laat, M. F., Lally, V., Lipponen, L., & Simons, P. R. J. (2006). Analysing student engagement with learning and tutoring activities in networked learning communities: A multi-method approach. *International Journal of Web-Based Communities*, *2*(4), 394–412. doi:10.1504/IJWBC.2006.011766

De Laat, M. F., Lally, V., Lipponen, L., & Simons, P. R. J. (2007). Patterns of interaction in a networked learning community: Squaring the circle. *International Journal of Computer-Supported Collaborative Learning*. doi:.doi:10.1007/s11412-007-9006-4

DeSanctis, G., & Poole, M. S. (1994). Capturing the complexity in advanced technology use: Adaptive structuration theory. *Organization Science*, *5*(2), 121–147. doi:10.1287/orsc.5.2.121

Dresner, M., & Worley, E. (2006). Teacher research experiences, partnerships with scientists, and teacher networks sustaining factors from professional development. *Journal of Science Teacher Education*, *17*, 1–14. doi:10.1007/s10972-005-9000-5

Engeström, Y. (2009). Expansive learning: Toward an activity-theoretical reconceptualization. In Illeris, K. (Ed.), *Contemporary theories of learning: Learning theorists ... in their own words* (pp. 53–73). London, UK: Routledge.

Erlandson, D. A., Harris, E. L., Skipper, B., & Allen, S. D. (1993). *Doing naturalistic inquiry: A guide to methods*. Newbury Park, CA: Sage Publications.

Gee, J. P. (2005). Semiotic social spaces and affinity spaces: From the age of mythology to today's schools. In Barton, D., & Tusting, K. (Eds.), *Beyond communities of practice: Language, power and social context* (pp. 214–232). Cambridge, UK: Cambridge University Press. doi:10.1017/CBO9780511610554.012

Granovetter, M. (1973). The strength of weak ties. *American Journal of Sociology*, *78*, 1360–1380. doi:10.1086/225469

Gruzd, A., & Haythornthwaite, C. (2011). Networking online: Cybercommunities. In Scott, J., & Carrington, P. (Eds.), *Handbook of social network analysis* (pp. 167–179). London, UK: Sage.

Haythornthwaite, C. (2001). Exploring multiplexity: Social network structures in a computer-supported distance learning class. *The Information Society*, *17*(3), 211–226. doi:10.1080/01972240152493065

Haythornthwaite, C. (2002a). Strong, weak and latent ties and the impact of new media. *The Information Society*, *18*(5), 385–401. doi:10.1080/01972240290108195

Haythornthwaite, C. (2002b). Building social networks via computer networks: Creating and sustaining distributed learning communities. In Renninger, K. A., & Shumar, W. (Eds.), *Building virtual communities: Learning and change in cyberspace* (pp. 159–190). Cambridge, UK: Cambridge University Press. doi:10.1017/CBO9780511606373.011

Haythornthwaite, C. (2005). Social networks and Internet connectivity effects. *Information Communication and Society*, *8*(2), 125–147. doi:10.1080/13691180500146185

Haythornthwaite, C. (2006). Learning and knowledge exchanges in interdisciplinary collaborations. *Journal of the American Society for Information Science and Technology*, *57*(8), 1079–1092. doi:10.1002/asi.20371

Haythornthwaite, C. (2010). Social networks and information transfer. In Bates, M. J., & Maack, M. N. (Eds.), *Encyclopedia of library and information sciences* (3rd ed., pp. 4837–4847). New York, NY: Taylor & Francis.

Haythornthwaite, C., & Andrews, R. (2011). *E-learning theory and practice*. London, UK: Sage.

Haythornthwaite, C., Bruce, B. C., Andrews, R., Kazmer, M. M., Montague, R., & Preston, C. (2007). New theories and models of and for online learning. *First Monday, 12*(8). Retrieved October 11, 2010, from http://firstmonday.org/issues/issue12_8/haythorn/index.html

Haythornthwaite, C., & De Laat, M. F. (2010). *Social networks and learning networks: Using social network perspectives to understand social learning.* Paper presented at the Networked Learning Conference, Aalborg, Denmark, May 2-3, 2010.

Hollingshead, A. B., Fulk, J., & Monge, P. (2002). Fostering intranet knowledge sharing: An integration of transactive memory and public goods approaches. In Hinds, P., & Kiesler, S. (Eds.), *Distributed work: New research on working across distance using technology* (pp. 335–355). Cambridge, MA: MIT Press.

Jenkins, H., Clinton, K., Purushotma, R., Robinson, A. J., & Weigel, M. (2006). *Confronting the challenges of participatory culture: Media education for the 21st century*. Chicago, IL: MacArthur Foundation.

Kazmer, M. M. (2006). Creation and loss of sociotechnical capital among information professionals educated online. *Library & Information Science Research, 28*, 172–191. doi:10.1016/j.lisr.2006.03.002

Kazmer, M. M. (2007). Community-embedded learning. In Andrews, R., & Haythornthwaite, C. (Eds.), *Handbook of e-learning research* (pp. 311–327). London, UK: Sage.

Lieberman, A., & Wood, D. (2002). From network learning to classroom teaching. *Journal of Educational Change, 3*, 315–337. doi:10.1023/A:1021286014650

Lin, N. (2001). *Social capital: A theory of social structure and action*. Cambridge, UK: Cambridge University Press.

McGrath, J. E. (1984). *Groups, interaction and performance*. Englewood Cliffs, NJ: Prentice-Hall.

McLaughlin, M. L., Osborne, K. K., & Smith, C. B. (1995). Standards of conduct on usenet. In Jones, S. G. (Ed.), *CyberSociety: Computer-mediated communication and community* (pp. 90–111). Thousand Oaks, CA: Sage.

Monge, P. R., & Contractor, N. S. (2003). *Theories of communication networks*. Oxford, UK: Oxford University Press.

Montague, R.-A. (2006). *Riding the waves: A case study of learners and leaders in library and information science education*. Unpublished doctoral dissertation. University of Illinois at Urbana-Champaign, Champaign, IL.

Orlikowski, W. J. (2002). Knowing in practice: Enacting a collective capability in distributed organizing. *Organization Science, 13*(3), 249–273. doi:10.1287/orsc.13.3.249.2776

Pachler, N., Bachmair, B., & Cook, J. (2009). *Mobile learning: Structures, agency, practices*. New York, NY: Springer.

Preston, C. J. (2008). Braided learning: An emerging process observed in e-communities of practice. *International Journal of Web Based Communities, 4*(2), 220–243. doi:10.1504/IJWBC.2008.017674

Putnam, R. D. (2000). *Bowling alone: The collapse and revival of American community*. New York, NY: Simon & Schuster.

Resnick, P. (2002). Beyond bowling together: Sociotechnical capital. In Carroll, J. (Ed.), *HCI in the new millennium* (pp. 247–272). Addison-Wesley.

Salomon, G. (Ed.). (1993). *Distributed cognitions: Psychological and educational considerations*. Cambridge, UK: Cambridge University Press.

Scott, J., & Carrington, P. (Eds.). (2010). *Handbook of social network analysis*. London, UK: Sage.

Star, S. L., & Strauss, A. (1999). Layers of silence, arenas of voice: The ecology of visible and invisible work. *CSCW*, *8*(1-2), 9–30.

Strijbos, J. W., & De Laat, M. F. (2010). Developing the role concept for computer-supported collaborative learning: An explorative synthesis. *Computers in Human Behavior*, *26*, 495–505. doi:10.1016/j.chb.2009.08.014

Timmermans, S., Bowker, G., & Star, L. (1998). The architecture of difference: Visibility, discretion, and comparability in building a nursing intervention classification. In Mol, A. M., & Berg, M. (Eds.), *Difference in medicine: Unraveling practices, techniques and bodies* (pp. 202–225). Raleigh, NC: Duke.

Wasserman, S., & Faust, K. (1994). *Social network analysis*. Cambridge, UK: Cambridge University Press.

Watts, D. J. (2004). The new science of network. *Annual Review of Sociology*, *30*, 243–270. doi:10.1146/annurev.soc.30.020404.104342

Wegner, D. (1987). Transactive memory: A contemporary analysis of the group mind. In Mullen, B., & Goethals, G. (Eds.), *Theories of group behavior* (pp. 185–208). New York, NY: Springer-Verlag.

Wellman, B. (1999). The network community: An introduction to networks in the global village. In Wellman, B. (Ed.), *Networks in the global village* (pp. 1–48). Boulder, CO: Westview Press.

Wellman, B., & Berkowitz, S. D. (Eds.). (1997). *Social structures: A network approach* (pp. 19–61). Greenwich, CT: JAI Press.

Wenger, E. (1998). *Communities of practice: Learning, meaning, and identity*. Cambridge, MA: Cambridge University Press.

ADDITIONAL READING

Arya, B., & Lin, Z. (2007). Understanding collaboration outcomes from an extended resource-based view perspective: The roles of organizational characteristics, partner attributes, and network structures. *Journal of Management*, *33*(5), 697–723. doi:10.1177/0149206307305561

Aviv, R., Erlich, Z., & Ravid, G. (2003). Network analysis of knowledge construction in asynchronous learning networks. *Journal of Asynchronous Learning Networks, 7*(3), Article 1.

Aviv, R., Erlich, Z., & Ravid, G. (2005). Reciprocity analysis of online learning networks. *Journal of Asynchronous Learning Networks, 9*(4), Article 1.

Bennet, A., & Tomblin, M. S. (2006). A learning network framework for modern organizations: Organizational learning, knowledge management and ICT support. *Vine*, *36*(3), 289–303. doi:10.1108/03055720610703588

Bonamy, J., Charlier, B., & Saunders, M. (2001). Bridging tools' for change: Evaluating a collaborative learning network. *Journal of Computer Assisted Learning*, *17*(3), 295–305. doi:10.1046/j.0266-4909.2001.00184.x

Borgatti, S. P., & Cross, R. (2003). A relational view of information seeking and learning in social networks. *Management Science*, *49*(4), 432–445. doi:10.1287/mnsc.49.4.432.14428

Brolø, A. (2009). Innovative coopetition: The strength of strong ties. *International Journal of Entrepreneurship and Small Business*, *8*(1), 110–134. doi:10.1504/IJESB.2009.024108

Cho, H., Lee, J.-S., Stefanone, M., & Gay, G. (2005). Development of computer-supported collaborative social networks in a distributed learning community. *Behaviour & Information Technology*, *24*(6), 435–447. doi:10.1080/01449290500044049

Cross, R., Borgatti, S., & Parker, A. (2002). Making invisible work visible: Using social network analysis to support human networks. *California Management Review*, *44*(2), 25–46.

Cross, R., Nohria, N., & Parker, A. (2002). Six myths about informal networks – And how to overcome them. *MIT Sloan Management Review*, *43*(3), 67–75.

De Laat, M. F. (2006). *Networked learning*. Apeldoorn, The Netherlands: Politie Academie.

De Laat, M. F., Lally, V., Lipponen, L., & Simons, P. R. J. (2007). Online teaching in networked learning communities: A multi-method approach to studying the role of the teacher. *Instructional Science*, *35*(3), 257–286. doi:10.1007/s11251-006-9007-0

De Laat, M. F., Lally, V., Simons, P. R. J., & Wenger, E. (2006). A selective analysis of empirical findings in networked learning research in higher education: Questing for coherence. *Educational Research Review*, *1*(2), 99–111. doi:10.1016/j.edurev.2006.08.004

Dresner, M., & Worley, E. (2006). Teacher research experiences, partnerships with scientists, and teacher networks sustaining factors from professional development. *Journal of Science Teacher Education*, *17*, 1–14. doi:10.1007/s10972-005-9000-5

Earl, L., & Katz, S. (2007). Leadership in networked learning communities. *School Leadership & Management*, *27*(3), 239–258. doi:10.1080/13632430701379503

Goodyear, P., Banks, S., Hodgson, V., & McConnell, D. (2004). *Advances in research on networked learning, Norwell, Ma*. Kluwer Academic Publishers.

Harasim, L., Hiltz, R., Teles, L., & Turoff, M. (1995). *Learning networks: a field guide to teaching and learning online*. Cambridge, MA: MIT Press.

Haythornthwaite, C. (2001). Exploring multiplexity: Social network structures in a computer-supported distance learning class. *The Information Society*, *17*(3), 211–226. doi:10.1080/01972240152493065

Haythornthwaite, C. (2002). Strong, weak and latent ties and the impact of new media. *The Information Society*, *18*(5), 385–401. doi:10.1080/01972240290108195

Haythornthwaite, C. (2006). Learning and knowledge networks in interdisciplinary collaborations. *Journal of the American Society for Information Science and Technology*, *57*(8), 1079–1092. doi:10.1002/asi.20371

Haythornthwaite, C. (2008). Learning relations and networks in web-based communities. *International Journal of Web Based Communities*, *4*(2), 140–158. doi:10.1504/IJWBC.2008.017669

Jones, C. R., Ferreday, D., & Hodgson, V. (2008). Networked learning a relational approach: Weak and strong ties. *Journal of Computer Assisted Learning*, *24*(2), 90–102. doi:10.1111/j.1365-2729.2007.00271.x

Katz, S., & Hands, C. (2007). *Scaling up from one network to many: The establishment of networked learning communities within the district*. York: Region District School Board.

Knight, L. (2002). Network learning: Exploring learning by interorganizational networks. *Human Relations*, *55*(4), 427–454.

Levin, D. Z., & Cross, R. (2004). The strength of weak ties you can trust: The mediating role of trust in effective knowledge transfer. *Management Science*, *50*(11), 1477–1490. doi:10.1287/mnsc.1030.0136

Lieberman, A. (2000). Networks as learning communities shaping the future of teacher development. *Journal of Teacher Education*, *51*(3), 221–227. doi:10.1177/0022487100051003010

Liebowitz, J. (2005). Linking social network analysis with the analytic hierarchy process for knowledge mapping in organizations. *Journal of Knowledge Management*, *9*(1), 76–86. doi:10.1108/13673270510582974

O'Brien, M., Varga-Atkins, T., Burton, D., Campbell, A., & Qualter, A. (2008). How are the perceptions of learning networks shaped among school professionals and headteachers at an early stage in their introduction? *International Review of Education*, *54*(2), 211–242. doi:10.1007/s11159-008-9084-1

Reffay, C., & Chanier, T. (2003). How social network analysis can help to measure cohesion in collaborative distance-learning. In B. Wasson, S. Ludvigsen & U. Hoppe (Eds.), *Designing for change in networked learning environments. Proceedings of Conference CSCL 2003* (pp. 343-352). Dordrecht: Kluwer Academic Publishers.

Rusch, E. A. (2005). Institutional barriers to organizational learning in school systems: The power of silence. *Educational Administration Quarterly*, *41*(1), 83–120. doi:10.1177/0013161X04269546

Ryberg, T., & Larsen, M. C. (2008). Networked identities: Understanding relationships between strong and weak ties in networked environments. *Journal of Computer Assisted Learning*, *24*(2), 103–115. doi:10.1111/j.1365-2729.2007.00272.x

Steeples, C., & Jones, C. (Eds.). (2002). *Networked learning: Perspectives and issues*. London: Springer.

Suthers, D. D., & Chu, K.-H. (2010). Identifying mediators of socio-technical capital in a networked learning environment. In L. Dirckinck-Holmfeld, V. Hodgson, C. Jones, M. de Laat, D. McConnell & T. Ryberg (Eds.), *Proceedings of the 7th International Conference on Networked Learning* (pp. 387-395). Aalborg, Denmark.

van der Sluis, L. E. C., & de Jong, T. (2009). Hop, step, jump! Building social capital by learning through bridging, bonding and linking. *International Journal of Learning and Intellectual Capital*, *6*(3), 214–234. doi:10.1504/IJLIC.2009.025042

Vrasidas, C., & Glass, G. V. (Eds.). (2004). *Current perspectives in applied information technologies. Online professional development for teachers*. Greenwich, CT: Information Age Publishing.

KEY TERMS AND DEFINITIONS

Informed Design: The pro-active design of social and technical systems to support meaningful learning outcomes based on analysis of learning activity.

Learning Capital: Analogous to social capital, learning capital may be considered as the ability of a network to learn (i.e., to absorb and transform understanding based on network connections, and also as the learning and transformation that results as an outcome of network connections).

Network Positions: Structural positions in the network that have significance to the flow of resources in a network (e.g., a network star).

Network Roles: Roles that emerge in a network due to the specific kinds of interactions actors engage in with others (e.g., a technological gatekeeper).

Networked Learning: The use of computer networks and social relationships to promote collaborative or cooperative learning among learners, their tutors and learning resources.

Relations: The interaction, connection or mutual activity that form the basis of a tie between actors in a network.

Social Capital: Benefits that reside in and result from the network connections between people within a social group (e.g., knowledge held among network members that supports their ability to respond to economic, social, intellectual or informational need).

Social Network: The configuration of interconnections among a set of actors that results from patterns of communication, resource exchange, social support, work, learning and/or play.

Social Network Analysis: The collection and analysis of data describing patterns of interaction among interacting members of a network.

Chapter 19
Designing a Model for Enhanced Teaching and Meaningful E-Learning

Heli Ruokamo
University of Lapland, Finland

Päivi Hakkarainen
University of Lapland, Finland

Miikka Eriksson
University of Lapland, Finland

ABSTRACT

In this chapter, we describe the informed design of a specific pedagogical model in the context of higher education. We have developed the model of Enhanced Teaching and Meaningful e-Learning to design, implement, and evaluate the use of educational technology. Although a great number of pedagogical models already exist, we argue that development of new models remains crucial. Despite decades of development, teachers still need functional examples of how to use educational technology in a pedagogically meaningful way. In this chapter, we present a theoretical framework for our model design, taking into account previous models and characteristics of meaningful learning. We then present our research strategy along with the research questions we have posed. Additionally, we describe the course we have designed and implemented as well as the participants in this course. We follow this with an evaluation of successes, both in the course implementation, as well as the model design. Next, this chapter will present our data collection and analysis methods, as well as the research results. Finally, at the end of the chapter, we present future research trajectories of the model and recommendations for how to further develop the course.

DOI: 10.4018/978-1-61350-080-4.ch019

INTRODUCTION

In this chapter, we provide a description of this research, which aims to create a pedagogical model for designing, implementing and evaluating meaningful e-learning in higher education. More specifically, our aim is to transform an existing pedagogical model (the pedagogical model for teaching and meaningful learning [TML]) into a model for enhanced teaching and meaningful e-learning. In order to achieve this aim, we conducted a design-based research (DBR) study that focused on the national Finnish inter-university e-learning course *Pedagogical and Learning Theoretical Approaches to Educational Use of ICTs* (4 ECTS, European Credit Transfer System credits). Participants of the study were 22 students from three Finnish universities. This e-learning course builds on the principles of the TML model and, thus, offers a framework with which to study the modification of the model as a teaching and meaningful e-learning model. Our aim is to develop the course further and to design a model that functions as a theoretical foundation for the informed design of educational technology in higher education.

We argue that development of pedagogical models (see Joyce & Weil, 1980) is still crucial, as teachers are not yet fully aware of how to use technology in pedagogically appropriate ways. An effective pedagogical model will make teachers aware of the different means available to them, it will help in the designing, implementation, and evaluation of e-learning and it will ensure that students benefit from a more meaningful learning experience.

THEORETICAL BACKGROUND

The researchers engaged in this study have been developing pedagogical models for network-based education since the beginning of 2000, starting with the development of the integrated model for network-based education (see Tissari, Vahtivuori-Hänninen, Vaattovaara, Ruokamo, & Tella, 2005). The concept of a network refers here to both collaborative and technological networks. Over the past ten years, we have further developed the models based on previous research findings. In this study, the pedagogical model for teaching and meaningful learning (TML, see Figure 1) (Hakkarainen, 2007, 2009; in press; Hakkarainen, Saarelainen, & Ruokamo, 2007, 2009) guided the design, implementation, and evaluation of the e-learning course *Pedagogical and Learning Theoretical Approaches to Educational Use of ICTs.*

The Pedagogical Model for Teaching and Meaningful Learning (TML)

The development of the TML model was based on the integrated model of network-based education, which has its foundational roots in the ideas of meaningful learning put forward by Ausubel (1963) and Jonassen (1995). Ausubel presented the significance of meaningful learning in his cognitive learning theory (Ausubel, 1963, 1968; Ausubel, Novak, & Hanesian, 1978), while Ausubel et al. (1978) later distinguished between logical meaning and psychological meaning, which is the product of a meaningful learning process. Meaningful learning depends on the student's ability to relate new concepts and propositions to what they already know. Ausubel et al. (1978) combine the concepts of meaningfulness and personal significance, which has become a common practice in the field of education (Yrjönsuuri & Yrjönsuuri, 2005). In the TML model, meaningful learning includes the additional aspect of personal significance, which is conveyed by including the characteristic of the "individual" in the model.

The TML model consists of teaching and meaningful learning, which is defined in terms of 17 procedural characteristics and their expected outcomes, including domain-specific and generic knowledge and skills. The model also includes pedagogical models or approaches (e.g.,

Figure 1. The TML Model (Hakkarainen, 2007, 2009, in press; Hakkarainen, Saarelainen, & Ruokamo, 2009)

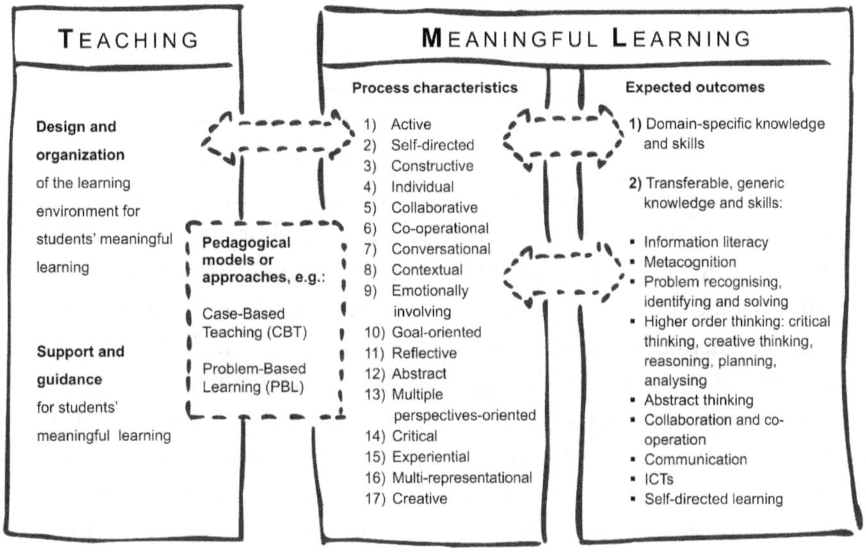

case-based teaching and problem-based learning), which cover both teaching and the learning processes (Figure 1). The relationships between the components of the model are reciprocal and conditional; in the TML model, a dashed two-way arrow indicates this relationship. Central to the application of the model is that not all of the 17 characteristics of meaningful learning processes need to be present at any given time. Moreover, the characteristics can be intertwined, interdependent, interactive, partly overlapping, and synergetic (Jonassen, 2000).

The broad and general nature of the TML model can be considered as both its strength and its weakness (Hakkarainen, 2007; Hakkarainen et al., 2009). The model's strength lies in its ability to provide a general framework from which to design, implement and assess educational technologies, instructional practices and learning outcomes within different subject areas and pedagogical models. As compared to other pedagogical e-learning models (see, e.g., Gabbagh, 2005), the procedural characteristics of meaningful learning provide a broad theoretical foundation for informed design of educational technologies. The model also stresses the meaning of students' emotional involvement in learning (until the last 10 to 15 years emotions have been an under-researched part of learning despite their integral meaning) (Kort & Reilly, 2002; Linnenbrink, 2006; Pekrun, Goetz, Titz, & Perry, 2002; Schutz, Hong, Cross, & Osbon, 2006).

The TML model does not describe specific instructional strategies. Instead, such instructional strategies are derivatives of the TML model itself (see also Gabbagh, 2005). The model represents what are generally understood as good teaching and learning processes and outcomes in the 2000s, but it cannot be considered all-inclusive (Hakkarainen, 2007; Hakkarainen et al., 2009).

The model is, however, fairly complex, suggesting that the number of process characteristics and expected outcomes of meaningful learning might be reduced (Hakkarainen et al., 2009). In this research, our aim is to study whether it is possible to group together the 17 process characteristics of meaningful learning, rather than making the list of characteristics longer. We, therefore, attempt to decipher which characteristics are similar to each other in the specific context of higher education e-learning.

Teaching

Anderson, Rourke, Garrison and Archer (2001) have influenced the conceptualization of teaching by proposing the concept of "teaching presence" for e-learning settings that use computer conferencing. They define teaching presence as the "design, facilitation and direction of cognitive and social processes for the purpose of realizing a personally meaningful and educationally worthwhile learning outcome" (p. 5). Anderson et al. (2001) describe this in terms of three categories: (1) design and organization (e.g., designing methods, utilizing media effectively), (2) facilitating discourse (e.g., encouraging student contributions, setting the climate for learning, drawing in participants) and (3) direct instruction (e.g., presenting content/ questions, diagnosing misconceptions, providing assessment and feedback).

In the TML model, teaching and meaningful learning are viewed as processes triggered by various pedagogical models or approaches, such as case-based teaching or problem-based learning. A pedagogical model or approach is understood, following Joyce and Weil (1980), as "a plan or pattern that can be used to shape curricula (long-term courses of studies), to design instructional materials, and to guide instruction in the classroom and other settings" (p. 1).

Process Characteristics of Meaningful Learning

The process characteristics of meaningful learning have been selected from the work of Jonassen (see, e.g., 1995; 2000), Ruokamo and Pohjolainen (2000), Ruokamo (see, e.g., 2001), and Ruokamo, Tella, Vahtivuori, Tuovinen & Tissari (2002). The list also draws on the characteristics of purposive studying presented by Vahtivuori et al. (2003), Vahtivuori-Hänninen et al. (2004), and Vaattovaara, Tissari, Vahtivuori-Hänninen, Ruokamo, & Tella (2005) and Soini's (1999) characteristics of good learning situations.

The influence of Ausubel et al. (1978) is clearly visible in the active, constructive, individual and goal-oriented characteristics of meaningful learning. For example, Ausubel et al. claimed that the cooperative and emotionally-involving aspects of learning could be explored, but that not too much weight should be given to them. It can be argued that the process characteristics of meaningful learning in the TML model represent an updated version of the Ausubel et al. position — an interpretation of meaningful learning for the 2000s, as it were (Hakkarainen, 2007).

We will next present a brief overview of the process characteristics of meaningful learning (see also Hakkarainen et al., 2009).

1. *Active*. In active learning "learners are engaged by the learning process in a mindful processing of information, where they are responsible for the result" (Jonassen, 1995, p. 60). Students are encouraged to ask questions, acquire information, critically evaluate information, and express new ideas and models of thinking (Ruokamo et al., 2002) and to use different productivity tools and cognitive tools in their learning environments (Jonassen, 1995, 2000).
2. *Self-directed*. Self-direction in learning refers to "a process in which a learner assumes primary responsibility for planning, implementing, and evaluating the learning process" (Brockett & Hiemstra, 1991, p. 24). The concept intertwines with the characteristics of activeness, goal-orientedness, and reflection.
3. *Constructive*. Constructive learning means that learners accommodate new ideas into their prior knowledge in a process of mean-

ing making, not of knowledge reception (Jonassen, 1995, 2002).

4. *Individual.* Individuality means that learners have individual learning styles and strategies and that students' prior knowledge, conceptions, and interests always influences learning (Ruokamo et al., 2002).
5. *Collaborative.* Working collaboratively makes it possible for students to exploit each other's skills and to provide social support and modeling for other students (Jonassen, 1995, 2002). Collaboration is collaborative knowledge construction where the group is the subject of learning (see, e.g., Repo-Kaarento, 2004).
6. *Co-operative.* Co-operative learning entails using groups as tools for enhancing individual learning. The learners' individual responsibility is the characteristic that most clearly sets the approach apart from collaborative learning (Repo-Kaarento, 2004); however, the concepts are sometimes used synonymously.
7. *Conversational.* Conversational learning is a dialogue, that is, a process of internal and social negotiation (Jonassen, 1995, 2002).
8. *Contextual.* Contextual learning refers to learning tasks that are situated either in meaningful, real world tasks, or simulated through a case-based, or problem-based learning environment (Jonassen, 1995, 2000).
9. *Emotionally involving.* According to university students' perceptions, emotional involvement is a highly important feature of a good learning environment (Soini, 1999). The emotions that students experience in academic settings play a central role in their motivation to learn, self-regulate, and achieve academically (Pekrun et al., 2002; Pekrun, 2007). Positive emotions predict high achievement, and negative emotions predict low achievement, with the exception that a successful learning process may also include occasional negative emotions (Op't Eynde, De Corte, & Verschaffel, 2001; Pekrun et al., 2002; Pekrun, 2007).
10. *Goal-oriented.* In a goal-oriented learning process, students work actively to achieve a cognitive goal, and can define their own learning objectives (Jonassen, 1995; Ruokamo & Pohjolainen, 2000).
11. *Reflective.* Intertwined with goal-orientation is the process of reflection (Jonassen, 1995, 2000). In a reflective learning process, students express what they have learned and examine the thinking practices required during the process (Jonassen, 1995; Ruokamo & Pohjolainen, 2000).
12. *Abstract.* Abstract learning can be defined as the construction of new ideas at an abstract level, where the development of theoretical ideas reach from practical experience to a deeper level (Lehtinen, 1997; Ruokamo et al., 2002).
13. *Multiple perspectives-oriented.* Learners are presented with information from multiple perspectives and case studies that present diverse examples (Spiro, Feltovich, Jacobson, & Coulson, 1992). Students experience learning situations that lead to an awareness of multiple perspectives as good and real learning situations (Soini, 1999).
14. *Critical.* Critical thinking is a general critical attitude toward knowledge and knowing, described by Cottrell (2005) as "holding open the possibility that what you know at a given time may only be part of the picture" (p. 2). In addition to a general attitude, critical thinking is a set of practices aimed at exploring evidence in a critical way. It focuses on messages being conveyed through speech, writing, performance, or media (Cottrell, 2005).
15. *Experiential.* Experiential characteristics mean that students can use their own experiences as a starting point in the learning process and that they are able to apply

their own practical experiences throughout the course. "Experiences" are understood first as referring to students' prior practical knowledge, and second as the aim of learning. Learning should integrate theoretical knowledge with practical knowledge in order to create experiential knowledge (Poikela, 2006).

16. *Multi-representational.* Effective learning processes should make use of the careful combination and integration of multiple representational modes (e.g., texts, still/moving pictures, and voice) (see, e.g., Dekeyser, 2000; Mayer, 2003; Spiro et al., 1992).
17. *Creative.* According to Novak (1998), "the creative person sees how to make the right connections between concepts in two domains of knowledge that were previously regarded as unrelated, or in some cases even contradictory" (p. 78). According to Novak, creativity should be viewed as a search for high levels of meaningful learning.

Expected Learning Outcomes

The expected outcomes of meaningful learning processes in the TML model include: (1) domain-specific knowledge and skills, and (2) transferable, generic knowledge and skills such as metacognitive skills and higher-order thinking skills. Transfer of learning refers to the ability to extend what has been learned from one context into others. Transfer of learning is central to helping students approach new situations in a flexible manner and in the development of adaptive expertise (Bransford, Brown, & Cocking, 2000). In the light of previous findings (see Brandsford et al., 2000), it can be argued that the self-directed, contextual (but not overly contextualized), abstract, and reflective characteristics of meaningful learning processes, in particular, can lead to transferable knowledge and skills (Hakkarainen, 2007).

However, learning outcomes in the TML model are considered very complex issues. The relationship between learning processes and their outcomes is represented in the TML model (Fig. 1) as dashed two-way arrows between the two components (Hakkarainen, 2007). One of the most important reasons for this complexity is that students cannot learn simply by deciding to learn something. Even if people cannot determine what they will learn or how well they will learn it, they can develop knowledge and skills to *enhance* their learning (Yrjönsuuri & Yrjönsuuri, 2005).

Although the TML model is based on the argument that each component has critical importance, the research we present in this chapter focuses mainly on students' perceptions about the realization of teaching and the process characteristics of meaningful learning. It is not possible to include all viewpoints and components of the instructional process in the design of a particular study (see Kansanen & Meri, 1999).

RESEARCH STRATEGY AND QUESTIONS

This research was a design-based research (DBR) process (see also Hakkarainen, 2007, 2009, in press). DBR involves developing, testing, investigating, and refining learning environment designs and theoretical constructs) such as the pedagogical models that support learning (as well as illustrating and predicting how learning occurs (Barab & Squire, 2004; Design-based Research Collective, 2003). A DBR process proceeds through iterative cycles of design and implementation, and according to Wang and Hannafin (2005), design-based research leads to "contextually-sensitive design principles and theories" (p. 7). DBR aims to improve simultaneously, both theory and local practices.

In this research, our aim is to find out which of the 17 process characteristics of meaningful learning are close to each other and how these processes are realized in the specific context of higher education e-learning. Based on our findings, we will also discuss how the course can be developed effectively. Our aim is also to design and describe the model for enhanced teaching and meaningful e-learning. Our research questions in this study are as follows:

- **RQ1:** How can the characteristics of meaningful learning be grouped to design a model for Enhanced Teaching and Meaningful e-Learning (ETMeL)?
- **RQ2:** From the student perspective, how is teaching and meaningful learning realized in *the Pedagogical and Learning Theoretical Approaches to Educational Use of ICTs* course?

Participants and Course Description

Participants in this study were students enrolled in the Finnish national inter-university e-learning course *Pedagogical and Learning Theoretical Approaches to Educational Use of ICTs* (four ECTS credits) in autumn 2009. The aim of the course is for students to acquire a basic understanding of the use of ICTs in teaching and learning. In addition, the students are expected to develop an understanding of the pedagogical and theoretical learning concepts related to the field. In total, 29 students participated in this course. Participants (N=22) of this study were from three universities in Finland: University of Lapland (N=17), University of Helsinki (N=2) and University of Turku (N=3). Ages of the participants varied from 19 to 36 years, 18 (82%) were females and four (18%) were males. Thirteen (59%) of the students had no previous experience of e-learning, while nine (41%) had previous experience. Twenty-one students (96%) owned a laptop, two (9%) had desk computers and one (5%) had a mobile phone with Internet connection.

The timeline of the course was 11 weeks. The first six weeks included active participation from students and during the following five weeks, the teachers (N=5) prepared written feedback for the students. The course began with a 60-minute introductory, online meeting through *Adobe Connect Pro* web conferencing software. During this meeting, the 17 characteristics of meaningful learning were presented and discussed with students. Following this, the students familiarized themselves with the course literature and engaged in online discussions in groups of five to 15 students. As their learning assignment, students discussed the topics of the course either through chat discussions or through asynchronous discussions. In addition, they wrote essays individually or as a pair assignment. The course used the *Moodle* learning management system to provide guidance for the students, group conversations, delivering the course materials, submitting the essays, and for the teachers' written feedback.

The design of the course did not draw on a distinct pedagogical model such as case-based teaching, case-based reasoning, or problem-based learning. However, several of the characteristics of the TML model were taken into special consideration while designing the course. The course materials were developed and presented in multi-representational modes including text, graphics, still images and video clips. The aim of the online discussions was to support *active*, *constructive*, *collaborative*, *co-operational*, *conversational*, *contextual*, *experiential*, *multiple perspectives -oriented* and *reflective* learning. The teachers' role was designed to support and guide students' *individual* learning, to provide assessment and explanatory feedback through online discussions, and especially through the written feedback. It has been demonstrated that in e-learning settings, the students particularly appreciate the teachers' feedback (see also Chang & Petersen, 2005). The pedagogical rationale for the essay was specifically to support the *abstract, self-directed, critical, contextual,* and *experiential characteristics* of meaningful learning. Our intention in this study was to develop a model for enhanced teaching and meaningful e-learning to be used in this course and in future courses.

Data Collection and Analysis

Authors of this chapter devised and used a 138-item online questionnaire, which the students completed at the end of the course after receiving written feedback from the teachers. In this chapter, we will present part of the resulting data collected by the questionnaire. In order to receive the completed questionnaires from students, three reminder e-mails were sent. The author devised and used the questionnaire in previous research (see Hakkarainen, 2007, 2009, in press; Hakkarainen et al., 2007, 2009). The questionnaire included, for example, 26 five-point Likert scale statements concerning the meaningfulness of the learning process, five statements enquiring about the effects of different course structures on learning, five statements enquiring about the effects of teacher activities on studying and learning, and 36 statements concerning the practical realization (e.g., locations and the use of technologies) of students' learning processes. The response rate was reasonably high: 22 out of 29 course participants completed the questionnaire (76%).

We analyzed the data using several quantitative analysis methods, such as frequencies, means, standard deviations, and percentages. Students' experiences of teaching and meaningful learning were analyzed using principal component analyses (PCA) for Likert scale variables and calculated Cronbach's Alphas. To support the content interpretation, varimax rotation with Kaiser normalization was also performed. When interpreting results, we must take into account the relatively small number of respondents (N=22) in this study. Therefore, using PCA is not a reliable method without careful consideration of the resulting groupings with respect to the theoretical model used in this research, that being the TML model.

RESULTS

The first research question of this study was: How can the characteristics of meaningful learning be grouped to design a model for Enhanced Teaching and Meaningful e-Learning (ETMeL). To answer this question, we used principal component analysis (PCA) taking into account its limitations in this research due to the small number of participants.

A Model for Enhanced Teaching and Meaningful e-Learning (ETMeL)

To simplify the TML model to ETMeL, we used principal component analysis (PCA). In total, 26 individual items were included (a segment of them describing the practical realization of the meaningful learning process and segment of them describing the outcomes of these processes in the course). Results from the principal component analysis are presented in Table 1. Because the sample size was relatively small, the results of the analyses are not very reliable. Therefore, we also estimated the internal consistency of the resulted groupings by calculating Cronbach's Alpha (see last row of the Table 1) that takes values from 0 (indicating no correlation) to 1 (indicating identical results) (Cronbach, 1951). Alpha values of about 0.7 or above, are considered as evidence of acceptable internal consistency (Nunnally, 1978). Only the two last factors with more than one item had Alpha values below the acceptable level. Therefore, discussions of the groupings of the factor analyses are concerned only with the first four factors and the sixth one. Items in the other factors are treated as single items.

The first factor was named '*flexible and individual studying*' as the two most highly loaded items included the possibility to study when and where it best suited the student. In addition to the two items that described the practical realization of the meaningful learning process, the possibility to choose the topic of the course essay was also included in this factor. The other items de-

Table 1. Results of the principal component analysis (PCA)

	Flexible and Individual studying?	Constructive studying	Collaborative studying	Learning outcomes	Multi-representational	Reflective studying	Emotionally involving: challenging	Practical and Experiential
The course helped me to understand different perspectives related to the topics under study.	.537							
The studying enabled the achievement of my personal goals.	.705							
The course deepened my understanding of what I had learned before.	.722							
I was able to influence the topic of my essay.	.587							
I was able to study at times suitable to me.	.859							
I was able to study flexibly at places suitable to me	.880							
I was able to apply my own practical experiences during the course.		.841						
I was able to utilize my prior knowledge about the course topics.		.813						
Students' role was to actively acquire, evaluate, and apply information.		.570						
The studying developed my problem solving skills.		.541						
The studying developed my creative thinking.		.600						
The students were committed to collaboration.			.682					
Teachers "actions" supported my learning			.712					
Studying with fellow students supported my learning.			.727					
I was able to influence the topic and progress of online discussions.			.538					
The studying developed my collaboration and communication skills.			.687					
I can use knowledge and skills learned in other contexts.				.510				
The course promoted the learning of skills and knowledge needed in working life.				.675				
The studying developed my understanding in the subject matter of the course.				.764				
The studying developed my critical thinking skills.				.761				
The targets of learning were examined through several forms of presentation (text, diagrams, pictures, video, etc.).					.846			
It was possible for me to study according to my own personal style that suits me.						.709		
I was able to evaluate my own learning during the course.						.900		
Online discussions were challenging.							.849	
Writing the essay was challenging.							.645	
On the course practical examples were studied in a theoretical framework.								.797
I was able to utilize my own experiences as the starting point of learning.								.598
Cronbach's Alpha	0.893	0.862	0.850	0.764	-	0.728	0.560	0.590

scribed the outcomes of these processes: the achievement of one's personal goals, understanding different perspectives related to the topics under study and deepened understanding of what one had learned before. However, whether the occurrences these items describe are really the outcomes of flexible studying cannot be reliably estimated based on this data. The flexible and individual studying factor, therefore, represents several process characteristics of the TML model.

The second factor, '*constructive studying,*' includes three items describing the practical realization of the course. The item describing the application of one's own practical experiences during the course was the most highly loaded item, followed closely by the possibility to utilize one's prior knowledge about the course topics. The student's active role in the learning process (the basis of constructivist learning) fits well into the same category. Outcomes of the process included in this factor were the development of problem solving skills and creative thinking that fit well within the category of constructive learning. Moreover, the second factor represents more than one process characteristic of the TML model.

The third factor '*collaborative studying,*' includes items that describe the collaborative side of the course, including teachers' actions during the course and the students' possibility to influence the topic and progress of online discussions. One outcome of the studying process, 'studying with fellow students supported my learning,' was the most highly loaded item within this factor. Items in this factor clearly represent the collaborative characteristics of the TML model, which also highlights the teachers' active role in collaborative studying.

The fourth factor '*learning outcomes,*' includes only outcomes of the learning process. The two most highly loaded items included the development of understanding of the subject matter and the development of one's critical thinking. Furthermore, the usability of the acquired skills or knowledge in other areas of life and the promotion of skills and knowledge needed in working life were represented. This factor, therefore, also describes the applicability of the skills and knowledge outside of the educational context (cf. *Transfer*).

The sixth factor '*reflective studying*' includes only two items: the possibility to study according to one's own personal style, and the ability to evaluate one's own learning. Both items, therefore, represent the individual process characteristics of the TML model.

On the basis of the principal component analyses and careful consideration, whether each group of items (factor) form a logical and rational aggregate, we developed the following model for teaching and meaningful learning (see Figure 2). We named the model Enhanced Teaching and Meaningful e-Learning (ETMeL). This model presents how the characteristics of meaningful learning can be grouped together in the *Pedagogical and Learning Theoretical Approaches to Educational Use of ICTs* course as it was carried out in autumn 2009. We will describe how we formed the characteristics of enhanced teaching later in this chapter.

Our second research question of this study was: From the student perspective, how is teaching and meaningful learning realized in the *Pedagogical and Learning Theoretical Approaches to Educational Use of ICTs* course? To answer this question we used means, standards deviations and percentages.

Teaching and Meaningful Learning in the Pedagogical and Learning Theoretical Approaches to Educational Use of ICTs Course from the Student Perspective

Table 2 presents the data focusing on the practical realization of the process characteristics of meaningful learning. The data indicate that, according to the students, the course approach supported most

Figure 2. The model for enhanced teaching and meaningful e-learning

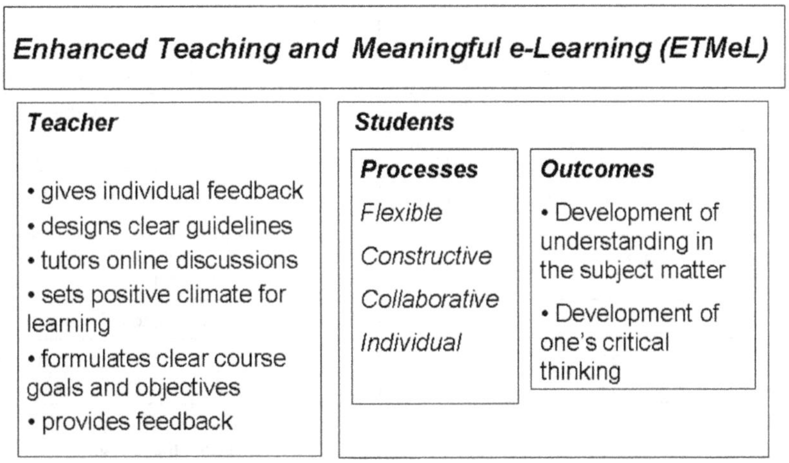

strongly the *active*, *self-directed*, *constructive*, *individual*, *reflective*, *abstract*, *multiple perspectives-oriented*, *critical*, and *multi-representational* characteristics of meaningful learning. Fifty-five (N=12) to eighty-two (N=18) percent of the respondents agreed, or moderately agreed, with the statements focusing on these characteristics. Two exceptions to this were students' ratings on the statement 'The studying enabled the achievement of my personal goals,' to which only 32% (N=7) of the students agreed or moderately agreed, and students' ratings of the statement 'I was able to influence the topic and progress of online discussions', to which 46% (N=10) agreed or moderately agreed.

The percentage of students who agreed with the statements focusing on the *collaborative, co-operational, conversational, contextual, goal-oriented,* and *creative* process characteristics of meaningful learning ranged from 32% (N=7) to 55% (N=12). Promoting these characteristics is therefore a development challenge for this course.

Student perspectives on teaching activities were measured using six statements in the questionnaire. We extracted the mean values, standard deviations, and percentages of the students' ratings of the teaching activities performed by the teachers of the *Pedagogical and Learning Theoretical Approaches to Educational Use of ICTs* course. Table 3 presents the questionnaire data focusing on the practical realization of teaching activities. These activities are presented in the model of Enhanced Teaching and Meaningful e-Learning (see Figure 2.) earlier in this chapter.

Thirty-two (N=7) to eighty-two (N=18) percent of the respondents agreed, or moderately agreed, with these statements. This indicates that the students' perception of teaching activities was positive. The students rated the significance of clear guidelines and individual feedback about their essays for their learning process and outcomes favourably. However, only 32% (N=7) of the respondents agreed or moderately agreed that the teachers supported their learning process and outcomes by "providing feedback and advice in a sufficiently timely manner" (M=3.27, SD=1.03).

FUTURE RESEARCH DIRECTIONS

The results of this research are purely descriptive in nature, therefore, the designed ETMeL model

Table 2. The students' ratings of the practical realization of the meaningful learning process and outcomes in the Pedagogical and Learning Theoretical Approaches to Educational Use of ICTs course

Group characteristics	Meaningful learning process and outcomes	Mean value	Standard deviation	Moderately agree/agree %	Statement in the questionnaire focusing on the learning process characteristics and outcomes
Flexible and Individual Studying	Individual	4.05	0.95	81.8	I was able to study flexibly at places suitable to me.
	Individual	4.05	0.84	77.3	I was able to study at times suitable to me.
	Constructive	3.41	0.73	50.0	The course deepened my understanding of what I had learned before.
	Individual and goal-oriented	3.09	1.07	31.8	The studying enabled the achievement of my personal goals.
	Self-directed	3.36	1.14	59.1	I was able to influence the topic of my essay.
	Multiple perspectives –oriented	3.68	1.04	77.2	The course helped me to understand different perspectives related to the topics under study.
Constructive Studying	Individual	3.32	1.13	59.1	I was able to apply my own practical experiences during the course.
	Constructive	3.41	1.22	68.2	I was able to utilize my prior knowledge about the course topics.
	Creative	3.23	0.92	50.0	The studying developed my creative thinking.
	Active	3.59	1.14	68.2	Students' role was to actively acquire, evaluate, and apply information.
	Active, Constructive, Creative	3.00	1.02	40.9	The studying developed my problem-solving skills.
Collaborative Studying	Co-operational	3.36	1.05	54.6	Studying with fellow students supported my learning.
	Co-operational	2.95	1.36	40.9	Teachers' actions supported my learning.
	Conversational	3.36	0.95	54.5	The studying developed my collaboration and communication skills.
	Collaborative	2.86	1.08	31.8	The students were committed to collaboration.
	Self-directed	3.00	1.31	45.5	I was able to influence the topic and progress of online discussions.
Learning Outcomes	Domain-specific knowledge	3.86	0.83	81.8	The studying developed my understanding in the subject matter of the course
	Transferable, generic knowledge and skills	3.64	0.95	63.6	The studying developed my critical thinking skills.
	Transferable, generic knowledge and skills	3.23	0.87	40.9	The course promoted the learning of skills and knowledge needed in working life.
	Transferable, generic knowledge and skills	3.70	0.75	77.3	I can use the knowledge and skills learned in other contexts.
Reflective Studying	Reflective	3.23	0.97	81.8	I was able to evaluate my own learning during the course.
	Individual	3.73	0.88	72.7	It was possible for me to study according to my own personal style that suits me.

n = 22 5-point scale: 1 = disagree, 2 = moderately disagree, 3 = neither disagree or agree, 4 = moderately agree, 5 = agree

Table 3. The students' ratings of the practical realization of the teaching activities in the Pedagogical and Learning Theoretical Approaches to Educational Use of ICTs course

Statement on the questionnaire focusing on teaching activities	M Mean value	S Standard deviation	M Moderately agree / agree %
Teachers supported my learning process and learning outcomes significantly by:			
(1) giving individual feedback about my essay	44.00	00.93	077.3
(2) designing clear guidelines for the course	43.86	01.08	081.8
(3) tutoring online discussions	43.64	01.14	063.6
(4) setting positive climate for learning	43.41	01.10	050.0
(5) formulating clear course goals and objectives	33.27	01.35	059.1
(6) providing feedback and advice in a sufficiently timely manner	43.27	01.03	031.8

n = 22 5-point scale: 1 = disagree, 2 = moderately disagree, 3 = neither disagree or agree, 4 = moderately agree, 5 = agree

is tentative as there was a relatively small number of respondents (N=22) in this study. Therefore, using PCA is not a reliable method without careful consideration. To develop the designed model, more participants and new design-based research cycles are necessary. In autumn 2011, we are going to put this tentative ETMeL model into use in the *Pedagogical and Learning Theoretical Approaches to Educational Use of ICTs* course and will carry out the next DBR cycle. Since autumn 2010, we have had more participants in this course since it is now obligatory in the new 2010–2012 curriculum for teacher education students (intake: 64 students/year) at the University of Lapland.

In the future, we are interested in examining the teacher's perspectives on this course. We will study what kind of experiences the course teachers have had, first with regard to designing and organizing the learning environment for students' meaningful learning, and second, with regard to supporting and guiding students' meaningful learning processes. From their own perspective, we are interested in studying how course teachers feel when enhanced teaching is realized.

CONCLUSION

The results of this study indicate a need to develop the e-learning course *Pedagogical and Learning Theoretical Approaches to Educational Use of ICTs*. To conclude, we will present some recommendations dealing with the informed design of the course and the ETMeL model. In the future, the model and the course should be designed so that they can better enable students to achieve their personal goals. Furthermore, students should have more influence over the topics and the progress of online discussions.

Promoting the *collaborative, co-operational, and conversational* characteristics has proven to be a development and refinement challenge for this course. It can be argued that the learning assignments of the course provided somewhat limited opportunities for these characteristics to be realized. As their first learning assignment, students discussed the topics of the course in online discussions and secondly, wrote essays either individually or as a pair assignment. However, if we understand collaboration as collaborative knowledge construction in which the group is the subject of learning (see, e.g., Repo-Kaarento, 2004), we can refine the course by making the course assignments more collaborative. Students should be obliged to collaborate with each other and teachers should support them more in these collaborative processes.

If we consider the fact that the collaborative, co-operational, and conversational characteristics are a development challenge for this course, together with the fact that the *contextual* characteristics of learning were not fully realized according to the students, it is possible to refine the course by designing a collaborative learning assignment that is situated in meaningful, real world, case-based tasks (see Jonassen, 1995, 2000) that are generated by the students. A collaborative analysis of a real world case, dealing with the topic of the course (i.e. educational use of ICTs), decided by the students themselves, could increase the students' commitment to collaboration. The course should put more emphasis on promoting the learning of skills and knowledge necessary for working life.

Furthermore, more support should be provided for the development of students' problem-solving skills and creative characteristics of meaningful learning. We should encourage students to make connections between concepts in previously unrelated domains of knowledge (cf. Novak, 1998, 78). Despite a decade of development work, there is still a lot to do in the future.

REFERENCES

Anderson, T., Rourke, L., Garrison, R., & Archer, W. (2001). Assessing teaching presence in a computer conferencing context. *JALN Journal of Asynchronous Learning Networks, 5*(2), 1−17. Retrieved from http://www.aln.org/publications/jaln/v5n2/pdf/v5n2_anderson.pdf

Ausubel, D. (1963). *The psychology of meaningful verbal learning*. New York, NY: Grune and Stratton.

Ausubel, D. (1968). *Educational psychology: A cognitive view*. New York, NY: Holt, Rinehart & Winston.

Ausubel, D. P., Novak, J. D., & Hanesian, H. (1978). *Educational psychology: A cognitive view* (2nd ed.). New York, NY: Holt, Rinehart and Winston.

Barab, S., & Squire, K. (2004). Design-based research: Putting a stake in the ground. *Journal of the Learning Sciences, 13*(1), 1–14. doi:10.1207/s15327809jls1301_1

Bransford, J. D., Brown, A. L., & Cocking, R. R. (Eds.). (2000). *How people learn. Brain, mind, experience, and school* (Expanded ed.). Washington, DC: National Academy Press.

Brockett, R. G., & Hiemstra, R. (1991). *Self-direction in adult learning: Perspectives on theory, research, and practice*. London, UK: Routledge.

Chang, N., & Petersen, N. J. (2005). Cybercoaching: An emerging model of personalized online assessment. In Williams, D. D. (Ed.), *Online assessment, measurement and evaluation: Emerging practices* (pp. 110–130). Hershey, PA: Information Science Publishing. doi:10.4018/978-1-59140-747-8.ch008

Cottrell, S. (2005). *Critical thinking skills: Developing effective analysis and argument*. Basingstoke, UK: Palgrave Macmillan.

Cronbach, L. J. (1951). Coefficient alpha and the internal structure of tests. *Psychometrika, 16*(3), 297–334. doi:10.1007/BF02310555

Dekeyser, H. M. (2000). Student preference for verbal, graphic or symbolic information in an independent learning environment for an applied statistics course. In K. Littleton (Series Ed.) & J. F. Rouet, A. Biardeau, & J. J. Levonen (Eds.), *Advances in learning and instruction series: Multimedia learning, cognitive and instructional issues* (pp. 99−109). Amsterdam, The Netherlands: Pergamon.

Design-Based Research Collective. (2003). Design-based research: An emerging paradigm for educational inquiry. *Educational Researcher, 13*(1), 1–14.

Gabbagh, N. (2005). Pedagogical models for e-learning: A theory-based design framework. *International Journal of Technology in Teaching and Learning, 1*(1), 25–44.

Hakkarainen, P. (2007). *Promoting meaningful learning through the integrated use of digital videos*. Doctoral dissertation, University of Lapland. Acta Universitatis Lapponiensis 121. Rovaniemi, Finland: University of Lapland, Faculty of Education.

Hakkarainen, P. (2009). Designing and implementing a PBL course on educational digital video production: Lessons learned from a design-based research. *Educational Technology Research and Development, 57*(2), 211–228. doi:10.1007/s11423-007-9039-4

Hakkarainen, P. (in press). Promoting meaningful learning through video production-supported PBL. *Interdisciplinary Journal of Problem-based Learning.*

Hakkarainen, P., Saarelainen, T., & Ruokamo, H. (2007). Towards meaningful learning through digital video-supported case-based teaching. *Australasian Journal of Educational Technology, 23*(1), 87–109.

Hakkarainen, P., Saarelainen, T., & Ruokamo, H. (2009). Assessing teaching and students' meaningful learning processes in an e-learning course. In Spratt, C., & Lajbcygier, P. (Eds.), *E-learning technologies and evidence-based assessment approaches* (pp. 20–36). Hershey, PA: IGI Global. doi:10.4018/978-1-60566-410-1.ch002

Jonassen, D. H. (1995). Supporting communities of learners with technology: A vision for integrating technology with learning in schools. *Educational Technology, 35*(4), 60–63.

Jonassen, D. H. (2000). *Computers as mindtools for schools. Engaging critical thinking*. New Jersey: Prentice-Hall.

Joyce, B., & Weil, M. (1980). *Models of teaching* (2nd ed.). New Jersey: Prentice/Hall International.

Kansanen, P., & Meri, M. (1999). The didactic relation in the teaching–studying–learning process [Electronic version]. In B. Hudson, F. Buchberger, P. Kansanen, & H. Seel (Eds.), *Didaktik/Fachdidaktik as science(-s) of the teaching profession. The Thematic Network of Teacher Education in Europe (TNTEE) Publications, 2*(1), 107–116. Retrieved from http://tntee.umu.se/publications/v2n1/pdf/2_1complete.pdf#page=113

Kort, B., & Reilly, R. (2002). Analytical models of emotions, learning, and relationships: Towards an affective-sensitive cognitive machine. *Proceedings of the ITS 2002 – Intelligent Tutoring Systems Conference* (pp. 955–962). June 2002, Biarritz, France. Retrieved from http://web.media.mit.edu/~reilly/its2002.pdf

Lehtinen, E. (1997). Tietoyhteiskunnan haasteet ja mahdollisuudet oppimiselle. [Challenges and possibilities for learning in the information society] In Lehtinen, E. (Ed.), *Verkkopedagogiikka* (pp. 12–40). Helsinki, Finland: Edita.

Linnenbrink, E. A. (2006). Emotion research in education: Theoretical and methodological perspectives on the integration of affect, motivation, and cognition. *Educational Psychology Review, 18*(4), 307–314. doi:10.1007/s10648-006-9028-x

Mayer, R. E. (2003). *Multimedia learning*. New York, NY: Cambridge University Press.

Novak, J. D. (1998). *Learning, creating, and using knowledge: Concept maps as facilitative tools in schools and corporations*. Mahwah, NJ: Lawrence Erlbaum Associates.

Nunnally, J. C. (1978). *Psychometric theory* (2nd ed.). New York, NY: McGraw-Hill.

Op't Eynde, P., De Corte, E., & Verschaffel, L. (2001). What to learn from what we feel: The role of students' emotions in the mathematics classroom. In Volet, S., & Järvelä, S. (Eds.), *Motivation in learning contexts. Theoretical advances and methodological implications* (pp. 149–167). Amsterdam, The Netherlands: Pergamon.

Pekrun, R. (2007). Emotions in students' scholastic development. In Perry, R. P., & Smart, J. C. (Eds.), *The scholarship of teaching and learning in higher education: an evidence-based perspective* (pp. 553–610). Dordrecht, the Netherlands: Springer. doi:10.1007/1-4020-5742-3_13

Pekrun, R., Goetz, T., Tizt, W., & Perry, R. P. (2002). Academic emotions in students' self-regulated learning and achievement: A program of qualitative and quantitative research. *Educational Psychologist, 37*(2), 91–105. doi:10.1207/S15326985EP3702_4

Poikela, E. (2006). Knowledge, knowing and problem-based learning—Some epistemological and ontological remarks. In Poikela, E., & Nummenmaa, A. R. (Eds.), *Understanding problem-based learning* (pp. 15–31). Tampere, Finland: Tampere University Press.

Repo-Kaarento, S. (2004). Yhteisöllistä ja yhteistoiminnallista oppimista yliopistoon — Käsitteiden tarkastelua ja sovellutusten kehittelyä [Introducing collaborative and cooperative learning at university — Looking at the concepts and developing applications] [The Finnish Journal of Education]. *Kasvatus, 35*(5), 499–515.

Ruokamo, H. (2001). The Solver learning environment and anchored instruction on mathematical word problem-solving. In C. Montgomerie & J. Viteli (Eds.), *Proceedings of ED-MEDIA 2001 - World Conference on Educational Multimedia, Hypermedia & Telecommunications* (pp. 1595–1600) [CD-ROM]. Association for the Advancement of Computing in Education.

Ruokamo, H., & Pohjolainen, S. (2000). Distance learning in multimedia networks project: Main results. *British Journal of Educational Technology, 31*(2), 117–125. doi:10.1111/1467-8535.00142

Ruokamo, H., Tella, S., Vahtivuori, S., Tuovinen, H., & Tissari, V. (2002). Pedagogical models in the design and assessment of network-based education. In P. Barker & S. Rebelsky (Eds.), *Proceedings of ED-MEDIA 2002 - World Conference on Educational Multimedia, Hypermedia & Telecommunications* (pp. 1676–1681) [CD-ROM]. Association for the Advancement of Computing in Education.

Schutz, P., Hong, J., Cross, D., & Osbon, J. (2006). Reflections on investigating emotion in educational activity settings. *Educational Psychology Review, 18*(4), 343–360. doi:10.1007/s10648-006-9030-3

Soini, H. (1999). *Education students' experiences of learning and their conceptions about learning disabilities. Towards a comprehensive theory of learning*. Doctoral dissertation, University of Oulu. Acta Universitatis Ouluensis Scientiae Rerum Socialium 40. Oulu, Finland: Oulu University Press.

Spiro, R. J., Feltovich, P. J., Jacobson, M. J., & Coulson, R. L. (1992). Cognitive flexibility, constructivism and hypertext: Random access instruction for advanced knowledge acquisition in ill-structured domains. In Duffy, T. M., & Jonassen, D. H. (Eds.), *Constructivism and the technology of instruction: A conversation* (pp. 57–75). Hillsdale, NJ: Lawrence Erlbaum Associates.

Tissari, V., Vahtivuori-Hänninen, S., Vaattovaara, V., Ruokamo, H., & Tella, S. (2005). Applying pedagogical models in network-based education: Research findings from the Finnish HelLa project case studies. *Proceedings of ED-MEDIA 2005 - World Conference on Educational Multimedia, Hypermedia & Telecommunications* [CD-ROM] (pp. 656–662). Association for the Advancement of Computing in Education.

Vaattovaara, V., Tissari, V., Vahtivuori-Hänninen, S., Ruokamo, H., & Tella, S. (2005). Perspectives of some salient characteristics of pedagogical models in network-based education. In H. Ruokamo, P. Hyvönen, M. Lehtonen & S. Tella (Eds.), *Proceedings of the 12th International Networks-Based Education (NBE) Conference (Former PEG) 2005* (pp. 95). Rovaniemi, Finland: Lapland University Press. Retrieved from http://wanda.uef.fi/mathematics/MathDistEdu/Animations-2MentalModels/RovaniemiNBE2005/NBE2005.pdf#page=102

Vahtivuori, S., Tella, S., Tissari, V., Tuovinen, H., Ruokamo, H., & Vaattovaara, V. (2003). First evaluations of network-based education: Preliminary findings of the ICT programs evaluation project. In D. Lassner & C. McNaught (Eds.), *Proceedings of ED-MEDIA 2003 Conference - World Conference on Educational Multimedia, Hypermedia & Telecommunications* (pp. 3177–3183) [CD-ROM]. Association for the Advancement of Computing in Education.

Vahtivuori-Hänninen, S., Tissari, V., Vaattovaara, V., Rajala, R., Ruokamo, H., & Tella, S. (2004). Opetus, opiskelu ja oppiminen didaktisessa verkkoympäristössä [Teaching, studying and learning in a didactic network environment]. In *HelLa-projektin loppuraportti — Helsingin ja Lapin yliopistojen tieto- ja viestintätekniikan opetuskäytön tutkimus- ja kehittämisprojekti 2001–2003* (pp. 7–25). Retrieved December 12, 2006, from http://www.edu.helsinki.fi/media/hellaraportti.pdf

Wang, F., & Hannafin, M. J. (2005). Design-based research and technology-enhanced learning environments. *Educational Technology Research and Development*, *53*(4), 5–23. doi:10.1007/BF02504682

Yrjönsuuri, Y., & Yrjönsuuri, R. (2005). *Intentionality and learning*. Hamina, Finland: Oppilo.

KEY TERMS AND DEFINITIONS

Design-Based Research (DBR): The central goals of designing learning environments and developing theories or "prototheories" of learning are intertwined; development and research take place through continuous cycles of design, enactment, analysis, and redesign; research on designs must lead to sharable theories that help communicate relevant implications to practitioners and other educational designers; research must account for how designs function in authentic settings. It must not only document success or failure but also focus on interactions that refine our understanding of the learning issues involved; the development of such accounts relies on methods that can document and connect processes of enactment to outcomes of interest. (Design-Based Research Collective 2003).

E-Learning: E-learning is most frequently used to refer to computer-based training which incorporates technologies that support interactivity beyond that which would be provided by a single computer. There are 3 kinds of definition, E-Learning can refer to: 1) A conceptually simple form of content-based computer-based training and the addition of some e-tutoring components, 2) Distance education or similar forms of formal open learning making use of technology and 3) Any form of pedagogical model that makes use of information and communication technology.

Educational Technology: Educational technology is the use of technology to improve education. It is a systematic, iterative process for designing instruction or training used to improve performance. Technology should facilitate learning processes and increase performance of the educational system(s) as it regards to effectiveness and/or efficiency.

Meaningful Learning: Meaningful learning has its foundational roots in the ideas of meaningful learning put forward by Ausubel (1963) and Jonassen (1995). Ausubel presented the significance of meaningful learning in his cognitive learning theory (Ausubel, 1963, 1968; Ausubel, Novak, & Hanesian, 1978), while Ausubel et al. (1978) later distinguished between logical meaning and psychological meaning, which is the product of a meaningful learning process. Meaningful learning depends on the student's ability to relate new concepts and propositions to what they already know. Ausubel et al. (1978) combine the concepts of meaningfulness and personal significance, which has become a common practice in the field of education (Yrjönsuuri & Yrjönsuuri, 2005).

Pedagogical Model: A pedagogical model or approach is "a plan or pattern that can be used to shape curricula (long-term courses of studies), to design instructional materials, and to guide instruction in the classroom and other settings" (Joyce & Weil 1980, 1).

Chapter 20
An Ecological Approach to Instructional Design:
The Learning Synergy of Interaction and Context

Paul Resta
The University of Texas at Austin, USA

Debby Kalk
The University of Texas at Austin, USA

ABSTRACT

The confluence of collaborative and social technologies, with the phenomenon of digital natives, creates new opportunities for learning environments, which, in turn, demand innovative instructional design strategies. An ecological approach to instructional design can yield rich learning environments that provide learners with authentic experiences. These learning experiences can be challenging, engaging, and effective, and provide students with deep appreciation of underlying processes, principles, and relationships. It's a learner-centered design that features collaboration, authentic experiences, and complex environments. Designing for these complex systems requires thinking outside the boxes of traditional approaches. The ecological approach requires identifying the key contextual factors and interactions that are central to understanding and performing complex intellectual tasks. This non-linear process involves selecting appropriate technologies and social interactions, appropriate levels of scaffolding and support, and giving learners increasing levels of responsibility for their own successful outcomes.

DOI: 10.4018/978-1-61350-080-4.ch020

Figure 1. Ecology of traditional context for instructional design

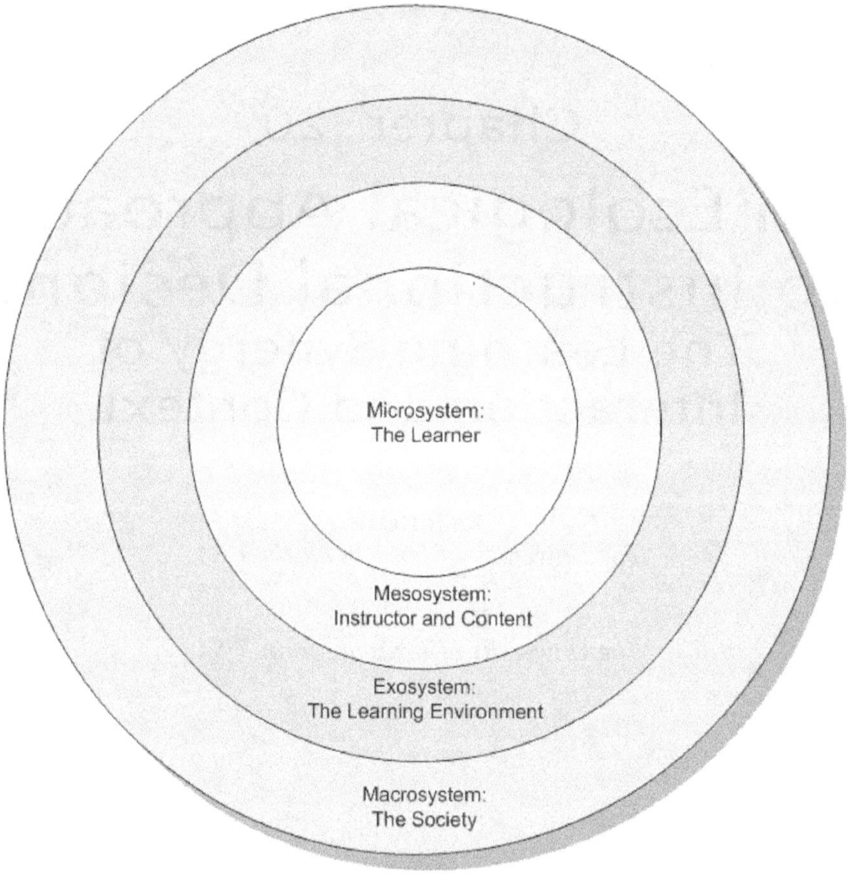

INTRODUCTION

Traditionally, the instructional designer's task was to devise a solution in which the learner was situated in a bounded environment that was linear and self-enclosed. The setting provided the designer with a static certainty about the learners, instructor, location, timeline, and resources. Drawing on Bronfenbrenner's bioecological system theory framework (Bronfenbrenner, 1979, 1989, 1995; Bronfenbrenner & Ceci, 1994; Bronfenbrenner & Morris, 1998), this traditional approach can be seen as a series of nested systems, each wholly contained and unchanging (Figure 1). The learner could be clearly identified, and each concentric circle representing expanding layers of the context for learning could be clearly defined. For instructional designers, this ecological landscape allowed for a systematic approach to design:

- The microsystem is the learner who brings a set of knowledge and aptitudes to the classroom.
- The mesosystem is the classroom, which includes the instructor and content forming the immediate context for the class.
- The exosystem is the learning environment of the school and its resources.
- The macrosystem is the society in which the learning environment is located.

The above static and linear approach stands in contrast to today's rapidly changing, technology and knowledge-based global society that

Figure 2. Dynamic context for ecological approach to instructional design

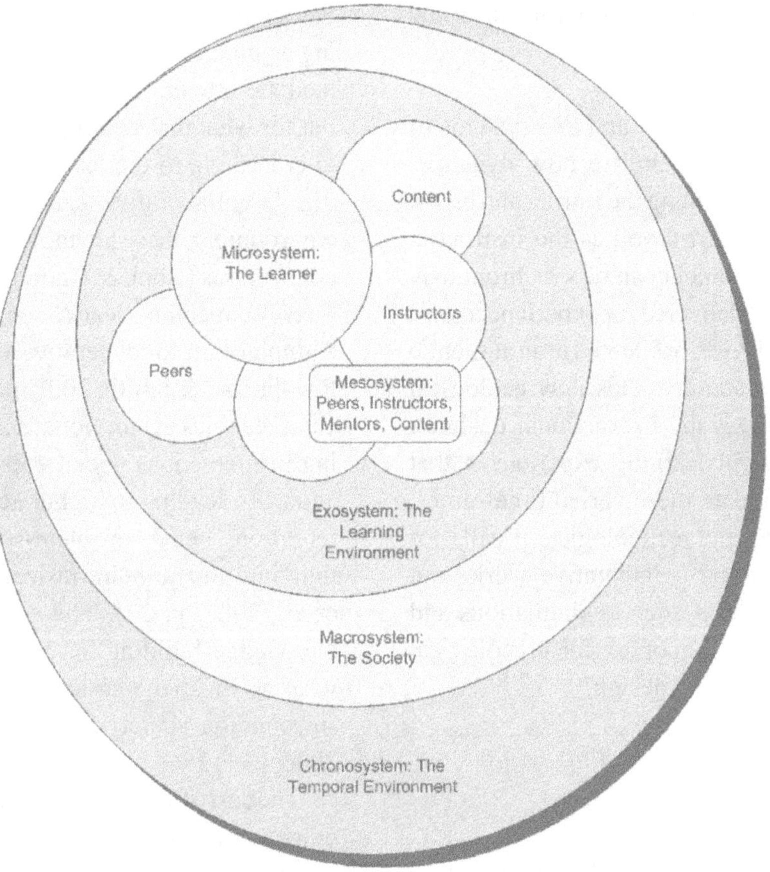

represents features of nonlinear dynamic systems such as adaption and plasticity. Today's college students are also changing. They are immersed in technological environments that provide ubiquitous access to rich information resources. Social networks allow almost continuous interactions with others across the globe, providing more opportunities for self-organization of their learning, even within a closed instructional system. Now, with the dynamic and unpredictable nature of the evolving digital landscape, the ecology of learning design has also evolved, reflected in the model in Figure 2:

- The microsystem is still focused on the learner but the learner is now immersed in an environment that interacts with the meso- and exo-systems.
- The mesosystem expands beyond a classroom and includes peers and mentors, in addition to instructors and content. All interact with the learner and with each other.
- The exosystem shifts from a brick-and-mortar school to a dynamic learning environment that might be online or a blend of physical and virtual spaces.
- The macrosystem remains the surrounding society, though it may include more than a single society since learners may hail from a broad spectrum of countries and cultures.
- The chronosystem includes the temporal factor of changes over time. Changes include technological changes as well as innovations

in the structure of education and the blurring of distinctions between formal and informal education.

The fixed micro-, meso-, and exo-systems of the traditional environment are now dynamic. There is engagement among the learner and peers, content, and mentors, as well as the instructor. The learning environment can be synchronously or asynchronously delivered, or experienced on a laptop or mobile device, or situated in an authentic and collaborative activity. This new ecological landscape challenges the instructional designer to devise successful learning experiences that flexibly accommodate these varied timeframes, delivery channels, and technologies. It calls for authentic experiences, collaborative work, and complex environments, such as simulations and virtual worlds. This is the context for an ecological approach to instructional design.

FRAMEWORK

When Dewey (1916) proposed that education should provide an experiential component to make education accessible and directly relevant, he was challenging the premise that teachers were there to present and students were there to absorb. He made the distinction between passive learning, which he characterized as "undergoing," and experiential learning, which he described as "trying." Thus, learning requires doing, the acquisition of learning occurring through that effort (Dewey, 1916). More recent advocates of "learning by doing" include Shank who, with Berman and Macpherson, claim that when students "are pursuing goals in a topic that they care about, they are motivated to pay attention to the information that is required to accomplish that goal" (1999, p. 181).

The social and collaborative elements of the ecological approach are informed by the work of Vygotsky (1978) who proposed that we can only understand each individual person by examining the societal context in which that person lives. Salomon and Perkins (1997) conceive of learning as inherently socially mediated, "learning to mediate others' learning not only for their sake but for what that will teach oneself, and learning to contribute to the learning of a collective" (p. 21). As collaborative learning moves to an online environment, these technologies can foster social connections (Bonk & Cunningham, 1998, p. 43). These connections lead to social interdependence and contribute to cooperative learning (D. Johnson, R. Johnson, & Smith, 2007, p. 16). This develops competencies in individual accountability, meaningful interactions, social skills, group processing, and trust, leading to higher achievement, greater retention, better problem-solving and critical thinking, and more intrinsic motivation (Johnson et al., 2007, p. 24). This further contributes to knowledge building, as learners "connect with what is most dynamic and meaningful in the surrounding society" (Scardamalia & Bereiter, 2006, p. 113).

The cost of technology production tools is dropping dramatically and, in some cases, these tools are free. While the costs have declined, the quality and usability has greatly improved. Taken together, low cost and high quality have lowered barriers to creating effective learning environments. This moves sophisticated technology systems from production by design and production specialists to educators and students. In fact, the vision of Web 2.0 technology is one populated by user-generated material (O'Reilly, 2005). New Web 2.0 tools and immersive environments are creating fresh digital ecologies that represent new and dynamic learning spaces. Instructional designers need to understand the affordances of these tools and the attributes of digital environments. They must determine how learners interact with, are shaped by, and, in turn, shape the methods through which they access, create, and share ideas, learning resources, and cultural knowledge.

For the ecological approach to yield effective learning results, instructional designers must design powerful, yet easy-to-use, flexible tools and learning systems. The structure of the learning tasks requires appropriate supports, including strong scaffolding, easily accessible resources, and effortless social connections. Poor usability creates cognitive load that interferes with optimal learning. Karweit (1993) emphasizes the importance of context in learning and defines contextual learning as design so that students can carry out activities and solve problems in a way that reflects the nature of such tasks in the real world. In addition, there is an extensive body of research that supports the effectiveness of learning in meaningful contexts (Carraher, Carraher & Schleimer, 1985; Lave, Smith & Butler, 1988).

THE MICROSYSTEM: THE LEARNER'S EXPERIENCE

Informed, ecological design recognizes the need to develop strategies and systems to accommodate 21st century learners. These are young people who have grown up immersed in technology and whose social connections are technology-mediated. The fact that digital natives (people born into a wired world) find the online environment second nature makes the case for online learning environments particularly compelling (Prenksy, 2005; Dede, 2005). For instructional designers, the tasks require thinking about learning outcomes in terms of learning environments. Instead of being passive or reactive consumers of lectures, readings, and assignments, learners take greater responsibility for their own success. Optimal design exploits the affordances of technology and engages learners with authentic experiences. These experiences run the continuum from immersive games to case studies that situate the problem with authentic elements. Tools, such as simulations, shared documents, team workspaces, social networking, and communications channels, lower barriers to cooperative and collaborative work. This level of engagement requires students to interact directly with and within a complex learning system. The combination of technology and social connections both demands and entices learners to stretch, reaching for the appropriate level of challenge that Vygotsky called the zone of proximal development (1978).

While the range of designs varies broadly, the confluence of technology and interactions typically includes authentic experiences, simulations, social interactions, and immersive environments. Individually, and in combination, these components can provide deeply engaging learning experiences that build deep understanding of complex content. The ecological approach to instructional design requires that instructional designers consider the ways different aspects and levels of context relate to each other and to the learning goals and objectives. To envision how learning occurs in an authentic, collaborative, immersive environment, think of the process in six stages (see Figure 3). These stages share elements in common with the legacy cycle developed by Bransford, Brown, and Cocking (2003).

Learners enter the initial state, with their prior knowledge, interests, goals, and their self-efficacy. They begin a collaborative learning task in which they are responsible for effective performance of specific roles and tasks, including being an active and supportive member of the learning team. Upon completion, each student assesses his or her contributions, as well as those of team members. They reflect on the feedback from these assessments, which enables them to adjust and improve their work both individually and as part of the group.

Self and peer assessment are critical to the success of this model, which is validated by the growing use of these assessments in both online and face-to-face collaborative learning environments. Instructors find that this self- and peer-analysis contributes to the learning experience. Self-assessment requires learners to take responsibility for monitoring and making judgments about aspects of their own learning. It requires learners

Figure 3. Learning cycle of authentic learning environment

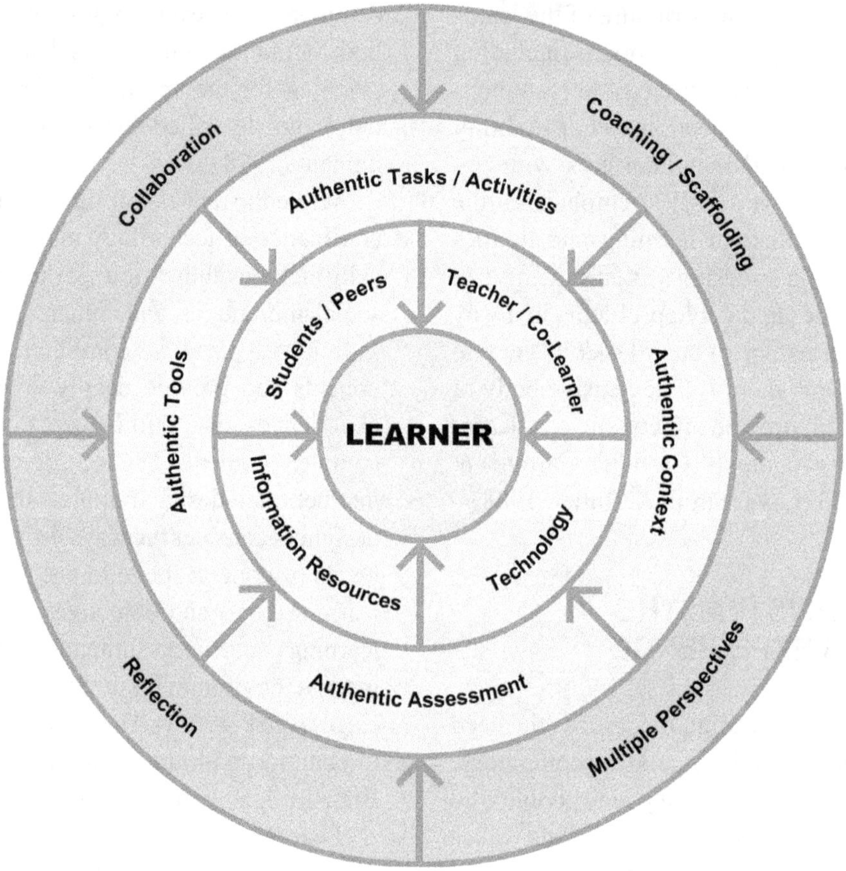

to think critically about what they are learning, to carefully consider appropriate standards of performance, and to apply these standards to their own work. The power of self-assessment lies in an individual's ability to reflect on his own activities and performance in the same way as he reflects on those of his peers. Individuals receive valuable feedback from team members, which they can compare to their own self-assessments (Resta & Lee, 2010).

Similarly, peer-assessment involves the responsibility to make critical judgments about how peers have contributed to the team and applying the standards to the work of these peers (Sluijsmans & Moerkerke, 1999). As noted by Heron (1988), "Peer assessment makes a vital contribution through the fostering of interdependent learning where students work collaboratively rather than competitively; and by necessity develop affective and interpersonal competence" (p. 86).

DESIGN DECISIONS FOR THE MESOSYSTEM AND EXOSYSTEM

The Learner of the Microsystem engages with the elements of the Mesosystem. These include the content, instructors, peers, mentors, and other participants in the Exosystem, which is the Learning Environment. This environment can be a complex setting that includes learning technologies, instructional strategies, and social interactions. Combinations of these elements produce a range of learning outcomes, such as mastery and ac-

Table 1. Elements of the ecological approach to instructional design

Elements	Examples	Outcomes
Instructional Strategies	Self-discovery Collaboration Cooperative learning Authentic experiences Authentic assessment Constructionist Social constructionist	Accelerated learning Social competence Mastery learning Deep understanding of complex content Learner confidence Collaborative skills Portfolio production
Social Interactions	Peers, instructors, mentors Meetings Shared documents Email Discussion board Chat Web/telephone discussions	
Learning Technologies	Simulations Immersive environments E-learning Webinars Shared workspaces Virtual environments	

celerated learning, developing social competence and collaborative skills, producing a portfolio, and developing deep understanding of complex content (see Table 1).

In a linear and closed system approach to instructional design, it is easy for the instructional designer to ignore the ways that the elements related to the micro-, meso-, and exosystem interact and the way those interactions may impact the learning environment. Activity systems theory (AST) (Engeström, 1987) may be a useful tool to help the instructional designer carefully consider the interactions that occur at the different system levels that may impact the designed learning environment. AST represents a comprehensive framework developed by Engeström that characterizes practical human activity and learning (Engeström, 1993; Engeström, 1987), and is based on the cultural/historical psychology of Vygotsky and the activity theory of Leont'ev. As does cultural/historical psychology and activity theory, AST assumes a material and social basis for thought and action. The initial constructs assumed by the theory are the individual, the population, and the environment. Each of these is viewed as affecting the other in what is usually represented schematically as a triangular relationship. This framework recognizes that each of the elements may significantly impact the others and is another conceptual way to look at the relationships and interactions between the micro-, meso-, and exosystems. An illustration of this approach is shown in Figure 4.

In this approach, the designer must understand the characteristics of the learner (Subject) and have a clear view of the desired student competencies and knowledge (Outcomes) to be fostered by the design. The designer must also understand all of the tools, processes, and information to be provided (Artifacts) as well as the tasks and work to be done by all elements of the learning system including the student, instructor, tutor, and others (Division of Effort). In addition, the design must be in accord with the university's or department's academic policies and norms (Rules). Lastly, all of this must take place in an academic context with many players, including fellow students, faculty members, administrators, technical support

Figure 4. Activity systems theory model

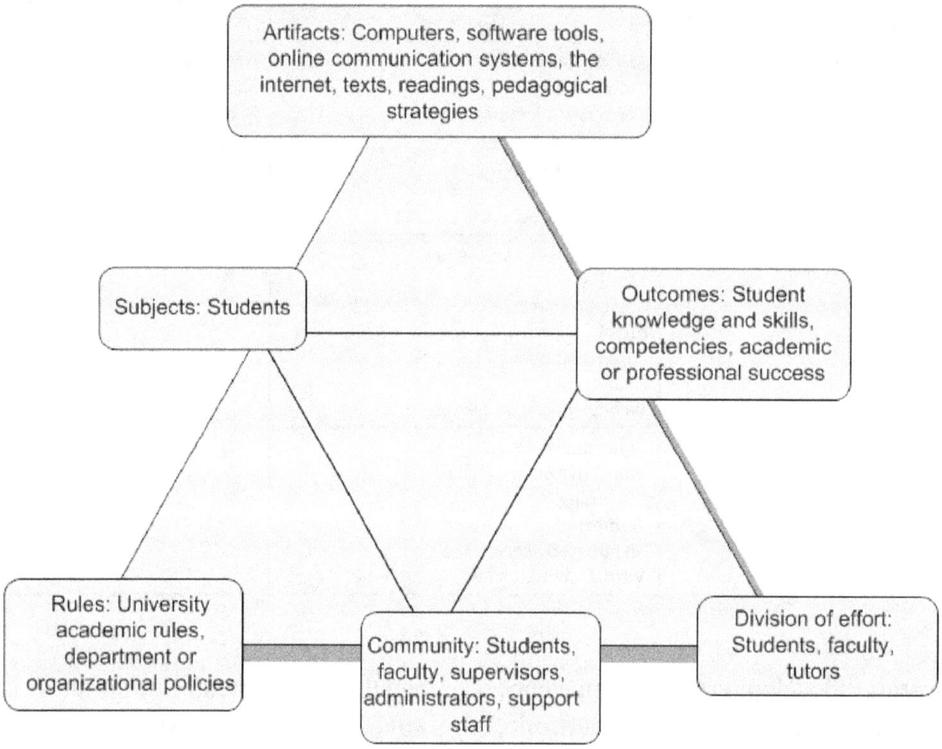

staff, and others (Community). The Activity Systems Theory conceptual model is useful in helping the designer to look more carefully at the inter-relationships and ways the micro-, meso-, and exosystem interact and affect each other.

Instructional Strategies

Traditionally, the designer begins by considering the instructional strategies that are likely to be effective. However, in some situations, the learning technologies may be a given, or the social interactions may have the priority in the design. The designer must begin where it makes sense, yet consider each option carefully. In analyzing the learning goals, what elements seem most appropriate for individual work, and which lend themselves to collaborative work? If the concern is that learners may enter the course with differing skill levels, the designer might decide to have them complete individual work until all reach a level of pre-requisite knowledge. On the other hand, pairing individuals with varying levels of skills can be effective for both learners. Consider what will work best for collaborative tasks and design for that outcome.

Is there a way to construct an authentic experience? Assign the appropriate instructional strategy to each of the learning goals. The level of realism may depend on the learning technologies that are available. However, even with limited technology, it is possible to create a highly effective experience. The authentic experience is most effective when the tasks are representative of actual tasks, using actual tools, and using assessment that is also representative of the manner in which assessment takes place in an authentic setting.

Social Interactions

Many interactions are possible using online technologies in the service of collaborative and authentic learning experiences. These interactions can include exchanges with peers, instructors, mentors, and others, perhaps clients or outside experts. The designer needs to consider what interactions are likely to yield important experiences. Depending on the target learners, the designer can require some interactions, or can make options available as part of the resources in the course.

Where individuals serve specific, unique functions on a team, they may have different needs for interactions and for using communication tools. For example, a project manager will need to communicate with all team members, and individuals may need to consult with other individuals, experts, or mentors. Teams have several options for meeting, including using online tools, conference calls, and meeting face-to-face. Online tools support web meetings and webinars, which support sharing audio, video, desktops, and documents. These tools are often available at no or low cost.

Learning Technologies

Simulations and virtual environments, such as Second Life, provide an experience that can feel realistic or react in realistic ways. They can be complex to design and to produce, but can create experiences that can't be presented in any other way. They are particularly useful in giving learners a fuller appreciation of complex relationships and sequences over time.

Authentic tools are important in creating the authenticity requisite of such activities. These might be out of reach due to cost or exclusivity of a professional standing. Where feasible to incorporate, or to approximate with other tools, they enhance and extend the learning experience.

The designer can decide to make these tools fully available, or to introduce them in a specific sequence; to make them required, or to make them optional. Some designers have had success by introducing complex tools in succeeding assignments to ensure that students learn to use them. In other settings, learners are considered to be fairly versant in the tools and can select those that meet their own needs.

PUTTING THE ECOLOGICAL APPROACH IN PRACTICE

Whether these principles and elements seem lofty or logical, they only work when instructional designers can apply them in real situations with real learners. In this section, the authors present several examples of actual projects and provide the context for their design decisions. These draw on the theoretical models of established educational frameworks. There is never a single solution for any set of requirements, and there is never an obvious solution. All projects present different sets of constraints and opportunities, and the designer's job is to exploit the opportunities and minimize the impact of the constraints.

Example: Creating Authentic Experience

The Design Problem

Let's say that you are an instructional designer who is designing a graduate school course. The target learner is a graduate student enrolled in an Instructional Technology program. The goal of the course is to develop competency in the planning and implementation of instructional technology resources in an educational setting. One strategy for designing this course would be to develop a syllabus of lectures, a reading list of relevant journal articles, and assignments for papers, presentations, and perhaps an exam. This course would no doubt provide students with a lot of information about school technology planning. As these students move into their careers, this course might prepare them well to discuss trends, to find data, and to speak authoritatively about technology tools. However, could they take the knowledge they acquired in this class and apply it in developing an actual technology plan?

The Solution

Backing up, let's reconsider the premise of the course. Why not design the course to provide students with an authentic experience (that of actually designing a school technology plan). In thinking through your task, you decide to invent a fictional school district but to incorporate actual data from a real district to make the experience plausible and engaging. The data includes student performance data, an equipment inventory for each school, budgets from previous years, teacher self-evaluations of level of technology competency and use, and other data. To enhance the experience, you create characters for the district superintendent, principals, teachers, parents, and staff. To conserve production costs, you ask colleagues to portray these characters. You snap photos and use a small recorder to capture them speaking brief "viewpoints" that you've written up (if budgets allow in a future year, you could add video vignettes). You can also use an ordinary digital camera and free software to create a virtual tour of a real school that will represent the school in your program. You organize these materials on a course website. Student teams use shared workspaces and collaborative documents to develop their group's technology plan. This was the direction the designer of this course took in developing this richly authentic environment.

Authentic learning tasks should approximate the type and complexity of tasks encountered in real world settings. The advantage of this approach is that it facilitates the transfer of learning from the instructional learning environment to a real world context.

The designer focused on the most salient contextual elements relevant to the learning task. To build their technology plan, learners were provided with student performance data for the school from the previous five years; data on technology competency levels of the teachers in the school; budgets for the past five years plus the projected budget for the coming year; and partially completed hardware and software inventories.

To further enhance the experience, the designer used a number of tools to create a more realistic school environment. Using a digital still camera and panorama and object movie software tools, the designer created a virtual school. The virtual school served a greater purpose than simply providing an enhanced visual experience. Learners used the virtual school to complete the hardware inventory for three of the school's classrooms. Once in a classroom, the learner could zoom in on each device that then became an object movie in which the student could obtain information on the type of platform. Using an authentic tool used by schools to manage inventory, students entered the information they collected. With these additional entries, the equipment survey was updated, providing the student with a complete inventory, which they needed to complete their assignment. Designers who consider this level of technology use beyond their capability, should note that this free software tool was relatively simple to learn to use effectively. The designer, who does not have graphics expertise, acquired the imagery for the virtual tour of a school in one afternoon.

Importantly, the competencies required for success in this course mirror those required for success in a real educational setting. In addition to producing the technology plan, students learned about the trade-offs and compromises that feed into budgetary decisions. They came to appreciate the difficulty in working with multiple decision-makers and competing visions. They contended with how to manage their own expectations about what technology can realistically accomplish. The interactions with peers in negotiating the work required students to test their ideas, defend them, revise them, and come to consensus. These deeper understandings can only develop through the complex challenges of such authentic experiences.

Example: Creating a Simulation

The need for highly engaging, authentic, and collaborative activities that also allow for multiple, dynamic outcomes leads to devising a simulation. A simulation allows students to explore the world, "to sample and analyze data and to make connections among these explorations (Dede, et al., 2005)."

The Design Problem

Students in American history courses rarely appreciate the complexity and precariousness involved in surviving for one year in a colony in the New World. In most American history courses in the US, this standard lesson is presented as a set of names, facts, and figures—who landed when and where. Additionally, most American students have been exposed to these lessons with little variation throughout many years of education. The instructional designers for this curriculum felt their solution needed to provide a new perspective on a topic that had grown stale and bland.

The Solution

The design team decided to develop a computer-based simulation that would give students a sense of the difficult decisions, relationships, and luck that factored into a settlement's chance of survival. Similar to the SimCity programs, students working through this simulated colony had to make numerous decisions, none of which were clearly superior to others. Students could run the program multiple times, experiencing a range of outcomes. By varying their decisions on what to build, where to plant, when to harvest, and how to interact with Native Americans, student groups learned which elements tended to lead to success.

To design this simulation, designers worked with a full production team to find cost-effective yet realistic methods of presenting the environment. The interface for the simulation was a topographic map of an area. As students rolled over specific locations on the map, they could learn about the soil conditions, prevailing winds, water sources, and other features. With this information, they could use their time to seek out and meet with Native Americans, go hunting or fishing, build buildings, or clear land for a farm. They planned where and what to build, and in what order, which could include a church, a fort, or homes. They could choose where, when, and what to plant, and when to harvest. They also encountered random events, such as an occasional hurricane or epidemic. By working through the simulation several times, students could build a deeper appreciation for the complexities of survival in a difficult environment. They identified relationships among factors and gained insight into the precariousness of the enterprise.

Example: Situated Learning

Authentic experiences provide what Brown, Collins, and Duguid have identified as "know how" and "know what" (1989) and called situated learning, or learning in context.

The Design Problem

The goal for this course was to accelerate training for pre-professional engineers so that they would be better prepared to assume more complex duties. While their education equipped them to accomplish many tasks, they did not have the skills and experience to integrate these tasks in order to design and manage complex projects. They also did not have many experiences with collaborative learning, though collaborative practice is standard in the industry.

The Solution

The course designers focused on how to accelerate knowledge building. They decided that the goal was for students to work collaboratively to produce authentic work in as authentic a work environment as possible. This design draws on the principles of Computer-Supported Collaborative Learning, or CSCL (Scardamalia et al., 2006). Modeling the course environment on those widely found in many businesses today, they designed an immersive environment that supported a range of communication channels. It facilitated collaboration and made both information and personnel resources readily available. The class included both online and face-to-face components. The design specified that learners would work in teams of four. Each team focused on specific, real world applications, and worked with a group of experienced industry mentors who had subject matter expertise in applicable areas. The online, immersive environment served as the central hub for learners, instructors, and mentors. The hub included tools for blogs, wikis, webinars, collaborative documents, podcasts, and social networking.

The designers identified 25 competencies that learners needed to master, which they did through self-paced, online modules. As they completed each competency, they worked with their peers to apply this learning to a realistic application. Mentors provided each team with feedback on how well they applied these competencies to their application. The teams accomplished their work using shared, online workspaces and communications tools. A document management system handled version control and made documents available to all team members at all times. Teams also interviewed their mentors, recording these interviews on video or audio to create podcasts, which they added to their knowledge management system.

This intensive program was measured at several levels. Individuals were measured using objective assessment on the core competencies. Teams used rubrics to assess their project deliverables. The instructor and mentors also used these rubrics to provide feedback. Each participant in the learning environment did self-assessment and assessment of peers. This also included mentors and the instructor. This data was used to make modifications to subsequent deliveries of this course.

DESIGN OF COMPLEX ENVIRONMENTS

All of the instructional design examples cited here represent actual instructional programs developed by the authors of the chapter. They represent an ecological approach to instructional design in which the designers analyzed the key contextual factors and interactions that are central to understanding and performing complex intellectual tasks and then, within the time, funding, and resource constraints, strove to incorporate these elements into the online learning environment. The goal was always to engage the learner in authentic learning tasks in an authentic context using authentic tools, resources, and forms of assessment.

Evaluation and Iteration

The designer's goal is to develop a learning experience that delivers successful outcomes for learners, with the designer's success measured by the learners' success. Yet in designing a complex program, there are many opportunities for less-than-optimal decisions leading to unhappy results. If it were easy to design effective learning experiences, there wouldn't be so many poor examples. The antidotes to this are strong project management and the incorporation of a strong evaluation program into the design and development process (Baker & Alkin, 1973).

If the entire project is developed by one resourceful person, that person must have excellent organization and time-management skills. However, many instructional design projects require a team of specialists. The work of these team members must be coordinated by a project manager. Projects that are stretched for resources or rushed because of poor time management are more likely to produce poor results. There are software tools that provide some elements of project management, such as scheduling and budgeting, and there are online services that maintain version control for project documents. However, these tools are not a substitute for a person whose job is to keep things on track. The manager must have excellent skills in communication, organization, flexibility, and resourcefulness.

There are two types of evaluation: formative and summative. Formative evaluation occurs during development, in other words, while the curriculum is still in formation. Summative evaluation is the process of assessing effectiveness after the program's completion. Plans for both types of evaluation should be developed before starting production.

Formative evaluation requires testing the material with representatives of the target audience, and then revising the material based on the evaluation outcomes. Designers can select from a range of evaluation methods. One strategy that is frequently used is for online materials involves producing a "rapid prototype" of a small section of the total program. For this, online tools may be useful in capturing usage and feedback from prototype participants.

In addition to evaluation, include regular, ongoing reviews throughout the design and development process. Instructional design is inherently iterative. Think of reviews and revisions as part of the cycle for each stage in design and development. In addition to learners, look to peers, subject matter experts (SMEs), the production team, and others for important perspectives on the project. During the design process, build in steps for making documents and files available for review. Provide specific direction to reviewers, explaining how to provide effective feedback. First, subject matter experts (SMEs) should review materials to catch and correct any content inaccuracies. Next, involve design and production peers in reviews. When implementing complex technology systems, or planning sophisticated media components, the entire project team must participate throughout the design stage. While a programmer or a graphic artist may not have expertise in instructional design, these professionals provide the design team with guidance in implementing their designs. This team involvement is essential in ensuring the viability of the project. These strategies can keep projects on track and prevent any serious errors in design and effectiveness.

Following delivery, summative evaluation can provide perspective on the longer-term efficacy of learning outcomes. If a course is delivered online, be sure to include contact information that makes it easy for learners to provide feedback. Solicit feedback from adopters, such as individual instructors and institutions. Also, since content and technology can change rapidly, regular post-course evaluations will monitor the ongoing effectiveness of the program.

FUTURE RESEARCH DIRECTIONS

While evidence points to the efficacy of these essential elements of instructional design within an ecological approach, most studies have considered one, or only a few elements, at a time. Not unexpectedly, considering the time and cost required, few studies have examined a richly immersive environment with many "moving parts." Also, these are relatively new technologies and new cultural experiences. However, these areas are increasingly attracting researchers and we expect to see many studies emerge in coming years. Additionally, a meta-review of existing studies would be a useful resource. This could provide instructional designers with clear, or clearer, direction on the most effective strategies in developing environments with these complex sets of tools.

CONCLUSION

The ecological approach to instructional design calls for learners to be immersed in authentic experiences, building deep understanding through technology-mediated interactions with peers and mentors, in an environment that is at once comfortable yet challenging. To design these experiences, instructional designers need to look beyond the traditional, systematic sequence of design steps to think in non-linear ways about creating high levels of engagement. The process begins, as all instructional design projects begin, with an understanding of the learner and the learning need. It proceeds to envision the authentic tasks that could provide levels of engagement and collaboration that would yield meaningful understanding. With this understanding of the learner, the designer anticipates where learners may need guidance and scaffolding, and where they are likely to work productively without support or constraints. The environment is one that supports learning goals while being open-ended to accept serendipitous discoveries. This ecological approach taps the environmental systems of technology and social learning to create transformational learning.

REFERENCES

Baker, E., & Alkin, M. (1973). Formative evaluation of instructional development. *AV Communication Review*, *21*(4), 389–418.

Bonk, C., & Cunningham, D. (1998). Searching for learner-centered, constructivist, and socio-cultural components of collaborative educational learning tools. In Bonk, C. J., & King, K. S. (Eds.), *Electronic collaborators: Learner-centered technologies for literacy, apprenticeship, and discourse* (pp. 25–50). Mahwah, NJ: Erlbaum.

Bransford, J., Brown, A., & Cocking, R. (2003). *How people learn: Brain, mind, experience, and school*. Washington, DC: National Academy of Science.

Bronfenbrenner, U. (1979). *The ecology of human development: Experiments by nature and design*. Cambridge, MA: Harvard University Press.

Bronfenbrenner, U. (1989). Ecological systems theory. In Vasta, R. (Ed.), *Six theories of child development: Revised formulations and current issues* (pp. 187–250). Greenwich, CT: JAI Press.

Bronfenbrenner, U. (1995). Developmental ecology through space and time: A future perspective. In Moen, P., Elder, G. H. Jr, & Luscher, K. (Eds.), *Examining lives in context: Perspectives on the ecology of human development* (pp. 619–647). Washington, DC: APA Books. doi:10.1037/10176-018

Bronfenbrenner, U., & Ceci, S. J. (1994). Nature-nurture reconceptualized in developmental perspective—A bioecological model. *Psychological Review*, *101*(4), 568–586. doi:10.1037/0033-295X.101.4.568

Bronfenbrenner, U., & Morris, P. A. 1998. The ecology of developmental processes. In W. Danon (Series Ed.) & R. M. Lerner (Vol. Ed.), *Handbook of child psychology: Vol. 1. Theoretical models of human development* (5th ed., pp. 993–1028). New York, NY: Wiley.

Brown, J. S., Collins, A., & Duguid, P. (1989). Situated cognition and the culture of learning. *Educational Researcher*, *18*(1), 32–42.

Carraher, T., Carraher, D., & Schliemann, A. (1985). *Social competence in developmental perspective* (Schneider, B., Nadel, J., & Weisbord, R., Eds.). New York, NY: NATO/Springer.

Dede, C. (2005). Planning for neomillennial learning styles: Implications for investments in technology and faculty. In Oblinger, J., & Oblinger, D. (Eds.), *Educating the net generation* (pp. 1–22). Boulder, CO: EDUCAUSE.

Dede, C., Clarke, J., Ketelhut, D., Nelson, B., & Bowman, C. (2005). *Students' motivation and learning of science in a multi-user virtual environment*. Harvard Graduate School of Education. Retrieved on October 29, 2010 from http://muve.gse.harvard.edu/rivercityproject/documents/motivation_muves_aera_2005.pdf

Dewey, J. (1916). *Democracy and education*. New York, NY: McMillan. Retrieved on December 2, 2007, from http://www.ilt.columbia.edu/publications/dewey.html

Engeström, Y. (1987). *Learning by expanding: An activity-theoretical approach to developmental research*. Helsinki, Finland: Orienta-Konsultit Oy.

Engeström, Y. (1993). Developmental studies of work as a testbench of activity theory: The case of primary care practice. In Chaiklin, S., & Lave, J. (Eds.), *Understanding practice: Perspectives on activity and context* (pp. 64–103). Cambridge, UK: Cambridge University Press. doi:10.1017/CBO9780511625510.004

Heron, J. (1988). Assessment revisited. In Boud, D. (Ed.), *Developing student autonomy in learning* (pp. 77–90). London, UK: Kogan Page.

Johnson, D., Johnson, R., & Smith, K. (2007). The state of cooperative learning in postsecondary and professional settings. *Educational Psychology Review, 19*, 15–29. doi:10.1007/s10648-006-9038-8

Karweit, D. (1993). *Contextual learning: A review and synthesis*. Baltimore, MD: The Center for Social Organization of Schools, Johns Hopkins University.

Lave, J., Smith, S., & Butler, M. (1989). Problem solving as an everyday practice. In Charles, R. I., & Silver, E. A. (Eds.), *The teaching and assessing of mathematical problem solving* (pp. 61–81). Hillsdale, NJ: Lawrence Erlbaum Associates.

O'Reilly, T. (2005). *What is Web 2.0: Design patterns and business models for the next generation of software*. O'Reilly Media, Inc. website. Retrieved on September 7, 2008, from http://www.oreillynet.com/pub/a/oreilly/tim/news/2005/09/30/what-is-web-20.html

Prensky, M. (2005). Learning in the digital age. *Educational Leadership, 63*(4), 8-13. Retrieved on March 12, 2009 from http://www.ascd.org/authors/ed_lead/el200512_prensky.html

Resta, P., & Lee, H. (2010). Self and peer assessment. In Ubell, R. (Ed.), *Virtual teamwork: Mastering the art and practice of online learning and corporate collaboration* (pp. 45–64). Hoboken, NJ: Wiley. doi:10.1002/9780470615782.ch3

Salomon, G., & Perkins, D. (1997). Individual and social aspects of learning. *Review of Research in Education, 23*(1), 1–24. doi:10.3102/0091732X023001001

Scardamalia, M., & Bereiter, C. (2006). Knowledge building. Theory, pedagogy, and technology. In Sawyer, R. K. (Ed.), *The Cambridge handbook of the learning sciences* (pp. 97–118). New York, NY: Cambridge University Press.

Shank, R. C., Berman, T. R., & Macpherson, K. A. (1999). Learning by doing. In Reigeluth, C. M. (Ed.), *Instructional-design theories and models: A new paradigm of instructional theory* (*Vol. II*, pp. 161–182). Mahwah, NJ: Lawrence Erlbaum.

Vygotsky, L. (1978). *Mind in society: Development of higher psychological processes* (14th ed.). Cambridge, MA: Harvard University Press.

ADDITIONAL READING

Anderson, T. (2009). Toward a theory of online learning. In T. Anderson (Ed.), *The theory and practice of online learning* (2nd ed., pp. 33-60). Athabasca: Athabasca University Press.

Azevedo, R., Moos, D., Greene, J., Winters, F., & Cromley, J. (2008). Why is externally-facilitated regulated learning more effective than self-regulated learning with hypermedia? *Educational Technology Research and Development, 56*, 45–72. doi:10.1007/s11423-007-9067-0

Bandura, A. (1989). Regulation of cognitive processes through perceived self-efficacy. *Developmental Psychology, 25*(5), 729–735. doi:10.1037/0012-1649.25.5.729

Bereiter, C., & Scardamalia, M. (1986). Educational relevance of the study of expertise. *Interchange, 17*(2), 10–19. doi:10.1007/BF01807464

Bonk, C., & Cunningham, D. (1998). Searching for learner-centered, constructivist, and socio-cultural components of collaborative educational learning tools. In Bonk, C. J., & King, K. S. (Eds.), *Electronic collaborators: learner-centered technologies for literacy, apprenticeship, and discourse* (pp. 25–50). Mahwah, NJ: Erlbaum.

Borgatti, S., & Cross, R. (2003). A relational view of information seeking and learning in social networks. *Management Science, 49*(4), 432–445. doi:10.1287/mnsc.49.4.432.14428

Browne, E. (2003). Conversations in cyberspace: a study of online learning. *Open Learning, 18*(3), 245–259. doi:10.1080/0268051032000131017

Buraphadeja, V., & Dawson, K. (2008). Content analysis in computer-mediated communication: Analyzing models for assessing critical thinking through the lens of social constructivism. *American Journal of Distance Education, 22*, 130–145. doi:10.1080/08923640802224568

Cameron, B., Morgan, K., Williams, K., & Kostelecky, K. (2009). Group projects: Student perceptions of the relationship between social tasks and a sense of community in online group work. *American Journal of Distance Education, 23*, 20–33. doi:10.1080/08923640802664466

Cegarra-Navarro, J., & Sabeter-Sánchez, R. (2005). E-learning: organizational requirements for successful feedback learning. *Journal of Workplace Learning, 17*(5/6), 276–290. doi:10.1108/13665620510606715

Cennamo, K., & Kalk, D. (2005). *Real world instructional design*. Belmont, CA: Wadsworth/ Cengage Publishers.

Cho, H., Gay, G., Davidson, B., & Ingraffea, A. (2005). Social networks, communication styles, and learning performance in a CSCL community. *Computers & Education, 49*, 309–329. doi:10.1016/j.compedu.2005.07.003

Collis, B., & Margaryan, A. (2004). Applying activity theory to computer-supported collaborative learning and work-based activities in corporate settings. *Educational Technology Research and Development, 5*(4), 38–52. doi:10.1007/ BF02504717

De Smet, M., Van Keer, H., & Valcke, M. (2008). Blending asynchronous discussion groups and peer tutoring in higher education: An exploratory study of online peer tutoring behaviour. *Computers & Education, 50*, 207–223. doi:10.1016/j. compedu.2006.05.001

De Smet, M., Van Keer, H., & Valcke, M. (2009). Cross-age peer tutors in asynchronous discussion groups: A study of the evolution in tutor support. *Instructional Science, 37*(1), 87–105. doi:10.1007/s11251-007-9037-2

Dewey, J. (1916). *Democracy and education*. New York: McMillan.

Fahy, P. (2003). Indicators of support in online instruction. *International Review of Research in Open and Distance Learning, 4*(1), 1–16.

Flowers, J., & Cotton, S. (2007). Impacts of student categorization of their online discussion contributions. *American Journal of Distance Education, 21*(2), 93–104. doi:10.1080/08923640701299058

Gomez, E., Wu, D., & Passerini, K. (2010). Computer-supported team-based learning: The impact of motivation, enjoyment and team contributions on learning outcomes. *Computers & Education, 55*, 378–390. doi:10.1016/j.compedu.2010.02.003

Hara, N., Bonk, C., & Angeli, C. (2000). Content analysis of online discussion in an applied educational psychology course. *Instructional Science, 28*, 115–152. doi:10.1023/A:1003764722829

Hrastinksi, S. (2008). What is online learner participation? A literature review. *Computers & Education, 51*, 1755–1765. doi:10.1016/j.compedu.2008.05.005

Johnson, D., Johnson, R., & Smith, K. (2007). The state of cooperative learning in postsecondary and professional settings. *Educational Psychology Review, 19*, 15–29. doi:10.1007/s10648-006-9038-8

Jones, S. (1998). *Cybersociety 2.0: revisiting computer-mediated communication and community*. London: Sage.

Ke, F. (2010). Examining online teaching, cognitive, and social presence for adult students. *Computers & Education, 55*, 808–820. doi:10.1016/j.compedu.2010.03.013

LaPointe, D., & Gunawardena, C. (2004). Developing, testing and refining of a model to understand the relationship between peer interaction and learning outcomes in computer-mediated conferencing. *Distance Education, 25*(1), 83–106. doi:10.1080/0158791042000212477

Lavooy, M., & Newlin, M. (2008). Online chats and cyber-office hours: Everything but the office. *International Journal on E-Learning, 7*(1), 107–116.

Lee, J.-S., Cho, H., Gay, G., Davidson, B., & Ingraffea, A. (2003). Technology acceptance and social networking in distance learning. *Journal of Educational Technology & Society, 6*(2), 50–61.

Liebeskind, J., Oliver, A., Zucker, L., & Brewer, M. (1996). Social networks, learning, and flexibility: Sourcing scientific knowledge in new biotechnology firms. *Organization Science, 7*(4), 428–443. doi:10.1287/orsc.7.4.428

Mabrito, M. (2006). A study of synchronous and asynchronous collaboration in an online business writing class. *American Journal of Distance Education, 20*(2), 93–107. doi:10.1207/s15389286ajde2002_4

Nicol, D., Minty, I., & Sinclair, C. (2003). The social dimensions of online learning. *Innovations in Education and Teaching International, 40*(3), 270–280. doi:10.1080/1470329032000103807

Offir, B., Bezalel, R., & Barth, I. (2007). Introverts, extroverts, and achievement in a distance learning environment. *American Journal of Distance Education, 21*(1), 3–19. doi:10.1080/08923640701298613

Prensky. M. (2005). Learning in the digital age. *Educational Leadership website, 63*(4), 8-13. Retrieved on March 12, 2009 from http://www.ascd.org/authors/ed_lead/el200512_prensky.html.

Puzziferro, M. (2008). Online technologies self-efficacy and self-regulated learning as predictors of final grade and satisfaction in college-level online courses. *American Journal of Distance Education, 22*, 72–89. doi:10.1080/08923640802039024

Richardson, T. E., Long, G., & Woodley, A. (2003). Academic engagement and perceptions of quality in distance education. *Open Learning, 18*(3), 223–244. doi:10.1080/0268051032000131008

Russo, T., & Koesten, J. (2005). Prestige, centrality, and learning: A social network analysis of an online class. *Communication Education, 54*(5), 254–261. doi:10.1080/03634520500356394

Schroeder, J., & Greenbowe, T. (2009). The Chemistry of Facebook: Using social networking to create an online community for the organic chemistry laboratory. *Innovate 5*(4). Retrieved on March 31, 2009 from http://www.innovateonline.info/index.php?view=article&id=625.

Seo, K. (2007). Utilizing peer moderating in online discussions: Addressing the controversy between teacher moderation and nonmoderation. *The American Journal of Distance Learning, 21*(1), 21–36. doi:10.1080/08923640701298688

Shen, D., Nuankhieo, P., Huang, X., Amelung, C., & Laffey, J. (2008). Using social network analysis to understand sense of community in an online learning environment. *Journal of Educational Computing Research, 39*(1), 17–36. doi:10.2190/EC.39.1.b

So, H., & Brush, T. (2008). Student perceptions of collaborative learning, social presence and satisfaction in a blended learning environment: Relationships and critical factors. *Computers & Education, 51*, 318–336. doi:10.1016/j.compedu.2007.05.009

Tu, C.-H. (2002). The measurement of social presence in an online learning environment. *International Journal on E-Learning, 1*(2), 34–45.

Tu, C.-H., & McIsaac, M. (2002). The relationship of social presence and interaction in online classes. *American Journal of Distance Education, 16*(3), 131–150. doi:10.1207/S15389286AJDE1603_2

Van der Pol, J., van den Berg, B., Admiraal, W., & Simons, P. (2008). The nature, reception, and use of online peer feedback in higher education. *Computers & Education, 51*, 1804–1817. doi:10.1016/j.compedu.2008.06.001

Warschauer, M. (1998). Online learning in sociocultural context. *Anthropology & Education Quarterly, 29*(1), 68–88. doi:10.1525/aeq.1998.29.1.68

Whipp, J., & Lorentz, R. (2009). Cognitive and social help giving in online teaching: an exploratory study. *Educational Technology Research and Development, 57*(2), 169–192. doi:10.1007/s11423-008-9104-7

Whipp, J. L., & Chiarelli, S. (2004). Self-regulation in a web-based course: A case study. *Educational Technology Research and Development, 52*(4), 5–22. doi:10.1007/BF02504714

KEY TERMS AND DEFINITIONS

Activity Theory: Theorizes that when individuals engage and interact with their environment, production of tools results. These tools are "exteriorized" forms of mental processes, and as these mental processes are manifested in tools, they become more readily accessible and communicable to other people, thereafter becoming useful for social interaction.

Authentic Learning: Involves the design of learning activities and the use of materials and tools that are framed around "real life" contexts in which they would be used. The underlying assumption of this approach is that material is meaningful to students and therefore, more motivating and deeply processed.

Collaborative Learning: Is a joint activity of two or more learners engaged in a mutual goal to produce work for an educational purpose. It is through their engagement with each other in performing the work that the learners understand the material.

Ecological Approach: Draws on a biological framework to understand the environmental context of learning as a series of nested and interconnected systems, including the learner, peers, instructors, and larger systems of the school, neighborhood, and society.

Instructional Design: Is the meaningful application of learning theories and practices to create learning experiences that can be replicated for similar audiences using a systematic approach of aligning objectives, assessment, and instructional activities.

Learning Technologies: Are the hardware and software tools that can provide a platform for the design and delivery of learning experiences.

Mentoring: Refers to an activity in which a more experienced or more knowledgeable person helps a less experienced or less knowledgeable person in the acquisition of knowledge or skills

Scaffolding: Refers to the provision of specialized instructional supports for novice learners that are gradually removed as the learners gain knowledge, skill and confidence to cope with the full complexity of the context.

Chapter 21
Multi-Faceted Professional Development Models Designed to Enhance Teaching and Learning within Universities

Donald E. Scott
University of Calgary, Canada

Shelleyann Scott
University of Calgary, Canada

ABSTRACT

In this chapter we advocate the reconceptualisation of pedagogical focused professional development to a more flexible and systematic approach and present two technology-oriented models. This chapter is of interest to a range of educational stakeholders including university professional developers, academics, leaders, students, and support staff. Two mixed method case studies of students' and academics' experiences of online and blended teaching and learning informed the design of the models. These multi-faceted models are designed to promote effective pedagogically-focused professional development, the scholarship of teaching and learning, social and professional networking, and supportive university leadership all aimed at improving teaching and learning. We articulate how the integration of technology can facilitate all of these important activities. It is anticipated that, if implemented, these models will result in a more pedagogically- and techno- efficacious academy; more satisfied and successful graduates; more informed, involved, and trusted leaders; greater sustainability for programmes; and the enhancement of institutional reputation.

DOI: 10.4018/978-1-61350-080-4.ch021

INTRODUCTION

The objectives of this chapter are to 1) present descriptions of effective university teaching within ICT-facilitated learning environments drawn from the research within the higher education context; 2) articulate the lessons learned about teaching and learning (T&L) from two case studies involving students' and academics' perceptions of T&L within online and blended modes, and 3) present and advocate for new conceptualisations of pedagogical and ICT-facilitated professional development for all academics aimed at enhancing university teaching and learning.

The research that supports this chapter is reported in two mixed method case studies where we present students', perspectives about learning experiences and the instructors', and administrator's perceptions about the instructional design, teaching, and assessment within predominantly online courses. The first case involves an international undergraduate cohort of learners studying an Australian degree within the discipline of Commerce and encompasses issues of facilitating learning for students within a blended mode. The second case reports on online postgraduate (Master and Doctoral) students studying within the education discipline at a Canadian university. The similarities and differences between the students' perceptions of their learning experiences and of instructor T&L capacities within ICT-mediated learning environments are explored.

In order to enhance T&L in universities, educational stakeholders must first understand what constitutes effective teaching practice that supports student learning outcomes and the contextual factors influencing academics' capacity and willingness to engage with the 'quality T&L agenda' in order to create effective professional development opportunities. To this end this chapter is structured to outline research findings about effective teaching in the literature review presented in the 'background'. The case studies in the section 'Technology for University Teaching and Learning' describe how technology was used to facilitate T&L, and while not necessarily representing exemplars, they do provide insights into real classrooms and pragmatic orientation of contemporary students and instructors.

BACKGROUND

Teaching and learning in universities is a complex topic and involves quite different stakeholders with differing perspectives. For example, university academics are content or discipline specialists but who also need to be able to teach their students effectively. Academics' focus is on effective teaching, but is also consumed by institutional expectations such as research, service, and/or leadership. Academics are very important as they select the curriculum, design the learning experiences, and assess students' learning. Students are also important as they are the other half of the educational equation, as recipients of the learning experiences. Leaders are influential as they have the opportunity, and indeed the responsibility, to monitor the effectiveness of teaching and promote professional development that can enhance teaching and learning. This section introduces key aspects of T&L at universities: an overview of the impact of technology on universities, descriptions of effective pedagogies, the importance of structuring for active learning in the design of courses, and the importance of assessment for effective learning. The chapter does not explore curriculum or content as it is well understood that all academics are experts in their field and therefore should have an excellent command of their discipline upon which they can draw for teaching purposes. We explore the 'how' and 'why' of effective university teaching and propose models for professional development designed to enhance academics' capacity to teach within their disciplines, particularly as it relates to contemporary ICT-rich learning landscapes.

ICT-Rich Learning Landscapes

Information is power, particularly if it can be gathered, harnessed, and disseminated. More so than at any other time in history, the power inherent in obtaining and leveraging information has evolved and morphed largely due to the impact of technology on society. The way school and university educators conceptualise knowledge creation and its mobilisation has radically altered in the past two decades due to the influence of technology. Universities were early adopters of technology for financial, student services, learning management systems (LMS), and library systems although many academics were still coming to terms with this technological age and its application to teaching and research (de la Harpe & Radloff, 2008; Laurillard, 2008). Even though many faculty are receptive to technology particularly if these represent ways to increase efficiencies in their work, some remain resistant, or indeed resentfully technophobic, clinging to the slower, more methodical era of their early university life. The university context has changed though, with a new generation of students who think, communicate, work, and play technologically (Tapscott, 1999, n.p.). Black (2010) referred to the youth born between 1981 and 2001 as "Generation Y" or "Gen Y" (p. 92). She described them as "digital natives" (p. 92) proficient and largely dependent on technology perceiving it as an "extension of their brains" (p. 95), "more demanding consumers with customer expectations of immediate service," "assertive and confident" (p. 94) and yet sometimes lacking an awareness of etiquette and the social responsibility required for sensitive online communication. Therefore, for universities to be considered still relevant and desirable, academics must engage with developing ICT-rich learning landscapes facilitated by a 'techno-efficacious' academy. So how do teaching academics cater to meet the needs of these wired students? In responsive universities it is not unusual to find learning experiences incorporating a range of technologies. For example, it is increasingly common to find the use of iPhones™ and software like Twitter™, Facebook™, YouTube™, research databases, Skype™ and Elluminate Live™ being employed for teaching and learning, research, and communication. Academics now need to become efficacious with both effective pedagogies and technology in order to educationally engage these Gen Y students.

Effective Pedagogies in Higher Education

Unlike the K-12 context, research about T&L in higher education has only become popular over the past three decades. Chickering and Gamson's (1987; 1991; 1999; Chickering, Gamson, & Barsi, 1989) research of university teaching provided foundational understandings about the undergraduate teaching context. Building and expanding on their work were other researchers including Ramsden (1998b, 2003; Ramsden & Martin, 1996; Ramsden, Prosser, Trigwell, & Martin, 2007), Prosser and Trigwell (Prosser, 2010; Prosser & Barrie, 2000; Prosser, Martin, Trigwell, Ramsden, & Middleton, 2008; Prosser, Ramsden, Trigwell, & Martin, 2003; Prosser & Trigwell, 1999a; 1999b), Biggs (1993; 2001), Marsh (Marsh & Roche, 1994; Marsh & Dunkin, 1992), and Centra (1979; 1989; 1993). These scholars' research into various aspects of T&L at universities spanned Australia, Hong Kong, United Kingdom, and the USA. With the advent of technology and its potential for use in T&L further research has emerged examining the impact and significance of educational technology. Researchers in this emergent field include Aragon (2003), Ascough (2002), Laurillard (1993, 2008, 2009), Levine and Sun (2002), Oliver and his associates (1998), Palloff and Pratt (1999, 2005), Roxå and Mårtensson (2009), and Smith and Ragan (2005). These researchers' contexts are representative of the globalised higher education sector. They investigated aspects of T&L within the university context, however, only a few have provided an overview of the principles or guidelines for effective teaching.

In the late 1980s Chickering and Gamson (1987) researched undergraduate teaching and proposed a set of seven principles of good practice. They, and later with Ehrmann (1996), Payne and Poitras (2001), expanded their 'principles' in the mid to late 1990s largely due to the influence of technology. Ramsden's research in articulating and promoting effective university T&L spanned the 1990s through to the present. He also presented an overview of effective teaching. In this section we explore these two main foundational overviews and identify the aspects of overlap and difference.

Chickering, Gamson and their associates specified the following seven principles of good undergraduate teaching which they distilled from their research with academics and students. These included: 1) encouraging contact between students and faculty; 2) respecting diverse talents and ways of learning; 3) communicating high expectations; 4) emphasising time on-task; 5) providing prompt feedback; 6) encouraging active learning; and 7) developing reciprocity and cooperation among students. The following outlines the impact of ICT on these principles:

- *Encourage contact between students and faculty:* Technology for communication purposes has become embedded into everyday life for most in society. Email, web pages, bulletin boards and online discussions (synchronous and asynchronous) are now additional modes of interaction available to university instructors (Chickering & Ehrmann, 1996). Although some academics perceived technological communication to be a burden, with the expectation of constant availability, technology also offered some streamlining of academics' work whereby the face-to-face commitment was reduced and the convenience of broadcast communication avoided unnecessary repetition (Woods, 2002).
- *Develop reciprocity and cooperation among students:* This principle resonated with the research of Johnson, Johnson and Smith (1998, 2007) who reported cooperative learning outcomes as sharper cognitive processes and deeper learning. ICT facilitated greater opportunities for collaboration and dialogue regardless of time, space, and locality.
- *Encourage active learning:* This principle dovetailed with the literature on increasing student engagement through variation in teaching strategies (Joyce, Weil, & Calhoun, 2008). It also embodied principles from the adult learning literature which emphasised the importance of active and relevant learning experiences (Knowles, Holton III, & Swanson, 2005; Merriam, 2001). Chickering and Ehrmann (1996) highlighted three groupings of ICTs that promoted activity: resources and tools for learning-by-doing (e.g., simulations), time-delayed exchange of written materials (e.g., forums and bulletin boards), and more recently real-time Voice-over-Internet-Protocol (VoIP) conversation where individuals and groups can communicate using Internet media (e.g., Skype™, Elluminate Live™).
- *Provide prompt feedback:* Formative and summative feedback was and remains essential to support the ongoing learning of students. Assessment remains a contentious aspect of university life with much research being undertaken to establish in-depth guidelines to support enhancement of academics' assessment practices (James, McInnis, & Devlin, 2002; Knight, 2002; Yorke, 2003). Technology supports clarity of feedback with 'tracked changes' options in MSWord, and increases the speed of return of feedback through email,

while streamed video and digital recording offers opportunities to accurately capture students' work for later reflection and critique by both students and instructors.

- *Emphasise time on-task:* Organisational skills and time management have become essential capabilities for the employment market but they are also key to academic success (Business Higher Education Round Table, 2002; DEST, 2002, 2007). These skills along with active learning and cooperative learning (Bender, 2003; Palloff & Pratt, 2005) must be scaffolded through careful instructional design of learning experiences, materials and resources, and assessment tasks (Moore & Kearsly, 1996; Simonson, Smaldino, Albright, & Zvacek, 2006; Smith & Ragan, 2005). There could be numerous examples of how technology can engage "digital native" students (Black, 2010, p. 93), for example, the emergence of online research databases have decreased time wasted commuting to institutional libraries and therefore translated into less time wasted and more on-task time.
- *Communicate high expectations:* Articulating high academic expectations for students encourages student to rise to the challenge. Expectations must be explicitly communicated to students. Instructional design principles outline the importance of communicating academic expectations through documentation.
- *Respect diverse talents and ways of learning:*Chickering and Gamson (1987) acknowledged that all students were unique and therefore required a variety of learning experiences to facilitate their learning. This principle aligned with Gardner's (1999) theory of multiple intelligences and the field of learning styles (Dunn & Griggs, 2000; Kolb, 1976). Therefore, instructors who have adopted a range of teaching strategies promote the successful learning of all students. This also linked with Galbraith's (2004), Long's (2004), and Wlodkowski's (2004) research involving motivating and engaging the discerning adult learner. Technology promotes variety in teaching strategies for varied learning outcomes:

Technological resources ... [allow for] powerful visuals ... direct, vicarious, and virtual experiences; and [development of] analysis, synthesis, and evaluation ... [and] self-reflection and self-evaluation [capacities]. ... Technologies can help students learn in ways they find most effective and broaden their repertoires for learning. They can supply structure for students who need it and leave assignments more open-ended for students who don't. Fast, bright students can move quickly through materials they master easily and go on to more difficult tasks; slower students can take more time and get more feedback and direct help from teachers and fellow students. Aided by technologies, students with similar motives and talents can work in cohort study groups without constraints of time and place. (Chickering & Erhmann, 1996, p.5)

From his research with academics and students, Ramsden (1995; 1996; 2003; 2007) posited there was no "'best way'" to teach but presented thirteen "important properties of good teaching" (Ramsden, 2003, pp. 86-7): 1) a desire to share your love of the subject with students; 2) an ability to make the material being taught stimulating and interesting; 3) facility for engaging with students at their level of understanding; 4) a capacity to explain the material plainly; 5) commitment to make it absolutely clear what has to be understood, at what level, and why; 6) showing concern and respect for students; 7) commitment to encouraging student independence; 8) an ability to improvise and adapt to new demands; 9) using teaching methods and academic tasks that require students to learn thoughtfully, responsibly, and cooperatively; 10) using valid assessment methods; 11) a focus on key concepts, and students' misunderstandings of them, rather than on covering the ground; 12) giving the highest-quality feedback on student work; and 13) a desire to learn from students about the effects of teaching and how it can be improved.

Comparing Ramsden's "important properties" with Chickering and Gamson's work revealed significant alignment but also some interesting additions. Ramsden identified academics' content expertise in his first property 'sharing your love of the subject with students', however, Chickering's principles do not include curriculum content expertise, as it was likely assumed that academics with doctoral level qualifications should have deep content knowledge. Alignment was evident in Ramsden's "showing concern and respect for students" and Chickering's "respects diverse talents and ways of learning," although Chickering's point was broader taking account of diverse learning styles and talents. Similarly, Ramsden's "using teaching methods and academic tasks that require students to learn thoughtfully, responsibly, and cooperatively" linked with Chickering's "develops reciprocity and cooperation among students" although the notion of responsibility tied into promoting student independence and empowerment. Further alignment was evident in the importance of providing effective and timely feedback. Ramsden's thirteenth property drew upon his research about student evaluation of teaching and its value in improving teaching integrating metacognition for academics, as well as students. Both Ramsden and Chickering identified 'expectations' as an element. However, there were slight variations in intent. Ramsden highlighted the importance of clear expectations, the level of the content, and rationale for including it into the course; whereas, Chickering's principle focused on simply communicating high expectations for students. Ramsden's point on expectations also resonated with Smith and Ragan's (2005) and Bender's (2003) instructional design research as a key factor for student success in online learning environments.

Instructional Design for Active Learning

The key goal of an instructor is to facilitate and support the learning of his/her students. Instructional design, or the understanding of how learning occurs, what conditions support learning, and how to maximise students' learning potential are important elements of being an effective university teacher. Smith and Ragan (2005) referred to instructional design as "the systematic and reflective process of translating principles of learning and instruction into plans for instructional materials, activities, information resources, and evaluation" (p. 4). Instructional design is important for face-to-face teaching but is imperative for online learning environments, as students may have less formalised contact with their instructors and therefore become more reliant on the educational materials and resources. As Chickering, Gamson, Ehrmann, and Ramsden articulated, the academic's responsibility is to develop an environment that supports active learning strategies and employ methods that enhance learning. Woods and Baker (2004) stated "interaction is at the heart of online learning experience" (p. 2). He referred to Moore's (1989) transactional distance theory which highlighted the importance of communication in the construction of knowledge through learner-content, learner-instructor, and learner-learner interaction. As Laurillard (2009) stated "New kinds of social networking, collaborative, mobile, and user-generated-design technologies are creating exciting opportunities for supporting collaborative learning online" (p. 5).

There are overt linkages between instructional design principles for active learning and Chickering's, Ramsden's principles of effective teaching involving reciprocity and cooperative learning. Cooperative learning researchers Johnson, Johnson and Smith (1998, 2007) found that certain conditions must be established for successful educational outcomes. That is, there must be careful structuring of the learning activities (instructional design) to ensure individual accountability, equal participation, team-based orientations and loyalties (positive interdependence), and simultaneous interactions (Kagan, 1994). Even though there is considerable evidence that cooperative learning yields both social and academic gains, many university students dislike cooperative activities, particularly if it incorporates an assessment component. Their concerns include "free-riding" and "social loafing" behaviours of group members who are content to share the successes without doing their share of the work (Caspersz, Skene & Wu, 2002, n.p.). Therefore, activities and assessment tasks must be well planned to incorporate individual accountability and equal participation, as well as, a range of collaborative technologies.

Instructional Design for Sound Assessment Practices

As previously identified, teaching incorporates three main components: curriculum content, learning experiences and activities, and assessment. Ensuring alignment between all three is crucial for course coherence (James, McInnis & Devlin, 2002). So far we have established that academics are content experts who should be able to ensure their course curriculum is relevant and research informed. We have also established a range of broad principles from the literature that can guide academics design of optimal learning experiences; however, assessment has been and remains a problematic and a frequently trivialised aspect of T&L within higher education (Knapper, 2010). The fact that both Chickering and Ramsden included assessment aspects into their guidelines underscores the concerns with assessment in universities. Yorke (2003) and Knight (2002) explored issues with formative and summative feedback respectively, and called for professional development to improve assessment practices. "Assessment should not only measure student learning but also make a contribution to it" (James, McInnis & Devlin, 2002, p. 1). James and his associates described changes to assessment in universities as the move to criterion referenced assessment, provision of clearer statements of criteria that aligned with learning outcomes, and more strategic assessment that integrated the knowledge, and the provision of more timely formative and summative feedback. James and his associates' (2002) sixteen indicators of effective assessment served as guides for instructional design processes. They recommended further development on minimising plagiarism, online assessment, group-based projects, and assessing large classes with the view to ensuring fairness, equity, consistency, and parity.

To summarise, this literature review highlighted a sampling of the knowledge base in relation to teaching, learning, and assessment within higher education and presented the tensions and constraints that academics are facing in meeting the demands of their teaching role within a technological society. Two cases are now presented that outline undergraduate and postgraduate online learning in two culturally different contexts. These cases are not necessarily exemplars, although there were many elements of effective T&L practices and instructional design actively incorporated into many of the courses within the three described programmes. They are illustrative of how students and academics perceive and respond to the integration of ICT-facilitated T&L within undergraduate (Bachelor of Commerce) and postgraduate (Masters in Education and Doctoral) programmes. Analysis of our research findings from different disciplines, namely, Commerce and Education, and different cultural contexts (e.g., Canada and Australia) facilitated the identification of globalised similarities from which we synthesised our conceptualisation of multi-faceted models for academic professional development.

TECHNOLOGY FOR UNIVERSITY TEACHING AND LEARNING

Issues, Controversies, Problems

The Australian case explores Commerce undergraduate students' perspectives of their learning within a technological mode, while the Canadian case study draws upon the experiences of master's and doctoral students in an Education faculty. Additionally, insights about instructional design, teaching, and assessment are offered by the teaching academics in both contexts.

The Australian case study was drawn from doctoral research that used a mixed methodology employing student feedback questionnaires (n= 76), student journals (n= 84), student (n=16) and faculty interviews (n=3). In the Canadian case, data were collected through interviews with four doctoral students, formal master's course evaluations (n=83), personal journaling as participant observers (n=2), and an interview with an experienced supervisor.

Australian Case Study: Undergraduate

This case study was an evaluation of a pilot integration of synchronous VoIP technology within a capstone course in a Bachelor of Commerce degree programme. Students were undertaking an Australian degree but were physically located in Singapore. The offshore teaching arrangements in this case involved the Australian course coordinator conducting half of the teaching course hours (12 hours) in an intensive face-to-face mode in Singapore (Friday evening, Saturday and Sunday). The complement of the course was conducted in situ with the local instructor through synchronous VoIP (Elluminate Live!™) virtual classroom and asynchronous modes (e.g., Blackboard™ LMS and email). Prior to implementing the virtual classroom, teaching in this degree had been only conducted face-to-face. The instructor travel and accommodation expenses had become prohibitive which had raised issues related to ongoing programme viability and necessitated the exploration of alternative ways to deliver overseas programs. The trial of the Elluminate Live!™ virtual classroom was proposed as a potential technological solution.

The capstone course aimed to provide a mandatory final coalescing experience wherein students worked in multi-disciplinary (e.g., accounting, business law, economics and finance, information systems, management, and marketing) teams in a simulation of a real commercial enterprise within a software programme called, Capsim®. Each team represented a 'company' with the compilation of teams representing a 'market place'. Capsim®, was a commercially available programme which emulated a software development company within a competitive industry market. To be successful in the course "students had to work collaboratively in their teams to make sound business decisions which were uploaded each week into the Capsim® programme" (course outline). The software provided output on the success of the teams' decisions with information on why decisions were successful or not within the virtual 'marketplace'. The class sessions were dedicated to debriefing the decisions in relation to the theories.

There were two Australian academics responsible for the course design and grading, with a local (Singapore based) instructor who undertook half of the course facilitation. There were 84 students in the research cohort, with the majority (93%) in the 20-30 years of age range. Over half (54%) were working at least part time in the areas of Commerce.

As student satisfaction with learning experiences can be highly subjective and variable it was important to establish the criteria upon which student satisfaction and instructional design were to be measured. These criteria included the structuring for deeper rather than surface learning approaches; incorporating relevant discipline knowledge and expertise required by the profession and employers; promoting active engagement with the content; demonstrating alignment between the content objectives, learning experiences and the assessment tasks that measured learning; ensuring students' had a clear understanding of expectations and processes; motivating students to engage with the content and activities; developing metacognitive capacities; challenging students and providing learning experiences which are meaningful; providing variation enabling students to learn in diverse ways; and encouraging reciprocal engagement with peers and experts.

Perceptions about the Learning

Students provided fair and balanced feedback about the instruction, the learning environment, their own learning abilities and the instructors' capacities. They indicated that the course was difficult and yet they reported enjoying the challenge. In their self-reflections students were candid about their strengths and weaknesses and reflected on their personal and professional development as a result of the course activities. They expressed increased confidence and pride in their capacity to meet the challenges.

The team work environment contributed to students' professional growth both in the knowledge and skills dimensions. Students enjoyed the group work, even though they had been discomforted by the instructor-initiated creation of multi-disciplinary groups. Many students stated they were accustomed to being teamed with friends and found teaming with peers who they did not know to be uncomfortable. They blamed the instructor even though it was a necessary aspect of the course design. Even so, almost all students described motivations of genuine commitment to making their team effective and successful. In reporting what skills had been developed in this course, student cited critical and creative thinking, namely, analytical, problem-solving and decision-making due to them being core to the activities within the simulation. Team work and leadership were also key skills that were developed. Students reported an increased awareness of the importance of the professional skills to their long-term career success as a result of this course.

Students preferred interacting face-to-face, and as they were all located in the same city they met both in face-to-face and in VoIP meetings. Even so, the majority of students favourably viewed VoIP and indicated they would have liked to see this used more innovatively rather than simply as a lecturing device. All students had had experience with synchronous interaction modes, albeit texting not voice. They reported feeling comfortable with the VoIP environment after two class sessions and recommended more extensive use of VoIP in the university programme. They wanted greater control over and access to the VoIP environment so that they could organise their own meeting times rather than having a prescribed meeting schedule. They did like the convenience of using VoIP to reduce the travel to the university and preferred formal instruction to be conducted via VoIP. Some of their reasons included were that they were able to get instant feedback, have miscommunications cleared up because they could talk it through and they could have their doubts clarified. They favourably compared the instant nature of this form of synchronous communication over that of email.

Reported problems encountered with the VoIP learning environment included problems with access to a computer with some sharing a computer with team members during class times. Some indicated that there was a temptation to become distracted while class was in session with one saying she undertook household chores while class was in session. Some felt that there was a loss of non-verbal cues and lack of intimacy in the online environment and this was at times uncomfortable in being unable to "read the tone of the conversation." Overall though they indicated VoIP had real potential in university programmes but teaching staff needed more training to fully utilise the range of functions available. They disliked the use of the VoIP classroom for a lecture with little opportunity for interaction which limited the experience. Contrastingly, the instructor reported frustration with students use of the synchronous 'text chat' facility in preference to 'voice' communication options when he was trying to get verbal discussions underway.

Perceptions about the Teaching and Instructional Design

The administrator (a pedagogical expert) and a discipline expert collaborated to design and write the course materials and to develop the learning experiences. This course was created with a handbook of supporting teaching documentation, lecture PowerPoints, and assessment tasks and associated rubrics. Additionally, students had a handbook with content information, materials, assessment information and rubrics, and other supporting documentation. Curiously the instructor experienced difficulties in encouraging students to read the materials as they wanted him to simply explain it all to them, although they did like having the assessment materials provided to them at the start of the course.

The course coordinator opted to be in the trial perceiving it as exciting and personally strategic for career development. Professional development was conducted, albeit limited, with staff and students to support the technical implementation. The professional development focused on the various functions of the Elluminate™ environment and how they could be used for various T&L activities. It was conducted a week prior to the course roll out and consisted of three two-hour sessions. Technical support was provided during the first week of classes.

The offshore instructor was a highly experienced face-to-face teacher within the Business discipline; however, online teaching was completely new and unfamiliar. He reported that the rapid implementation of the course caused him considerable discomfort. He wanted to further explore functions in the programme which could promote greater student interaction. He indicated that with more experience would come more comfort, and he would be more willing to try other strategies and functions to structure for more engagement and interaction.

Voice-over-Internet-Protocol represented emergent technologies with the potential to provide increased convenience and flexibility for adult learners within the university context. The negative aspects of VoIP recognised by staff and students were easily rectifiable in subsequent semesters and did not outweigh the advantageous dimensions of this innovative medium. The findings in this case endorsed Price and Kirkwood's (2008) perception that effective pedagogy should shape how online learning experiences were structured and supported. Attention needed to be given to ensure that learning experiences within the VoIP environment were active, interactive, reflective, and engaging. As Aragon (2003) stated the instructor needed to create a psychologically "safe" space which promoted a "social presence" (p. 57). Social presence was linked with student satisfaction in the online classroom. Professional development of instructors, in relation to exploring sound pedagogical practices and their underlying philosophies, was crucial to the successful implementation and ongoing effectiveness of learning experiences within the VoIP classrooms.

Canadian Case Study: Postgraduate

This study was an exploration of master's and doctoral students' experiences and perspectives of studying within a fully online mode. Data was obtained from formal student evaluations (n=83) from the Master's in Education programme. The qualitative data included interviews with four doctoral students. The doctoral students were all mature age, ranging from late 30s to early 50s in age and all had or were current educators with three of them being school administrators. The academic perspective was gleaned from participant-observation and an interview with an experienced academic supervisor. The technologies that were involved in supporting the doctoral programme at this Western Canadian university included Blackboard™ LMS (e.g., resource materials and asynchronous modes of communication such as bulletin boards, forums, and email), telephone, and VoIP synchronous modes (e.g., Skype™ and Elluminate Live!™).

Students in both master's and doctoral programmes reported the quality of coursework was highly variable with some academics using the VoIP technologies to advantage by actively engaging students in discussion, problem solving and presentations, while others simply lectured. Their preference was for the active engagement as this encouraged them to think more deeply, and expand their ideas as a result of the discussions with others. They enjoyed course materials if these were made available through links to the library but resented the time it took to "go hunting" in the library databases. Some indicated their reliance on online resources was extreme and found accessing hardcopy text materials at a distance to be difficult, time consuming, and expensive. Assessment was highly contentious as many received almost no feedback from instructors but appreciated those who provided useful feedback. Students frequently experienced difficulties in contacting faculty and this exacerbated their sense of isolation and frustration with studying online. Additionally, the relevance of some tasks was questionable. Students reported that some faculty were nervous of the technology and were not prepared to alter their embedded practices to fully integrate technological advantages. For example, some academics required online students to send hardcopy assignments to the university and to provide a self-addressed envelope for the return feedback, rather than returning graded assignments electronically with 'track change' comments. Students liked group work as this reduced the isolation inherent in online studies but found the pragmatics of organising online meetings to be problematic. They did use the VoIP software to organise meetings. They were quite intrigued at the sense of camaraderie that had developed in many courses with peers they had only met face-to-face briefly in the orientation class.

Students indicated that a higher level of self-discipline was required to undertake doctoral studies in an online mode. They had to be pro-active in requesting regular meetings with their supervisor. They felt VoIP media like Skype™ and Elluminate™ more closely mirrored face-to-face meetings. Connectivity was a problem for one doctoral student who was situated in a rural community with unstable Internet services; hence, meetings were conducted by telephone in conjunction with reviewing her documentation on the computer. Students preferred meeting synchronously to discuss feedback as they were able to obtain clarification and deeper understandings of the comments when there was a live conversation. Studying online provided all these students with the flexibility of continuing to work while still accessing postgraduate studies unlike other face-to-face or on-campus programmes. One student indicated she would have been precluded from doctoral studies as she was in a remote location not within commuting distance to any university. All students articulated enjoying the freedom and flexibility that online studies allowed.

Supervisors perceived online supervision as comparable in educational quality to that of face-to-face modes, if conditions were met. For example, time had to be structured to build personal and positive relationships between supervisor and student so that students felt they were important, and their lives and views mattered to their supervisor. Allowing sufficient time in meetings for personal discussions before addressing academic concerns was deemed essential. Online studies meant that students' written communication became the predominant focus as there were fewer opportunities for students to explain the meaning verbally; hence, stronger written dissertations resulted. A disadvantage was that written instructions had to be more comprehensive due to less frequent synchronous contact with students. One faculty member indicated that providing in-depth comments on track changes was difficult as he did not have sufficiently proficient typing skills for this to be a comparable option to handwritten feedback. He was now becoming proficient with Dragon Speak™, a voice recognition software programme enabling him to provide written feedback by verbally articulating it into the computer. Additionally, a significant problem was that weak, lazy, or hesitant students could use the technology interface to become passive or to avoid regular discussions and accountability processes. A common problem was the expectation of instant replies to email queries regardless of the time of day or whether or not it was the weekend. Therefore, establishing explicit expectations with students was crucial to establishing positive relationships. Being prepared to try out new programs and hone new technological capacities was an imperative mindset to being an effective academic. Technology professional development was important, however, it was not always available.

Solutions and Recommendations

Key findings across both case studies indicated students' preferences for online learning were greater at the postgraduate level. Technology-mediated learning was perceived to be desirable for its convenience, capacity to provide increased access to education regardless of physical location, and enabled more flexible modes of learning. It also increased access to more widely ranging information, resources, and experts than prior to the advent of the Internet. All students preferred clarity in materials and resources, communication, and expectations for assessments. When the instructor designed and structured for both synchronous and asynchronous forms of interaction, reflection, and activity, the result was a more cohesive, supportive, and engaged learning community than when communication was left to chance. From the results of the two cases it appears that the academics in the Faculty of Education were better prepared to teach than their counterparts in the Business School. Even so, there were no guarantees that pedagogical knowledge ensured good practice as students had reported considerable variability in quality even within the Education faculty. This means there was a need for academics to undertake professional development about pedagogies as this was a primary issue for students in the Business School, but also professional development on the effective and ethically appropriate use of technology for T&L purposes or 'techno-pedagogies'. Additionally, there needed to be incentives or rewards for academics to engage with the quality T&L agenda. Both cases demonstrated that the instructional design was important to students and when these were educationally sound students responded positively and were more successful in their learning.

Professional development should be focused on enhancing university teachers' understanding of effective pedagogies (the why), include the what (curriculum), the how (designing optimal learning experiences and assessment) and particularly, how these translate in their discipline. Professional development must provide opportunities for academics to hone their practices in relation to instructional design, teaching, assessing, and integrating ICT into rich T&L landscapes.

FUTURE RESEARCH DIRECTIONS

No longer will exchange of ideas be limited by time, distance, and local community. We have learned that using technology to support networks around a shared purpose enhances professional development and provides fertile ground for professional learning communities. (Chesbro & Boxler, 2010, p. 49)

Pathways to the academy are usually through research not teaching. Hence, many academics

Figure 1. Macro conceptualisations of webs of enhanced practice within dynamic, competitive universities

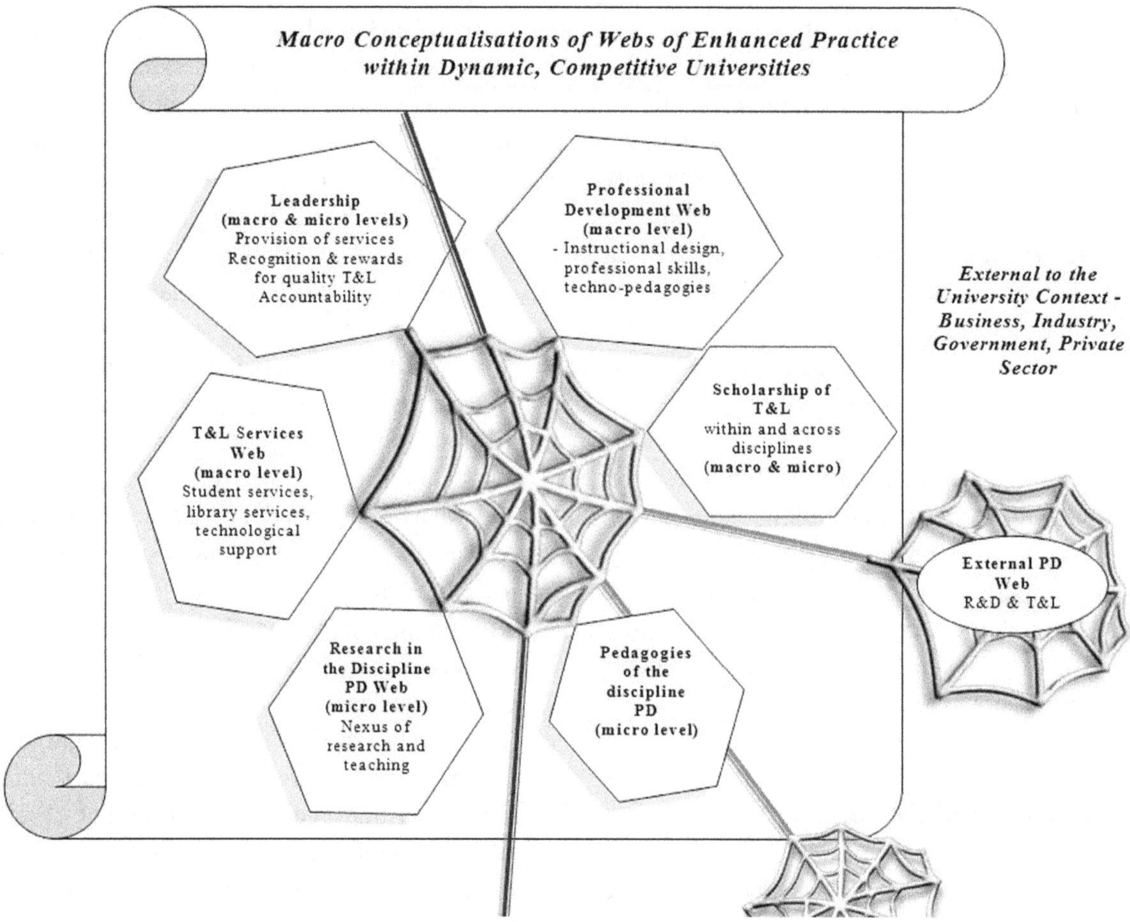

are ill prepared to teach well other than being experts in a discipline (Scott & Scott, 2010b). Simply have a doctorate in the discipline "does not mean that they are all excellent teachers, but it means that most of the time they believe in what they do, or at least they try to make the best of it" (Roxå & Mårtensson, 2009, p. 548). Additionally, the complexity of T&L in universities has been compounded since the 1990s due to the influence of technology (Laurillard, 1993, 2008). Technological innovations in university courses present a range of challenges to academics who have limited pedagogical knowledge and limited expertise with a range of technologies that can support learning (Price & Kirkwood, 2008). Therefore, professional development is also needed about techno-pedagogies - how to effectively integrate a range of technologies to enhance T&L activities. As Chesbro and Boxler (2010) rightly identified, ICT now also provides new and different opportunities for professional growth for university academics. However, university leadership is needed to support the quality T&L agenda as it has long been acknowledged that what is rewarded most in universities is research, not teaching (Laurillard, 2008; Ramsden, 1998a; Ramsden, Margetson, Martin, & Clarke, 1995; Scott & Scott, 2010b). Unfortunately, much

Figure 2. Micro conceptualisations of webs of enhanced practice in universities (modified from Scott, 2009)

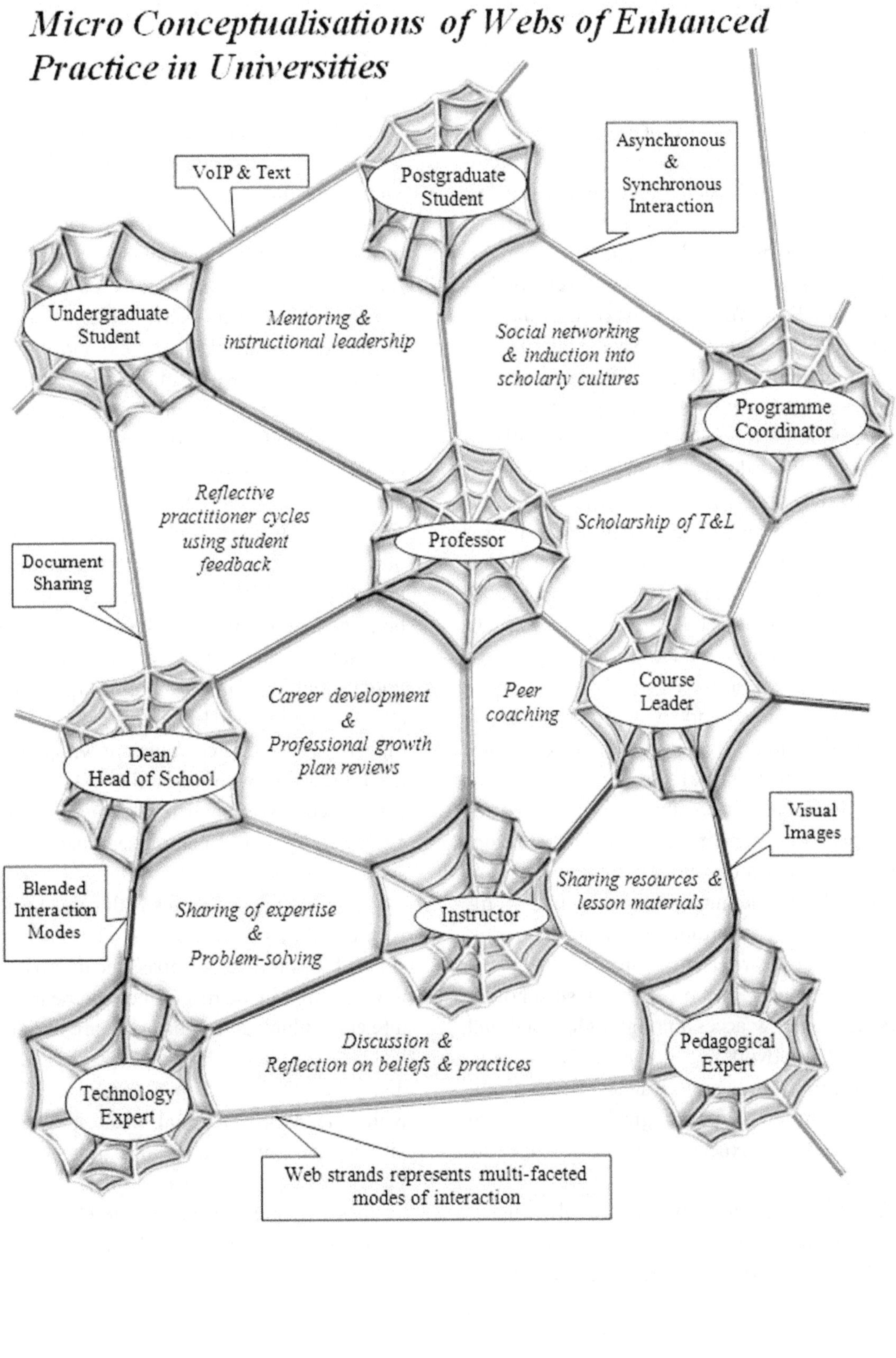

of what is offered to academics in the way of pedagogically-focused professional development is fragmented, non-contextually relevant, and with few incentives for academics to engage. Leaders must address the professional development needs of their staff, what is offered, as well as the format, to ensure the most effective learning experiences for them. This support is more than simply funding centralised professional development centres; rather it requires a multi-faceted approach to enhancing teaching and learning.

We propose two models using Webs of Enhanced Practice (WoEP) at a macro or whole university level (see Figure 1) and at the micro level, or within faculties (see Figure 2). These models, if implemented, would facilitate the interactions and learning between the following educational stakeholders: academics, leaders, support staff, students, technical experts, content experts, and pedagogical experts. The models advocate for flexible, multi-modal delivery opportunities to promote these stakeholders' learning about pedagogy, technology, their discipline, and to facilitate a social networking arena that encourages positive organisational cultures.

In our previous work we defined WoEP as representing "innovation in the use of technology for teacher professional development." It included four main dimensions: multi-faceted interaction, social and professional networking, technology, and multi-modal delivery (Scott & Scott, 2010a). The multi-faceted interaction dimension offers opportunities for academics to dialogue and learn from multiple sources. It overtly recognises the diversity of stakeholder perspectives now accessible through social and professional networking. This means that academics can learn from their colleagues, leaders, support staff, students, pedagogical and technical experts, and even experts external-to-the-university.

The technological dimension involves using a range of technologies to support professional development and interaction. The emphasis though is not on the technology itself as a means to an end, rather, it is about ensuring the greatest delivery flexibility. The multi-modal delivery dimension involves using asynchronous, synchronous, face-to-face, and blended modes of communication. These variations provide the innovation of facilitating academic learning in ways that are convenient, timely, and which acknowledge differences in preference and style. It also recognises the pressures in academic lives in juggling competing demands; hence, finding time for learning is likely to be curtailed if only one mode of delivery is available.

In this chapter we have expanded the conceptualisation of WoEP in the university context to include two levels: the macro or overview of support and professional development at the centralised university level (see Figure 1); and at the micro or faculty level webs (see Figure 2).

Figure 1 is a representation of a web of support webs within the centralised level of the university. For example, there is leadership at both the macro and micro levels, that is, leadership at the chancellery level supports a range of policies and systems promoting and rewarding quality teaching, and leadership at the micro level involves promoting engagement with the quality teaching agenda within faculties and departments; centralised professional development; centralised T&L services; and centralised leadership and support to coordinate the scholarship of T&L (research about pedagogies within the discipline) within and across disciplines. The other dimensions of the model encompass the micro levels of how research in the disciplines can be integrated into curriculum; and again at the micro or faculty level the exploration of deeper pedagogies of the discipline. Displayed in Figure 1 are linkages with other WoEP external to the university environs. These may include research webs and/or T&L webs with other institutions, organisations, businesses, or government whereby social and professional networking and learning can occur.

In the macro conceptualisation of WoEP the different webs appear to be separate and distinct and yet in reality there would be relationships and linkages between faculty and support staff in each web. Ideally, there would also be relationships and some overlap between the webs at the macro or centralised level with those at the micro or faculty levels. Indeed some staff in the macro webs would be charged with facilitating and supporting webs within the micro or faculty setting. For example, researchers within the scholarship of T&L web within the central university (macro) would coordinate and participate in interdisciplinary research as well as support faculty members' research (micro) into 'pedagogies of the discipline'. Additionally, professional developers within the centralised professional development web (macro) would facilitate programmes as well as coordinate and support faculty-based (micro) professional development.

Macro Conceptualisations of Webs of Enhanced Practice within Dynamic, Competitive Universities

Leadership

Leaders in universities are charged with ensuring the quality of education and research as the two main outcomes of academics' work. Unfortunately, tensions exist between these two academic roles. Frequently, academics are presented with mixed messages from administrators about prioritising T&L developments when institutional recognition and rewards are for research quality and magnitude of output. This means faculty leaders must be clear and realistic about the goals they are setting for their staff and actively support all to focus on T&L priorities. Many deans are discipline experts, hence are poorly equipped to lead in pedagogical matters. Even so, they can promote professional development, provide support and recognise the efforts of engaged academics, overtly promote T&L goals within their faculty, all with the view to nurturing a community of learners committed to enhancing institutional quality.

The academy responds to the reward structures in universities. Good teaching in some institutions is included in promotion criteria and academics are more likely to obtain tenure and promotion if their teaching and research portfolios are balanced with positive outcomes. As an intrinsic reinforcement, if academics are perceived to be receptive to innovations in technology, content, and pedagogies, students are more likely to respond positively to them and the learning experiences designed by their instructors (Scott, Issa, & Issa, 2008). If instructors are receiving positive feedback from students, this can influence instructor self-efficacy and empowerment over their teaching duties (Scott & Dixon, 2009). Empowered academics contribute to positive academic cultures which increases student satisfaction with educational quality and ultimately to enhancing institutional reputation. Hence, direct linkages can be identified from improving the quality of T&L to enhancing institutional reputation. This underlines the importance of leadership in enhancing teaching and learning.

Professional Development Web

Most universities that are engaging with 'raising the quality of T&L' agenda have established some form of professional development support centre. These centres offer in workshops or short courses generally focused on generic teaching skills. While these are important, professional developers need to expand their repertoire of offerings to include the principles of instructional design which not only relate to teaching within a technological medium but also serve to promote more systematic and comprehensive approaches and resources within face-to-face and blended modes.

Techno-pedagogies should also be incorporated into professional development to promote academic techno-efficacy. Gen Y students expect more integration of technology in T&L environments and this means the need to support academics in exploring what is available, how to use it effectively and responsibly to increase student motivation, and to ensure that their integration of technology is educationally optimal.

Scholarship of Teaching and Learning Web

The scholarship of T&L is research about teaching within and across faculties, done by practitioners for practitioners. It is an emerging dimension in contemporary universities with Ramsden (2003) and Laurillard (2009) reporting the scholarship of T&L as highly effective for improving teaching. Support for the research about T&L can be through funding grants and in the coordination of research projects within and across faculties (Macdonald & Black, 2010). These research projects would also serve to raise the profile of 'pedagogies of the discipline' research to that commensurate with 'research in the discipline' and provide increased opportunities for implementing more systematic, positive, and evidence-based curriculum changes.

Pedagogies of the Discipline' Professional Development Web

Teaching science subjects can be quite different to teaching in the arts; hence, there needs to be support for professional development for teaching in the discipline. This would occur within faculties and is also incorporated into the micro conceptualisations of the webs of enhanced practice (see Figure 2). Academics who engage in webs of enhanced practice can draw upon the pedagogical, discipline, technological expertise of their colleagues within and across the university to improve their own practice and to expand their repertoire of teaching and assessment strategies.

Research in the Discipline Web

Research in the discipline is usually the primary activity of all scholars. Research in the discipline can also positively influence teaching when research findings flow back into university curriculum. When there is a nexus between research and teaching, the curriculum is cutting edge and relevant to the profession which ensures the dissemination and mobilisation of knowledge garnered through scholarly research.

Teaching and Learning Services Web

Included in the macro conceptualisation of WoEP are the centralised T&L services web which involves student services, technical support for ICT, library services, and the bookshop. These services all have ICT infrastructure and systems which must remain cutting edge in order to maintain the highest quality services imperative for student success and satisfaction with the learning environment. This is particularly important for those studying online who have fewer opportunities to travel to the university campus to resolve problems and seek assistance. Leaders cannot underestimate the importance of these service areas in promoting quality T&L outcomes.

Micro Conceptualisations of Webs of Enhanced Practice

The micro conceptualisations of WoEP (see Figure 2) focus on establishing sound professional development about T&L, increasing technological expertise, and social and professional networking opportunities within faculties and departments. The participants would be academics, experts, technicians, leaders, support staff, and students. Academic perspectives would span all levels from dean or head of school, professors, programme coordinators, course leaders, and instructors. Postgraduate students would be included as some are also instructors and mentors for undergraduate classes. Undergraduate perspectives would also be included through student feedback which provides valuable data to inform T&L developments.

In faculty-based WoEP, educational stakeholders would communicate in multi-faceted interactive modes using a range of technological media to facilitate conversations. Work life in the university context is increasingly hectic, hence, reserving professional and course development conversations to face-to-face modes is simply no longer viable. This model presents a multi-modal delivery dimension whereby stakeholders can engage with each other using a range of synchronous and asynchronous technologies such as email, video conferencing, bulletin boards and forums, VoIP, text, document and resource sharing, as well as, face-to-face modes. This provides greater freedom for the evolution of learning communities, that is, academics working collaboratively focused on expanding their knowledge about pedagogy; interrogating their personal teaching and techno-pedagogical philosophies; exploring innovations in teaching; solving real problems; and sharing resources and developing cutting edge curriculum, learning experiences, and assessments.

Including technological experts into the WoEP enables academics to become exposed to, and comfortable with, a range of technologies for their own learning and that of their students. Learning through technology can also facilitate their comfort with a range of technologies. In turn, this familiarity promotes faculty members' techno-efficacy (their capacity to effectively and appropriately integrate a range of technologies to promote optimal teaching and research activities). This presents opportunities to decrease the digital divide between the Gen X academics and the Gen Y student body.

These WoEP facilitate wider-ranging relationships with stakeholders who have varied knowledge, expertise, and perspectives. Anticipated outcomes of this model include the enhancement of content and pedagogical knowledge, and technological expertise, as well as, faculty cultures by reducing the isolation inherent in the academy. It is also designed to provide opportunities for peer coaching, mentoring, instructional leadership, and indeed friendships between members of the academy. It has the potential to promote career development; greater accountability for improving T&L through the conversations between leaders and their staff about faculty professional growth plans; peer accountability by working in collegial teams; and the use of student feedback to promote reflective practitioner cycles for improving teaching and learning. Other anticipated outcomes include the induction of postgraduate students into scholarly cultures. Additionally, there would be greater empowerment of stakeholders, more collaborative and positive faculty cultures, and increased engagement with professional development due to peer accountability.

It is anticipated that these two models working in concert will result in: a more pedagogically and techno-efficacious academy; more satisfied and successful graduates; more informed, involved, and trusted leaders; greater sustainability for programmes; and enhancement of institutional reputation.

CONCLUSION

Traditionally, institutional reputation was based solely on research performance, however, now it is frequently measured through T&L quality performance indicators. Given that many university students are characteristic of the "digital native" Generation Y and are discerning consumers of education, universities and their teaching academics must engage with techno-pedagogies in order to facilitate satisfying, relevant, and effective learning experiences to maintain the sustainability of the institution (Black, 2010). This highlights the importance of professional development to enhance T&L within universities.

For many academics, focusing on improving T&L and techno-pedagogies is not a priority unless leadership at the macro and micro institutional levels fund, support, and reward engagement with multi-dimensional professional development. It is proposed that traditional conceptualisations of professional development are no longer yielding high quality T&L outcomes; therefore, more flexible and innovative models better suited to the contemporary context are required. Future research can be focused on implementing and evaluating the impact of these Webs of Enhanced Practice models of professional development on T&L outcomes and academics' efficacy.

The academy must engage in different ways to support students' learning in not only discipline knowledge acquisition but also social, technological, and professional outcomes. If we pay homage to lifelong learning, we academics must be prepared to continue our own learning in our disciplines, our pedagogical knowledge and expertise, and also in our techno-pedagogical exploration so that we can provide optimal learning experiences for students. As Black (2010) stated:

In a sense, little has changed: effective teaching has always focused on students' needs. The combination of the new generation and new digital tools, however, is forcing a rethinking of the very nature of education in both content and delivery. In understanding who Gen Y's members are and how they learn, faculty will be able to determine how to engage them in and beyond the classroom. (p. 100)

REFERENCES

Aragon, S. R. (2003). Creating social presence in online environments. *New Directions for Adult and Continuing Education, 100*, 57–68. doi:10.1002/ace.119

Ascough, R. S. (2002). Designing for online distance education: Putting pedagogy before technology. *Teaching Theology and Religion, 5*(1), 17–29. doi:10.1111/1467-9647.00114

Bender, T. (2003). *Discussion-based online teaching to enhance student learning*. Sterling, VA: Stylus Publishing.

Biggs, J. B. (1993). From theory to practice: A cognitive systems approach. *Higher Education Research & Development, 12*(1), 73–85. doi:10.1080/0729436930120107

Biggs, J. B. (2001). The reflective institution: Assuring and enhancing the quality of teaching and learning. *Higher Education, 41*, 221–238. doi:10.1023/A:1004181331049

Black, A. (2010). Gen Y: Who they are and how they learn. *Educational Horizons*, ▪▪▪, 92–101.

Business Higher Education Round Table. (2003). *Developing generic skills: Examples of best practice. Brunswick St.* Australia: Business Higher Education Round Table.

Caspersz, D., Skene, J., & Wu, M. (2002, 5-6 February). *Team members that bring you down dead: The antecedents of student willingness to participate in team projects*. Paper presented at the 11th Annual Teaching Learning Forum: Focusing on the Student, Perth: Edith Cowan University.

Centra, J. A. (1979). *Determining faculty effectiveness: Assessing teaching, research, and service for personnel decisions and improvement*. San Francisco, CA: Jossey-Bass.

Centra, J. A. (1989). Faculty evaluation and faculty development in higher education. In Smart, J. C. (Ed.), *Higher education: Handbook of theory and research* (pp. 155–179). New York, NY: Agathon.

Centra, J. A. (1993). *Reflective faculty evaluation*. San Francisco, CA: Jossey-Bass.

Chesbro, P., & Boxler, N. (2010). Weaving the fabric of professional development in the 21st century through technology. *Journal of Staff Development, 31*(1), 48–53.

Chickering, A., & Ehrmann, S. C. (1996). Implementing the seven principles: Technology as lever. *AAHE Bulletin, 49*(2), 3–6.

Chickering, A. W., & Gamson, Z. F. (1987). Seven principles for good practice in undergraduate education. *AAHE Bulletin, 39*(7), 3–7.

Chickering, A. W., & Gamson, Z. F. (1991). Seven principles for good practice in undergraduate education. In Chickering, A. W., & Gamson, Z. F. (Eds.), *Applying the seven principles for good practice in undergraduate education: New directions for teaching and learning* (pp. 63–69). San Francisco, CA: Jossey-Bass.

Chickering, A. W., & Gamson, Z. F. (1999). Development and adaptations of the seven principles for good practice in undergraduate education. *New Directions for Teaching and Learning*, (80): 75–81. doi:10.1002/tl.8006

Chickering, A. W., Gamson, Z. F., & Barsi, L. M. (1989). *Principles for good practice in undergraduate education*. Racine, WI: Johnson Foundation.

Chickering, A. W., Payne, C., & Poitras, G. (2001). Teaching and technologies for human development. *Educational Technology, 41*(5), 46–51.

de la Harpe, B., & Radloff, A. (2008). Institutional support for quality learning and teaching. In Scott, S., & Dixon, K. (Eds.), *The globalised university: Trends and development in teaching and learning* (pp. 19–50). Perth, Australia: Black Swan Press.

DEST. (Department of Education, Science and Training). (2002). *Employability skills for the future* (pp. 1-74). Canberra, Australia: Department of Education, Science and Training.

DEST. (Department of Education, Science and Training). (2007). *Graduate employability skills* (p. 60). Business, Industry and Higher Education Collaboration Council.

Dunn, R., & Griggs, S. A. (2000). *Practical approaches to using learning styles in higher education*. Westport, CT: Bergin & Garvey.

Galbraith, M. G. (2004). Becoming an effective teacher of adults. In Galbraith, M. G. (Ed.), *Adult learning methods* (3rd ed., pp. 3–19). Malabar, India: Krieger Publishing Company.

Gardner, H. (1999). *Intelligence reframed: Multiple intelligences for the 21st century*. New York, NY: Basic Books.

James, R., McInnis, C., & Devlin, M. (2002). *Assessing learning in Australian universities: Ideas, strategies and resources for quality in student assessment* (pp. 1–62). Canberra, Australia: Centre for the Study of Higher Education. The University of Melbourne.

Johnson, D. W., Johnson, R. T., & Smith, K. A. (1998). Cooperative learning returns to college: What evidence is there that it works? *Change, 30*(4), 26–35. doi:10.1080/00091389809602629

Johnson, D. W., Johnson, R. T., & Smith, K. A. (2007). The state of cooperative learning in post-secondary and professional settings. *Educational Psychology Review, 19*, 15–29. doi:10.1007/s10648-006-9038-8

Joyce, B., Weil, M., & Calhoun, E. (2008). *Models of teaching* (8th ed.). New York, NY: Allyn & Bacon.

Kagan, S. (1994). *Cooperative learning*. San Juan Capistrano, CA: Kagan Cooperative Learning.

Knapper, C. (2010). Changing teaching practice: Barriers and strategies. In Christensen Hughes, J., & Mighty, J. (Eds.), *Taking stock. Research on teaching and learning in higher education* (pp. 229–242). Kingston, ON: School of Policy Studies, Queens University.

Knight, P. T. (2002). Summative assessment in higher education: Practices in disarray. *Studies in Higher Education, 27*(3), 275–286. .doi:10.1080/03075070220000662

Knowles, M. S., Holton, E. F. III, & Swanson, R. A. (2005). *The adult learner: The definitive classic in adult education and human resource development* (6th ed.). Amsterdam, The Netherlands: Elsevier.

Kolb, D. (1976). *Learning styles inventory: Technical manual*. Boston, MA: McBer and Company.

Laurillard, D. (1993). *Rethinking university teaching. A framework for the effective use of educational technology*. London, UK: Routledge.

Laurillard, D. (2008). Technology enhanced learning as a tool for pedagogical innovation. *Journal of Philosophy of Education, 42*(3-4), 521–533. doi:10.1111/j.1467-9752.2008.00658.x

Laurillard, D. (2009). The pedagogical challenges to collaborative technologies. *Computer-Supported Collaborative Learning, 4*, 5–20. .doi:10.1007/s11412-008-9056-2

Levine, A., & Sun, J. C. (2002). *Barriers to distance education*. Washington, DC: American Council on Education.

Long, H. B. (2004). Understanding adult learners. In Galbraith, M. W. (Ed.), *Adult learning methods: A guide for effective instruction* (3rd ed.). Florida, USA: Krieger Publishing.

Macdonald, J., & Black, A. (2010). Disciplinary knowledge practices in distance education: Testing a new methodology for teaching enhancement in history. *Arts and Humanities in Higher Education, 9*, 69–87. .doi:10.1177/1474022209349828

Marsh, H. W., & Roche, L. A. (1994). *The use of students' evaluations of university teaching to improve teaching effectiveness*. Canberra, Australia: Department of Employment, Education and Training.

Marsh, W. H., & Dunkin, M. (1992). Students' evaluations of university teaching: A multidimensional perspective. In Smart, J. C. (Ed.), *Higher education: Handbook on theory and research* (*Vol. 8*, pp. 143–234). New York, NY: Agathon.

Merriam, S. B. (2001). Andragogy and self-directed learning: Pillars of adult learning theory. In Merriam, S. B. (Ed.), *The new update on adult learning theory* (*Vol. 89*, pp. 3–13). San Francisco, CA: Jossey-Bass.

Moore, M. (1989). Three types of interaction. *American Journal of Distance Education, 3*(2), 1–6. doi:10.1080/08923648909526659

Moore, M. G., & Kearsly, G. (1996). *Distance education: A systems view*. Belmont, CA: Wadsworth Publishing Company.

Oliver, R., Omari, A., & Herrington, J. (1998). Investigating implementation strategies for WWW-based learning environments. *International Journal of Instructional Media, 25*(2), 121–138.

Palloff, R. M., & Pratt, K. (1999). *Building learning communities in cyberspace: Effective strategies for the online classroom*. San Francisco, CA: Jossey-Bass.

Palloff, R. M., & Pratt, K. (2005). *Collaborating online: Learning together in community*. San Francisco, CA: Jossey-Bass.

Price, L., & Kirkwood, A. (2008). Learning and teaching and technology. In Scott, S., & Dixon, K. (Eds.), *The globalised university: Trends and development in teaching and learning* (pp. 83–113). Perth, Australia: Black Swan Press.

Prosser, M. (2010). Faculty research and teaching approaches: Exploring the relationship. In Christensen Hughes, J., & Mighty, J. (Eds.), *Taking stock: Research on teaching and learning in higher education* (pp. 129–137). Montreal & Kingston, ON: McGill-Queen's University Press.

Prosser, M., & Barrie, S. C. (2000). Using a student-focused learning perspective to strategically align academic development with institutional quality assurance. In Blackwell, R., & Blackmore, P. (Eds.), *Towards strategic staff development in higher education* (pp. 195–202). Buckingham, UK: Open University Press.

Prosser, M., Martin, E., Trigwell, K., Ramsden, P., & Middleton, H. (2008). University academics' experience of research and its relationship to their experience of teaching. *Instructional Science: An International Journal of the Learning Sciences*, *36*(1), 3–16.

Prosser, M., Ramsden, P., Trigwell, K., & Martin, E. (2003). Dissonance in experience of teaching and its relation to the quality of student learning. *Studies in Higher Education*, *28*(1), 37–48. doi:10.1080/03075070309299

Prosser, M., & Trigwell, K. (1999a). *Understanding learning and teaching, on deep and surface learning*. Society for Research into Higher Education and Open University Press.

Prosser, M., & Trigwell, K. (1999b). *Understanding learning and teaching: The experience in higher education*. Buckingham, UK: Open University Press.

Ramsden, P. (1998a). *Learning to lead in higher education*. London, UK & New York, NY: Routledge. doi:10.4324/9780203278116

Ramsden, P. (1998b). Managing the effective university. *Higher Education Research & Development*, *17*(3), 347–370. doi:10.1080/0729436980170307

Ramsden, P. (2003). *Learning to teach in higher education* (2nd ed.). London, UK: Routledge Falmer.

Ramsden, P., Margetson, D., Martin, E., & Clarke, S. (1995). *Recognising and rewarding good teaching in Australian higher education*. Canberra, Australia: Committee for the Advancement of University Teaching.

Ramsden, P., & Martin, E. (1996). Recognition of good university teaching: Policies from an Australian study. *Studies in Higher Education*, *21*(3), 299–315. doi:10.1080/03075079612331381231

Ramsden, P., Prosser, M., Trigwell, K., & Martin, E. (2007). University teachers' experiences of academic leadership and their approaches to teaching. *Learning and Instruction*, *17*, 140–155. doi:10.1016/j.learninstruc.2007.01.004

Roxå, T., & Mårtensson, K. (2009). Significant conversations and significant networks - Exploring the backstage of the teaching arena. *Studies in Higher Education*, *34*(5), 547–559. .doi:10.1080/03075070802597200

Scott, D. E., & Scott, S. (2010a). Innovations in the use of technology and teacher professional development. In Lindberg, J. O., & Olofsson, A. D. (Eds.), *Online learning communities and teacher professional development: Methods for improved education delivery* (pp. 169–190). Hershey, PA: IGI Global.

Scott, D. E., & Scott, S. (2010b). *Faculty perceptions of teaching and learning at the University of Calgary*. Calgary, Canada: University of Calgary's Institutional Learning and Teaching Plan Committee.

Scott, S., & Dixon, K. C. (2009). Partners in a learning organisation: A student-focused model of professional development. *The Educational Forum*, *73*(3), 240–255. doi:10.1080/00131720902991319

Scott, S., Issa, T., & Issa, T. (2008). Closing the loop. The relationship between instructor-reflective practice and students' satisfaction and quality outcomes. *International Journal of Learning, 15*(3), 109–120.

Simonson, M., Smaldino, S., Albright, M., & Zvacek, S. (2006). *Teaching and learning at a distance: Foundations of distance education* (3rd ed.). Upper Saddle River, NJ: Pearson Merrill Prentice Hall.

Smith, P. L., & Ragan, T. J. (2005). *Instructional design* (3rd ed.). New York, NY: Wiley Publishing Inc.

Tapscott, D. (1999). Educating the net generation. *Educational Leadership, 56*(5), 6–11.

Wlodkowski, R. J. (2004). Strategies to enhance adult motivation to learn. In Galbraith, M. W. (Ed.), *Adult learning methods: A guide for effective instruction* (3rd ed., pp. 91–112). Florida, USA: Krieger Publishing.

Woods, R. H. (2002). How much communication is enough in online courses? Exploring the relationship between frequency of instructor-initiated personal email and learners' perceptions of and participation in online learning. *International Journal of Instructional Media, 29*(4), 377–394.

Woods, R. H., & Baker, J. D. (2004). Interaction and immediacy in online learning. *International Review of Research in Open and Distance Learning, 5*(2), 1–13.

Yorke, M. (2003). Formative assessment in higher education: Moves towards theory and the enhancement of pedagogic practice. *Higher Education, 45*, 477–501. doi:10.1023/A:1023967026413

ADDITIONAL READING

Bork, A. (2001). What is needed for effective learning on the Internet? *Journal of Educational Technology & Society, 4*(3), 139–143.

Lindberg, J. O., & Olofsson, A. D. (Eds.). (2010). *Online learning communities and teacher professional development: Methods for improved education delivery*. Hershey, PA: IGI Global.

Scott, S., & Dixon, K. (Eds.). (2008). *The globalised university: Trends and development in teaching and learning*. Perth: Black Swan Publishing.

Scott, S., & Issa, T. (2006). *Lessons learned from using students' feedback to inform academic teaching*. Paper presented at the 15th Annual Teaching and Learning Forum: Experience in Learning, University of Western Australia.

Scott, S., & Issa, T. (2006). *Team work skills do not come naturally even for adult learners! Embedding structure and scaffolding into the university program are essential for optimal results*. Paper presented at the paper presented at the British Educational Research Association conference, Warwick University.

KEY TERMS AND DEFINITIONS

Effective Learning Experiences: Formal and informal, structured and unstructured experiences which support and promote optimal learning.

Good Teaching: Teaching which demonstrates alignment between teacher beliefs, understanding of the principles of good practice, and excellence in practice. It encompasses considerations related to content, students' needs, optimal learning experiences, assessment and feedback, communication and interaction, structuring for collaboration, and practitioner reflection and improvement.

ICT-Facilitated Learning Environments: Learning environments including formal and informal which utilise information communication technologies for the instructional delivery, participant interaction, and/or supply of learning materials.

Models: Conceptualisations, illustrations, or representations of processes, practices, people, objects, and/or relationships encompassed within a system.

Professional Development: Any activity which is designed to facilitate improvement and enhancement of a teachers' knowledge and practices with the view to improving student outcomes.

Scholarship of Teaching and Learning: Individual or collaborative research focused on extending understandings and enhancing effective pedagogies within and across disciplines.

Social and Professional Networking: A social structure comprised of individuals who are linked through various relationships (including friendships, common interests, collegial, hierarchical positions, and professional affiliations) focused on knowledge creation and mobilisation, and the nurturing of constructive interactions and organisational cultures.

Techno-Efficacy: An individual's capacity to effectively and appropriately integrate a range of technologies to promote optimal teaching and research activities.

Techno-Pedagogies: The effective and ethically appropriate use of technology for teaching and learning purposes

Webs of Enhanced Practice: Models advocating for flexible, multi-modal delivery opportunities to promote stakeholders' learning about pedagogy, technology, their discipline, and to facilitate a social networking arena that encourages positive organisational cultures.

Section 5
Changing Educational Practices Through Informed Choices of Design

There is a constant need for well-informed decisions to change educational practices and activities embraced by educational technologies in higher education. In this fifth and last section of the book, three different approaches for promoting successful changes in educational technology rich contexts are presented. The chapters all communicate a rational for change through informed design.

Chapter 22
The Design of Learning Materials within Small Scale Projects:
What is the Value of an Action Research Approach?

Michael Hammond
University of Warwick, UK

Jie Hu
University of Chongqing, China

ABSTRACT

This chapter discusses the design of learning materials in the context of small scale projects within higher education. It describes the enduring appeal of instructional material and its growing use following the take up of virtual learning environments (VLEs) / learning platforms in teaching and learning. It suggests that action research approaches may be of value in the design of instructional material as they offer systematic, formative feedback at an early stage in the design process and prioritise user participation. A case study is provided of a broadly action research approach to the design of instructional material to support academic reading skills at one university. The case exemplifies the strengths of action research but also highlights the tensions and difficulties, in particular that of securing the engagement of stakeholders. The implications for further research are brought out.

DOI: 10.4018/978-1-61350-080-4.ch022

INTRODUCTION

In a world in which technology provides opportunities for immersive and more deeply participatory learning than ever before (e.g., Ijsselsteijn, 2005) discussion of the design of instructional materials has an outdated feel. Indeed instructional material under the banner of computer based learning (CBL) or courseware is associated with first forays into the use of computers in teaching and learning. The lasting criticism of CBL, and of courseware in general, is that is not adaptable in the same way as face to face instruction. CBL became critiqued as electronic page turning both in its heavy text input and lack of interaction (see contributions to Stephenson, 2001) and, in particular, it was not seen as establishing a conversational framework of learner and tutor (Laurillard, 1993) or the wider networking of learners (e.g., Thorpe, 2001). But this is not the end of the matter. A revisionist view is to see something valuable within the history of courseware with, for example, Rushby & Seabrook (2008) arguing that early designers engaged seriously with understanding learners' needs. More recently the idea of instructional material framed by learning objectives, and reinforced by repeated practice and testing, has been revisited within the context of 'learning platforms' or virtual learning environments (VLEs) now widely used within higher education.

VLEs, of course, offer opportunities for discussion and other forms of collaborative activity such as WIKIs, forums and blogs but of central importance is the opportunity they provide for repositories of materials, instructional support and online formative summative assessment all of which can be accessed 'any time / anywhere' (JISC undated). Online learning material can allow learners to reinforce what they have covered through other means (Martín-Blas & Serrano-Fernándeza, 2009; Ramos & Yudko, 2008; Salaway et al., 2008) and self-assessment can provide feedback on learning across educational sectors (e.g., Angus & Watson, 2009; Gill & Greenhow, 2008; Gvozdenko & Chambers, 2007; Martin, Klein & Sullivan, 2007; Oxford Brookes University, 2004, Park & Choi, 2008). The introduction of VLEs has provided opportunities for university teachers to develop a wider repertoire of roles including that of 'do-it-yourself designer' of learning materials complete with formative and summative testing. Yet university teachers often find it difficult to take on this role and much of what is produced within a VLE may appear half finished or poorly designed. There are various reasons why this might be the case. One needs to consider the competing demands made on university teachers (e.g., Lingard, 2007); limitations in support and training (e.g., Morón-Garcia, 2006); and perhaps the wider activity system in which innovation takes place (e.g., Kirkup & Kirkwood, 2005). These are difficulties that need addressing at a wider level (JISC, 2009) but it is striking that while there is plentiful advice on, say, the pedagogy involved in design (e.g., Mayes & De Freitas, 2004) or issues of quality in e-learning (e.g., Swedish National Agency for Higher Education, 2008) the design process—the steps an individual tutor or small team of tutors might undertake to produce material within a VLE to support learning—has remained under-reported.

With the above points in mind this chapter looks at the contribution that action research can make as an approach to instructional design within small scale innovations using learning platforms or VLEs. The context is the development of learning material containing guidance and interactive feedback. This chapter is addressing three key questions:

- What is an action research approach to design?
- What is the appeal of an action research approach to design?
- What are the tensions within an action research process?

BACKGROUND

Action research is capable of broad definition (e.g., Elliot 1993; Lewin 1946; McNiff 1993) but a common theme is that it offers a systematic approach to improving professional practice through cycles of reflection and action. As with Analysis, Design, Development, Implement, Evaluate (Addie) models, to which some conceptions of action research appear similar, it is flexible in application.

The case for using action research within the instructional design process has been put forward by several writers including Reigeluth & Frick (1999) whose key concern was to 'factor in' formative feedback within the design process. Such feedback would, it was argued, lead to a better fit of product to user and provide a more efficient approach to product development. Action research has been taken up by many small scale developers with different intentions. For example Chen (2007) borrows from action research to develop a formative approach to the design of virtual reality learning environments. Along similar lines Cook & Crawford (2008) argue that rapid prototyping allows a deeper engagement with users and further suggest that action research seeks to understand the context in which adoption of new technology takes place. This is reinforced by Parrish & Wilson (2009) who argue that action research has a special relevance at a time when there is increasing attention to understanding user needs and a range of innovative approaches to accessing and evaluating those needs. In this sense an action research approach calls for a change of perspective within the design process (the expert designer is one among many in collaborative teams).

The strengths of action research are widely recognized but the approach is not without tensions [T] which have been covered both in the more general literature on action research and in that pertaining to instructional design:

(T1) Action research is very often small scale in nature and descriptive in reporting. This makes it very difficult to generalise processes and findings to a wider audiences. On one hand this may not be a problem—knowledge produced through action research is by its nature personal, practical and essentially context-specific (Levy, 2006)—but can what is learnt in one context be of value to other action researchers?

(T2) While action research may lead to more 'efficient' outcomes it is not clear whether practitioners really have the time to engage with it. Even those supportive of the approach (e.g., Johnston 1994) question whether action research is 'doable' without the impetus of external involvement and wonder just how systematic and detailed 'research' should be to inform action.

(T3) This raises a further tension concerning the depth of collaborative involvement needed within the process. While Elliot (1993) stresses the collaborative, consensus-seeking nature of action research Waters-Adams (1994) is less certain this can always be secured.

(T4) While action research is closely aligned to a belief in the experiential nature of learning (for example Collis & Margaryan, 2005, describe the work undertaken in action research teams as explicitly promoting real-world problem solving) this is not always taken for granted. Others see action research as a series of steps to be taken within an enquiry without any a priori assumptions about pedagogy. The parallel here is with instructional design (ID) itself and whether ID should be focused on pedagogy as well as process.

(T5) Models of action research are contested. Some researchers, for example, draw on original work by Lewin (1946) to describe cycles of planning; reflecting; acting and observing. Others develop more colloquial 'heuristics' such as 'look, think and act' (Stringer, 1996) and Kemmis & McTaggart (1988) who suggest the process is one of repeated cycles of 'plan, act, observe'. While all commentators see the process as an iterative one there is disagreement over the number and nature of those 'iterations' and how action research methodology should be modelled.

The chapter now turns to a case study in order to identify the strengths of an action research approach in one particular instructional design context and to expose tensions and difficulties.

THE CASE STUDY

The main focus of this chapter is on the development of online material to support study skills within a full time one year Masters in Education course which attracts around 30 students each year. Nearly all these students are international students: many from East Asian countries and with English as an additional language (EAL). Many international students encounter difficulties of academic adjustment particularly when from very different cultural backgrounds (Wu, Hammond & Barnes, 2009) and find proficiency in the English language a key concern as it is central to academic success and social integration (Badur, 2003; Bamford, 2008; Heikinheimo & Shute, 2005). In the institution concerned, students received F2F and print based language and study skills support but there was felt to be an opportunity for providing further support online. An area which had most potential was that of academic reading as this seemed to pose lower technological barriers than designing materials to support listening, speaking or writing. The authors were interested in the context due to their participation in the Masters programme teaching (MH) and as part of the target audience for the material and later as a focus for PhD research (JH). The development of the product took place over the period 2006 – 2008 -fitted in around numerous other commitments. The context

Figure 1. Action research hybrid model

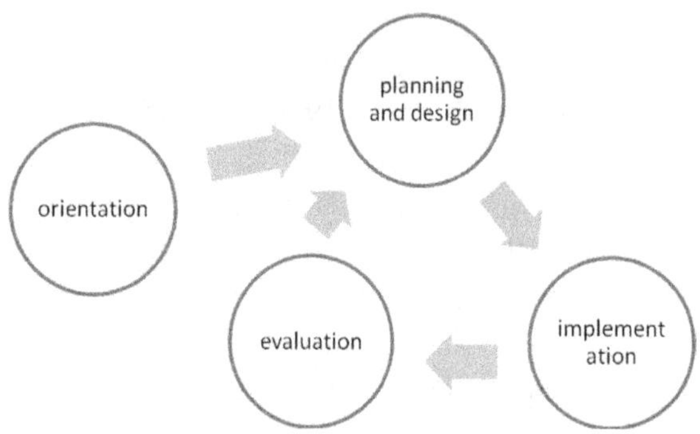

is specific to a department of education but is a familiar one in higher education: a small 'team' with an open ended brief to explore an opportunity opened up by technology and is reported here as a kind of designed case (Yin, 2009).

Action research provided the developers with a cyclical open ended framework useful for exploration of a problem (that of providing adequate support for international students with EAL) and an opportunity (access to online technology). However, rather than take an off the shelf approach, a hybrid version of action research was constructed which took the idea of iterative cycles within a process of design, implementation and evaluation following on from an extended orientation (Figure 1).

The *orientation* phase within the model focused on understanding the nature and scope of the problem. Put simply it was asking, 'where are we and where do we want to go?'. Orientation had an obvious association with 'needs analysis' in more conventional ID approaches, however, it offered a more open and exploratory approach and a wider frame of reference. It sought to access the voice of the users and engage 'stakeholders' in the process from the start. It generated varied sources of evidence to compare and contrast. The orientation consisted of: first, a review of the literature on academic reading; second, a web review of sites which support academic reading; third, interviews with students taking the programme; fourth, interviews with their tutors. Only a sample of students (14 out of a total cohort of 32) was interviewed but one that was broadly representative of the wider body in background, gender and age. Twelve interviewees were from East Asian countries and nine out of the 14 were female. The six tutors interviewed taught different modules on the programme. Findings from all four sources of data were grouped around key themes including the nature of difficulties that EAL created for learners and tutors, the strategies used to overcome these difficulties and specific issues related to academic reading.

The *design* phase within the model sought to turn the findings from the orientation into a set of goals for implementation. These findings were systematically organised and the implications set out for: the scope of the courseware; the texts; the questions about texts; the feedback; and the user interface. This is described in Table 1 although for reasons of space only a excerpt of this work is provided.

Table 1. An excerpt from the organization of data generated during the orientation phase

Themes	Orientation phase				Design phase	
	It was found that	Sources			This suggests that the resources should:	More specifically we should aim to:
		Preliminary interviews	Literature review	Web review		
About the scope of the courseware	International students have cultural backgrounds which are different from the L1 community and face problems of academic adjustment	√	√	-	clarify academic expectations	provide an academic rather than a general L2 reading support focus
	Students may lack appropriate reading strategies	√	√	-	cover reading strategies	provide both practice and explanation
	Fluent academic reading requires knowledge of context as well as of language	√	-	-	be subject related	identify and adapt texts used in modules
	Writing is the output of reading and it can assess the effectiveness of reading.	-	√	-	consider writing extension	provide opportunity for writing
	Reading speed can be improved.	√	√	√	promote speed reading	offer timed reading exercises
	Students may lack knowledge of reading skills such as skimming and scanning.	√	√	√	explain skimming and scanning	provide explanation and back up practice
	Students may lack knowledge of grammar.	√	√	√	consider grammatical explanations	provide explanation and back up practice
	Students may lack vocabulary, especially academic vocabulary.	√	√	√	identify key academic vocabulary	provide practice and explanation of meaning in context.
	Students may be unaware of text structure and discourse organisation.	√	√	-	demonstrate essay structure	provide explanation of structure
	Students might not understand keywords in academic use.	√	√	-	identify academic titles and keywords	provide explanation
	Students might not be able to use library resources effectively and may lack confidence and skills in selecting relevant texts.	√	-	-	consider use of library resources	provide explanation
	Students may have problems understanding the organisation of references.	√	-	√	consider use of referencing	provide explanation and practice

Figure 2. An example of feedback to students

The main emphasis in these passages is:

- ○ methods and methodology in educational research
- ● the value of scientific research in education
- ○ building models and theories
- ○ developing a science of behaviour

0 out of 3
Wrong. Although the article covers the value of scientific research in education its mains focus is methods and methodology. Many academic papers make clear primary or principle concerns and secondary subsidiary concerns. Tips: Please see Appendix 8: Structuring an Essay.

Design and planning can be differentiated as two separate stages—by way of analogy an architect may design a house and then hand over to a clerk of works for the planning of week by week operations—but in smaller scale studies such as this, design and planning are integrated more closely. Here decisions over planning concerned choices over the software to be used, the texts to be selected and the presentation of texts and questions. At the time the institution did not have a VLE as such but used a mix of software to create a learning platform (Becta, 2008) offering the similar functionality. The programme Questionmark Perception was part of that platform and was freely available and supported by the university IT services.

The *implementation* phase consisted of the production of the courseware and the collection of data as specified within the planning for evaluation. The courseware product consisted of a log-in page and four texts taken from different course modules with associated questions, feedback on each answer and support within nine appendices containing guidance on reading skills and vocabulary extension. The first page was designed to allow the selection of texts so that students could choose which ones were relevant for them. These four texts were provided by tutors, on the basis that they were widely used in sessions and students would have to access them during the year. The texts were followed by different types of question including: multiple-choices, filling-in-blanks, and multiple matching and open-ended questions.

Feedback was offered after each question (Figure 2). This provided an explanation as to why the response was right / wrong and signposted additional support within nine appendices covering reading skills and strategies

After the materials had been tested and thoroughly revised, they were saved and made available over the university network. Students were then able to log in to access them.

In the *evaluation* phase of the process the materials were initially trialled with six volunteer students from the course. These again were broadly representative in age and gender: all had EAL and four were from East Asian countries. Evaluation sessions lasted from 45 – 55 minutes with a structured schedule to record behaviour when using the material. Afterwards students were interviewed on: their general impressions of the material; whether they felt it supported their reading of academic texts; the valuable / not so valuable features of tests, questions and feedback. Test scores were collected to identify which questions student found easier / more difficult. These different sources of evaluation data were then compared and contrasted (as seen in

Table 2. Summary of evaluation findings

	Sources		
	Interview	Observation	Score
What was learnt about students and reading:			
Students were motivated to learn online.	√√	√	-
Students could flexibly use the courseware materials.	√√	-	-
Students would have valued more specific study skills support.	√√	-	-
Past experience of learning was varied. They had wide range of learning strategies.	√√	-	-
Previous study skill training was not systematic.	√	-	-
Reading was not necessarily the most important issue, but it was a major issue for students.	√√	-	-
Students' productive skills were a concern.	√	-	-
Positive features of the materials			
The level of the texts was appropriate.	√√	-	√
The language used in the sections was at an appropriate level.	√√	√	√
The descriptions were clearly understood and easy to follow.	√√	√	-
The programme was friendly to use.	√	√	-
The navigation of the programme was interactive and easy to be managed.	√	√	-
The colour of the texts was dull, but usable.	√	-	-
The screen page layout was structured.	√	-	-
The students had the flexibility to choose which sections they would like to take.	√	-	-
The texts were identified as authentic and subject related .	√	√	-
The question types were generally liked by the students, but not the open question.	√	√	-
The online feedback was instant and helpful—better than in previous online support.	√√	√√	-
The materials were appreciated by the students	√	-	-
The students were willing to use the products in the future.	√	-	-
How could be the product be improved?			
More guidance on reading skills.	√√	-	-
The texts should be 'more interesting'.	√√	√	-
Some texts were not seen as relevant—students would accept more generic texts to illustrate study skills.	√	√	-
Signposting to other useful websites should be provided.	√	-	-
The scoring should be more balanced.	√√	√	√
The interface should be modified to be more attractive (*e.g.*, adding graphics and animation).	√	-	-

("√√" refers to strongly indicated, "√" refers to indicated, "-" refers to inconclusive)

Table 2) though the interviews felt to be of most value in reaching judgments.

A Second Round of Development

To address some of the shortcomings in the first product a second round of development was undertaken following a similar pattern of designing, implementing and evaluating as described above. For reasons of space this is described briefly with some key steps in the process highlighted. A key requirement was to deal systematically with findings from the initial evaluation and to

Table 3. Scope for revision following the first round feedback

Themes	Scope for revision
About the material in general	• Making the materials more accessible to better illustrate specific reading skills support. • Revising the scoring system.
About the texts	• Selecting more accessible texts which contain fewer subject knowledge obstacles. • Focusing on reading skills improvement. • Recognising study skills resources as helpful sources.
About the questions	• Providing more accurate descriptions of questions. • Abandoning open writing tasks • Continuing to use the four question types and adding other types of question.
About the feedback	• Continuing to use specific and contextually clarified feedback. • Continuing to provide appendices. • Considering creating paper versions of the appendices, if possible.
About the user interface	• Improving the visual appeal of the screen. • Adding extra design elements to increase the interest of the texts; colour schemes and additional figures, for example.

identify amendments concerning all features of the materials (Table 3).

A key concern was to reconsider the texts used and the modelling of reading skills. Ideally a bank of texts would be provided but there was not the time to do this and more generic texts (some on the topic of academic adjustment and role of study skills) were selected. Each text was preceded with guidance on topics including skimming and scanning text; speed reading and an introduction to the more holistic Survey, Question, Read, Recite, and Review (SQ3R) approach to reading. 'Guidance-exercise-feedback' became central to the material with guidance now foregrounded. Question types and feedback, which were positively reviewed by students, would remain though new 'drag and drop' formats were created and the open question scrapped as it had not been feasible to provide appropriate feedback.

The planning process included further consideration of software. The university had by now created online question forms within its content authoring system and for the sake of consistency it was decided to use these. Redesigned welcome and instruction pages were created alongside a summary of the reading skills the material was going to address. Greater care was taken over the consistency of the routes students should follow and the text was presented in a less cluttered manner. Six sections of material were created following the pattern of guidance-exercise-feedback though the feedback was similar in detail as within the earlier version.

Evaluation was again based on interviews, observations and computer generated scores. Trials were initially conducted with 14 volunteers from the programme from January 2008 to June 2008. Again these were broadly representative of the wider intake, more were female (12) than male and ten were East Asian. All had EAL. For reasons of space the findings are not reproduced in full here but an overall conclusion from the evaluation was that the materials were well received in that the guidance given was helpful; the texts were largely seen as relevant and interesting to read; the questions were at an appropriate level; the feedback was useful and easy to understand; and the user interface was clear and uncluttered. However, there were difficulties indicating that a further round or rounds or development would be needed. In particular there needed to be personalised routes through the materials (this was confirmed when analysis of data showed those with the highest and lowest test scores were less positive about the material than those within the middle range). This suggested that, albeit implicitly, the material had been produced with the 'average student' in mind. For this reason branching options would be provided as and when time and resources were available.

ISSUES, PROBLEMS, AND RECOMMENDATIONS

It was suggested earlier that there was a tension (T1) between the essentially practical reporting of small scale action research projects and the drawing out of general questions for wider consideration. The stance taken here is that there are lessons to be learnt from this highly contextualised case study which are worthy of further discussion. In particular the study suggests that there are strengths within each phase of the action research process which are of general interest.

First the orientation phase. Here there was an attempt to gain a systematic understanding of the views of students, tutors and the experiences of others in a wide ranging review of literature and courseware products. This confirmed that what was felt to be a problem really was a problem and that addressing the problem could lead to an ICT based solution. The orientation enabled a holistic description of the nature and scope of student difficulties and avoided a premature commitment to a particular vision of a 'product'. Participative designers talk of 'building bridges with users' and this is a useful metaphor even if, as in this case, PD is not taken up. In contrast other ID models can prejudge the specification of outcomes and minimise the complexity of planning, leaving it difficult to imagine how a product can be 'fit for purpose'. Orientation in this study continued up to the point where the designers felt that there were patterns in the data – the analogy is with data saturation in social science research. The temptation many designers feel within a project is to get started on implementation right away in a bid to be seen as doing something productive. However this can lead to a greater loss of time in the long run if the product is not fit for purpose, with technology rather than pedagogy driving the project (Carswell 1998).

The obvious advantage of design on a small scale is that what is lost in sophistication through 'diseconomies of scale' is gained through 'fine tuning' to a particular set of users – in this case through the choice of specialist but relevant texts and a pedagogy with which students were comfortable. However orientation should not limit itself to the target users and here orientation included literature and web review. Without this wider range of reference it would not have been possible to identify useful skills such as skimming and scanning and strategies such as SQ3R; in other words there is a limit on the kinds of solutions generated by users themselves and a sense in which users 'do not know what they do not know'. Systematic orientation can help the designer move more confidently into a design stage within which further exploration of context can take place (for example the search for the most suitable software and sources of help).

Turning to evaluation, a strength in this and in many other cases of action research was that user feedback was welcomed and again dealt with systematically. A further strength was that evaluation criteria were contextualised—the materials were not assessed against an expert check list of desirable features (though such checklists were occasionally consulted) but against the behaviours and views of the students studying this particular course. This had the effect of prioritising the appeal of the product (as suggested within Parrish & Wilson, 2009) and learner readiness to engage with the material. This, in turn, provided an interesting comparison between the subject of study (the comprehensibility of academic texts) and the evaluation of the materials (the comprehensibility of a learning environment). In both contexts the reader must seek personal meaning, fluent application of lower-level knowledge (i.e. learning and linguistic process) and higher-level knowledge (i.e. efficient, interactive and strategic processes) (Carrell, Devine & Eskey, 1988; Grabe, 2009). Comprehension involves the texts themselves *and* about the reader's motivation, goals, and background knowledge and language abilities. Evaluation is, however, only valuable if it is acted on and a strength in this case study was the designers' commitment to iterative development. This resulted in a product that was considerably improved over two cycles of development - the second version was seen as more accessible, easier to navigate and offering a wider range of support. By implication, through acting on feedback, a third product would be better still.

Notwithstanding the above strengths the case study also illuminated some tensions. First, there were limits on the engagement of users (T2) and in the level of collaboration within the design (T3). For example, orientation focused on user representatives and this can be contrasted to participatory design (PD) which emphasises the active involvement of all. Further, the engagement of 'stakeholders' in the wider sense was not secured. In particular it was assumed that as the product was well received it would automatically be taken up by students (in practice this did not happen as the materials had not been integrated clearly enough into the advice and guidance offered to students by course leaders). The lack of wider ownership of the product was very largely due to structural constraints. The users were sojourners and even if involved as stakeholders in the early stages of design would have returned to their home countries by the time implementation took place. Meanwhile the intense demands on tutors meant they had very little time to engage with the project beyond providing texts and expressions of support. This presents a familiar difficulty. The literature on e-learning applications (e.g., Arias et al, 2002; Kieslinger, Pata and Fabian, 2009; Light & Luckin, 2008; Whitworth, 2007; Zaphiris et al, 2004) as well as the literature on organisational change (e.g., Sax et al, 2007) highlights the importance of engaging stakeholders and it is precisely in this area that action research has so much to offer (e.g., Cook & Crawford, 2008). Yet understanding the need is not the same as being able to deliver the engagement and action researchers are always working in a context of constraint as well as opportunity.

A further tension in this study was the lack of fit between the cognitive instructional principles upon which the product was designed and the experiential learning principles of action research (T3). An explanation here is that as designers we drew too heavily on 'traditional' models of teaching reading. This may have been because one of the designers held on to implicit 'traditional' beliefs about teaching (cf Ertmer, 2005) and while the other may have over compensated for the divergence between users' views of pedagogy and his own. These problems could have been mitigated by offering very explicit alternatives to the product (e.g., the use of discussion forums, productions Wikis, workshops) to be discussed with all stakeholders with appropriate mock ups. However action research cannot wish away the problem that user voice may lead to the directions in which the designer may not want to go.

A final tension lies in the modelling of the design process (T5). In this case the model was useful as it focused attention on the holistic nature of design not simply the production phase of the process. The model was easy to follow and drew attention to pre design orientation and to iterative development. However it neglected to make explicit mini cycles of implementation (Elliot 1993) and might be amended. However there is a trade off here between accessibility and sophistication.

FUTURE RESEARCH DIRECTIONS

The dearth of practitioner reporting of action research case studies was noted at the start of the chapter and more studies such as this are needed to illustrate the strengths of the approach and the difficulties it throws up. Key issues to cover are the modelling the design process; the nature of pedagogical assumptions within the process and the engagement of stakeholder. Such work would value from a cross disciplinary approach in which the designer is deeply concerned with both the content of the product and the methodology followed in its production.

CONCLUSION

The chapter began by asking:

- What is an action research approach to design?
- What is the appeal of an action research approach to design?
- What are the tensions within an action research process?

It was found that action research was a broad concept but implied a systematic approach to improving a situation through iterative cycles of development and evaluation. In this example a distinguishing feature of the process was a wide and systematic orientation to the problem / opportunity. Further, it was found that the appeal of an action research approach lay in its concern for its attention to user needs; the collection of diverse data; and a commitment to iterative development. Action research requires a deep understanding of context. Evaluation of materials should be based on their fitness for purpose. Finally, it was found that the tensions in the action research process lay in securing the engagement of users and other stakeholders; the level of commitment to experiential learning design and the modelling of the design process. These are tensions which cannot easily be addressed and only capable of best fit solutions.

REFERENCES

Angus, S., & Watson, J. (2009). Does regular online testing enhance student learning in the numerical sciences? Robust evidence from a large data set. *British Journal of Educational Technology*, *40*(2), 255–272. doi:10.1111/j.1467-8535.2008.00916.x

Arias, E. G., Eden, H., Fischer, G., Gorman, A., & Scharff, E. (2002). Transcending the individual human mind: creating shared understanding through collaborative design. In Carroll, J. M. (Ed.), *Human-computer interaction in the new millennium* ((pp. 347–372). New York, NY: ACM Press.

Badur, G. (2003). *International students' perspectives on their cross-cultural adjustment to American higher education.* Unpublished doctoral dissertation, Illinois State University, Illinois.

Bamford, J. (2008). *Strategies for the improvement of international students' academic and cultural experiences of studying in the UK. Hospitality, leisure, sport and tourism network.* York, UK: HEA Academy.

Becta. (2008). *What is a learning platform?* Coventry, UK: Becta.

Carrell, P., Devine, J., & Eskey, D. (Eds.). (1988). *Interactive approaches to second language reading.* Cambridge, UK: Cambridge University Press.

Carswell, L. (1998). Possible versus desirable in instructional systems: Who's driving? *ALT-J*, *6*(1), 70–80. doi:10.1080/0968776980060111

Chen, C. J. (2007). *Formative research on the instructional design process of virtual reality based learning environments*. Paper presented at Ascilite Singapore 2007, Singapore. Retrieved November 1, 2010, from www.ascilite.org.au/conferences/singapore07/procs/chen.pdf

Collis, B., & Margaryan, A. (2005). Merrill Plus: Blending corporate strategy and instructional design. *Educational Technology*, *45*(5), 54–58.

Cook, R., & Crawford, C. (2008). Combining quality and expediency with action research in e-learning instructional design. *The Journal of Educators Online*, *5*(2), 1–34.

Elliott, J. (1993). *Action research for educational change*. Milton Keynes, UK: Open University Press.

Ertmer, P. (2005). Teacher pedagogical beliefs: The final frontier in our quest for technology integration? *Educational Technology Research and Development*, *53*(1), 25–39. doi:10.1007/BF02504683

Gill, M., & Greenhow, M. (2008). How effective is feedback in computer-aided assessments? *Learning, Media and Technology*, *33*(2), 207–220. doi:10.1080/17439880802324145

Grabe, W. (2009). *Reading in a second language: Moving from theory to practice*. Cambridge, UK: Cambridge University Press.

Gvozdenko, E., & Chambers, D. (2007). Beyond test accuracy: Benefits of measuring response time in computerised testing. *Australasian Journal of Educational Technology*, *23*(4), 542–558.

Heikinheimo, P., & Shute, J. (1986). The adaptation of foreign students: Students' views and institutional implications. *Journal of College Student Personnel*, *27*(5), 399–406.

Ijsselsteijn, W. A. (2005). Social presence in e-learning. *International Journal of Technology and Human Interaction*, *1*(1), 85–87.

JISC. (2009). *Introducing managed learning environments (MLEs)*. Bristol, UK: JISC.

JISC. (n.d.). *Effective use of virtual learning environments*. Bristol, UK: JISC. Retrieved November 1, 2010, from http://www.jiscinfonet.ac.uk/InfoKits/effective-use-of-VLEs

Johnston, S. (1994). Is action research a natural process for teachers? *Educational Action Research*, *2*(1), 39–48.

Kemmis, S., & McTaggart, R. (1988). *The action research planner* (3rd ed.). Melbourne, Australia: Deakin University Press.

Kieslinger, B., Pata, K., & Fabian, C. (2009, June). *Participatory design methods for learning and knowledge sharing activities in networked organizations*. Paper presented at The International Conference on E-Learning in the Workplace, New York. Retrieved November 1, 2010, from http://www.intelleo.eu/uploads/tx_abdownloads/files/ICELW2009-Kieslinger_final.pdf

Kirkup, G., & Kirkwood, A. (2005). Information and communications technologies (ICT) in higher education teaching -A tale of gradualism rather than revolution. *Learning, Media and Technology*, *30*(2), 185–199. doi:10.1080/17439880500093810

Laurillard, D. (1993). *Rethinking university teaching: A framework for the effective use of educational technology*. London, UK: Routledge.

Levy, P. (2006). Living theory: A pedagogical framework for process support in networked learning. *ALT-J. Research in Learning Technology*, *14*(3), 225–240. doi:10.1080/09687760600837025

Lewin, K. (1946). Action research and minority problems. *The Journal of Social Issues*, *2*(4), 34–46. doi:10.1111/j.1540-4560.1946.tb02295.x

Light, A., & Luckin, R. (2008). *Designing for social justice: people, technology, learning*. Bristol, UK: Futurelab.

Lingard, M. (2007). *Why don't all lecturers make use of VLEs? What can the so-called laggards tell us*. London, UK: Institute of Education, University of London.

Martin, F., Klein, J., & Sullivan, H. (2007). The impact of instructional elements in computer-based instruction. *British Journal of Educational Technology, 38*(4), 623–636. doi:10.1111/j.1467-8535.2006.00670.x

Martin-Blas, T., & Serrano-Fernandeza, A. (2009). The role of new technologies in the learning process: Moodle as a teaching tool in Physics. *Computers & Education, 52*(1), 35–44. doi:10.1016/j.compedu.2008.06.005

Mayes, T., & De Freitas, S. (2004). *Review of e-learning theories, frameworks and models: Commissioned review report as part of the JISC-funded e-pedagogy desk study on e-learning models*. Bristol, UK: JISC.

McNiff, J. (1993). *Teaching as learning: An action research approach.* London, UK: Routledge. doi:10.4324/9780203187999

Morón-García, S. (2006). What lecturers say helps and hinders their use of a virtual learning environment to support face-to-face teaching. In O'Donoghue, J. (Ed.), *Technology supported learning and teaching: A staff perspective* (pp. 34–50). London, UK: Information Science Publishing. doi:10.4018/978-1-59140-962-5.ch003

Oxford Brookes University. (2004). *Effective practice with e-learning: Assessing your learning.* Bristol, UK: JISC.

Park, J., & Choi, B. (2008). Higher retention after a new take-home computerised test. *British Journal of Educational Technology, 39*(3), 538–547. doi:10.1111/j.1467-8535.2007.00752.x

Parrish, P., & Wilson, B. (2009). *A design and research framework for learning experience.* Working paper presented at the AECT 2008 Conference. Retrieved October 1, 2010, from http://homes.comet.ucar.edu/~pparrish/papers/ExperienceFramework13.doc

Ramos, C., & Yudko, E. (2008). Hits (not discussion posts) predict student success in online courses: A double cross-validation study. *Computers & Education, 50*(1), 1174–1182. doi:10.1016/j.compedu.2006.11.003

Reigeluth, C. M., & Frick, T. W. (1999). Formative research: A methodology for creating and improving design theories. In Reigeluth, C. M. (Ed.), *Instructional-design theories and models – A new paradigm of instructional theory* (pp. 633–652). New Jersey: Lawrence Erlbaum.

Rushby, N., & Seabrook, J. (2008). Understanding the past—Illuminating the future. *British Journal of Educational Technology, 39*(2), 198–233. doi:10.1111/j.1467-8535.2008.00816.x

Salaway, G., Caruso, J., & Nelson, M. (2008). *The ECAR study of undergraduate students and information technology* (Research Study, Vol. 8). Boulder, CO: Educause Center for Applied Research.

Sax, H., Allegranzi, B., Uckay, I., Larson, E., Boyce, J., & Pittet, D. (2007). My five moments for hand hygiene: A user-centred design approach to understand, train, monitor and report hand hygiene. *The Journal of Hospital Infection, 67*(1), 9–21. doi:10.1016/j.jhin.2007.06.004

Stephenson, J. (2001). *Teaching and learning online: Pedagogies for new technologies.* London, UK: RoutledgeFalmer.

Stringer, E. (1996). *Action research.* Thousand Oaks, CA: Sage.

Swedish National Agency for Higher Education. (2008). [*R E-learning quality: Aspects and criteria for evaluation of e-learning in higher education.* Stockholm, Sweden: Swedish National Agency for Higher Education.]. *Report, 2008*, 11.

Thorpe, M. (2001). From independent learning to collaborative learning: new communities of practice in open, distance and distributed learning. In Lea, M., & Nicoll, K. (Eds.), *Distributed learning: Social and cultural approaches to practice* (pp. 64–82). London, UK: Routledge.

Waters-Adams, S. (1994). Collaboration and action research: a cautionary tale. *Educational Action Research*, *2*(2), 195–210. doi:10.1080/0965079940020205

Whitworth, A. (2007). Researching the cognitive cultures of e-learning. In Andrews, R., & Haythornthwaite, C. (Eds.), *The Sage handbook of e-learning research* (pp. 1–52). London, UK: Sage.

Wu, W.-L., Hammond, M., & Barnes, A. (2009). Strategies for learning English in a cross-cultural learning environment: East Asian students in one UK university. *Journal of English as an International Language*, *4*, 166–179.

Yin, R. (2009). *Case study research: Design and methods*. California: SAGE.

Zaphiris, P., Zacharia, G., & Rajasekaran, M. (2004). Distributed construction through participatory design. In Ghaoui, C. (Ed.), *E-education applications: Human factors and innovative approaches* (pp. 164–179). Hershey, PA: Idea Group. doi:10.4018/9781931777926.ch009

ADDITIONAL READING

There are many general guides to action research some written more with the school sector in mind (e.g., McNiff, 1993) and some cross sector (e.g., Somkeh, 2005).

Carr & Kemmis (1986) provide grounding in the philosophical principles that lie behind the action research as an approach. There are many reports of taking an action research within higher education though not surprisingly, given the association with experiential learning, their focus is often on more enquiry approaches to learning rather than the design of instructional material per se (e.g., Levy, 2006; Farren, 2008).

Action research has long been suggested as an approach to staff development (e.g., Zuber-Skerritt 1996). Within the field of instructional design Reigeluth & Frick (1999) remain an important point of reference as does Laurillard (1983).

A perspective on 'design research' is offered by Reeves et al (2004; 2005). For those with an interest in study skills - the focus of this chapter - both Cottrell (2003) and the freely available Open University (undated) provide basic introductions.

Carr, W. & Kemmis, S. (1986). *Becoming critical. Education, knowledge and action research.* Lewes: Falmer. Cottrell, S. (2003). *The study skills handbook.* Basingstoke: Palgrave Macmillan.

Farren, M. (2008). eLearning and action research as transformative practice. *Innovate, 5*(1). Retrieved November 1, 2010, from http://innovateonline.info/pdf/vol5_issue1/

Laurillard, D. (1993). *Rethinking university teaching: A framework for the effective use of educational technology*. London: Routledge.

Levy, P. (2006). `Living′ theory: a pedagogical framework for process support in networked learning. *ALT-J. Research in Learning Technology*, *14*(3), 225–240. doi:10.1080/09687760600837025

McNiff, J. (1993). *Teaching as learning: An action research approach.* London: Routledge. doi:10.4324/9780203187999

Reeves, T., Herrington, J., & Oliver, R. (2004). A development research agenda for online collaborative learning. *Educational Technology Research and Development*, *52*(1), 53–65. doi:10.1007/BF02504718

Reeves, T., Herrington, J., & Oliver, R. (2005). Design research: A socially responsible approach to instructional technology research in higher education. *Journal of Computing in Higher Education*, *16*(2), 96–115. doi:10.1007/BF02961476

Reigeluth, C. (Ed.), *Instructional-Design theories and models – A new paradigm of instructional theory*. New Jersey: Lawrence Erlbaum.

The Open University. (undated) *OpenLearn learning space*. Milton Keynes: Open University. Retrieved November 1 from http://openlearn.open.ac.uk/course/category.php?id=12

Zuber-Skerritt, O. (1996). *Professional development in higher education: A theoretical framework for action research*. London: Kogan Page.

KEY TERMS AND DEFINITIONS

Action Research: A term with contested definitions but generally signifying a systematic approach to improving a situation through cycles of reflection and action.

Addie: An approach to instructional design based on a cycle of Analysis, Design, Development, Implement, Evaluation. As an approach it is capable of broad interpretation.

Design: Used to describe the process of making a product (for example the design process may cover planning, implementation and evaluation) but can also refer, as here, to describe the process of turning findings from orientation into a set of goals for implementation.

Evaluation: Assessing the value of the product. This may encompass a range of strategies including observation, testing and interview. Evaluation typically covers concerns such as usability, effectiveness and affective appeal. In this case evaluation was primarily focused on the user appreciation of the material and was formative - used to inform further development.

Orientation: Used in action research to describe a phase of understanding the nature and scope of a problem or opportunity. Mixed methods of data collection are often used to address the question 'where are we and where do we want to go?'

Stakeholder: A general term to describe anyone with an interest in the product that is being designed. In an educational context this would typically include students, teachers and possibly administrators. The term usually conveys an aspiration that users will have some ownership (or stake) in the product.

Virtual Learning Environment (VLE): Typically a single item of software offering learners online access to: course administration; learning material; testing; discussion including email, forums and chat; and online collaboration tools such as Wikis and blogs. VLEs generally have differentiated access rights and often include spaces exclusive to tutors. Learning platforms offer the same functionality as VLEs but this may be achieved using a combination of software.

Chapter 23
Instructional Technical and Pedagogical Design:
Teaching Future Teachers Educational Technology

Anne T. Ottenbreit-Leftwich
Indiana University, USA

Mark O. Millard
Indiana University, USA

Peter van Leusen
Indiana University, USA

ABSTRACT

This chapter described a case study of informed educational technology design. The chapter discussed how a conceptual guide for technology teacher experiences (Ottenbreit-Leftwich, Glazewski, & Newby, 2010) informed educational technology design in a course intended to prepare future teacher students to use technology. These students are introduced to various technologies and create materials for their future classrooms. They are also exposed to cases wherein they are required to make decisions on which technologies are most pedagogically appropriate. Therefore, the technology and pedagogy selected for this course are particularly important, as course instructors need to model appropriate decision-making.

INTRODUCTION

Experts and policymakers advocate technology integration as an essential tool in K-12 education. Research studies conducted in the United States have indicated that although schools are currently equipped with adequate technological resources, teachers are still not utilizing those resources in their classrooms (CDW-G, 2010; Project Tomorrow, 2008). This could be due, in part, to a lack of teacher training with regards to technology (Kleiner, Thomas, & Lewis, 2007). To encourage teacher education students to transfer knowledge gained during technology experiences to their future classrooms, teacher education programs

DOI: 10.4018/978-1-61350-080-4.ch023

may need to improve on the instructional design of those technology experiences (Ottenbreit-Leftwich, Glazewski, & Newby, 2010).

Many teacher education programs have recognized the difficulties associated with developing teachers' abilities to use technology in the classroom and have proposed original, innovative approaches to use technology. "Extensive time and money has been spent developing strategies and programs to help preservice teachers use technology effectively… collaboratively crafted to address the technology needs of preservice teachers" (Kay, 2006, p. 392). The U.S. Department of Education funded a program (Preparing Tomorrow's Teachers to Use Technology) to support the development of teacher technology learning experiences, spending over $750 million on projects with new methods for preparing future teachers to effectively integrate technology into their teaching (Pellegrino, Goldman, Bertenthal, & Lawless, 2007). However, there is little empirical evidence regarding which methods are the most effective (Mims, Polly, Shepard, & Inan, 2006; Polly, Mims, Shepard, & Inan, 2010). In fact, after a meta-analysis of 68 studies discussing various strategies for incorporating technology into preservice teacher education programs, Kay (2006) concluded that "…only a handful of studies have carefully and rigorously pursued the evaluation process. The jury is still out on which strategies work best…" (p. 395).

Therefore, the *Conceptual Guide for Technology Teacher Experiences* (Ottenbreit-Leftwich et al., 2010) can help direct informed educational technology design for individual institutions. Depending on the institution, there may be different resources or expectations that influence how effective technology experiences are designed. This chapter will discuss how informed educational technology design, specifically utilizing the *Conceptual Guide,* assisted in selecting appropriate technology and pedagogy for technology experiences required in one teacher education program.

BACKGROUND

To become a teacher in the United States, preservice teachers (students who want to be teachers), must undergo a rigorous preparation and certification system that includes various assessments. These assessments include performance assessments from field experiences in classrooms, state-mandated tests, and completed accredited program from a higher education institution. While teacher certification requirements might slightly differ from state to state, most states require teachers to be proficient at using technology. To address this proficiency requirement, the higher education institution requires preservice teachers to complete a three-credit hour course related to technology use for teachers for three hours per week for one semester.

The only required educational technology experience in the teacher education program is a stand-alone, 3-credit hour course. This course is a pre-requisite requirement for being accepted into the teacher education program; admittance into the teacher education program depends on successfully completing the course. Approximately 400 students register for the course each semester, ranging in majors (early education, elementary education, secondary math education, secondary science education, secondary language arts education, secondary social studies education, foreign language education, physical/health education, music education, art education, and many other education-related fields).

The course is chronologically divided into three units. The first unit covers why teachers should use technology, hopefully conveying the rationale for using technology in their classrooms to these preservice teachers. Particular importance is placed on the pedagogical aspects of technology use based on the National Educational Technology Standards for Teachers published by the International Society for Technology in Education (ISTE 2008); meaning that technology should only be used when it is an effective, efficient, or enhancement to a particular teaching or learning activity. The second unit shows them how the use subject-specific technology tools for their future classrooms. Each week, we review and apply different hardware and software. The third unit covers technology issues associated with using technology in the classroom (e.g., assistive technology, digital divide, plagiarism, cyber-bullying). Throughout the course, there are three main assignments: Weekly Review and Application of Different Software/Hardware, Cases, and ePortfolio Reflection.

Weekly Review and Application of Different Software/Hardware

Each week, preservice teachers are introduced to new technology tools and examples of how to use these tools in their future classrooms. Depending on the major of preservice teachers, the application of a specific technology tool during that week will vary. For example, one week we discuss communication technology tools. Elementary majors may investigate ePals or PikiWiki, while foreign language majors may investigate Skype or LiveMocha. Preservice teachers are required to produce deliverables (that target their future classrooms) with a new technology tool each week.

Case Analyses

The preservice teachers are required to complete three cases. The cases are from inservice teachers, describing an instructional situation that they believe could benefit from technology. For example, one secondary history teacher described that her high school students need constantly updated resources for current events. Preservice teachers analyze the case, and then create artifacts for the inservice teacher (see Figure 1). The case assignments begin in the middle of the course. Over the last six weeks of the course, preservice teachers complete one case analysis or artifact each week (e.g., Case Analysis #1 in week six, Case Artifact #1 in week seven).

Figure 1. Case study artifact

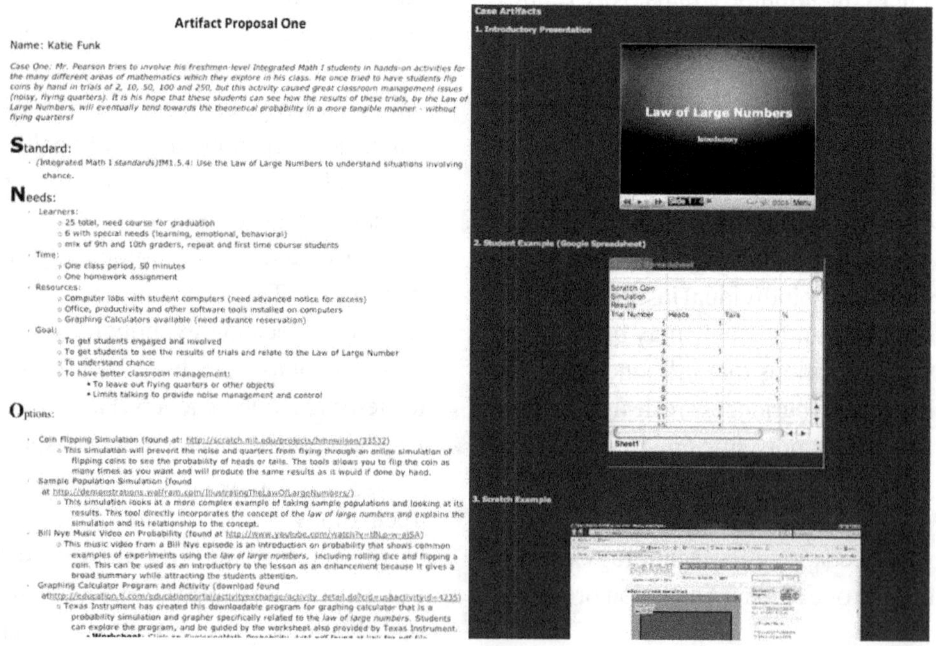

E-Portfolio Reflection

The final assignment is the ePortfolio. The ePortfolio present all the assignments completed during the course including the weekly assignments and cases. Preservice teachers describe how they met the national teacher standards and reflect on their development, using the assignments as evidence. The ePortfolio is developed over the 15 weeks of the course; it is the final product to holistically assess preservice teachers' educational technology knowledge.

Instructional Design Process

An important part of the instructional design process is assessment and evaluation that helps guide instructional decisions (Sadler, 1989). Formative evaluation includes two stages: data collection and revision (Weston, McAlpine, & Bordonaro, 1995). Although anecdotal evaluation data is collected on a weekly basis through instructor meetings, evaluation data is primarily collected and analyzed at the end of each semester to improve the course holistically. Since the course is mandated to follow a course syllabus presented at the beginning of the semester, only small changes can be made during the course Therefore, throughout the course, various assessments and evaluations are used to improve the course for the following semesters (see Table 1).

Each semester, formative and summative evaluation is conducted to improve the course. Formative and summative evaluation of the pedagogy and technology implemented in the course are conducted through a variety of sources for triangulation: midterm and final course evaluations, weekly assessments (quantitative and qualitative), projects, rubrics, electronic portfolios, end-of-course evaluations, and instructor meetings. Perhaps the most significant form of evaluation is through an online program: Profiler Pro (see Figure 2). At the beginning of the semester, students are asked to rate their abilities/skills. If students rate their abilities as high, the pink color will expand further. The examples (shown in Figure 2) illustrate the differences between approximately 400 students at the beginning of the semester and the improvements in their self-rated abilities at the end of the semester.

Due to the administrative constraints, the instructional design process for this course encountered many challenges including the large number of students, variance in majors, and the lack of students' pedagogical and content knowledge. To facilitate informed educational technology design, the *Conceptual Guide for Technology Teacher Experiences* (Ottenbreit-Leftwich et al., 2010) is continuously applied to this course. The guide presents four steps to assist instructors in designing technology experiences for teacher education programs: (1) understanding the broader context,

Table 1. Assessments used for informed educational technology design

Assessment	Description
Demographics Pre-Survey	Students self-rated their comfort and attitude with regards to technology on a scale from 1 to 10 (10 being comfortable/positive attitude). Students also indicated majors and year in school.
Profiler Pro Survey (2 - pre and post)	72-item survey using a 5-point Likert scale (1-strongly disagree, 2-disagree, 3-neutral, 4-agree, 5-strongly agree) to self-assess their technology skills and knowledge of NETS-T (national education technology standards for teachers).
Rubrics	Rubrics evaluating how students completed cases and other assignments.
End of Course Evaluations	Anonymous closed- and open-ended questions answered by students regarding the course and suggestions for improvement.
Instructor Meetings	All instructors met weekly, as well as at the end of the semester to discuss the strengths and weaknesses of the course. Notes were taken during meetings to document suggestions.

Figure 2. Profiler Pro: Students' self-reported technology skills

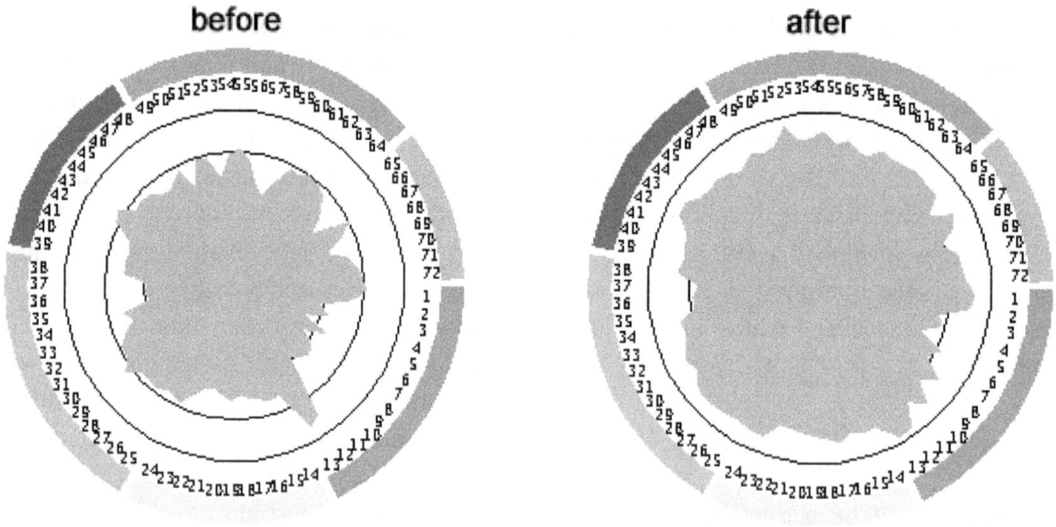

(2) establishing technology content goals that address the needs specific to the broader context, (3) selecting appropriate instructional approaches to meet the technology content goals with the broader context in mind, and (4) designing practical activities based on the instructional approaches selected. Each step informs the next step in the process. In the following section, each step is discussed in relation to one teacher education program.

CONTEXT

Technology Experiences in Teacher Education Program

The first step is to consider how the technology experiences are situated within the broader context of the teacher education program. Some of the elements to consider are the available resources (What types of equipment and support are available?), format (Where does technology fit within the teacher education curriculum?), and the current skills of those involved (e.g., What level of technology and teaching skills do preservice teachers have when they receive their technology experience?).

In this situation, there are ample resources available. The School of Education has several computer labs that are accessible by students. Each lab has 30 computers with Internet access and a wide range of software (e.g., Microsoft Office, Open Office, KidPix, Kidspiration, Inspiration, Inspiredata, Google Earth, Geometer SketchPad, Kurzweil, etc.). Each lab also has a teacher computer and projector. There is also a separate computer lab called the Technology Teaching Lab (TTL); this lab is open daily with support staff and is designated to help education majors with technology. The TTL also contains equipment available for check-out (e.g., science probes and sensors, LeapPads, FlyPens, etc.). The resources and support available adds significantly to the broader context and potential for various methods. Even with the significant amount of resources, the large number of students can place strain on resources and staff.

The format for the technology experiences is facilitated through a stand-alone, 3-credit

Figure 3. Year in teacher education program

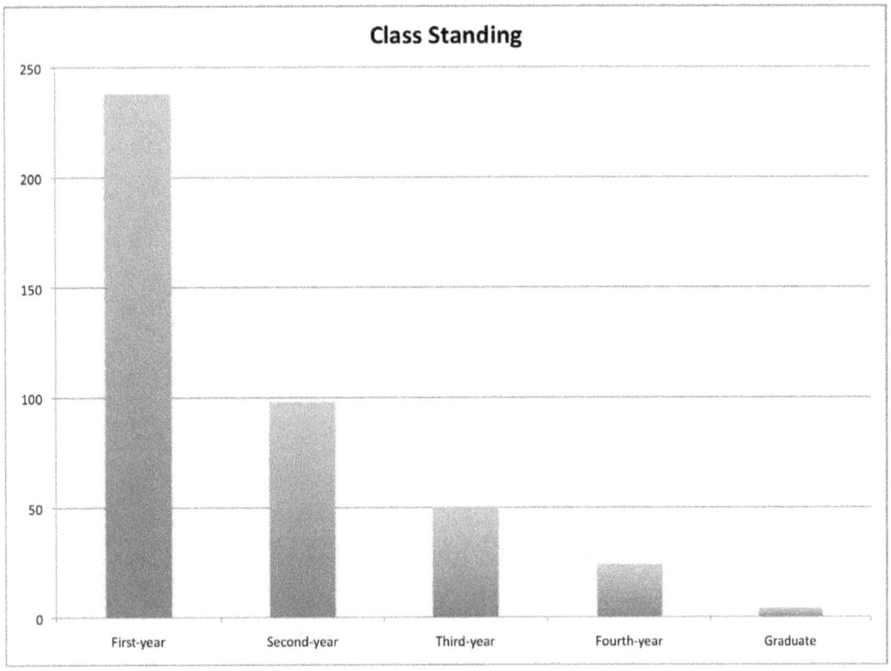

hour course that is a pre-requisite for applying to the School of Education. Because this course is a pre-requisite, this impacts the skills, such as prior knowledge and abilities of the students. This is the first education course students complete in the teacher education program. The prior knowledge of these future teachers is based on their experiences as K-12 students. This can be problematic because most students are unaware of how to design instruction and have not developed a teachers' persona. Based on the survey at the beginning of the course, more than half of the students are in the first year of their teacher education programs (see Figure 3). These students may also bring additional considerations as they are new to the college environment and Indiana University in general.

There are many other variables associated with this course. As previously stated, the course has approximately 400 students enrolled and ten instructors teaching the 15 sections of the course at the beginning of each semester. Each section has approximately 28 students and one instructor. The course is required for all future teacher students, which results in a wide variety of focus ranging from early education teachers to secondary math teachers to physical education teachers. Therefore, all content areas (math, science, etc…) need to be addressed, as well as all grade levels (preK to 12th grade) (see Figure 4).

In order to further assess the broader context to impact the course design, several online questionnaires assisted in collecting baseline information (e.g., overall self-rated technology skills, overall self-rated technology attitude, self-assessment of understanding related to the NETS-T standards) at the beginning of the course. On average, students rated their attitude toward technology slightly higher ($M = 6.92$, $SD = 1.99$) than their technology skills ($M = 5.84$, $SD = 1.48$). This may indicate that students were willing to learn about technology, even if their skills were not exceptional.

The broader context is important to consider for developing technology content goals that are appropriate for students. In addition, the broader

Figure 4. Students' majors

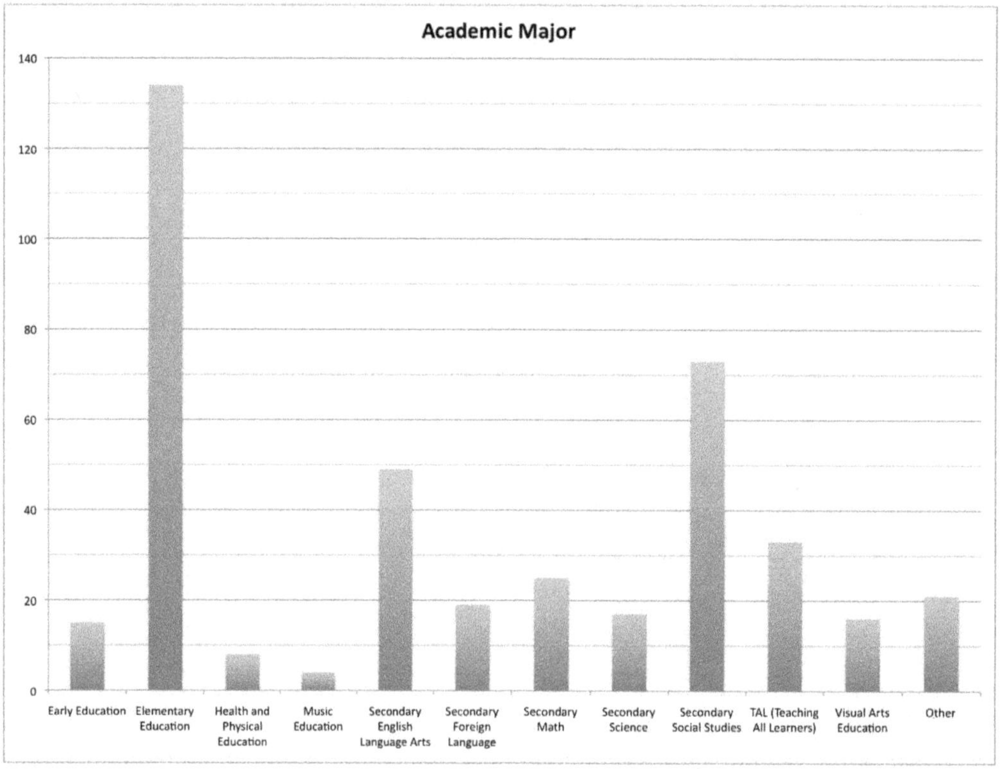

context will be considered when designing appropriate activities.

Technology Content Goals

The second step is to establish the technology content goals. The primary technology content goal for our future teacher students was to be able to make appropriate technology integration decisions. The United States National Education Technology Standards for Teachers (NETS-T) (ISTE, 2008) focuses on digital technology, with less emphasis on media. Therefore, appropriate technology integration decisions focused on digital technology integration decisions, specifically concentrating on computers.

In order to achieve this main goal, sub-goals were established from national teacher technology standards and research-based practices.

1. Given certain goals and limitations, analyze the strengths and weaknesses of various technologies to make appropriate selections for instructional purposes.
2. Make good technology integration decisions and being able to explain reasons behind decision.
3. Design uses of various emerging digital technologies to create instructional activities for future K-12 students.
4. Increase personal software/hardware technology skills.
5. Develop positive attitude toward technology.
6. Acknowledge how technology can be used in specific subject areas.

Based on students' pre-questionnaire responses, each class has students with different needs: technology abilities, technology attitudes, and subject areas that they will be teaching. Due to the range of student needs, the course needs to be flexible enough to address these differences while ensuring that all students meet the technology content goals. For example, a secondary math teacher with low technology abilities will require different software (e.g., Geometer Sketchpad) and more assistance than an elementary teacher with high technology abilities to use elementary-focused software (e.g., KidPix).

An additional consideration based on the limitations associated with the broader context is the lack of students' prior pedagogical knowledge. Since the majority of these students are at the beginning of their teacher education programs, they lack teaching experience and pedagogical knowledge. Therefore, instructional design and high levels of integration may extend too far beyond the limitations associated with one course. Instead, computer-based applications and alignment with the ISTE NETS-T standards, is a better focus for technology content goals (Betrus & Molenda, 2002).

Selecting Appropriate Approaches

The next step is to select appropriate approaches to meet the technology content goals, while also considering the limitations and affordances of the broader context. There are six approaches teacher education programs typically used to develop preservice teacher technology abilities were identified: (1) information delivery (how the instructor of the course delivers important information on technology integration), (2) hands-on technology skill building activities (step-by-step procedures to learn a specific technology skill set), (3) practice with technology integration in the field (test strategies, visually see consequences of practice, gain feedback, and adapt their practice to better integrate technology into K-12 classrooms), (4) technology integration observation or modeling sessions (show students good teaching with technology examples), (5) authentic technology integration experiences (opportunities to encounter a wide range of messy and ambiguous problems that students are likely to encounter with technology in their future classrooms), and (6) technology integration reflections (encourages preservice teachers to think about their current beliefs and pedagogy). Each of these approaches has their strengths and weaknesses (Ottenbreit-Leftwich et al., 2010).

The approaches selected for this teacher education program were selected based on the previously identified technology content goals, while also considering the broader context (see Table 2). For example, authentic experiences were selected as appropriate approaches for many of the technology content goals (TCG#1, TCG#2, TCG#3). Authentic experiences provide students with the opportunity to encounter a wide range of messy and ambiguous problems that they are likely to encounter with technology in their future classrooms (Rosaen & Bird, 2005). During these experiences, students identify specific problems, analyze various strategies to use within the situation, establish recovery mechanisms, and revise their practices for when they encounter a similar problem in the future (Kim & Hannafin, 2009). One strong advantage of authentic experiences is that students encounter real-world problems they may face in their future classrooms. Authentic experiences were selected for the first three goals because this approach would enable students to analyze authentic problems in a non-threatening environment (see Table 2). In other words, students can take their time and fully evaluate different solutions for the problem. This was an important consideration as students lack pedagogical and technical knowledge (broader context); they may need a significant amount of time and support to achieve the first three technology content goals. After authentic teacher technology experiences, students have shown improvement in their abilities to identify instructional problems, consider multiple perspectives, create solutions, consider the consequences of those solutions, identify potential issues, and synthesize final solutions

Table 2. Appropriate approaches selected for specific technology content goals

Specific Technology Content Goal (TCG)	Appropriate Approaches
1. Given certain goals and limitations, analyze the strengths and weaknesses of various technologies to make appropriate selections for instructional purposes.	Observations and Modeling Authentic Experiences Reflections
2. Make good technology integration decisions and being able to explain reasons behind decision.	Authentic Experiences Reflections
3. Design uses of various emerging digital technologies to create instructional activities for future K-12 students.	Authentic Experiences
4. Increase personal software/hardware technology skills.	Information Delivery Hands-on Skill Building Activities
5. Develop positive attitude toward technology.	Hands-on Skill Building Activities
6. Acknowledge how technology can be used in specific subject areas.	Information Delivery Reflections

and conclusions (Beck, King, & Marshall, 2002; Kim & Hannafin, 2009).

Reflections were also selected as activities for three of the goals (TCG#1, TCG# 2, TCG#6). One of the weaknesses of authentic experiences is that students tend to focus on the surface level problems (Hsu, 2004). This could be due to their lack of expert knowledge needed to solve the problem and overlook the main dilemma (Brush, 1998). Reflection experiences can encourages students to think more critically about their instructional decisions and choices as future teachers (Lasley & Matczynski, 1995). Therefore, by asking students to reflect on the different options for technology, or on the reasons why they made a particular technology integration decision, this may encourage students to focus on the problems and solutions with more depth. In the case of technology content goal number six, after students are exposed to different ideas for how technology can be used in their own specific subject areas, they can individually reflect on how they would use technology. This is important for each individual student to consider because they consider their teaching practices in a way that may challenge their current beliefs and necessitate change (Ertmer, 2005); this is especially true with technology.

Designing Activities

The fourth and final step is to design the activities. The three previous design decision steps (broader context, technology content goals, and approaches) converge to guide the design of activities that will intentionally address the specific technology content goals (see Table 3). By reviewing these goals and appropriate approaches, activities were designed to address multiple goals. In order to address the technology content goals within the broader context, weekly reviews of software/hardware, cases, and an electronic portfolio were designed. Each of these activities will be briefly discussed.

Activity #1: Weekly Review and Application of Different Software/ Hardware

As students entered the class with little to no prior knowledge regarding how technology could be used in the classroom, it was necessary to introduce them to different hardware and software. There is so much hardware/software available to teachers and needs to be covered in 15 weeks. Some of the hardware/software topics covered included the following: Google applications (Google Earth, Google Docs, Google Sites), Web 2.0 applica-

Table 3. Alignment of specific technology content goals, appropriate approaches, and assignments

Specific Technology Content Goal	Appropriate Approaches	Assignments
1. Given certain goals and limitations, analyze the strengths and weaknesses of various technologies to make appropriate selections for instructional purposes.	• Observations and Modeling • Authentic Experiences • Reflections	• Cases: Instructors model how to make appropriate decisions, application in case analyses (reflect on various options, analyzing strengths and weaknesses)
2. Make good technology integration decisions and being able to explain reasons behind decision.	• Authentic Experiences • Reflections	• Cases: application in case analyses (reflect on why decisions were made)
3. Design uses of various emerging digital technologies to create instructional activities for future K-12 students.	• Authentic Experiences • Hands-on Skill Building Activities	• Cases: Create artifacts based on analyses
4. Increase personal software/hardware technology skills.	• Information Delivery • Hands-on Skill Building Activities	• Weekly review and application of different software/hardware
5. Develop positive attitude toward technology.	• Reflections	• ePortfolio reflection on their growth
6. Acknowledge how technology can be used in specific subject areas.	• Information Delivery • Hands-on Skill Building Activities • Reflections	• Weekly review and application software/hardware (regarding different subject specific technology uses). • ePortfolio reflection on how technology can be used in their specific subject areas.

tions (wikis, blogs, podcasts, Wordle, Delicious), purchased software packages (Inspiration, KidPix, Inspiredata, Geometer Sketchpad), digital video recording and editing, classroom management software, and much more.

In addition to covering a large amount of technology, students also need to learn acknowledge how technology can be used in specific subject areas (TCG #6). As previously stated, covering the large number of different subject areas is the most difficult aspect of the course. Technology is used differently in the classroom depending on the subject area and/or grade level (Niederhauser & Lindstrom, 2006). Several studies have indicated that teachers are more likely to use technology if they can see the alignment with their own specific subject area. For example, the five English teachers in Hughes' (2005) study attributed their integration to discovering subject-specific applications of technology. If teachers perceived no value tied directly to their content area, they are less likely to use the technology (Ertmer & Ottenbreit-Leftwich, 2010; Hennessy, Ruthven, & Brindley, 2005; Hughes, 2005; Niess, 2005). While weekly readings are typical methods of information delivery activities, no textbooks would address all the various subject areas separately. Instead, students were asked to explore specific podcasts, articles, or websites (depending on the focus of the week) that discussed using technology in their specific subject areas.

In addition to information delivery activities, hands-on skill building activities help to increase personal software/hardware technology skills (TCG #4). Each week, students create subject-specific materials using technology covered during information delivery activities. By establishing a link between specific technology applications and curriculum, students may be more likely to apply these skills in their future classrooms (Koehler, Mishra, & Yahya, 2007).

Activity #2: Cases

The first three technology content goals required an authentic experience. In a review of literature on effective professional development for teachers, Hew and Brush (2007) found that technology skills and experiences need to be introduced within an educational context, and should be consistent

Figure 5. Cases by subject area

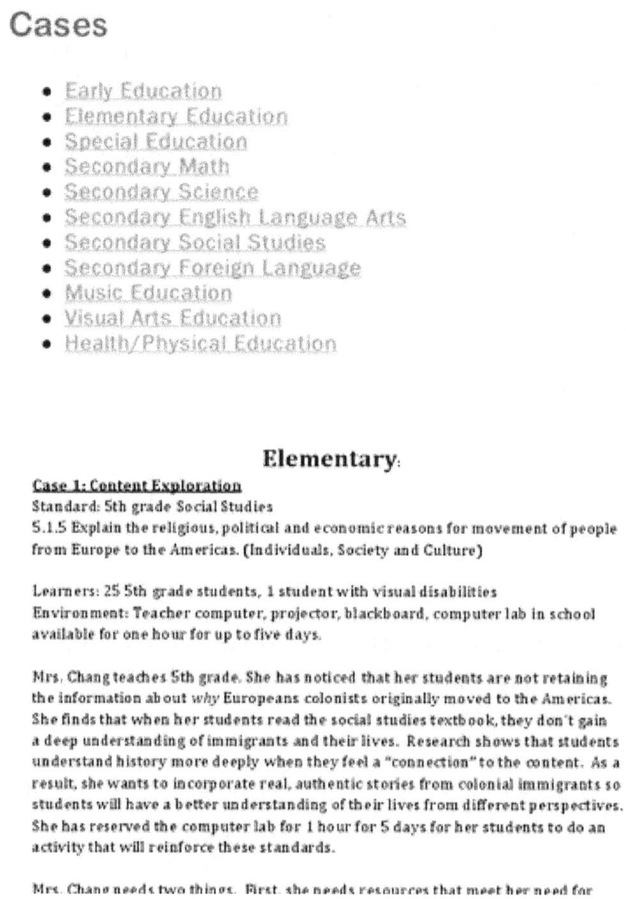

Cases

- Early Education
- Elementary Education
- Special Education
- Secondary Math
- Secondary Science
- Secondary English Language Arts
- Secondary Social Studies
- Secondary Foreign Language
- Music Education
- Visual Arts Education
- Health/Physical Education

Elementary:

Case 1: Content Exploration
Standard: 5th grade Social Studies
5.1.5 Explain the religious, political and economic reasons for movement of people from Europe to the Americas. (Individuals, Society and Culture)

Learners: 25 5th grade students, 1 student with visual disabilities
Environment: Teacher computer, projector, blackboard, computer lab in school available for one hour for up to five days.

Mrs. Chang teaches 5th grade. She has noticed that her students are not retaining the information about *why* Europeans colonists originally moved to the Americas. She finds that when her students read the social studies textbook, they don't gain a deep understanding of immigrants and their lives. Research shows that students understand history more deeply when they feel a "connection" to the content. As a result, she wants to incorporate real, authentic stories from colonial immigrants so students will have a better understanding of their lives from different perspectives. She has reserved the computer lab for 1 hour for 5 days for her students to do an activity that will reinforce these standards.

Mrs. Chang needs two things. First, she needs resources that meet her need for

with specific and authentic needs and problems teachers faced in their professional contexts. With authentic experiences selected as appropriate approaches for multiple technology content goals, case-based learning seemed to address all of these needs identified in the first step of broader context.

Case-based learning was selected for the authentic experiences because it could provide situated learning contexts for all majors, as well as incorporate reflection. Since students have a wide range of majors (see Figure 4), several cases were created for each major (see Figure 5).

There were two parts to the case assignments: case analysis and case artifacts. Students completed three case analyses and three case artifacts (see Figure 1). A template for the case analysis was used as a scaffold to guide novice students through the decision-making process.

As students lacked prior knowledge on making instructional decisions, students need to witness how to analyze technologies for strengths and weaknesses. Each week, the instructor modeled the case analysis process with a different situation. Through this modeling, students were able to take these observed actions, and mimic them in their case analyses, hopefully adding them to their eventual teaching repertoires and practices (Bennett, 1991). In the application of their own case analyses, students analyzed strengths and weaknesses of specific technology (TCG #1), made strong technology integration decisions, and provided rationale for those decisions (TCG

#2). Students were also asked to reflect on their technology decisions in the case analysis template.

After students decide which technology should be used, they create artifacts for the teacher using the proposed technology. With guidance from instructors, students designed uses of digital technologies to create instructional activities for future K-12 students (TCG #3). Because students had a wide range of technology skills, it was important to allow students to pursue options based on their own technology skills and comfort levels. Additional assistance was offered through the TTL to support students outside of class with difficult technology concerns or extra support.

When a link is established between specific technology applications and students' future curriculum, they are more likely to use this technology in their future classrooms (Koehler et al., 2007). As the cases are directly related to their future classrooms, the skills and artifacts gained from these authentic experiences may transfer to their future classrooms.

Activity #3: E-portfolio Reflection

Finally, electronic portfolios have been heavily utilized in teacher education (Britten, Mullen, & Stuve, 2003). Electronic portfolios provided students with an opportunity to reflect on teacher practices and review technology skills gained during the course (Lin, 2008). The electronic portfolio used in this class, allowed students to reflect on all the practices and skills they learned with regards to technology in their subject areas. Specifically, students reflect on their Profiler Pro pre- and post-survey (see Figure 6), as well as write narrative reflections on how technology can by used in their subject areas. During this process, students tend to witness their growth and develop a positive attitude toward technology (TCG #5) and feel confident in their abilities to describe how technology can be used in specific subject areas (TCG#6).

Perhaps one of the greatest difficulties associated with designing activities for this course is the variance in students. Students have different majors (e.g., secondary math, elementary education, etc.) that require different examples and software. In order for teachers to use technology, it becomes important to establish the link between specific technology applications and curriculum (Koehler et al., 2007). Several studies have indicated that teachers are more likely to use technology if they can see the alignment with their own specific subject area. For example, the five English teachers in Hughes' (2005) study attributed their integration to discovering subject-specific applications of technology. If they perceived no value tied directly to their content area, they were less likely to use the technology (Hughes, 2005; Niess, 2005). Teachers are reluctant to adopt technology that does not align with their subject's sub-culture (Hennessey et al., 2005; Ertmer & Ottenbreit-Leftwich, 2010). In order to create effective professional development that will change teacher practices, we need to investigate the technology uses that are relevant for teachers in different subject areas (Zhao, 2003).

RESULTS OF EVALUATION

While additional formative and summative evaluation of the pedagogy and technology implemented in the course were conducted through a variety of sources for triangulation (i.e., weekly assessments, projects, rubrics, and electronic portfolios), perhaps the most significant form of evaluation was derived from two self-assessments conducted by course participants following a one group pre-posttest design (Ohlund & Yu, 2009).

At the beginning and at the end of the semester, students enrolled in the educational technology course for pre-service teachers were asked to rate their technology skills and knowledge of NETS-T standards by completing an online questionnaire. The questionnaire included 72 questions address-

Figure 6. E-portfolio reflection

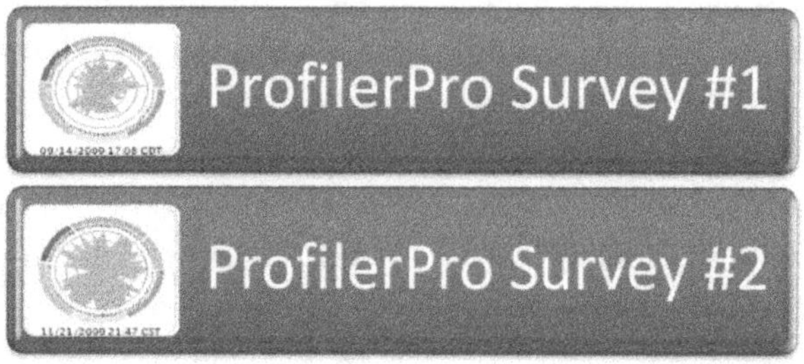

After taking the ProfilerPro survey for the first time at the beginning of this fall semester, I discovered that I knew little about technology, the various options and usages that it provides, and the opportunities I could create using it. I only had a vague familiarity with basic word processing software, search engines, computer etiquette, and communication tools. I now have retaken the same ProfilerPro survey, and my results have drastically changed. This survey showed my new strengths in the technological field. I once had no understanding of complex word processing, database, podcasting, movie editing, audio, image, spreadsheet, blogging, and as Photoshop (as shown in the red section) and remain unclear about what constitutes formative and summative assessments (as shown in the green section), but by looking at my results and seeing the progressive trends displayed, I believe it will not be long until I master such skills as I have since taking my first survey.

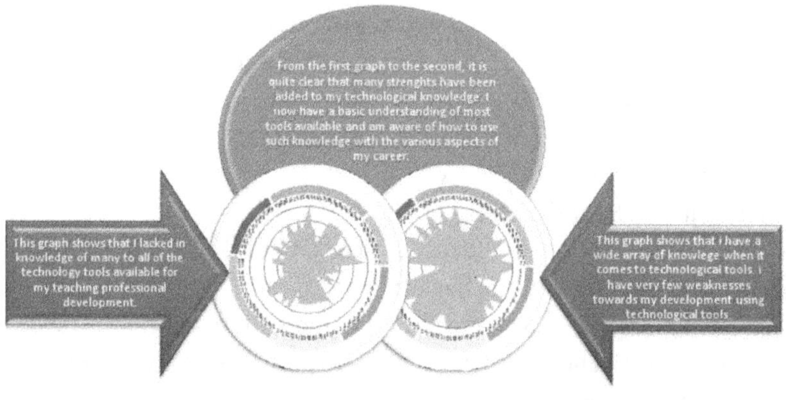

ing general technology skills and five NETS-T standards and was administered online as part of a homework assignment in the fall of 2009. The pretest was administered in the second week of classes and the posttest in the final week. Students responded to each item using a 5-point Likert scale (1-strongly disagree, 2-disagree, 3-neutral, 4-agree, 5-strongly agree) to self-assess their technology skills and knowledge of NETS-T.

Of the 388 students who completed the pretest, only 271 also completed the posttest (completion rate of 70%). This could be due to students withdrawing or failing the class, as well as technical problems with the system. Each of the 72 items on the questionnaire used a 5-point Likert scale and were based on a ISTE rubric to evaluate technology skills and NETS-T knowledge. To ensure face validity, a content expert reviewed the questionnaire before administration. Statistics

Table 4. Alignment of specific technology content goals and assessments

Specific Technology Content Goal (TCG)	Assessments
1. Given certain goals and limitations, analyze the strengths and weaknesses of various technologies to make appropriate selections for instructional purposes.	Profiler Pro Survey: NETS-T #2 Profiler Pro Survey: NETS-T #5 Case Analysis Rubric
2. Make good technology integration decisions and being able to explain reasons behind decision.	Profiler Pro Survey: NETS-T #2 Profiler Pro Survey: NETS-T #5 Case Analysis Rubric
3. Design uses of various emerging digital technologies to create instructional activities for future K-12 students.	Profiler Pro Survey: NETS-T #2 Profiler Pro Survey: NETS-T #3 Profiler Pro Survey: NETS-T #4 Profiler Pro Survey: NETS-T #5 Case Artifacts Rubric
4. Increase personal software/hardware technology skills.	Pre/post test: Technology skills Profiler Pro Survey: NETS-T #5
5. Develop positive attitude toward technology.	ePortfolio Rubric
6. Acknowledge how technology can be used in specific subject areas.	Profiler Pro Survey: NETS-T #1 Profiler Pro Survey: NETS-T #5 Case Analysis Rubric ePortfolio Rubric

were calculated for the overall results, technology skills as well as each NETS-T standard. Results indicated a significant improvement in each area. Each of the technology content goals was assessed during the course (see Table 4).

Areas of Significant Improvement

To determine areas of significant improvement, paired-samples t-tests were conducted to compare each area on the pre- and posttests of the ProfilerPro survey. Results showed a significant difference in pre- and posttest scores suggesting an overall improvement in learning. In addition, significant differences were found in pre-service teachers' technology skills and knowledge about NETS-T standards. While all areas showed significant increases, technology skills showed the largest improvement. As the technology content goals for this course were based on the NETS-T standards, the improvement on all of these standards indicates that the technology content goals were addressed by the activities in this course. The measurement used a Likert-scale to have preservice teachers self-assess their technology skills and knowledge of NETS-T on a scale of one to five, one meaning they felt weak and five meaning they felt strong.

Technology Skills

This section specifically asked about technology hardware and software and their abilities. They rated themselves on a scale of one to five (five meaning they strongly agreed with the statement). One sample item for this section was "I am highly skilled at using podcasting software (e.g., iTunes, Podcaster)." There was a significant difference in the pretest score for technology skills ($M = 3.05$, $SD = .55$) and the posttest score for technology skills ($M = 4.11$, $SD = .45$), $t(270) = -33.66$, $p < .05$. These results suggest that the course had an effect (Hedges $g = 2.04$) on student learning regarding technology skills. Specifically, the results indicate that when students complete the course, the students' technology skills increase. This indicates that technology content goal #4 (Increase personal software/hardware technology skills) was met through the activities in this course.

NETS-T #1: Facilitate and Inspire Student Learning and Creativity

This section focused on their abilities to facilitate student learning through the use of technology. They rated themselves on a scale of one to five (five meaning they strongly agreed with the statement). One sample item for this section was "I can design technology-based learning activities." There was a significant difference in the pretest score for NETS-T#1 (M = 3.17, SD = .65) and the posttest score for NETS-T#1 (M = 4.26, SD = .43), $t(270) = -27.87$, $p < .05$. These results suggest that the course had an effect (Hedges g= 1.68) on student learning for NETS-T#1. Specifically, the results indicate that when students complete the course, the students' increase their knowledge "of the subject matter, teaching and learning, and technology to facilitate experiences that advance [their future] student learning, creativity, and innovation" (ISTE, p. 1, 2008). This indicates that technology content goal #6 (Acknowledge how technology can be used in specific subject areas) was met through the activities in this course.

NETS-T #2: Design and Develop Digital-Age Learning Experiences and Assessments

This section evaluated preservice teachers' abilities to design and develop technology-based learning activities. They rated themselves on a scale of one to five (five meaning they strongly agreed with the statement). One sample item for this section was "I know how to help students use technology tools to research and collect information online." There was a significant difference in the pretest score for NETS-T#2 (M = 3.25, SD = .56) and the posttest score for NETS-T#2 (M = 4.14, SD = .47), $t(270) = -23.55$, $p < .05$. These results suggest that the course had an effect (Hedges g = 1.43) on student learning for NETS-T#2. Specifically, the results indicate that when students complete the course, the students' increase their knowledge to "design, develop, and evaluate authentic learning experiences and assessment incorporating contemporary tools and resources to maximize content learning in context and to develop the knowledge, skills, and attitudes identified in the NETS-S" (ISTE, p. 1, 2008). Specifically, this analysis indicates that students achieved several of the technology content goals (TCG#1, TCG#2, TCG#3).

NETS-T #3: Model Digital-Age Work and Learning

This section measured their abilities to create work and model learning using technology. They rated themselves on a scale of one to five (five meaning they strongly agreed with the statement). One sample item for this section was "I know the best ways to use digital tools to communicate and collaborate with peers, students, and parents." There was a significant difference in the pretest score for NETS-T#3 (M = 3.41, SD = .62) and the posttest score for NETS-T#3 (M = 4.41, SD = .49), $t(270) = -19.13$, $p < .05$. These results suggest that the course had an effect (Hedges g = 1.16) on student learning for NETS-T#3. Specifically, the results indicate that when students complete the course, the students' increase their knowledge to "exhibit knowledge, skills, and work processes representative of an innovative professional in a global and digital society" (ISTE, p. 1, 2008). This difference indicates students are able to design uses of various emerging digital technologies to create instructional activities for future K-12 students (TCG#3).

NETS-T #4: Promote and Model Digital Citizenship and Responsibility

This section measured their abilities to teach and learn within a technology-based society; in particular, it focused on the issues associated with integrating technology into the classroom. They rated themselves on a scale of one to five (five meaning they strongly agreed with the statement). One sample item for this section was "I know how to handle cyberbullying in the classroom." There was a significant difference in the pretest score for NETS-T#4 (M = 3.38, SD = .53) and the posttest score for NETS-T#3 (M = 4.23, SD = .43), t(270)= -25.86, $p < .05$. These results suggest that the course had an effect (Hedges g = 1.56) on student learning for NETS-T#4. Specifically, the results indicate that when students complete the course, the students' increase their knowledge to "understand local and global societal issues and responsibilities in an evolving digital culture and exhibit legal and ethical behavior in their professional practices" (ISTE, p. 1, 2008). This increase is important for future teachers because they need to be aware of digital citizenship and responsibility in order to design uses of various emerging digital technologies to create instructional activities for future K-12 students (TCG#3).

NETS-T #5: Engage in Professional Growth and Leadership

This final section investigated their abilities to engage in technology-enhanced professional development, and to continue to build their skills in using technology for teaching and learning. They rated themselves on a scale of one to five (five meaning they strongly agreed with the statement). One sample item for this section was "I can investigate and reflect on research and professional practice for using digital tools and resources to support student learning." There was a significant difference in the pretest score for NETS-T#5 (M = 3.23, SD = .58) and the posttest score for NETS-T#3 (M = 4.08, SD = .51), t(270)= -23.49, $p < .05$. These results suggest that the course had an effect (Hedges g = 1.43) on student learning for NETS-T#5. Specifically, the results indicate that when students complete the course, the students' increase their knowledge to "continuously improve their professional practice, model lifelong learning, and exhibit leadership in their school and professional community by promoting and demonstrating the effective use of digital tools and resources" (ISTE, p. 1, 2008). Consistent improvement is an important skill for future teachers to learn. By developing this skill, future teachers can continue to investigate technologies that will apply to their classrooms in order to improve teaching and learning (TCG#1, TCG#2, TCG#3, TCG#4, TCG#5).

Other Forms of Evaluation

Case Analysis and Artifacts

All six case analyses and artifacts were graded using rubrics. The Case Analysis rubrics measured how well they explored different technologies used for their subject areas (TCG#6), the technology selected, and rationale for selecting that technology (TCG#1, TCG#2). The Case Artifact rubrics measured their use of technology skills (TCG#4) and their abilities to design technology activities (TCG#3). In general, the scores associated with the cases did not significantly improve over the course of the semester (see Table 5). This could be due to the fact that instructors raised their expectations as the semester continued. In order to increase these scores and better prepare students to make educational technology decisions and materials, scaffolds such as template and instructions need to be improved. All materials can be found on the course website: http://www.indiana.edu/~educw200.

At the end of the semester, all instructors (n=9) for the course reflected upon, and discussed how to improve the educational technology design for the course using our experiences and the evaluation data. One of the common problems identified was that several of the cases resulted in poorer case analyses and artifacts. This could be due, in part, to the lack of authenticity. Cases were created by course instructors - not K-12 teachers in the field. Currently, the cases are being refined by K-12 teachers. However, course evaluations and the end-of-semester instructor meeting helped inform what should be included in the course for next semester. Throughout the course evaluations, students discussed the importance of the cases; this activity helped students develop computer skills and technology integration abilities by creating technology materials to address a subject-specific authentic situation. For example, when asked to describe the most valuable aspects of the course, students overwhelming mentioned the case analysis and artifacts: "I liked working with the teacher for our Case because I was able to incorporate technology into a real lesson," "I think the case studies were the most valuable because they gave me insight on real-life experiences that I will have some day in my future teaching career," and "I think the case studies and the artifacts were the most valuable thing because it put what we are learning in class and into an actually classroom setting." The end-of-semester instructor meeting further confirmed the positive impact of the cases activities on students' abilities and attitudes towards technology.

E-Portfolio

The ePortfolio reflection required preservice teachers to reflect on their Profiler Pro pre- and post-surveys (see Figure 5). In addition, preservice teachers wrote narrative reflections on how technology can by used in their subject areas. The rubrics measured preservice teachers abilities to summarize their strengths and weaknesses, their current attitudes toward technology (TCG#5), and how technology can be used in their future classrooms (TCG#6). Overall, preservice teachers in this course received an average score of 245/250 points on the ePortfolio rubric. Preservice teachers described how their future development could also factor in, as shown in the following excerpt of one preservice teacher's ePortfolio reflection: "During the beginning of my undergraduate teacher training, I completed a survey to see how well I knew different technology programs and skills. My results, shown on my Profiler Pro Pre-Survey, were not horrible, but I did realize what technologies I needed improvement on. My areas of weakness were how to use tools such as Google Forms, Dreamweaver, and Professional Development resources; knowing what cyberbullying was and how to handle it in a classroom; and how to incorporate formative and summative assessments within a classroom. To improve upon these weaknesses, I addressed each one during the class. I have retaken the original survey to see where I stand. The results, shown on my Profiler Pro Post-Survey, show much improvement. It is much more smooth, and does not pass the second inner circle, which means that I did not have any skills in which I had any weak knowledge of. This shows a strong improvement, for in my Pre-Survey, the results appear jagged and show only 1-2 skills in which I have a strong knowledge of. The results of the second survey show several strong areas, and very few weaknesses. The areas which show gaps are:

Table 5. Rubrics for case analyses and artifacts

	N	Mean	Standard Deviation
Case Analysis #1	357	39.94/45	4.88
Case Analysis #2	351	40.65/45	4.89
Case Analysis #3	347	40.41/45	5.49
Case Artifact #1	343	44.23/50	6.87
Case Artifact #2	341	44.68/50	6.83
Case Artifact #3	340	44.82/50	6.54

(7) using audio editing software (Audacity), (35-37) formative and summative assessments, and (50) copyright rules as they apply to teachers. To ensure that I will understand which technology is better to use in my future math class, I will first research them each online. After researching, I will evaluate each and determine which one will be used in my future secondary math classroom. Based on which one is more effective for my specific subject area, I will explore and accumulate the tools on my iGoogle and Delicious accounts as proof, as well as a resource I can use in the future to create assessments and further develop. Lastly, one long term goal I hope to achieve is to continue discovering educational tools such as Wordle, Scatch, Glogster, etc. to better enhance my students learning and understanding through technology. To achieve this I will need to continue exploring sources and join teacher blogs and sharing sites, such as Delicious, Teacher Blogger etc., in order to find these tools. As I find them, I will put them into my Delicious or iGoogle account in order to keep track of them, as well as share them with other educators."

FURTHER RESEARCH DIRECTIONS

Informed educational technology design demands constant revision due to the constant updates in technology and pedagogy. In order for informed educational design to be effective, we need to continue to update ourselves on new technologies and pedagogies which challenge our current design, and instill this need for continual improvement and evaluation in our students. Therefore, this requires a consistent plan for revision and evaluation. In particular, more research is needed to provide a better understanding and further conceptualize the activities and practices discussed in this chapter in order to further formalize methods and models for developing such authentic reflective practices in students and teachers when it comes toward selecting and utilizing educational technologies in various educational contexts. Future research may develop better guides or models when considering new technologies and pedagogies for instruction.

CONCLUSION

This chapter described a case study of informed educational technology design. The chapter discussed how a conceptual guide for technology teacher experiences (Ottenbreit-Leftwich, Glazewski, & Newby, 2010) informed educational technology design in a course intended to prepare future teacher students to use technology. It is critical to consider the broader context and technology content goals before selecting an appropriate approach. The continuous evaluation and improvement of this course is particular important as technology is constantly changing.

Based on the evaluations used to assess teacher growth, the six technology content goals were targeted throughout the course. By selecting various approaches, the preservice teachers were introduced to technology through multiple paths (information delivery, modeling, authentic experiences, hands-on skill building activities, and reflections). The three primary assignments were the weekly reviews of software/hardware, cases, and an electronic portfolio. The Profiler Pro pre- and post-survey showed that preservice teachers indicated feeling more competent in technology skills and the national educational technology standards for teachers (NETS-T). In addition, although the case analysis and artifacts rubrics did not show a significant increase, preservice teachers still mentioned the assignments as one of the most valuable aspects of the course. At the end of the course, in the ePortfolio reflections, preservice teachers discussed an improvement in their attitudes regarding technology and described how technology could be used in their future classrooms.

REFERENCES

Beck, R. J., King, A., & Marshall, S. K. (2002). Effects of video case construction on preservice teachers' observations of teaching. *Journal of Experimental Education, 70*(4), 345–355. doi:10.1080/00220970209599512

Bennett, C. (1991). The teacher as decision maker program: An alternative for career-change preservice teachers. *Journal of Teacher Education, 42*(2), 119–130. doi:10.1177/002248719104200205

Betrus, A. K., & Molenda, M. (2002). Historical evolution of instructional technology in teacher education programs. *TechTrends, 46*(5), 18–21, 33. doi:10.1007/BF02818303

Britten, J., Mullen, L., & Stuve, M. (2003). Initial reflections: The benefits of using a continuous portfolio development in preservice teacher education. *Teacher Educator, 39*(2), 79–94. doi:10.1080/08878730309555332

Brush, T. (1998). Teaching pre-service teachers to use technology in the classroom. *Journal of Technology and Teacher Education, 6*(4), 243–258.

CDW-G. (2010). *The 2010 CDW-G 21st century classroom report: Preparing students for the future or the past*? Retrieved March 28, 2010, from http://newsroom.cdwg.com/features/

Ertmer, P., & Ottenbreit-Leftwich, A. (2010). Teacher technology change: How knowledge, confidence, beliefs, and culture intersect. *Journal of Research on Technology in Education, 42*(3), 255–284.

Ertmer, P. A. (2005). Teacher pedagogical beliefs: The final frontier in our quest for technology integration? *Educational Technology Research and Development, 53*(4), 25. doi:10.1007/BF02504683

Hennessy, S., Ruthven, K., & Brindley, S. (2005). Teacher perspectives on integrating ICT into subject teaching: Commitment, constraints, caution, and change. *Journal of Curriculum Studies, 37*, 155–192. doi:10.1080/0022027032000276961

Hew, K., & Brush, T. (2007). Integrating technology into K-12 teaching and learning: Current knowledge gaps and recommendations for future research. *Educational Technology Research and Development, 55*(3), 223–252. doi:10.1007/s11423-006-9022-5

Hsu, S. (2004). Using case discussion on the web to develop student teacher problem solving skills. *Teaching and Teacher Education, 20*, 681–692. doi:10.1016/j.tate.2004.07.001

Hughes, J. (2005). The role of teacher knowledge and learning experiences in forming technology-integrated pedagogy. *Journal of Technology and Teacher Education, 13*, 277–302.

International Society for Technology in Education [ISTE]. (2008). *NETS for teachers.* Retrieved on April 23, 2010, from http://www.iste.org/Content/NavigationMenu/NETS/ForTeachers/2008Standards/NETS_for_Teachers_2008.htm

Kay, R. H. (2006). Evaluating strategies used to incorporate technology into preservice education: A review of the literature. *Journal of Research on Technology in Education, 38*(4), 383–408.

Kim, H., & Hannafin, M. (2009). Web-enhanced case-based activity in teacher education: A case study. *Instructional Science, 37*, 151–170. doi:10.1007/s11251-007-9040-7

Kleiner, B., Thomas, N., & Lewis, L. (2007). *Educational technology in teacher education programs for initial licensure* (NCES 2008-040). Washington, DC: National Center for Education Statistics, Institute of Education Sciences, U.S. Department of Education.

Koehler, M., Mishra, P., & Yahya, K. (2007). Tracing the development of teacher knowledge in a design seminar: Integrating content, pedagogy and technology. *Computers & Education, 49*(3), 740–762. doi:10.1016/j.compedu.2005.11.012

Lasley, T. J., & Matczynski, T. J. (1995). Reflective teaching. In Ornstein, A. C. (Ed.), *Teaching: Theory into practice* (pp. 307–321). Needham Heights, MA: Allyn & Bacon.

Lin, Q. (2008). Preservice teachers' learning experiences of constructing e-portfolios online. *The Internet and Higher Education, 11*(3-4), 194–200. doi:10.1016/j.iheduc.2008.07.002

Mims, C., Polly, D., Shepherd, C., & Inan, F. (2006). Examining PT3 projects designed to improve preservice education. *TechTrends, 50*(3), 17–24. doi:10.1007/s11528-006-7599-5

Niederhauser, D., & Lindstrom, D. (2006). Addressing the NETS for students through constructivist technology use in K-12 classrooms. *Journal of Educational Computing Research, 34*(1), 91–128. doi:10.2190/E0X3-9CH0-EE2B-PLXG

Niess, M. L. (2005). Preparing teachers to teach science and mathematics with technology: Developing a technology pedagogical content knowledge. *Teaching and Teacher Education, 21*(5), 509–523. doi:10.1016/j.tate.2005.03.006

Ohlund, B., & Yu, C. (2009). *Threats to validity of research design*. Retrieved on April 23, 2010, from http://www.creative-wisdom.com/teaching/WBI/ threat.shtml

Ottenbreit-Leftwich, A., Glazewski, K., & Newby, T. (2010). Preservice technology integration course revision: A conceptual guide. *Journal of Technology and Teacher Education, 8*(1), 5–33.

Ottenbreit-Leftwich, A., Glazewski, K., Newby, T., & Ertmer, P. (2010). Teacher value beliefs associated with using technology: Addressing professional and student needs. *Computers & Education, 55*(3), 1321–1335. doi:10.1016/j.compedu.2010.06.002

Pellegrino, J., Goldman, S., Bertenthal, M., & Lawless, K. (2007). Teacher education and technology: Initial results from the what works and why project. *Yearbook of the National Society for the Study of Education, 106*(2), 52–86. doi:10.1111/j.1744-7984.2007.00115.x

Polly, D., Mims, C., Shepard, C., & Inan, F. (2010). Evidence of impact: Transforming teacher education with preparing tomorrow's teachers to teach with technology (PT3) grants. *Teaching and Teacher Education, 26*, 863–870. doi:10.1016/j.tate.2009.10.024

Project Tomorrow. (2008). *21st century learners deserve a 21st century education: Selected national findings of the Speak Up 2007 Survey.* Retrieved March 28, 2009, from http://www.tomorrow.org/speakup/ speakup_congress_2007.html

Rosaen, C., & Bird, T. (2005). Providing authentic contexts for learning information technology in teacher preparation. *Journal of Technology and Teacher Education, 13*(2), 211–231.

Sadler, D. R. (1989). Formative assessment and the design of instructional systems. *Instructional Science, 18*(2), 119–144. doi:10.1007/BF00117714

Weston, C., McAlpine, L., & Bordonaro, T. (1995). A model for understanding formative evaluation in instructional design. *Educational Technology Research and Development, 43*(3), 29–48. doi:10.1007/BF02300454

Zhao, Y. (2003). Introduction: What teachers need to know about technology? Framing the question. In Zhao, Y. (Ed.), *What should teachers know about technology: Perspectives and practices* (pp. 1–14). Greenwich, CT: Information Age Publishing.

ADDITIONAL READING

Anderson, S. E., & Maninger, R. M. (2007). Preservice teachers' abilities, beliefs, and intentions regarding technology integration. *Journal of Educational Computing Research, 37*(2), 151–172. doi:10.2190/H1M8-562W-18J1-634P

Angeli, C., & Valanides, N. (2009). Epistemological and methodological issues for the conceptualization, development, and assessment of ICT-TPCK: Advances in technology and pedagogical content knowledge (TPCK). *Computers & Education, 52*, 154–168. doi:10.1016/j.compedu.2008.07.006

Angers, J., & Machtmes, K. (2005). An ethnographic-case study of beliefs, context factors, and practices of teachers integrating technology. *Qualitative Report, 10*, 771–794.

Brantley-Dias, L., Kinuthia, W., Shoffner, M. B., DeCastro, C., & Rigole, N. (2007). Developing pedagogical technology integration content knowledge in preservice teachers: A case study approach. *Journal of Research on Computing in Teacher Education, 23*, 143–149.

Britten, J., Mullen, L., & Stuve, M. (2003). Initial reflections: The benefits of using a continuous portfolio development in preservice teacher education. *Teacher Educator, 39*(2), 79–94. doi:10.1080/08878730309555332

Brzycki, D., & Dudt, K. (2005). Overcoming barriers to technology use in teacher preparation programs. *Journal of Technology and Teacher Education, 13*(4), 619–641.

Ertmer, P. A., Conklin, D., Lewandowski, J., Osika, E., Selo, M., & Wignall, E. (2003). Increasing preservice teachers' capacity for technology integration through use of electronic models. *Teacher Education Quarterly, 30*(1), 95–112.

Grove, K., Strudler, N., & Odell, S. (2004). Mentoring toward technology use: Cooperating teacher practice in supporting student teachers. *Journal of Research on Technology in Education, 37*(1), 85–109.

Hew, K., & Brush, T. (2007). Integrating technology into K-12 teaching and learning: Current knowledge gaps and recommendations for future research. *Educational Technology Research and Development, 55*(3), 223–252. doi:10.1007/s11423-006-9022-5

Howard, J. (2002). Technology-enhanced project-based learning in teacher education: Addressing the goals of transfer. *Journal of Technology and Teacher Education, 10*(3), 343–364.

Hsu, S. (2004). Using case discussion on the web to develop student teacher problem solving skills. *Teaching and Teacher Education, 20*, 681–692. doi:10.1016/j.tate.2004.07.001

Hughes, J. (2004). Technology learning principles for preservice and in-service teacher education. *Contemporary Issues in Technology & Teacher Education, 4*(3), 345–362.

Hughes, J. (2005). The role of teacher knowledge and learning experiences in forming technology-integrated pedagogy. *Journal of Technology and Teacher Education, 13*(2), 277–302.

Kariuki, M., & Duran, M. (2004). Using anchored instruction to teach preservice teachers to integrate technology in the curriculum. *Journal of Technology and Teacher Education, 12*(3), 431–445.

Kay, R. H. (2006). Evaluating strategies used to incorporate technology into preservice education: A review of the literature. *Journal of Research on Technology in Education, 38*(4), 383–408.

Kleiner, B., Thomas, N., & Lewis, L. (2007). *Educational technology in teacher education programs for initial licensure (NCES 2008–040). National center for education statistics, institute of education sciences, U.* Washington, DC: S. Department of Education.

Lawless, K., & Pellegrino, J. (2007). Professional development in integrating technology into teaching and learning: Knowns, unknowns, and ways to pursue better questions and answers. *Review of Educational Research, 77*(4), 575–614. doi:10.3102/0034654307309921

Li, Q., Guy, M., Baker, M., & Holen, J. (2006). Partnering prospective and practicing teachers to create technology-supported learning opportunities for students. *Journal of Educational Technology Systems, 34*(4), 387–399. doi:10.2190/C12C-992H-UMJE-WLLE

Pope, M., Hare, D., & Howard, E. (2002). Technology integration: Closing the gap between what preservice teachers are taught to do and what they can do. *Journal of Technology and Teacher Education, 10*(2), 191–203.

Rosaen, C., & Bird, T. (2005). Providing authentic contexts for learning information technology in teacher preparation. *Journal of Technology and Teacher Education, 13*(2), 211–231.

Zheng, D., & Young, M. (2006). *Comparing instructional methods for teaching technology in education to preservice teachers using logistic regression.* Paper presented at the International Conference on Learning Sciences, 873-879. Bloomington, Indiana

KEY TERMS AND DEFINITIONS

Case Analysis and Artifacts: Preservice teachers receive a case study from their focused major.

End of Course Evaluations: A summative paper or electronic questionnaire administered to students in order to evaluate the instruction and quality of a given course. Typically utilized to provide useful feedback to teachers and schools in order to improve quality of instruction.

ePortfolio: A compilation of student work made up of documents and artifacts displayed electronically, usually accessible on the Web. Such electronic evidence may include inputted text, electronic files, images, multimedia, blog entries, and hyperlinks.

Inservice Teacher: In the United States, inservice teachers are currently teaching in the classroom.

NETS-T Standards: The ISTE NETS for Teachers (NETS-T) focus on preservice teacher education and define the fundamental concepts, knowledge, skills, and attitudes for applying technology in educational settings. The NETS-T standard is related to and builds on the NETS for Students.

Profiler Pro: A web-based educational technology tool that allows individuals assess and compare their skills, and improve these skills around a general topic. Results are automatically and immediately generated and allows users to track results over a period of time with Profiler badges and graphs.

Preservice Teacher: In the United States, preservice teachers (college students who want to be teachers) must undergo a rigorous preparation and certification system that includes various assessments, such as student teaching, state-mandated tests, and complete an accredited program at an institution of higher education.

Rubric: A systematic scoring guideline to evaluate behaviors, documents or performance through the use of detailed performance standards.

Chapter 24
Priorities in the Classroom: Pedagogies for High Performance Learning Spaces

Robert Emery Smith
Stanford University, USA

Helen L. Chen
Stanford University, USA

Menko Johnson
Stanford University, USA

Alyssa J. O'Brien
Stanford University, USA

Cammy Huang-DeVoss
Stanford University, USA

ABSTRACT

Innovative and informed design for higher education must begin with attention to teaching, not with shopping lists for digital media tools or blueprints for high performance spaces. The outcomes of the action research program embodied in Wallenberg Hall, a "socio-technical system" at Stanford University created to explore the futures of classroom learning, demonstrate the merit of this perspective. Framed in terms of an evolved implementation of the Technology, Pedagogy and Content Knowledge (TPACK) model of course design and presenting a three level categorization of teaching innovation, this chapter discusses a collection of course case studies to argue that the most innovative and informed design happens by keeping well-supported pedagogy at the forefront of higher education.

DOI: 10.4018/978-1-61350-080-4.ch024

INTRODUCTION

In 2001, Mark Prensky noted a fundamental change in the nature of students since the emergence of digital media technology, calling it a "singularity" that gave birth to a generation he dubbed "Digital Natives." These students were born to a world of digital media, and the effects of the consumption of that media, he claimed, had changed the very neural pathways of their brains. Clearly they could not be expected to succeed in schools based in old media and methods; education had to change.

Responding to these perceptions, educational institutions began bringing technology-based tools into classrooms. For example, by 2007 most primary and secondary schools in Britain equipped classrooms with interactive whiteboards, which seemed to enhance student attention (Willingham, 2010). However, subsequent studies indicated that, despite continued enthusiasm for interactive whiteboards (IWB), better learning was not taking place. Achievement measured against control schools was slightly better in the first year but did not sustain first-year gains. "The literature review has revealed a clear preference for IWB use by both teachers and pupils. It remains unclear, however, as to whether such enthusiasm is being translated into effective and purposeful practice" (Higgins et al, 2005).

This is a problem facing higher education today. How do we best serve our students through providing better learning environments and experiences and leveraging new tools without privileging the latest technological tools as the primary means to improving education?

We note that teaching and learning are the reasons why our educational system exists. We may choose to design new classroom experiences and methods and equip them with a variety of information and communication technology (ICT) tools, but the priority should be clear: learning goals must come first in designing or redesigning classes, followed by pedagogy, then the actual design of the class, and finally the identification of appropriate technological tools. In other words, to best serve our students and enhance their learning, we should not ask what pedagogies are afforded by a particular technology, but instead ask how, in the context of a particular teacher and course, a pedagogy might be enhanced by which particular tools.

Thus this chapter is an account of some experiences and findings from the action research program in Wallenberg Hall. Our experiences lead us to argue that innovative and informed design for higher education must begin with attention to teaching, not with shopping lists for digital media tools or blueprints for learning spaces. The successes of the action research program of Wallenberg Hall, a learning center at Stanford University devoted to innovative teaching, provide a number of case studies demonstrating the merit of this perspective.

BACKGROUND

It is common to encounter articles in the literature today that isolate a technology to investigate how it might be used in an educational setting (Lloyd, 2010). Beginning with projectors, then interactive whiteboards and laptops, and recently with video lecture capture and Web 2.0 tools, the march of products aspiring to bring education out of the presumed dark ages of the twentieth century has continued. Meanwhile, educational scholars such as Abbott (2000) have argued persuasively for a re-evaluation of the use of digital technologies in the classroom based on their increasing prevalence as a mode of communication within an international context.

Indeed, technology is an important item on the docket of most school districts and colleges because computers and other ICT tools are generally regarded as a necessity, representing a significant cost of operations and a comparatively short useful life as an investment. A five-year-old classroom table is practically new; a five-year-old computer is a relic: not only slow, but in some cases unable to cope with current operating systems and applications. If concern about being up-to-date drives the adoption of these tools for classrooms, it is clear that the same concern demands continuing expenditures to deliver on the promises of educational technologies.

Further, there is an entirely understandable desire to ensure that the teachers who will use these tools are sufficiently competent to realize the promise of classroom technology. Traditionally, teaching faculty have grappled with two distinct areas of expertise: content and pedagogy. Shulman (1986) recognized that the intersection of content knowledge and pedagogy creates a unique type of knowledge which he termed Pedagogical Content Knowledge (PCK). The heart of this specific knowledge goes beyond content expertise and general pedagogical strategies: PCK represents the blending of content and pedagogy into an understanding of specific challenges within subject matter and insights into suitable pedagogical strategies to teach that material.

Building on this model, Mishra and Koehler (2006) propose that technology's increasing prominence and widespread use in classrooms situate it as a third area of expertise that should be integrated into the PCK model. Their new model Technology, Pedagogy and Content Knowledge (TPACK) posits that true technology integration in the classroom happens when teachers comprehend and interweave all three of the expertise areas and attain an understanding and insight that supersedes expertise in technology, pedagogy or content alone, as illustrated in Figure 1.

In the TPACK model, teachers who combine deep content knowledge with pedagogical insights and a sense of what technologies and media will best support the pedagogy are identified as peak performers. This might lead some educators and institutions to require that acquisition of the latest classroom technologies be accompanied by with appropriate training for teaching staff.

The challenge inherent in this model is attaining and sustaining expertise in three quite different fields, when the technology field continues to change in both evolutionary and revolutionary ways at a very rapid pace, a pace that may as well be reflected in a teachers's primary area of content expertise.

The classroom teaching program in Wallenberg Hall is guided by an action research process (Kemmis & McTaggart, 1988; Laurillard, 2008) that has evolved over the past eight years. We have come to rely on a model of collaboration that implements the TPACK ideal not in individuals of superhuman capabilities, but in a community of practice, where professors partner with staff with expertise in pedagogy and instructional design as well as technology experts with specific interests in pedagogy and classroom learning.

This team-based, collaborative approach offers a different way of addressing the goal of enhancing learning. Our experience leads us to argue that the selection of tools should be the final, not the first, step in support of an educational design. Our experiences in Wallenberg Hall, designing and supporting a high-performance learning space with innovative technology tools, have taught us that we need to first begin with a clear understanding of the teacher's learning objectives and preferred pedagogical strategy for the students, and then consider which specific technological tools might support that teacher's course.

Our metric for increased efficacy of classroom activities has been a survey measure of student engagement. Student engagement is a multi-dimensional concept with a long intellectual history developed by Pace (1998), Astin, (1975, 2003), and continued by George Kuh (2007) and the comprehensive research program of the National Survey for Student Engagement (2010). Data from the 1,400 institutions who have participated in the NSSE program since 2000 demonstrate the positive impact of student engagement on such outcomes as students' grades and their persistence to graduation (Kuh, 2007). The design of the

Figure 1. TPACK: Technological Pedagogical Content Knowledge, (http://tpack.org/, used with permission)

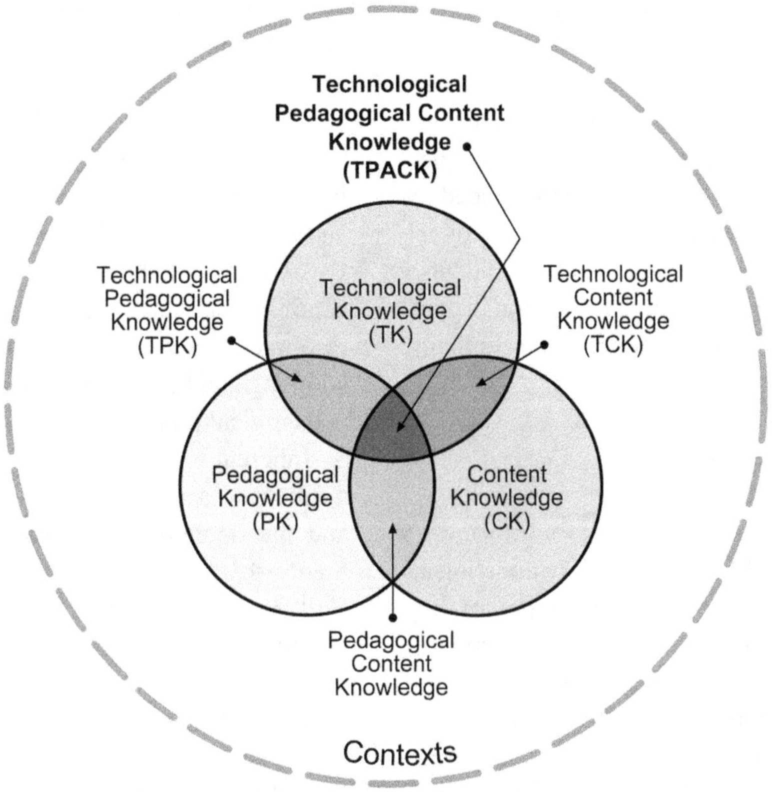

NSSE instruments and resulting research findings show how institutional practices can lead to high levels of student engagement (Kuh et al., 1991; Pascarella & Terenzini, 1991).

While descriptions of student engagement are varied (ranging from study-skill strategies to how students allocate attentional, cognitive, and affective resources in the classroom), our guiding research question is focused on how the learning environment contributes to both student engagement and faculty engagement in learning and teaching. We collaborate with faculty to document and understand how the choices they make about curricular content, instructional practices and assessment practices influence the educational experiences of their students. (Chen, 2010)

It's important to note that simple acknowledgement or inclusion of each of the three regions of TPACK in a course design is not, in our experience, sufficient for success: the class design must balance appropriate contributions from all regions. Several classes undertaken in Wallenberg Hall failed to increase student engagement, a result that can be attributed to an imbalance in implementation.

For example, a few teachers have approached Wallenberg Hall facilities as a modern setting for a class otherwise unchanged from the way they've always taught. Such classes can be thought of as a context for introducing the potential contribution of tech tools, while leaving the pedagogy and content regimes unchanged. Students (in their independent, anonymous reviews of the class, published for the benefit of other students) have characterized such classes as missed opportunities.

Other instructors have demonstrated an enthusiasm for the use of the available tech tools, when perfectly ordinary methods would have been sufficient to the need. Students have disparaged this extreme in their reviews as well.

Still other classes have leveraged the availability of tools to foster some activity, but failed to design the course activities and assessments in such a way as to make such activities desirable and/or necessary. One such class experienced a breakdown of the intended course structure over the course of the quarter as a result of students correctly surmising that their participation in one major activity didn't impact their learning or their assessment.

Wallenberg Hall: A Design for Stanford

In 2000, Stanford University began remodeling a major building on campus with the support of the Wallenberg Foundations.[1] The goal was to support global research in the advancement of learning. To that end, Wallenberg Hall's classrooms were developed with demands for teaching and learning at the forefront of all design considerations. They provide a technology-rich environment for faculty and students, equipped with small group tables and chairs on wheels so the space can easily be reconfigured and offer a range of interactive teaching tools that encourage group work. Yet the classrooms are more than rooms with digital tools: we call them high-performance learning spaces.

Many classrooms in a modern university have some mix of hardware and software facilities. What makes the classrooms in Wallenberg Hall different is their design, implementation, and the associated staff. Instructional designers, technical staff and assessment researchers work closely with Stanford faculty and instructors to match content, learning theories, and pedagogical vision with the room facilities in order to reinforce the objectives and activities of each class. Wallenberg Hall's high performance learning spaces can thus be said to be the home of a sophisticated "socio-technical system" (Marshall, 1998) that supports and enhances the classes and learning experiences that take place. By characterizing Wallenberg Hall as a socio-technical system, we are referring specifically to the social and technical factors that influence how the organization is able to support innovation in teaching and learning. Wallenberg Hall possesses staff expertise in educational technology, instructional design, and assessment which is unique to our campus. By actively collaborating with faculty using an action research approach, we bring the "social" resources to address the technical challenges of adopting and integrating technological tools into pedagogical practice.

Inherent to this system's operation is a commitment to accommodate the needs of the user and the domain, in this case, the teacher and Stanford University. The design of Wallenberg Hall derived from explicit specifications from faculty and from an implicit understanding by the design team of human interface preferences and the cultural context of Stanford University itself.

Design Born of Collaboration

Stanford University's Design program in the School of Engineering has a long history of success employing user-centered design techniques for a wide variety of design solutions, and design practitioners from this tradition (from IDEO, as well as Stanford staff) employed this approach for this project. Wallenberg Hall's first-generation classrooms were designed in an iterative, scenario-based design process with an advisory group of Stanford faculty members from across the campus including education, mechanical engineering, computer science, languages and writing and rhetoric.[2] The design process privileged the teaching and learning we hoped would take place in the new spaces, not the technological tools we expected to use. Thus, the design born of collaboration rested on the following assumptions:

The quality of the users' experience (teachers and students) has the highest priority

The tools in these rooms should be entirely configurable by the instructor, with no need for an external operator

The interface should take advantage of users' prior experience and training

The human social aspects of classes should be supported by the classroom and its tools, not the reverse.

Working closely with the faculty advisory group was a team with a range of expertise (information technology, audio visual, human interface design, human factors) with prior experience creating formal spaces at Stanford (the Bechtel Conference Center and the Hewlett Teaching Center), a space planning consultancy (IDEO/ San Francisco) and the architect for the building (Skidmore Owings Merrill, LLP). This team regarded the design of new 20- to 25-person class spaces as a genuine, complex design challenge rather than an opportunity to simply replicate a "Classroom" template from their files. In a very real sense, the rooms were designed with a commercial product design approach: we wanted faculty and students to *want* to use these rooms, and for their experiences to reinforce that desire. The path to that desire was seen to be genuine utility, not mere novelty or "flash."

Streamlining the design process, we decided the rooms would all have very similar facilities; we designed the four regular-size classrooms as variants on one design. This minimized the burden on our faculty collaborators and provided us with a fairly well-optimized general-purpose classroom design rather than four designs optimized for different subject areas. This decision has paid dividends in the form of easier scheduling (as the rooms are, to a large degree, almost interchangeable) and has subsequently simplified our planning for promulgating some of the tools from these rooms to other classrooms on campus. A larger multipurpose central space (dubbed the "Learning Theater") was designed in parallel as a community space, gesturing both to the open architecture of the original 1900 building and to public squares in European villages.

Student input was gathered in multimedia forms created by the students themselves: a large group of students from every academic level in the university was provided with cameras and asked to document where they and their peers work, play, collaborate and reflect. The resulting library of images and supplementary survey information was analyzed and used to shape the design of the public, informal learning spaces of Wallenberg Hall.

In the iterative design process, five members of the faculty were provided with a draft design specification, sketches, and an operations description for a technologically agile classroom and asked to reflect on how they might use the tools provided, what features might be adjusted, and what tools were missing. We wanted to know what they might use such a room for and what things they might want to do that were not supported by the room described.

That input was collected, reviewed by the rest of the team, and the base design adjusted to accommodate the information provided, resulting in a new room plan and operational description, which was then submitted for a new round of faculty review and feedback. We completed multiple iterations of this process.

Prototyping was also part of our room design process. For example, when questions about the best lighting solution emerged, we built a full-sized mockup of the classroom ceiling as designed and used that to select the lighting instruments, ensuring the light intensity at the desktop was more than adequate, and that the architectural diffusion of the light was sufficient to largely eliminate shadows in the rooms, both reducing eye strain for occupants and easing the task of capturing video for videoconferences or ethnographic research in these spaces.

Wallenberg Hall Classroom and Features

Most classrooms are designed by architects, not teachers. – Robert Siegel

In addition to designing the rooms in an architectural sense, the five faculty advisors guided the collaborative team to attend to features that would best serve the needs of teachers in the space. These include attention to seemingly banal "tools" such as furniture, walls, and writing surfaces, as well as the more sophisticated digital technology systems for high-performance learning.

Flexibility: One of the features of the Wallenberg classrooms often noted by visitors is the comfort and flexibility of the furniture. The chairs are lightweight and ergonomically outstanding, providing comfortable accommodation for their still-growing users. In two of our larger rooms, the chairs are stackable, facilitating their use in standard rows for lectures and presentations, while lightweight to allow for easy reorganization for other activities. In the other four classrooms, a variant of the chair with a swivel/caster base is used, allowing free and rapid reconfiguration of the room for different activities in the course of a single class session.

The rooms have six to ten medium-sized rectangular tables, also on casters, which can fold to a small, stackable footprint when unneeded, allowing the desktop workspace of each room to vary from the maximum that floor space allows to none at all, with very little overhead.

When furniture is easily moved, a class can have multiple layouts in the same session, from a horseshoe seminar shape for a media-supported discussion to rows for an orienting lecture or presentation to islands for small group work. Classroom layout changes can easily be performed by the students quickly, with these momentary reorganizations underscoring transitions between activities while providing the best available configuration of the room for the work at hand.

Writeable Surfaces: Each room has a collection of small, lightweight, double-sided whiteboards called Huddleboards. These are about the scale of a meeting marker pad and easel, and there are two racks of five Huddleboards in each classroom. These provide a comparatively large drawing/writing surface for collaborative notes, idea mapping or presentation diagrams.

Whiteboards and other writeable surfaces line the perimeter walls of the classrooms. The whiteboards are vitreous enamel over a steel substrate, allowing both the use of magnets to affix documents and easy clean-up should a permanent marker be mistakenly used. Large windows with internal frosting increase the available "whiteboard" area in some rooms; the smooth surfaces of these translucent windows both transmit light and can be drawn on with whiteboard dry erase markers.

Capture And Share Information: Two whiteboards have a capture scanner mounted above them, situated to capture the contents of that board, or content on three Huddleboards hung from a rail in front of that board. This content is transferred to a dedicated gallery website.

Group Computing: Each room has two or more in-room computers driving large interactive displays (or, in the case of the "Learning Theater," three 4-meter diagonal measure front-projection screens), and a wireless gyro mouse and keyboard. The choice to use multiple separate machines and interactive displays was quite intentional: for maximum flexibility of use, we wanted all of the screens to be able to be used independently. This is useful for student work in the classroom and for presentation of material by the teacher.

The fluent operation of these machines and their displays is provided by the use of iROS (interactive Room Operating System). This cross-platform facility allows virtual keyboard and mouse control over the public machines from the room laptops. It differs from a more common Virtual Networking Computing (VNC)-style system (e.g., Apple's Remote Desktop, SMART Technology's Sync

Classroom Management software) by maintaining separate functional identities for all participating machines. The large room displays do not display the contents of a selected student's laptop screen, but rather are a central public display space that can host the content that the student has directed to that public space. Each individual laptop keyboard and mouse can be easily directly mapped to control the larger screen, according to the social norms and practices that pertain to a verbal classroom conversation.

To participate in this environment, each classroom has 10 to16 laptops with appropriate applications installed; these laptops are stored in mobile carts within each room where they recharge while not in use.

Connectivity: Each room also has multiple channels of wireless network access, all configured to minimum transmission power so each wireless access hub covers an area only a bit larger than the classroom it serves, minimizing network management issues over the five classrooms on the first floor of the building.

Collaboration Stations: In addition to the base configuration, two rooms have five collaboration stations to facilitate group work around a 34" plasma screen. These stations also serve as useful machines for a variety of other applications (workshops, project presentation events, collaborative writing, etc).

Communications: Classroom communication tools include teleconferencing and a range of studio-style videoconferencing platforms. In addition, we support the major video chat applications and a video collaboration platform called Marratech, developed originally in Luleå, Sweden.

An Engaged Model of Support

While creating the space and selecting tools based on faculty guidance about the teaching to take place is a necessary part of building a systems approach to enhanced learning, it is not sufficient to guarantee effective learning or even productive use of the facilities. Thus, the educational technology team in Wallenberg Hall have identified and refined three elements of a support model that have served us well to sustain and generate new kinds of classroom learning.

An Open Invitation to Teach in Wallenberg Hall

First, we designed the space to be open to all. Wallenberg Hall classrooms are available for use at no cost by any teacher from any school or department at Stanford University. Since opening in 2002, we have not explicitly advertised our services, as we have been more than fully subscribed each quarter through faculty word-of-mouth referrals alone. The distribution of use across the schools (see Table 1) is partially due to the nature of these social networks (any given social network rarely if ever includes the entire faculty community), academic calendar differences (the Graduate School of Business, Law School and Medical School calendars are slightly offset from the main campus Academic Calendar), and the availability of domain-specific facilities (wet labs, etc.).

Faculty expressing interest in teaching a class in Wallenberg Hall are first encouraged to meet with our course design/academic technology specialist with whom they discuss the teacher's goals for their class in the broadest sense: what experiences do they want to provide for their students? What would be a measure of success for their class? What have they seen or experienced recently that inspired them?

In this way, we offer consultation about pedagogy for teachers who approach Wallenberg Hall as a potential teaching space. The Wallenberg Hall staff bring pedagogical, technical and production capabilities to these meetings, as well as experience supporting hundreds of earlier classes given in these spaces. This knowledge of prior efforts is invaluable: many times, an activity or technique used in a class for an entirely different subject area can be translated for the purposes of a new class.

Table 1. Number of courses taught in Wallenberg Hall from 2002-2010 by school

School	Number of Courses (%)
Law and Business	5 (1%)
Education	97 (13%)
Engineering	104 (14%)
Humanities and Sciences (including Earth Sciences)	265 (34%)
Medicine	25 (3%)
Program in Writing and Rhetoric	261 (34%)
Continuing Studies	14 (2%)
TOTAL	771

* Percentages are rounded

Once a course has been mapped out and scheduled, Wallenberg Hall's educational technology staff prepare specific requirements. These may be as simple as installing particular software on the computers in the classroom or setting up a complex audio/visual configuration.

Fostering Community

The second element of the support model is the facilitation of our teaching and learning community. Each quarter, Wallenberg Hall hosts a lunch for faculty, and we invite both those who are currently teaching there and those who have taught there in the past. The agenda is simple: introductions, brief updates on the status of the facilities and future plans, then discussion from the individual faculty of their experiences teaching in the space. Instructors and support staff all ask questions, offer suggestions, and share observations and expertise. This supports a continuing community of practice among the teachers at Wallenberg Hall.

Visible Means of Support

Third in our model of support is a deep commitment to discussions of learning, not just to fixing technology tools. Wallenberg Hall's support staff are clear that their job is to support the learning taking place in the classrooms, not just the hardware or software resident there. This clarifies many situations: the support goal is not to fix a technical problem for some future use, but rather to keep a particular class on track. To that end, we have been very fortunate to have a group of support staff who enjoy learning, understand something of the world of the teachers, and regard an opportunity to assist in a classroom a desirable break from daily responsibilities to be undertaken with enthusiasm.

More specifically, Wallenberg Hall staff confirm the proper functioning of room systems on a daily basis, and can be seen between and during classes on the first floor, greeting teachers and students, helping out as they can. The teachers know Wallenberg staff on sight and have developed a collegial relationship, which serves to lower barriers to asking questions or asking for support.

In addition, the home page on the browsers installed on the in-room machines is a room help screen. Both that home page and a small sign on the wall have a phone number that rings the entire support staff when called. Whoever is available to help answers the call, and thus owns the question or problem being reported until explicitly handed off to another support staff member.

Whenever possible, we try to respond to a problem in person, even if it might be resolved remotely. We find addressing a problem on a face-to-face basis most satisfying for all parties, reinforcing the collegiality we seek, and allowing the support staff to confirm that whatever problem they resolved really did enable the teacher and the class to carry on.

The commitment to high visibility and in-person support from Wallenberg Hall staff has produced a deeply collaborative model of education such that as support staff, we are also resources for the students in the Wallenberg classrooms. We have the opportunity to get to know the teachers very well, understanding a wide range of teaching styles. Moreover, we have come to categorize the teaching facilitated by the design, features and support of Wallenberg Hall through a particular theoretical lens that has wide implications for other institutions.

A Three-Level Model of Technology Integration

Based on our collaborations with faculty and our observations of technology-augmented courses over the years of operation at Wallenberg Hall, as well as in consultation with our peers at similar educational facilities, we have developed a conceptual framework to categorize the different levels of technology integration in classes into three broad categories, shown below in Table 2.

The first category of technology integration we call *Traditional+* (Traditional-plus). These are courses that use technology tools to streamline, accelerate or enhance activities and assignments, where the core curriculum and instructional strategies remain unchanged. For example, consider reviewing the online version of a magazine photo essay on a large screen rather than distributing copies of the magazine to the class. A traditional classroom activity has been enhanced in some dimension by the use of a technological affordance. For a course being redesigned, this type of change is the simplest to make and has the smallest burden on course planning for faculty. In the following case studies, we discuss two examples from the Traditional+ category.

The next category, *Transitional*, differs from the first in that the integration of some technology significantly impacts the class process, creating new activities and learning opportunities that were not part of an earlier version of the course. For example, consider a literature professor teaching a class dealing with eighteenth century writing. Traditionally, he would ask students to research a topic and write a paper about it—a common learning activity. However, in his Transitional class, the professor creates an eighteenth century timeline in Google Documents and has each of the students pick topics and develop them collaboratively online. This allows students to see each other's work, understand the historical context that each of the literary works was written in, and situate their own work in a larger context, providing a deeper engagement and learning experience for all the students. While the content has not changed and the product is still a written paper, the activity is significantly altered through collaborative technology. In the following case studies, we discuss two examples from the Transitional category.

In the third category, *Transformational*, the entire class turns on the use of a particular facil-

Table 2. Characteristics of three levels of technology integration

Paradigm	Characteristics	Amount of Change in Course Design
Traditional+	Increase in efficiency or effectiveness, but pedagogy remains the same	Low
Transitional	Extend existing pedagogy in new direction through use of tools	Medium
Transformational	Create new pedagogy that was not possible before the use of tools	High

ity to solve some logistic or pedagogic problem, resulting in an entirely different kind of instruction. In one instance, a rhetoric class might use a video collaboration environment to bring students from Stanford together with students from another cultural context to work together on a rhetorical analysis. Careful selection of the rhetorical object discussed can result in bringing the cultural presumptions and biases of the student teams involved into sharp relief, a powerful learning experience. In another example, the discourse of a communications or sociology class might be partially supported by the very social media tools being studied, blending the review and creation of media in an instructive interplay of activities. In the following case studies, we present three examples from the Transformational category, one more than the other categories, as this level of innovation creates the greatest diversity of results.

These categories presume a preexisting course as a basis rather than creating an entirely new course. In the latter situation, the integration of technology occurs from the very beginning and is a salient component that is addressed in all consultations with the instructor.

CASE STUDIES

We offer the following seven case studies from Stanford as case study examples of the kinds of courses that informed the development of the framework delineated above. The next section will present two Traditional+, two Transitional and three Transformative courses, chosen to illustrate the breadth of innovative strategies employed by our faculty colleagues.

Traditional+: A History Seminar

Margaret O'Mara was looking for a flexible seminar room and found one in Wallenberg Hall. She prefaced each quarter's seminar with an orienting lecture framing the goals of the course and providing an overarching context. Students were then asked to pair up and were assigned to organize and lead each of the subsequent weekly course discussions. O'Mara had met with Wallenberg staff before the quarter started and decided to use the dual interactive displays to provide a richer and more nuanced introductory lecture, using imagery, web-based materials and contrasting elements in her presentation.

Without any suggestion or training to do so, the students in the course also incorporated these tools and techniques into their weekly framing presentations, juxtaposing images, displaying maps alongside statistics, displaying timelines next to newspaper headlines, etc.

This is an excellent example of a Traditional+ technology integration. Using the dual screens as a rhetorical presentation device (enabling text/context and compare/contrast modalities of display and discussion) increased the richness of class presentations, analysis and discussions, while implicitly training the students in the class around the effective utilization of such a presentation resource, all stemming from the unremarked modeling of these methods by the teacher.

Traditional+: Chinese Language Classes

Sik Lee Dennig came to Wallenberg Hall looking for a flexible classroom space with networked in-room laptops where she could implement her vision for her conversational Chinese classes.

Learning a language for conversation relies heavily on the auditory channel as a primary means of improving fluency beyond memorizing vocabulary. It requires the learner to understand how the instructor's pronunciation of each word compares to their own pronunciation of the word through practice in dialog with an expert and their peers.

A typical class includes introducing the vocabulary words for the day and students engaging in dialog and conversations with each other and the instructor. Students would then have a homework assignment to perform in a language lab, where they would listen to native speakers and respond to the recording. Even in small language courses with fewer than 20 students, live, real-time interaction is limited.

Dennig attended a session at a Summer Institute at Wallenberg Hall led by Howard Rheingold (another Wallenberg Hall instructor) on the topic of social media creation, and subsequently incorporated social media tools in her classes.

I want them to feel [like] a community. You know, they're learning as a community. They're supporting each other. And also, I always try to address the individual differences, too. Within the same class, I have a very wide range of proficiency levels. (Dennig)

In order to increase interaction time between herself and students as well as between peers, Dennig moved this activity out of the language lab. A course management system and content repository were created to organize the class, resources being shared with students and other language instructors via a wiki, and a blog used for student reflection. Students downloaded audio files for the class from iTunesU.

Dennig's class used VoiceThread[3], a web-based tool that allows easy sharing of multimedia content, to post assignments online and to allow students to respond with audio recordings that are subsequently shared with other students in the class for peer and instructor review. Dennig was able to provide both written and recorded spoken feedback for these assignments, in effect increasing the amount of individual student-teacher interaction time for these classes, while the web-accessible audio recording tool allowed her to keep her time commitment at a sustainable level.

This course features multiple innovative elements: recorded verbal response to assignments, written and audio feedback to students, interaction between students to create the recorded dialogs, etc. While the number of activities is high, any of them could conceivably be implemented in another fashion; the role of technology in this class is to greatly increase efficiency (allowing more instructional time), so we regard it as Traditional+ in our categorization.

Transitional: Coaching Research Methods in Genomics

Doug Brutlag wanted to use the dual large displays in a Wallenberg Hall classroom to scale a one-on-one advising technique up to a full classroom activity. Brutlag is a professor of biochemistry and medicine in the Medical School and teaches undergraduate classes in genetics.

In the undergraduate class, he addressed the material in a combination lecture/seminar format. For lectures, he loaded materials onto the Wallenberg Hall NAS (Network Attached Storage) from his office, and then opened them on the two host machines in the classroom.

For seminars, Brutlag assigned research topics to the students, making them responsible for leading a seminar on their topic later in the course. Brutlag provided some demonstration of productive online research techniques, made himself available in person and via email for coaching, but the left the work of preparing the seminar to the students. Some of Brutlag's coaching focused on research techniques:

Normally, when I would teach a graduate student, the graduate student would come into my office, and we would sit and talk, and I'd have my computer there with two screens, usually one for me and one for him, and I would show him how to do an experiment on the Web or how to access a database on the Web. I wanted to have a classroom where I could do exactly the same thing, and that's what this Wallenberg [classroom] has allowed me to do. (Brutlag)

This is a close-coaching interaction but the locale is a full class. At one level, it is very much like an elementary school teacher coaching a student at a blackboard through the process of long division, with the classroom of peers all receiving the benefit of that coaching.

Brutlag was not teaching a mechanistic algorithm, however, but instead the real-time assessment and evaluation of complex information as well as the evaluation of source validity. Each of the students had similar tasks to perform, and all benefitted from the coaching being received by their peers, thereby collapsing the content of what would otherwise be the very lengthy and individualized coaching of an individual's efforts into an exceptional shared research experience.

Because the activities in this class translate one-on-one coaching to a productive group activity, we regard this case as Transitional: the benefits achieved by scaling a one-to-one interaction to a classroom scale are different in kind than simple increasing the efficiency of a traditional classroom activity.

Transitional: Layering Representations in Shakespeare

Larry Friedlander used Wallenberg Hall to teach a variety of classes on the plays of Shakespeare as literature. He welcomed students to approach the theatrical works in the manner of a company of actors, warming up before class, sharing dramatic readings. Then Friedlander furthered their textual understanding by engaging large-scale presentation of media.

Theatre exists as a set of possibilities for multiple realizations and representations in different modes. In life, on film or in video, in a text, through a discussion. And, theatre itself is made up of endless variations on these representations so that I can show students five, six, ten versions of Hamlet. But the trick is not only for them to see different versions, but be able to precisely extract and review and analyze small segments of those performances next to each other. Because that's when I can see the difference between Ian McKellen and Lawrence Oliver saying, 'To be or not to be.' And then the students can then work on small elements. So this gives them a sense of process of how something is created and of the field of possibilities that are generated by any text. (Friedlander)

Friedlander held his classes in the largest of the Wallenberg Hall classrooms, the Peter Wallenberg Learning Theater. This is a large, two-story, flat-floored classroom with the same lightweight, movable furniture as the other classrooms. It also features a video capture system and three 4 meter diagonal screens with bright, high-resolution projectors, enabling the screens to be used as presentation screens for review of performances of the texts under consideration and to be used as backdrops for student-interpreted performances of those texts. The video capture system records performances for later review and reuse.

For example in theatre, using two screens, we can show two different versions of a scene done by different companies. Then the students can rehearse and create their own scene and they can put it on another scene so that there's a way of not only producing something, but of, kind of comparative analysis of visual and time based events as opposed to simply watching a movie or reading a play.

What I've always been interested in is ... finding [a] way that students can not only study and analyze, but also participate and actually make theatre. So in our classes we used those spaces to move easily from a discussion format where we can analyze and review and argue about text to actually trying out different configurations in space and then moving towards more formal presentations where we use the large screens as a background; as kind of stage scenery for student work.

What's very important for me is that these rooms allow a very easy flow of back and forth from these different modalities. In other words, you don't have to go to another space. And the students can break out at any moment, work on something, come back and show it. We can capture it and then use it again. Or the students can use the rooms as rehearsal space and as actual theatrical presentation spaces. (Friedlander)

Taking advantage of presentation and capture technologies in a mutable space, Friedlander's Shakespeare classes went beyond a Traditional+ integration of technology to a new level of classroom experience. We regard Friedlander's Shakespeare classes collectively as Transitional classroom experiences.

Transformational: Class Focus and Layered Gesture Transform the Classics

In *The Poetry of Horace* course, Richard Martin used the ancient odes as a vehicle for exploring how a classicist analyzes and thinks about texts by bringing that process to the classroom.

Typically, he would bring the text of the ode into class as a double-spaced Microsoft Word file, loading it onto one of the large public display machines. He then used the interactive capability of those displays to annotate his analysis of the grammar and construction of a stanza with a digital pen. Then it was the students' turn:

I would display a text of the poem in the original Latin on one screen. This would become the arena (to use a Roman word) for translation. In turn - sometimes in teams - the students, who had for homework read the poem and tried to work out its meaning, would come up, stylus in hand, and "perform" their understanding. By that I mean, they would translate live, pointing out to me and other students the syntactical connections between subject and verb, what words went with what, and so on, as they translated. And all this could be highlighted - even using different stylus marker colors. So at the end of a few minutes, the class as a whole had a clearly visible "map" or 3-D image of the inner workings of the Horatian Ode. We could debate the fine points of translation, of image, of meaning all sharing the same digital whiteboard. (Martin)

In contrast to more typical classics classes, Martin's use of the interactive screens meant that a single "page" had the students' attention, rather than each engaging their individual copies of the text. The central display of this one page enabled meaningful group annotation of that text (using both digital pen and the room laptops) and produced a clear gestural layer of communication and meaning ("*this* adjective agrees with *that* noun" or "what is *that* word doing in the sentence?") in group analysis.

Martin employed the second interactive screen to display maps, images, concordances and translations for the text under examination, an excellent example of displaying simultaneous text and context. He would also break up the larger group into two-person teams, each with text to analyze and a Huddleboard portable whiteboard to record their efforts, which would then be reviewed with the rest of the class.

In sharing the process of professional analysis of texts with his students, Martin created what we regard as an excellent example of a Transformational class. His use of the interactive screens and the room collaboration system to share the work of annotating and translating a single instance of a text produced an interaction around those documents that was immediate, immersive, interactive and collaborative, and almost inevitably engaging.

Transformative: Rhetoric on a Global Scale

As teachers exploring transformative course designs, Christine Alfano and Alyssa O'Brien sought the resources of Wallenberg Hall to teach students hands-on learning with visual rhetoric and multimedia texts for courses in the required writing curriculum at Stanford. With funding from the Wallenberg Global Learning Network, they developed a cross-cultural rhetoric course that required innovative re-design of classroom spaces and the acquisition and implementation of new technology tools to meet their pedagogical vision. This one course evolved into the Cross-Cultural Rhetoric Project (CCR).[4] Alfano and O'Brien now support up to 30 courses (10 to 20 teachers) a year in transformative teaching situations using the spaces and resources of Wallenberg Hall for a global pedagogy that connects Stanford students with students in classes across five continents through the use of video conferences, collaborative blogs, and other forms of global communication (O'Brien & Alfano, 2009). In this way, students learn first-hand the essential skills in international collaboration and communication while they also develop new understandings of diverse cultural perspectives around the world.

The original research team for these courses consisted of faculty from Orebro University in Sweden (Brigitte Mral, Anders Eriksson, and Eva Magnusson) and from Stanford University (Andrea Lunsford, Alfano, and O'Brien). Envisioning a curriculum in global learning, they sought to use persuasive technologies to make the rhetorical situation of writing real to their students (O'Brien, Alfano, & Magnusson, 2007). They wanted their students not to create work in a vacuum but to exchange their writing and ideas with other students from around the world.

To support this pedagogical vision, the Wallenberg Hall staff had to think creatively about the learning space and collaborative tools that would foster this new kind of active global learning. The first step was to set up class-to-class video conferencing, but the positioning of the equipment prevented students from making direct eye contact with each other, significantly degrading the ideal collaboration and making small group work impossible. This failure drove the design of collaboration stations, in which teams of students sit at a large plasma screen equipped with a webcam and echo-cancelling microphone to allow for proximity and transparency. In the first iteration of this design, all the student groups remained in one room with sound dividers. Unfortunately, the sound bounced off the walls of the dividers and interfered with the learning and work of students in each group. We then distributed the groups among smaller conference rooms in the basement and top floors of Wallenberg Hall. Redesigning the space of the class, breaking it out of the standard classroom, made possible the vision for global pedagogy desired by the teaching team, which focuses on creating an "international contact zone" as a site of "global negotiation" (O'Brien & Eriksson 2009).

A student's reflection reveals the power of this global pedagogy:

I learned to not just think about the perspective of American society but also of other societies across the globe. In addition, it helped to be able to bounce my ideas around with my peers and hear their sincere thoughts. The diversity of opinions provided by the international students really helped me to expand my topic and consider ideas I had not thought of or considered looking into and researching. (O'Brien, 2007)

In pursuing the technological tools to make the CCR pedagogy possible, we decided to rely upon a video collaboration tool called Marratech, developed originally at Luleå University in Sweden. It allows a number of remote stations (up to 30 in Stanford's system) to connect with real-time audio (allowing normal conversations, including simultaneous speakers), along with standard resolution lip-synched video of all of the participants. It also provides a large "whiteboard" where students can share images, collaborate on the creation of texts, indicate and annotate areas of interest, and engage in the development of a common document in response to the pedagogical activity.

Alfano and O'Brien have written about the implications for course design on a global scale (O'Brien & Alfano, 2009). Their ongoing research explores whether it is necessary that two interacting classes be focused on the same topic area, and whether class interactions may be limited to a single point activity between otherwise dissimilar courses, and still produce a significant sensitizing impact on the students involved.

The CCR classes are an excellent example of a Transformative use of technology. Cross-cultural studies are becoming more prevalent in university education today, with an increasing number of actual global connections made possible by advances in video-conferencing, blogging, and remote communication. Alfano and O'Brien's work designing activities, training and supporting CCR instructors, and preparing their students for live intercultural exchanges has helped pave the way for a new generation of transformative courses. Students' experience of deep learning combined with the social interaction using advanced videoconferencing tools makes these classes truly representative of an entirely new and exceptionally effective style of university instruction.

Transformational: Parallel Activities in Health Policy

"Technology works best when we're not trying to design the curriculum around the technology."
-Robert Siegel

Stanford University offers a special program for returning second-year students every fall called Sophomore College. It returns students to campus three weeks before classes begin to engage in an intensive class led by a senior faculty member.

Robert Siegel taught a three-week microbiology seminar called "Smallpox: Past, Present, and Future." The class met daily to explore a series of case studies related to the evolutionary origins of smallpox, its relationship to public health policy, sociocultural changes from its eradication, research funding, and implications for gene therapy. The course activities featured guest speakers, field trips, lectures, discussions and student presentations. Students also contributed to a class blog.

The class met for about four hours each day, a long session for any class. Siegel constantly monitored the state of the students' attention: in a session as intensive and as long as his, student (and faculty) attention and focus will eventually flag. He addressed this by using the Learning Theater's three projections screens to simultaneously show multiple streams of information in the classroom.

One screen held a Twitter stream that the students were invited to use as a back-channel for commentary, annotations, and feedback. Another held his lecture presentation for reference. The third featured multiple open windows, including a class calendar (noting upcoming activities and deadlines in a color-coded format), the class blog (where students were assigned to post "new and hot" items from their assigned out-of-class research), and a web browser for real-time investigations or reference.

Following the idea that "a change is as good as a break," Siegel used the multiple streams to shift class focus when he sensed the need to refresh the students. For example, if in the course of a lecture on epidemiology he sensed that attention was fading, he would switch to the class blog and ask students to present some of the material they had posted to it.

In addition, Siegel felt that the students should provide some real contribution to world knowledge based on their experiences in his class, and his assignments reflected that expectation. His students wrote Wikipedia articles on viruses and posted book reviews on Amazon.com. Multiple classes over the years created web pages describing the evolution of various virus families.

The use of Twitter in Siegel's course stemmed from his belief that students need to know how to observe the world and respond to their observations. Through Twitter, students provided one-line observations about a particular reading, lecture, etc. Those observations provided Siegel with a good barometer of how students were doing in the course and also identify areas where additional clarification and expansion were needed.

Siegel's course highlights how creating, organizing, and referencing the materials for a lecture in a classroom with multiple screens differs from a single-screen presentation. His use of multiple channels of information and embrace of on-the-fly feedback and student commentary combined with lectures, real-world experts, and other resources mark his class as a Transformative experience. This class would simply not be possible without the recruitment and very effective use of the range of technology tools available.

Wallenberg Hall's role is to create new opportunities in advanced resource classrooms and invite faculty to experiment. Once they have invested time in these new environments, they may so integrate these tools into their teaching practice that they are unwilling to teach in facilities that do not provide those resources.

FUTURE DIRECTIONS

In the fall of 2010, Wallenberg Hall classrooms moved into its next phase of operations with a transfer of operations responsibility for those classrooms to the Office of the Registrar, which is responsible for the maintenance and operation of most classrooms on the Stanford campus. The Wallenberg classrooms represent an increase in complexity over most classrooms for this organization's staff, so the coming year will be one of growth and accommodation by the Registrar's Office, even as the rooms are being updated and extended in capability in consultation with faculty and research organizations on campus. The Registrar has moved the offices of two classroom tech support staff into Wallenberg Hall to facilitate quick support and continued visibility of the agents of classroom support.

The Wallenberg community will be increasingly supported by organizations on campus that are concerned with the quality of teaching and learning at Stanford University, including the Center for Teaching and Learning and others.

The transition in organizational leadership for Wallenberg Hall represents an opportunity to explore how the emphasis on pedagogical innovation as supported by technological tools cultivated in individual faculty and courses within the laboratory of Wallenberg Hall can be scaled and sustained at the campus-wide level. The Registrar's Office is supportive of these research efforts and collaborations with other institutions including the University of Minnesota and colleagues at several Swedish universities. Going forward, surveys focusing on the role of learning environments in fostering both student and faculty engagement will continue to be administered by staff associated with Wallenberg Hall.

CONCLUSION

Many things have changed since the Prensky's coining of "Digital Native." As recently as the summer of 2010, cognitive scientists were reporting that student thinking is actually not fundamentally different than in years past, the conceit of multitasking not bearing up under scientific scrutiny (Ophir, Nass & Wagner, 2009). Willingham (2010) notes that research shows that classroom technology on its own has little real impact on learning; these tools are only productive when they align with the teacher's practice (or vice versa). Moreover, Abbott (2010) recently contended that "Too often, the research can be accused of a technologically determinist perspective which takes insufficient account of the social and cultural contexts which support the technology use."

Since Wallenberg Hall opened in 2002, its mission has been to understand the social and cultural contexts in which the best teaching and learning occurs. To date, we have hosted 306 Stanford instructors teaching a total of 781 classes as well as more than a thousand special events supporting every school in the University, including videoconferences, lectures, workshops and receptions.

As described above, the facility was designed in collaboration with Stanford faculty, who kept the work focused on the teaching and learning intended to take place in those spaces. The collaboration between Wallenberg Hall staff and the faculty who teach there has maintained this focus, always returning to the unique learning goals and strategy of the individual teacher and their class. For this reason, the unavoidable challenges and disappointments with classroom technology have not been felt as keenly here: keeping the tools subservient to the teaching mission has kept "the horse before the cart."

We have argued that any facility supporting such collaborations is by its very nature as much a social system as any kind of technical system. Intentionally engaging in the support and furthering of the social dynamic is productive, sustaining participation and contribution of participants over time, and sustaining a welcoming and supportive environment for individuals or working groups to explore new ways of teaching and working.

In the theoretical background section of this chapter, we noted the TPACK model of course design and the need for teacher expertise in multiple domains. Our perspective is that asking a professional academic to be expert in the field of available technology (a fast-paced, constantly changing landscape) is perhaps a bit too ambitious. On the other hand, if the teacher is working in a social context that hosts a wide range of experience in technology, and also in complementary content areas and pedagogies (represented by fellow teachers), perhaps that collegial *group* can efficiently realize the goal of merged expertise.

Indeed, perhaps the easiest way for the TPACK ideal to be realized is at an institutional level in a collaborative environment such as Wallenberg Hall, where teachers have an interest and enthusiasm for the new opportunities provided and supported by technology, and the resident consulting technologists have an interest and enthusiasm for pedagogical issues. Their shared interests establish a comfortable basis for continuing dialog, with all parties contributing from their areas of strength and benefitting from the expertise of their colleagues.

The case studies presented here are the result of a collaborative process that started with the teachers' ideas and goals, and proceeded to the design of powerful learning opportunities which were in turn supported by carefully selected tools and educationally informed staff. This process keeps the classroom priorities on the pedagogy, not on the latest digital device. Our hope is that this collaborative model experimented with in Wallenberg Hall for designing and equipping high performance learning spaces can offer other institutions an alternative approach to serving student learners, one that avoids the disadvantages of leading with tool acquisition. We recommend that future enhanced spaces for learning apply a socio-technical systems approach to the challenge of educating the next generation. In this way, we may come closer to meeting the goal of supporting and enhancing classes and learning experiences in ways and contexts that we cannot yet even imagine.

REFERENCES

Abbott, C. (2000). *ICT: Changing education*. London, UK: Routledge.

Abbott, C. (2010). *E-inclusion: Learning difficulties and digital technologies*. Retrieved July 11, 2010, from https://www.spectronics.com.au/conference/ 2010/ pdfs/ E-inclusion - Learning Difficulties and Digital Technologies.pdf

Astin, A. W. (1975). *Preventing students from dropping out*. San Francisco, CA: Jossey-Bass.

Astin, A. W. (2003). From number crunching to spirituality. In Smart, J. C. (Ed.), *Higher education: Handbook of theory and research* (*Vol. 28*, pp. 1–56). Boston, MA: Kluwer Academic. doi:10.1007/978-94-010-0137-3_1

Chen, H. L. (2010, April 12). Wallenberg Hall learning spaces: For course innovation. *Speaking of Computers, 83*. Retrieved October 30, 2010, from http://speaking.stanford.edu/ highlights/ Wallenberg_Hall_Learning_Spaces.html

Hasso Plattner Design Institute. (2010). *Stanford design thinking workbook*. Retrieved October 28, 2010, from http://www.scribd.com/ doc/ 37607571/ Stanford-Design-Thinking-Workbook

Higgins, S., Falzon, C., Hall, I., Moseley, D., Smith, F., Smith, H., & Wall, K. (2005). *Embedding ICT in the literacy and numeracy strategies*. Newcastle upon Tyne, UK: Newcastle University. Retrieved July 11, 2010, from http://www.ecls.ncl.ac.uk/ publications/ Clark%5E2005 -IWBreport.pdf

Kemmis, S., & McTaggart, R. (1988). *The action research planner*. Geelong, Victoria, Australia: Deakin University Press.

Kemmis, S., & McTaggart, R. (2000). Participatory action research. In Denzin, N. K., & Lincoln, Y. S. (Eds.), *Handbook of qualitative research* (2nd ed., pp. 567–605). Thousand Oaks, CA: Sage.

Koehler, M. J., & Mishra, P. (2008). Introducing technological pedagogical knowledge. In American Association of Colleges of Teacher Education (AACTE) Committee on Innovation and Technology (Ed.), *The handbook of technological pedagogical content knowledge for educators*. London, UK: Routledge/Taylor & Francis Group.

Kuh, G. D. (2007, June 15). How to help students achieve. *The Chronicle of Higher Education, 53*(41), B12–B13.

Kuh, G. D., Kinzie, J., & Schuh, J. H. Whitt., E. J., & Associates. (2005). *Student success in college: Creating conditions that matter*. San Francisco, CA: Jossey-Bass.

Kuh, G. D., Schuh, J. H., & Whitt, E. J. (1991). *Involving colleges: Successful approaches to fostering student learning and personal development outside of the classroom*. San Francisco, CA: Jossey-Bass.

Laurillard, D. (2008). The teacher as action researcher: Using technology to capture pedagogic form. *Studies in Higher Education, 33*(2), 139–154. doi:10.1080/03075070801915908

Laurillard, D. (2009). The pedagogical challenges to collaborative technologies. *International Journal of Computer-Supported Collaborative Learning, 4*(1), 5–20. doi:10.1007/s11412-008-9056-2

Lloyd, M. (2010, April 28). 18 Web 2.0 tools for instruction. *Campus Technology*. Retrieved July 15, 2010, from http://campustechnology.com/ articles/ 2010/05/ 01/ 18-web-20-tools-for-instruction.aspx

Marshall, G. (1988). Socio-technical system. In *A dictionary of sociology*. Retrieved July 15, 2010, from http://www.encyclopedia.com/ doc/ 1O88-sociotechnicalsystem.html

Mishra, P., & Koehler, M. J. (2006). Technological pedagogical content knowledge: A new framework for teacher knowledge. *Teachers College Record, 108*(6), 1017–1054. doi:10.1111/j.1467-9620.2006.00684.x

O'Brien, A. (2007). *Data analysis of Örebro-Stanford cross-cultural rhetoric project*. White paper.

O'Brien, A., & Eriksson, A. (2009). Cross-cultural connections: Intercultural learning for global citizenship. In M. Alagic & G. Remington (Eds.), *Intercultural communication competence: Educating the world citizen* (pp. 1-20). Retrieved July 14, 2010, from https://www.stanford.edu/ group/ ccr/ archive/ articles/ Cross_cultural_connections.pdf

O'Brien, A. J., Alfano, C., & Magnusson, E. (2007). Improving cross-cultural communication through collaborative technologies. In de Kort, Y., IJsselsteijn, W., Midden, C., Eggen, B., & Fogg, B. J. (Eds.), *Lecture Notes in Computer Science 4744: Persuasive technology* (pp. 125–131). Berlin, Germany: Springer.

O'Brien, A. J., & Alfano, C. L. (2009). Connecting students globally through video-conference pedagogy. *Journal of Online Learning and Teaching, 5*(4). Retrieved July 14, 2010, from http://jolt.merlot.org/ vol5no4/ obrien_1209.htm

Ophir, E., Nass, C., & Wagner, A. D. (2009). Cognitive control in media multitaskers. *Proceedings of the National Academy of Sciences of the United States of America, 106*(37), 15583–15587. doi:10.1073/pnas.0903620106

Pace, C. R. (1998). Recollections and reflections. In Smart, J. C. (Ed.), *Higher education: Handbook of theory and research* (*Vol. 13*, pp. 1–34). New York, NY: Agathon Press. doi:10.1007/978-94-011-3971-7_1

Pascarella, E. T., & Terenzini, P. T. (2005). How college affects students: *Vol. 2. A third decade of research*. San Francisco, CA: Jossey-Bass.

Prensky, M. (2001) *Digital natives, digital immigrants*. Retrieved July 15, 2010, from http:// www.marcprensky.com/ writing/ Prensky%20 -%20Digital%20Natives,%20 Digital %20Immigrants%20-%20Part1.pdf

Shulman, L. (1986). Those who understand: Knowledge growth in teaching. *Educational Researcher, 15*(2), 4–14.

Suggs, E. (2010, January 19). Bills seek ban on texting while driving. *The Atlanta Journal-Constitution*. Retrieved July 15, 2010, from http:// www.ajc.com/ news/ georgia-politics-elections/ bills-seek-ban-on-278266.html

TPCK. (n.d.). *Technological Pedagogical Content Knowledge*. Retrieved July 14, 2010, from http:// tpack.org

Willingham, D. T. (2010). Ask the cognitive scientist: Have technology and multitasking rewired how students learn? *American Educator*, (Summer): 23–28, 42.

ADDITIONAL READING

Hasso Plattner Design Institute. (2010). *Stanford design thinking workbook*. Retrieved October 28, 2010, from, http://www.scribd.com/ doc/ 37607571/ Stanford-Design-Thinking-Workbook

JISC InfoNet. *Planning & designing technology-rich learning spaces*. Retrieved October 30, 2010, from, http://www.jiscinfonet.ac.uk/ infokits/ learning-space-design

Oblinger, D. G. (Ed.). (2006). *Learning spaces*. EDUCAUSE. Retrieved October 30, 2010, from, http://www.educause.edu/ LearningSpaces

Van Note Chism, N., & Bickford, D. J. (Eds.). (2002). *New directions for teaching and learning: The importance of physical space in creating supportive learning environments, 92 (Winter)*. San Francisco, CA: Jossey-Bass.

KEY TERMS AND DEFINITIONS

Action Research: Action research is a systematic form of inquiry that is collective, collaborative, self-reflective, critical, and undertaken by the participants of the inquiry (McCutcheon & Jung, 1990). Our approach has followed the model of participatory action research proposed by Kemmis and McTaggart (1988) defined as "collective, self-reflective enquiry undertaken by participants in social situations in order improve the rationality and justice of their own social...practice" (p.5).

Cross Cultural Rhetoric: A method that fosters efficient learning of core writing, communication, and rhetoric skills to enable students can learn to communicate with intercultural audiences in rhetorically effective ways. Some examples of these approaches include attention to the rhetorical concepts of audience, context, medium, message, and argument as well as concrete strategies for writing, speaking, active listening, peer review response, and collaboration across a range of cultural and university settings. (http://ccr.stanford.edu)

Digital Natives: Coined by Mark Prensky (2001), this term refers to individuals (typically young persons or students who are currently entering college and university), who have grown up with digital technology and are facile with using technology in all aspects of their lives. The term is often used in comparison to "Digital Immigrants," referring to individuals who was introduced to digital technology later in life. Digital Natives are also often referred to as Millennials (individuals born after 1982) and the Net Generation.

High Performance Learning Space: Environments that support learning with a combination of human factors considerations (suitable architecture/infrastructure, comfortable/flexible furnishings) and rich information/media resources.

Socio-Technical System: By characterizing Wallenberg Hall as a socio-technical system, we are referring specifically to the social and technical factors that influence how the organization is able to support innovation in teaching and learning. Wallenberg Hall possesses staff expertise in educational technology, instructional design, and assessment which is unique to our campus. By actively collaborating with faculty using an action research approach, we bring the "social" resources to address the technical challenges of adopting and integrating technological tools into pedagogical practice.

Student Engagement: Definitions of this multi-dimensional concept range from study-skill strategies to how students allocate attentional, cognitive, and affective resources in the classroom and can include such concepts as time on task, quality of effort, student involvement, and good practices in undergraduate education. Our use of this term is specifically focused on how the technology-augmented learning environments contribute to outcomes and evidence related to students' learning and understanding.

TPACK: A model of instructional skills that intersect content knowledge, pedagogy, and classroom technology. http://tpack.org

ENDNOTES

1 The work represented in this chapter was funded by the Knut and Alice Wallenberg Foundation, the Marcus and Marianne Wallenberg Foundation, and the President and Provost of Stanford University. Special thanks to Andrea Lunsford of the Program for Writing and Rhetoric, to our colleague Dan Gilbert, and to all of the extraordinary educators who have allowed us to learn from them since 2002. You can learn more about Wallenberg Hall, and see clips from the faculty interviews cited in this chapter at http://wallenberg.stanford.edu/

2 The faculty advisory team consisted of Larry Leifer of Mechanical Engineering Design, Momoyo Kubo Lowdermilk of Japanese Language, Andrea Lunsford of the Program

for Writing and Rhetoric, Jan Borschers of Computer Science, and Laura Donohue of Political Science.

3 http://www.voicethread.com

4 See http://ccr.stanford.edu for a history of the project, its objectives and learning goals, and reports on implementation of technology for courses connecting the US and Sweden.

About the Contributors

Anders D. Olofsson, PhD, is an Associate Professor, working at the Department of Education, Umeå University, Sweden. From a philosophical hermeneutical approach his research is aimed at understanding the meaning of social processes of teaching, learning, and ethics in higher education contexts being embraced by educational technology. Over the years Dr. Olofsson has developed a deep research interest in the field of informed design of educational technology practices. He is the scientific leader for a research group titled LICT (Learning & ICT). In addition he is a teacher and researcher involved in several development- and research projects focused on educational technology in medical education. He has contributed with numerous book-chapters, journal articles, and papers to conference proceedings on these specific topics. For example has Dr. Olofsson, together with Dr. J. Ola Lindberg, co-edited the book *Online Learning Communities and Teacher Professional Development: Methods for Improved Educational Delivery*. A list of publications may be found at http://www.pedag.umu.se/om-institutionen/personal/olofsson-d-anders

J. Ola Lindberg is presently a postdoctoral research fellow at the Department of Education, Mid Sweden University, and his primary research interest lies in teachers' professional development (TPD) and distance education supported by ICT. His research departs from a philosophical hermeneutical approach with an overall aim at understanding social and ethical processes of teaching and fostering. In TPD and distance education his focus is on how participants negotiate meaning and learn using technology. Between 2008 and 2010 he has been the scientific leader of the project "Technology Enhanced Teachers Professional Development in Sweden and in China," a joint research project between Mid Sweden University and South China Normal University. He has contributed with book-chapters, conference-papers, and journal articles; for example has Dr. Lindberg, together with Dr. Anders D Olofsson, co-edited the book *Online Learning Communities and Teacher Professional Development: Methods for Improved Educational Delivery*.

* * *

Serena Alvino is Consulting Professor in the Educational Sciences Faculty of the University of Genoa for the "E-learning for adults and organizations" course. Serena Alvino has been collaborating with the Institute for Educational Technologies of the Italian National Research Council since 2002 on a number of projects about Computer Supported Collaborative Learning (CSCL) and online learning instructional design. She received a PhD in "Languages, Cultures and ICTs" from the University of Genoa in 2008, discussing the thesis "Computer Supported Collaborative Learning & reusability: an approach to the integration of reusable resources in collaborative learning processes." Her interests and activities mainly focus on learning objects, learning design models, educational metadata models, instructional design for CSCL, ontologies, and folksonomies supporting online learning and resource sharing.

Tel Amiel is Researcher at the Center for Informatics Applied to Education (*Núcleo de Informática Aplicada à Educação; NIED*) and a visiting Professor at the School of Education, both at the State University of Campinas (UNICAMP). Since 2003 he co-directs collaborative student-exchange projects between the United States and Brazil through grant programs focused on culture, education, and technology. He was a visiting fellow at the University of Wollongong in 2007. Current research interests revolve around educational change, open educational resources, new media, and technological resources in public schools.

Gary J. Anglin serves as a faculty member and Program Coordinator of the Instructional Systems Design Program at the University of Kentucky. His educational background includes degrees in mathematics and degrees in instructional systems technology from Indiana University. He teaches graduate classes in the areas of instructional design, instructional theory, distance learning, and foundations of instructional technology. Dr. Anglin has served as president of the Research and Theory Division, and the Division of Instructional Development, and currently chairs the Robert M. Gagne Award Committee for Outstanding Graduate Student Research, Association for Educational Communications and Technology. He is also a past president of the Instructional Technology Interest Group (IT-SIG) of the American Educational Research Association. His recent publications have been in the area of distance learning, and he is editor of the forthcoming book (in press), *Instructional Technology: Past, Present and Future* (3rd edition).

Leonor Barroca, PhD, is a Senior Lecturer in Computing at The Open University. Previously she has taught at the Universidade do Minho, Portugal. Her research is in the software engineering area where she has published in international conferences and journals and has been a member of international conferences programmes committees; she has recently been also carrying out research in the area of research skills development in distance education. Leonor has co-chaired the Virtual MPhil in Computing since its beginning. In teaching, she has been involved with the production and teaching of many undergraduate and postgraduate distance education courses in software engineering.

Claire Bradley is a Research Fellow at the Learning Technology Research Institute at London Metropolitan University. She has a Master's degree in Interactive Multimedia. For the past 14 years she has worked on a number of UK and European research projects involved in e-learning, m-learning, online communities, multimedia, and in the general application and evaluation of e-learning in teaching and learning. She has co-authored a number of journal articles and papers in these areas. Prior to working as a researcher, she worked for 12 years developing and producing distance learning materials for adult learners at The Open College.

Urban Carlén specializes on continual professional development organised in online learning communities (OLC). His dissertation in Applied Information Technology at the IT-faculty, University of Gothenburg examined how Swedish general practitioners build an OLC within the specialist subject of general/family medicine by using an e-mailing list. His academic background started in the interdisciplinary fields of behavioural studies and computer science. Much of his work is related to issues of how people participate over the Internet. Research interests consider analysis of text based communication, social network analysis, Internet cultures, and design for online participation. Currently he lectures in IT and learning at the teacher training programme at University of Skövde.

Helen L. Chen, Ph.D., is a research scientist at the Center for Design Research and the Stanford Center for Innovations in Learning within the Human Sciences and Technologies Advanced Research Institute at Stanford University. She earned her undergraduate degree from UCLA and her PhD in Communication with a minor in Psychology from Stanford University in 1998. Through collaborations with national and international portfolio researchers, she co-led the development of Folio Thinking, a reflective practice that situates and guides the effective use of learning portfolios. Helen is a founding member and co-facilitator of EPAC, a community of practice focusing on pedagogical and technological issues related to e-portfolios broadly defined. She most recently co-authored a publication for the Association of American Colleges and Universities on Electronic Portfolios and Student Success. Helen's current research interests relate to e-portfolios, engineering education, and designing approaches to document and evaluate the innovations in teaching and learning occurring in the technology-augmented classrooms.

John Cook is Professor of Technology Enhanced Learning (TEL) at the Learning Technology Research Institute, London Metropolitan University. He has over 8 years project management experience, which includes AHRB, BECTA, HEFCE (CETL Manager 2005-2008), and EC work. Furthermore, John has been part of research and development grant proposals that have attracted £4 million in competitive external funding. In addition, he has published/presented around 230 refereed articles and invited talks in the area of TEL, having a specific interest in four related areas: informal learning, mobile learning, augmented contexts for development, and work-based learning. He was Chair/President of the Association for Learning Technology (2004-06); he is currently the Chair of ALT's Research Committee. John sits on various journal editorial boards and conducts assessor and review work for the EU, UK Research Councils, and Science Foundation of Ireland.

Maarten de Laat is member of management staff of the Ruud de Moor Centrum and Director of the Networked Learning research programme. He coordinates about 20 projects on teacher professional development, lifelong learning, and workplace learning. His research concentrates on professional development, knowledge creation, and sharing through social networks and communities. He has published and presented his work extensively in research journals, books, and conferences. He is currently a member of the local organizing committee of the EARLI conference in Exeter (2011) as well as the organizing committee of the international Networked Learning conference hosted at the Open University of the Netherlands in 2012.

Mats Deutschmann, PhD, is Associate Professor in Language Didactics at the Department of Language Studies, Umeå University, Sweden. He has over ten years' experience in the field of online language learning and over the past five years he has worked extensively in virtual worlds. His research includes didactic design for collaborative language learning in online contexts, the language pragmatics of online education, and the use of innovative technology for raising engagement and active participation.

He is currently involved in a number of international telecollaborative projects, some of which involve the use of virtual worlds in language learning, for example "Access to Virtual and Action Learning live Online" (AVALON), an EU-funded project with the aim of developing new methods for language learning in virtual worlds. He has published extensively in the field and is co-editor of the book "Learning and Teaching in the Virtual World of Second Life," (2009) eds. Molka-Danielsen, J. & Deutschmann, M., Tapir Academic Press, Trondheim.

Pierre Dillenbourg is Professor of computer science and pedagogy at Swiss Federal Institute of Technology in Lausanne (EPFL). A former teacher in elementary school, Pierre graduated in educational science (University of Mons, Belgium). He started to conduct research in learning technologies in 1984. He obtained a PhD in computer science from the University of Lancaster (UK), in the field of educational applications of artificial intelligence. He is past president of the International Society for the Learning Sciences. His work covers various domain of CSCL, ranging from novel interfaces for face-to-face collaboration (interactive furniture, tangibles, paper computing) to more cognitive projects on dual eye tracking and mutual modelling.

Jan Arild Dolonen holds a Master's in Information Science from the University of Bergen, Norway. He has more than six years of experience as a systems designer and programmer, and almost three years of experience as a research assistant at InterMedia, University of Oslo. He had the role as a technical consultant in the DLC, DLP, and Calibrate projects. Currently, he is PhD candidate at InterMedia, focusing on Information Systems design research. His research interests are design and use of net–based environments. In his PhD project he uses a socio-cultural perspective to study the social processes inside a co-design project of a mathematical tool and how this tool is used in the classrooms of Norwegian high schools.

Miikka J. Eriksson is a Project Manager and Researcher in the Centre for Media Pedagogy at University of Lapland (Finland). He received his MS and PhD degrees in Biology from the University of Joensuu (Finland) in 2003 and 2007, respectively. Since his graduation he has also been working as a biology and geography teacher in comprehensive and secondary school and as a researcher at the Finnish Forest Research Institute. In educational context he has previously studied the use of laptops in higher education. His current research interests include the use of mobile technologies, social media tools, and virtual worlds and the development of pedagogical models to enhance and inform the use of these tools in both secondary and tertiary education.

Charles R. Graham is an Associate Professor of Instructional Psychology and Technology at Brigham Young University with interest in technology-mediated teaching and learning. Charles studies the design and evaluation of blended learning environments and the use of technology to enhance teaching and learning.

Päivi Hakkarainen is Senior Lecturer in media education at the Centre for Media Pedagogy at the University of Lapland's Faculty of Education. She teaches both face-to-face courses and inter-university online courses. Previously she worked as project manager and researcher in several national and international research and development projects encouraging the educational use of ICTs. She received her

PhD from the University of Lapland, Finland, in 2007. Her doctoral thesis focused on the educational use of digital videos for supporting meaningful learning. Her research interests include higher education pedagogy, meaningful learning, pedagogical models, ICTs and media in teaching and learning, and internet in older adults' everyday life. She has published her research in international scientific journals and compilation works. For further information, please visit: http://paivihakkarainen.wordpress.com/

Michael Hammond is Associate Professor in new technology at the Institute of Education, University of Warwick. He teaches several courses on the use of new technology in teaching and learning, many of which follow an action research methodology. He co-ordinates the Centre for New Technologies Research in Education at the Institute and is director of research degree students. He has written widely on the topic of new technology in professional and academic journals and has subsidiary interests in the experience of overseas students in high education and in research methodology.

Trond Eiliv Hauge is Professor of Education at the Department of Teacher Education and School Research, University of Oslo, Norway, and Visiting Professor at the Department of Education, Umeå University, Sweden. He is leading the research group *Teacher Professionalism and Educational Change: Practices, Purposes, and Policies* (TEPEC) at the Faculty of Educational Sciences, University of Oslo. He is researching in the fields of ICT and learning, teacher professional learning, school leadership, and school development. In recent years, he has been involved in international projects like: *Calibrating eLearning in Schools* (EU) and *Knowledge Practices Laboratory* (EU) and the *International School Effectiveness Project.*

Caroline Haythornthwaite is Director, School of Library, Archival and Information Studies, University of British Columbia. She joined UBC in August, 2010 after 14 years at the University of Illinois at Urbana-Champaign, where she was Professor in the Graduate School of Library and Information Science. In 2009-10, she was Leverhulme Trust Visiting Professor at the Institute of Education, University of London presenting and writing on learning networks. Her research concentrates on information and knowledge sharing through social networks and the impact of computer media and the Internet on work, learning and social interaction. Major publications include The Internet in Everyday Life (2002, with Barry Wellman); Learning, Culture and Community in Online Education (2004, with Michelle M. Kazmer), the Handbook of E-learning Research (2007, with Richard Andrews), and E-learning Theory and Research (2011, with Richard Andrews).

Jan Herrington is Professor of Education at Murdoch University in Perth. The last 20 years of her professional life have been devoted to the promotion and support of the effective use of educational technologies in learning in schools and universities. Jan's current research focuses on mobile learning, design-based research, authentic learning, and the use of authentic tasks as a central focus for e-learning courses. She has published over 150 refereed journal articles, conference papers, and chapters, and several books including a recently co-edited book entitled Authentic Learning in Higher Education and a co-authored book (with Thomas C Reeves and Ron Oliver) A Guide to Authentic e-Learning in 2010. She was a Fulbright Scholar in 2002 at the University of Georgia, USA, and has won many awards for her research including the Association for Educational Communication and Technology award for new researchers.

Jie Hu is Lecturer and Course Director at the College of Foreign Languages at the University of Chongqing, China. Her interests cover using technology to enhance students' English language skills, pedagogies of English language teaching, and students' English language learning experiences. She completed her PhD on online language learning for international students at the University of Warwick, UK. She continues to research in the field of language learning with a special interest in the experiences of learners using networked technology.

Camillan Huang-DeVoss, Ph.D., is a Lecturer in the departments of Human Biology and of Surgery, division of Anatomy and the Director of instructional technology and digital media for the Center for the Support of Excellence in Teaching K-12 at Stanford University. She was previously the director of the Wallenberg Global Learning Network at Stanford leading a multi-institutional international faculty grants program in ICT and K-12 education and the project director for the Virtual Labs interactive education media project. Her expertise is in global project management, interactive media production for education, human-computer interaction, instructional design, curriculum development with technology and science, and faculty and teacher professional development. Dr. Huang holds a PhD in Molecular and Cell Biology (neurobiology) from the University of California, Berkeley.

Su-Ling Hsueh holds a PhD degree in Instructional Psychology & Technology from Brigham Young University. She is currently an Assistant Dean to oversee and develop language technology at the Defense Language Institute Foreign Language Center. Her research interests include technology integration, faculty technology training, and technology assisted 2nd language learning and teaching, and related topics.

Lars O. Häll, MSc, is a doctoral student at the Umeå University Department of Education. His research focus is learning with educational computer-assisted simulations in health care education, with a developing interest for informed, practical models to support teachers and researchers in analysis and design. Research for his coming thesis has been performed within the research and development projects Learning Radiology in Simulated Environments and Nordic Safety and Security (NSS). A member of the Learning & ICT (LICT), and Learning in Simulated Environments research (LiSE) groups.

Jimmy Jaldemark is a Lecturer and Researcher at the Department of Education, Mid Sweden University, Härnösand, Sweden. He reached the PhD-grade in Education early 2010 with the thesis "Participation in a boundless activity: Computer-mediated communication in Swedish higher education;" a project that comprised four papers analysing different aspects of participating in online education. Influenced by other ideas developed within eco-psychological, pragmatist, and socio-cultural perspectives and theories, his research takes a transactional approach to human action. Research interests include studies within the fields of computer-mediated communication, distance education, educational communication, educational design, learning, online communities, online settings of higher education, and power.

Menko Johnson is Director of Technology at the Fremont Union High School District focused on effective integration of technology in teaching spaces emphasizing collaboration and flexibility. As a former technology teacher and professional development expert, he is dedicated to helping teachers become more effective, engaging teachers through innovative pedagogies and prudent use of technology. Currently he is part of design team creating a new vision for teaching and learning in the district through innovative spaces, technology and teaching. Formerly at Stanford's Wallenberg Hall, Menko was a member of a team that was investigating the impact off flexible learning spaces on faculty and student learning experiences. Menko's research focus is on how technology mediates and creates innovative teaching pedagogies. Menko has an M.A. in Instructional Technology and an M.Ed in Elementary Education. He previously helped launch San Jose State's Academic Success Center and managed the Incubator Classroom from 2006-2008.

Michael C. Johnson is a Senior Instructional Designer at Brigham Young University's Center for Teaching & Learning. His research interests include the moral dimensions of teaching and learning, distance education, and the instructional use of technology and social media. He holds a Master's degree in Instructional Technology from Utah State University and a PhD in Instructional Psychology & Technology from Brigham Young University.

Christopher R. Jones is a Reader in the Institute of Educational Technology at the Open University. He teaches on the Master's programme in Online and Distance Education (ODE) and coordinates the ODE strand of the Doctorate in Education. His research focuses on networked learning and the utilization of the metaphor of networks to the understanding of learning in tertiary education. Chris has an interest in collaborative and cooperative methods of teaching and learning and in Communities and Networks of Practice. Chris was the principal investigator for a UK Research Council funded project "The Net Generation encountering e-learning at university." He was previously co-leader of the European Union funded Kaleidoscope Research Team "Conditions for productive networked learning environments". Chris has published two edited collections (most recently *Analysing Networked Learning Practices in Higher Education and Continuing Professional Development*, 2009, Sense Publishers), over 60 refereed journal articles, book chapters, and conference papers connected to his research.

Debby Kalk is an Instructional Designer, Project Manager, and e-learning Consultant with extensive experience in developing training and education programs for a broad range of institutions and audiences. As CEO of Cortex Interactive, she worked with educational publishers to produce award-winning learning technology products for secondary and higher education curricula in disciplines including foreign language education, mathematics, business management, and engineering. She is co-author of the college textbook, *Real World Instructional Design* (2005), published by Wadsworth/Cengage. She has worked on the design and delivery of instructional design courses and has investigated strategies for training instructional designers. Her current research interests include the social dimensions of distance learning, the efficacy of collaborative learning tools, and the design of complex and blended learning programs.

Maged N. Kamel Boulos, PhD, SMIEEE, originally a medical doctor, is currently Associate Professor in Health Informatics at the University of Plymouth, UK. He was previously Lecturer in Healthcare Informatics at the University of Bath, and worked before that at City University London. Maged has >90 peer-reviewed publications on a specialized range of medical and public health informatics topics. He is Co-Chair of WG-IV/4 (Virtual Globes) within the International Society for Photogrammetry and Remote Sensing Commission IV, 2008-2012. He is the Founder and Editor-in-Chief of International Journal of Health Geographics (http://ij-healthgeographics.com/). He also serves on the editorial boards of other peer-reviewed publications. His research has been partly funded by UK and international bodies, including UK TSB KTP Programme, UK Arts & Humanities Research Council, WHO EMRO, and European Commission. He has delivered invited keynotes at a number of international events and his work has received wide media coverage in the UK and abroad.

Adrian Kirkwood (B.A. [London] M.Ed. [Manchester]) is a Senior Lecturer at the UK Open University. He has been monitoring and evaluating developments in media-based teaching and learning for almost 25 years, both within the UK Open University and in other education and training organisations. His primary interest is in student learning with media - with an emphasis on learning to a greater extent than on media technologies *per se*. Adrian has a long record of supporting professional development for staff at the UK Open University. Specifically, this has taken an evidence-based approach to making the most effective use of media technologies for learning and teaching in courses developed for independent adult students. He has also led professional development workshops on the selection, use, and evaluation of media technologies for academic staff in universities in the UK, Europe, and other parts of the world.

Agnes Kukulska-Hulme is Professor of Learning Technology and Communication in the Institute of Educational Technology at The Open University, and Programme Leader for the Next Generation Distance Learning research programme. She is President of the International Association for Mobile Learning. Agnes has been working in mobile learning since 2001, leading numerous research projects investigating learning innovation across the UK and in Europe. She is co-editor of two books on mobile learning: *Researching Mobile Learning: Frameworks, Tools and Research Designs* (2009) and *Mobile Learning: A Handbook for Educators and Trainers* (2005). Her work includes co-editing special issues of the *Journal of Interactive Media in Education* (2005), *ReCALL* (2008), *ALT-J* (2009) and *Open Learning* (2010). Agnes's original discipline background is in foreign language teaching and learning, and from this perspective, she has a longstanding research interest in effective communication with technology and the experiences of non-technical users.

Berner Lindström's overarching research interest is geared to learning and teaching, especially communication and learning with media and information and communication technologies (ICT). His methodological interests lie in the relationship between learning and development in the individual and social, institutional, and material/technological conditions. Specific research areas are learning from multimedia representations, spatial cognition, learning styles and learning strategies, distance education and open/flexible education, and functions of information and communication technologies in changing educational practices. In terms of subject matter, his research focuses on mathematics and science. Berner teaches at the postgraduate and Master's levels in areas like educational psychology, learning, communication and IT, distance education and flexible learning, and analysis of interaction.

Eunice Luyegu is a Faculty Member at Franklin University, Columbus, OH where she teaches courses in the Master's in Science in Instructional Design and Performance Technology program. In addition to teaching, Eunice works with other faculty members at Franklin University on developing interactive and dialogic approaches to teaching and learning, in both virtual and face-to-face environments. She has a Ph.D. in Instructional Design and Development. Her research interests are in the integration, use, and evaluation of information communication technologies in teaching, learning, and assessment.

Colleen M. McLinn is an Extension Associate and Instructional Designer in the Education Program at the Cornell Lab of Ornithology. She oversees curriculum development and faculty outreach for the Online Research in Biology project, which strives to create feasible opportunities for undergraduate research about behavior and ecology in diverse classroom settings. McLinn has a doctorate in Ecology, Evolution, and Behavior, along with substantial expertise in application of information and communication technologies in science teaching. Current interests include: (1) scaffolding effective use of multimedia and databases in inquiry, (2) supporting faculty in articulating and assessing student learning outcomes, and (3) creating interactive online courses for free-choice learning about bird behavior.

Mark O. Millard is the Learning Design and Technology Specialist for the Department of Engineering Professional Development in the College of Engineering at University of Wisconsin-Madison. Mark is also a doctoral student in the School of Information Science at Indiana University. His professional and research interests include the areas of social and educational informatics, learning technologies, computer-mediated communication, computer-supported collaborative learning, HCI, ubiquitous computing, and ICT Literacy.

Shailey Minocha, PhD, is a Reader in Computing in the Department of Computing at The Open University, UK. The focus of her research is understanding users' interactions with technology and investigating the factors that affect usability, user experience, and user adoption of technology-enabled systems. Her recent research projects have involved investigating the role of social software and 3D virtual worlds in virtual team working, socialisation, collaborative learning, and community building. She has also been investigating the role of 3D virtual worlds and gaming environments for non-teaching, research purposes, either where the behaviour of the gamers becomes the object of study, or where the 3D environment is used to investigate or simulate other behaviours, such as wayfinding and navigation. Shailey's website has details of her activities and publications: http://mcs.open.ac.uk/sm577

David Morse, PhD, is a Senior Lecturer in the Computing Department at the Open University, UK. He studied for his undergraduate and doctoral degrees at the University of York before moving to the University of Kent where he taught computing at undergraduate and postgraduate level in the face-to-face context. On moving to the Open University he began teaching via distance-learning. At the OU, David has taught on a number of courses using a variety of approaches, from those which follow a supported open learning model, to those which are wholly online. In the latter category, David has been chairing a course on virtual teamworking since 2003. He has published extensively on collaboration in virtual teams.

Gary R. Morrison received his doctorate in Instructional Systems Technology from Indiana University and is a Professor and graduate program Director in the instructional design and technology program at Old Dominion University. His research focuses on cognitive load theory, instructional strategies, K-12 technology integration, and distance education. He is author of two books: Morrison, Ross, & Kemp's *Designing Effective Instruction* (6th Edition) and Morrison & Lowther's *Integrating Computer Technology into the Classroom* (4th Edition). He has written over 25 book chapters and over 40 articles on instructional design and educational technology. Gary is the editor of the *Journal of Computing in Higher Education.* He has worked as instructional designer for three Fortune 500 companies and the University of Mid-America. Gary is a past president of Association for Educational Communication and Technology's (AECT) Research and Theory Division and Design, Development Division, and Distance Learning Division.

Jari Multisilta is the Professor of multimedia in University of Helsinki, Information Technology at Pori, Finland. He got his M. Sc from the University of Tampere in 1992 in Mathematics and his Dr. Tech. at Tampere University of Technology in 1996. The title of his doctoral thesis was "Hypermedia Learning Environment for Mathematics." Prof. Multisilta has studied learning and modern communication and Information Technologies and has taken part in several research projects on this area. Currently, his research interests include networked and mobile learning and mobile social media. Professor Multisilta has published over 100 international conference papers and journal articles on his research area. He was a Visiting Fellow at Nokia Research Center on 2008-2009. Multisilta has also been a Visiting Scholar at Stanford University, H-STAR Institute for summers in 2007 and 2008 and six months in 2010.

Alyssa J. O'Brien, Ph.D., is a lecturer at Stanford University, where she teaches writing, public speaking, and cross-cultural communication in the Program in Writing and Rhetoric. Since arriving at Stanford in 2001, Alyssa has written or co-authored three writing textbooks and three adjacent instructor's manuals (Pearson Longman, 2004; 2008; 2010; Bedford St. Martin's, 2003, 2008, 2010). She directs the Stanford Cross-Cultural Rhetoric project, a research endeavor originally funded by the Wallenberg Global Learning Network that now connects students across five continents through video-conference technology and blogs. Dr. O'Brien won the Phi Beta Kappa Outstanding Teaching Award in 2006. She has been an invited speaker in Asia, Europe, and the Middle East on subjects such as global learning, communication for leadership, visual rhetoric, and "mapping a change in writing."

Anne T. Ottenbreit-Leftwich is an Assistant Professor of Instructional Systems Technology at Indiana University – Bloomington. Dr. Ottenbreit-Leftwich's expertise lies in the areas of the design of digital curriculum resources, the use of technology to support pre-service teacher training, and development/implementation of professional development for teachers and teacher educators. Dr. Ottenbreit-Leftwich has experience working on large-scale funded projects, including projects supported by the U.S. Department of Education and the Indiana Department of Education. Her primary research focuses on teachers' value beliefs related to technology and how those beliefs influence teachers' technology use, adoption, and integration. She is currently working on a FIPSE grant developing technology-based scaffolds for preservice teachers to create problem-based learning units.

Simon Pratt-Adams is Head of the Department of Teacher Education at Anglia Ruskin University. Anglia Ruskin is one of the leading providers of Initial Teacher Education in the East of England. He has researched and lectured in the area of urban education. His second book on the subject - 'Changing Urban Education' - was published by Continuum International Publishers in 2010. Recent articles have included 'Improving the English urban primary school: questions of policy,' 'Urban Primary School Headship in England: an emotional perspective,' and 'Urban Education, Equality and Inequality' with Professor Meg Maguire. He has a contract with Continuum as series editor for Contemporary Issues in Education Studies with Dr. Richard Race and to date has seven books commissioned in this series.

Linda Price (MSc [CS Ed], Ad Dip FE, Ph.D, FHEA) has worked at the UK Open University since 1995 promoting pedagogically driven uses of new technology in higher education. She coordinates staff development activities across the university and has developed evidence-based professional development programmes that promote student-centred learning for Open University faculty and external bodies, such as the UK Higher Education Academy. Her professional development activities draw upon institutional, national, and international research on the student experience to promote the synergy between research and practice. Linda was an early pioneer of e-learning (particularly electronic assignment and assessment support) and has conducted many evaluations of e-learning in various settings. Her research concentrates on investigating how variations in context relate to students' conceptions of learning and perceptions of their educational experience, particularly in relation to new technology.

Lucia Rapanotti, PhD, is a Senior Lecturer in the Computing Department at the Open University, UK, where she has worked on a variety of programmes at undergraduate and graduate levels, with roles which span from educational software designer to academic author, to chair of production and delivery of innovative educational initiatives. She is a Member of the Editorial Board of Expert Systems and a Member of the British Computing Society (BCS). Previously she was a researcher at Newcastle upon Tyne and Oxford Universities, Editor-in-Chief of Expert Systems, and Secretary of the BCS Requirements Engineering Specialist Group. Her main research focus is problem solving in design and engineering. She has published widely in international conferences and journals, has delivered keynotes at international conferences, and is a member of numerous international programme committees. For more information, please see http://mcs.open.ac.uk/lr38/.

Paul E. Resta holds the Ruth Knight Milliken Centennial Professorship in Instructional Technology and serves as Director of the Learning Technology Center at The University of Texas at Austin. His current work focuses on the research and development of web-based learning environments, computer-supported collaborative learning strategies and tools, and online teacher professional development. He served as President of the International Council of Computers in Education and is the Founding President of the International Society for Technology in Education. He currently serves as President of the International Jury for the United Nations Educational, Scientific and Cultural Organization (UNESCO) King Hamad Bin Isa Al-Khalifa Prize for the Use of Information and Communication Technologies in Education. He also serves as Chair of the Association for Teacher Educators National Commission on Technology and the Future of Teacher Education.

Heli Ruokamo is a Professor of education, specialty media education, and Director of the Centre for Media Pedagogy in the Faculty of Education at University of Lapland, Finland. She is also Docent of Media Education at University of Helsinki and Docent of network-based learning environments at University of Turku. Last semester (2009-2010) she was working as a Visiting Scholar for six months in the H-Star Institute at Stanford University in California, US. Heli Ruokamo is a member of several boards in her field; e.g. CICERO Learning, the Graduate School of Multidisciplinary Research on Learning Environments, InnoSchool Consortium, TravED, and MediPeda projects [see: www.ulapland.fi/cmp]. She is also a member of Collegium at University of Lapland. Her research interests are in meaningful learning, pedagogical models, ICTs and media in teaching and learning, mobile learning, VR and simulation-based learning, and playful learning environments. She has published approximately 150 scientific publications in these areas. For further information, see: http://heliruokamo.wordpress.com/

Donald E Scott is the Coordinator of ICT for Learning in the Office of Professional and Community Engagement, Faculty of Education, University of Calgary. Dr. Scott is a highly experienced educator and professional developer. His expertise spans both educational and technical expertise in the areas of: information communication technologies; adult learning; professional development; and teaching, learning, and assessment. He has held the roles of teacher, network administrator, senior administrator, and university professor. He teaches in the postgraduate programmes and manages ICT learning projects. Dr. Scott has been an Information Technology consultant to business and government organisations. Dr. Scott's research interests encompass: explorations into the role of technology to support optimal learning for both teachers and students and to increase organisational effectiveness and culture; investigations into students' and teachers' techno-efficacy; and examinations of the viability of technological solutions to increasing communication between agencies and schools to provide better support of at-risk youth.

Shelleyann Scott is the Director of Professional Graduate Programs within Professional and Community Engagement, Faculty of Education, University of Calgary. Dr. Scott teaches in the postgraduate leadership programmes and supervises doctoral and Master's students. She is an experienced tertiary and secondary educator with expertise in professional development, simple and complex instructional strategies, curriculum and programme design and evaluation, and information communication technology as it applies to learning environments. Her research interests include: establishing and evaluating professional development within education, business, and government contexts; the creation and maintenance of learning communities; the use of technology to support educational experiences for students and teachers; and developing and supporting quality teaching and learning improvement cycles. Dr. Scott has an established publishing record within national and international journals and conferences. She is an experienced professional developer and has designed and facilitated programmes in Australia, Canada, Hong Kong, Indonesia, Malaysia, Philippines, Singapore, and Sri Lanka.

Carl Smith (PGDip, MA) is a Developer and Researcher for the Learning Technology Research Institute. His recent work has concentrated on exploiting the various ways that computer-based modelling can be used in the design, construction, and generation of learning environments and resources. His primary research involves the investigation of these micro forms of learning from the point of view of their units of construction – to see across the whole range of constituent parts, schemas, and key narratives involved in their successful development and application. He uses visualization techniques to produce interactive and engaging learning resources for both the Web and mobile devices. His other research interests include: augmented reality, intermediality, visualization as interface, open source learning, and the emerging practice within the arts and sciences that merges digital virtual experiences and technologies with physical spatial experiences. His was previously employed at the Humanities Computing departments at Glasgow and Sheffield Universities. Further info can be found at: http://learning.londonmet.ac.uk/TLTC/carl/index.htm

Robert Emery Smith is the Director of Technology Services at Stanford University's Wallenberg Hall. He works with faculty, instructors, IT professionals, and engineers to design, implement, and support the use and evaluation of technology-supported classroom activities. Bob has a long history in commercial technological product design, and returned to Stanford University to lead the design team that created Wallenberg Hall, where he has overseen classroom research operations since the facility opened in 2002. He participated in a wide variety of events and projects, including the Wallenberg Global Learning Network program High Performance Learning Spaces, facilitating rich ethnographic research in the classrooms and enabling a cross-continental live music performance. He continues to support faculty at Stanford and other institutions in their experiments with classroom augmenting technologies.

Tor Söderström, PhD, is an Associate Professor at the Department of Education, Umeå University. He supervises doctoral and Master's students. His prime field of expertise concerns technology enhanced learning and simulation based training and learning. He is leading research projects on learning in and design of simulated environments (e.g. medical training, firemen training). He is involved in several development and research projects within the field of learning in simulated environments. Over the years, has he contributed with book-chapters, journal articles, and papers to conference proceedings on the topic learning and information and communication technology.

Maureen Tam is currently Associate Professor in the Department of International Education and Lifelong Learning and Deputy Director of the Centre for Research and Development of Lifelong Learning with the Hong Kong Institute of Education. Before joining the Institute, Dr. Tam had occupied senior positions in higher education management as Dean of the Community College and Further Education of Lingnan University, and as Director of the Teaching and Learning Centre of the same university in consecutive periods responsible for teaching and learning development, quality assurance, and assessment of student experience. Dr. Tam's research interests are wide-ranging, including: elderly education, lifelong learning, professional and vocational education, quality assurance, outcomes-based education, instructional design, educational technology, teaching, and learning and assessment in higher education.

Nancy M. Trautmann, as Director of Education at the Cornell Lab of Ornithology, leads a team that creates educational resources and experiences for people of all ages, in person and online. Drawing on the lab's extensive Web resources and citizen science opportunities, these efforts aim to spark curiosity, build science skills, and inspire conservation action. Dr. Trautmann holds a joint appointment between the Lab of Ornithology and Cornell University's Department of Natural Resources. Her academic interests focus on developing and assessing techniques for engaging students in scientific research and citizen science, supporting effective university science outreach, and exploring the potential of educational technology in supporting collaboration and project-based learning for all students, including those who might not otherwise succeed in school.

Guglielmo Trentin is Senior Researcher and Project Manager at the Institute for Educational Technology (ITD) of the Italian National Research Council (CNR). His studies have largely focused on the use of network technology in formal and informal learning. In this field he has managed several projects and scientific activities, developing technological applications and methodological approaches to support networked collaborative learning. Since 2002, he teaches Network Technology, Knowledge Flow, and Human Resources Development at the University of Turin. He has authored several papers and some books on the themes of technology enhanced learning. Since 1999 he is contributing editor of *Educational Technology* (USA). He is presently the principal investigator of *WISE (Wiring Individualized Special Education)*, a strategic research project funded by Italy's Ministry of Universities and Research that studies the use of network technology in homebound special education.

Peter van Leusen is the Assistant Director of the Office of Instructional Consulting in the School of Education at Indiana University, Bloomington. He is a doctoral student in the Department of Instructional Systems Technology at Indiana University. His research interests focus on the integration of technology into teaching and faculty development in higher education. He has taught face-to-face and online courses in the university and K-12 setting.

Rui Zeng has a Ph.D. in Instructional Technology. She is Manager of Distance Education at the School of Biomedical Informatics at The University of Texas Health Science Center at Houston. She oversees distance education and outreach program development and implementation of health informatics. She is actively involved in instructional design and development projects and research including social media, Second Life, and mobile learning. Her research interests include strategies for effective learning in healthcare, emerging technologies in teaching and learning, and evaluation.

Index

Symbols

A

B

C

D

E

F

G

H

I

O

P

Q

R

S

www.ingramcontent.com/pod-product-compliance
Lightning Source LLC
LaVergne TN
LVHW062136200926
848484LV00007B/1818